READERS PRAISE PREVIOUS EDITIONS OF THIS BOOK

"You saved my life with your book! Your book has been **EXACTLY** what I've been looking for!"

—Steven D. McKenna

"The author's explanations remain at a very comprehensible level even when he's talking about complicated topics. That's the way to teach. **Just two words: Thank You. Your book is very clear and well done.** Good job."

—Alberto Fanelli

"I have been looking for this type of book for some time, and so far it has been perfect. **The book has been everything I have been looking for**. It is filling in the gaps that I have."

—Jeff Koski

"**I cannot express how valuable your new book has been to me!** I could not have been more rewarded and justified in buying your book. It almost seems like every example, tip, or code listing that you cite is exactly what I needed to know. No other reference on database access using VB has provided me with such competent information and clear examples.
Your delivery of the necessary concepts is top-notch! Thank you for your clear writing and masterful production. Your text has truly been worth its weight in gold. Maybe even platinum!"

—AJ Phillips

"It was as though this book was written just for me: detailed where I needed detail and practical in its examples. **Without reservation, I can say that this book is the most helpful book this database programmer has ever bought.**"
—Bob Dozier

"I have found *Database Access with Visual Basic* very useful. In fact, having pretty thoroughly researched the subset of data access books available for VB, I think it is fair to say that this is not just the **best book on the market for database programming, but really the only one in its class.**"
—Ron Kincaid

DATABASE ACCESS WITH VISUAL BASIC® 6

DATABASE ACCESS
WITH
VISUAL BASIC® 6

Jeffrey P. McManus

201 West 103rd Street, Indianapolis, IN, 46290, USA

Database Access with Visual Basic® 6

Copyright © 1999 by Sams Publishing

International Standard Book Number: 0-672-31422-3

Library of Congress Catalog Card Number: 98-87577

Printed in the United States of America

First Printing: January 1999

02   01   8   7   6

Trademarks

Warning and Disclaimer

Executive Editor
Tracy Dunkelberger

Acquisitions Editor
Tracy Dunkelberger

Development Editor
Sean Dixon

Managing Editor
Jodi Jensen

Project Editor
Maureen McDaniel

Copy Editors
Maryann Steinhart
Bart Reed

Indexer
Bruce Clingaman

Proofreader
Eddie Lushbaugh

Technical Editor
Debra Schnedler

Software Development Specialist
Michael Hunter

Team Coordinator
Michelle Newcomb

Interior Design
Gary Adair

Cover Design
Anne Jones

Layout Technicians
Brian Borders
Susan Geiselman
Amy Parker

Contents at a Glance

TABLE OF CONTENTS

ABOUT THE AUTHOR

Jeffrey P. McManus is the author of *How To Program Visual Basic Control Creation Edition, Visual Basic Components Sourcebook for Developers,* and *Database Access with Visual Basic*. He's a contributing editor and columnist for *Visual Basic Programmer's Journal* and has written for *PC Computing*. In addition to being a Visual Basic developer, he's trained thousands of developers in corporate environments.

DEDICATION

For Plaiddy

TELL US WHAT YOU THINK!

As the reader of this book, *you* are our most important critic and commentator. We value your opinion and want to know what we're doing right, what we could do better, what areas you'd like to see us publish in, and any other words of wisdom you're willing to pass our way.

I welcome your comments. You can email or write me directly to let me know what you did or didn't like about this book—as well as what we can do to make our books stronger.

Please note that I cannot help you with technical problems related to the topic of this book, and that due to the high volume of mail I receive, I might not be able to reply to every message.

When you write, please be sure to include this book's title and author as well as your name and phone or fax number. I will carefully review your comments and share them with the author and editors who worked on the book.

E-mail: `feedback@samspublishing.com`

Mail: Linda Engelman
           Sams Publishing
           201 West 103rd Street
           Indianapolis, IN 46290 USA

INTRODUCTION

Welcome to the second edition of *Database Access in Visual Basic*. This book contains coverage of all the database access technologies available to the Visual Basic developer out of the box, as well as some that aren't available. My goal for this book is to emphasize the important aspects of database access . . . the plumbing.

It's clear that in Visual Basic 6, the bulk of new features revolve around database access. You now get ActiveX Data Objects out of the box, instead of as an awkward after-the-fact download. In addition, you get a number of enhancements to the development environment, such as the Data View window and the Data Environment designer, to make connecting to and working with databases easier than ever.

If you're not quite ready to move up to Visual Basic 6, no problem. Easily 95% of the topics in this book work equally well with Visual Basic 5 and 6. The fact that the database library doesn't care which version—or language—of your development environment you use, is a testament to the interoperability standards upon which ADO and other database technologies are built.

INSTALLING THE EXAMPLE FILES

The code files for use with this book are contained in a Setup application. This application is on the CD-ROM that accompanies this book. To install the files on your computer, launch the file Setup.exe by double-clicking it in Windows Explorer. Note that this setup application doesn't install any libraries, change your system configuration, or overwrite any files. It simply installs the code examples used in the book, as well as the large example database used in the examples.

The Setup application installs the files on any drive and directory you want; however, if you choose the default directory (c:\vbdb), your file locations will always be in synch with the examples in the book. If you do something to alter or delete the files, you can always re-install them by running the Setup application again.

INSTALLING THE SOFTWARE

As with the first edition of this book, we've included a number of trial editions of software you might find useful. The following software is included on the CD-ROM:

> VideoSoft VSREPORTS 1.1 (Chapter 4)
>
> VideoSoft VSVIEW 3.0 (Chapter 4)
>
> Apex TrueDB Grid Pro(Chapter 13)
>
> VideoSoft VSFLEX 4.0 (Chapter 14)
>
> Sheridan DataWidgets 3.11 (Chapter 15)
>
> Winzip
>
> Microsoft Internet Explorer 4.0 SP-1
>
> Aivosto Oy Project Analyzer
>
> Aivosto Oy DBLock
>
> Aivosto Oy DB to VB Wizard
>
> Gridlinx VB DocuMentor
>
> Gridlinx VB Builder
>
> 4Developers COM Explorer
>
> Spectrum Access Developer Utilities

These are trial versions of the software. Some of them are time-limited, and others display a screen encouraging you to register them. To register them, contact the appropriate vendor.

All of these trials have their own installation procedures. They are contained in their own subdirectories of the `\3rdParty` directory on the book's CD-ROM.

CONTACTING THE AUTHOR

I love to hear from my readers with comments, questions, and suggestions. If you have something you'd like to share, please let me know via email at `jeffreyp@sirius.com`. I may not be able to get back to you right away, but I do read every email I get. (What choice do I have?)

I wanted to extend a special thanks to everyone who sent me email with questions and compliments from the first edition of the book. Your contributions made this edition a better book.

This book has a Web site located at `http://www.redblazer.com/vbdb/`. For the first edition of the book, I posted supplemental articles with procedures and code examples that came out after the book went to press. I'll do the same for this edition, so be sure to check the site regularly.

This edition of this book was written in the summer and fall of 1998 in San Francisco, California; Paducah, Kentucky; Scottsdale, Arizona; London, England; Richardson, Texas; Madison, Wisconsin; and Austin, Texas.

Thanks for picking up this book. I hope you find it useful!

Jeffrey

Database Basics

WHAT IS A DATABASE?

USING THE DATA VIEW WINDOW

CREATING A DATA ENVIRONMENT DESIGNER

CREATING A USER INTERFACE USING A
DATA CONTROL

A database lies at the core of many business software applications. Databases are prevalent in the world of business because they permit centralized access to information in a way that's consistent, efficient, and relatively easy to set up and maintain. This chapter covers the basics involved in setting up and maintaining a database for a business, including what a database is, why databases are useful, and how you can use databases to create business solutions.

If you've used Visual Basic (VB) before or done any database programming, you might find this chapter to be rather basic; however, it will bring you up to speed on some jargon terms that can vary from one database system to another.

Although database concepts tend to be the same from one database system to another, things tend to have their own names from one vendor implementation to the next. What's referred to as one thing in one vendor's system is called something completely different in another. For example, many client/server programmers refer to queries stored in the database as views; Visual Basic and Access programmers refer to them as queries or QueryDefs. The two are basically the same thing.

If you're upgrading to Visual Basic 6 from a previous version—particularly if you're coming from Visual Basic 3—you need to know several new things about database programming using Visual Basic. Visual Basic includes the latest version of the Jet database engine (which Visual Basic shares with Microsoft Access). This version of Jet includes several new additions to the database engine, which are introduced in this chapter and referred to throughout the rest of this book. Also, the addition of ActiveX Data Objects (ADO), as well as a number of ADO-related tools in the development environment, represent major changes for VB database developers. If you're familiar with database development in 32-bit Visual Basic, you might want to jump ahead to Chapter 10, "ActiveX Data Objects," for information on what's new in VB6.

WHAT IS A DATABASE?

A *database* is a repository of information. While there are several different types of databases, this book is primarily concerned with *relational databases*, the most commonly used type of database in the world today. A relational database:

▶ Stores data in *tables*, which are in turn composed of *rows*, also known as *records*, and *columns*, also known as *fields*

▶ Enables you to retrieve (or *query*) subsets of data from tables

▶ Enables you to connect (or *join*) tables together for the purpose of retrieving related records stored in different tables

WHAT IS A DATABASE ENGINE?

The basic functions of a database are provided by a *database engine*, a software system that manages how data is stored and retrieved.

One database engine covered in this book is called Microsoft Jet. Jet isn't a commercial product; rather, it is a subsystem used by several Microsoft products. Microsoft first included this engine with Visual Basic 3 and Microsoft Access 1; it has been revised and expanded since its introduction. The version of Jet covered in this book is Jet 3.51, which ships with both Microsoft Visual Basic and Microsoft Access.

> **Note:** There are many other database engines besides Jet, but because Visual Basic supports Jet natively, this book focuses much of its attention on that engine. Additionally, Jet can support other database engines as if they were Microsoft Access-style databases, so much of the discussion of Jet databases pertains to other database engines as well. Chapter 5, "Getting Started with SQL Server," discusses a completely different database engine: that of Microsoft SQL Server 6.5.

Business Case 1.1: Introducing Jones Novelties Incorporated   Many computer books consist of long laundry lists of software features with hastily scribbled explanations of how they work. If you're lucky, the discussion of software includes some kind of discussion that relates the software to the real world.

However, the mission of this book is to present the software in terms of business solutions. Accordingly, each chapter contains several business cases, in which a fictional company pursues the elusive goal of office automation in the face of real-world business problems.

The business cases in this book follow the merry exploits of Jones Novelties Incorporated, a small business just breaking into the retail souvenir, novelty, and party-tricks business.

The company's CEO, Brad Jones, recognizes that for the business to succeed it must automate large parts of the company's transactions. Jones must implement customer contacts, inventory, and billing systems in a way that is both tailored to the business and flexible enough to endure change over time.

Brad recognizes that the company will rise or fall on the basis of its access to information, so he decides to use a relational database system to manage the company's information. The design and functionality of that database is the focus of the rest of this chapter.

TABLES AND FIELDS

Databases are composed of *tables*, which represent broad categories of data. If you were creating a database to handle the accounts for a business, for example, you might create one table for customers, another for invoices, and another for employees. Tables have a predefined structure; they contain data that fits into this structure.

Tables, in turn, contain records, which are individual pieces of data within the broad category they represent.

Records, in turn, contain fields. A field represents a subdivision of data in a record. A record that represents an entry in an address book, for example, might consist of fields for first and last name, address, city, state, ZIP code, and telephone number.

You can use Visual Basic code to refer to and manipulate databases, tables, records, and fields.

Designing Your Database   To create a database, you must first determine what information it will keep track of. You then design the database, creating tables composed of fields that define the types of data you'll store. After you create this database structure, the database can store data in the form of records. You can't add data to a database that has no table or field definitions, because the database has nowhere to store the data. So the design of the database is crucial, particularly because it can be difficult to change the design of a database once you've implemented it.

This book represents tables in a standard format, with the table's name at the top of the diagram and the list of field names beneath, as follows:

tblMyTable
ID
FirstName
LastName
...

The ellipsis (…) in the last field indicates that this table has one or more fields that the book is omitting for the sake of brevity.

If you're new to the world of database programming, but you have used other computer applications before, you might be surprised that a database application makes you go through so much trouble before you can even start entering data. A word-processing application, for example, just enables you to type; the details of how the file is saved is the bailiwick of the application itself. The reason for designing databases ahead of time is efficiency. If a computer application knows exactly how much and what kinds of data to store, it can store and retrieve them in an optimal manner. As you'll learn after you create your first 100,000-record multiuser database, speed is of paramount importance in the database world. Anything you can do to make the process of adding and retrieving information from the database quicker is worthwhile.

In addition to efficiency, another guiding principle behind database table design is to put fields related to the same category of data in the same table. All the customer records go in a Customer table, the orders that those customers place should go in an Orders table, and so forth.

Just because these sets of data go into different tables doesn't mean you can't use them together; quite the contrary. When the data you need is spread across two or more tables in a relational database, you can access that data by using a relationship. This book discusses relationships later; for now, we'll just focus on the table design.

Business Case 1.2: Designing Tables and Relationships Brad Jones has determined that Jones Novelties requires a way to store information about customers. He's pretty sure that most of his business will be repeat business, so he wants to be able to contact customers to send them catalogs twice a year.

So Brad scribbles a basic database schema on a cocktail napkin. "Here's what the business needs to keep track of," he says:

▶ The customer's name, address, city, state, ZIP code, and phone number

▶ The customer's region of the country (Northwest, Southwest, Midwest, Northeast, South, or Southeast)

▶ The date of the customer's last purchase

Brad figures that he should easily fit all this information in a single table and keep the database nice and simple.

Brad's intrepid team of database developers tell him that might be possible, but that he would end up with a database that is inefficient, disorganized, and extremely inflexible.

The information that Brad wants to include doesn't all directly map to database fields. For example, because the region is a function of a person's state of residence, it doesn't make sense to have a State field and a Region field in the same table. Doing so would mean that a data-entry person would have to enter similar information on a customer twice. Instead, it would make much more sense for the database to store a State field in the Customer table and store information pertaining to regions in a Region table. If the Region table always knows which states map to which regions, the data-entry people don't have to enter a region for each customer. Instead, they will just enter the state, and the Customer table can work with the Region table to determine the customer's region.

Similarly, splitting up the Name field into FirstName and LastName fields will make it easier to sort on those fields once data has been entered into them. This aspect of the design might seem trivial when you consider it, but it's surprising how many database designs don't take this kind of thing into consideration — and it's awfully hard to recover from this design flaw once it makes its way into your database.

So Brad and his intrepid team determine that Jones Novelties' customers should be stored in a table, called tblCustomer, that contains the following fields:

tblCustomer
ID
FirstName
LastName
Company
Address
City
State
Zip
Phone
Fax
Email

Data pertaining to the customer's region of the country should be stored in a table called tblRegion. This table has the following fields:

tblRegion
State
RegionName

There is a relationship between the two tables through the State field. Note that this field exists in both tables. The relationship between the Region table and the Customer table is a one-to-many relationship; for each record in tblRegion there can be none, one or many matching records in tblCustomer. (The sections on relationships later in this chapter discuss in more detail how to take advantage of such a relationship when retrieving records.)

Notice how the designer of the database named the tables and fields in her preliminary table designs. First, she named each table with the prefix "tbl." This enables her to distinguish, at a glance, that this is a table rather than another type of database object that can store records. Next, notice that each field name consists of full words (instead of abbreviations) and doesn't contain spaces or other special characters such as underscores.

Although the Microsoft Access database engine enables you to name database objects with spaces, underscores, and other nonalphanumeric characters, it's a good idea to eschew their use, because using them makes it difficult to remember the exact spelling of the field name later. (You won't have to remember whether the field is named FirstName or FIRST_NAME, for example.) Although this guideline seems like a trivial distinction now, when you start writing code against a database consisting of 50 tables and 300 fields, you'll appreciate having named things consistently the first time.

One last thing is missing from Brad's wish list: the answer to the question, "When did this customer last purchase something from us?" The database developer decides that this information can be determined from date values in the table that stores data pertaining to customers' orders. This table has the following layout:

tblOrder
ID
CustomerID
OrderDate
ItemID
Amount

In this table, the ID field uniquely identifies each order. The CustomerID field, on the other hand, connects an order with a customer. To attach an order to a customer, the customer's ID is copied into the Order table's CustomerID field. That way, it's easy to look up all the orders for a particular customer (as we'll demonstrate later).

WHAT IS A RECORDSET?

Once you have the ability to create tables, you'll need a way to manipulate them. Manipulating tables involves entering and retrieving data from tables, as well as inspecting and modifying the structure of tables. To manipulate the structure of a table, you use data-definition commands (covered in Chapter 2, "Queries") or a *TableDef object* (introduced in Chapter 3, "Data Access Objects"). To manipulate the data in a table, you use a recordset.

A *recordset* is a data construct that typically represents a subset of records retrieved from the database. It is conceptually similar to a table, but includes some important distinctive properties of its own.

Recordsets are represented as objects, conceptually similar to the user-interface objects (such as command buttons and text boxes) that you might have worked with in Visual Basic in the past. Just like other types of Visual Basic objects, recordset objects have their own properties and methods.

> **For more information:** You can write code to create and use recordsets in any of three data access libraries—Data Access Objects (DAO), Remote Data Objects (RDO), and ActiveX Data Objects (ADO). For more on DAO, see Chapter 3. For information on RDO, see Chapter 6, "Open Database Connectivity and Remote Data Objects." To learn about ADO, see Chapter 10.

DATA TYPES

If you've programmed in virtually any language before, you're probably accustomed to the use of data types. Visual Basic is a weakly typed language, which (for the purposes of this discussion) means that you aren't usually required to declare the data types of the variables you work with, as you would have to do in a strongly typed language. If you choose not to type your variables explicitly, they simply default to the Variant data type, which is an easy (although inefficient) method to use.

Here's an example of weakly typed Visual Basic code that does not declare variable types, thus allowing the data types to revert to their default:

```
Private Function MySquareLoop()

For x = 1 To 10000
    TheValue = TheValue + (x ^ 2)
Next x

MySquareLoop = TheValue

End Function
```

Visual Basic gives you the option of strongly typing the variables in your code. Here's a revised version of the MySquareLoop function that declares all its variable types:

```
Option Explicit
```

```
Private Function NewSquareLoop() As Single

Dim x As Integer, TheValue As Single

For x = 1 To 10000
    TheValue = TheValue + (x ^ 2)
Next x

NewSquareLoop = TheValue

End Function
```

There's not much difference between the first and second versions of this function, except that NewSquareLoop runs about 50 percent faster than MySquareLoop. That's the whole point of declaring your variable types: Strongly typed data executes much more quickly, particularly in situations where you have to perform repetitive actions on data.

The same is true for databases. When you design your tables, one of the steps in setting up the fields is to declare the type of each field, which enables the database engine to save and retrieve data much more efficiently. The only difference between data typing in conventional Visual Basic programming and data typing in database programming is that you must strongly type the database fields you create.

Visual Basic's native database format, known as Jet, provides 21 different types of data. Table 1.1 lists the data types available to you in a Visual Basic database application.

Table 1.1 Data Types Available in Visual Basic Databases	
Data Type	**Description**
Binary	Used to store large chunks of data such as graphics and digitized sound files.
Boolean	A true or false value.
Byte	A single-byte integer value from 0 to 255.
Currency	A numeric field that has special properties to store monetary values accurately.
Date/Time	An eight-byte value representing a date or time from January 1, 100 to December 31, 9999.

continues

Table 1.1 Data Types Available in Visual Basic Databases (Continued)	
Data Type	**Description**
Double	An eight-byte, double-precision numeric data type.
GUID	A 128-byte number, also called a globally unique identifier. You can use this number to identify a record uniquely; this number is typically used in replication (see Chapter 9, "Multiuser Jet Databases").
Integer	A two-byte whole number from –32,768 to 32,767.
Long	A four-byte whole number from –2,147,483,648 to 2,147,483,647. You can set this field to be an automatically incrementing field.
Long Binary	A large-value field that can store binary data structures such as images or files.
(OLE Object)	OLE Objects embedded in your database can be up to 1 gigabyte.
Memo	A large-value field that can store up to 65,535 characters. You do not need to declare the length of this field in advance.
Single type.	A four-byte, single-precision numeric data
Text	A fixed-length data type, which requires that you declare the size of the field when you declare its data type. Text fields can be from 1 to 255 characters long.
VarBinary	A piece of variable binary data (used with ODBCDirect).

There is not a one-to-one correspondence between Visual Basic's variable data types and database field data types. For example, you cannot set a database field to a user-defined type or a Visual Basic–style Object variable. Also, if you use Microsoft Access to create databases for use with your VB applications, note that some data types that are usable in your VB application don't appear in the Microsoft Access table designer. This is because Visual Basic supports programming databases other than those created in Microsoft Access.

CREATING A DATABASE SCHEMA

Although creating a list of tables and fields is a good way to nail down the structure of the database, you may also want a way to look at the tables and fields in a graphical format. Then you not only can see which tables and fields are available to you, but also how they relate to each other. To do this, you create a *schema*.

A schema is a road map to your database. The schema diagrams all the tables, fields, and relationships in your database. It's important to include a database schema as a part of your software design process because it gives you a quick way to see what's going on in your database.

Schemas are important long after the database design process is complete. You'll need the schema to perform multitable queries on the data. A good graphical schema answers such questions as, "Which tables do I need to join together to list all the orders greater than $50.00 that came in from customers in Minnesota in the last 24 hours?"

> **For more information:** For more on how to create queries based on more than one table, see Chapter 2.

There is no one official way to create a database schema, although there are many tools you can use to create them. The drawing tool Visio is flexible, fast, and easy to use. Furthermore, it integrates well with other Windows applications, particularly Microsoft Office.

> **For more information:** The section of this chapter that covers Visio is intended to show how to use a drawing program to document a database. But you can use Visio as a development tool as well. With Visio Professional you can design databases graphically. The product has the ability to take your graphical design and actually create the database for you. Visio Professional can also document existing databases, essentially reverse-engineering them and generating a graphical schema—even if you didn't use Visio to design the database.

> You can learn more about the Visio family of drawing tools at the Visio Web site, located at `http://www.visio.com`.

You're not limited to using Visio when you're creating a graphical database schema. You can use whatever drawing tool feels comfortable. Microsoft Windows Paint is a viable option, as are Microsoft Word's drawing features.

Business Case 1.3: Using Visio to Create a Schema   Now that you have your table and field design in place, it's time to create a graphical representation of the database tables, fields, and relationships. This is not the same as creating the tables themselves; for right now, you're
just drawing a diagram of how the tables will relate to each other after they're created. To do so, follow these steps:

1. Start Visio. The New dialog box appears.

2. Select Basic Template, then click OK. The basic Visio drawing window appears, as shown in Figure 1.1.

Figure 1.1
In the basic Visio drawing window, the drawing template appears on the left and your drawing area on the right; you create drawings by dragging items from the template onto your drawing area.

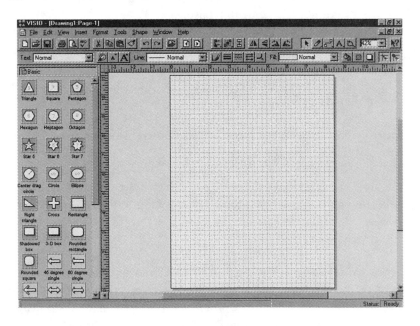

3. In the drawing template, click the Rectangle shape and drag it into the drawing area. A rectangle shape appears, as shown in Figure 1.2.

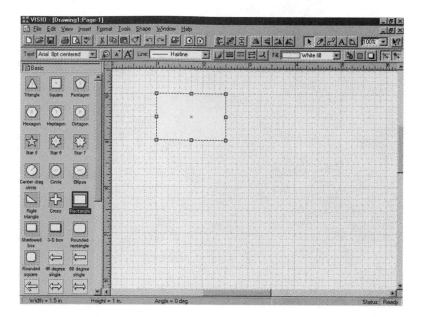

Figure 1.2
*You create a rec-
tangle in the
drawing area by
click-dragging.*

4. Click-drag on the rectangle's handles so it is 1.5 inches wide and 0.25 inches tall.

5. Type the name of the table, **tblCustomer**, into the rectangle.

6. From the template, drag another rectangle into the drawing area.

7. Type the names of the fields (shown in Figure 1.3) for this table into the rectangle. Because you still have the Text tool selected, you should be able to begin typing immediately.

8. When you're done typing field names, use the pointer tool to resize the rectangle's handles so it is large enough to display all the fields clearly. When you're done, the graphic should look like Figure 1.3.

Now that you've created your first table drawing, you can draw additional tables to display the relationships between them. The easiest way to do this is to duplicate the graphic you already have. To do so, follow these steps:

1. From the Visio menu, choose Edit, Select All. Then choose Edit, Duplicate.

2. A duplicate tblCustomer appears. Using the mouse, click-drag the duplicate out of the way so it doesn't overlap the original tblCustomer.

3. Click the duplicate field's name rectangle. Using the Text tool, change the field's name to tblOrder.

Figure 1.3
*Here is how a com-
pleted table
design using Visio
rectangles looks.*

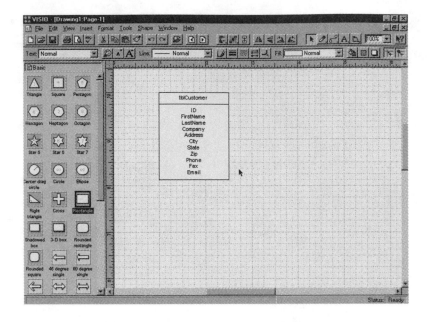

4. Click tblOrder's field rectangle. Using the Text tool, change the field's list of fields so it matches your design.

5. Click-drag the bottom handle of the field rectangle to make it shorter. The drawing should look like Figure 1.4.

Figure 1.4
*Two tables are
now in the Visio
database schema.*

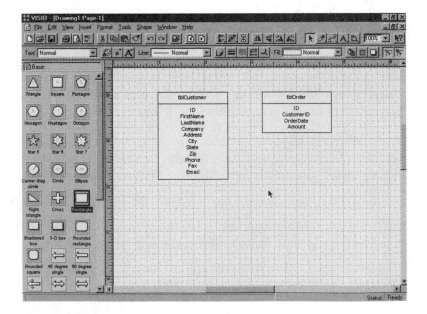

Now that your schema displays both tables in your design, you need to display the relationships between them. The relationship indicates that for a record that exists in one table, there can be one or many related records in another table. Each table in a relationship must share a field in common with the other tables it's related to. A real-world analogy for this process is, for example, when you put a green dot on all the file folders that are supposed to be filed in the green file drawer. By storing a matching piece of information on both the file folder and the file drawer, you ensure that nothing gets misplaced. The same applies to records in a database relationship.

We'll discuss more about relationships later in this chapter; for now, create the relationship in your schema by following these steps:

1. In the Visio toolbar, click the Line tool.

2. Click-drag from the ID field in tblCustomer to the CustomerID field in tblOrder. If you click-drag more than once, you can create a line that bends in several places.

Your schema should now look like Figure 1.5.

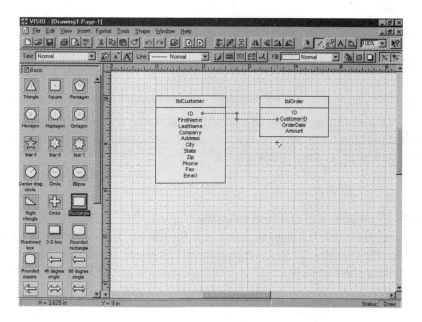

Figure 1.5
The schema now displays a relationship between the two tables..

Note: This is a very simple method of creating a database schema; there are more involved methodologies that might suit your purposes better. In fact, the professional edition of Visio has a number of specialized templates for entity relationship diagrams, which are a more detailed kind of schema diagramming system than the one used in this book.

Often, creating a graphical database schema will reveal flaws in your design. For example, the database design that you have so far enables the business to store information on customers and orders. But orders consist of items taken from the company's inventory and sold to the customer. If an order consists of more than one item, there's no way to store it in the database; you would have to create separate orders for each item.

The solution to this problem is to create a new table for line items associated with an order. The design of this new table looks like the following:

tblOrderLineItem
ID
OrderID
ItemID
Quantity
Cost

There is a one-to-many relationship, then, between the tblOrder table and the tblOrderLineItem table. This can be extended to encompass additional tables and relationships, as shown in Figure 1.6.

Code Example: You can find this drawing Visio file in the directory `\vbdb\code\01-Basics\schema.vsd`. For information on how to install the sample files on the CD that accompanies this book, see the section "Installing the Example Files" in the introduction at the beginning of this book.

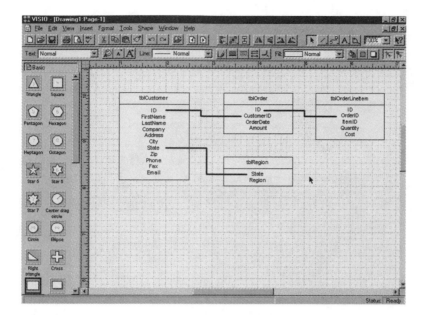

Figure 1.6
*The evolved data-
base schema shows
relationships
among four tables
in the database.*

Displayed in Microsoft Access, the data entered into this one-to-many relationship looks like that shown in Figure 1.7.

For more information: Don't confuse the process of developing a database schema with a software design methodology. Most successful software development organizations have a design methodology in place that
dictates such things as what business problems the software is supposed to
solve, how the software application will look, and how it will be built. You
should consider all these issues before you design the database.

If you're looking for more information on the design process, particularly as
it relates to the world of Visual Basic programming, check out Deborah
Kurata's *Doing Objects in Visual Basic 6* (Sams, 1999). In addition to serving
as a great introduction to the object-oriented programming techniques discussed in Chapter 7 of this book, "Database Access with Classes," Kurata's
book will give you some great ideas about developing software in Visual
Basic in general.

Figure 1.7
When data is entered in a one-to-many relationship, for every ID in the Orders table, there's one (or many) corresponding OrderID field in the OrderLineItem table.

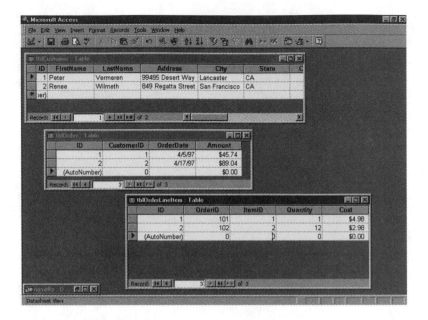

CREATING A DATABASE USING VISUAL BASIC

After creating your schema and refining your design, it's time to create the actual database. To create a Jet database using Visual Basic, you can use a utility called Visual Data Manager. This utility, which comes with the Professional and Enterprise Editions of Visual Basic, enables you to create databases that are compatible with Microsoft Access.

Note: Because Visual Basic and Microsoft Access 97 share the same database engine, you can use either Visual Basic or Access to create a database; the resulting database files created with the two systems are essentially identical. So if you're more comfortable working with Access, you can feel free to use it to create databases. For information on how to create databases using Microsoft Access, see the "Creating a Database Using Microsoft Access" section later in this chapter.

To launch the Visual Data Manager, follow these steps:

1. From the Visual Basic menu, choose Add-Ins, Visual Data Manager. The Visual Data Manager window appears.

2. From the Visual Data Manager menu, choose File, New. From the submenu, choose Microsoft Access, Version 7.0 MDB. A file dialog box appears.

Note: A "Version 2.0 MDB" is the version of Jet compatible with 16-bit versions of Access and Visual Basic.

3. Select the folder in which you want to save the new database, then type its name. (For the purposes of subsequent demonstrations in this book, you might want to call the database novelty.mdb.)

4. Click the Save button. The new database is created, and the Visual Data Manager displays several windows that enable you to work with the database, as shown in Figure 1.8.

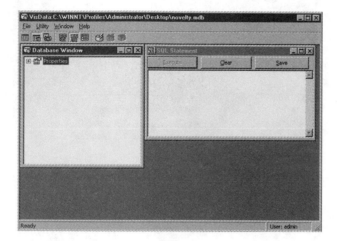

Figure 1.8
Visual Database Manager has just given birth to a brand new database.

Using the Database Window   Visual Data Manager's Database window stores all the components of the database. In this window, you can view properties, inspect the tables and other elements, and add new components of the database.

To view the properties of the database you just created, click the plus sign to the left of the Properties item in the outline. The outline then expands, as shown in Figure 1.9.

Creating a Table   One idiosyncratic thing about the Visual Data Manager is that it doesn't give you an obvious way to create a new table in the database you've created. This is because the elements that appear in Visual Data Manager's Database window are sensitive to right-clicks. But once you get used to right-clicking, creating a new table is easy. For example, to create a new table, follow these steps:

1. In Visual Data Manager's Database window, right-click Properties. The window's context menu appears.

2. Select New Table. The Table Structure dialog box appears, as shown in Figure 1.10.

Figure 1.9
Visual Data Manager's expanded outline shows default database properties.

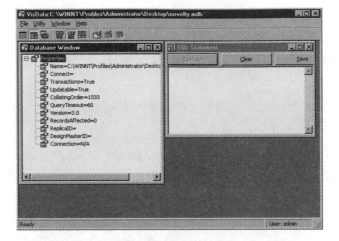

Figure 1.10
Visual Data Manager's Table Structure dialog box enables you to create the structure of a new table.

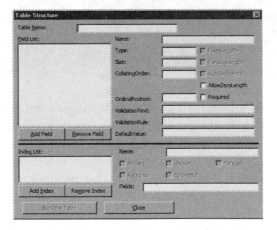

In the Table Structure dialog box, you can create the structure of a table, specifying fields, data types, and indexes. For this example, you'll create the structure of a table to store customers. To do so, follow these steps:

1. In the Table Name box, type **tblCustomer**.

2. Click the Add Field button. The Add Field dialog appears, as shown in Figure 1.11.

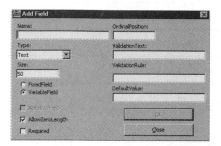

Figure 1.11
The Add Field dialog box enables you to add a field to a table created with Visual Data Manager's Table Structure dialog box.

3. In the Name text box, type **FirstName**. This will be the name of the field you're creating in the customer table.

4. In the Size text box, type **25**. This specifies that first names can be up to, but not more than, 25 characters long, but also means that the database will store names more efficiently.

5. Choose Fixed Field to indicate that this is not a variable-length field, then click OK. (Note that it's difficult to make a change to a field once you've created it, so make sure you've got everything set correctly.) The field is added to the database structure. The text boxes in the Add Field dialog box are cleared, permitting you to immediately add another field.

6. You can now continue to add additional fields to your table structure. Using the Add Field dialog box, add fields to tblCustomer so you wind up with these fields:

Name	Data Type	Size	Fixed
FirstName	Text	25	Yes
ID	Long, AutoIncr Field = True	N/A	N/A
LastName	Text	45	Yes

continues

Name	Data Type	Size	Fixed
Company	Text	100	Yes
Address	Text	100	Yes
City	Text	100	Yes
State	Text	2	Yes
Zip	Text	9	Yes
Phone	Text	25	Yes
Fax	Text	25	Yes
Email	Text	255	Yes

Note: You can't specify a size or a fixed value for the ID field because these attributes only apply to Text fields.

7. Be sure to check the AutoIncrField box when creating the ID field to ensure that every customer you create will have a unique identification number. Because the database engine increments the number in the field automatically, your database application won't have to generate the unique number.

8. When you're done entering fields, click the Close button. The Table Structure dialog box should now look like Figure 1.12.

Figure 1.12
The table structure of tblCustomer in the Table Structure dialog box looks like this after you've added fields.

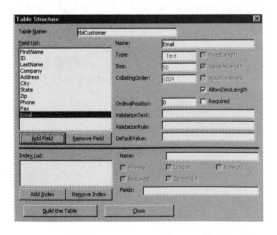

Designating Indexes and the Primary Key Now that you've created the basic table, one thing remains: You must designate *indexes*. An index is an attribute you can assign to a field to make it easier for the database engine to retrieve data based on information stored in that field. For example, in your database that tracks customers, your application will probably tend to look up customers by last name, ZIP Code, and individual ID number. So it makes sense to create indexes on each of these fields to make the process of retrieving records based on these fields faster.

Once you've realized the benefits of indexes in database design, you might ask yourself the following question: If indexes make lookups faster, why not place an index on every field in every table? The answer is that there's a diminishing return with indexes. Indexes make your database physically larger, so if you have too many indexes, they will consume a ton of memory and disk space, actually making your computer run more slowly. And this obviously nullifies the benefit of having an index in the first place. There's no hard and fast rule for how many indexes each table should have, but in general, you should create indexes based on the fields that you envision will be used in queries most often. (For more information on how to use the information in a field as a query criterion to retrieve sets of records, see Chapter 2.)

A primary key is a special type of index. A field that is designated as a table's primary key serves to uniquely identify the record. So, unlike other types of indexes, no two records in the same table may have the same value in its primary key field. Also, when you designate a field as a primary key, no record may contain an empty, or null, value in that field. When you designate a field in a table as that table's primary key, you can create relationships between that table and other tables in your database.

Every table you create should at least have a primary key, and it should also be indexed on those fields you expect will be queried the most. In the case of the tblCustomer table, as with many database tables, the primary key will be the ID field. The secondary indexes will be the LastName and FirstName fields.

To create indexes and primary keys, follow these steps:

1. In the Table Structure dialog box, click the Add Index button. The Add Index dialog box appears, as shown in Figure 1.13. First, you'll create a primary key for the table.

2. In the Name text box, type **PrimaryKey**.

3. Double-click the ID field in the list of available fields. ID is added to the list of indexed fields. The check boxes Primary and Unique should already be checked by default.

4. Click OK. The text boxes clear and the primary key is added to the table design. Note that indexes have names just like fields do (although if you're accustomed to using Microsoft Access, you may not know this, since Access hides index names from you in its user interface). It's useful to have access to the name of a field for certain programming purposes; we'll revisit this topic in Chapter 3.

Figure 1.13
Use the Add Index dialog box to add an index to a field in the table you're creating.

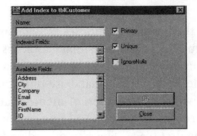

Now you can create two more indexes, for the FirstName and LastName fields. To do so, follow these steps:

1. Type the index name **FirstNameIndex** in the Name text box.

2. Double-click the FirstName field in the list of available fields. FirstName is added to the list of indexed fields.

3. *Uncheck* the check boxes for Primary and Unique, then click OK.

   Caution: If you leave the Unique check box selected, you won't be able to add two people with the same first name to the database.

4. Repeat the process for the LastName field, creating an index called LastNameIndex.

5. Click the Close button. You return to the Table Structure dialog box, which now looks like Figure 1.14.

6. To create the table, click the Build the Table button. The table is created and added to the Visual Data Manager Database window, as shown in Figure 1.15.

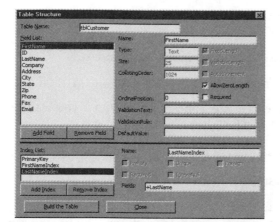

Figure 1.14
*The Table
Structure dialog
box looks like this
after all the fields
and indexes have
been designated.*

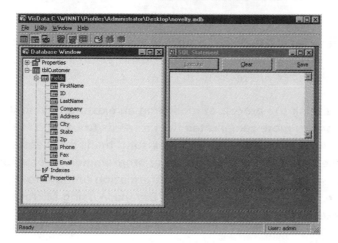

Figure 1.15
*A table is added
to the Database
window, and you
can click the plus
sign to expose
subitems in the
outline.*

Changing Existing Field Properties The Visual Data Manager makes it rather difficult to change most of the important properties of a table (unlike Microsoft Access, which enables you to change almost any part of a table's structure at any time). Generally, when you want to change the properties of a field using the Visual Data Manager, you must delete the field and re-create it.

Suppose that you want to change the length of the LastName field. To do so, follow these steps:

1. In Visual Data Manager's Database window, right-click tblCustomer.

2. From the context menu, choose Design. The Table Structure dialog box appears.

To remove the LastName field, you must first remove its index. To do so, follow these steps:

1. Click the LastNameIndex in the list of indexes.

2. Click the Remove Index button.

3. When the message box appears asking you if you want to remove the index, click Yes. The index is removed.

Now you can remove the field. To do so, follow these steps:

1. Click the LastName field in the list of fields.

2. Click the Remove Field button. When the message box appears asking you if you want to remove the field, click Yes. The field is removed from the table.

Now, finally, you can make the change to the field by adding it again to the table, this time with a field length of 50. Don't forget to add the field's index back to the table after you re-create it.

> **Tip:** If you think the process of modifying an existing field in Visual Data Manager seems more complicated than it needs to be, you're right. In Microsoft Access, making changes to existing fields is far easier. For this reason, the astute Visual Basic database programmer keeps a copy of Access lying around, just in case. For information on how to design a database using Access, see the "Creating a Database Using Microsoft Access" section later in this chapter.

Creating an Interface Using Visual Data Manager   One advantage that Visual Data Manager has over Microsoft Access is its ability to create Visual Basic *forms* based on the data structures you create. If you've never used Visual Basic before, a form is the basis of the user interface of your application—just about everything in the way of a user-interface is based in some way on the Visual Basic form, and on the user-interface controls that are placed on a form.

> **Note:** Although the Visual Data Manager's form-building capabilities are adequate to get started, in time you'll want to build your own interfaces with VB's powerful visual design facilities and third-party add-in tools. Chapters 12 through 15 of this book cover building a customized data access user interface in more depth.

Suppose you're happy with the design of tblCustomer and you want to add a Visual Basic form to your project based on the table design. To do so, follow these steps:

1. From the Visual Data Manager menu, choose Utility, Data Form Designer. The Data Form Designer dialog box appears.

2. In the Form Name text box, type **Customer**.

3. In the RecordSource combo box, choose tblCustomer. The Data Form Designer fills in the Available Fields list with the fields found in tblCustomer, as shown in Figure 1.16.

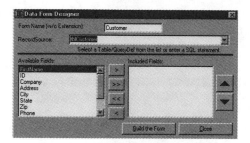

Figure 1.16
The Data Form Designer now displays a list of the fields available in your table.

4. Click the right-arrow button until all the available fields *except for ID* are added to the form. (There's no point in adding the ID field to a data-entry form because the user cannot edit the ID field.)

5. Click the fields and the up- and down-arrow buttons so that you arrange the fields in a way that makes sense, as shown in Figure 1.17.

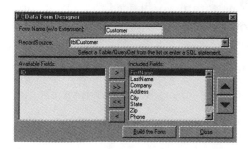

Figure 1.17
Fields have been added and arranged in the Data Form Designer.

6. Click the Build the Form button. The form is created in Visual Basic.

7. Click Close.

Next you'll want to exit the Visual Data Manager to see what your form looks like. But you might want to return later to add new elements to your database, or to make changes to what you've already done. To tell the Visual Data Manager that you want it to reopen your database the next time you return to it, follow these steps:

1. Choose Utility, Preferences. From the submenu, choose Open Last DataBase on Startup.

2. Exit the Visual Data Manager by choosing File, Exit. You are returned to Visual Basic; you should see a new form, called frmCustomer, as shown in Figure 1.18.

Figure 1.18
The new form created by the Data Form Designer has an interface for all the fields you selected, arranged in the order you selected them, and it also includes code that enables you to add and delete records.

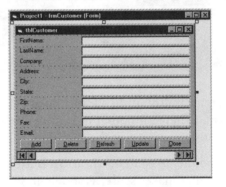

To work with this new form, you'll need to make it your project's startup form. To do so, follow these steps:

1. From Visual Basic's Project menu, select Project1 Properties. The Properties dialog box appears, as shown in Figure 1.19.

2. In the Startup Object combo box, select frmCustomer, then click OK.

3. From Visual Basic's Run menu, select Start. The application runs, displaying the data-entry interface in frmCustomer.

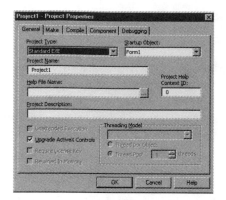

You can now enter data into the interface that Visual Basic has provided for you. To do so, follow these steps:

1. Click the Add button. You'll notice that the application gives you absolutely no visual feedback to indicate that anything has changed. However, rest assured that you are, in fact, now editing a new record.

2. Enter data in each text box in the form.

3. When you're done, click Update. The record is saved; the only visual feedback you get is that the data control displays "Record 1," as shown in Figure 1.20.

The basic data-entry interface created by the Data Form Designer gives you a sense of the code you must write to make a robust application using the Data control. Even though the Data control is supposed to be a "no-code" solution, if you need to extend its functionality (to perform such actions as lookups and deletion of records) the code can be non-intuitive to a beginner. We'll get to more information on this code, how it works, and how you can modify it to create a more full-featured application later.

CREATING A DATABASE USING MICROSOFT ACCESS

Microsoft Access has a much more sophisticated and easier-to-use interface for creating database objects. To demonstrate this, you'll use Access to create another table for your database. This table will track information pertaining to your business's inventory.

Note: This section assumes you're using Microsoft Access 97. If you have another version of Access, the instructions are basically the same; however, the database you create with Visual Basic's Visual Data Manager might not be compatible with the version of Access you're using.

To add a new Inventory table to your database using Microsoft Access, follow these steps:

1. Start Microsoft Access 97. The Access file dialog box appears.

2. Select More Files, then locate the database novelty.mdb that you created with the Visual Data Manager. (If you didn't use the Visual Data Manager to create the file in the previous section, you'll need to create a new database instead.) The Microsoft Access Database window appears, as shown in Figure 1.21.

Figure 1.21
The Microsoft Access Database window shows the existing table in the novelty database.

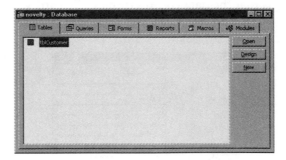

3. To create a new table, click the New button. The New Table dialog box appears. Select Design View and click OK. The Access table design window appears, as shown in Figure 1.22.

4. In the first row of the Field Name column, type the first field name, **ID**.

5. Press Tab to move to the next column.

6. Change the data type to AutoNumber. This creates a long integer field that automatically populates itself with a unique number each time you create a new record.

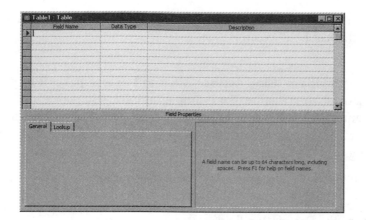

Figure 1.22
You're ready to create a new table in the Microsoft Access table design window.

7. To make this field the primary key of this table, choose Edit, Primary Key, or click the Primary Key button from the Access toolbar, as shown in Figure 1.23.

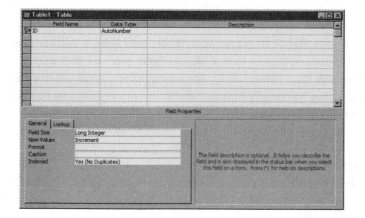

Figure 1.23
You can set a field's primary key in Access with a single click on a toolbar button.

8. Create the remaining fields in the table:

Field	Data Type
Product	Text (50 characters)
CatalogNumber	Text (50 characters)
WholesalePrice	Currency
RetailPrice	Currency
SupplierID	Number (Long Integer)
Description	Text (100 characters)

9. Close the table. Microsoft Access asks whether you want to save it. Save it with the name tblInventory.

Changing a Database Using Access   Microsoft Access makes it easy to change an existing database structure. For example, suppose you realize after creating the tblInventory table that your Description field needs to be larger than 100 characters. If you simply change its data type, Access takes care of converting any existing data to that new data type. To do so, follow these steps:

1. In the Access Database window, select tblInventory and click the Design button. The tblInventory table appears in Design view.

2. Change the Description field's data type to Memo.

3. Save the table by choosing File, Save. This command automatically converts the field to the new type.

4. Close the table.

Note: A Memo field can store much more text than a conventional text field. The disadvantage is that a Memo field can't be indexed, so it's inefficient to search on a Memo field. For more information on the data types available in the Microsoft Access/Jet database engine, see the "Data Types" section earlier in this chapter.

RELATIONSHIPS

A *relationship* is a way of formally defining how two tables relate to each other. When you define a relationship, you tell the database engine which two fields in two related tables are joined.

The two fields involved in a relationship are the primary key, introduced earlier in this chapter, and the foreign key. The foreign key is the key in the related table that stores a copy of the primary key of the main table.

For example, suppose you have tables for departments and employees. There is a one-to-many relationship between a department and a group of employees. Every department has its own ID, as does each employee. In order to denote which department an employee works in, however, you must make a copy of the department's ID in each employee's record. So, in order to identify each employee as a member of a department, the Employees table must have a field—possibly called DepartmentID—to store the ID of the department to which that employee belongs. The DepartmentID field in the Employees table is referred to as the foreign key of the Employees table, because it stores a copy of the primary key of the Departments table.

A relationship, then, tells the database engine which two tables are involved in the relationships and which foreign key is related to which primary key. The Access/Jet engine doesn't require that you explicitly declare relationships, but it's advantageous for you to do so because it simplifies the task of retrieving data based on records joined across two or more tables (discussed in more detail in Chapter 2).

In addition to matching related records in separate tables, you also define a relationship to take advantage of referential integrity, a property of a database engine that keeps data in a multitable database consistent. When referential integrity exists in a database, the database engine prevents you from removing a record when there are other records related to that record in the database.

After you define a relationship in your database, the definition of the relationship is stored until you remove it.

Note: You can't create a database relationship using the Visual Data Manager; however, you can create a relationship using either Microsoft Access or by writing code.

To see how to create a database relationship using Microsoft Access, see "Creating a Database Using Microsoft Access" earlier in this chapter. For more information on how to create relationships in a Jet database using Data Access Objects (DAO), see Chapter 3.

Using Referential Integrity to Maintain Consistency   When tables are linked through relationships, the data in each table must remain consistent with that in the linked tables. Referential integrity manages this task by keeping track of the relationships among tables and prohibiting certain types of operations on records.

For example, suppose that you have one table called tblCustomer and another table called tblOrder. The two tables are related through a common ID field, as shown in Figure 1.24.

Figure 1.24
The tblCustomer and tblOrder tables are related through the CustomerID field, and referential integrity prohibits the deletion of a customer that has related data in the tblOrder table.

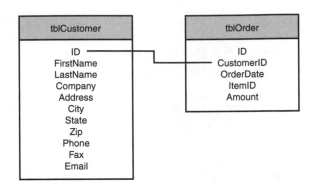

The premise here is that you create customers that are stored in tblCustomer, then create orders that are stored in tblOrder. But what happens if you run a process that deletes a customer who has outstanding orders stored in the order table? Or what if you create an order that doesn't have a valid CustomerID attached to it? An order without a CustomerID can't be shipped, because the shipping address is a function of the record in tblCustomer. When data in related tables suffers from this kind of problem, it is said to be in an inconsistent state.

Because it's so important that your database not become inconsistent, the Jet database engine provides a way for you to define formal relationships among tables. When you formally define a relationship between two tables, the database engine monitors the relationship and prohibits any operation that would violate referential integrity. Referential integrity works by generating errors whenever you perform an action that would leave data in an inconsistent state. For example, in a database with referential integrity activated, if you attempt to create an order that contains a customer ID for a customer who doesn't exist, you'll get an error and the order won't be created.

Creating a Relationship Using Microsoft Access   Microsoft Access enables you to define the relationships among tables. When you define a relationship, the database engine enforces referential integrity among the related tables.

Now that you have a database with two related tables, you can demonstrate how to set up a relationship between the tblCustomer and tblOrder tables. To do so, follow these steps:

1. Create a new table in the database called tblOrder. This table will be related to tblCustomer and should have the following fields and data types:

Field	Data Type
ID	LongInteger, AutoIncrement
CustomerID	LongInteger
OrderDate	Date/Time
Amount	Currency

2. In Microsoft Access, choose Tools, Relationships. The Show Table dialog box appears.

3. Double-click tblCustomer, double-click tblOrder, then click Close.

4. Click-drag between the ID field in the tblCustomer table and the CustomerID field in the tblOrder table. The Relationships dialog box appears, as shown in Figure 1.25.

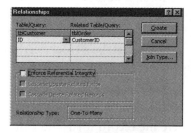

Figure 1.25
The Microsoft Access Relationships dialog box shows the relationship you have chosen.

5. Click the Enforce Referential Integrity check box. The Cascade Update and Cascade Delete check boxes become available.

6. Select the Cascade Update Related Fields and Cascade Delete Related Records check boxes.

7. Click Create. Access creates the relationship, as shown in Figure 1.26.

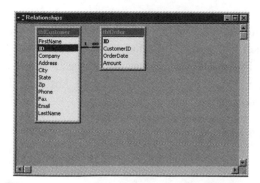

Figure 1.26
The relationship is successfully created in Access, and it's designed to look like a graphical schema (discussed earlier in this chapter).

To test how the relationship works, follow these steps:

1. Close and save the Relationship window.

2. Open the tblOrder table and attempt to enter a record for a customer who you know isn't in the tblCustomer table.

The database engine generates an error. Because this error is generated at the database engine level, the same kind of error is generated whether the referential integrity problem takes place in Access or in a Visual Basic application that utilizes this database.

Cascading Updates and Cascading Deletes   Cascading updates and cascading deletes are useful features of the Jet database engine. They cause the following things to happen in your database:

▶ With *cascading updates*, when you change a value in a table's primary key, the related data in the foreign keys related to that table change to reflect the change in the primary key. Therefore, if you change the ID of Halle's Hockey Mart in the tblCustomer table from 48 to 72, the CustomerID field of all the orders generated by Halle's Hockey Mart in the tblOrder table automatically change from 48 to 72 as well.

▶ With *cascading deletes*, when you delete a record in a table, all the records related to that record in related tables are automatically deleted as well. Therefore, if you delete the record for Halle's Hockey Mart in the tblCustomer table, all the orders in the tblOrder table for Halle's Hockey Mart are automatically deleted.

Note: You want to be cautious when setting up relationships that perform cascading updates and cascading deletes in your data designs. If you aren't careful, you could wind up deleting (or updating) more data than you expected.

Cascading updates and cascading deletes work only if you've established a relationship between two tables. If you always create tables with AutoNumber primary keys, you'll probably find cascading deletes more useful than cascading updates, because you can't change the value of an AutoNumber field (so there's no "update" to "cascade").

CREATING A DATABASE USING MORE EXOTIC TECHNIQUES

You can create a database structure entirely in code. You would want to do this in situations where your application needs to create or update data structures. Additionally, you may want to give users of your applications the ability to create their own data structures within the context of your existing data design.

There are two ways of creating Jet databases and database objects in Visual Basic: using Data Definition Language (DDL) commands and using DAO code.

For more information: For more on queries using Data Definition Language, see Chapter 2. For more on DAO, see Chapter 3.

NORMALIZATION

Normalization is a concept that is related to relationships. Basically, the principle of normalization dictates that your database tables will eliminate inconsistencies and minimize inefficiency.

Databases are described as being inconsistent when data in one table doesn't match data entered in another table. For example, if half of your staff thinks that Arkansas is in the Midwest and the other half thinks it's in the South, and if both factions of your staff handle their data entry accordingly, your database reports on how things are doing in the Midwest will be meaningless.

An inefficient database doesn't enable you to isolate the exact data you want. A database that stores all its data in one table might force you to slog through a slew of customer names, addresses, and contact history just to retrieve one person's current phone number. A fully normalized database, on the other hand, stores each piece of information in the database in its own table, and further identifies each piece of information uniquely by its own primary key. Normalized databases enable you to reference any piece of information in any table given that information's primary key.

You decide how to normalize a database when you design and initially set up a database. Usually, everything about your database application—from table design to query design, from the user interface to the behavior of reports—stems from the manner in which you've normalized your database.

Note: As a database developer, sometimes you'll come across databases that haven't been normalized for one reason or another. The lack of normalization might be intentional, or might be a result of inexperience or carelessness on the part of the original database designer. At any rate, if you choose to normalize an existing database, you should do so early in your development effort (because everything else you do in database development depends on the table structure of the database). Additionally, you will find *action queries* (discussed in Chapter 2) to be useful tools in getting a deficiently designed database in order. Action queries enable you to move fields from one table to another as well as add, update, and delete records from tables based on criteria you specify.

As an example of the normalization choices you make at the database design phase, consider the request made by Brad Jones in business case 1.2, "Designing Tables and Relationships." Brad's business needs a way to store the customer's state of residence, as well as the region of the country in which the customer lives. The novice database designer might decide to create one field for state of residence and another field for region of the country, like this:

tblCustomer
ID
FirstName
LastName
Address
Company
City
State
Zip
Phone
Fax
Email
Region

This structure might initially seem rational, but consider what would happen when someone tries to enter data into an application based on this table. The data-entry interface for tblCustomer would look like Figure 1.27.

Figure 1.27
The user interface for the non-normalized version of tblCustomer can lead to inconsistencies.

If you were entering data into this form, you'd have to get the normal customer information—name, address, and so forth—but then, after you'd already entered the customer's state, you'd have to do some thinking to determine the customer's region. Is Arkansas in the Midwest or the South? What about a resident of the U.S. Virgin Islands? You don't want to put these kinds of decisions in the hands of your data-entry people, no matter how capable they might be, because if you rely on the record-by-record decisions of human beings, your data will ultimately be inconsistent. And defeating inconsistency is one of the primary reasons for normalization.

Instead of forcing your data-entry people to make a decision each time they type in a new customer, you want to instead store information pertaining to regions in a separate table. You might call this table tblRegion, which would have the following design:

tblRegion
State
Region

The data in a table with this design would look like this:

State	Region
AK	North
AL	South
AR	South
	continues

State	Region
AZ	West
...	...

In this refined version of the database design, when you need to retrieve information about a region, you perform a two-table query with a join between the tblCustomer and tblRegion tables, with one supplying the customer's state and the other providing the region information based on that state. Joins match records in separate tables that have fields in common. See Chapter 2 for more information on how to do this.

Storing information pertaining to regions in a single table of its own has several advantages:

▶ If you decide to carve out a new region composed of an existing region, it is simple to alter a few records in the tblRegion table to reflect the change. Then you need to change only those few records in the tblRegion table, not the thousands of records that might exist in the tblCustomer table.

▶ Similarly, if you started doing business in regions other than the 50 states, it is easy to add a new region to accommodate changes in how your business is structured. Again, you need to add only a single record for each new area to the tblRegion table, and that record then becomes available immediately throughout your system.

▶ If you need to use the concept of regions again somewhere else in your database (to denote that a sales office located in a particular state served a particular region, for example), you could reuse the tblRegions table without modification.

In general, then, you should always plan on creating distinct tables for distinct categories of information. Devoting time to database design before you actually build the database will give you an idea as to which database tables you'll need and how they relate to each other. As a part of this process, you should map out the database schema, as discussed in the section "Creating a Database Schema" earlier in this chapter.

One-to-One Relationships Say your human resources database contains tables for employees and jobs. If you assign a single employee to a job, the relationship between employees and jobs is a *one-to-one relationship*, because for every employee in the database there is at most one job. One-to-one relationships are the easiest kind of relationships to understand and implement, because in such relationships, a table usually takes the place of a field in another table; the fields involved are easy to identify. However, a one-to-one relationship is not the most common relationship you find in most mature database applications. This is for two reasons:

▶ You can almost always express a one-to-one relationship without using two tables. You might do this to improve performance, although you lose the flexibility of storing related data in a separate table. In the previous example, instead of having separate employees and jobs tables, you could instead have all of the fields related to jobs stored in the employees table.

▶ Expressing a one-to-many relationship is nearly as easy as (and far more flexible than) expressing a one-to-one relationship, for reasons we'll go into in the next section.

One-to-Many Relationships   More common than a one-to-one relationship is a *one-to-many relationship*, in which each record in a table can have none, one, or many records in a related table.

For example, suppose that you decide to assign each customer to a specific salesperson. To do this, you'd need a table for salespeople with the following fields:

ID
FirstName
LastName
Department

Because each salesperson is responsible for many customers, you would say that a one-to-many relationship exists between salespeople and customers.

To implement this relationship in your database design, you must copy the primary key of the "one" side of the relationship to the table that stores the "many" side of the relationship. Figure 1.28 shows the tables that implement this design.

Figure 1.28
*The design of a
one-to-many rela-
tionship includes
the primary key of
the "one" side
table duplicated in
the related table
on the "many"
side.*

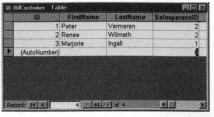

For more information: In a user-interface design, you'll commonly implement the process of copying the primary key of one table to the foreign
key of a related table with a list box or combo box. For more information
on how to implement this in your interface, see Chapter 12, "User-Interface
Controls."

Many-to-Many Relationships   A many-to-many relationship takes the one-to-
many relationship a step further. The classic example of a many-to-many relationship is the relationship between students and classes. Each student can have
multiple classes, and each class has multiple students. (Of course, it's also possible for a class to have one or no students, and it's possible for a student to have
one or no classes.)

To set up a many-to-many relationship, you must have three tables: the two
tables that store the actual data, and a third table, called a juncture table, that
stores the relationship between the two data tables. The juncture table usually
consists of nothing more than two foreign keys—one from each related table.

As an example of a multiple-to-multiple relationship, you can modify the
example in the previous section so the database can store multiple salespeople
per customer. Each salesperson can have multiple customers, and each customer
can have multiple salespeople. These tables would look like Figure 1.29.

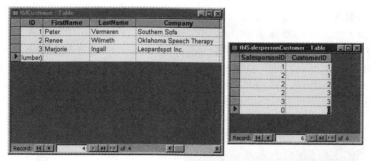

Figure 1.29
In this design of tables involved in a many-to-many relationship, tblSalespersonCustomer is the juncture table.

A user interface developed in Microsoft Access typically implements one-to-many or many-to-many relationships by using a subform. To a VB developer, an Access subform is like a form within a form; the main form displays the "one" side of a one-to-many relationship, while the subform displays the records on the "many" side. The advantage of a subform is that it doesn't require code to keep the relationship between the two tables consistent; you simply set properties to denote the primary and foreign keys.

Unfortunately, unlike Microsoft Access, VB doesn't provide subforms to automatically display all the records that are related to a particular record. Instead, Visual Basic applications typically require you to write some code to implement a user interface based on a many-to-many relationship. For more information on how this works, see Chapter 12.

USING THE DATA VIEW WINDOW

New to Visual Basic 6.0 is the Data View Window, which allows you to work with a database without having to use external tools or add-ins.

To use the Data View Window, follow these steps:

1. From Visual Basic's View menu, select Data View Window, or click the Data View button on VB's Standard toolbar.

2. The Data View Window appears. The window gives you two folders, Data Links and Data Environment Connections.

A data link is a way of connecting the Visual Basic development environment to a database of your choice. A data environment connection is a way of utilizing that database in a particular VB project. The difference between the two is that when you create a data link, it appears in the Data View window whenever the window is visible in Visual Basic, even if you close the current project and open a new one. The data environment connection designer, on the other hand, is specific to the project you're working on. It becomes part of the binary you create when you compile and can be shared across multiple projects.

To use the data link to browse data, follow these steps:

1. In the Data View window, right-click the Data Links folder. From the pop-up menu, select Add a Data Link.

2. The Data Link Properties window appears, as shown in Figure 1.30.

Figure 1.30
The Data Link Properties dialog box lets you create a connection to a database.

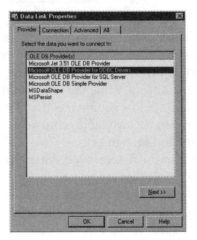

3. Click the Microsoft Jet provider, then click the Next button.

4. The Connection tab appears. Enter the full path and filename of the database you want to use. If you created the database novelty.mdb in the previous example, use that.

5. Click the Test Connection button at the bottom of the window. You should get a message indicating that the connection to the database succeeded. Testing the connection isn't a big deal with Access databases. But with client/server databases, it can be a lifesaver, since such systems often require a bunch of parameters to establish a connection.

6. Click OK. The data link is created, and the Data View window prompts you to type in the name of the link. Type the name **Novelty**, then hit Enter.

The data link provides an outline view of your data source. Once you've created the data link, you can browse by expanding its entry in the outline list. Do this by clicking the plus sign to the left of each item. The fully-expanded database in the data view window is shown in Figure 1.31. (Depending on which tool you used to create your database, you may see additional tables in the list.)

Figure 1.31
An expanded view of a database is displayed in the Data View window.

You should now be able to view live data. Do this by double-clicking the table tblCustomer in the Data View window. (Move the Data View window out of the way once you've opened the table.)

The initial view of the data isn't very impressive, since you haven't entered any records into the database yet. However, you can enter records by typing into the cells in the grid, as shown in Figure 1.32.

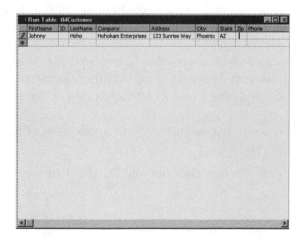

Figure 1.32
You can enter data through the Data View window's Run Table window.

At this point, you can either continue with the database you created earlier, or begin using the prefabricated `novelty.mdb` that was installed on your computer from the CD that accompanies this book. (By default, the path is `C:\vbdb\code\db\novelty.mdb`, although it may be different depending on which drive and folder you chose to install into). This database contains scads of data (including a 20,000-record table of customers and a 30,000-record table of orders), so it should be sufficient for any kind of testing you wish to perform. In addition, this database is the one used by all the examples in this book, so if you want your results to jibe with what's in these pages, you'll want to use this version of the database.

For information on how to install the database and VB code files contained on the CD accompanying this book, see "Installing the Example Files" in the Introduction.

CREATING A DATAENVIRONMENT DESIGNER

You can create a DataEnvironment designer to visually manage the connection to a database. When you have a DataEnvironment designer in your application, you can manage all of the information pertaining to the connection in one place, as opposed to traditional techniques that involve embedding database connection information in code. The DataEnvironment is included in your application's binary file at compile time, so there are no external dependencies to worry about.

> **Note:** New in VB6, the DataEnvironment designer is conceptually similar to the Remote Data Objects UserConnection designer you may have used in VB5. However, the DataEnvironment designer is based on ActiveX Data Objects and provides more functionality. If you have an existing application that uses RDO, you may want to continue using the UserConnection designer. RDO is discussed in Chapter 6.

This chapter covers how to create a database-driven user interface using the DataEnvironment designer. However, there are other things you can do with it. For more information on how to use a DataEnvironment designer in code, see Chapter 10.

To add a DataEnvironment designer to your application using the Data View window, follow these steps:

1. In the Data View window, click the Add DataEnvironment designer button.

2. The new DataEnvironment designer appears in your project. A default connection, called Connection1, appears in the designer, as shown in Figure 1.33.

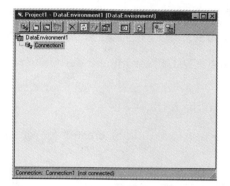

Figure 1.33
The DataEnvironment designer shows its default connection.

It's possible to manually adjust the default connection in the DataEnvironment designer so it points to your database. But if your database already exists in the Data View window, it makes more sense to simply drag and drop tables into the designer. To do this, follow these steps:

1. Starting in the Data View window, click a table in the Tables folder (such as tblCustomer).

2. Drag the table on top of the DataEnvironment designer.

3. A new connection, called Connection2, appears in the designer, with your table appearing under it.

At this point, you can drag additional tables onto the designer if you wish. When you're done, your designer should look like Figure 1.34.

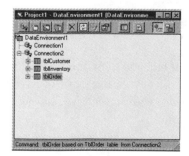

Figure 1.34
The DataEnvironment designer now contains the tables dragged from your Data View window.

CREATING A USER INTERFACE WITH THE DATAENVIRONMENT DESIGNER

You can create a quick user interface by using the DataEnvironment designer. The designer integrates with VB's forms engine, permitting you to use drag and drop to create a database-driven user interface. To do this, follow these steps:

1. Open the form you want to use as your user interface.

2. Click the table in the DataEnvironment designer (not the Data View window).

3. Drag the table onto the form.

A data-bound user interface should be created on the form, as shown in Figure 1.35.

Figure 1.35
An automatic user interface is built by dragging and dropping a table onto a form.

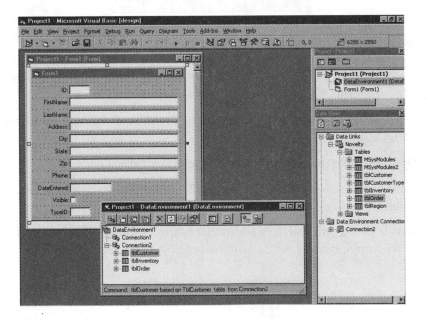

Running this application lets you view the first record in the database; however, no provision is made for navigating from one record to the next. To do this you either have to write code, as described in Chapter 10, or use a data control, described in the next section.

CREATING A USER INTERFACE USING A DATA CONTROL

You can use a data control to manage the connection between a Visual Basic form and a database. Data controls also provide basic data browsing functionality, enabling your application to navigate through a recordset and add and update records. Previous versions of VB provided two kinds of data controls: the Data Access Objects (DAO) Data control, usually used to connect to desktop databases such as Microsoft Access, and the Remote Data Control (RDC), used for client/server data. Visual Basic 6 adds a new data control, the ADO Data control, which lets you get access to all kinds of data, including desktop, client/server, and nonrelational data sources.

So which data control should you use? If you must use a data control in your application (and there are good reasons why you shouldn't), you should use the one that corresponds to the data access library used by your application. For more new database applications in VB6, you'll probably want to use ADO (introduced in Chapter 10). But you may need to use the older models, Data Access Objects (discussed in Chapter 3) or Remote Data Objects (covered in Chapter 6), in order to maintain an existing code base. Since the different types of data controls all operate similarly, this chapter covers the ADO data control only.

Note: The Data control is available in every edition of Visual Basic. In the Learning Edition of Visual Basic, the capabilities of the Data control are limited; for example, you can't use the Recordset object of a Data control to create other recordset objects.

Because of the limitations of the Data control in the Learning Edition, this book assumes that you're using the full version of the Data control found in the Professional and Enterprise Editions of Visual Basic. For more information on the differences between the Data control in the various editions of Visual Basic, see the *Visual Basic Guide to Data Access Objects*, part of the Visual Basic documentation (which is also available in Visual Basic Books Online).

Data controls are the simplest way of gaining access to databases in Visual Basic, whether the files are in Visual Basic's native format (shared with that of Microsoft Access), in an external format such as that of dBASE, or in a client/server database environment.

Figure 1.36 is a high-level diagram that demonstrates the way the ADO Data control connects your application to a database.

Figure 1.36
These are several components involved in connecting a Visual Basic application to a database through the ADO Data control.

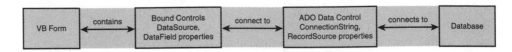

Note: Although the ADO Data control is an easy way to connect your application to a database, it's by no means the only way. After becoming more familiar with how database access works in Visual Basic, you'll almost certainly want to consider using code to manage the connection to the database. For more information on this, see Chapter 10.

CONNECTING TO A DATABASE AND WORKING WITH RECORDS

Creating an application that uses the ADO Data control is very simple—in fact, if all you're interested in doing is browsing the database, you don't even have to write a single line of code. It's a two-step process—setting the Data control's ConnectionString and RecordSource properties, then binding the control to user-interface controls. To do this, follow these steps:

1. Start a new Visual Basic project.

2. Using VB's Project Components menu, make a reference to Microsoft ADO Data Control 6.0 (OLEDB) by checking its entry in the list.

3. Click OK. The ADO Data control should appear in the Visual Basic toolbox. Double-click the control's icon to make an instance of the control appear on your form. Your screen should look like Figure 1.37.

4. Move and resize the control so it's in the lower-right corner of the form, taking up as little space as possible.

5. Right-click the control. From the pop-up menu, select ADODC Properties.

6. The control's Properties dialog box appears. Click the User Connection String option button, then click the Build button.

7. The Data Link Properties dialog box appears. This is the same dialog box you used to connect to the database in the example "Using the Data View Window" earlier in this chapter. Use the same steps to connect to the novelty database and click OK when you're done.

8. You should be back in the ADO Data control's Property Pages dialog box. Next you'll tell the control which table to use. Click the RecordSource tab, then select 2 - adCmdTable from the Command Type combo box.

9. Click the combo box labeled Table or Stored Procedure Name. The combo box should display a list of all the tables in the database. Select tblCustomer, then click OK.

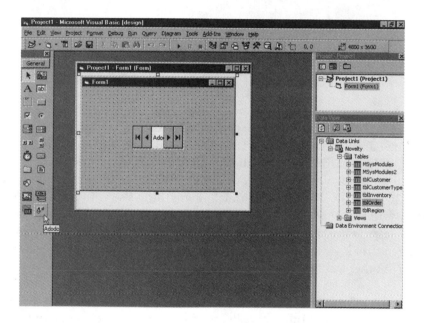

Figure 1.37
The ADO Data control appears in the Visual Basic toolbox and an instance of the control shows on the form.

The connection to the database takes place when the application runs. However, the connection isn't noticeable, because there's no way to display the data. To display data retrieved from a data control, you must create bound controls connected to the data control. To do so, follow these steps:

1. Create two text boxes on the form.

2. Set the text boxes' DataSource properties to ADODC1, the name of the data control.

3. Select the first text box and set its `DataField` property to a field in the database, such as FirstName. Again, as with the `RecordSource` property of the database, a bound control's `DataField` property displays a drop-down list that shows the list of what's available in the database.

4. Set the second text box's `DataField` property to the name of another field in the database, such as LastName.

5. Run the application. If you used the `novelty.mdb` database, you should see something like Figure 1.38.

Figure 1.38
An application displays two fields from a database with an ADO Data control; you can use the data control's buttons to navigate through the recordset.

Using the Data Control to Connect to a Database After you deposit the ADO Data control on a form, the user can navigate from one record to the next by clicking the control's buttons. The control displays four buttons.

Note that the data control does not by default enable the user to add or delete records. If you want the user to do much of anything else with the data control, you'll have to write code, as discussed in "Creating New Records Using the Data Control" later in this chapter. Fortunately, the code that you write to work with the data control is straightforward and similar to code you've probably written to perform other tasks in Visual Basic.

> **For more information: Several third-party ActiveX controls are designed to replace and extend the capabilities of the data controls provided with Visual Basic. For examples of third-party data controls, see Chapter 12.**

Updating Records Using the ADO Data Control You need not write any code to perform a database update using the ADO Data control. When a user changes a record displayed by the control, that record is updated as soon as the user moves to a new record (assuming the recordset is updateable). If you're familiar with the way that Microsoft Access updates records in its forms and datagrids, you should expect this behavior.

There are also ways to manipulate a recordset in code. The easiest way to do this is to change the values of user-interface controls that are bound to the data control; you can also manipulate the Recordset object contained by the data control to update its records.

CREATING A BASIC USER INTERFACE

Earlier in this chapter, you learned how to use the ADO Data control's property page to create a simple user interface. In this section, you create a user interface of your own, also using the ADO Data control, but manually setting up the properties that govern the connection to the database. This process enables you to customize the application and add additional functionality to it.

To connect a database-aware control to a data control, follow these steps:

1. Make sure your form contains an ADO Data control whose ConnectionString and RecordSource properties have been set to a valid data source. The minimal connection string you'll need to use is this:

```
Provider=Microsoft.Jet.OLEDB.3.51;Data
Source=c:\vbdb\code\db\novelty.mdb
```

2. Set the database-aware control's DataSource property to the name of the Data control. (When you use the Visual Basic Properties window to do this, the DataSource property conveniently displays the names of all the Data controls on the current form.)

3. If the database-aware control has a DataField property, set it to the name of the field you want the control to represent. Again, you'll notice that if everything is set up properly, a list of available fields drops down in the DataField property when you click it in the Visual Basic Properties window.

Note: Most data-aware controls have DataField properties, but not all do. The DataGrid control included with Visual Basic, for example, doesn't have a DataField property, because the control can display all the fields in a data source.

Data-Aware Controls   A *data-aware* control is any control that has a DataSource property. The DataSource property refers to a data control; this property connects the user-interface control to the data control (which in turn connects, or "binds" the user interface to the database). The user-interface control is therefore said to be *bound* to the database through the data control.

Several data-aware controls come with Visual Basic; the following list introduces these controls. Chapter 12 provides more information on how to use these and other data-aware controls:

▶ *Check box.* This control displays a true/false condition. It is typically bound to a Boolean, or yes/no, field in a database.

▶ *ComboBox.* This is the standard Visual Basic drop-down combo box. You usually don't use this control for data access purposes, since its list portion can't be bound to a data source, only its text portion. If you want to use a bound UI control for this purpose, you'll want to consider using the more robust DBCombo control instead.

▶ *DBCombo.* This data-aware control sports a drop-down list that is similar to the standard Visual Basic combo box control, but it can populate its list of choices from a database table.

▶ *DataGrid.* This grid can display database data in rows and columns. The commercial version of this control is the Apex True DB Grid control, which Chapter 12 covers.

▶ *DateTimePicker.* This control can bind to a date or time field in a database. It makes it easy for users to select a particular date or time graphically.

▶ *DBList.* This list box control is similar to the standard Visual Basic list box control, but it can populate its list of choices from a database table.

▶ *Hierarchical FlexGrid.* Similar to the FlexGrid control that appeared in VB5, this control lets you manipulate multiple related recordsets in a single grid control.

▶ *Image.* This image display control is similar to the PictureBox control, but lacks some of its features.

▶ *Label.* This control enables you to display text from a database field, but prevents the user from editing it.

▶ *ListBox.* This is the standard Visual Basic list box. You don't usually use this control for data-access purposes; use the more robust DBList control instead.

▶ *MaskedEdit.* This control is similar to a text box, but provides some intrinsic validation functionality as well as a default display that gives users a cue as to what to enter in the text box.

▶ *MSChart.* The MSChart control is the standard graphing control that has shipped with VB for years. New to VB6 is the ability to bind the chart control directly to a data control.

▶ *MSFlexGrid.* The MSFlexGrid control gives you the ability to display database data in a grid format. You can also use the control to pivot data, grouping it and arranging it in ways that let you see trends in your data. The commercial version of this control is the VideoSoft VSFLEX control. Chapter 12 covers the MSFlexGrid and VSFLEX controls in depth.

▶ *OLE.* The OLE container control displays documents created by other OLE-compliant applications.

▶ *PictureBox.* This control displays a graphical image. In previous versions of Visual Basic, the control could display graphics only in Visual Basic's BMP format; now, however, the control can also display images in GIF and JPG format.

▶ *TextBox.* This ubiquitous control enables the user to enter data in a straightforward way.

Third-Party Data-Aware Controls   In addition to the data-aware controls that come with Visual Basic, there is a third-party market for such controls. Usually, when a control is data-aware, a third-party control vendor promotes the control as "data-aware" or "bound," indicating it can be bound to a data control.

For More Information: If you're looking for a fascinating overview of third-party controls that you can use with Visual Basic, check out the *Visual Basic Component Sourcebook for Developers* (Ziff-Davis Press, 1997). The book contains information on more than 600 controls, including more than 100 database-aware controls.

If you want to create your own controls in Visual Basic, you'll want to peruse *How to Program Visual Basic Control Creation Edition* (Ziff-Davis Press, 1997). This is a full-color, step-by-step guide to creating ActiveX controls in any edition of Visual Basic.

Conveniently, both of these books are written by the author of the book you're reading right now. So if you like this book, you won't have to go through the trouble of acclimating yourself to another author's writing style. There are Web pages for both of these books at `http://www.redblazer.com/books`.

MANIPULATING RECORDS WITH THE ADO DATA CONTROL

In addition to enabling you to navigate through the recordset, the ADO Data control also enables you to perform actions on data. Many of these actions don't require you to write much code. You can use code with the data control to navigate through records one by one, delete records, and create new records.

Most of the code you write when working with the data control is centered around the concept of the Recordset object. A Recordset object becomes available after you've set the data control's ConnectionString and RecordSource properties. To access a property or method of the data control's Recordset object in code, you reference the data control, then reference the Recordset object, then reference the property or method of the Recordset object in which you're interested.

For example, to move to the first record of the recordset stored by the data control named ADODC1, you'd write the following code:

```
ADODC1.Recordset.MoveFirst
```

If you haven't written an extensive amount of code involving objects in Visual Basic, this code might seem a bit hard to understand. Why don't you just say datCustomer.MoveFirst instead? The answer lies in the fact that the data control isn't the same as the data; instead, the data control contains the data, in the form of a Recordset object. The properties of the data control itself pertain to its appearance and behavior, while the Recordset object has its own set of properties and methods pertaining to the actual data.

Creating New Records Using the Data Control   To create a new record using the data control, you have two options:

▶ Set the data control's EOFAction property to 2 - AddNew. This solution has the appeal of not requiring you to write any code.

▶ Use the AddNew and Update methods of the data control's Recordset object. This approach is more complicated, but gives you greater control over what happens when the user wants to create a new record. It is also appropriate in situations where you have hidden the data control from the user.

To enable the data control to create new records without writing code, do the following:

1. In your Data control project, set the Data control's EOFAction property to 2 - AddNew.

2. Run your project.

3. Click the Data control's Move Last button, then click the Next button. Instead of moving to the last record in the recordset, the data control creates a new record. You can tell that the record is new because all the bound controls on the form are blank.

4. Enter data in the bound controls.

5. Using the Data control's Previous button, move to the previous record. The new record is saved in the database.

To use the AddNew and Update methods to create a new record, do the following:

1. Add buttons or other controls to your interface to represent the AddNew and Update methods.

2. In the AddNew button's Click event, enter the following code:

```
ADODC1.Recordset.AddNew
```

3. In the Update button's Click event, enter the following code:

```
ADODC1.Recordset.Update
```

4. When a user is entering data, she has the option of clicking Update record to commit the new record to the database. She can also simply move off the record in order to save it, as is the case with updated records.

It's important to understand that when a user creates new records in a data-entry interface that uses the data control, many operations are not valid because there is no current record.

For example, if your application enables a user to create a new record by setting the data control's EOFAction property to AddNew, and then enables the user to perform the Delete method on the current record, that application will generate a runtime error.

This error occurs because there's no record to delete. To avoid this situation, you have several options. If you've worked with Visual Basic before, the obvious option might be simply to trap the error and disallow the Delete method. But there's an even better way to avoid the problem: Disable the Delete button to prevent the user from clicking it in the first place. A perfect way to do so is to use one of the data control's events, as described in the next section.

Using the *MoveComplete* Event to Update the User Interface   You can use the MoveComplete event of the ADO Data control to initiate changes in the application as the user moves from one record to the next.

The MoveComplete event is triggered after a new record becomes current. It is one of several events triggered when the control moves from one record to the next. Other events include the WillChange events, which are triggered when the control is about to move from one record to the next or about to change a record, and the RecordChangeComplete event, which happens when a record is successfully altered in the database as a result of an action in the data control.

You typically use the RecordChangeComplete event to do the following:

▶ Run a query of records related to a main record—what Microsoft Access refers to as a "main/subform" interface

▶ Calculate a value derived from one or more values in the record—for example, a total amount based on a subtotal multiplied by a sales tax constant

▶ Manage user-interface issues that respond to the state of the data control's recordset, performing tasks such as hiding or disabling certain features in the absence of a valid record

> **Note: The DAO Data control provides events similar to those described here. The ADO Data control's "Will" events (such as WillMove and WillChange) are roughly analogous to the DAO Data control's Validate event, whereas the ADO Data control's "Complete" events (such as RecordChangeComplete and MoveComplete) are analogous to the DAO Data control's Reposition event.**

For example, say you're interested in determining which region of the country each of your customers resides in. You can write a set of rules dividing up the country state by state, assigning each state to a region. You refer to the states in which you don't do business as "unassigned." You can display the region of each record on the form using the ADO Data control by following these steps:

1. On the form of the data control application you created in the previous examples, create a label control and name it lblRegion.

2. In the ADO Data control's MoveComplete event procedure, write the following code:

```
Private Sub ADODC1_MoveComplete(ByVal adReason As ADODB.EventReasonEnum, _
                                ByVal pError As ADODB.Error, _
                                adStatus As ADODB.EventStatusEnum, _
                                ByVal rs As ADODB.Recordset)

    Dim strSt As String
    Dim strRegion As String

    strSt = rs.Fields("State")

    ' Display region.
    Select Case strSt
        Case "VT", "NH", "NY", "CT"
        strRegion = "Northeast"

        Case "NC", "KY", "AR"
        strRegion = "South"

        Case "OK", "MN", "MI", "OH"
        strRegion = "Midwest"

        Case "MT"
        strRegion = "West"

        Case Else
        strRegion = "Unassigned"

    End Select

    lblRegion.Caption = strRegion

End Sub
```

3. Run the application. You should be able to see that the region is displayed
   as you move from record to record, as shown in Figure 1.39.

Figure 1.39
This application computes the region of the country in which a customer lives based on the state in which he resides.

Code Example: You can find the code discussed in this section in the sample project ADOData.vbp, located in the directory \vbdb\code\01-Basics\ADOData. For information on how to install the sample files on the CD that accompanies this book, see the section "Installing the Example Files" in the introduction at the beginning of this book.

Deleting Records Using a Data Control   To delete records in an application using the data control, you use the Delete method of the data control's Recordset object, as follows:

```
ADODC1.Recordset.Delete
```

There's an important caveat related to using the Delete method of a Recordset object with the Data control. When you delete a record, no current record appears to take its place; your recordset is essentially nowhere. So, to resolve this problem, you must move to another record in the recordset (typically by using recordset methods such as MoveNext or MoveLast).

Note: As discussed in the previous sections on creating new records and using data control events, you must make sure that there is a current record in the data control's recordset when you execute the Delete method, or your application will raise an error. To avoid this error, you should set up your user interface so that users can't delete records that aren't there. One good way to do that is to inspect the EOF and BOF properties of the recordset before proceeding with the Delete method; if either BOF or EOF are true, then the Delete method will fail.

Ensuring That Data Is Valid Using the *WillChangeRecord* Event   In database programming, *validation* ensures that data entered into the system conforms to rules defined by the design of your application. These rules are called *validation rules*. One way to implement validation when you're programming with the ADO Data control is to write code in the control's WillChangeRecord event. This event is triggered just before the record displayed by the data control is about to be altered for any reason. In a typical scenario, the user triggers the event by attempting to move to a new record after changing or creating a new record.

Business Case 1.4: Client-Side Validation While developing a data-entry interface for the Inventory application, Jones Novelties' database developer realizes that it might be problematic if an item in the product inventory is entered without a name—how would we be able to display or look up names of items?

The database developer decides to validate data entry in the WillChangeRecord event of the data control. In the Inventory example application, the code to perform this type of validation looks like this:

```
Private Sub ADODC1_WillChangeRecord(ByVal adReason As ADODB.EventReasonEnum, _
                                    ByVal cRecords As Long, _
                                    adStatus As ADODB.EventStatusEnum, _
                                    ByVal pRecordset As ADODB.Recordset)

    If txtName.Text = "" Then
        MsgBox "Sorry, friend. The product must have a name.", _
        vbExclamation + vbOKOnly, _
        "Validation Error"
        adStatus = adStatusCancel
    End If

End Sub
```

When this code exists in the data control's WillChangeRecord event and the user tries to enter a record without a product name, or attempts to delete a product name from an existing record, the result looks like Figure 1.40.

Unlike previous versions of Visual Basic, which used the DAO Data control,

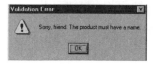

Figure 1.40
The validation rule is triggered, displaying a message box and rejecting the edit. Because the ADO Data control generates a WillChangeRecord event, you can include any code in the event you want—not just message boxes.

Unlike previous versions of Visual Basic, which used the DAO Data control, the ADO Data control raises distinct errors for each type of action taken by the Data control. The DAO Data control only raised a `Validate` event and a `Reposition` event, which could be triggered for a variety of reasons. Your code had to do additional work to determine why the events were triggered.

Validation at the Database Engine Level　In addition to doing ad hoc validation at the time your data is entered, remember that you can also do validation at the database engine level. Such validation is usually more reliable, because the validation is applied no matter what process changes the data. You do not have to remember to implement the validation rule in every application that accesses a particular table. But validation at the database engine level is less flexible because it's nearly impossible to override. Additionally, you can perform validation at the database engine only at the field level; you can't have database engine validation rules that, for example, are based on a comparison between two fields.

Database engine validation is a function of database design. For Jet databases, it's easiest to create database engine validation rules in the table design view of Microsoft Access.

For example, suppose that you want to make sure that a piece of inventory is never entered into the Inventory table without a catalog number. To do this, you set up a database engine level validation rule, as follows:

1. In Microsoft Access, open the table definition in design view.

2. Click the CatalogNumber field to select it.

3. In the Allow Zero Length setting in the window's bottom pane, select No. The table definition window looks like Figure 1.41.

Figure 1.41
Setting validation rules at the database engine level ensures that the contents of the CatalogNumber field are never empty, no matter what process performs the data entry.

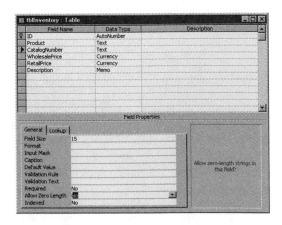

Note: This demonstration assumes that you're creating a new Novelty database. If you're using the prefabricated version of the Novelty database installed from the CD that accompanies this book, you'll find that the validation rule and validation text has already been set.

You can create more sophisticated validation rules at the database engine level as well. For example, suppose every item in your inventory has a catalog number that must begin with a letter from A through M. In this case, "F123" would be a valid catalog number, but "Z3875" would not. To implement this as a database engine validation rule, do the following:

1. In the table definition window for the Catalog Number field in the Inventory table, go to the `Validation Rule` property.

2. In the `Validation Rule` property, enter the following expression:

   ```
   Like "[A-M]*"
   ```

   The `Like` keyword indicates that you want a validation rule that permits any data that is like the expression that follows it. The expression that follows the `Like` keyword is a pattern; data that matches the pattern is valid, whereas data that doesn't match the pattern causes a validation error.

For more information: Like statements are most commonly used as criteria in queries. For more information on how Like expressions work, see Chapter 2.

So, in the case of this expression, `[A-M]` means "any letter of the alphabet between A and M, inclusive," whereas the asterisk means "anything else." So with this rule, "A34584" fits the validation rule, but "W34" does not, nor does "9039."

Data access operations are compared against database-engine validation rules first, before they are compared against any local validation that might exist in your application's `Validate` event. In your Visual Basic application, if you attempt to enter data that violates a database engine validation rule, the user gets a message box, as shown in Figure 1.42 (generated by the database engine).

Making Validation Clearer with Validation Text Because an inexperienced data-entry user might have trouble understanding the syntax of a validation rule violation message generated by the database engine, you can specify a more friendly message to display when the user enters a bad value. You do this in the `Validation Text` property of the table definition window.

Figure 1.42
A generic database engine validation message could be a little cryptic; it might not be appropriate for inexperienced users.

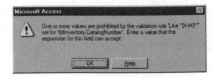

For example, to provide a more user-friendly message when the user violates the CatalogNumber's validation rule, do the following:

1. In Access, open the table definition for the tblInventory table.

2. In the CatalogNumber field's `Validation Text` property, type the following:

> `Look, dude. You gotta type a catalog number whose first character is a letter between A and M.`

3. Save and close the table definition and return to your Visual Basic application.

If you attempt to change a value in the Catalog Number field to an invalid value—for example, change the catalog number to "Z12"—an error message appears, as shown in Figure 1.43.

Figure 1.43
Validation text that is set in Access's table definition window appears in your Visual Basic application.

OTHER IMPORTANT PROPERTIES OF THE ADO DATA CONTROL

The ADO Data control has several additional properties that govern its behavior. You can set most of these properties at design time, so you don't have to write any code to take advantage of them.

The *CommandType* Property   The `CommandType` property determines what kind of command the ADO Data control issues against the data source to retrieve records. The examples in this chapter have all used the `CommandType` of 2 - adCmdTable to open and work with tables directly. However, you can use text commands or stored procedures to provide data to the data control.

A text command is a string, typically generated in your application's code, and submitted to the database engine for processing. For relational databases (such as Microsoft Jet, as well as many other systems), this string is typically composed in Structured Query Language (SQL). However, ADO permits you to use any language understood by the data source as a text command. For information on how to use SQL to perform queries, see Chapter 2.

A stored procedure is a query or other command that is embedded in the database itself. You typically create stored procedures to take advantage of centralized management of database access procedures, as well as to enhance query performance. Microsoft Jet databases provide a very basic form of the stored procedure called a QueryDef, discussed in Chapter 2. Microsoft SQL Server provides a complete set of extensions to SQL to allow you to program sophisticated stored procedures. These are discussed in Chapter 5.

The *EOFAction* Property   The EOFAction property determines what the data control does when the user moves to the end of the recordset. If you set the property to 2 - Add New, the control creates a new record when the user moves one record past the last one in the current recordset. (In other words, the setting causes the interface just to work like a Microsoft Access form.) But bear in mind that this setting is not the default behavior of a Visual Basic data control; you must change the property at design time to ensure that the control behaves this way.

To create a new record when the data control's EOFAction property is set to AddNew, you click the MoveLast button, then click the MoveNext button.

Controlling Access to Data Using the *Mode* Property   By setting the Mode property of the ADO Data control, you have control over whether other users can access the database when your application is running. For example, by setting the Mode property to 12 - adModeShareExclusive, your application gains exclusive access to the data—no other user can gain access to it as long as your application is running.

You can also open a data source in read-only mode by setting Mode to 1 - adModeRead; your application gains read-only access to the data. The advantage of this setting is that performance improves, because the database engine doesn't have to worry about such problems as record locking and multi-user contention that can occur if more than one application can access the same record.

SUMMARY

This chapter covered the basics of databases in general, as well as the easiest ways of connecting your Visual Basic applications to Microsoft Access databases.

It's important to remember that although Visual Basic and Microsoft Access share a database engine, Access-style databases aren't your only option in Visual Basic. Chapter 5 describes how to set up and use Microsoft SQL Server. Throughout the book I'll also use technologies such as ODBC and OLE DB, Windows technologies that enable you to get to databases of all kinds from a Visual Basic application without regard for the differences between them.

QUESTIONS AND ANSWERS

Q. Given the fact that the Visual Data Manager isn't as powerful or easy to use as Access, is there any reason why I should use it?

A. Yes—if you don't have Microsoft Access, for one thing. Also, some developers like to have a working familiarity with the Visual Data Manager in case they're stuck in a situation where they don't have access to Access. But in general, it's easier to design tables and queries using Access, so it's a good idea to use Access if you have it.

Q. What about the DAO Data control?

A. The DAO Data control was covered more extensively in the first edition of this book. In this edition, I decided to focus on the ADO version of the control because it's somewhat more powerful than its DAO predecessor. There are a few things you can do in DAO that you still can't do in ADO, though. For a more complete discussion of that, including a few tricks involving the DAO Data control, see Chapter 3.

Q. The data controls seem easy to use, but they also seem limited in what they can do and a little cumbersome. Are there other ways of doing database stuff in Visual Basic?

A. Absolutely. Microsoft originally provided the DAO Data control (way back in Visual Basic 3.0) as a way to provide a no-code solution to the problem of database access. Until VB6 came out, data controls were the only way to exploit the wealth of database-aware ActiveX controls. But the limitations of the data control, combined with its inefficiency, lead many developers to disdain its use. In all likelihood, you'll come to the point where production database applications will use either a combination of one or more data controls and code, or code by itself.

Q. Is there a way to use data-aware controls without using a data control?

A. Yes, although if you do not use a data control, you'll either have to write code to manage the database connection manually or use a DataEnvironment designer (as demonstrated in "Creating a User Interface with the DataEnvironment Designer" earlier in this chapter). This is not impossible to do, but it can be tricky. You'll use object code (either in DAO, RDO, or ADO) to handle retrieving and updating records in this scenario. (You can also use this kind of code to enable non-data-aware controls, such as the Visual Basic TreeView control, to display data from a database.)

Q. Data controls expose a Recordset object. Does that mean I can use that recordset for other purposes?

A. As long as you remember to use your newfound powers only for good and never for evil, yes. The Recordset object exposed by the ADO Data control is exactly the same as any other kind of Recordset object in ADO. And you can assign a recordset you generate in ADO code to the Recordset object of an ADO Data control. See Chapter 10 for more on how to create recordsets using pure code in ADO.

Q. Is it possible to have a primary key composed of more than one field?

A. Yes. Although not often done, in the database world this is known as a *concatenated key*. You might use such a key if you know that all the people in your database are going to have unique first and last names. You choose to make the FirstName and LastName fields the concatenated primary key so that users can never enter the same name twice in the database. The Visual Data Manager, as well as Microsoft Access, let you designate more than one field in a key.

Queries

The discussion of database and table structure in Chapter 1, "Database Basics," demonstrated how to create a database using Visual Basic and Microsoft Access. This chapter is concerned with manipulating data in tables, as well as creating and changing the structure of tables by using *Structured Query Language (SQL)*.

SQL queries give you the ability to retrieve records from a database table, match related data in multiple tables, and manipulate the structure of databases. They pertain to the applications you saw demonstrated in Chapter 1 in the sense that certain types of SQL queries can populate a data control. SQL queries are also used when you manipulate databases in code, using the DAO, RDO, or ADO object models, discussed in later chapters.

SQL is a standard way of manipulating databases. It's implemented in various forms by many relational database systems, including Microsoft Access and SQL Server. Generally, SQL is used for creating queries that extract data from databases, although a large subset of SQL commands perform other functions on databases, such as creating tables and fields.

Generally, SQL commands are broken down into two categories:

▶ *Data Definition Language (DDL) commands*, which enable you to use SQL queries to create components of the database, such as tables, fields, and indexes

▶ *Data Manipulation Language commands*, designed to retrieve records from databases

While this chapter discusses how to use both types of SQL commands, you may find it easier to use an object model instead of SQL to create database structures in Visual Basic applications. Data Access Objects (DAO) permits you to do this for Microsoft Access databases. Using DAO to create database structures is covered in Chapter 3, "Data Access Objects."

What Is a Query?

A *query* is a database command that retrieves records. Using queries, you can pull data from one or more fields from one or more tables. You can also subject the data you retrieve to one or more constraints, known as *criteria*, that serve to limit the amount of data you retrieve.

Queries in Visual Basic are typically based on SQL. SQL is a fairly standard language for retrieving and otherwise manipulating databases; it's easy to learn and is implemented across many different databases, so you don't have to learn a totally new query language if you, for example, migrate your Jet database application to Sybase or Oracle.

At least that's the theory. In practice, as with so many other "industry standards," every database vendor has its own way of implementing a standard, and Microsoft is certainly no exception. Though Jet's implementation of SQL isn't radically different than other vendors' implementations, you should be aware as you learn the language that other dialects of SQL exist.

And if that isn't enough, in VB6, you're not limited to using SQL for performing queries. Using ActiveX Data Objects, data sources can expose their functionality through query languages other than SQL. For more information on ADO, see Chapter 10, "ActiveX Data Objects."

Where SQL Is Useful

It's intuitive that you'd need to have a way to retrieve records from a database in order to write a database application in Visual Basic. It's not always intuitive where you actually stick the queries you need to retrieve records, however.

The rule of thumb in VB is that any place where you'd use a reference to a table, you can instead use a SQL statement or a reference to a stored query (which is, in turn, based on a SQL statement). The most obvious place to put a SQL statement, based on the limited data access techniques discussed in this book so far, would be the RecordSource property of a data control.

So instead of setting the RecordSource property to the name of a table (such as tblCustomer), you can instead set it to the name of a stored query (such as qryCustomerSorted, for example) or a SQL statement (such as SELECT * FROM tblCustomer ORDER BY State). This gives you a great deal of flexibility when choosing a record source.

Other contexts in which the use of SQL statements are used include the following:

▶ The *source* argument of the OpenRecordset method of a DAO Database object. You use this method most commonly when you are querying records from an Access database in code.

▶ The Source property of an ADO Recordset object, or the *source* parameter of the Recordset object's Open method.

▶ The *source* argument of the Execute method of a DAO Database or QueryDef object. You use the Execute method when you are running an action query. The analogous operation in ADO is the Execute method of the Command object.

▶ The SQL property of a DAO QueryDef object. You generally use this method when you are defining a query that is to be stored in the database.

All these techniques are discussed in more detail in Chapter 3 and Chapter 10.

TESTING QUERIES WITH THE DATA VIEW WINDOW

The Data View window is a useful tool for trying out the concepts described in this chapter. Use the steps here to build a query in the Data View window that you can use to test SQL statements as you work through this chapter.

Note: As an alternative to using the Data View window, you may want to consider simply using the Visual Data Manager or Microsoft Access to experiment with SQL. For my money, using Access to develop queries is the best option, if you have it, since Access has a graphical query-by-example feature that lets you create complex SQL queries without actually having to write SQL code. Additionally, while you can create queries embedded in your VB application using Data Environment designers, you can't create queries in Access databases using the Data View window. You can create views and stored procedures for Oracle and SQL Server databases using the Data View window, however. Creating SQL Server views is covered later in this chapter; creating stored procedures is discussed in Chapter 5, "Getting Started with SQL Server."

To create a query using the Data View window, follow these steps:

1. In Visual Basic, create a new EXE project.

2. From VB's View menu, select Data View Window. The Data View window appears, as shown in Figure 2.1. Note that you can dock the Data View window to the edge of the VB window, just like the Project Explorer and Properties window.

Figure 2.1
The Data View window lets you connect to data sources and run queries.

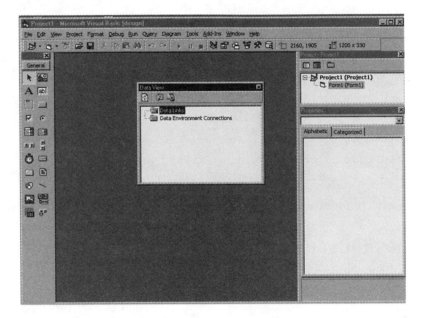

To query a data source, you need to first create a data link. A data link provides information about how to connect to the data source. Here's how to create a data link:

1. In the Data View window, right-click the Data Links window.

2. From the pop-up menu, select Add a Data Link. The Data Link Properties dialog box appears, as shown in Figure 2.2. (The list of drivers may be different on your machine depending on what you have installed.)

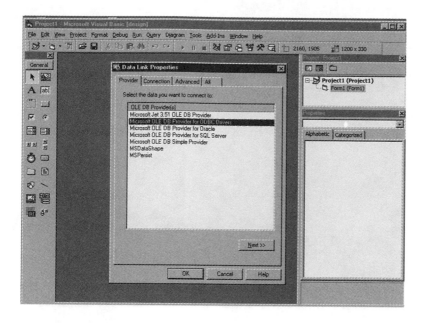

Figure 2.2
Select Add a Data Link to get the Data Link Properties dialog box.

3. You'll be connecting to a Microsoft Access database, so choose Microsoft Jet 3.51 OLE DB Provider and then click Next.

4. The Connection tab appears. Select a database by clicking the button to the right of the text box labeled "Select or enter a database name."

5. After you've selected a database, click the Test Connection button. You should get a message box indicating that the database was opened.

6. Click OK. A new data link to the database appears. Type a name for the new data link—**Novelty** will do. The new data link is shown in Figure 2.3.

Code Example: The database used to test the queries in this chapter is called `novelty.mdb`. This database is ideal for testing because it contains thousands of records in its tables of customers and orders. It is located in the directory `\vbdb\code\DB`. For information on how to install the sample files on the CD that accompanies this book, see the section "Installing the Example Files" in the introduction at the beginning of this book.

Figure 2.3
The Data View window contains a new link to the Novelty database.

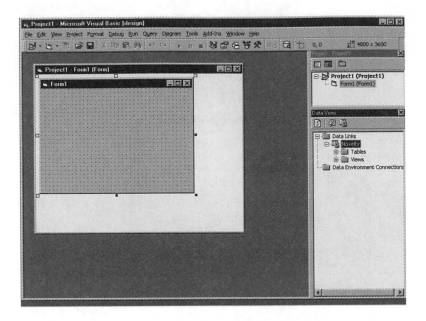

The data link will persist in the Visual Basic design-time environment until you get rid of it. It's not attached to any particular VB project—it will always come up whenever you're in VB. This is handy if you need to write lots of applications against the same database.

(You can manipulate data links by right-clicking them. For example, if you want to delete a data link after you've created it, right-click it; then from the pop-up menu, select Remove.)

Now that you've created a data link, you can create a SQL query against the database. To do this, you need to create a Data Environment designer. To do this, follow these steps:

1. From the Project window, select Add Data Environment.

2. A new Data Environment designer appears, as shown in Figure 2.4.

3. Click-drag the tblCustomer table from the Data View window onto the Data Environment designer. A new connection appears, containing the table.

4. In the Data Environment designer, right-click the table. From the pop-up window, select Properties.

5. The Table Properties dialog box appears. Click SQL Statement.

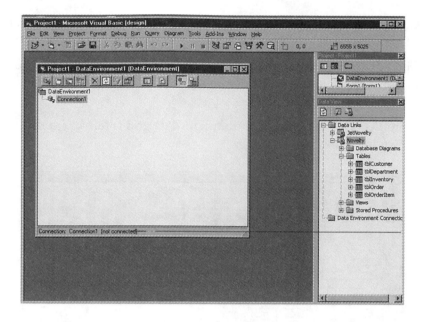

Figure 2.4
*Here's a new Data
Environment
designer in the
design-time envi-
ronment.*

6. Click the SQL Builder button. The Query Design window appears, as
shown in Figure 2.5.

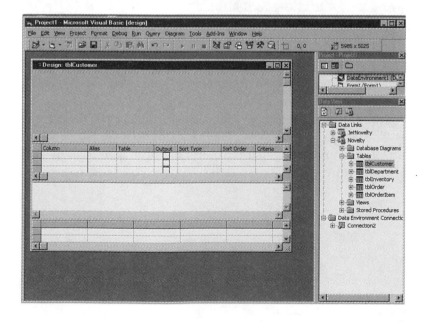

Figure 2.5
*You build your
SQL query in the
Design window.*

7. Click-drag the table tblCustomer from the Data View window to the top pane of the query window.

8. Click-drag the FirstName, LastName, and Address columns from the table to the query window's grid. You can see that the SQL query is built as you drag fields to the grid.

9. From VB's Query menu, select Run. The data grid is filled with data, as shown in Figure 2.6.

Figure 2.6

The Design window is filled after the query has been run.

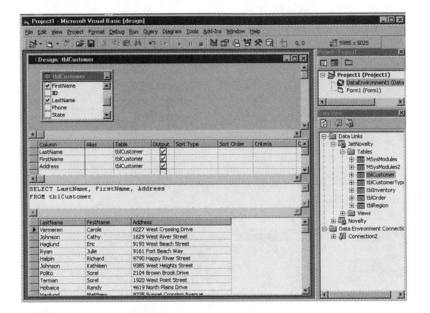

10. From the File menu, select Save tblCustomer; then close the query window. The table icon in the Data Environment designer has been changed to a SQL icon, indicating that the object has been converted to a query, as shown in Figure 2.7.

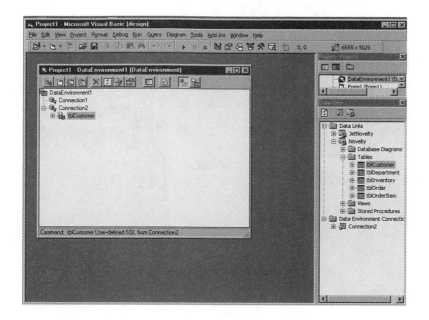

Figure 2.7
The SQL query looks like this in a Data Environment designer.

CREATING SERVER-SIDE QUERIES USING THE DATA VIEW WINDOW

If your data source is Microsoft SQL Server, you can create a server-side query, known as a *view*, using the Data View window. Such queries are more easily managed and can execute more quickly than client-side queries.

> **Note: The Enterprise Edition of Visual Basic ships with a copy of Microsoft SQL Server. For more information on setting up and using SQL Server, see Chapter 5.**

To create a view using the Data View window, follow these steps:

1. Create a data link to a SQL Server database using the procedure described earlier in this chapter.

2. Click the plus sign to the left of the data link name to expose its object folders. There should be four folders, as shown in Figure 2.8.

3. Right-click the Views folder. From the pop-up window, select New View.

4. The New View window appears, as shown in Figure 2.9.

Figure 2.8
*Display of a SQL
Server data source
in the Data View
window.*

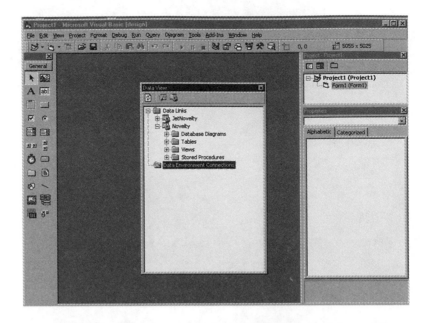

Figure 2.9
*The New View
window.*

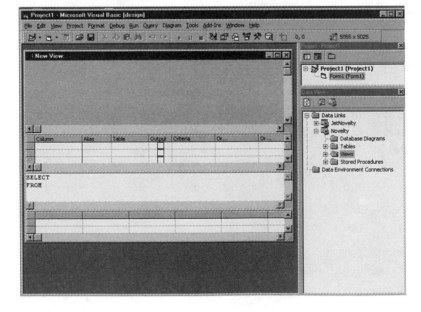

5. Click-drag the tblCustomer table from the Data View window onto the New View window. The query window changes to reflect the addition, as shown in Figure 2.10. (You can also see that a SQL statement is built for the table.)

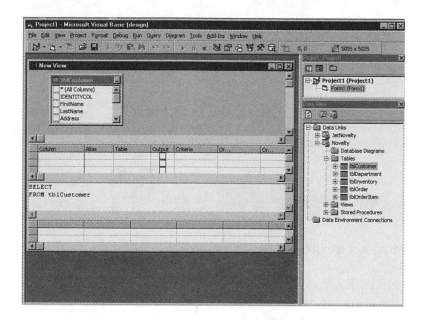

Figure 2.10
A table looks like this after it's been added to the New View window.

6. To indicate that you want to see all the columns in tblCustomer, drag the (All Columns) item from the table to the column grid. The data from the table is retrieved, as shown in Figure 2.11.

Now that the view is constructed, you can save it in the database. Once it's saved, it exists on the server and can be used by any process. To save the view, follow these steps:

1. From Visual Basic's File menu, select Save View.

2. The Save View dialog box appears. (This dialog isn't a file dialog because you aren't saving the view as a file—you're saving it as an object within the server.) Name the new view `qryCustomer` and click OK. The view is stored in the database on the server.

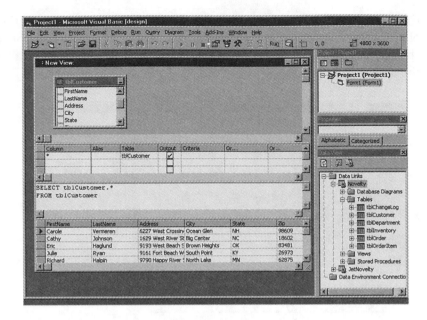

USING DATA ENVIRONMENT QUERIES

The cool thing about the Query Designer window is that it will enable you to
run any valid SQL SELECT statement against any table in the database with a minimum of fuss. You can do this by right-clicking a query command in the Data
Environment designer and then choosing Design from the pop-up menu. Once
the query designer window appears, you can enter any SQL command you want
in the SQL pane of the window.

For example, try entering the SQL statement given in Listing 2.1.

**Listing 2.1   A *SELECT* Query That Populates a Column with the
Results of a Calculation**

```
SELECT Product, 'WholesalePrice' * 1.4 AS 'NewPrice'
FROM tblInventory
```

After you've typed in the SQL statement, run the query by selecting the menu
command Query, Run. (You can also right-click the topmost pane of the query
designer window and select Run from the pop-up menu.) The grid displays all
the items in the inventory with a 40 percent increase over their wholesale prices,
as illustrated in Figure 2.12.

You can use the Query Designer to experiment with the SQL code introduced in the rest of this chapter.

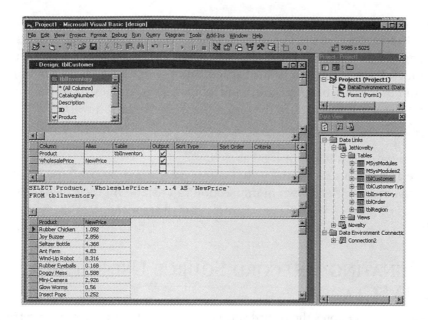

Figure 2.12
The Design window displays the results of a SQL query containing a calculation.

RETRIEVING RECORDS USING THE *SELECT* CLAUSE

The SELECT clause is at the core of every query that retrieves data. It tells the database engine what fields to return.

A common form of the SELECT clause is

```
SELECT *
```

This clause means "return all the fields you find in the specified record source." This form of the command is handy because you don't need to know the names of fields to retrieve them from a table. Retrieving all the columns in a table can be inefficient, however, particularly in a situation in which you only need two columns and your query retrieves two dozen.

So, in addition to telling the database engine to return all the fields in the record source, you also have the ability to specify exactly which fields you want to retrieve. This limiting effect can improve the efficiency of a query, particularly in large tables with many fields, because you're only retrieving the fields you need.

A SELECT clause that only retrieves the contents of the first and last names stored in a table looks like this:

```
SELECT [FirstName], [LastName]
```

Note that in Microsoft Jet SQL, you conventionally enclose field names in square brackets because field names in Microsoft Jet (unlike many other database engines) can contain embedded spaces and other undesirable characters.

Though I avoid using embedded spaces and the like in the field names I create, I still use square brackets around field names because it sometimes makes the SQL statements clearer. In the preceding SQL example, however,

```
SELECT FirstName, LastName
```

would have been perfectly legal as well.

Note also that a SELECT clause is not complete without a FROM clause (so the SELECT clause examples shown in this section can't stand on their own). For more examples of the SELECT clause, see examples for the FROM clause in the next section.

DESIGNATING A RECORD SOURCE USING THE *FROM* CLAUSE

The FROM clause denotes the record source from which your query is to retrieve records; this record source can be either a table or another stored query.

You also have the ability to retrieve records from more than one table; see "Joining Related Tables in a Query" later in this chapter for more information on how that works.

The FROM clauses work with SELECT clauses. For example, to retrieve all the records in tblCustomer, you use the SQL statement in Listing 2.2.

Listing 2.2   A Basic *SELECT* Query

```
SELECT *
FROM tblCustomer
```

This query retrieves all the records and all the fields in the tblCustomer table (in no particular order). The SQL statement produces the following resultset:

ID	FirstName	LastName	Address	City	State	Zip	Phone
1	Carole	Vermeren	6227 West Crossing Drive	Ocean Glen	NH	98609	6034485994
2	Cathy	Johnson	1629 West River Street	Big Center	NC	18602	9193669205
4	Eric	Haglund	9193 West Beach Street	Brown Heights	OK	83481	4059310689
......	...	...		...	...	...	...

(Note that your query should return many more records and columns than this; the ellipses indicate data that's omitted to save space.) To retrieve only the customers' first and last names, you use the SQL statement in Listing 2.3.

Listing 2.3   A *SELECT* Query That Limits the Number of Columns It Retrieves

```
SELECT FirstName, LastName
FROM tblCustomer
```

This command produces the following resultset:

FirstName	LastName
Carole	Vermeren
Cathy	Johnson
Eric	Haglund
…	…

For reasons of efficiency, it's always best to use this technique to limit the number of fields in a SELECT clause to only those fields you know your application will need. Also bear in mind that the Novelty database installed on your computer contains about 30,000 records—queries against that data set will take a long time to return unless you make judicious use of the WHERE clause, as described in the next section.

Note that records returned by a SELECT FROM query are returned in no particular order. Unless you specify a sorting order (using the ORDER BY clause discussed later in this chapter), the order in which records is returned is always undefined.

SPECIFYING CRITERIA USING THE *WHERE* CLAUSE

A WHERE clause tells the database engine to limit the records it retrieves according to one or more criteria you supply. A *criterion* is an expression that evaluates to a true or false condition; many of the same expressions of equivalence to which you're accustomed in Visual Basic (such as >0 and ='Smith') exist in SQL as well.

For example, let's say you want to return a list of only those customers who live in California. You might write a SQL query as shown in Listing 2.4.

Listing 2.4   A Basic *SELECT* Query with a *WHERE* Condition Limiting the Records Retrieved

```
SELECT FirstName, LastName, State
FROM tblCustomer
WHERE State = 'CA'
```

This query produces the following resultset:

FirstName	LastName	State
Marjorie	Kranyak	CA
Mark	Ruzich	CA
Steve	Lemay	CA
…	…	…

Once again the resultset is returned in no particular order unless you supply an ORDER BY clause; this clause is discussed later in this chapter.

Note also that the delimiter for a text string in a WHERE clause is a single quotation mark. This marker is convenient, as you'll see later, because the delimiter for a string in Visual Basic is a double quotation mark, and SQL statements must sometimes be embedded in VB code.

You can create more sophisticated WHERE clauses by linking two or more criteria together with AND and OR logic. For example, let's say you want to retrieve all the customers who live in Big River, Washington (as opposed to those customers who live in cities called Big River in other states). To do this, you need to denote two criteria linked with an AND operator, as you can see in Listing 2.5.

Listing 2.5 A Basic *SELECT* Query with a Pair of *WHERE* Conditions Linked with *AND*

```
SELECT FirstName, LastName, City, State
FROM tblCustomer
WHERE City = 'Big River' AND State = 'WA'
```

The resultset produced by this query looks like this:

FirstName	LastName	City	State
Jennifer	Townsend	Big River	WA
Katie	Savarese	Big River	WA
Gavin	Newton	Big River	WA
Sorel	Newton	Big River	WA

If you are interested in seeing information on people who live in cities called Big River in Washington as well as California, you use an OR clause to link the two criteria, as in the code in Listing 2.6.

Listing 2.6 A Basic *SELECT* Query with Multiple *WHERE* Conditions Linked with *AND* and *OR*

```
SELECT FirstName, LastName, City, State
FROM tblCustomer
WHERE City= 'Big River' AND (State='WA' OR State='CA')
```

The resultset of this query might look like the following:

```
FirstName    LastName    City        State
Jennifer     Townsend     Big River    WA
Katie        Savarese     Big River    WA
Peter        Worth        Big River    CA
Angela       Newton       Big River    CA
```

So you can see that you can pretty much go insane linking WHERE criteria together with AND and OR conditions to extract data from a table.

Note: One key to successful client/server development is to develop tactics for ensuring that client applications don't retrieve too many records at once. This will ensure that your applications run quickly and don't do bad things like cause users' computers to run out of memory. One of your most basic weapons you can use to avoid these unfortunate results is the WHERE clause.

OPERATORS IN *WHERE* CLAUSES

You can use the operators listed in Table 2.1 when constructing a WHERE clause.

Table 2.1 Operators for Use in *WHERE* Clauses	
Operator	**Function**
<	Less than
<=	Less than or equal to
>	Greater than
>=	Greater than or equal to
=	Equal to
<>	Not equal to
BETWEEN	Within a range of values
LIKE	Matching a pattern
IN	Contained in a list of values

The operators of equality and inequality work exactly the same in SQL as they do in Visual Basic.

The *BETWEEN* Operator

The BETWEEN operator returns all the records values that are between the limits you specify. For example, to return all the orders placed between June 1 and June 5, you would write the SQL statement shown in Listing 2.7.

Listing 2.7   A Basic *SELECT* Query with a *BETWEEN* Clause

```
SELECT *
FROM tblOrder
WHERE [OrderDate] BETWEEN #6/1/97# and #6/5/97#
```

This query produces the following resultset:

ID	CustomerID	OrderDate	Amount
813	8746	6/5/97	158.53
1250	2008	6/5/97	231.03
1372	1036	6/5/97	3.02

(In the sample database novelty.mdb, this query should return about 45 records.) Note that date values in SQL are delimited with pound signs (#). The boundaries of a BETWEEN operator are inclusive, meaning that if you ask for all the orders that were placed between June 1 and June 5, the resultset will include records that were placed *on* June 1 and June 5 as well.

The *LIKE* Operator and Wildcard Characters

The LIKE operator matches records to a pattern you specify. This pattern is often a "wildcard" character, such as the * or ? characters with which you may be familiar from working with the MS-DOS or Windows file systems.

The percent(%) character indicates a partial match. For example, to retrieve all the records in the tblCustomer table whose last names begin with the letter B, you'd use a query like the one in Listing 2.8.

Listing 2.8   A Basic *SELECT* Query That Matches a Pattern Based on a *LIKE* Expression

```
SELECT ID, FirstName, LastName, Address, City, State
FROM tblCustomer
WHERE [LastName] LIKE 'B%'
```

This query produces the following resultset:

ID	FirstName	LastName	Address	City	State
20	Marjorie	Bassett	5610 Golden Point Avenue	Sunset River	VA
57	Christian	Bassett	6068 Blue Glen Highway	South Heights	RI
229	Joe	Bassett	1670 Dead Man's Crossing Circle	Ocean Glen	ID

You can also create wildcard matches using the underscore character. The underscore takes the place of a single character in a pattern. For example, to locate all of the customers with five-digit ZIP codes beginning with the number 9, you use the SQL code in Listing 2.9.

Listing 2.9   A Basic *SELECT* Query That Uses Question Mark Wildcards in Its *LIKE* Clause

```
SELECT ID, FirstName, LastName, Address, Zip
FROM tblCustomer
WHERE 'Zip' LIKE '9____'
```

This query produces the following resultset:

ID	FirstName	LastName	Address	Zip
1	Carole	Vermeren	6227 West Crossing Drive	98609
155	Brad	Townsend	5477 Dead Man's Heights Street	99677
30	Randy	Nelson	5930 Dead Man's Lake Circle	90257

You can also use a LIKE operator that returns a range of alphabetic or numeric values. For example, to return a list of customers whose last names begin with the letters A through C, you use the SQL statement given in Listing 2.10.

Listing 2.10   A Basic *SELECT* Query That Returns a Range of Values with a *LIKE* Operator

```
SELECT ID, FirstName, LastName
FROM tblCustomer
WHERE [LastName] LIKE '[A-C]%'
```

This query returns the following resultset:

ID	FirstName	LastName
20	Marjorie	Bassett
22	Joe	Chideya
23	Katie	Chideya
24	Terri	Allen

Note: The wildcard characters in Microsoft Jet SQL are different than the wildcards in ANSI SQL. In Jet SQL, you use an asterisk instead of a percent sign to match any number of characters, and you use a question mark instead of an underscore to match any single character. In ANSI SQL, you use an underscore to match any number of characters, and you use a percent sign to match any single character. Queries you build in the Data View window use ANSI SQL. Queries you run using Data Access Objects, on the other hand, use Jet's own wildcard characters.

The *IN* Operator

You use the IN operator to retrieve records that match a list of values. For example, to retrieve all the customers in either Wyoming or Vermont, use the SQL statement shown in Listing 2.11.

Listing 2.11   A Basic *SELECT* Query That Matches Items in a List Using an *IN* Clause

```
SELECT FirstName, LastName, State
FROM tblCustomer
WHERE 'State' IN ('VT', 'WY')
```

This query produces the following resultset:

FirstName	LastName	State
Cathy	Vermeren	VT
Amy	Vermeren	WY
Randy	Polito	WY
Sorel	Jones	VT

SORTING RESULTS USING *ORDER BY*

The ORDER BY clause tells the database engine to sort the records it retrieves. You can sort on any field, or on multiple fields, and you can sort in ascending or descending order.

To specify a sort order, you include the ORDER BY clause at the end of a normal SELECT query, followed by the field or fields by which you wish to sort. For example, to return a list of customers sorted by last name, you use the SQL statement shown in Listing 2.12.

Listing 2.12   A Basic *SELECT* Query That Sorts on a Single Field

```
SELECT ID, FirstName, LastName
FROM tblCustomer
WHERE City LIKE 'Big L%'
ORDER BY LastName
```

This query produces the following resultset:

ID	LastName	FirstName
9361	Eric	Allen
5215	Daryl	Allen
17688	Katie	Bassett
12359	Marjorie	Chideya

SORTING IN DESCENDING ORDER

To sort in descending order, use the DESC keyword after the field by which you're sorting. For example, to retrieve records from the tblOrder table according to who placed the most recent order, you'd use the SQL statement given in Listing 2.13.

Listing 2.13   A Basic *SELECT* Query That Sorts on a Single Field in Descending Order

```
SELECT *
FROM tblOrder
WHERE OrderAmount > 250
ORDER BY OrderDate DESC
```

This produces the following resultset, displaying the most recent orders first:

ID	CustomerID	OrderDate	OrderAmount
7916	11525	5/2/99	250.51
872	9866	5/1/99	250.52
22757	12022	4/26/99	250.82

To sort on multiple fields, you list the fields one after the other immediately following the ORDER BY clause. For example, to sort the tblCustomer table by last name and then by first name, the SQL would be as shown in Listing 2.14.

Listing 2.14   A Basic *SELECT* Query That Sorts on Two Fields

```
SELECT FirstName, LastName, City, State
FROM tblCustomer
WHERE City LIKE 'Dead%'
ORDER BY LastName, FirstName
```

Here's the resultset of this query:

FirstName	LastName	City	State
Amy	Allen	Dead Man's Village	ID
Amy	Allen	Dead Man's Beach	TN
Angela	Allen	Dead Man's Lake	CT
Angela	Allen	Dead Man's Glen	IA
Brad	Allen	Dead Man's Bluffs	MI

DISPLAYING THE TOP OR BOTTOM OF A RANGE USING *TOP*

You use the TOP keyword to display only the top or bottom few records in a large recordset. In queries, the TOP keyword is combined with a sort clause to limit the number of records to a set number of records or a percentage of records in the resultset.

For example, let's say you want to view the largest orders in tblOrder. To do this, you'd write a SQL statement as in Listing 2.15.

Listing 2.15 A Basic *SELECT* Query That Sorts in Descending Order on a Single Field

```
SELECT ID, OrderDate, OrderAmount
FROM tblOrder
ORDER BY OrderAmount DESC
```

Note that the DESC keyword causes the resultset to be sorted in descending (biggest to smallest) order. This SQL produces a resultset that looks like this:

ID	OrderDate	OrderAmount
13388	11/21/97	251
7931	12/11/98	250.99
15804	10/13/98	250.98
27897	1/22/99	250.98
15776	1/3/99	250.97

This is fine, except that in a database that stores every order you've ever fulfilled, you might have to pass thousands of records back to the client when all you're really interested in are the top three outstanding orders. So instead of Listing 2.15, try the SQL statement in Listing 2.16.

Listing 2.16 A Query That Returns the Top Three Orders, Sorted in Descending Order by Amount

```
SELECT TOP 3 *
FROM tblOrder
ORDER BY OrderAmount DESC
```

This query provides the following resultset, composed of only four records:

ID	CustomerID	OrderDate	OrderAmount
13388	10407	11/21/97	251
7931	3046	12/11/98	250.99
15804	7608	10/13/98	250.98
27897	4976	1/22/99	250.98

Why does the query return four records when you specifically asked for three? It is not guaranteed that only three records will be returned in a TOP 3 query. It's possible that none, one, or two records will be returned if your table has only that many records. And if two or more records are tied for last place in your result list, it's possible that four or more records will be returned.

There is no such thing as "BOTTOM *N*" in SQL syntax, but it is possible to return the last few records in a table. To create such a query, you simply sort in ascending (smallest to biggest) order, as shown in Listing 2.17.

Listing 2.17   A *SELECT* Query That Returns the Top Three Items in the tblOrder Table

```
SELECT TOP 3 *
FROM tblOrder
ORDER BY OrderDate
```

This query shows you the three oldest orders in your database.

Sorting data in ascending order is implicit in SQL; there's no need to use the ASC keyword (to denote ascending sort order) unless you really want to.

This query produces the following result:

ID	CustomerID	OrderDate	OrderAmount
13875	7494	6/5/94	221.52
17326	11923	6/5/94	243.73
13057	10036	6/5/94	213.2
23025	4006	6/5/94	119.46

Note, again, that this query returns four records because four records were tied for last place. You can see how this type of query might be a problem if you didn't pay attention to what you are doing, because the TOP *N* query actually returns the "BOTTOM *N*" results from the table unless you remember to sort the field in question in descending order.

Note: The query design window handled *TOP N* queries inconsistently in the initial shipping version of VB6. I assume this is a bug that will be fixed in a future service pack. The bug happens when you run a *TOP N* query. The query window displays an error message indicating that the *TOP N* SQL query can't be parsed; then it goes ahead and executes the query anyway. I guess this is because the *TOP N* syntax is specific to the Microsoft Access dialect of SQL, but who knows. Basically, *TOP N* will work as advertised, even if the query window doesn't recognize it.

CREATING TOP PERCENTAGE QUERIES

You can write queries that return a percentage of records in a table. For example, if you have a table with 1000 records, and you wish to return the top one percent of records, 10 records will usually be displayed. (It's possible that more than 10 records will be displayed in a top percentage query if more than one record stores the same value; this is also the case with a TOP N query.)

To return the top records in a resultset according to their percentage of the total records in your table, you use the TOP N PERCENT clause. For example, to return the top ten percent of outstanding orders in the tblOrder table, you use the SQL in Listing 2.18.

Listing 2.18   A *SELECT* Query That Returns the Top Ten Percent of Orders

```
SELECT TOP 10 PERCENT *
FROM tblOrder
ORDER BY OrderAmount DESC
```

This query produces the following resultset:

ID	CustomerID	OrderDate	Amount
13388	10407	11/21/97	251
7931	3046	12/11/98	250.99
15804	7608	10/13/98	250.98
27897	4976	1/22/99	250.98
15776	6485	1/3/99	250.97

JOINING RELATED TABLES IN A QUERY

You use a *join* to retrieve related information from more than one table.

To create a join in a query, you must designate the primary and foreign keys of the tables involved in the join. (These concepts were introduced in Chapter 1.) For example, consider two related tables with the following designs:

tblCustomer
ID
FirstName
LastName
Address
City
State
Zip
Phone
DateEntered
Preferred
TypeID

tblOrder
ID
CustomerID
OrderDate
OrderAmount

Though the tblOrder table stores information about orders and the tblCustomer table stores information about customers, it's likely that you'll want to retrieve a recordset showing information about customers' orders, like the following:

FirstName	LastName	OrderDate	Amount
Katie	Woodruff	5/6/97	$57.96
Jill	Davidson	6/1/97	$12.92
Gavin	Edwards	5/19/97	$164.04
Gavin	Edwards	6/4/97	$84.08

Retrieving a resultset like this is easy to do with a join, even though the data is stored in separate tables. As long as you inform the database engine that the primary key in tblCustomer (ID) is related to the foreign key (CustomerID) in tblOrder, the correct data will be returned.

Note: You'll notice that in this joined recordset, the same customer is displayed more than once, even though his name was only entered in the database once. This reflects the fact that the individual customer has multiple orders. It's a nice feature, since it means we never have to enter the customer's data in the database twice, but it sometimes means we get more information back in a query than we want.

EXPRESSING A JOIN IN SQL

In Microsoft Jet SQL, you can set up a join as an expression of equivalence between two fields, as in the following example:

```
SELECT FirstName, LastName, OrderDate, OrderAmount
FROM tblCustomer, tblOrder
WHERE tblCustomer.ID = tblOrder.CustomerID
```

This SQL returns information on all the customers who have related orders in the tblOrder table. It returns four columns of data—the FirstName and LastName fields from tblCustomer, as well as the OrderDate and Amount fields from tblOrder.

Note that in a query that includes a join, when the same field appears in two tables, you must include a reference to the base table as well as field name (such as tblOrder.ID rather than simply ID) to denote which table you're talking about.

You can also designate a join between two tables by using the INNER JOIN clause. The syntax is different, but the data returned is the same. For example, the join between the two tables described in the previous example might also be expressed with the SQL shown in Listing 2.19.

Listing 2.19   A Query Based on a Join Between the tblOrder and tblCustomer Tables

```
SELECT FirstName, LastName, OrderDate, OrderAmount
FROM tblCustomer
INNER JOIN tblOrder ON tblCustomer.ID = tblOrder.CustomerID
```

While the INNER JOIN syntax is supported by both Microsoft Jet and SQL Server, it was only recently added to the body of SQL syntax. Accordingly, not every database will support it. (Every ANSI-compliant database should support the older equivalence syntax, but this syntax is a bit harder to read—it's not obvious unless you think about it that the query is doing a join.)

Creating joins using the INNER JOIN syntax provides an important bonus— when you use INNER JOIN instead of a WHERE clause to join tables in a query, the resultset produced by the query can be updateable. For this reason, queries you create using visual query tools (particularly Microsoft Access) will almost invariably use the INNER JOIN clause to join two tables in a query.

   Note that again, the full *tablename.fieldname* syntax is used in the last clause of the joined query. This syntax is required because two ID fields are involved in this query: the ID field belonging to the tblCustomer table and the ID field belonging to the tblOrder table. However, you can use this full syntax whenever you want in your queries (see Listing 2.20).

Listing 2.20   Another Way of Expressing the Same Query, This Time Using Full Syntax

```
SELECT tblCustomer.FirstName, tblCustomer.LastName,
       tblOrder.OrderDate, tblOrder.OrderAmount
FROM tblCustomer
INNER JOIN tblOrder ON tblCustomer.ID = tblOrder.CustomerID
```

USING THE QUERY DESIGNER TO CREATE JOINS

Because creating joins can be the most complicated part of queries—particularly when more than two tables are involved—you might find it useful to have some help when creating them. Fortunately, you can use the Visual Basic Query Designer to create a query composed of a join between multiple tables. Using the Query Designer means that you don't have to memorize complicated SQL join syntax—instead, you can create the join graphically. To do this, follow these steps:

1. Start with a VB Data Environment designer. Right-click the connection icon and select Add Command.

2. A new command object appears, labeled Command1. Right-click the command object and then select Properties.

3. The properties dialog box appears. Click the option button labeled SQL Statement and then click the SQL Builder button.

4. A blank Query Designer window appears. From the Data View window, drag in the tblCustomer and tblOrder tables. Your query window should look like Figure 2.13.

Figure 2.13
Dragging tables into the Design window will create a join.

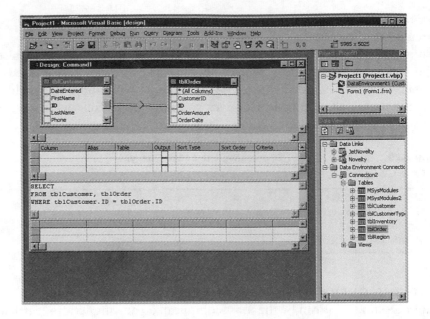

You can see that the Query Designer automatically creates a join between the two tables. However, the wrong fields are connected in the join—the ID field in tblCustomer is connected to the ID field in tblOrder. Joins are supposed to match data in the primary key of one table to a *foreign* key of another table. To fix this, follow these steps:

1. Right-click the join line connecting the two tables.

2. From the pop-up menu, select Remove.

3. The join line disappears. Now click-drag from the ID field in tblCustomer to the CustomerID field of tblOrder.

4. The join line reappears and the SQL expression is updated. The Query Designer window should look like Figure 2.14.

5. Next add fields to the output of the query. To do this, click the check boxes to the left of the FirstName and LastName fields in tblCustomer; then check the OrderDate and OrderAmount fields in tblCustomer.

6. To limit the number of records returned by the query (and speed up its execution), enter a criterion in the Criteria column for the OrderAmount field. Enter the value >**230**, indicating you only want to see orders for more than $230.

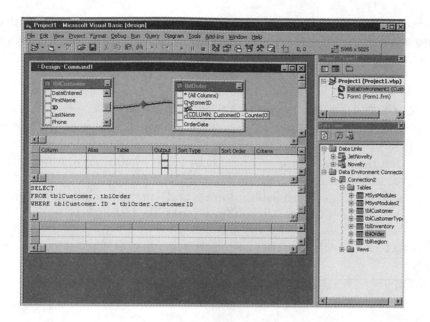

Figure 2.14
You can adjust the join line used to join two tables.

7. From VB's Query menu, select Run. The query returns data based on the relationship between customers and orders, as shown in Figure 2.15.

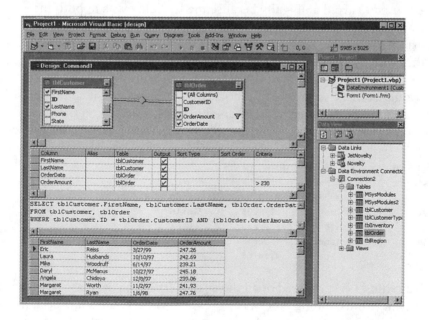

Figure 2.15
Data is returned from a joined query in the Design window.

Note: You have two additional weapons available in your query-constructing arsenal: the Visual Data Manager and Microsoft Access. Techniques for building queries using these tools are discussed later in this chapter.

USING OUTER JOINS TO RETURN MORE DATA

An inner join returns records from two tables in which a value in one table's primary key matches a value in a related table's foreign key. But suppose you want to return all the records on one side of a join whether or not there are related records? In this case, you must use an *outer join*.

For example, a query that lists customers and orders—including customers who do not have any orders outstanding—looks like Listing 2.21.

Listing 2.21   A Left Join That Lists Customers Regardless of Whether They Have Orders

```
SELECT FirstName, LastName, OrderDate, OrderAmount
FROM tblCustomer LEFT JOIN
    tblOrder ON tblCustomer.ID = tblOrder.CustomerID
WHERE LastName LIKE 'N%'
```

Note the `tablename.fieldname` syntax used in the LEFT JOIN clause. This longer name is used to avoid ambiguity because the ID field exists in both the tblCustomer and tblOrder tables. The fact that it's a LEFT JOIN means that tblCustomer, the table on the "one" side of the one-to-many relationship, is the one that will display all of its data. (If you were to change this to a RIGHT JOIN, the output would include all of the orders whether or not they had customers. This wouldn't make sense to do in most circumstances, but it could be useful if you were attempting to recover orphaned records—records on the "many" side of the relationship for which there are no corresponding records on the "one" side.)

This query returns the following resultset:

FirstName	LastName	OrderDate	Amount
Randy	Nelson	9/16/98	192.69
Randy	Nelson	10/5/98	215.16
Mikki	Newton	(NULL)	(NULL)
Julie	Nelson	(NULL)	(NULL)
Michelle	Nelson	4/14/98	62.97

This resultset is composed of all the customers in the database whether or not they have outstanding orders. For those customers without orders, *null* values appear in the OrderDate and Amount fields. A null value is a special value indicating the absence of data. In Visual Basic, `Null` is a keyword that represents a value that is different than zero or the empty string (which are also used to represent empty values in VB). For example, an arithmetic expression that contains a null value anywhere in the expression always evaluates to null.

A right join is the same as a left join, except that it returns all the records from the second table in the join (the right-side table), whether or not there are any matching records in the first table (the left-side table). Other than that, the same data can be returned whether you're using a left join or a right join.

As an example, say you have divided up the country into regions. Each region is assigned a salesperson, but you don't have enough salespeople to cover the whole country—some states don't have salespeople of their own. Accordingly, some states belong to a region, while other states belong to no region. (This is reflected in the table tblRegion.)

You want to develop a query to view your customers, whether or not they belong to a region. You accomplish this with a right join between tblCustomer and tblRegion, displaying all the states and regions whether or not they have any customers associated with them. The SQL to perform this query looks like Listing 2.22.

Listing 2.22 A Right Join That Lists All the Customers Whether or Not They Have Been Assigned a Region

```
SELECT FirstName, LastName, tblRegion.State, Region
FROM tblCustomer RIGHT JOIN
    tblRegion ON tblCustomer.State = tblRegion.State
WHERE City LIKE 'Ocean Glen' AND tblRegion.State IN ('CO', 'AL')
```

To further limit the number of records that come back in this query, we've provided a WHERE clause that only retrieves customers in the cities of Ocean Glen, Colorado and Ocean Glen, Alabama. (Never mind that Colorado is a landlocked state.)

Also note that the `tablename.fieldname` syntax is once again used to avoid ambiguity in situations where a field name exists in both tables involved in the join (in this case, the State field).

This query returns the following resultset:

FirstName	LastName	State	Region
Brad	Davidson	AL	(NULL)
Angela	Vermeren	AL	(NULL)
Cat	Johnson	AL	(NULL)
Steve	McClusky	CO	West
Rick	Hobaica	CO	West

The rows that contain nulls in the Region field indicate that the customer resides in a state that has not been assigned to a region.

DISPLAYING ZEROS INSTEAD OF NULLS IN A JOINED QUERY

It's very common—particularly when you're creating a query that will be used as the basis of a report—to create a query based on a join that displays zeros instead of nulls. To accomplish this, you can replace the reference to the field with a calculation.

In this case, the calculation involves the IIf function. IIf takes three arguments: an expression, a value to return if the expression is true, and a value to return if the expression is false.

For example, to return a string that flags whether an order is more than or less than $50, you would write the following IIf expression:

```
IIf([Amount] > 50, 'Big order', 'Small order')
```

So to use IIf to replace nulls with zeroes, you use the IsNull function to inspect the value of the field. If IsNull returns false, the field already has something in it, so you return whatever's in the field. But if it returns true, that means the field is null, so you return a zero instead. You can see an example of SQL code that accomplishes this in Listing 2.23.

Listing 2.23   A Query Based on a Join That Returns Zeros Instead of Nulls

```
SELECT FirstName, LastName, OrderDate,
       IIf(IsNull(OrderAmount), 0, OrderAmount) AS TotalAmount
FROM tblCustomer LEFT JOIN
    tblOrder ON tblCustomer.ID = tblOrder.CustomerID
WHERE OrderDate = #6/5/1998#
```

This query returns the following resultset:

FirstName	LastName	OrderDate	TotalAmount
Mike	Woodruff	6/5/98	198.58
Katie	Woodruff	6/5/98	0
Michelle	Husbands	6/5/98	52.33
Mark	Chideya	6/5/98	34.51
Kathleen	Woodruff	6/5/98	246.43
Michelle	Woodruff	6/5/98	0
Katie	Doberstein	6/5/98	44.53

Note: Queries with columns based on calculations generally return results significantly more slowly than queries based on fields.

When I was testing the preceding query in the Query Designer's SQL Window, I received the same warning message I received when attempting to run the TOP N query earlier in this chapter. Don't worry about it, though—this is a problem with the Query Designer, not with your SQL statement. The query runs as expected.

ALIASING FIELD NAMES USING *AS*

As you saw in the preceding example, you have the ability to *alias*, or rename, a field in a query. You might do this for two reasons:

▶ The underlying table has field names that are unwieldy, and you want to make the field names in the resultset easier to deal with

▶ The query you're creating produces some sort of calculated or aggregation column that requires a name

Whatever your reason for wanting to alias a field name, it's easy to do using the AS clause in SQL. For example, let's say you're doing a complex series of calculations on the OrderAmount field in the tblOrder table. You want to refer to that column as the Subtotal field to remind yourself that you're working with a subtotal rather than an extended total. To do this, you write the SQL code in Listing 2.24.

Listing 2.24   Renaming a Field in a Query Using the *AS* Clause

```
SELECT CustomerID, OrderDate, OrderAmount AS SubTotal
FROM tblOrder
```

This query produces the following resultset:

CustomerID	OrderDate	SubTotal
7548	5/25/99	112.78
4629	8/1/97	220.58
12925	1/17/99	192.92
…	…	…

The field that was formerly called Amount is referred to in this resultset as SubTotal. As far as this resultset is concerned, the Amount field doesn't exist, although the Amount field still exists in the underlying recordset. (Of course, this query isn't actually doing any subtotaling, it's just renaming the field.)

Although using the AS clause can be helpful in situations in which you're trying to simplify field names, aliasing fields is more commonly done when you're performing calculations on fields. For example, say you need to write a query that calculates sales tax on subtotals in tblOrder. Such a query might look like Listing 2.25.

Listing 2.25   A Query with Multiple Calculations: Each Calculated Field Is Named Using the *AS* Clause

```
SELECT ID, OrderDate, OrderAmount,
       (OrderAmount * 0.0825) AS SalesTax,
       (OrderAmount * 1.0825) AS Total
FROM tblOrder
WHERE OrderAmount > 250
```

The sales tax calculation assumes a sales tax of 8.25 percent. Here's the result-set of this query:

ID	OrderDate	Amount	SalesTax	Total
364	10/8/98	250.04	20.6283	270.6683
693	4/8/98	250.55	20.6704	271.2204
724	10/29/97	250.27	20.6473	270.9173
733	12/17/97	250.93	20.7017	271.6317
872	5/1/99	250.52	20.6679	271.1879

Note that the SalesTax and Total fields aren't stored in the database; they're calculated on the fly. Because they aren't stored in fields in the database structure, you should name them using the AS clause or you won't have any way of referring to them in code later. If you experiment with this, you can see that the Query Designer window will insert temporary names for calculated fields (such as "Expr1003") if you forget to supply a name using the AS clause.

QUERIES THAT GROUP AND SUMMARIZE DATA

Frequently, you'll need to create queries that answer questions like "how many orders came in yesterday?" In this scenario, you don't care exactly *who* ordered stuff, you only want to know how many orders came in. You can do this using group queries and aggregate functions.

Group queries summarize data according to one or more fields in common. For example, if you're interested in seeing the total number of orders that came in yesterday, you'd group by the OrderDate field (and supply a criterion limiting the data returned to yesterday only). Such a query would look like Listing 2.26.

Listing 2.26   A Query That Groups and Performs an Aggregate Count Function on a Field

```
SELECT OrderDate, Count(CustomerID) AS TotalOrders
FROM tblOrder
GROUP BY OrderDate
HAVING OrderDate=#6/30/1998#
```

(The HAVING clause is equivalent to the WHERE clause for grouped queries.)

The resultset produced by this query follows:

```
OrderDate    TotalOrders
6/30/98      30
```

Note the use of the AS clause in the SQL expression. This is used to give the column containing the result of the aggregate function a name, because it's calculated rather than stored in the database.

You could use a simpler version of this query to return a report of sales activity on a day-by-day basis. Such a query would simply eschew the HAVING criterion, as in Listing 2.27.

Listing 2.27   A Query That Groups and Sorts, This Time Without a Limiting Criterion

```
SELECT OrderDate, Count(CustomerID) AS TotalOrders
FROM tblOrder
GROUP BY OrderDate
```

Note that to refer to the field that results from the aggregate grouping, you need to name the new column. You do this by using the AS clause.

This query produces the following resultset:

```
OrderDate    TotalOrders
6/5/97       44
6/6/97       46
6/7/97       49
6/8/97       36
6/9/97       35
```

Note that this resultset does not generate records for dates on which no orders were taken.

THE *SUM* FUNCTION

You're not limited to simply counting records in aggregate functions. Using the SUM function, you can generate totals for all the records returned in numeric fields.

For example, to create a query that generates a day-by-day total of your company's sales, you would write the SQL code in Listing 2.28.

Listing 2.28   A Query That Performs an Aggregate *SUM* Function on the Amount Field

```
SELECT OrderDate, Sum(OrderAmount) AS TotalOrderAmount
FROM tblOrder
GROUP BY OrderDate
```

This query produces the following resultset:

OrderDate	TotalOrderAmount
6/5/97	6074.8
6/6/97	5440.38
6/7/97	7049.02
6/8/97	4277.99
6/9/97	5119.87

SUMMARY OF AGGREGATE FUNCTIONS

Table 2.2 lists all the aggregate functions available to you in SQL.

Table 2.2 Jet SQL's Aggregate Functions	
Function	**Result**
AVG	The average of all values in the column
COUNT	The count of the number of records returned
FIRST	The first value in the field
LAST	The last value in the field
MAX	The maximum (or largest) value in a column
MIN	The minimum (or smallest) value in a column
STDEV	The standard deviation
SUM	The total of all values in the field
VAR	The variance

The syntax of these aggregate functions is essentially the same as the syntax for COUNT, which I discussed in the previous section. For example, to calculate the average order in the tblOrders table on a day-by-day basis, you'd use the SQL query in Listing 2.29.

**Listing 2.29   A Query That Performs an Aggregate *AVG*
Function on the Amount Field**

```
SELECT OrderDate, Avg(OrderAmount) AS AverageOrderAmount
FROM tblOrder
GROUP BY OrderDate
```

This query produces the following resultset:

OrderDate	AverageOrderAmount
6/5/97	138.0636
6/6/97	118.2691
6/7/97	143.8576
6/8/97	118.8331
6/9/97	146.282

You must group on at least one field for an aggregate function to work.

CREATING ACTION QUERIES

An *action query* is a query that has the ability to alter records. Action queries do not return resultsets; instead, they make permanent changes to data.

You generally use action queries when you need to make changes to large amounts of data based on a criterion. For example, if you need to initiate a 10 percent across-the-board price increase in your products, you'd use an update query (a type of action query) to change the prices of all the items in your inventory.

> **Note:** The SQL examples in this section alter data in the database. If you're using the `novelty.mdb` database on the CD that accompanies this book, you might want to make a copy of it on your hard disk before attempting the examples in this section. If you hopelessly mangle the data, though, never fear—you can always reinstall it from the CD.

UPDATE QUERIES

An *update query* has the ability to alter a group of records all at once. An update query has three parts:

▶ The UPDATE clause, which specifies which table to update

▶ The SET clause, which specifies which data to change

▶ Optionally, the WHERE criteria, which limits the number of records affected by the update query

For example, to increase the wholesale price of all the items in your inventory, you'd use the update query shown in Listing 2.30.

Listing 2.30   An Update Query That Increases All the Values in the WholesalePrice Field by 10 Percent

```
UPDATE tblInventory
SET WholesalePrice = WholesalePrice * 1.1
```

The contents of the relevant fields in the tblInventory before you run the update query are as follows:

ID	Product	CatalogNumber	WholesalePrice
1	Rubber Chicken	AC5	$0.78
2	Joy Buzzer	BB1	$2.04
3	Seltzer Bottle	AZ401	$3.12
...	...	...	...

The contents after you run the update query are as follows:

ID	Product	CatalogNumber	WholesalePrice
1	Rubber Chicken	AC5	$0.86
2	Joy Buzzer	BB1	$2.24
3	Seltzer Bottle	AZ401	$3.43
...	...	...	...

To limit the number of records affected by the update query, you simply append a WHERE clause to the SQL query. For example, to apply a price increase only to big-ticket items that sell for more than $100, you'd alter the SQL as Listing 2.31 shows.

Listing 2.31   An Update Query That Increases the Values More Than $100 in the RetailPrice Field by 10 Percent

```
UPDATE tblInventory
SET [RetailPrice] = [RetailPrice] * 1.1
WHERE [RetailPrice] > 100
```

This query increases the retail price of items currently priced at more than $100 by 10 percent.

DELETE QUERIES

A *delete query* has the ability to delete one or more records at once.

For example, to delete all the orders that were placed before (but not on) last Halloween, you'd use the SQL statement shown in Listing 2.32.

Listing 2.32   A Delete Query That Deletes All the Records in the tblOrder Table Created Before October 31, 1998

```
DELETE *
FROM tblOrder
WHERE [OrderDate] < #10/31/98#
```

Note: Since this query will delete about two-thirds of the records in the Novelty database, you'll probably want to back up the database before trying out this query. (For the rest of the query examples in this chapter to make sense, you'll need all the original data.) If you didn't make a backup and you want to go back to the original version of the database, you can reinstall it from the CD.

APPEND QUERIES

You use an *append query* for two purposes:

▶ Adding a single record to a table

▶ Copying one or more records from one table to another

To create an append query, use the SQL INSERT clause. The exact syntax of the query depends on whether you're inserting a single record or copying multiple records.

For example, a single-record append query that adds a new order to the tblOrder table might look like Listing 2.33.

Listing 2.33   An Append Query That Inserts a Single Record into the tblOrder Table

```
INSERT INTO tblOrder (CustomerID, OrderDate, OrderAmount)
VALUES (119, #6/16/97#, 145.94)
```

Executing this query creates a new order for Customer 119 in the amount of $145.94 in tblOrder.

Note: In this append query, you don't append anything for the tblOrder table's ID field because it is an AutoNumber field. Attempting to do so would generate an error. The contents of an AutoNumber field can only be generated by the database engine itself.

To create the kind of append query that copies records from one table to another, you use an INSERT clause with a SELECT clause. For example, let's say that instead of deleting old orders, you archive them by periodically copying them to an archive table called tblOrderArchive, which has the same structure as the tblOrder table. (For this to work, you'll first need to create tblOrderArchive, making sure it has the same structure as tblOrder.)

The SQL statement to copy old records from the tblOrder table to the tblOrderArchive table might look like Listing 2.34.

Listing 2.34   An Append Query That Copies Multiple Records from One Table to Another

```
INSERT INTO tblOrderArchive
SELECT * FROM tblOrder
WHERE [OrderDate] < #6/10/97#
```

Executing this statement will copy all the records with order dates before June 10, 1997, into the tblOrderArchive table.

MAKE-TABLE QUERIES

A *make-table query* is similar to an append query, except that it can create a new table and copy records to it in one fell swoop.

To create a make-table query, you use the SELECT INTO clause. For example, in Listing 2.34 you copied records from the tblOrder table to an tblOrderArchive table. This presupposes that the tblOrderArchive actually exists, however. Instead, to copy the same records into a new table with the same structure as the original, you use the SQL action query given in Listing 2.35.

Listing 2.35   A Make-table Query That Copies All the Records from the tblOrder Table into a New Table

```
SELECT * INTO tblOrderArchive
FROM tblOrder
```

Note: Executing this query copies all the records from tblOrder into a new table called tblOrderArchive. However, if the query is run in Visual Basic, you'll receive an error if the table already exists. If tblOrderArchive already exists when the query is run in an Access query window, the original table is deleted and replaced by the database engine with the contents of the copied records.

You can apply selection criteria (using a WHERE clause) in the same way you apply criteria to an append query, as illustrated in the previous section on append queries. Doing so enables you to copy a subset of records from the original table into the new table you create with a make-table query.

UNION QUERIES

A *union query* merges the contents of two tables that have similar field structures. It's useful in situations in which you need to display potentially unrelated records from multiple record sources in a single resultset.

For instance, in the previous examples involving make-table queries and append queries, I described a procedure to store old orders in a table of their own, called tblOrderArchive. Because of the way your archiving system is set up, the records are physically located in two separate tables. This might be useful for efficiency—it's faster to query a small table than a large one. But it's possible that at some point you'd want to view all of the current records and the archived records in a single, unified resultset. A union query lets you do this.

Let's say you now need to view the old records in tblOrderArchive in the same resultset as the new records in tblOrder. The union query you write to accomplish this shown in Listing 2.36.

Listing 2.36   A Union Query That Displays the Contents of the tblOrder and tblOrderArchive Tables

```
SELECT *
FROM tblOrder
UNION
SELECT *
FROM tblOrderArchive
```

The resultset of this query combines old and new orders in a single resultset. The output would look exactly like the original table before it was archived.

By default, union queries do not return duplicate records (this would be useful if your record-archiving system did not delete records after it copied them to the archive table). You can cause a union query to intentionally display duplicate records by adding the ALL keyword, as in Listing 2.37.

Listing 2.37   A Union Query That Displays the Contents of the tblOrder and tblOrderArchive Tables Without Suppressing Duplicate Records

```
SELECT *
FROM tblOrder
UNION ALL
SELECT *
FROM tblOrderArchive
```

CROSSTAB QUERIES

A *crosstab query* is a way of grouping data in two dimensions at once. It is a great way to see summaries of data in a very compact resultset. Crosstab queries are commonly used in database reporting and charting.

Crosstab queries are similar to queries that perform grouping and aggregation. With a conventional grouping query, you group on a single field and perform an aggregate function on another field. An example of this might be a query that shows day-to-day sales figures for a week-long period, as in the following resultset:

```
OrderDate    TotalSales
6/1/97       $1,224.35
6/2/97       $269.04
6/3/97       $83.85
6/4/97       $267.68
6/5/97       $45.97
6/6/97       $178.90
6/7/97       $2.34
```

But this is a one-dimensional resultset—it only displays sales. What if you wanted to see how much each customer purchased on each day? With a crosstab query, you can do this easily, because crosstab can group on two separate fields.

To create a crosstab query that shows how much each customer spends per day, you use the SQL statement given in Listing 2.38.

Listing 2.38   A Crosstab Query That Shows Customer Sales Broken Down by Day and by Customer

```
TRANSFORM Sum(OrderAmount) AS TotalSales
SELECT CustomerID
FROM tblOrder
WHERE ((OrderDate) Between #6/5/98# And #6/7/98#)
GROUP BY CustomerID
ORDER BY CustomerID, OrderDate
PIVOT OrderDate
```

This statement produces the following resultset:

CustomerID	6/5/98	6/6/98	6/7/98
10	(NULL)	91.12	(NULL)
183	(NULL)	(NULL)	127.52
300	(NULL)	(NULL)	235.43
311	112.89	(NULL)	(NULL)
576	197.36	(NULL)	(NULL)
614	(NULL)	(NULL)	187.58

Note: Crosstab queries are not part of ANSI SQL, although they are supported in both Access and SQL Server. This means that you should not expect your crosstab queries to function when you migrate your application to another database back end.

Even if you understand crosstab queries pretty well, it makes sense to use a tool like Microsoft Access to create them if you can, because even the simplest crosstabs can be quite complicated to write. Access has an outstanding facility for creating crosstab queries graphically. For more information on how to create queries using Access, see "Creating Stored Queries Using Microsoft Access" later in this chapter.

SUBQUERIES

A *subquery* is a query whose result serves as a criterion for another query. Subqueries take the place of normal WHERE expressions. Because the result generated by the subquery takes the place of an expression, the subquery can only return a single value (as opposed to a conventional query, which returns multiple values in the form of rows and columns).

The only syntactical difference between a subquery and any other type of expression placed in a WHERE clause is that the subquery must be enclosed in parentheses.

For example, let's say you want to create a query that shows your biggest orders. You define a big customer as a customer that places a larger-than-average order. Because you can determine the value of a larger-than-average order (by performing an aggregate function on the Amount field in the tblOrder table), you can use this value as a subquery in the larger query. The SQL to do this is shown in Listing 2.39.

Listing 2.39 A Subquery That Provides a *WHERE* Condition to the Main Query

```
SELECT OrderDate, CustomerID, OrderAmount
FROM tblOrder
WHERE OrderAmount > (SELECT AVG(OrderAmount) FROM tblOrder)
```

In this case, the query and the subquery happen to be querying the same table, but this doesn't have to be the case. Subqueries can query any table in the database as long as they return a single value.

The SQL statement in Listing 2.39 returns the following resultset:

OrderDate	CustomerID	Amount
8/1/97	4629	220.58
1/17/99	12925	192.92
3/27/99	790	247.26
8/21/98	1942	147.86
10/29/97	1324	159.46

USING QUERIES STORED IN THE DATABASE

So far you've seen how to create queries on the fly, composed and executed at runtime by your Visual Basic application. In real Visual Basic database access applications, it's likely that your application will have dozens or even hundreds of SQL queries. To make it easier to maintain and reuse the queries you create, the database engine gives you the ability to permanently store a query definition in the database. This section describes how to create such queries.

> **Note:** In the parlance of Data Access Object programming, queries stored in a database are also referred to as *QueryDefs*. In the world of client/server programming, queries stored in the database are sometimes referred to as *views*. In this book, I'll generally refer to such queries as *stored queries* to make my discussion of them consistent and less jargonish.

Database programmers frequently ask why one would go about storing SQL statements in a compiled executable rather than storing them in a database. The answer isn't always clear-cut, but, in general, it's easier and more efficient to embed your queries in the database. There are also some valid situations in which you'd want to compose your query in Visual Basic code at runtime, however. Table 2.3 highlights the advantages and disadvantages of the two techniques.

Table 2.3 Advantages of Stored Queries Versus Queries in Executables	
Stored Query	**Query in Executable**
Executes quickly because it's compiled ahead of time by the database engine	Executes more slowly because it must be interpreted at the time it is run
Requires a change to the to install	Requires a recompilation and database redistribution of that executable
Moderate degree of flexibility (mainly through the use of parameterized queries)	High degree of flexibility (can include parameterized queries as well as concatenated SQL statements generated from any Visual Basic process, including variables, If...Then statements, and other queries)
Easier to maintain because it's stored in the database	Harder to maintain because it's embedded in code

BUSINESS CASE 2.1: STORED QUERIES VERSUS QUERIES GENERATED ON THE FLY

Queries that you store in the database let you modify the way your application works without breaking existing code. For example, let's say you have a payroll application that stores data in tblEmployee. If the application generates its queries on the fly in Visual Basic code, it would interact with the database as illustrated in Figure 2.16.

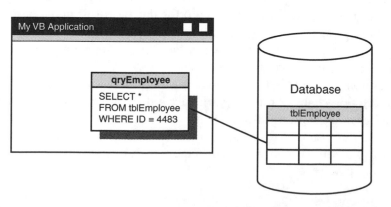

Figure 2.16
Here's an application that generates its own database queries on the fly.

This application might be functional, but it would have the following problems:

▶ It would be extremely difficult to change, because the SQL code would be scattered throughout your code.

▶ The queries scattered throughout your code might be inconsistent—for example, one query might recognize a particular status field in the database while others might ignore it.

▶ It would run less efficiently because queries stored in Visual Basic EXEs aren't compiled by the database engine. This is the case whether you're using Jet or SQL Server.

A better technique is to store the query in the database, as illustrated in Figure 2.17.

Figure 2.17
Here's the same database application, this time with the query stored in the database.

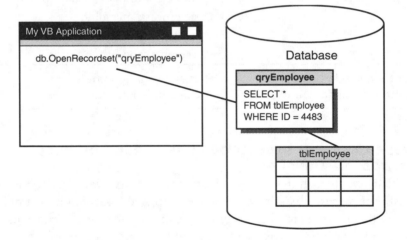

In addition to reducing complexity in your VB application by moving the SQL code out of your application and into the database, this design also inoculates your design against change. If a component of the database design changes, you don't have to change your VB code (which would force you to recompile and redistribute your application).

For example, say you alter your database design to accommodate a Hide field in the tblEmployee table. Employees who are hidden are currently inactive—perhaps they don't work for the company anymore, or they haven't been hired yet. You don't want to delete them, because you need to retain information about them indefinitely, but you need to hide them so your system doesn't keep issuing them paychecks.

The database design that describes this change is illustrated in Figure 2.18.

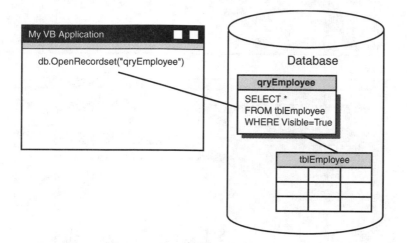

Figure 2.18
The database design looks like this after a change has been made, and no change in the VB application was necessary.

As long as you don't change field names or remove a column from the result-set of the query, you can use the same query again and again in your application. Your application's code remains unchanged, while your database has the ability to adapt to whatever changing business conditions happen to come along.

CREATING STORED QUERIES USING VISUAL DATA MANAGER

You have the ability to create queries stored in a Jet database using the Visual Data Manager add-in included with Visual Basic. To do this, follow these steps.

1. In Visual Basic, select the menu command Add-Ins, Visual Data Manager.

2. The Visual Data Manager appears. In the Visual Data Manager's File, Open DataBase menu, select Microsoft Access. From the file dialog box, locate and select the database `novelty.mdb`.

3. The database opens. In the Visual Data Manager's toolbar, select the Use DBGrid Control On New Form button, as illustrated in Figure 2.19.

4. In the Visual Data Manager's SQL Statement window, type the SQL statement shown in Listing 2.40.

Listing 2.40   A Basic Select Query

```
SELECT FirstName, LastName
FROM tblCustomer
WHERE State = 'OR'
ORDER BY LastName, FirstName
```

Figure 2.19
A Visual Data Manager's toolbar selection displays query results in a grid format.

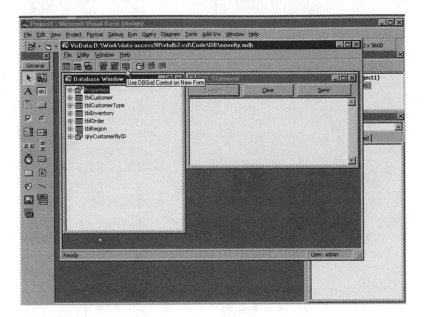

Note: In Visual Data Manager, pressing Enter when you're entering a SQL statement indicates that you want to execute the query. If you're instead looking to insert a line break in the SQL statement, press Shift+Enter.

5. When you're done typing the SQL statement, click Execute.

6. The message box "Is this a SQLPassThrough Query?" appears. Because SQL pass-through queries are only relevant in client/server development, click No.

The query executes, as illustrated in Figure 2.20.

Note: Every time you run a query using the Visual Data Manager, it asks this question—even for Access databases, which don't support pass-through. There's no way that I know of to suppress this needlessly irritating behavior.

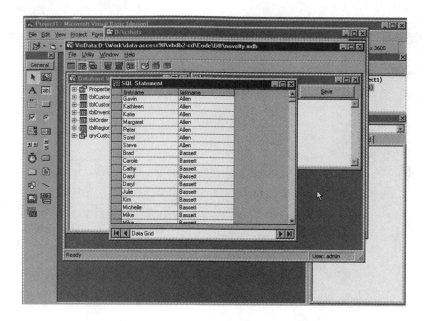

Figure 2.20
The product of a query in the Visual Data Manager is displayed in a grid.

7. Now that you know the query works properly, close the query window.

8. In the SQL Statement window, click the Save button.

9. In the Enter QueryDef Name dialog box, type **qryOregonCustomers** and then click OK.

10. The message box "Is this a SQLPassThrough QueryDef?" appears. Because this is not a client/server database, click the No button.

The query is stored in the database. It also appears in the Database window, as illustrated in Figure 2.21.

You can rerun the query at any time by double-clicking the query definition in Visual Data Manager's Database window. Now that you've saved it in the database, you can refer to qryOregonCustomers just as you would refer to any table in the database.

> **Note:** You've probably noticed already that in this book, tables are named with the "tbl" prefix and stored queries are named with the "qry" prefix. Now you know why—the fact that the database engine treats tables and queries almost interchangeably means that it can become difficult for developers to know what they're dealing with.

Figure 2.21
*A query saved in
the database is
seen in Visual Data
Manager's
Database window.*

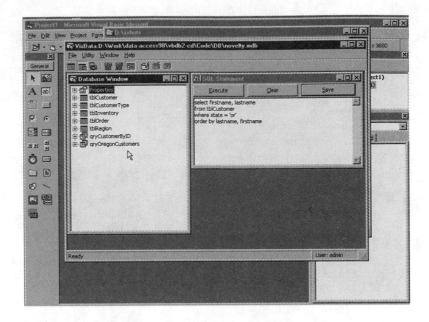

USING THE VISUAL DATA MANAGER QUERY BUILDER

You can use Visual Data Manager's Query Builder to create a SQL statement that serves as the basis of a query. Using the Query Builder can be easier than writing the SQL yourself because the Query Builder presents lists of choices. To create a query using the Query Builder, follow these steps:

1. From Visual Data Manager's Utility menu, select Query Builder.

2. From the list of tables, click tblCustomer.

3. The Fields to Show list is populated with a list of fields in tblCustomer. From that list, select tblCustomer.FirstName, tblCustomer.LastName, and tblCustomer.State.

The Query Builder looks like Figure 2.22.

Next, you'll specify a criterion for this query to limit the number of records it will return.

1. From the Field Name combo box, select tblCustomer.State.

2. In the Operator combo box, make sure that the equal sign is selected.

3. Click the List Possible Values beneath the Value combo box. A list of possible values that can match the field you chose is added to the combo box. Select the value CO to list customers from Colorado.

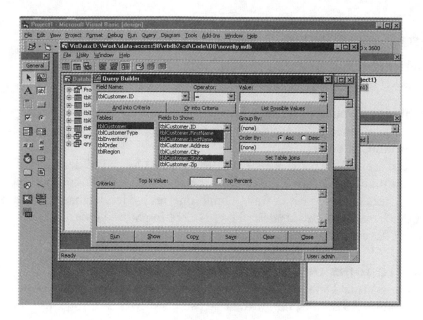

4. Click the And Into Criteria button to add the criterion you just constructed to the query definition.

The query looks like Figure 2.23.

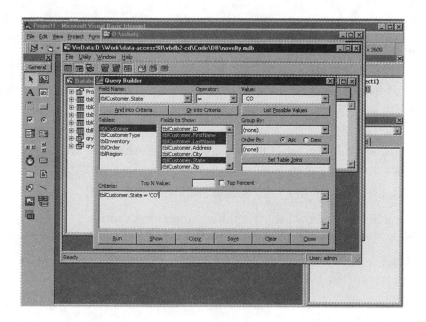

Figure 2.23
The Query Builder now contains a query that has a criterion associated with it.

5. Run the query by clicking the Run button. The ultra-annoying "Is this a SQLPassThrough Query?" message box appears. Click No.

6. The query runs. Only those records for customers in Colorado are displayed in the grid.

At this point, you can save the query in the database if you wish. To save the query you've defined, click the Save button and then enter the name **qryColoradoCustomers**.

You can see that by using Visual Data Manager's Query Builder, you can save a significant amount of time developing queries—particularly, complicated queries. There's an even easier way to build queries for Jet databases, however: by using Microsoft Access, as described in "Creating Stored Queries Using Microsoft Access" later in this chapter.

CREATING JOINS IN VISUAL DATA MANAGER

You can use Visual Data Manager to create a query based on a join between two or more tables. To do this, follow these steps:

1. If the Query Builder dialog box is visible, click the Clear button to clear out the previous query. If it's not visible, select Query Builder from the Visual Data Manager's Utility window. The Query Builder dialog box appears.

2. In the list of tables, click tblCustomer and tblOrder.

3. Click on the Set Table Joins button.

4. The Join Tables dialog box appears. Click tblCustomer and tblOrder. The list of fields in both tables appears in the dialog's list boxes, as illustrated in Figure 2.24.

5. In the first column, select the primary key of the tblCustomer table, ID. In the second column, select the foreign key in the tblOrder table, CustomerID.

6. Click the Add Join to Query button and then click Close.

7. In the Fields to Show list, click tblCustomer.FirstName, tblCustomer.LastName, tblOrder.OrderDate, and tblOrder.OrderAmount.

8. Click the Run button. The "Is this a SQLPassThrough query?" message box appears; answer No.

9. The query is run and the result is displayed, as illustrated in Figure 2.25.

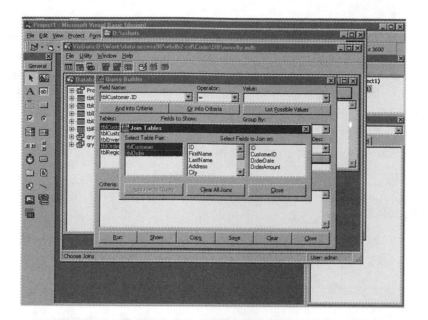

Figure 2.24
Lists of fields in selected tables appear in the arduous process of creating a join in the Visual Data Manager.

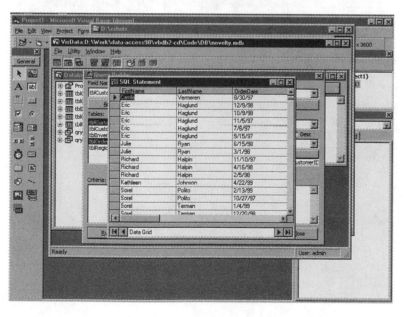

Figure 2.25
The product of a query joining two tables in the Visual Data Manager is displayed.

At this point, if you wish to save the query, you can do so (by clicking the Save button in the Query Builder). When you're done with the Query Builder, close it by clicking its Close button.

CREATING STORED QUERIES USING MICROSOFT ACCESS

Microsoft Access has a much slicker interface for creating queries than that of the Visual Data Manager. You can use Access to create very complicated joins very quickly. As an added bonus, Access has the ability to translate a graphical query into a SQL string in the same way the Query Designer window does. As a result, many developers prefer to use Access to build and test queries.

To create a query using Microsoft Access, follow these steps:

1. Launch Access and open the database you wish to work with. The Database window appears.

2. Click the table on which you wish to base your query. In this example, I'll use tblCustomer.

3. From the Insert menu, select Query.

4. The New Query dialog box appears. Choose Design View.

   The query design window appears, as illustrated in Figure 2.26.

Figure 2.26
The Microsoft Access graphical query design window looks like this.

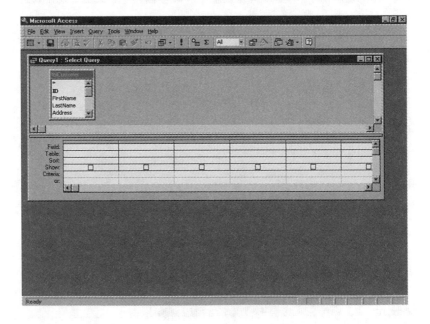

5. For this query, you want to display the customer's first and last name, address, city, and state. To do this, click-drag those fields from the list of fields to the grid at the bottom of the query design window. The query looks like Figure 2.27.

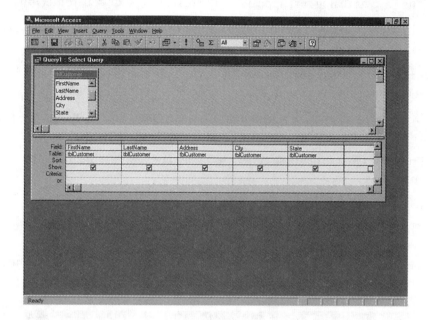

Figure 2.27
Fields are dragged from the table to the Access query design window.

6. To sort the query output, click the Sort row underneath the FirstName and LastName fields. Select Ascending for both fields.

7. Click the LastName field to select it. Then click-drag the field so it appears in the leftmost column in the query design grid. Doing this will ensure that it is sorted first, before the FirstName field.

8. Run the query by selecting the menu command Query, Run. The resultset appears.

9. Go back to design view by selecting the menu command View, Design View.

Now you'll specify a criterion to limit the number of records returned by the query:

1. Type the word **Jones** in the Criteria row under the LastName field.

2. Run the query. Only records for customers named Jones are returned.

You can save the query you're working on at any time. To save a query you're working on in Access, follow these steps:

1. From the File menu, select Save.

2. The Save As dialog box appears. In the dialog, type **qryCustomerJones**.

3. Click OK. The query definition is saved in the database.

Creating Joins in Microsoft Access   It's extremely easy to create a query based on two or more joined tables in Microsoft Access. To do this, follow these steps:

1. If you need to, open qryCustomerJones, the query you created in the previous example. Make sure you open this query in design view.

2. From the Query menu, select Show Table. The Show Table dialog box appears.

3. Double-click tblOrder, and then click the Close button.

4. The table tblOrder appears in the query. If you defined a relationship between tblCustomer and tblOrder in your database in the example in Chapter 1, you should be able to see the relationship expressed graphically, as illustrated in Figure 2.28.

Figure 2.28
You can see two joined tables in the Microsoft Access query design window.

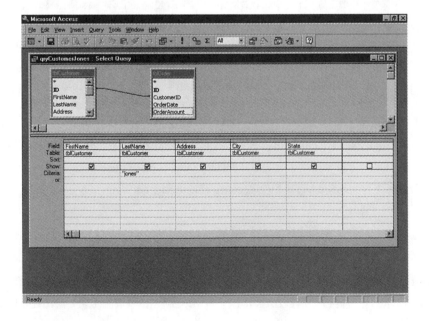

Note: Access is smart enough to know that a predefined relationship exists between two tables when you build a query based on those tables. This capability saves you some steps because you don't have to create the joins in each query you build; it also keeps you from having to remember which fields to connect in the tables.

5. If Access does not automatically create a join between the two tables, draw one manually by click-dragging from the ID field in tblCustomer to the CustomerID field in tblOrder.

6. Click-drag the fields OrderDate and OrderAmount from tblOrder into the query design grid.

7. Run the query. You should be able to see the data from both fields, as illustrated in Figure 2.29.

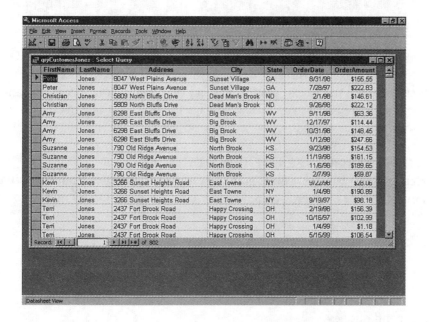

Figure 2.29
The output of the multitable query created in Microsoft Access is displayed.

Using SQL Code Generated by Access   You can view the SQL behind a query you develop in Access at any time. To do this, select SQL View from the Microsoft Access View menu. The query output window changes in a SQL view window, as illustrated in Figure 2.30.

Figure 2.30
*Microsoft Access
gives you the ability to view the SQL
behind a stored
query.*

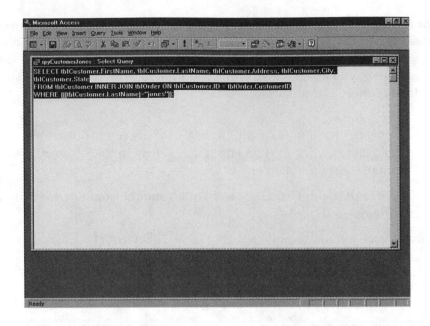

You can edit this SQL directly, if you wish. In most cases, you can switch back and forth between the Access graphical query designer, recordsheet view, and SQL view. This ability lets you take advantage the power of SQL as well as Microsoft Access's ease of use.

CREATING OTHER TYPES OF QUERIES IN ACCESS

By default, Access assumes you're going to create a SELECT query, but you can easily change the type of query you're writing. Using Access's Query menu, you can create these types of queries:

▶ Crosstab queries

▶ Make-table queries

▶ Update queries

▶ Append queries

▶ Delete queries

▶ A category of queries Access refers to as *SQL-specific queries*, which includes Union queries, pass-through queries, and Data Definition Language (DDL) commands

The SQL syntax for creating all of these queries is discussed earlier in this chapter.

There is no graphical user interface for creating "SQL-specific" queries in Microsoft Access or the Visual Data Manager; you must type in the code for these queries manually. For more information on Data Definition queries, see "Using Data Definition Language" later in this chapter.

CREATING STORED QUERIES AT RUNTIME

You have the ability to create queries in code at runtime using Data Access Objects (DAO). You'd do this in situations in which some component of the query depends on some other processing performed by your application.

For example, say you are writing a Visual Basic application that acts as a report generator for a particular database. This application must have the ability to output data from any table in the database, constrained by any one of a number of criteria, and sorted any way the user wishes. To avoid hard-wiring any of this information, yet permit the user to return to queries she defined earlier, you might use a dynamically-generated query.

To create queries dynamically at runtime, you use the OpenRecordset method of the DAO QueryDef object. For more on dynamically generated queries using Data Access Objects, see Chapter 3.

USING DATA DEFINITION LANGUAGE

Data Definition Language (DDL) commands are SQL statements that enable you to create, manipulate, and destroy elements of the database structure. Using DDL, you can create and destroy tables and alter the definition of tables.

Data Definition Language commands are perhaps the most seldom-used statements in Microsoft Jet SQL, mainly because there are so many good tools (such as Microsoft Access and the Visual Data Manager) that help you perform chores such as creating tables, fields, and indexes. It's also more Visual Basic–like to perform these kinds of tasks using one of the data access libraries such as DAO (discussed in Chapter 3) or ADO (Chapter 10). If you're coming from a client/server environment, however, you might be more comfortable with using DDL to create the structure of your database. If you use ADO, you'll pass DDL commands to the ADO Command object regardless. (Bear in mind that Microsoft Jet doesn't support the use of DDL commands on non-Jet databases.)

Like action queries, Data Definition Language commands do not return resultsets (which is why they're referred to as "commands" rather than "queries").

There is no support for DDL commands in the graphical user interface of either Microsoft Access or the Visual Data Manager. To execute a DDL command, you must type the SQL directly. In the Visual Data Manager, you type the SQL into the SQL Statement window; in Access, you type the SQL into the SQL view of a query definition window.

CREATING DATABASE ELEMENTS USING *CREATE*

You create new database elements using the SQL CREATE clause. To create a table, you use the CREATE TABLE command, followed by the fields and data types you wish to add to the table, delimited by commas and enclosed in parentheses.

For example, to create a new table, you can use the SQL statement in Listing 2.41.

Listing 2.41   A Query that Creates the tblRegionNew Table

```
CREATE TABLE tblRegionNew
([State] TEXT (2),
[Region] TEXT (50))
```

The data type "TEXT (2)" tells the database engine to create a text field that can store a maximum of two characters; "TEXT (50)" creates a field 50 characters long.

This query creates a table with the following schema:

tblRegionNew
State
Region

Table 2.4 shows a list of the data types of fields you can denote using Microsoft Jet DDL and the CREATE clause.

Table 2.4 Data Types of Fields Available in Jet		
Data Type	**SQL**	**Comments**
AutoNumber (Long Integer)	COUNTER	This is the most commonly used AutoNumber field
AutoNumber (Replication ID)	GUID	Generally used only for replication
Currency	CURRENCY	

Data Type	SQL	Comments
Date/Time	DATETIME	
Hyperlink	LONGTEXT	Stored the same as a Memo field
Memo	LONGTEXT	
Number (Byte)	BYTE	
Number (Double)	DOUBLE	
Number (Integer)	INTEGER	
Number (Long Integer)	LONG	The most commonly used integer field
Number (Single)	SINGLE	
OLE Object	LONGBINARY	
Text	TEXT	You must supply the length of the field; for example, TEXT (50)
Yes/No	BOOLEAN	

ADDING CONSTRAINTS TO TABLES

You can add constraints at the time you create a table. A *constraint* is similar to an index, but it's used to designate a unique key, a primary key, or a foreign key.

You create a constraint by using the SQL CONSTRAINT clause. The CONSTRAINT clause takes two parameters: the name of the index and the name of the field or fields you're interested in indexing. You can declare the index to be UNIQUE or PRIMARY, in which case the index designates that the field can only accept unique values or that a field or fields serves as the table's primary key.

> **Note:** The concept of indexes having names might seem a little strange to you if you're accustomed to Microsoft Access; this is because Access buries the names of indexes in its user interface. You can get access to the name of an index programmatically, however.

For example, as an enhancement to the tblRegionNew table created in the previous example, you might add a unique index to the State field because it is used in joins. The SQL to create this table with a CONSTRAINT clause looks like Listing 2.42.

Listing 2.42 A SQL Command That Creates a Table with a Constraint That Forces the State Field to Be Unique

```
CREATE TABLE tblRegionNew
([State] TEXT (2),
[Region] TEXT (50),
CONSTRAINT StateIndex UNIQUE ([State]))
```

This query creates the table with a unique index called StateIndex on the State field.

Though this example indexes the State field, it might make more sense to make the State field the table's primary key. Doing so will index the field, ensure that no values are duplicated in the State field, and ensure that no null values appear in the State field. The SQL to create the tblRegionNew table with the State field as its primary key is in Listing 2.43.

Listing 2.43 A SQL Command That Creates a Table with a Primary Key

```
CREATE TABLE tblRegionNew
([State] TEXT (2),
[Region] TEXT (50),
CONSTRAINT PrimaryKey PRIMARY KEY ([State]))
```

DESIGNATING FOREIGN KEYS

To designate a field as a foreign key, you use the FOREIGN KEY constraint.

For example, let's say that in your database design, there is a one-to-many relationship between the State field in the tblRegionNew table and a corresponding State field in the tblCustomer table. Given this fact, the code that you'd use to create a tblCustomer table in code might look like Listing 2.44.

Listing 2.44 SQL Code That Creates a Table with a Relationship, Including a Primary and Foreign Key

```
CREATE TABLE tblCustomer
([ID] COUNTER,
[FirstName] TEXT (20),
[LastName] TEXT (30),
```

```
[Address] TEXT (100),
[City] TEXT (75),
[State] TEXT (2),
CONSTRAINT IDPrimary PRIMARY KEY ([ID]),
CONSTRAINT StateForeign FOREIGN KEY ([State])
REFERENCES tblRegionNew ([State]))
```

Note that designating a foreign key in a CREATE TABLE command doesn't create an index on that foreign key; it only serves to create a relationship between the two tables.

CREATING INDEXES WITH *CREATE INDEX*

In addition to creating indexes at the time you create your table (using the CONSTRAINT clause), you can also create indexes after you've created the table (using the CREATE INDEX clause). This is useful when you want to create an index on a table that already exists (as opposed to the CONSTRAINT clause, which only lets you create indexes on tables at the time you create the table).

To create an index on an existing table, you use the SQL in Listing 2.45.

Listing 2.45   A SQL Command That Creates an Index on the tblCustomer Table

```
CREATE INDEX StateIndex
ON tblCustomer ([State])
```

To create a unique index, you use the UNIQUE keyword, as in Listing 2.46.

Listing 2.46   A SQL Command That Creates a Unique Index on the State Field In the tblRegionNew Table

```
CREATE UNIQUE INDEX StateIndex
ON tblRegionNew ([State])
```

To create an index that does not permit null values, you use the DISALLOW NULL clause, as in Listing 2.47.

Listing 2.47   A SQL Command That Creates a Unique Index on the State Field and Does Not Allow Nulls

```
CREATE UNIQUE INDEX StateIndex
ON tblRegionNew ([State])
WITH DISALLOW NULL
```

To create a primary key on an existing table, you use the SQL in Listing 2.48.

Listing 2.48   A SQL Command That Designates the State Field as the Primary Key in the tblRegion Table

```
CREATE UNIQUE INDEX PrimaryKey
ON tblRegionNew ([State])
WITH PRIMARY
```

DELETING TABLES AND INDEXES USING *DROP*

You can delete database elements using the DROP clause. For example, to delete a table, you use the SQL statement shown in Listing 2.49.

Listing 2.49   A SQL Command That Deletes a Table

```
DROP TABLE tblRegionNew
```

You can also drop an index in a table using the DROP clause, as in Listing 2.50.

Listing 2.50   A SQL Command That Removes an Index on a Field in the tblRegion Table

```
DROP INDEX PrimaryKey ON tblRegionNew
```

Note that to delete a primary key, you must know the primary key's name. If you're not sure of a key's name, you can access it using DAO Indexes collection. For more information on that, see Chapter 3. You might not know the internal name of a table's index if you built the table in Microsoft Access, since Access shields implementation details like index names from the database designer.

You have the ability to drop individual fields within tables. To do that, you use a DROP clause within an ALTER TABLE clause, as discussed in the next section.

Note: In the client/server world, you also have the ability to drop a database using DDL commands. This doesn't work in the Microsoft Jet world—in Jet, to "drop" a database, you simply delete the .mdb file from disk. You can delete a file in Visual Basic code using VB's Kill statement.

MODIFYING A TABLE'S DEFINITION USING *ALTER*

You can alter the definition of a field in a table by using the ALTER clause. For example, to add a CustomerType field to the tblCustomer table, you use the SQL statement given in Listing 2.51.

Listing 2.51   A SQL Command That Adds the CustomerType Column to the tblCustomer Table

```
ALTER TABLE tblCustomer
ADD COLUMN CustomerType LONG
```

To remove a field from a database, you use the DROP COLUMN clause along with an ALTER TABLE clause, as in Listing 2.52.

Listing 2.52   A SQL Command That Removes the CustomerType Column from the tblCustomer Table

```
ALTER TABLE tblCustomer
DROP COLUMN CustomerType
```

You also have the ability to add constraints to a table by using the ALTER TABLE clause. For example, to create a relationship between the tblCustomer and tblOrder tables using ALTER TABLE, you use the SQL given in Listing 2.53.

Listing 2.53   A SQL Command That Designates the CustomerID as the Foreign Key in the tblOrder Table

```
ALTER TABLE tblOrder
ADD CONSTRAINT OrderForeignKey
FOREIGN KEY ([CustomerID])
REFERENCES tblCustomer ([ID])
```

Remember, adding a constraint doesn't create a conventional index on a field, it just makes a field unique, designates a field as a primary key, or creates a relationship between two tables.

SUMMARY

This chapter covered the query technologies available to you in a Visual Basic database access application. Queries that return records as well as queries that create and change database structures were covered.

Much of what's covered in this chapter doesn't stand on its own—it will make much more sense when you start programming with one of the database libraries such as DAO or ADO, introduced in Chapters 3 and 10 respectively.

QUESTIONS AND ANSWERS

Q. Given the fact that you can either generate queries dynamically at runtime or use queries that are stored in the database, which technique should you use?

A. It depends on your application, but it's generally better to embed queries in the database, if you can. Doing so reduces complexity in your application, causes queries to execute more efficiently, and opens the possibility of multiple procedures in your application sharing the same query resources. In a multiuser application, storing queries in the database also means that when you need to alter a query, that alteration doesn't necessarily break the client applications that depend on it. You don't have to redistribute new versions of a compiled executable to all your users just because one of your queries now returns five fields instead of four.

Q. Why would one use straight SQL—as opposed to a visual query-building tool such as Visual Data Manager or Microsoft Access—to build database tables or stored queries?

A. Having the ability to create database components in code is useful if you are writing an application that creates database elements at runtime. In this case, your application has no access to the design-time tools provided by the Visual Data Manager or Microsoft Access. Having a handle on the underlying SQL is also very helpful when you move into Data Access Objects programming, because many DAO commands take SQL statements as arguments.

It's also useful to write your database using straight SQL code if you need to document everything that went into creating the database. This way, if you need to replicate the design of all or part of the database at some point in the future, you don't have to go digging through Microsoft Access's GUI to figure out what you did to create the database.

Q. This chapter refers to Data Access Objects (DAO) and ActiveX Data Objects (ADO). I already understand SQL pretty well—why would I want to use these data access libraries when I already know SQL?

A. If SQL is what you know, and you can get by using SQL alone, by all means do so. The fact that the Visual Basic documentation focuses so much on DAO and ADO at the expense of straight SQL is one of the reasons why this chapter covers SQL so thoroughly.

That said, SQL is just one part of the equation. You'll need a programmability model provided by a database access library to actually program the database from VB. it's also important to understand that in Visual Basic, DAO and ADO give you a far more robust and flexible way to get access to data than straight SQL does. And many Visual Basic developers find DAO or ADO much easier to deal with than SQL, because they express many common database operations in terms of VB's object/property/method/event paradigm. You still need to know at least a little SQL to be a successful database developer in Visual Basic, but the choice of how much SQL to use will depend on what you want to do and what you feel comfortable with.

Data Access Objects

USING THE DAO OBJECT MODEL

USING DAO TO WORK WITH DATA

CREATING OBJECTS THAT MANIPULATE THE
STRUCTURE OF A DATABASE

You can manipulate databases in Visual Basic code using Data Access Objects (DAO). Using DAO, you can run queries, update values in database tables, and create the structure of databases, including tables, stored queries, and relationships among tables.

If you're accustomed to using the features of SQL to perform these tasks in your applications, DAO will represent something of a paradigm shift. But after you ascend the learning curve, you'll find that DAO's programming interface is extremely robust and easy to use. With Microsoft Jet databases, DAO also gives you access to features not available with SQL by itself—or by ActiveX Data Objects (ADO), the more recent replacement for DAO (covered in Chapter 10, "ActiveX Data Objects").

DAO was once used by VB developers for gaining access to both desktop and client/server databases. But with the advent of ADO, it's now appropriate for use mainly with Jet databases only. (Coverage of the ODBCDirect mode of DAO is included in this book for those developers who need to continue to use DAO code to manage existing client/server projects; for new client/server development you'll almost certainly want to take advantage of ADO).

Although it may seem as if there is some overlap between DAO and SQL (described in Chapter 2, "Queries"), you'll actually find that as you become more experienced with using databases in Visual Basic, you use SQL and DAO together. The OpenRecordset method of the Database object, for example, can take a SQL statement as its parameter. If you're familiar with SQL already, this familiarity enables you to leverage your existing knowledge and transfer it into the world of object-oriented programming.

USING THE DAO OBJECT MODEL

The DAO object model is complex, with hundreds of elements. Dozens of types of collections own dozens more objects, each of which in turn has properties, methods, and subordinate objects of its own. The model can be a lot to grasp.

Figure 3.1 is a simplified version of the DAO object hierarchy.

Figure 3.1
The DAO hierarchy, showing relationships among database objects.

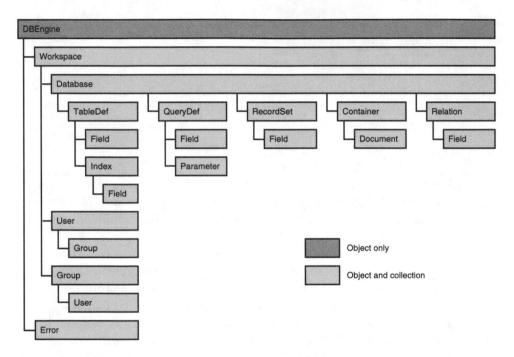

One way to digest the complexity of DAO's object model is to start with the Database object and consider its collections. Collections are related sets of objects; the Database object has the collections of objects shown in Figure 3.2.

Through the collections owned by the Database object, you can manipulate data and the structure of a database, create new database objects, and inspect the structure and data contained in a database.

Within DAO programming, there is a core set of commonly used techniques used in nearly every program. These include the following:

▶ Retrieving data by running a select query

▶ Iterating through the records in a recordset, one record at a time

▶ Running an action query (including update, delete, and append queries)

▶ Altering the structure of the database

▶ Handling errors generated by database access

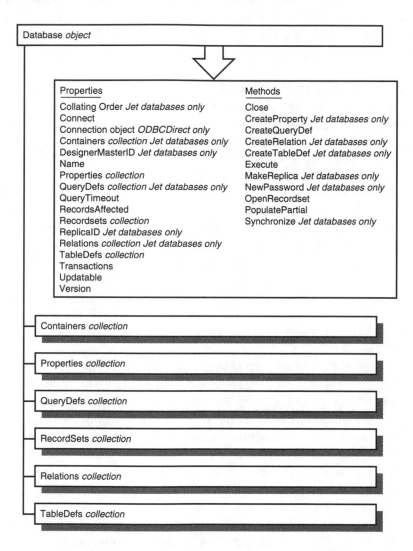

Figure 3.2
The collections owned by the Database object in the DAO object hierarchy.

Database *object*

Properties	Methods
Collating Order *Jet databases only*	Close
Connect	CreateProperty *Jet databases only*
Connection object *ODBCDirect only*	CreateQueryDef
Containers *collection Jet databases only*	CreateRelation *Jet databases only*
DesignerMasterID *Jet databases only*	CreateTableDef *Jet databases only*
Name	Execute
Properties *collection*	MakeReplica *Jet databases only*
QueryDefs *collection Jet databases only*	NewPassword *Jet databases only*
QueryTimeout	OpenRecordset
RecordsAffected	PopulatePartial
Recordsets *collection*	Synchronize *Jet databases only*
ReplicaID *Jet databases only*	
Relations *collection Jet databases only*	
TableDefs *collection*	
Transactions	
Updatable	
Version	

Containers *collection*

Properties *collection*

QueryDefs *collection*

RecordSets *collection*

Relations *collection*

TableDefs *collection*

This chapter serves as a cookbook for these commonly used code constructs, providing typical code examples that work with any kind of database. Bear in mind that these techniques work best with Microsoft Access databases; although DAO will work with client/server databases, ADO, covered in Chapter 10, is a better choice for most purposes.

To gain access to the features provided by DAO, you'll need a handle on how to code against an object library. If you're an experienced Visual Basic programmer and you have experience working with object libraries, you can skip the next section on programming with objects. But if you're relatively inexperienced with Visual Basic, you'll want to peruse the next few sections carefully because they're crucial to successful programming against the DAO object model.

PROGRAMMING WITH OBJECTS

One of the reasons that object-oriented programming is easier than procedural programming is that it describes computer-based abstractions in real-world terms. For example, a procedural program that handles invoices might call one procedure to open the database, another to read invoice data, another to save invoice data, and another procedure to print.

An object-oriented program might perform the same task by creating an Invoice object with properties of Invoice Date, Customer ID, and Due Date. The object also has methods that pertain to actions that an Invoice object is expected to do—a Print method, a Save method, and so forth.

If you're not familiar with object-based programming, it might seem like just another coding philosophy, a different way of looking at putting code together. But the more you use objects, the more you realize that they're easier to code against—at least once you understand what objects are available to you and how they relate to one another. Because objects present themselves consistently, after you learn how to program a particular set of objects, you begin to have a handle on how to use all the objects related to that object. Such is the case with DAO, as well as the other two database object models provided by VB, Remote Date Objects (RDO), and ADO.

Another advantage to using an object model to get to your database is that DAO serves as a layer of abstraction on top of your specific database implementation. This means that when you're doing database programming in Visual Basic, you don't write code that talks to the database directly. Instead, you write code that talks to the object library, which in turn translates your code into something the database engine understands. This means that you can, in many cases, write one set of code that works with any database. You can think of an object library, then, as something that stands between your program and the specific database implementation, standardizing your access to the database and giving you a consistent, Visual Basic-style set of objects to work with.

All objects have the following items:

▶ *Properties.* The data pertaining to the object. Properties can be conventional data types, such as strings and integers, but they can also be objects or collections—for example, the `Fields` collection of a `Recordset` object is also a property of the `Recordset` object.

▶ *Methods.* The actions that the object can perform. These can act similar to functions (which return data) or subroutines.

▶ *Events.* Messages the object can send to the application that uses the object. If you've programmed in Visual Basic at all, you should be accustomed to assigning code to event procedures; DAO has its own event model that you can write code against.

The process of manipulating a database in code using DAO, then, entails your determining which object is appropriate to use, and then executing its methods and setting and retrieving its properties.

There isn't much difference between manipulating the properties and methods of a DAO and programming the properties and methods of a conventional user interface control, such as a text box. With DAO, however, you must instantiate objects you use (because DAO objects aren't visual, you can't just draw them on a form as you'd draw a list box or a command button).

Additionally, unlike user interface objects, DAOs belong to a hierarchy called an object model. This hierarchy dictates that objects own other objects. To gain access to a table, for example, you must understand that a database object owns the table object; the process of creating a table object dictates that you first create a database object.

Using Object Variables   In Visual Basic, you begin using objects by creating an *object variable.* An object variable stores a reference to an object.

In Visual Basic, you must always declare an object variable (even if you're not using Option Explicit, the Visual Basic statement that forces you to declare all variables). This is because objects are often complicated constructs that require more memory than other types of variables; the process of dimensioning a variable in Visual Basic tells the computer to set aside memory for the variable.

You declare an object variable using the `Dim` statement, as shown in Listing 3.1.

Listing 3.1   Creating a *Database* Object Variable Using the *Dim* Statement

```
Dim db As Database
```

When you assign a value to an object variable, you must use the set statement. This is in contrast to conventional Visual Basic assignment statements (such as x = 538) that simply require a variable, an operator, and a value. Listing 3.2 shows an example of an object variable declaration and assignment.

Listing 3.2   Dimensioning and Assigning the Value of an Object Variable Using the *Set* Statement

```
Dim db As Database
Set db = OpenDatabase("..\..\db\novelty.mdb")
```

This code example uses the OpenDatabase to create a Database object. The Set statement assigns this object to the object variable db. At this point, you can program against the object variable db, executing its methods and setting and retrieving its properties.

There's more information about the properties and methods of the Database object later in this chapter.

Working with Collections in Code   One of the most daunting things for new programmers to overcome when learning DAO programming is DAO's object model. Learning this model seems to be particularly tricky for programmers who are accustomed to a more procedural programming model, such as that provided by SQL.

Think of a collection as a type of object that stores a set of references to other objects. You can think of a book's table of contents as a collection because it stores a set of references to chapters and their page numbers. A phone directory is also a collection because it stores a set of references to people and businesses. The advantage of having such a set of references is that you can iterate through them quickly and consistently. Iterating through a collection entails acting on all its members one after another; scanning a table of contents, checking off items on a to-do list, and flipping through a phone directory are examples of iterating through a collection.

Although collections you create can contain references to many types of objects, collections typically store references to one type of object; this is the case for all the DAO collections.

Table 3.1 summarizes all the collections available in DAO 3.5 programming, and what they represent.

Table 3.1 DAO Collections		
Collection	**Represents**	**Interface**
Workspaces	Represents the open connections to the database engine; normally you'll have only one workspace active at a time	Count property; Append, Delete, and Refresh methods
Databases	All the databases open in a particular Workspace; normally you'll have only one database open at a time	Count property; Refresh method
TableDefs	All the table definitions available in a database	Count property; Append, Delete, and Refresh methods
QueryDefs	All the query definitions available in a database	Count property; Append, Delete, and Refresh methods
Recordsets	All the recordsets open in the context of a single database	Count property; Refresh method
Parameters	The parameters available in a particular QueryDef	Count property; Refresh method
Relations	The relationships defined in a particular database (Jet databases only)	Count property; Append, Delete, and Refresh methods
Connections	The connections to the database owned by a Workspace object; this is the ODBCDirect equivalent of the Database object (ODBCDirect databases only)	Count property; Refresh method

continues

Table 3.1   DAO Collections (Continued)

Collection	Represents	Interface
Indexes	The index that belongs to a particular TableDef	Count **property**; Append, Delete, **and** Refresh **methods**
Fields	The fields that exist in a data construct (such as a TableDef or Recordset)	Count **property**; Append, Delete, **and** Refresh **methods**
Groups	The security groups owned by the database; for information on groups, see Chapter 9, "Multiuser Jet Databases" (Jet databases only)	Count **property**; Append, Delete, **and** Refresh **methods**
Users	The list of users identified by the security features of the database; for information on users, see Chapter 9 (Jet databases only)	Count **property**; Append, Delete, **and** Refresh **methods**
Errors	The errors generated by a particular DAO operation; it's important to note that in DAO, this is a collection rather than a single object, as it is in Visual Basic	Count **property**; Refresh **method**
Containers	A group of predefined document objects stored in the database (Jet databases only)	Count **property**; Refresh **method**
Documents	Databases, tables, and Relations are examples of Document objects (Jet databases only)	Count **property**; Refresh **method**

Collection	Represents	Interface
Properties	The properties of a DAO object; all DAO objects (except for Error and Connection) have a properties collection; properties can either be user-defined or built-in	Count property; Append, Delete, and Refresh methods

If you're experienced with object-oriented programming in Visual Basic, you might have created your own collection classes. One important difference between collections provided by DAO and collections you create yourself is that DAO classes (along with most other collections provided by Visual Basic) are zero based. Therefore, the first element in a DAO collection is numbered zero. The ordinal number of an item in a collection is called its *index*.

You can retrieve an element from a collection by using its index. For example, to display the value of the first field in the current record in a Recordset object, use the following code:

```
MsgBox MyRecordset.Fields(0).Value
```

You aren't required to access values in fields by their index number in DAO; this example just shows how you might go about it. Normally, when you know the name of a field, you access it by its name, as in the following code:

```
MsgBox MyRecordset.Fields("LastName").Value
```

The unique textual identifier that designates an element of a collection is called its *key*. To refer to an element of a collection, you can use either its index or its key. (For this reason, keys must always be strings; if they weren't, Visual Basic wouldn't know whether you were trying to access the item whose key is 12 or the 12th item in a collection.) In the previous example, LastName is the key you use to access a Field object from the Fields collection.

Accessing a member of a collection by index and by key is a technique that is common to programming all collection objects, whether such objects are created by you or provided for you by Visual Basic. For a complete discussion of accessing values in fields, see the sections on the Recordset and Field objects later in this chapter.

For more information: To understand more about how collections can be useful, including how to create your own collection classes, check out Deborah Kurata's *Doing Objects in Visual Basic 6* (Sams Publishing, 1998). This book gives you much more detail on how collections work and how you can create collections to manipulate data in your Visual Basic applications.

Using Default Collections and Default Properties to Simplify Code   Objects can have *default collections*. These collections make it easier to code against a complicated object model because you don't have to make references to the most commonly used collections; instead of explicitly referring to a default collection, you can instead use an exclamation point (!) to refer to it.

For example, consider the previous code example, designed to retrieve a value from the LastName property of a recordset:

```
MsgBox MyRecordset.Fields("LastName").Value
```

The code works because you have a Recordset object that has a Fields collection. That Fields collection has a property called LastName, which has some value (which would be a textual value; the name Smith, for example).

But it so happens that the Fields collection is a Recordset object's default collection. So, as a shorthand technique for determining the value of the LastName field, you could instead write the following code:

```
MsgBox MyRecordset!LastName.Value
```

You can make this code even less complicated by taking advantage of the fact that a Field object's Value property is its default property. You don't have to make reference to a default property of an object at all. So instead of using the techniques demonstrated in the previous two examples, you could write the following code:

```
MsgBox MyRecordset!LastName
```

All three ways of referring to a value of a field return the same result.

Some argue that taking advantage of default collections and default properties is bad—the rationale is that code readability comes from making as few implicit assumptions as possible. You don't want to do anything invisibly or rely on defaults because when you go back months later to debug your code , you won't be able to remember what those defaults are. Consequently, you'll have a hard time figuring out what's going on in your code.

This argument might hold water in general, but in DAO programming, it makes sense to take advantage of default collections and properties when you can. This is because it's extremely common to retrieve the `Fields` collection from a recordset and somewhat uncommon to retrieve anything else.

In this chapter, the code examples generally spell out references to default collections where it makes the conceptual explanations easier to follow. But later in the book, as you move into more complicated code, the examples use more defaults to make the code less complicated overall.

USING THE DAO DATA CONTROL

You can use the DAO Data control to connect to a Microsoft Jet database. Although the reasons for doing this are diminishing with the advent of the superior ADO Data control (introduced in Chapter 1, "Database Basics"), there are still reasons to use the classic DAO Data control. Among these is the ability to connect to data sources such as dBASE files, text files, and Excel spreadsheets without having to use open database connectivity (ODBC).

Note: The basic premise of the DAO Data control is the same as the ADO Data control; only the details are different. To use the control, you assign the name of a database file to the control's `DatabaseName` property and then select a table or other data source in its `RecordSource` property. Finally, you bind user interface controls such as text boxes to the control by setting each user interface control's `DataSource` and `DataField` property.

USING THE *CONNECT* PROPERTY OF THE DAO DATA CONTROL TO ACCESS EXTERNAL DATA SOURCES

The `Connect` property determines the type of database to which the Data control is connected. By default, this property is set to Microsoft Access, but you can change the setting if you are interested in connecting to a non-Access data type. Such data types are referred to as *external data types*.

Note: Don't confuse external data types with client/server databases such as Microsoft SQL Server and Oracle; those are better supported through the Remote Data control or the ADO Data control. You can access several databases not directly supported by Jet by using these other data controls. The ADO Data control was introduced in Chapter 1. For more information on both the Remote Data control and ODBC, see Chapter 5 "Getting Started with SQL Server."

Jet supports the following types of desktop databases:

▶ dBASE III, IV, and 5.0

▶ Excel versions 3.0, 4.0, 5.0, and 8.0

▶ FoxPro versions 2.0, 2.5, 2.6, and 3.0

▶ Lotus spreadsheets in WK1, WK3, and WK4 formats

▶ Paradox versions 3.*x*, 4.*x*, and 5.*x*

▶ Delimited ASCII text files

One of the easiest ways to test how this works is to connect to an Excel spreadsheet. You can do this whether or not Excel is installed on your computer; simply use the file EXCEL-DB.XLS found on this book's companion CD. To do so, follow these steps:

1. Set up a Visual Basic form with a Data control.

2. Set the Data control's Connect property to the following:

```
Excel 5.0;
```

3. Set the Data control's DatabaseName property to the name of the Excel spreadsheet, excel-db.xls.

4. Set the Data control's RecordSource property to Sheet1$. You can now create bound controls on your Visual Basic form as you normally would.

The Excel spreadsheet that stores the data resembles Figure 3.3.

Figure 3.3
The Excel spread-sheet as a Data control–compatible data source. Note that in Excel, field names are entered as the first row of the data.

	FirstName	LastName	Address	City	State	Zip
	Angela	Chideya	9408 North Center Highway	Sunny Point	UT	64479
	Rick	Eves	4167 Old Crossing Circle	East Bluffs	ND	02922
	Jill	Husbands	1978 Sunny Center Way	South Plains	SC	72412
	Kathleen	Jones	3619 Golden Beach Drive	Sunset Crossing	DE	31283
	Morgan	Polito	7254 Sunny Brook Boulevard	South Point	NE	07700
	Mikki	Chideya	5101 Ocean Point Way	Happy Valley	KY	25127
	Kevin	Kadrey	5169 Golden Glen Boulevard	Ocean Plains	MI	13960
	Carole	Kranyak	2175 Happy Ridge Court	South Ridge	KS	91608
	Eric	Jones	3050 Ocean Plains Circle	West Center	WY	72268
	Laura	Ruzich	9139 New Glen Avenue	West Glen	NV	62664
	Suzanne	Johnson	678 Fort Beach Way	Happy Ridge	CO	75130
	Mikki	Polito	6303 Fort Ridge Way	Sunset Valley	AZ	64893
	Sorel	McClusky	6627 Blue Brook Court	Sunset Towne	OR	75853
	Terri	Terman	1699 Sunset Plains Way	Brown Farm	TN	66380
	Katie	Davidson	6637 Fort Beach Circle	Old Brook	NE	22667
	Kathleen	Rosenthal	3926 Happy Towne Road	South Brook	DC	47348
	Matthew	Savarese	8845 South Bluffs Road	East Ridge	NY	12004
	Suzanne	Marshall	3323 Dead Man's Farm Court	Fort Beach	IA	66518

Code Example: You can find the project described in this section in the
`\Code\03-DAO\ExcelDB` folder. For information on how to install the sample
files on the CD that accompanies this book, see the section "Installing the
Example Files" in the introduction at the beginning of this book.

Bear in mind that DAO doesn't support some operations on external databases. In particular, such databases do not support DAO procedures that create
databases, fields, and query definitions, nor do they support DAO's security-
related objects (the User and Group objects). Those are used for Jet databases only.

USING DAO TO WORK WITH DATA

DAOs are most commonly used to manipulate data in an existing database.
Running queries, updating records, and performing database maintenance are
DAO's bread and butter.

Although DAO's object model is vast, you can start creating solutions using
DAO even if you understand only a few properties and methods of the most
important objects in DAO: the Database, Recordset, and Field objects, and the like-
named collections that contain them. The next sections describe how to get
started programming these objects.

CONNECTING TO A DATABASE USING THE *DATABASE* OBJECT

The Database object is where your application normally begins most of its database access. To use a Database object, you begin by making a reference to
Microsoft DAOs in Visual Basic's Project References menu. This enables your
project to gain access to all the objects provided by DAO.

To do this, follow these steps:

1. From the Visual Basic Project menu, select References.

2. The References dialog box appears. From the list of libraries, check
   Microsoft DAO 3.51 Object Library.

3. Click OK. You can now use the objects provided by the DAO object
   library.

The next step is to dimension, or declare, a database object variable in code:

```
Dim db As Database
```

If your application is designed to work with a single database, it makes sense
for you to dimension the Database variable at the module level of your application's main form.

However, if many forms in your application need access to the same database, it might make sense for you to create a class to manage the connection to the database, instantiate an object from that class when the application starts, and terminate the object when the application ends. For more on this, see Chapter 7, "Database Access with Classes."

You assign the `Database` object variable to a database using the `OpenDatabase` method, as described in the next section.

Using the *OpenDatabase* Method to Create a *Database* Object   You create a `Database` object by using the `OpenDatabase` method. `OpenDatabase` is a method that returns a `Database` object (therefore, before you use `OpenDatabase`, you must declare an object variable of type Database to store in the return value of the method). This technique is shown in Listing 3.3.

Listing 3.3   Creating a *Database* Object Using the DAO *OpenDatabase* Method

```
Dim db As Database
Set db = OpenDatabase("..\..\db\novelty.mdb")

MsgBox "The database " & db.Name & " is now open."
```

The `OpenDatabase` method takes one required argument—the name of the database you want to open. (This name can also be the name of an ODBC data source; for more information on ODBC, see Chapter 6, "Open Database Connectivity and Remote Data Objects.")

`OpenDatabase` also has several optional parameters. The following is the full syntax of `OpenDatabase`:

```
OpenDatabase(dbname, [options], [readonly], [connect])
```

Table 3.2 describes the optional parameters of the `OpenDatabase` method.

Table 3.2   Optional Parameters of the *OpenDatabase* Method

Parameter	Description
options	If this argument is `True`, the database opens in exclusive mode; no other users can open a database when you open it in exclusive mode. If the value is `False`, other users can open the database.
	When you're opening a database using ODBCDirect, this option can take other values. For more information, see Chapter 5.

Parameter	Description
readonly	If this argument is `True`, you can't make changes to the database.
connect	A string that specifies how to connect to the database; the string is usually used for client/server and ODBC data sources only. For more information on using the connect argument, see Chapter 5.

There are significant performance benefits to opening a database in read-only and exclusive modes. If you're building an application that is designed to analyze data, for example, it is appropriate for such an application to open the database in read-only mode.

Note: Although the `OpenDatabase` method may not seem similar to this method because it doesn't appear to be attached to an object, rest assured that it is, in fact, a method. (It's actually a method of the DAO `Workspace` object.) You don't have to refer to this `Workspace` object because Jet assumes you're using a default, invisible `Workspace` object if you don't explicitly refer to one. This is partly to maintain backward compatibility with previous versions of DAO, which did not contain the `Workspace` object, but also to make your code simpler. You can find more information on the `Workspace` object later in this chapter.

Using the *Execute* Method to Run Action Queries You use the `Execute` method of the `Database` object to execute a SQL command against the database. This method shouldn't be used in all cases, though. You use the `Execute` method to run SQL code that does the following:

▶ Updates, deletes, or copies records (known in Access/Jet as an *action query*)

▶ Modifies the structure of the database (known as a Data Definition Language command)

Note: Previous versions of DAO called the `Execute` method `ExecuteSQL`.

Conventional select queries (the kind that return records) are typically run using the Database object's OpenRecordset method. For more on this, see the section on the OpenRecordset method later in this chapter.

Listing 3.4 demonstrates a typical use of the Execute method. This code runs an update query against the table called tblInventory, increasing the retail price of all the items in the table by 10 percent.

Listing 3.4   An Update Query That Alters All the Records in a Particular Table

```
' References: Microsoft DAO 3.51 Object Library
'
Dim db As Database

Private Sub Form_Load()

    Set db = OpenDatabase("..\..\DB\novelty.mdb")

End Sub

Private Sub cmdExecute_Click()

    db.Execute "UPDATE tblInventory " & _
            "SET RetailPrice = [RetailPrice]*1.1"

End Sub
```

Code Example: The preceding code example is in the directory \vbdb\code\03-DAO\Execute\Execute.vbp. For information on how to install the sample files on the CD that accompanies this book, see the section "Installing the Example Files" in the introduction at the beginning of this book.

A Data Definition Language (DLL) command using the Execute method works much the same way, as shown in Listing 3.5.

Listing 3.5   A DDL Command That Creates the Supplier Table Using the *Execute* Method

```
Private Sub cmdCreate_Click()

    db.Execute "CREATE TABLE tblSupplier " & _
            "([Name] TEXT (50), [Address] TEXT (40))"

End Sub
```

When you run a query or DDL command using the Execute method of the database, it executes immediately. Note, too, that QueryDef objectss have Execute methods as well; you use Execute in this context when the QueryDef is a stored update query or DDL command and you want to run it.

Note: Chapter 2 explains the different types of SQL queries and their syntax.

Using the *DBEngine* Object to Control Database Access   Although you'd think that the Database object would be at the top of the object hierarchy of DAO, it isn't. (It can be useful to think of the Database object as being at the top, because it's where you start coding most of the time.) But in fact, the highest-level object in the DAO object model is the DBEngine object.

Figure 3.4 shows the position of the DBEngine object in the DAO hierarchy.

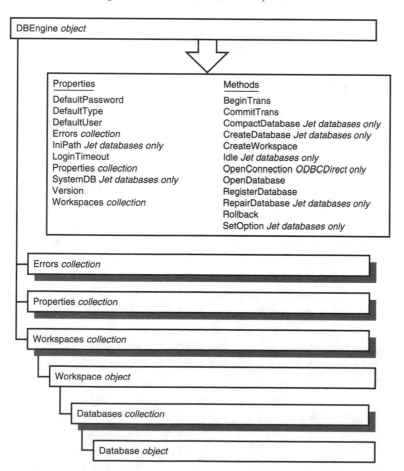

Figure 3.4
The DBEngine object and the objects beneath it in the DAO hierarchy.

The DBEngine object is a singleton object; there's only one such object available, and you can't create new instances of DBEngine objects.

You use the DBEngine object to determine which type of Workspace objects you create. You typically do this in situations where your application uses ODBCDirect (because Jet workspaces are the default). To set the default type of workspace to ODBCDirect, set the DBEngine's DefaultWorkspace property to dbUseODBC.

For more on ODBCDirect, see Chapter 6.

You can also use the DBEngine to set other types of defaults in your workspaces. For example, suppose that your application accesses a secured database, and it always accesses that database using the same user name and password. If you want your application to always create Workspace objects based on a particular combination of user name and password, you can set the DBEngine's DefaultUser and DefaultPassword properties to whatever the user supplies. That way, every Workspace object you create starts with the same default user name and password.

For more information on users, passwords, and the databases that love them, see Chapter 8, "Remote Database Access."

USING THE *RECORDSET* OBJECT

You use the Recordset object to manipulate records in DAO. Recordset objects provide an object-oriented interface to the relational database model involving tables divided into records and fields.

Figure 3.5 shows the position of the Recordset object within the DAO hierarchy, as well as its properties and methods.

To create a recordset, you typically use the OpenRecordset method, as described in the next section.

Creating a *Recordset* Object Using the *OpenRecordset* Method   You create a Recordset object by using the OpenRecordset method. In DAO, the Database, Connection, QueryDef, TableDef, and Recordset objects have OpenRecordset methods. All are used for the same purpose: to get access to the data stored in a database.

If you used data access under previous versions of Visual Basic and Microsoft Access, particularly the 16-bit versions of Visual Basic or Access, you'll probably find recordsets easier to deal with under Jet 3.51. One reason for this is that you don't have to worry about what kind of recordset you're dealing with. In Jet 3.51, the database engine enables you to create a generic recordset object instead of having to specify what kind of recordset object you want. (In previous versions of Jet, there were separate Dynaset, Snapshot, and Table objects; these objects are now obsolete.) These recordset types still exist, they just aren't represented by their own objects.

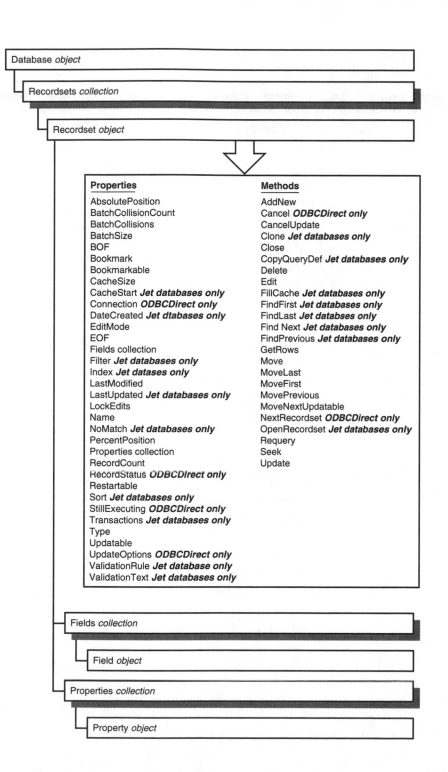

Figure 3.5
The Recordsets collection and the Recordset object within the DAO object hierarchy.

Database *object*

Recordsets *collection*

Recordset *object*

Properties	**Methods**
AbsolutePosition	AddNew
BatchCollisionCount	Cancel *ODBCDirect only*
BatchCollisions	CancelUpdate
BatchSize	Clone *Jet databases only*
BOF	Close
Bookmark	CopyQueryDef *Jet databases only*
Bookmarkable	Delete
CacheSize	Edit
CacheStart *Jet databases only*	FillCache *Jet databases only*
Connection *ODBCDirect only*	FindFirst *Jet databases only*
DateCreated *Jet dtabases only*	FindLast *Jet databases only*
EditMode	Find Next *Jet databases only*
EOF	FindPrevious *Jet databases only*
Fields collection	GetRows
Filter *Jet databases only*	Move
Index *Jet datases only*	MoveLast
LastModified	MoveFirst
LastUpdated *Jet databases only*	MovePrevious
LockEdits	MoveNextUpdatable
Name	NextRecordset *ODBCDirect only*
NoMatch *Jet databases only*	OpenRecordset *Jet databases only*
PercentPosition	Requery
Properties collection	Seek
RecordCount	Update
RecordStatus *ODBCDirect only*	
Restartable	
Sort *Jet databases only*	
StillExecuting *ODBCDirect only*	
Transactions *Jet databases only*	
Type	
Updatable	
UpdateOptions *ODBCDirect only*	
ValidationRule *Jet database only*	
ValidationText *Jet databases only*	

Fields *collection*

Field *object*

Properties *collection*

Property *object*

Table 3.3 outlines some advantages and disadvantages of using the various types of recordsets in Jet 3.5.

Table 3.3 Advantages and Disadvantages of Recordset Types in Jet 3.5		
Recordset Type	**Advantages**	**Disadvantages**
Table	Editable. Can locate and return records quickly because tables can be indexed.	Can't represent the results of a multitable query.
Dynaset	Updateable. Efficient because it represents a set of references to the data in the underlying query (rather than the actual data). Can return records from more than one table through the use of a join, even when those tables are linked from multiple databases. Such recordsets are, in many cases, updateable.	Because a table can utilize an index, searches on a dynaset aren't always as fast as searches on a table.
Snapshot	Can be faster than tables and dynasets, particularly for smaller recordsets. Can return records from more than one table through the use of a join. Such recordsets are, in many cases, updateable.	Not updateable under Microsoft Jet; possibly updateable under Open Database Connectivity (see Chapter 6). Unlike dynasets, which return a set of references to the records in a table, a snapshot returns a copy of the data, which can make large snapshots slower than dynasets.

Recordset Type	Advantages	Disadvantages
Forward-Only	Faster than, but similar to, a snapshot. Can return records from more than one table through the use of a join.	Same as those of a snapshot; you can move forward only.
Dynamic	Updateable. Can return records from more than one table through the use of a join. Particularly well suited to multiuser databases because they can update themselves when other users change records contained by them.	Not as efficient as a dynaset.

Note: The `OpenRecordset` method replaces the `OpenSnapshot`, `OpenTable`, and `OpenDynaset` methods that existed in previous versions of DAO. These methods are now obsolete; they still work, but you should use `OpenRecordset` instead. Additionally, the `Snapshot`, `Dynaset`, and `Table` objects are obsolete; to get access to a structure that contains data, you use the `Recordset` object.

Because the `OpenRecordset` method is really a function that returns a `Recordset` object, you need to dimension a `Recordset` object before you use `OpenRecordset`. The code to do this typically resembles the code shown in Listing 3.6.

Listing 3.6   A Typical Example of an *OpenRecordset* Method Applied to a *Database* Object

```
Dim db As Database
Dim rs As Recordset

Set db = OpenDatabase("..\..\DB\novelty.mdb")
Set rs = db.OpenRecordset("tblCustomer")
```

The single required argument of the `OpenRecordset` method is the data source. This is a text string, typically the name of a table or a stored query definition. But it can also be a SQL SELECT statement, as demonstrated in Listing 3.7.

Listing 3.7   Creating a *Recordset* Object Using the *OpenRecordset* Method

```
Dim db As Database
Dim rs As Recordset

Set db = OpenDatabase("..\..\DB\novelty.mdb")
Set rs = db.OpenRecordset("SELECT * " & _
                          "FROM tblCustomer " & _
                          "ORDER BY [LastName]")
```

After creating a Recordset object, you can access the data in it by using code that accesses the object's properties and methods. Examples of this are littered throughout the rest of this chapter and the rest of this book.

Avoiding the Great *OpenDatabase* Quotation Mark Caper   A common problem among programmers using the OpenRecordset method is determining how to delimit a text string embedded in the SQL statement. For example, how do you submit the SQL statement in Listing 3.8 to the database engine using OpenRecordset?

Listing 3.8   A SQL *SELECT* Statement That Includes a Text Parameter in Quotations

```
SELECT *
FROM tblCustomer
WHERE [LastName] = "Smith"
```

The problem lies in the fact that you can't include double quotation marks in the parameter of an OpenRecordset method. If you did, the code would resemble Listing 3.9.

Listing 3.9   The Problem with Trying to Embed a SQL Statement That Includes Quotation Marks in an *OpenRecordset* Method

```
Dim db As Database
Dim rs As Recordset

Set db = OpenDatabase("..\..\DB\novelty.mdb")
Set rs = db.OpenRecordset("SELECT * " & _
                          "FROM tblCustomer " & _
                          "WHERE [LastName] = ""Smith""")
```

This code would cause a compile error because Visual Basic can't parse the two pairs of double quotation marks around the word *Smith*.

The solution to the problem is to change the double quotation marks to single quotation marks, as shown in Listing 3.10.

Listing 3.10   Code That Overcomes the Great *OpenDatabase* Quotation Mark Caper

```
Dim db As Database
Dim rs As Recordset

Set db = OpenDatabase("..\..\db\novelty.mdb")
Set rs = db.OpenRecordset("SELECT * " & _
                          "FROM tblCustomer " & _
                          "WHERE [LastName] = 'Smith'")
```

If the value for the WHERE clause is not hard coded (as is often the case), the solution gets even more complicated. For example, suppose that instead of the name *Smith*, you want to create a Recordset object based on the name the user enters in a text box called txtLastName. Your code would then resemble Listing 3.11.

Listing 3.11   A Query Generated from a SQL String Concatenated with User Input

```
Dim db As Database
Dim rs As Recordset

Set db = OpenDatabase("..\..\db\novelty.mdb")
Set rs = db.OpenRecordset("SELECT * " & _
                          "FROM tblCustomer " & _
                          "WHERE [LastName] = '" & txtLastName.Text & "'")
```

The key here is not to forget that you must delimit string data in quotation marks, even when the data is part of a big, ugly concatenated expression.

One alternative I sometimes like to use is a function that encloses the parameter in quotation marks, similar to this:

```
Function Quote (strValue As String) As String
    Quote = Chr(34) & strValue & Chr(34)
End Function
```

This function encloses in double quotation marks (ASCII value 34) whatever string it's passed. This way, you can cleanly enclose any parameter in quotes at any time, using code similar to this:

```
Set rs = db.OpenRecordset("SELECT * " & _
                          "FROM tblCustomer " & _
                          "WHERE [LastName] = " & Quote(txtLastName.Text))
```

This simplifies things somewhat. But because this kind of code can be so difficult to read and debug, it can make more sense to instead create a parameterized query stored in the database. (In addition to making this code easier to maintain, replacing SQL code in your Visual Basic code with stored queries in the database can make your queries run faster as well.) For information on how to do this, see the section "Manipulating Stored Queries Using the QueryDef Object" later in this chapter.

Setting Recordset Options   The Options argument of the OpenRecordset method determines several things about how records can be manipulated. Table 3.4 outlines the legal values for this argument.

Table 3.4 Values for the *Options* Argument of the *OpenRecordset* Method	
Constant	**Meaning**
dbOpenTable	In a Microsoft Jet workspaces, creates a table-style Recordset object
dbOpenDynamic	In an ODBCDirect workspace, opens a dynamic-type Recordset object
dbOpenDynaset	Opens a dynaset-type Recordset object
dbOpenSnapshot	Opens a snapshot-type Recordset object
dbOpenForwardOnly	Opens a Recordset object whose cursor can scroll forward only

Chapter 6 covers dynamic recordsets in ODBCDirect. You can also create dynamic recordsets in ActiveX Data Objects, as discussed in Chapter 10.

MANIPULATING FIELDS USING THE *FIELD* OBJECT

The Field object represents a field in a data structure. TableDef, Recordset, Relation, and Index objects all contain collections of fields.

You can retrieve the value of a field by inspecting the Value property of a Field object. (Because the Value property is the Field object's default property, you need only make reference to the Field object; you never have to explicitly reference the Value property.)

Note: The Fields collection replaces the ListFields method that existed in previous versions of DAO. This method is now obsolete; it still works, but you should use the Fields collection instead.

Figure 3.6 shows the `Field` object's place in the DAO hierarchy.

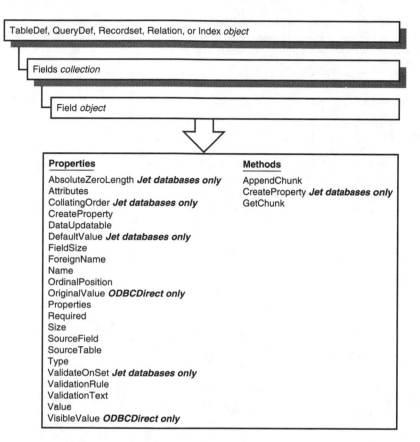

Figure 3.6
The Fields Collection and the Field Object in the DAO hierarchy.

Business Case 3.: Creating a Database Browser   The Jones Novelties customer database has begun to grow. The users of the database are now requesting a quick browser application that enables them to choose customers from a list and then view the complete details of a customer's data.

You can use a combination of the DAO `Database`, `Recordset`, and `Field` objects to create a database browser application. This application consists of pure DAO code. The benefit is that the application does not require the Data control, so the application is fast and flexible.

This application consists of two forms: frmMain and frmSingle. The main form displays a list of all the customers in the database; the form frmSingle displays the details for a single customer.

Listing 3.12 shows the code that initializes the application's main form.

Listing 3.12   Code That Initializes the Database Browser Application

```
' References: Microsoft DAO Object Library 3.51

Dim db As Database

Const DBPath = "..\..\db\"

Private Sub Form_Load()

    Dim rs As Recordset

    Set db = OpenDatabase(DBPath & "novelty.mdb")
    Set rs = db.OpenRecordset("SELECT ID, LastName, FirstName " & _
                              "FROM tblCustomer " & _
                              "WHERE ID > 18000 " & _
                              "ORDER BY LastName, FirstName")

    ' Populate the list box
    Do Until rs.EOF
        lstCustomer.AddItem rs.Fields("LastName") & ", " & _
                            rs.Fields("FirstName") & _
                            " [" & rs.Fields("ID") & "]"
        lstCustomer.ItemData(lstCustomer.NewIndex) = rs.Fields("ID")

        rs.MoveNext

    Loop

    rs.Close
    Set rs = Nothing

End Sub
```

Note that this code uses the ItemData property of the list box control, which enables you to add an additional piece of numeric data to each item in the list box. In this case, you're adding the value of the ID field—tblCustomer's primary key—to the list box. This value populates the single-record form when the user double-clicks the list box.

After loading the form and running this code, the application resembles Figure 3.7.

Figure 3.7
*The Database
Browser applica-
tion after DAO
code populates its
list box.*

Listing 3.13 shows the code that reveals the detail of a record when a user
double-clicks a name in the list.

**Listing 3.13   Code That Causes a Form with Detailed Data to Appear when the User
Double-Clicks an Item in the List**

```
Private Sub lstEmployee_DblClick()
    Dim rs As Recordset
Dim f As frmSingle
    Dim lngID As Long

    Set f = New frmSingle

    lngID = lstCustomer.ItemData(lstCustomer.ListIndex)

    Set rs = db.OpenRecordset("SELECT * " & _
                              "FROM tblCustomer " & _
                              "WHERE ID = " & lngID)

    f.TextBox(0) = rs.Fields("FirstName")
    f.TextBox(1) = rs.Fields("LastName")
    f.TextBox(2) = rs.Fields("Address") & ""
    f.TextBox(3) = rs.Fields("City") & ""
    f.TextBox(4) = rs.Fields("State") & ""

    ' Show child form with frmMain
    ' as parent.
    f.Show vbModeless, Me

    rs.Close
    Set rs = Nothing

End Sub
```

The concatenated empty strings (" ") at the end of the field assignments are a trick designed to avoid a common error: A text box's Text property must be a string, but a database field can potentially return a special value known as known as Null. Null represents the absence of a value—a database field that has no data. When you attempt to assign a Null to a text box's Text property, an error occurs.

Even worse, the obvious solution to this problem doesn't work. When you use conventional means (for example, the CStr function) in an attempt to convert the Null field value into a string, the error still takes place because by definition the product of nearly any operation involving a Null value is Null.

Concatenating Null to an empty string always returns an empty string, but concatenating a nonempty string to an empty string gives you the string you started with. So by always concatenating an empty string to a field value whose value could be Null, you avoid the error. It's a goofy trick, but it works, and it's used commonly to weed out Null values in the world of Visual Basic database access programming.

Code Example: You can find the application described in this section in the directory \vbdb\code\03-DAO\Browser\Browser.vbp. For information on how to install the sample files on the CD that accompanies this book, see the section "Installing the Example Files" in the introduction at the beginning of this book.

USING NAVIGATIONAL METHODS WITH THE *RECORDSET* OBJECT

After creating a Recordset object, you can use navigational methods to move from one record to the next in the recordset. You typically do this in situations where you need to retrieve data from every record in a recordset, although you can also use them to permit users to simply browse from one record to the next.

The following are navigational methods of a Recordset object:

▶ The MoveFirst method moves to the first row in the recordset.

▶ The MoveNext method moves to the next row in the recordset.

▶ The MovePrevious method moves to the previous row in the recordset.

▶ The MoveLast method moves to the last row in the recordset.

▶ The Move method moves a specified number of records.

Bear in mind that there are recordsets with cursors that enable you to move forward only; in such recordsets, the MovePrevious and MoveFirst methods trigger errors.

Using *BOF* and *EOF* to Navigate Through Recordsets   In addition to these methods, the Recordset object provides two properties that let you know when you've moved to the beginning or end of the recordset:

▶ The EOF (end of file) property is True when you've moved beyond the last record in the recordset.

▶ The BOF (beginning of file) property is True when you've moved to a position before the first record in the recordset.

Instead of thinking of EOF and BOF as properties of the recordset, you might find it helpful to think of them as locations in the recordset, as shown in Figure 3.8.

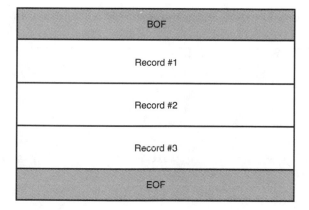

Figure 3.8
BOF and EOF in a recordset.

The code you typically use to iterate through a recordset, then, combines navigation methods along with BOF and EOF. In general, such code involves a loop of the following form:

```
Do Until EOF
    ' Perform action on the data or
    ' read values from fields
    rs.MoveNext
Loop
```

Note: While the navigational model of the `Recordset` object is useful, it's not always right for every situation. If, for example, you want to change the value of every record in a table, it's better to use a SQL UPDATE command (as described earlier in this chapter).

Business Case 3.2: Accessing Data in a Table Using Navigational Methods
Now that the Jones Novelties database system is beginning to shape up, you're realizing that it is somewhat lacking in performance. Rather than using the Data control, which can be somewhat inefficient and unwieldy to program, you decide to use pure DAO code to navigate through the recordset.

Listing 3.14 provides an example of navigational code that satisfies this requirement (and does something potentially useful). This code prints out the complete list of customers returned from a query of the tblCustomer table. (However, the code could just as well be sending this data to the printer or using it to populate a list box, for example.)

Listing 3.14   An Example of Iterating Through a Recordset Using Navigational Methods

```
' References: Microsoft DAO 3.51 Object Library
'
Dim db As Database
'

Private Sub Form_Load()

    Set db = OpenDatabase("..\..\db\novelty.mdb")

End Sub

Private Sub Command10_Click()

    Dim rs As Recordset
    Set rs = db.OpenRecordset("tblCustomer")

    Do Until rs.EOF = True
        Debug.Print rs.Fields("FirstName") & _
                    " " & rs.Fields("LastName")
        rs.MoveNext
    Loop

End Sub
```

Iterating through a table by using a loop is a very commonly used technique in the world of DAO programming. You can use such code to populate user interface controls, output data to a file or the printer, or export data to a file.

However, it's usually not appropriate to use this kind of code to change the values of a particular field in all the records in a table, for example, or to delete a particular set of records based on a particular criterion. You should use a SQL action query for those kinds of operations because using SQL for bulk update operations is usually faster than iterating through records using code.

Using *BOF* and *EOF* to Determine Whether a Recordset Is Empty   The BOF and EOF properties are always available, even in a recordset that has no records. In fact, the best way to see whether a recordset contains no records is to inspect the value of both BOF and EOF. If BOF and EOF are both True, the recordset has no records. Figure 3.9 illustrates this.

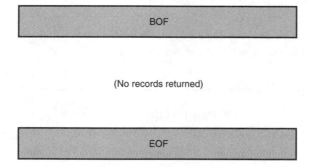

Figure 3.9
A recordset that has no records still has BOF and EOF properties.

Using the *RecordCount* Property to Determine the Number of Records in a Recordset   You use the RecordCount property to find out how many records are in a Recordset object. But it's important to remember that the value of the RecordCount property is not valid until you move to the end of the recordset.

This is the case because Jet handles queries in two stages. The first stage returns just enough data to enable your program to keep working without a noticeable delay in processing. The second stage executes in the background, retrieving all the data required to execute the query completely. Jet does this for performance reasons, so your application's execution isn't blocked while waiting to retrieve a large result set. You don't have direct control over how this process works, but you do need to know that it exists and how to get around it when, for example, you want to know exactly how many records are in a recordset.

An example of code that displays the number of records in a recordset is in Listing 3.15.

Listing 3.15   Code That Determines the Number of Records in a *Recordset* Object

```
' References: Microsoft DAO 3.51 Object Library
'
Dim db As Database
'


Private Sub Form_Load()

    Set db = OpenDatabase("..\..\db\novelty.mdb")

End Sub

Private Sub cmdCount_Click()

    Dim rs As Recordset

    Set rs = db.OpenRecordset("tblInventory")

    rs.MoveLast
    MsgBox "There are " & rs.RecordCount & _
            " items in inventory.", vbInformation

End Sub
```

Remember that if you are simply trying to determine whether there are zero records in a recordset, it is much easier (and faster) simply to inspect the BOF and EOF properties of the Recordset object, as described in the previous section.

Understanding the Types of Recordsets   It's important to understand that the OpenRecordset method can return several types of Recordset objects. The type of recordset has implications for what you can do with it (for example, snapshot-style recordsets are usually read-only).

Jet 3.51 features five types of recordsets. When using the DAO Data control, you set the type of recordset in the Data control's RecordsetType property. You set the type of recordset when you create the recordset in code.

You can determine the type of a particular Recordset object by inspecting the value of its Type property. Table 3.5 summarizes the possible values for this property.

Table 3.5 Values of a Recordset's *Type* Property		
Constant	Value	Type of Recordset
dbOpenTable	1	A table-style recordset (Microsoft Jet only)
dbOpenDynaset	2	A dynaset-style recordset
dbOpenSnapshot	4	A snapshot-style recordset
dbOpenForwardOnly	8	A snapshot-style recordset with a forward-only cursor
dbOpenDynamic	16	A recordset with a dynamic cursor (ODBCDirect only)

How do you control which type of recordset returns when you execute the OpenRecordset method? By supplying the appropriate constant in the type argument of the OpenRecordset method. (For more on this, see the "Creating a Recordset Object Using the OpenRecordset Method" section earlier in this chapter.)

Changing Values in a Record Using the *Edit* Method   You can edit the current record in an updateable Recordset object using the Edit and Update methods of the recordset. To edit the value of a field in a recordset, follow these steps:

1. Use the Recordset object's navigation methods to move to the record you wish to edit.

2. Execute the recordset's Edit method.

3. Assign values to the fields in the record using the Fields collection of the Recordset object:

```
rs.Fields("LastName") = "Smith"
```

Alternatively, because Fields is the default collection of the Recordset object, you can omit the explicit reference to the Fields collection when you're assigning a value to a field:

```
rs!LastName = "Smith"
```

4. Save the record to the database using the recordset's Update method.

Creating New Records Using the *AddNew* and *Update* Methods   You can create a new record in any updateable Recordset object using the AddNew and Update methods of the recordset. Creating a new record in a recordset is a three-step process:

1. Execute the recordset's AddNew method. This adds a new, blank record to the end of the recordset.

2. Assign values to the new record using the same kind of assignment statements you normally make to database fields.

3. Write the record to the database using the recordset's Update method.

Business Case 3.3: Creating a Data-Entry Application   Jones Novelties requires an application that enables employees to enter items into the product database. This application is written with DAO for maximum efficiency and flexibility. And because the application only needs to enter data, it requires only the Database and Recordset objects, along with the AddNew and Update methods.

The application's interface consists of text boxes, labels and buttons, not unlike the Data control applications described in the section "Using the Visual Basic Data Control" in Chapter 1. However, this application eschews the use of the Data control. Figure 3.10 shows the layout of the inventory Data-entry application.

Figure 3.10
The user interface of the inventory data-entry application.

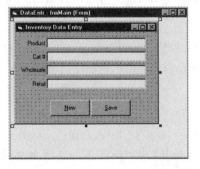

The code for the application starts with some module-level declarations, shown in Listing 3.16. The code defines indexes of a control array of text boxes and declares the DAO Recordset and Database objects.

Listing 3.16   Module-Level Declarations for the Inventory Data-Entry Application

```
Option Explicit

' References: Microsoft DAO 3.51 Object Library

Enum TextBoxes
    txtProduct = 0
    txtCatalogNumber = 1
    txtWholesalePrice = 2
    txtRetailPrice = 3
End Enum


Private db As Database
Private rs As Recordset
Private x As Integer
```

Next, the application's main form initializes the Database and Recordset objects when it's loaded, as shown in Listing 3.17.

Listing 3.17   The Database-Initialization Code That Runs when the Form Loads

```
Private Sub Form_Load()

    Set db = OpenDatabase("..\..\DB\novelty.mdb")
    Set rs = db.OpenRecordset("tblInventory")

    For x = txtProduct To txtRetailPrice
        TextBox(x).Enabled = False
    Next x

    cmdSave.Enabled = False
    cmdNew.Enabled = True

End Sub
```

The code that enables and disables the user interface controls ensures that the user doesn't do anything inappropriate (such as hit the Save button when there's no data to save). So when the application first launches, the only thing the user can do is hit the New button. (This is a contrived example; you will certainly be able to come up with a more inspired user interface in your DAO applications.)

When the user hits the New button, the code in Listing 3.18 executes.

Listing 3.18   Code That Creates a New Record in the *Recordset* Object and Sets Up the User Interface for Data Entry

```
Private Sub cmdNew_Click()

    ' Create a new record
    rs.AddNew

    ' Enable data entry controls
    For x = txtProduct To txtRetailPrice
        TextBox(x).Enabled = True
    Next x

    TextBox(txtProduct).SetFocus

    cmdSave.Enabled = True
    cmdNew.Enabled = False

End Sub
```

This code creates a new record in the Recordset object, enables all the text boxes on the form, and enables the application's Save button.

The only thing the user can do when the application is in this state is enter data and save a record. When the user is entering a record, the user interface resembles Figure 3.11.

Figure 3.11
The inventory data-entry application when a user is entering data.

Listing 3.19 shows the code for the Save button.

Listing 3.19   Code That Saves the Record Being Edited and Resets the User Interface

```
Private Sub cmdSave_Click()

    ' Map UI controls to fields
    rs.Fields("Product") = TextBox(txtProduct)
    rs.Fields("CatalogNumber") = TextBox(txtCatalogNumber)
    rs.Fields("WholesalePrice") = TextBox(txtWholesalePrice)
```

```
    rs.Fields("RetailPrice") = TextBox(txtRetailPrice)

    ' Commit data to database
    rs.Update

    ' Clear out UI
    For x = txtProduct To txtRetailPrice
        TextBox(x).Text = ""
        TextBox(x).Enabled = False
    Next x

    cmdSave.Enabled = False
    cmdNew.Enabled = True

End Sub
```

Code Example: You can find this project in the directory `\vbdb\code\`
`03-DAO\DataEntr\DataEntr.vbp`. For information on how to install the sample
files on the CD that accompanies this book, see the section "Installing the
Example Files" in the introduction at the beginning of this book.

This code assigns values to the fields in the new record using the `Fields` collection of the `Recordset` object. The `Fields` collection and `Field` object are discussed in more depth later in this chapter.

Remember also that because of the database engine–level validation rule for
the CatalogNumber field (set up in Chapter 1), the catalog number must begin
with the letters A through M.

This application isn't the most sophisticated in the world, but it's thoroughly
functional and reasonably bulletproof. You can probably think of several additions to add to the application, such as a procedure that automatically generates
a catalog number based on an algorithm applied to the name, and a setting that
enables a data-entry user to enter records one after another (without having to
go through the extra step of clicking the New button each time). All these additional features would be relatively trivial to add using Visual Basic code.

Appending Data to a Binary Field Using *AppendChunk*　You can store binary
data in your databases. Binary data includes such things as graphics or sound
files—anything you might need to store in a database that *isn't* a simple textual
or numeric value.

Note: Microsoft Access refers to binary fields as OLE Object fields. The rest of the database universe, however, consistently refers to them as *binary fields*, so that's the term I'll use here. Also, you can use the GetChunk technique described in this section to append data to a memo field as well as a binary field. The methods used to manipulate binary fields exist in nearly the same forms in all three data access object models—DAO, RDO, and ADO.

When you assign a value to a binary field in code, you need to perform some extra steps to get the data in the field. This is because binary data doesn't have a fixed length as other data types do; a single piece of binary data could conceivably take up megabytes or more.

So, to put a piece of binary data in the database, you must first break it into chunks. You do this using the GetChunk method of a recordset's Field object. After reading a chunk of binary data, you append it to the field using the AppendChunk method of the recordset's Field object.

For example, suppose that your salespeople make sales calls on customers frequently. It might be helpful if the database stored a little graphical map for each customer that shows where the customer's office is located. You could create this graphic in a paint program and display it in a picture box control. Because the graphic resides in a field in the tblCustomer table, the user can browse it alongside other data pertaining to the customer.

The challenge here is to come up with a way to create and save the information to the database. You use GetChunk and AppendChunk to do this.

Using these methods still poses a problem, however. In an application with user interface controls bound to a Data control, you can't use the PictureBox control to display the data; instead, you must resort to more creative tactics. See Chapter 12, "User-Interface Controls," for more information on enabling your users to access binary data in an application of this kind.

Closing the Recordset Using the *Close* Method   You close a recordset using the Close method. You should do this when your code finishes using a Recordset object:

```
rs.Close
```

It's particularly important to close a Recordset object if the object places a lock on the table (as described in Chapter 9). Closing a recordset releases the lock your application has placed on the database object, permitting other users to access it.

Note that in DAO, the `Workspace`, `Connection`, `Database`, and `QueryDef` objects also have `Close` methods.

SEARCHING FOR DATA IN RECORDSETS AND TABLES

After creating a database and making provisions for entering data, you want a way to locate individual records within a recordset. The process of locating an individual record in a recordset according to criteria you specify in code is called a *search*.

A search is different than a query in that a query returns a recordset. A search scrolls through records in an existing recordset to find a single record that satisfies a specific criterion.

There are several techniques for searching for data. The method that is appropriate to use depends on the kind of data structure you're accessing:

▶ If you're working with a recordset, you're limited to the `Find` methods—`FindFirst`, `FindNext`, `FindLast`, and `FindPrevious`.

▶ If you have direct access to a table-style recordset, you can use the `Seek` method to locate records. This method is harder to code, but it can be faster because you can use a table's index with the `Seek` method.

The following sections describe these two techniques for finding records.

Locating Records in a Recordset Using the *Find* Methods   To find a record in a recordset, you use the one of the four find methods of the `Recordset` object:

▶ `FindFirst`

▶ `FindLast`

▶ `FindNext`

▶ `FindPrevious`

The syntax of these four methods is the same— to use a find method, you pass an SQL `WHERE` clause to the method specifying the information you wish to find. After executing the method, the current record in the `Recordset` object becomes the record that matches the `WHERE` criteria. If the find method doesn't locate a record that matches your criteria, the `Recordset` object's `NoMatch` property is set to `True`.

The type of method you use determines how the record is found. For example, if you use the `FindFirst` method, the database engine will move to the first record in the recordset that matches your criteria. The `FindNext` and `FindPrevious` methods, in contrast, find records relative to the current record.

For example, suppose that you have a recordset composed of customers, and you're interested in finding the first customer whose last name is Smith. Use the following code:

```
rs.FindFirst "[LastName] = 'Smith'"
```

It's important to remember that unlike a SQL SELECT query, a search does not generate a recordset. When the database engine finds a match for the criterion you specify, it moves to that record; the record becomes the current record. If no match is found, the current record is unchanged and the Recordset object's NoMatch property is set to True.

Business Case 3.4: Creating a Customer Finder Application   Jones Novelties needs a small application that will quickly retrieve a customer's contact information when the customer's first and last names are provided. You can use DAO to do this using a dynaset-style Recordset object and the FindFirst method, or you can use a table-style Recordset object and the Seek method. This business case demonstrates an application that uses both techniques.

You start developing the Customer Finder application by creating its user interface. This can be as simple as a few text boxes and a command button, as shown in Figure 3.12.

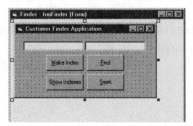

Figure 3.12
The design of the user interface of the Customer Finder application.

The application initializes its Database and Recordset objects when its main form loads, as shown in Listing 3.20.

Listing 3.20   The Initialization Code of the Customer Finder Application

```
' References MS DAO 3.51 Object Library

Private db As Database
Private rs As Recordset
'


Private Sub Form_Load()
```

```
    Set db = OpenDatabase("..\..\db\novelty.mdb")
    Set rs = db.OpenRecordset("tblCustomer", dbOpenDynaset)

End Sub
```

As the comment in the code indicates, you use the dbOpenDynaset argument of
the OpenRecordset method to ensure that Jet opens the query as a dynaset. This is
required for the use of the FindFirst method.

After the application runs, the user types in a customer first and last name in
the text boxes and then clicks the Find button. The button's Click event triggers
a simple validation on the search criteria (ensuring that the user entered both
first and last names) and then performs the search. The event then returns the
customer's name and address information in a message box. Listing 3.21 shows
the code that does this.

Listing 3.21   Code That Performs the Search in the Customer Finder Application

```
Private Sub cmdFind_Click()

    If txtFirstName.Text <> "" And txtLastName.Text <> "" Then

        rs.FindFirst "[LastName] = '" & txtLastName.Text & "' " & _
                     "AND [FirstName] = '" & txtFirstName.Text & "'"

        If rs.NoMatch Then
            ' not found
            MsgBox "No customer by that name was found.", vbExclamation
        Else
            ' return info
            MsgBox rs!Address & vbCrLf & _
                    rs!City & ", " & rs!State & " " & _
                    rs!Zip & vbCrLf & _
                    rs!Phone, _
                    vbInformation, _
                    rs!FirstName & " " & rs!LastName
        End If
    Else
        ' you must enter a first and last name
        MsgBox "Please enter a first and last name.", vbExclamation, "Error"

    End If
End Sub
```

When you run the application, enter a valid customer name, and click the Find button, the application returns that customer's address and phone number, as shown in Figure 3.13.

This application works well, but you could enhance it to use an index on the table. To do this, you must use the Seek method of the Recordset object, as described in the next section.

Code Example: You can find the application described in this section, including the modifications described in the next section, in the directory \vbdb\code\03-DAO\Finder\Finder.vbp. For information on how to install the sample files on the CD that accompanies this book, see the section "Installing the Example Files" in the introduction at the beginning of this book.

Performing Indexed Searches Using the *Seek* Method   You can perform searches on a table-type Recordset object more efficiently using the Seek method. This is because a Seek operation permits you to use indexes.

To perform a search on an index, the table first obviously must have an index. See "Creating Indexes Using the *Index* Object," later in this chapter, for information on how to create indexes using DAO code. You'll also need to know the name of the index, which can be tricky, particularly if you created the database in Microsoft Access, because Access hides the names of indexes from you behind its graphical user interface. (Visual Data Manager, on the other hand, forces you to supply a name for indexes, which still means that you have to keep track of the indexes' names.)

For this example, just assume that you have a tblCustomer table with an index on the LastName field. The name of the index is LastNameIndex. Listing 3.22 shows the code to retrieve a piece of information from this table using the Seek method.

Listing 3.22   An Indexed Search Using the *Seek* Method

```
' References MS DAO 3.51 Object Library

Private db As Database
Private rs As Recordset

Private Sub Form_Load()

    Set db = OpenDatabase("..\..\db\novelty.mdb")
    Set rs = db.OpenRecordset("tblCustomer", dbOpenTable)

End Sub


Private Sub cmdSeek_Click()

    rs.Index = "LastNameIndex"
    rs.Seek "=", txtLastName.Text
    If rs.NoMatch Then
            ' not found
            MsgBox "No customer by that name was found.", vbExclamation
    Else
            ' return info
            MsgBox rs!Address & vbCrLf & _
                    rs!City & ", " & rs!State & "  " & _
                    rs!Zip & vbCrLf & _
                    rs!Phone, _
                    vbInformation, _
                    rs!FirstName & "  " & rs!LastName
    End If

End Sub
```

Note that this code creates the `Recordset` object by using the `dbOpenTable` argument, instead of `dbOpenDynaset`, as in the previous examples. Opening a table-type recordset enables you to use the `Seek` method to do a fast indexed search.

Figure 3.14 shows the result of a search using this technique.

Bear in mind that the `Seek` method limits your options for searching on a field. In addition to the requirement that the field on which you're searching must be indexed, when you use `Seek`, the only operators you can use are listed in Table 3.6.

Figure 3.14
*The result of a
seek on a table-
type recordset.*

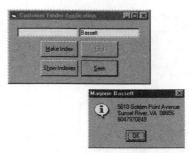

Table 3.6	Operators Available with the *Seek* Method
Operator	**Definition**
<	Less than
<=	Less than or equal to
>	Greater than
>=	Greater than or equal to
=	Equal to

Unlike the Seek method, which restricts you to indexed fields and a limited set of operators, the Find methods enable you to use any operators available with the SQL WHERE clause, including Like and In. (For more information on the operators that you can use with a SQL WHERE clause, see Chapter 2.)

Iterating Through a TableDef's *Indexes* Collection   When you're performing a Seek operation on a table-type recordset, it's useful to know what indexes are available. To determine which indexes exist in a given table, you can iterate through the TableDef object's Indexes collection. The code in Listing 3.23 shows how to do this.

Listing 3.23   Listing the Names of the Index Objects Belonging to a Particular TableDef

```
' References MS DAO 3.51 Object Library

Private db As Database
Private rs As Recordset

Private Sub Form_Load()
```

```
    Set db = OpenDatabase("..\..\db\novelty.mdb")

End Sub

Private Sub cmdShowIndexes_Click()

    Dim td As TableDef
    Dim ind As Index
    Dim f As Field

    Set td = db.TableDefs("tblCustomer")

    For Each ind In td.Indexes
        Debug.Print ind.Name

        For Each f In ind.Fields
            Debug.Print "   On field: " & f.Name
        Next

    Next

End Sub
```

Note: You can use code similar to this to iterate through other collections in DAO. For example, you can use code like this to view all the databases in a workspace, the QueryDefs in a database, or the fields in a TableDef.

Figure 3.15 shows the output of this procedure.

Figure 3.15
An application that displays all the indexes in a TableDef.

Code Example: You can find the application described in this section in the directory \vbdb\code\03-DAO\Finder\Finder.vbp. For information on how to install the sample files on the CD that accompanies this book, see the section "Installing the Example Files" in the introduction at the beginning of this book.

Remembering Your Place in a Recordset Using the *Bookmark* Property
When you're performing operations on a Recordset object, it's common to move hither and yon in the recordset, only to return to your starting place later. You use the Bookmark property of the Recordset object to hold your place so that you can return to a position in the recordset later.

The Bookmark property gives you an efficient way of zipping back and forth between two or more records in a recordset. It's much faster to use a bookmark than it is to repeatedly use find methods to move through the database.

Every record in a "bookmarkable" recordset has its own unique bookmark that you can retrieve and store at any time. However, bookmarks aren't stored with the database; they're generated automatically when a Recordset object is created and are discarded when the Recordset object is destroyed.

To use a bookmark, follow these general steps:

1. Move to the position in the recordset you wish to bookmark.

2. Assign the value of the Recordset object's Bookmark property to a string variable. This saves the unique bookmark for the current record.

3. When you wish to move back to the record, assign the recordset's Bookmark property to the value of the string variable. The current record will be changed to the bookmarked record.

Business Case 3.5: Browsing a Database Using Bookmarks   Jones Novelties' customer service representatives have noticed that they spend much time querying and requerying the database for information as they attempt to handle orders that deal with more than one customer at a time. They ask you to build an application that enables them to browse the database and store bookmarks for up to two customers at a time. Users of the customer browser then can bounce back and forth between many customers quickly.

Figure 3.16 shows the user interface of this application.

Figure 3.16
The user interface of the enhanced Customer Browser featuring bookmarks.

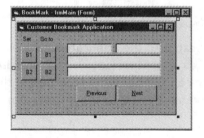

This application provides a database browser interface, enabling the user to move forward and backward in the recordset without the use of a Data control.

Listing 3.24 shows the code that initializes this application.

Listing 3.24   The Declarations and *Load* Event for the Enhanced Customer Browser

```
' References: MS DAO 3.51 Object Library

Private db As Database
Private rs As Recordset

Const DBPath = "..\..\db\"

Private Bookmark1 As String
Private Bookmark2 As String

Private Enum TextBoxEnum
    txtFirstName = 0
    txtLastName = 1
    txtAddress = 2
    txtPhone = 3
End Enum

Private Enum CmdButtonEnum
    cmdSetBookmark1 = 0
    cmdSetBookmark2 = 1
    cmdGoToBookmark1 = 2
    cmdGotoBookmark2 = 3
End Enum


Private Sub Form_Load()

    Set db = OpenDatabase(DBPath & "novelty.mdb")
    Set rs = db.OpenRecordset("tblCustomer")
    PopulateControls

End Sub
```

This code (and several other procedures in the application) call the PopulateControls subroutine. This subroutine simply takes text values from the current record in the recordset and uses the data to populate the application's text boxes. Listing 3.25 shows the code for this procedure.

Listing 3.25   The Code for the *PopulateControls* Subroutine

```
Private Sub PopulateControls()
On Error GoTo ErrHandler

    TextBox(txtFirstName).Text = rs!FirstName & ""
    TextBox(txtLastName).Text = rs!LastName & ""
    TextBox(txtAddress).Text = rs!Address & ""
    TextBox(txtPhone).Text = rs!Phone & ""

Exit Sub
ErrHandler:
    If Err = 3021 Then ' no current record
        Exit Sub
    Else
        MsgBox Err.Description
    End If

End Sub
```

This routine assigns values from the recordset to the Text properties of the text boxes on the form, but it doesn't assign those properties directly; instead, it concatenates those values to an empty string. The routine does this to coerce null values from the database into empty string values that the text box's Text property can accept. (If you didn't do this, an error would be generated every time the user scrolled to a record that contained no data in one of its fields.)

Listing 3.26 shows the code that enables the Next and Previous buttons.

Listing 3.26   DAO code That Enables the User to Move Forward and Backward in the Recordset

```
Private Sub cmdNext_Click()
On Error GoTo ErrHandler

    rs.MoveNext
    PopulateControls

Exit Sub
ErrHandler:
    If Err = 3021 Then ' no current record
        rs.MoveLast
        Exit Sub
    Else
        MsgBox Err.Description
    End If
```

```
End Sub

Private Sub cmdPrevious_Click()
On Error GoTo ErrHandler

    rs.MovePrevious
    PopulateControls

Exit Sub
ErrHandler:
    If Err = 3021 Then ' no current record
        rs.MoveFirst
        Exit Sub
    Else
        MsgBox Err.Description
    End If

End Sub
```

The error handlers in these procedures are based on the idea that errors occur when the user attempts to scroll outside of the boundaries of the recordset (that is, beyond BOF and EOF). It is possible to write another, more elegant version of these routines to inspect the values of BOF and EOF and disable the buttons when the values of these properties are True. But this version is good enough for now.

The bookmark-setting portion of the code is shown in Listing 3.27.

Listing 3.27   The Code That Sets Bookmarks in the Enhanced Customer Browser Application

```
Private Sub BookMark_Click(Index As Integer)

    Select Case Index
        Case cmdSetBookmark1
            Bookmark1 = rs.BookMark

        Case cmdSetBookmark2
            Bookmark2 = rs.BookMark

        Case cmdGoToBookmark1
            If Bookmark1 <> "" Then
                rs.BookMark = Bookmark1
                PopulateControls
```

continues

Listing 3.27 The Code That Sets Bookmarks in the Enhanced Customer Browser Application (Continued)

```
        Else
            MsgBox "That bookmark has not been set.", _
                    vbExclamation, "Error"
        End If

    Case cmdGotoBookmark2
        If Bookmark2 <> "" Then
            rs.BookMark = Bookmark2
            PopulateControls
        Else
            MsgBox "That bookmark has not been set.", _
                    vbExclamation, "Error"
        End If

    Case Else
        MsgBox "BookMark_Click: Something's terribly wrong.", _
                vbExclamation, "Error"

    End Select

End Sub
```

To understand this code, remember that in this application, the command buttons (similar to the text boxes) are in control arrays. Based on which button in the control array the user clicked, either the application saves a bookmark (that is, the application reads the bookmark into a variable) or the recordset moves to a previously set bookmark. Anytime the recordset repositions itself, the PopulateControls subroutine is called to update the data displayed in the text box controls.

To test this application, do the following:

1. Run the application. The database loads and the application displays the first record in the recordset.

2. Click the Next button a few times until you locate a record you like.

3. To bookmark the record, click the Set B1 button.

4. Move forward or backward a few more records; then click the Go to B1 button.

The previously bookmarked record is displayed.

Code Example: You can find the application described in this section, in the directory `\vbdb\code\03-DAO\Bookmark\BookMark.vbp`. For information on how to install the sample files on the CD that accompanies this book, see the section "Installing the Example Files" in the introduction at the beginning of this book.

Note: Not every type of `Recordset` object supports the `Bookmark` property. To determine whether you can bookmark a particular type of recordset, inspect the value of the recordset's `Bookmarkable` property. If the property is `True`, you can bookmark the recordset.

ACCESSING SESSION INFORMATION WITH THE *WORKSPACE* OBJECT

You establish a user session with the database engine using the `Workspace` object. This object governs everything related to how an individual user interacts with the database engine; accordingly, the `Workspaces` collection and `Workspace` object occupy a position in the DAO object model below the `DBEngine` object but above the `Database` object.

Figure 3.17 shows the `Workspace` object's place in the DAO hierarchy.

So far, you've seen plenty of code examples that don't require the use of the `Workspace` object. So why is the object necessary? One answer is that it's as necessary as your kidney—and you don't have to pay any attention to it, just as you don't have to pay any attention to your kidney. In other words, there's always a `Workspace` object, even if you're not aware of it, and you don't code against it.

To verify this, try this fun experiment: In code that creates a `Recordset` object, place a breakpoint on the line immediately after the one that contains the `OpenRecordset` method. Open the Immediate window and execute the following line of code:

```
Print Workspaces(0).Name
```

The Immediate window deftly responds with the following:

```
#Default Workspace#
```

Figure 3.17
The position of the Workspaces collection and Workspace object in the DAO hierarchy.

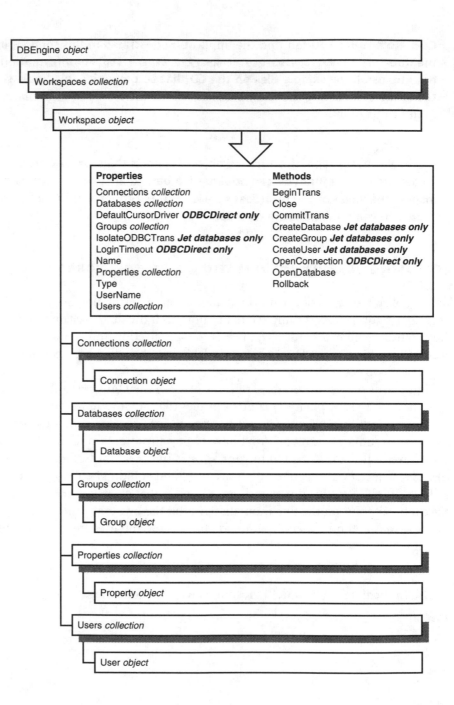

Surprise! You're the unwitting parent of a bouncing baby `Workspace` object.

In DAO programming, you wittingly create `Workspace` objects in the following situations:

▶ You want to perform *transactions* (multiple database operations that are grouped together and executed as one operation). The next section of this chapter describes transactions.

▶ You want to create or manipulate groups and users in the Microsoft Jet security system. The technique for doing this is coyly alluded to later in this chapter and described more fully in Chapter 9.

Creating Transactions Using the *Workspace* Object   A *transaction* is a unit of work performed by a database engine. Generally, transactions comprise two or more distinct operations, all of which must be successfully accomplished for any of the operations to be valid.

The oft-repeated example of a typical transaction is a financial transfer. For money to be debited from someone's account, it must be credited to some other account, or the bank's books won't balance. If some error condition takes place between the time the money is credited and the time it is debited, you have a serious problem—you've either lost the customer's money, or you've fabricated money out of thin air.

A transaction is used in this situation to ensure that one operation doesn't take place without the other. Either the debit and the credit are successful, in which case the transaction is successful and the change to the database is committed, or one of the operations fails, in which case the transaction is rolled back.

> **Note:** You can use transactions only on Microsoft Jet databases and on ODBC client/server data sources; you can't use transactions with "installable ISAM" data sources such as dBASE and Paradox.

In general, transactions are stored in memory until they are committed. However, for transactions composed of many operations, the transaction might need to write temporary data to disk. Jet handles this writing behind the scenes.

In previous versions of Microsoft Jet, there was a performance benefit to wrapping intensive data access code in transactions. Transactions usually take place in memory, and coding against constructs stored in memory in order of magnitude is more efficient than coding against a database stored on disk.

Current versions of Jet add performance enhancements to make this trick unnecessary.

You follow these general steps to create a transaction in DAO:

1. To initiate a transaction, use the Workspace object's BeginTrans method. This initiates a transaction and tells the database engine not to write to the database until the transaction is committed. Subsequent database operations are either cached in memory or stored in a temporary database.

2. If any of the database operations in your transaction fail, execute the Workspace object's Rollback method.

3. If all the database operations in the transaction succeed, execute the Workspace object's CommitTrans method.

When you initiate a transaction, that transaction is owned not by the database, but by the Workspace object. This is because the Workspace object manages your application's session with the database engine. (This makes sense because if a Database object owned the transaction, you couldn't perform transactions across databases.)

This gives you an interesting capability. Because the Workspace object owns a Databases collection, and the scope of a transaction spans every database owned by a workspace, you can perform transactions against multiple databases and then commit or roll them all back as a group. This can be useful, but it can be a trap—especially when you consider that the Workspace object is often referenced implicitly. If you initiate a transaction, perform updates on one database, perform updates in another database, and then roll back the transaction expecting only the changes to the second database to be rolled back, you're going to be in for a nasty surprise. Because both databases are part of the same workspace, everything gets rolled back.

If you want each database to be part of separate transactions, you create a new workspace for each database—using the CreateWorkspace method of the DBEngine object—and execute separate BeginTrans and CommitTrans methods against each workspace. That way, you can roll back a transaction against one database, but not against the other.

Business Case 3.6: Using Transactions to Impose Business Rules   Listing 3.28 is an example of code that runs a simple transaction. The business rule behind this transaction handles the creation of customers and orders: When a customer and an order are created at the same time, both customer and order must be created. If the order is created without the customer, you won't know where to ship the product. If the customer is created without the order, the order will be lost. Either way, any problem accessing either table will cause the transaction to be rolled back.

Listing 3.28   An Example of a Database Transaction Using the DAO *Workspace* Object

```
Dim db As Database

Private Sub Form_Load()
    Set db = OpenDatabase("..\..\db\novelty.mdb")
End Sub

Private Sub cmdTrans_Click()
On Error GoTo ErrHandler

    Dim rsCustomer As Recordset
    Dim rsOrder As Recordset

    Set rsCustomer = db.OpenRecordset("tblCustomer")
    Set rsOrder = db.OpenRecordset("tblOrder")

    Workspaces(0).BeginTrans
        rsCustomer.AddNew
        rsCustomer.Fields("FirstName") = txtFirstName.Text
        rsCustomer.Fields("LastName") = txtLastName.Text

        rsOrder.AddNew
        rsOrder.Fields("CustomerID") = rsCustomer!ID
        rsOrder.Fields("OrderDate") = txtOrderDate.Text
        rsOrder.Fields("OrderAmount") = txtAmount.Text

        rsCustomer.Update
        rsOrder.Update
    Workspaces(0).CommitTrans

Exit Sub

ErrHandler:
    Workspaces(0).Rollback
    MsgBox "There was an error saving the data."
End Sub

Private Sub Form_Unload(Cancel As Integer)
    db.Close
    Set db = Nothing
End Sub
```

Code Example: You can find the application described in this section in the directory `\vbdb\code\03-DAO\Trans\Trans.vbp`. For information on how to install the sample files on the CD that accompanies this book, see the section "Installing the Example Files" in the introduction at the beginning of this book.

When using transactions, it's helpful to remember that you can refer to the default `Workspace` object implicitly. Consider the following code:

```
Workspaces(0).BeginTrans

    ' [vital earth-shaking code goes here]

    Workspaces(0).CommitTrans
```

Instead of using this code, you can drop the references to `Workspaces(0)` and write code such as the following:

```
    BeginTrans

    ' [really important mind-blowing code goes here]

    CommitTrans
```

If you never use multiple workspaces, this technique can make your transactions easier to code.

Objects That Manage Users and Groups   In addition to handling transactions, `Workspace` objects are useful for managing users and groups. In a secured database, users identify individuals who have access to your database; groups contain collections of users.

`User` and `Group` objects are only available with Jet databases. Figure 3.18 shows the position of the `User` and `Group` objectss in the DAO object model.

Users and groups are part of the DAO object model for Microsoft Jet databases. But because users and groups aren't directly related to the construction of a database application, the DAO code that enables you to create users and groups is covered in more detail in Chapter 8, "Remote Database Access."

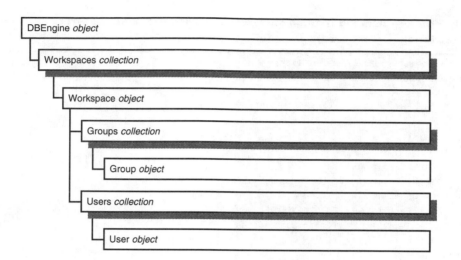

Figure 3.18
The User and Group objects in the DAO model.

HANDLING ERRORS USING THE *ERRORS* COLLECTION AND THE *ERROR* OBJECT

Your application can deal with errors in DAO by using the Error object and the Errors collection. The Errors collection exists because in database programming, a particular operation can generate more than one error. (This is particularly true in client/server programming, in which, for example, an ODBC driver bites the dust because a piece of middleware is hosed because the server is toast. All three components might generate their own unique and lovely error messages, but you'd never see them all unless you had a nice collection to iterate through.)

Having a collection of errors instead of a single Error object, then, enables you to iterate through all the errors in an effort to determine what went wrong.

Figure 3.19 shows the Error object's place in the DAO object hierarchy.

Note: You can't append or delete Error objects to the Errors collection.

Listing 3.29 gives an example of how to iterate through the DBEngine's Errors collection to see all the errors it generates.

Listing 3.29   Iterating Through the *Errors* Collection to See All the Error Descriptions

```
' References: MS DAO 3.51


Dim db As Database
Dim rs As Recordset
```

continues

Listing 3.29 **Iterating Through the *Errors* Collection to See All the Error Descriptions** **(Continued)**

```
Private Sub cmdBadFileName_Click()
On Error GoTo ErrHandler

    Set db = OpenDatabase("..\..\DB\slez.mdb")

Exit Sub
ErrHandler:
    Dim DBError As Error
    Debug.Print "Contents of DBEngine Errors Collection"
    Debug.Print "-------------------------------------"
    For Each DBError In DBEngine.Errors
        Debug.Print DBError.Description
    Next
End Sub
```

Figure 3.19
The Errors collection and the Error object in the DAO object hierarchy.

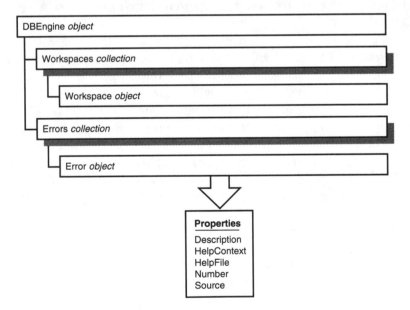

Note that the last error generated by the DBEngine Errors collection is raised to the Visual Basic Err object. In this case, because the operation generates only one error (Couldn't find file slez.mdb), the effect is the same as if you'd trapped the error at the Visual Basic level, using Visual Basic's Err object.

Code Example: You can find the application described in this section, including the modifications described in the next section, in the directory \vbdb\code\03-DAO\Error\Error.vbp. For information on how to install the sample files on the CD that accompanies this book, see the section "Installing the Example Files" in the introduction at the beginning of this book.

As you can imagine, it's tough to simulate a situation in which you'd generate multiple errors when you're working with a Jet database. However, it's easy to generate multiple errors in a client/server environment because so many components work together to establish the connection between the client and server. For more information on error handling in the world of client/server programming, see Chapter 8 and Chapter 10.

CREATING OBJECTS THAT MANIPULATE THE STRUCTURE OF A DATABASE

DAO gives you a rich set of procedures for creating databases, tables, fields, and query definitions. In addition, DAO enables you to create new types of custom data in your application, such as custom properties of database objects and new types of database documents.

CREATING A DATABASE

You create a Microsoft Jet database using the CreateDatabase method of the DBEngine object in DAO.

When you create a database, you must supply a filename (typically ending in a MDB extension) and a locale. The locale is a function of the language used by users of your application; it sets the collating order for your database. The collating order determines how text values in your database are sorted by default.

Note: The CreateDatabase method of the DBEngine object replaces the CreateDatabase statement that existed in previous versions of DAO. But because DBEngine is one of those DAO objects you never need to reference explicitly in code, you can continue using CreateDatabase the old way, without a reference to a DBEngine object in front of it. However, if you want to be 100 percent correct, you use DBEngine.CreateDatabase instead of just CreateDatabase.

Listing 3.30 gives an example of code that creates a database. In addition to creating the database, the code also appends a single table with two fields to the database. (The code used here is slightly different from the table-creating code listed in the next section, which describes TableDef objects.)

Listing 3.30   Creating a New Database Using the *CreateDatabase* Method of the *DBEngine* Object

```
' References MS DAO 3.51

Private db As Database
Private td As TableDef
Private f As Field

Private Sub cmdCreate_Click()
On Error GoTo ErrHandler

    Set db = DBEngine.CreateDatabase("..\..\DB\newdb.mdb", dbLangGeneral)
    Set td = New TableDef

    Set f = td.CreateField("LastName", dbText, 50)
    td.Fields.Append f

    Set f = td.CreateField("FirstName", dbText, 50)
    td.Fields.Append f

    td.Name = "tblSupplier"
    db.TableDefs.Append td

    Set db = Nothing

    MsgBox "The database newdb.mdb has been created."

Exit Sub
ErrHandler:
    If Err = 3204 Then
        MsgBox "Try deleting the database 'newdb.mdb' first, pal."
    Else
        MsgBox Err.Description
    End If
End Sub
```

Because the CreateDatabase method generates an error if the database already exists, this code contains error-handling that tells the user what to do if the database already exists. Also remember that you don't need to instantiate an instance of the DBEngine object. It's always available for your application to use.

Code Example: You can find the application described in this section, including the modifications described in the next section, in the directory `\vbdb\code\03-DAO\DBCreate\DBCreate.vbp`. For information on how to install the sample files on the CD that accompanies this book, see the section "Installing the Example Files" in the introduction at the beginning of this book.

MANIPULATING TABLES USING THE *TABLEDEF* OBJECT

You use the `TableDef` object to create and manipulate the structure of tables in your application. You can use the `TableDef` object to create new tables or change existing tables.

Figure 3.20 shows the position of the `TableDef` object in the DAO hierarchy, as well as the properties and methods of a `TableDef` object.

Note: In previous versions of DAO, you used the `ListTables` method of the `Database` object to get the names of the tables in the database. This method is obsolete; you now use the `TableDefs` collection to access all the tables in a database.

Creating a New Table Using the *TableDef* Object   To create a new table, you instantiate an object of type `TableDef` and then append it to the `TableDefs` collection using the collection's `Append` method. (This pattern is similar for many types of DAO objects that create persistent components of the database.)

Listing 3.31 is an example of code that uses the `TableDef` to create a new table. This code uses the `Field` object and `Fields` collection; these are discussed later in this chapter. Note that if you use this code to create a table that already exists, you'll get a runtime error; accordingly, if you already have a table called tblEmployee, you may wish to set the `Name` propertyy of the `TableDef` object to something similar to tblEmployeeNew.

Listing 3.31   Creating a New Table with a Single Text Field Using DAO Code

```
' References: Microsoft DAO 3.51 Object Library

Dim db As Database
                                                          continues
```

Listing 3.31 **Creating a New Table with a Single Text Field Using DAO Code (Continued)**

```
Private Sub Form_Load()
    Set db = OpenDatabase("..\..\db\novelty.mdb")
End Sub

Private Sub cmdCreate_Click()
On Error GoTo ErrHandler

    Dim td As TableDef
    Dim f As Field

    Set td = New TableDef
    Set f = New Field

    f.Name = "FirstName"
    f.Type = dbText

    td.Name = "tblEmployeeNew"

    td.Fields.Append f

    db.TableDefs.Append td

    MsgBox "Lo, the table has been created."

Exit Sub
ErrHandler:
    If Err.Number = 3010 Then
        MsgBox "You can't create the table twice, chief."
    Else
        MsgBox Err.Description
    End If
End Sub
```

Code Example: You can find the application described in this section, including the modifications described in the next section, in the directory `\vbdb\code\03-DAO\TblDef\TblDef.vbp`. For information on how to install the sample files on the CD that accompanies this book, see the section "Installing the Example Files" in the introduction at the beginning of this book.

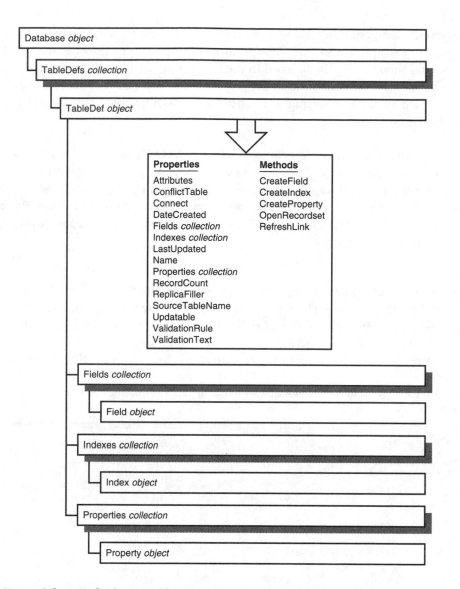

Figure 3.20
The TableDefs collection and TableDef object in the DAO object hierarchy.

You might not find yourself using DAO to create tables and fields on a regular basis. You have Microsoft Access and Visual Basic's Visual Data Manager for that. However, because you can create tables in code, you can write applications that treat database tables as documents.

For example, consider an application that enables an engineer to create a new type of product. The product might have properties that no one has ever thought of before. If your application enables the engineer to build tables to represent data pertaining to the new product, she could then create fields to represent each property of the new product. Each prototype the engineer created would then be a distinct record in the table, so that when the engineer came upon the correct combination of properties, the new product could then be built. Such an application might require that the user be able to create custom fields and tables.

> **Note:** Remember that you can also use SQL Data Definition Language (DDL) to perform many of the same types of operations on tables as you would using the TableDef object in DAO. However, using DAO gives you an object-oriented programming interface that is usually more similar to Visual Basic. For more information on using SQL to create and alter tables, see "Using SQL DDL" in Chapter 2.

Creating a *Field* Object Using the *CreateField* Method   You can create a Field object by using the TableDef's CreateField method. You typically do this to add a new field to a table or modify an existing field in a table. You can also create a field for other purposes, such as adding a field to an index.

Listing 3.32 demonstrates how to create a new field in an existing TableDef.

Listing 3.32   Adding a New Field to an Existing TableDef Using the *CreateField* Method

```
' References: Microsoft DAO 3.51 Object Library
'
Dim db As Database

Private Sub Form_Load()
    Set db = OpenDatabase("..\..\db\novelty.mdb")
End Sub

Private Sub cmdNewField_Click()
    Dim td As TableDef
    Dim f As Field

    Set td = db.TableDefs("tblEmployee")
    Set f = td.CreateField("MiddleName", dbText)

    td.Fields.Append f

End Sub
```

Code Example: You can find the application described in this section, including the modifications described in the next section, in the directory `\vbdb\code\03-DAO\NewField\NewField.vbp`. For information on how to install the sample files on the CD that accompanies this book, see the section "Installing the Example Files" in the introduction at the beginning of this book.

In this example, you're adding a totally new field to the table's structure. The field is permanently appended to the table's structure when you append the `Field` object to the TableDef's `Fields` collection.

Note: The `CreateField` method works in Jet workspaces only.

CREATING RELATIONSHIPS BETWEEN TABLES USING THE *RELATION* OBJECT

You use the `Relation` object to create a relationship in your database. You use this object with other DAO commands that create tables.

Figure 3.21 shows the place of the `Relation` object in the DAO hierarchy.

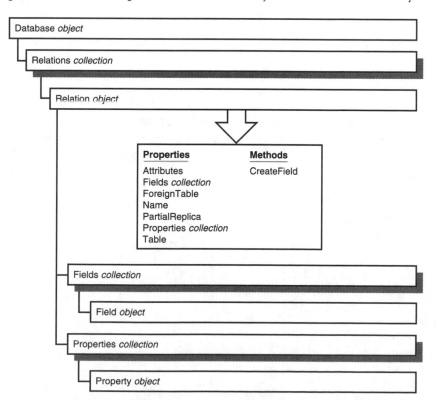

Figure 3.21
The Relations collection and the Relation object in the DAO hierarchy.

Recall from the discussion of relationships in Chapter 2 that a *relation* is a formal declaration of the relationship between two tables. For a relationship to exist, you must name two fields, one in each table: the primary key of one table and a foreign key in the related table.

You create a new relationship between two tables using the CreateRelation method of the Database object. To create a new relationship, you must specify the name of the new relationship, the tables involved in the relationship, and the type of relationship; you then append fields to the Relation object to specify which fields are linked in the relationship.

Here's the syntax of the CreateRelation method:

```
Set relation = db.CreateRelation ([name], [table], [foreigntable], [attributes])
```

▶ *relation* is the name of an object variable of type Relation.

▶ *db* is a Database object.

▶ *name* is the name of the Relation object you're trying to create.

▶ *table* is the name of the primary table involved in the relationship.

▶ *foreigntable* is the name of the foreign table involved in the relationship.

▶ *attributes* specifies any attributes assigned to the relationship (for example, whether you want the database to enforce cascading deletes).

Listing 3.33 shows an example of a DAO procedure that creates a relationship in an existing database.

Listing 3.33   Creating a New *Relation* Object Using DAO Code

```
' References MS DAO 3.51 Object Library

Private db As Database
Private rel As Relation

Private Sub cmdMakeRelation_Click()
On Error Goto ErrHandler

  Set db = OpenDatabase("..\..\db\novelty.mdb")

  Set rel = db.CreateRelation("CustomerOrder")

  With rel
    .Table = "tblCustomer"
    .ForeignTable = "tblOrder"
```

```
  End With

  rel.Fields.Append rel.CreateField("ID")
  rel.Fields("ID").ForeignName = "CustomerID"

  db.Relations.Append rel

  MsgBox "Voila. The relationship is created."

Exit Sub
ErrHandler:
  MsgBox "The relation can't be created " & _
         "or it already exists."
End Sub
```

Code Example: You can find the application described in this section, including the modifications described in the next section, in the directory `\vbdb\code\03-DAO\Relate\Relate.vbp`. For information on how to install the sample files on the CD that accompanies this book, see the section "Installing the Example Files" in the introduction at the beginning of this book.

This code creates a relationship between tblCustomer and tblOrder. It begins by creating a Relation object using the CreateRelation method of the Database object. It then creates a Field object (called ID) using the CreateField method of the Relation object. It does not matter that this field does not derive directly from the underlying table definition because the relationship requires only a Field object that contains the name of the field used in the relationship. You then set the ForeignName property of the Field object to the name of the foreign key, and finally append the whole works to the Relations collection.

When you create a Relation object in your database, you're also creating an index on the foreign key field. (In some client/server systems, it's impossible to create a join on two tables unless the primary key is indexed; Access creates this index for you automatically when you create the join.) For this reason, it's not necessary to explicitly create an index on the foreign key field yourself—unless you think you'll need to get programmatic access to the index later. You typically access an index programmatically when using the Seek method, as described in "Performing Indexed Searches Using the *Seek* Method" earlier in this chapter.

Note: Creating relationships in code is something that you probably won't do very often. (Instead, you'll typically use a utility such as the Visual Data Manager or Microsoft Access to create relationships.)

CREATING INDEXES USING THE *INDEX* OBJECT

You can create indexes on fields belonging to TableDefs by using DAO code with the `Index` object and the `CreateIndex` method of the `TableDef` object.

Figure 3.22 shows the place of the `Index` object in the DAO hierarchy.

Figure 3.22
The Indexes collection and the Index object in the DAO hierarchy.

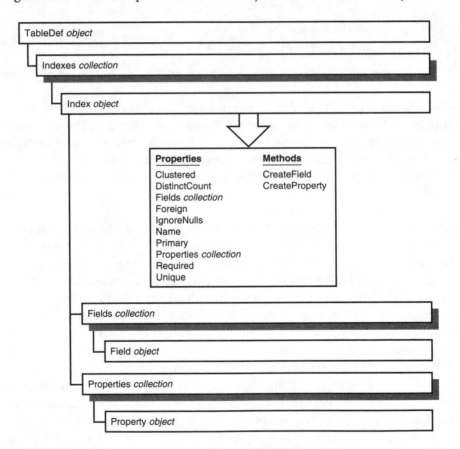

Note: The `Indexes` collection replaces the `ListIndex` method that existed in previous versions of DAO. This method is now obsolete; it still works, but you should use the Indexes collection instead.

To create an index on the LastName field of the tblCustomer table, you use the code in Listing 3.34.

Listing 3.34   Creating an Index on a Field in DAO Using the *Index* Object

```
' References MS DAO 3.51 Object Library

Private db As Database

Private Sub Form_Load()

    Set db = OpenDatabase("..\..\db\novelty.mdb")

End Sub


Private Sub cmdMakeIndex_Click()
On Error GoTo ErrHandler

  Dim td As TableDef
  Dim ind As Index

  Set td = db.TableDefs("tblCustomer")
. Set ind = td.CreateIndex("LastNameIndex")

  ind.Fields.Append td.CreateField("LastName")
  td.Indexes.Append ind

  MsgBox "Yippee, the index was created."

Exit Sub
ErrHandler:
  MsgBox "The index could not be created."

End Sub
```

Note that if another user, or another process in your application, has the table open while you attempt to create an index on it, the CreateIndex method generates an error. Also, if the index already exists, the method also fails.

MANIPULATING STORED QUERIES USING THE *QUERYDEF* OBJECT

You can create and alter stored queries using DAO's QueryDef object. In addition to creating stored queries, the QueryDef object also enables you to run parameterized queries; this is a common reason to access QueryDef objects using DAO code.

Note: The `QueryDefs` collection replaces the `OpenQueryDef` method of the `Database` object that existed in previous versions of DAO. This method is now obsolete; you should use the `QueryDefs` collection to manipulate `QueryDef` objects instead.

As an alternative to creating stored queries using DAO, you can also create stored queries using Microsoft Access or Visual Basic's Visual Data Manager. For more information on how to use Visual Data Manager, see Chapter 1.

Figure 3.23 shows the `QueryDef` object's place in the DAO hierarchy, along with its properties and methods.

You create query definitions in your database by using DAO's `QueryDef` object. Such definitions can either be temporary, in which case they disappear as soon as you are done with them, or permanent, in which case they are permanently stored in the database.

You create a `QueryDef` object using code similar to that shown in Listing 3.35.

Listing 3.35   Creating a New *QueryDef* Object in DAO Code

```
' References: Microsoft DAO 3.51 Object Library
'
Private db As Database
Private qd As QueryDef

Private Sub Form_Load()

  Set db = OpenDatabase("..\..\db\novelty.mdb")

End Sub


Private Sub cmdCreate_Click()
On Error GoTo ErrHandler

  Set qd = New QueryDef

  qd.Name = "qryCustomerSortName"
  qd.SQL = "SELECT * " & _
           "FROM tblCustomer " & _
           "WHERE LastName Like 'L*' " & _
           "ORDER BY LastName, FirstName"

  db.QueryDefs.Append qd

  MsgBox "Whaddya know, the query was created."
```

```
Exit Sub
ErrHandler:
  MsgBox "There was an error creating the QueryDef."
End Sub
```

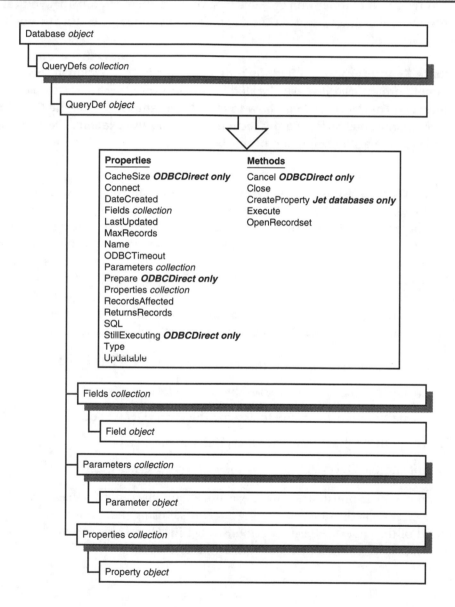

Figure 3.23
The QueryDefs collection and the QueryDef object within the DAO hierarchy.

You designate the name of the QueryDef you're creating using the QueryDef object's Name property. If you attempt to create a QueryDef that already exists, you trigger a trappable error.

Don't forget to give your new QueryDef a name; otherwise, you won't have a way to refer to it (and Jet won't be able to save it). Remember, too, that you can determine which queries exist in the database at any time by iterating through the QueryDefs collection.

Code Example: You can find the code discussed in this section in the sample project QueryDef.vbp, located in the directory \vbdb\code\03-DAO\ QueryDef. For information on how to install the sample files on the CD that accompanies this book, see the section "Installing the Example Files" in the introduction at the beginning of this book.

Running Queries Using the *QueryDef* Object   You can run (or execute) a query by using the methods of the QueryDef object. You typically do this in situations where you need to do something unusual to the query before running it, such as specifying a parameter, or when you need to execute an action query that updates, deletes, or changes records in the database. (To run a query normally, you use the OpenRecordset method of the Database object, as demonstrated earlier in this chapter.)

To execute a QueryDef, you use the OpenRecordset method of the QueryDef object (to run a SELECT query) or the QueryDef object's Execute method (to run an action query).

To execute a QueryDef, follow these steps:

1. Create an instance of a QueryDef object in code.

2. Create a SQL string that defines what the QueryDef will do when it is run.

3. Assign the SQL string to the QueryDef's SQL property.

4. Append the QueryDef to the Database object's QueryDefs collection.

Listing 3.36 demonstrates how to execute a QueryDef in a database. (This code is essentially the same as creating a recordset using the OpenRecordset method of the Database object, as demonstrated in "Creating a *Recordset* Object Using the *OpenRecordset* Method" earlier in this chapter.)

Listing 3.36   Executing a *QueryDef* Object in DAO Code

```
Private Sub cmdRun_Click()
On Error GoTo ErrHandler
  Dim rs As Recordset
  Dim qd As QueryDef

  Set qd = db.QueryDefs("qryCustomerSortName")
  Set rs = qd.OpenRecordset

  Do Until rs.EOF
    lstCustomer.AddItem rs!LastName & " " & _
                        rs!FirstName & " " & _
                        rs!Address

    rs.MoveNext
  Loop

Exit Sub
ErrHandler:
  MsgBox "There was an error running the query."

End Sub
```

The procedure uses a list box to display the customers it retrieves from the database. This code assumes you have declared and opened a Database object in your code. It also assumes you have a stored query in your database called qryCustomerSortName.

> **Code Example:** You can find the code discussed in this section in the sample project QueryDef.vbp, located in the directory \vbdb\code\ 03-DAO\QueryDef. For information on how to install the sample files on the CD that accompanies this book, see the section "Installing the Example Files" in the introduction at the beginning of this book.

Creating Queries Using *QueryDef* Objects   You can create a QueryDef programmatically using code. To create a QueryDef, you create a new QueryDef object using the Database object's CreateQueryDef method. This method lets you give the query a name and assign it an SQL string. Executing this method also saves the QueryDef permanently in the database.

Listing 3.37 gives an example of how to do this.

Listing 3.37 Creating a QueryDef Using Code

```
Dim db As Database
Dim qd As QueryDef


Set db = OpenDatabase("..\..\db\novelty.mdb")


Set qd = db.CreateQueryDef("qryIdahoCustomers", _
         "select * from tblCustomer where State = 'ID'")
```

Once you've created the QueryDef, you can manipulate it as you normally would in code. Giving the QueryDef a name is what determines whether the query is permanently stored in the database. If you ever want to create a QueryDef that isn't permanently stored in the database, simply pass an empty string in place of the first parameter of the CreateQueryDef method.

Creating Parameterized Queries Using the *Parameter* Object The Parameters collection of a QueryDef enables you to perform parameterized queries. These queries are built with one or more components (the parameter or parameters) intentionally omitted; these components must be filled in when the query is run.

You create parameterized queries because they execute much faster than queries you build in SQL on-the-fly in Visual Basic code. This is because the database engine compiles a query before you run it, which optimizes the query's execution.

Figure 3.24 shows the place of the Parameters collection and Parameter object in the DAO hierarchy, as well as the Parameter object's properties.

Figure 3.24
The Parameters collection and the Parameter object in the DAO object hierarchy.

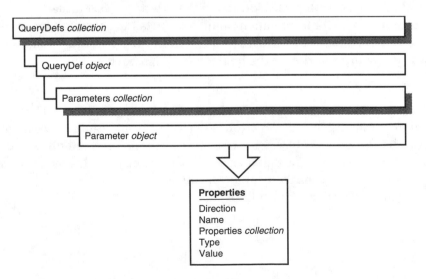

Note: The `Parameters` collection replaces the `ListParameters` method that existed in previous versions of DAO. This method is now obsolete; you should use the `Parameters` collection instead.

Chapter 2 describes the syntax of a parameterized query in SQL. To keep you from having to ruffle through pages to find it, Listing 3.38 contains another example of a parameterized query.

Listing 3.38   The SQL Code for a Parameterized Query

```
SELECT *
FROM tblCustomer
WHERE ID = pID
```

The parameter in this query is called pID. Under the syntax of the Jet dialect of SQL, pID is interpreted as a parameter because it doesn't correspond to the names of any fields or tables in the database.

For the query to run, you must supply a value for this parameter. You supply a parameter in code by setting the `Value` property of the appropriate `Parameter` object, as shown in Listing 3.39.

Listing 3.39   Returning a *Recordset* Object Using a Parameterized Query

```
' References MS DAO 3.5

Private db As Database
Private qd As QueryDef
Private rs As Recordset
'

Private Sub Form_Load()
   Set db = OpenDatabase("..\..\db\novelty.mdb")
   Set qd = db.QueryDefs("qryCustomerParam")
End Sub


Private Sub cmdQuery_Click()

   qd.Parameters("pID").Value = txtID.Text
   Set rs = qd.OpenRecordset
```

continues

Listing 3.39   Returning a *Recordset* Object Using a Parameterized Query (Continued)

```
If rs.EOF and rs.BOF Then
    MsgBox "Sorry, no customers with that " & _
            "ID are in the database."
Else
    MsgBox rs!Address & vbCrLf & _
            rs!Phone, _
            vbInformation, _
            "Info for " & rs!FirstName & _
            " " & rs!LastName
End If

End Sub
```

Code Example: You can find the code discussed in this section in the sample project `ParamQry.vbp`, located in the directory `\vbdb\code\ 03-DAO\ParamQry`. For information on how to install the sample files on the CD that accompanies this book, see the section "Installing the Example Files" in the introduction at the beginning of this book.

To find a customer with this application, the user enters the customer's ID in the text box. If the application finds a customer with that ID in the database, it displays the customer's address and phone number. If the application determines that there is no record in the database matching the parameter supplied, it informs the user.

Note: Because a QueryDef's parameters are a function of the SQL statement that defines the query, you can't add new parameters to the `Parameters` collection of a QueryDef the way you add other objects to collections in DAO.

COMPACTING AND REPAIRING A JET DATABASE

The DBEngine object gives you several methods that enable you to perform maintenance operations on Jet databases. These operations include the following:

▶ *Compacting* the database, which removes deleted data from the database, causing it to take up less space on disk

▶ *Repairing* the database, which is necessary when the database becomes damaged, usually as a result of something unusual, such as the computer losing power while trying to save data to the database

Note: The database maintenance procedures described in this section work only on Microsoft Jet databases; they don't work on client/server or IISAM data sources.

Using the *CompactDatabase* Method   You use the `CompactDatabase` method to shrink the size of a database after it's been in use for a while. The reason `CompactDatabase` is necessary has to do with how components of a database get deleted. When you delete a database object, instead of wiping out every bit and byte in the object you just deleted, Jet puts it in a bit bucket that's stored in an inaccessible place in the .MDB file. Compacting the database empties this bit bucket.

Note: The `CompactDatabase` method of the `DBEngine` object replaces the `CompactDatabase` statement that existed in previous versions of DAO. But because `DBEngine` is one of those DAO objects, you never need to reference it explicitly in code; you can continue using `CompactDatabase` the old way, without a reference to a `DBEngine` object in front of it. However, if you want to be 100 percent correct, you'll use `DBEngine.CompactDatabase` instead of just `CompactDatabase`.

The complete syntax of the `CompactDatabase` method is as follows:

```
DBEngine.CompactDatabase olddb, newdb, [locale], [options], [password]
```

Executing the `CompactDatabase` method creates a new copy of your database on disk. The *olddb* parameter is the current name of your database's .MDB file. The *newdb* parameter is the name of the file to which the Jet engine will copy the new, compacted database.

The *locale* parameter affects the sorting order of the database. (For example, text gets sorted in German differently from the way it gets sorted in English.) This parameter is relevant only if you're developing a database application for international use.

The *options* argument sets a locale for the database; it's the same as the options argument of the `CreateDatabase` method (discussed earlier in this chapter).

The next section shows an example of compacting the database.

Changing the Database's Version Using *CompactDatabase*   You can change the version of a Jet database using the `CompactDatabase` method. You do this in situations where you want to upgrade a database to a newer version of Jet.

This situation occurs when you want the new database file produced by the CompactDatabase method to be compatible with different versions of the Microsoft Jet database engine. Upgrading a database to a newer version gives you access to new features; for example, database replication (discussed in Chapter 8) became available in Jet 3.0.

However, you must be careful not to upgrade a database in situations where a client application (created in Visual Basic, Microsoft Access, or another development environment) uses an older version of the database engine. Doing so forces you to make changes to the application—at the very least, you'll need to set a reference to the new version of the database engine. (In Visual Basic, you do this in the Project References menu.)

For example, if you have a 16-bit application developed in Visual Basic 3.0 that uses a Jet 2.0 database created with Microsoft Access 2.0, and you convert the database to Jet 3.5 format using CompactDatabase, your application will break, and you won't be able to open the database in Microsoft Access 2.0. The moral of the story is that you should carefully prototype and test your client applications before converting and deploying a converted database.

> **Note:** Bear in mind that an application developed in an environment that uses Jet can access data created in any previous version of Jet.

To convert a database using CompactDatabase, you assign a version constant to the options parameter of the CompactDatabase method. (To convert the database to Jet 3.0/3.5, use the dbVersion30 argument.)

In the following example, the DAO constant dbVersion30 tells CompactDatabase to convert the database to a format that's compatible with Jet 3.0 and 3.5:

```
DBEngine.CompactDatabase strOldFile, _
                         strNewFile, _
                         dbLangGeneral, _
                         dbVersion30
```

The database can't be open when you run CompactDatabase on it; if it's open (by any user), the database engine generates an error.

Listing 3.40 gives an example of how to compact a database, including options for changing the version of the database. The code traps any errors that occur in the compacting process and notifies the user if something went wrong.

Listing 3.40 Using the *CompactDatabase* Method of the *DBEngine* object to Compact a Jet Database

```
'
'References MS DAO 3.51

Const DBPath = "..\..\DB"

' Enumerate members of the
' control array
Enum CmdButtonEnum
  cmdCompactNormal = 0
  cmdCompactVersion = 1
End Enum


Private Sub cmdCompact_Click(Index As Long)
On Error Resume Next

    Dim strOldFile As String
    Dim strNewFile As String
    Dim lngVersion As Long

  strOldFile = DBPath & "novelty.mdb"

  Select Case Index
    Case cmdCompactNormal
      strNewFile = DBPath & "nov-compact.mdb"
      lngVersion = dbVersion30

    Case cmdCompactVersion
      strNewFile = DBPath & "nov-20.mdb"
      lngVersion = dbVersion20

  End Select

' Delete the compacted file, if it exists,
' and ignore any errors
  Kill strNewFile
  Err.Clear

  DBEngine.CompactDatabase strOldFile, _
                           strNewFile, _
                           dbLangGeneral, _
                           lngVersion
```

continues

Listing 3.40   Using the *CompactDatabase* Method of the *DBEngine* object to Compact a Jet Database   (Continued)

```
If Err Then
  MsgBox "The compact was not successful. " & _
         "Make sure the database is not open.", _
         vbExclamation, _
         "Database Compact Error"
Else
  MsgBox "Database successfully compacted."
End If

End Sub
```

This code also renames the file and includes error trapping that takes care of situations where the database can't be compacted (most likely because it's open). It does not touch the original file.

Code Example: You can find the code discussed in this section in the sample project `Compact.vbp`, located in the directory `\vbdb\code\03-DAO\Compact`. For information on how to install the sample files on the CD that accompanies this book, see the section "Installing the Example Files" in the introduction at the beginning of this book.

Repairing the Database   You can repair a damaged database by using the `RepairDatabase` method of the `DBEngine` object. The `RepairDatabase` method requires only the name of the database as an argument:

```
DBEngine.RepairDatabase "..\..\DB\novelty.mdb"
```

`RepairDatabase`, like the `CompactDatabase` method, cannot run if any user has the database open. But unlike `CompactDatabase`, `RepairDatabase` doesn't create a copy of the database.

You should consider running `CompactDatabase` after you run `RepairDatabase` because the process of repairing the database can create the kind of useless temporary data chunks inside the database file that `CompactDatabase` gets rid of.

WORKING WITH DATABASE DOCUMENTS AND CONTAINERS

Database documents are a DAO construct that enable you to refer to elements of the database generically. They also provide for extensibility of the features of a Jet database. You access the properties of a database document through a `Container` object.

Figure 3.25 shows the position of the Containers collection and Container objects.

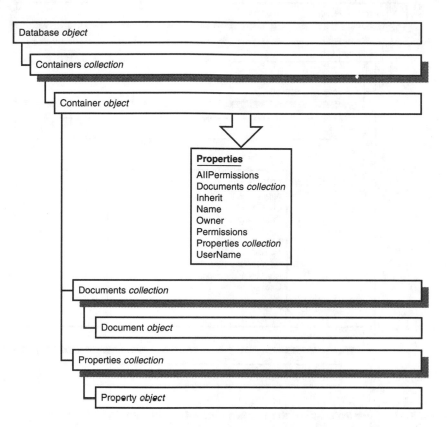

Figure 3.25
The Containers collection and the Container object in the DAO object hierarchy.

Container objects own sets of Document objects. Figure 3.26 shows the position of the Document object in the DAO object model, along with its properties and methods.

As with the many other objects available in DAO, you can use DAO code to iterate through containers and documents. Listing 3.41 shows the code to iterate through the Collection and Document objects in a Jet database.

Figure 3.26
The Documents collection and Document object in the DAO object hierarchy.

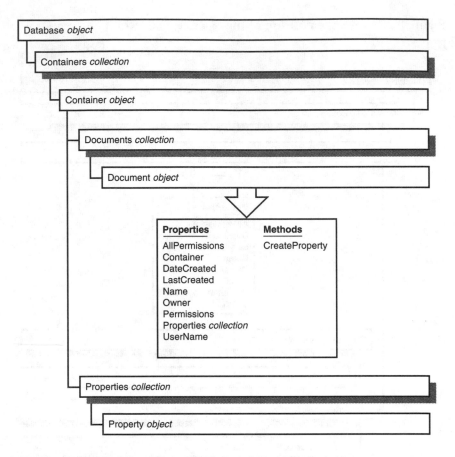

Listing 3.41   **Code to Display the Contents of a Database's *Containers* and *Documents* Collections**

```
' References DAO 3.51

Private db As Database
Private con As Container
Private doc As Document


Private Sub Form_Load()
  Set db = OpenDatabase("..\..\db\novelty.mdb")
End Sub



Private Sub cmdView_Click()
```

```
lstOutput.Clear

For Each con In db.Containers
  lstOutput.AddItem con.Name
  For Each doc In con.Documents
    lstOutput.AddItem "      " & doc.Name
  Next
Next

End Sub
```

Code Example: You can find the code discussed in this section in the sample project `Contain.vbp`, located in the directory `\vbdb\code\03-DAO\Contain`. For information on how to install the sample files on the CD that accompanies this book, see the section "Installing the Example Files" in the introduction at the beginning of this book.

For the database `novelty.mdb`, this code should produce output similar to the following:

```
Databases
  AccessLayout
  MSysDb
  SummaryInfo
  UserDefined
Forms
Modules
Relationships
  tblCustomertblOrder
Reports
  rptEmployees
Scripts
SysRel
  Admin
Tables
  ~sq_rrptEmployees
  MSysACEs
  MSysModules
  MSysModules2
  MSysObjects
  MSysQueries
  MSysRelationships
  qryAppendCustomer
  qryCustomer
```

```
qryCustomerParam
qryCustomerSortName
qryCustomerZip
qryNamesSorted
qryOrder
tblCustomer
tblEmployee
tblInventory
tblOrder
tblOrderArchive
tblRegion
```

(The elements highlighted in bold are containers; the indented elements are documents.)

It's important to understand the difference between database documents and DAO collections. A collection of TableDefs, for example, refers to all the TableDefs you've opened in your code. The `Tables` document, on the other hand, contains references to all the table documents in the database that you could open. In Jet, the `Tables` container includes documents such as stored queries and system tables (which begin with the prefix "MSys").

You use `Container` and `Document` objects in these situations:

▶ You want to assign security permissions to an object in a secured database. (See Chapter 8 for information on how to do this.)

▶ You want to create or retrieve custom properties for all the components of a database by iterating through collections. (See "Creating and Using Custom Properties of *Database* Objects" later in this chapter for more information on how to do this.)

In addition to inspecting the contents of existing database documents, DAO also enables you to define and create your own documents, which are stored in the database alongside the default documents.

Custom documents are included in the Jet object model to support extensibility. The general idea is to prevent the existing object model from inhibiting new features.

One example of how custom documents give you access to additional database functionality is *replication*, the ability of Jet databases to copy their contents to replica databases over a network. Replication is introduced in Chapter 9.

CREATING AND USING CUSTOM PROPERTIES OF *DATABASE* OBJECTS

You can refer to the properties of DAO generically. This allows for extensibility, enabling you to add your own properties and read the properties of existing objects whether you know what they're called or not.

You access the generic list of properties of a DAO through the Properties collection and Property object. You can create a new property by using the CreateProperty method of the Document object. The properties provided by the Properties collection are referred to as dynamic properties because they can be different from one database to another or one version of the database engine to another.

> Note: Just as the Document object is available only in Microsoft Jet databases, the Properties collection and Property object are unique features of Jet databases. They aren't available in other types of databases.

As an example of how the Properties collection works, Listing 3.42 shows a procedure that generates the list of default properties available in a database.

Listing 3.42   Code That Exports the Current Database's Properties to the Immediate Window

```
' References: Microsoft DAO 3.51 Object Library

Dim db As Database
Dim pr as Property



Private Sub Form_Load()
  Set db = OpenDatabase("..\..\DB\novelty.mdb")
End Sub



Private Sub cmdShow_Click()
On Error Resume Next

  lstOutput.Clear

  For Each pr In db.Properties
    With pr
      lstOutput.AddItem .Name & ": " & _
                        .Value
    End With
  Next

End Sub
```

Running this code generates the output shown in Figure 3.27.

Figure 3.27
Output generated by code that iterates through the Properties collection of a Jet database.

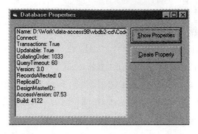

Code Example: You can find the code discussed in this section in the sample project `DBProps.vbp`, located in the directory `\vbdb\code\03-DAO\DBProps`. For information on how to install the sample files on the CD that accompanies this book, see the section "Installing the Example Files" in the introduction at the beginning of this book.

There are 13 default properties of a `Database` object available through the `Properties` collection, including such perennial favorites as `Name`, `Version`, and `Connect`, but also including properties that can't be accessed directly, such as `AccessVersion` and `Build` (both of which are undocumented in Visual Basic and Microsoft Access, but presumably pertain to the exact version of the Jet database engine used to create the database).

So, given that, you can just write code similar to this:

```
MsgBox db.Name
```

So why would you want to write code that accesses a database's properties similar to the following?

```
MsgBox db.Properties("Name")
```

The answer is that you can create your own custom properties and assign them to virtually any DAO (not only the `Database` object). Listing 3.43 shows code that creates a new property in your database.

Listing 3.43   Creating a New Property in the Database Using the DAO *Properties* Object

```
Private Sub cmdCreate_Click()
Dim prp As Property

  Set prp = db.CreateProperty("DateLastBackedUp", dbDate, Now)
  db.Properties.Append prp
  cmdShow_Click    ' Update list of properties

End Sub
```

The following is the full syntax of the CreateProperty method:

```
obj.CreateProperty(propertyname, [datatype], [value], [ddl])
```

▶ The *propertyname* argument is a string that denotes the name of the new property.

▶ The *datatype* argument specifies the data type of the new property.

▶ The *value* argument supplies an initial value for the property.

▶ The *ddl* argument is a Boolean value that specifies whether the new property is a data definition language object. I. If this is the case, users who lack permission to alter the database structure can't change the custom property.

To retrieve the value of your custom property after you've created it, you simply access it through the Properties collection of the Database object.

It would be nice if you could access your custom property using this syntax:

```
MsgBox db.DateLastBackedUp
```

However, this doesn't work because custom database properties are stored different from normal properties. You must go through the Properties object to set or retrieve your custom property.

SUMMARY

This chapter explained the grand, unified theory of DAO programming. If you have a good handle on the topics discussed in this chapter, you can perform most of the actions you will ever be called upon to do in the universe of Visual Basic database access. And if you plan on migrating to the more recent data access object models—RDO or ADO—you'll have a big head start because many of the techniques discussed in this chapter are essentially the same in those object models.

But before you take the plunge into the wonderful world of remote database access, there's one more major topic to cover: packaging and sending all this lovely data to some useful output format. Reporting and exporting data is covered in Chapter 4, "Reporting and Exporting Data."

Questions and Answers

Q. Is it appropriate to use DAO to do client/server programming?

A. It's *possible* to use DAO for client/server programming, but it's more appropriate to use ActiveX Data Objects (ADO), discussed in Chapter 10. ADO provides a programming interface similar to DAO, but with additional features (such as the ability to access non-relational data providers, asynchronous connects and queries, and a simpler object model). So if you learn DAO first, and spend some time experimenting on Jet databases, you will have a leg up on ADO because many of the basic concepts are the same.

Q. I'm creating an application based on Jet. Should I stick with DAO or migrate to ADO?

A. If your application works fine with DAO today, by all means, stick with it. Even if you don't have an existing DAO code base (or knowledge base) you're trying to preserve, you may still want to consider staying with DAO. It's the object model written with Jet databases in mind. ADO still doesn't do a number of important things that DAO lets you do. You can create Jet databases in DAO, for example—you can't do this in ADO. You can also get access to the security model (users and groups) using DAO. ADO doesn't let you do this, either. Until a version of the Jet OLE DB provider is released that supports all the functionality of DAO, it's going to be a tough call for Jet programmers as to whether they should migrate.

Q. I'm upgrading to VB 6.0 and DAO 3.5 from a 16-bit version of Visual Basic. Are there any big changes I should know about?

A. The most important change you'll want to be aware of is the fact that support for different types of records objects is dropped. For example, in DAO 3.5, there isn't a Dynaset or Snapshot object like there is in DAO 2.0. Other changes to the syntax are noted throughout this chapter.

If you need to continue to support DAO 2.5, there is a "DAO 2.5/3.0 Compatibility Library" that lets you continue to use the old objects you're accustomed to using (such as the Dynaset object). You might consider using this library if you need to move existing DAO 2.5 code into VB6 and DAO 3.5.

Reporting and Exporting Data

REPORTING USING THE VB DataReport
   DESIGNER

REPORTING USING MICROSOFT ACCESS

REPORTING USING CRYSTAL REPORTS

USING THE VISUAL BASIC PRINTER OBJECT

REPORTING USING VIDEOSOFT VSVIEW

EXPORTING TO TEXT USING THE MICROSOFT
   SCRIPTING RUNTIME LIBRARY

EXPORTING TO TEXT FILES USING VB'S CLASSIC
   FILE FUNCTIONS

EXPORTING TO MS OFFICE APPLICATIONS

A fter you've got your database up and running and you've populated it with data, you need a way to output information from it. This chapter discusses several options—some are easy to implement and will work with Visual Basic out of the box, some require third-party tools, and some are rather code-intensive. The method you use depends on your application's requirements, as well as how much flexibility you need (and how much code you're interested in writing).

Database reporting involves much more than simply printing data from your database. Most database reports involve additional operations on the data. Here are some examples:

▶ *Querying* the data in order to retrieve, display, and print just the data you want. In a report context, this is sometimes referred to as *filtering*.

▶ *Sorting* the data so it appears in an order that makes sense. (This is another facet of querying.)

▶ *Grouping* the data in order to display more concisely. For example, you wouldn't show your boss the cash register receipts for the entire year if she wanted to know how much money the company made; instead you'd show her the receipts grouped in some way—month by month or product by product, for example.

This chapter makes the distinction between reporting, which involves printing data as well as grouping and sorting it, and exporting, which involves converting the data in your database to another file format.

The Great Forward-Scrolling Cursor Caper

We haven't really discussed client/server systems in depth yet, but it's worth jumping ahead at this point. Visual Basic gives you access to some new client/server technologies that enable you to perform database access more efficiently—particularly when it comes to exporting or reporting data.

One technique involves the use of forward-scrolling cursors. A forward-scrolling cursor is a type of recordset that enables you to move forward only (that is, you can only do a `MoveNext` operation—you can't use recordset methods such as `MovePrevious` or `Find`). This kind of record is much easier for the database engine to keep track of and is therefore much more efficient to work with. It's ideal for generating reports, because you almost never need to scroll backward when you're outputting data.

When you're using Remote Data Objects (discussed in Chapter 6, "Open Database Connectivity and Remote Data Objects,") or ActiveX Data Objects (discussed in Chapter 10, "ActiveX Data Objects,"), you have the option of creating forward-scrolling recordsets.

Reporting Using the VB DataReport Designer

New to VB 6.0 is the DataReport designer, a visual way to create reports that are tightly integrated into the VB development environment. The DataReport designer provides very basic functionality—it isn't nearly as full-featured as several other reporting options discussed in this chapter. But the DataReport designer has the advantage of being extremely easy to use.

To create a DataReport designer, do the following:

1. In your VB project, select the menu command Project, Add Data Report.

2. A DataReport designer is added to your project, as shown in Figure 4.1

Figure 4.1
A new DataReport designer in a VB project looks like this.

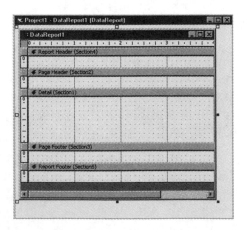

DataReport designers are composed of a number of sections, including the following:

▶ A *report header*, which prints once at the beginning of the report

▶ A *report footer*, which prints once at the end of the report

▶ A *page header*, which prints at the top of each page

▶ A *page footer*, which prints at the bottom of each page

▶ A *detail section*, which prints rows of data

▶ One or more *group headers* or *footers*, which print at the top or bottom of a group section

It's easiest to create a DataReport in conjunction with a DataEnvironment designer. When you use the DataEnvironment, many report-design operations can be accomplished using drag-and-drop. For more information on how to create a DataEnvironment designer, see Chapter 1, "Database Basics."

Designing DataReports

Once you create a DataReport designer, you must bind it to a database to display data. You do this through a special set of bound controls that only work within the context of the DataReport designer.

The DataReport designer's set of visual controls includes the following items:

▶ A label control

▶ A text box control

▶ An image control

▶ Line and shape controls

▶ A function control that permits you to insert summary calculations into a report

Since the DataReport controls are specially designed to work in the context of the DataReport designer, they have different names. For example, the formal class name of the text box control is RptTextBox; the name of the image control is RptImage.

It's possible to create a control, such as an RptTextBox, and bind it to a database field using the control's DataField property (similar to any other bound control). But it's much easier to use drag-and-drop to create the basic report. To do this, follow these steps:

1. Add a DataReport designer to your project by using the VB menu command Project, Add Data Report.

2. Create a DataEnvironment designer the way you normally would. (The technique for doing this is described in Chapter 1.)

3. Create a query in the DataEnvironment designer based on the tblCustomer table.

4. The DataEnvironment designer displays a list of fields in the tblCustomer table. Drag the FirstName field from the DataEnvironment designer to the Detail section of the DataReport designer.

5. A label and a text box bound to the FirstName field appear on the DataReport designer, as shown in Figure 4.2.

Figure 4.2
Drag and drop to add a field to the DataReport designer.

It makes a bit more sense if you drag the label to the Page Header section, so it only prints once per page (instead of once per record). Once you've done this for a number of fields, your report should look like Figure 4.3.

When you have multiple controls selected, resizing one control causes the other controls in the selection to be resized as well. This is handy when you want the label and the text box to be the same width or height. If you make a bound text box wider, you should be able to see that it displays the name of the table as well as the field to which it is bound.

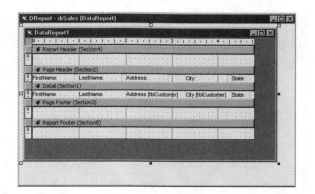

Although you'd think that dragging fields from a DataEnvironment designer onto the report would be enough to bind the controls to the data source, there's one more step—you must tell the DataReport designer which data source to bind to. Here's how to do this:

1. Make sure that the DataReport itself is selected (as opposed to any of the sections contained in the DataReport). The easiest way to do this is to select the DataReport from the drop-down at the top of VB's Properties window.

2. In the Properties window, set the DataReport's DataSource property to the name of the DataEnvironment designer (or other data source).

3. If you're using a DataEnvironment designer, set the DataReport's DataMember property to the data command you wish.

At this point, the report is connected to your data source, and you can run it.

Viewing and Exporting a DataReport

You can view a report in Print Preview mode by executing its Show method. For example, if your DataReport is called drCustomer, you can run it by executing the line of code:

```
drCustomer.Show
```

Running the application and executing this line of code produces the report in its own window, as shown in Figure 4.4.

Figure 4.4
A DataReport is shown running in a Visual Basic application.

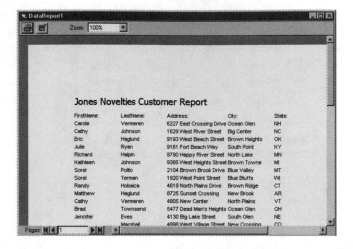

At this point, the user has several options. For example, she can admire the data in the window, paging through it using the navigation control at the bottom of the window. The user also has the option of zooming in or out on the data. Or the user can print or export the data, using the buttons at the top of the window.

When the user clicks the Export button, a file dialog box appears, permitting the user to specify a filename and format. The export formats provided by the DataReport designer are HTML text and plain text. A single page of data exported from the DataReport designer and displayed in a Web browser looks like Figure 4.5.

Code Example: You can find the database report discussed in this section in the project `DReport.vbp`, located in the directory `\vbdb\code\04-Report\DReport`. For information on how to install the sample files on the CD that accompanies this book, see the section "Installing the Example Files" in the introduction at the beginning of this book.

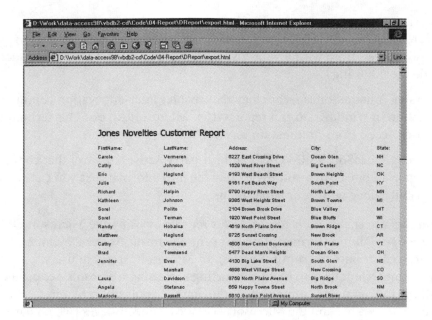

Figure 4.5
*The output of a
DataReport design-
er is viewed in a
Web browser.*

REPORTING USING MICROSOFT ACCESS

Microsoft Access enables you to write database reports. It sports an easy-to-use, visual interface that most Visual Basic programmers will feel very comfortable with. Like Crystal Reports (see "Reporting Using Crystal Reports" later in this chapter), Microsoft Access reports enable you to group and sort data, as well as include custom expressions in your reports.

This section is designed to give you an idea of Microsoft Access report-writing capabilities, but it's not a complete reference to reports in Access. Rather, this section is designed to give you an idea of how to integrate Access reports into your Visual Basic database access application.

This section describes two techniques for running Microsoft Access reports in your Visual Basic application:

▶ Using Automation to launch an instance of Microsoft Access, running the report directly from within that application

▶ Using the VideoSoft VSREPORTS product to enable users of your application to run Microsoft Access reports whether or not they have Microsoft Access installed on their computers

Running Microsoft Access Reports from Visual Basic

You can use several techniques to run database reports that were created in Microsoft Access from within your Visual Basic application. These techniques include the following:

▶ Using Automation, a technology that enables inter-application communication in Windows, to run reports from Microsoft Access. This technique uses Access as an Automation server.

▶ Using VideoSoft VSREPORTS, a third-party ActiveX control that converts reports from a Microsoft Access .MDB file into a format that you can redistribute along with your applications.

You can also enable users to run Access reports by using the Microsoft Office 97 Developer Edition (formerly known as the Microsoft Access Developer's Toolkit) to distribute the runtime version of Microsoft Access to users.

With this technique, you build a reporting tool using Microsoft Access, then install the tool on users' computers. Deploying the application requires installing an .MDB file and the Microsoft Access runtime libraries (which have significant size or resource requirements).

Because this solution transforms your project from a Visual Basic program to a Microsoft Access application, the technique goes beyond the Visual Basic–centric scope of this book. However, much of what this book discusses—particularly the information about querying and Data Access Objects (DAO)—pertains to development in Microsoft Access.

> **Note:** You can get more information on what's included in the Microsoft Office Developer Edition by visiting the Microsoft Office Developer Forum online at `http://www.microsoft.com/OfficeDev/Default.htm`.

Running Access Reports Using Automation

You can use a technology known as Automation to launch an instance of Microsoft Access from your Visual Basic application. Using this technique, you can program Microsoft Access the same way you program other objects (such as Data Access Objects or an ActiveX control) in Visual Basic.

The disadvantage of this technique is that it forces users to run an instance of Microsoft Access every time they want to view or print a report. Obviously, it also requires that they have Microsoft Access loaded on their machines. If you are interested in overcoming these drawbacks but you still want to use Access reports as part of your Visual Basic application, you might consider a reporting solution based on VideoSoft VSREPORTS, discussed later in the section "Running Access Reports Using VideoSoft VSREPORTS."

To program Microsoft Access through Automation, you begin by making a reference to Access in your Visual Basic application. Do this by using VB's Project References menu to make a reference to Microsoft Access 8.0 Object Library.

Bear in mind that the Microsoft Access 8.0 Object Library creates a reference to Microsoft Access 97. If you're using an earlier version of Access, you can still use Automation; however, the object library will be called something else.

Avoiding Early Binding with Automation

You might be familiar with Automation from the days when it was called *OLE Automation*; most of the techniques described in this section worked way back in the days of Visual Basic 3.0 and Microsoft Access 2.0.

If you've used Automation before, you should know that there's one important difference between the Automation technique described in this section and the Automation technique you might be familiar with. In Visual Basic, you want to avoid defining Automation objects as the generic Object data type. For example, in Visual Basic 3.0, you might write code that looks like this:

```
Dim appAccess As Object
Set appAccess = CreateObject("Access.Application")
```

This code worked fine in Visual Basic 3.0, and it actually still works, but there's a better way to do it now. Instead of using the generic Object data type, you should define the Automation object as whatever object data type the Automation server provides (Access.Application, in the case of Microsoft Access). Making an explicit reference to the object server's library and then explicitly creating objects using its data types is more efficient. This is because Visual Basic doesn't have to run a query on the Automation server each time you access it in an attempt to determine what kind of object you're trying to create. This technique, known as *late binding*, is now appropriate in only two situations:

▶ You don't know what kind of Automation server object your application is going to create when writing the code (a situation which will probably occur rarely, if ever).

▶ You're using an application development environment that does not support early binding, such as VBScript and/or Active Server Pages.

Because Visual Basic does support early binding, the use of late binding in modern Visual Basic applications happens very infrequently. In fact, it makes sense for you to upgrade your existing Visual Basic applications to take advantage of early binding—particularly for processor-intensive calls to Microsoft Office Automation servers—because of the performance benefits provided by early binding.

Running Automation Code to Control Microsoft Access

After creating a reference to Microsoft Access from within your Visual Basic application, you can start writing code to instantiate objects provided by it. You'll notice that after you make a reference to an external object server, Visual Basic integrates that server's object model into the Auto List Members feature.

Because programming against hostile, alien object models can be such a daunting task, integration into Auto List Members is a beautiful thing, as Figure 4.6 illustrates.

Figure 4.6
View members of the Microsoft Access object model with Visual Basic's Auto List Members feature.

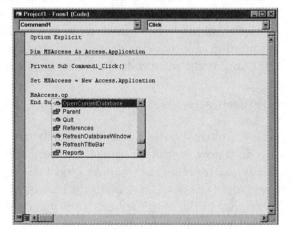

Note: Remember, too, that you can view all the members of any hostile, alien object model by using Visual Basic's Object Browser.

Listing 4.1 shows how to create an instance of Microsoft Access from within Visual Basic. This code uses Automation to execute methods of Access' DoCmd object; this object is used to issue commands to the Microsoft Access application through Automation.

Listing 4.1   Programming Microsoft Access From Visual Basic Using Automation

```
' References MS Access 8.0 Object Library (this
' code will work with any version of Access that
' supports Automation)

Dim MSAccess As Access.Application


Private Sub cmdReport_Click()

    Set MSAccess = New Access.Application

    MSAccess.OpenCurrentDatabase ("c:\vbdb\Code\DB\novelty.mdb")

    MSAccess.DoCmd.OpenReport "rptEmployee", acViewNormal
    MSAccess.CloseCurrentDatabase
    Set MSAccess = Nothing

End Sub
```

Note that the acViewNormal constant passed to the OpenReport method tells Access to open the report and print it immediately to whatever default printer you've designated in Access.

Knowing When to Use Automation with Access

Remember to consider the advantages and disadvantages of solutions based on Automation. The disadvantage of such solutions is that they require that users have Access installed on their computers. There is also a significant performance hit associated with launching the entire Microsoft Access application.

As an alternative to running Access reports through Automation, you can run reports created in Microsoft Access by using the VideoSoft VSREPORTS product discussed in the next section.

Running Access Reports Using VideoSoft VSREPORTS

You can use the VSREPORTS tool to run database reports created in Microsoft Access in your Visual Basic application. VSREPORTS is implemented in two parts:

▶ A conversion utility that takes an Access .MDB file and creates a report file from report objects stored in the Access database

▶ An ActiveX control that's responsible for opening the report file and running it in your Visual Basic application

If this architecture sounds familiar, it's because VSREPORTS is similar to Crystal Reports (discussed later in this chapter). With both systems, you must first create a report file, then add a control and code to your application to make the report file print. Each time you make a change in the basic report, you must save and redistribute the report file to users.

There are many differences between Crystal and VSREPORTS—not the least of which is the fact that Crystal Reports has its own report-writing facility, whereas VSREPORTS uses that of Microsoft Access. The product that is best for you is a matter of personal preference and feature-set robustness.

If you want to use Microsoft Access reports, one advantage of using VSRE-PORTS over the Automation technique described in the previous section is that users don't have to start a new instance of Access each time they run reports. In fact, with VSREPORTS, users don't even have to have Access loaded on their computers. This fact can come in handy if you're responsible for managing a large, database-driven organization with all kinds of users. If you can't be certain that users will have the latest version of Access on their computers, you can give them a VSREPORTS file that will work no matter what the users have.

> **For more information: VideoSoft frequently releases maintenance updates to its products to fix bugs and add features. You can read about the latest version of VSREPORTS and download a trial version from VideoSoft's Web site at `http://www.videosoft.com`. A trial version of VSREPORTS is also on this book's companion CD, in the folder `\SOFTWARE\VIDEOSFT\VSREPORT`.**

Converting Microsoft Access Reports Using VSREPORTS

To begin the process of integrating a Microsoft Access report in your application, you first create a report in Microsoft Access, then run the VSREPORTS translator on it. The product of the translator is a file that you can use with the VSREPORTS ActiveX control inside your application.

There are actually two translator utilities:

▶ TRANS95.EXE, for converting reports created in Microsoft Access 95

▶ TRANS97.EXE, for reports created in Microsoft Access 97

These utilities are installed into the folder you chose when you first installed VSREPORTS.

Business Case 4.1: Creating an Application Using VideoSoft VSREPORTS

In its ever-widening search to create custom software systems incorporating as many different types of technologies as possible, the human resources staff of Jones Novelties has begun to generate reports using Microsoft Access. The staff approaches you with the department's work, asking whether you can integrate the staff's report-writing work with its existing custom employee-tracking application. Because not every person in the human resources department has Microsoft Access on his or her computer, you determine that VSREPORTS is the ideal way to give everyone in the department access to the employee information reports.

The version of the Jones Novelties database installed from the CD accompanying this book contains a report called rptCustomer. You can use the VSREPORTS translator to convert this report into a file that you can use in a Visual Basic application. To do this, follow these steps:

1. Locate and launch VSREPORTS' Access 97 translator utility, TRANS97.EXE. This file can be found in the folder where you originally installed VSREPORTS.

The translator launches, as shown in Figure 4.7.

Figure 4.7
The VSREPORTS translator utility looks like this.

2. Double-click More Files to display a file dialog box.

3. From the file dialog box, select the Novelty database from the CD that accompanies this book.

4. The translator opens the database and displays a list of reports. Choose rptCustomer by selecting it, then clicking on the right-arrow button at the center top of the dialog box. Click the Next button to move to the next step.

In the next step, the translator asks you to supply a path and filename for the output file. You can either choose the path and filename it suggests or choose your own. You can also change the output filename at this time if you wish.

5. Click Translate. The translator generates a .VSR file that contains the definition of your report.

Note: **To run the translator under Windows NT 4.0, VideoSoft recommends that you apply Windows NT Service Pack 2 to your system. (I applied Service Pack 3, which was the latest Service Pack as of this writing, and it worked fine for me.) You can get the latest Windows NT Service Pack from the Microsoft Windows NT Server Web site, located at** `http://www.microsoft.com/ntserver/`.

The VSREPORTS translator generates a report definition file that ends in a .VSR extension. This file contains all the information used to print your report. You'll use the file in the next step to add the report to your Visual Basic application.

Code Example: **You can find an example of the report definition file** `rptCustomer.vsr` **in the directory** `\vbdb\code\04-Reports\VSReport`**. For information on how to install the sample files on the CD that accompanies this book, see the section "Installing the Example Files" in the introduction at the beginning of this book.**

Running Microsoft Access Reports with the VSREPORTS ActiveX Control
Now that you've created a report file using the VSREPORTS converter, you can integrate it into your project. You do this by using the VSREPORTS ActiveX control. This control is invisible at runtime; its sole purpose is to read and output .VSR files created with the VSREPORTS translator utility.

Caution: **It's important to understand that there are two versions of the VSREPORTS ActiveX control. The one that's installed on your computer by default,** `VSREPORT.OCX`**, is appropriate for use with Jet 3.0. Another version of the control,** `VSREP351.OCX`**, is appropriate for use with Jet 3.5. If you attempt to connect to a database and get the error message "ActiveX component can't create object," the problem is probably that you have the wrong flavor of the VSREPORTS control installed.**

To install the DAO 3.5 version of the VSREPORTS control, do the following:

1. Install the VSREPORTS update files from the CD-ROM that accompanies this book, or download it from the VideoSoft Web site at `http://www.videosoft.com`.

2. Make sure that the file `VSREP351.OCX` is in your Windows system directory.

3. Register the new OCX file using the regsvr32 utility. This utility is included with Visual Basic; it's on the Visual Basic CD Disc 1 in the `\OS\SYSTEM` folder. If your machine's Windows system directory is `C:\WINDOWS\SYSTEM`, the command line you must execute to register the OCX file is as follows:

   ```
   regsvr32 c:\windows\system\vsrep351.ocx
   ```

   You can execute this command line from the Run command located in the Windows Start menu. Also, note that the Windows system directory is not necessarily the same on all computers; for example, the file may be located in the \WINDOWS\SYSTEM32 directory if you're using Windows NT.

4. When you add the control to your project using the Project Components menu, you should see entries for two vsReport controls: one for the Jet 3.0 version, and another for the Jet 3.5 version. Choose the Jet 3.5 version.

For More Information: VideoSoft maintains an excellent and frequently updated Web page containing the latest technical information on VSREPORTS. The page is at `http://www.videosoft.com/faqrept.html`.

Business Case 4.2: Creating a VSREPORTS Solution (Continued)
Now that you've created a report definition file from the Access report that the human resources department brought to you, you can integrate the file into your human resources application.

To do this, follow these steps:

1. In your Visual Basic project, use the Project Components menu to add the vsReport control to your project.

2. The vsReport control appears in your project's toolbox. Double-click the vsReport tool in the toolbox to add an instance of the vsReport control to your project's main form. This control will be invisible at runtime, so it doesn't matter where you place it on the form.

3. Set the vsReport control's ReportFileName property to the name of the .VSR file you created previously. Then set the control's DatabaseName property to the name of your .MDB file. You can do this either in Visual Basic's property sheet or in code. Listing 4.2 shows how to do this with code.

Note: You'll notice that, annoyingly, the ReportFileName property does not provide a filename browse button, nor does the vsReport control provide a custom property page that enables you to browse files. Perhaps a future version of VSREPORTS will provide this functionality.

4. Execute the control's PrintReport method to run the report. You have the option of sending output either to the screen or to the printer, depending on the setting of the control's PrintDevice property.

When you've set up the application for print preview (that is, you've set the PrintDevice property to vsrPrintDeviceScreen), the report looks like Figure 4.8.

Figure 4.8
The sample application containing the vsReport ActiveX control displays a report written in Microsoft Access.

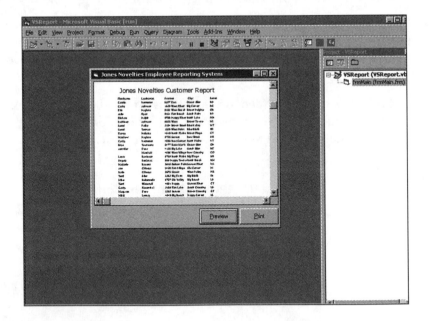

In this demonstration application, everything is done in code. Listing 4.2 shows the code behind the application's print and print preview features.

Listing 4.2   Code to Preview and Run Database Reports Using the VSREPORTS ActiveX Control

```
Option Explicit

' Requires Jet 3.5 version of VSREPORTS (vsrep351.ocx)

Private Sub Form_Load()
    vsReport1.ReportFileName = App.Path & "\rptCustomer.vsr"
    vsReport1.DatabaseName = "..\..\DB\novelty.mdb"
End Sub


Private Sub cmdPreview_Click()
    vsReport1.PrintDevice = vsrPrintDeviceScreen
    vsReport1.Zoom = 50    ' Percent
    vsReport1.PrintReport
End Sub


Private Sub cmdPrint_Click()
    vsReport1.PrintDevice = vsrPrintDevicePrinter
    vsReport1.PrintReport
End Sub


Private Sub vsReport1_LoadingDoc(ByVal Page As Integer, _
                                ByVal Of As Integer, _
                                Cancel As Boolean)
    Debug.Print "Loading: " & Page & " of " & Of
End Sub
```

The LoadingDoc event procedure at the end of the code listing suggests how you might take advantage of the events provided by the VSREPORTS control to provide status information to your users in your application.

Code Example: You can find an example of running a report created with VSREPORTS in the project VSReport.vbp, located in the directory \vbdb\code\04-Report\VSReport. For information on how to install the sample files on the CD that accompanies this book, see the section "Installing the Example Files" in the introduction at the beginning of this book.

Creating Advanced Reporting Applications with VSREPORTS

The VSREPORTS package has several other features that enable you to create more robust reporting applications. You can use these advanced features of the vsReport control to provide advanced functionality:

▶ *The* zoom *property.* This property, demonstrated previously in Listing 4.2, enables you to zoom in and out by percentages. If your user interface allows it, you can let users determine the zoom percentage, giving them full flexibility to view the report the way they want.

▶ *Printer properties.* You can set the Collate, ColorMode, Copies, Duplex, Pages, PaperBin, PrintQuality, and PrintRange properties to control how the report is printed. You can also use the Device property to determine which printer will print the report and the Port property to determine which printer port to use.

▶ *Support for browsing through multipage reports.* You can enable users to move from one page to the next in a multipage report by setting the PreviewPage property.

▶ *Integration with the DAO* Database *object.* Instead of assigning a DatabaseName to the control, you can assign a DAO Database object to the control. This solution might be appropriate if your application already uses DAO to get to a database and you don't want to make an explicit reference to the database from within the vsReport control. To assign a Database object to the vsReport control, you set the control's DatabaseAccessMode property to 1 - vsrDatabaseObject. You can then assign a DAO Database object to the DatabaseObject property of the vsReport control.

In addition to these properties, reports run with the vsReport control can trigger events, just like Microsoft Access reports do. This enables you to write code to respond to events that take place while the report is printing. The event model for the vsReport control is different than that provided by Access, however, so you'll want to prototype your existing Access reports carefully before attempting to port them to VSREPORTS.

REPORTING USING CRYSTAL REPORTS

Crystal Reports permits you to create database reports in your Visual Basic applications. It consists of two major parts—a report designer that lets you determine the data that will be included in a report and how it should look and an ActiveX control that permits you to run, display, and print the control at runtime.

For many Visual Basic programmers, Crystal Reports is the be-all end-all when it comes to database reporting. This is because a version of Crystal Reports comes with Visual Basic and it's extremely easy to use.

There are two steps to creating a report for your application using Crystal Reports: creating the report and adding the Crystal Reports ActiveX control to your project. You create the report using the Crystal Reports Designer application. This application creates report documents that you can run from within your Visual Basic applications. You open report documents in your Visual Basic application using the Crystal ActiveX control.

Installing Crystal Reports

Unlike previous versions of Visual Basic, Crystal Reports isn't installed automatically when you install VB. You must install it separately.

> **Note:** If you installed Crystal Reports when you installed VB 5.0, you don't have to install it again. The version that ships with VB 6.0 is exactly the same.

To install Crystal Reports, launch the installer file `crystl32.exe`, located in the directory `\COMMON\TOOLS\VB\CRYSREPT` on your VB 6.0 CD Disc 1. The appropriate files will be copied to your system and registered. You'll then be able to use Crystal Reports in your VB applications.

Creating a Report Using Crystal Reports

Before you can use a report in your Visual Basic application, you must first create it. You can't create reports in code; you must instead use Crystal Reports' own application for building reports. After building your report, you save it as a file on disk and distribute it to users along with your application.

To launch the Crystal Reports designer, follow these steps:

1. Launch the Report Designer, CRW32.EXE.

> **Note: On my computer, the Report Designer was installed in the folder** \Program Files\Microsoft Visual Studio\Common\Tools\REPORTS. **Your installation, of course, may be different. If Report Designer isn't available at all, you might have neglected to install it. Follow the instructions earlier in this chapter to install Crystal Reports' Report Designer.**

2. The Crystal Reports designer launches.

3. From Crystal Reports' File menu, choose New. The Create New Report dialog box appears, as shown in Figure 4.9.

Figure 4.9
The Create New Report dialog box in Crystal Reports looks like this.

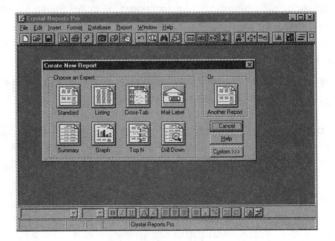

From this dialog box, Crystal Reports offers you several report templates you can use to output data; you can also use your own reports as templates as well as create custom reports that aren't based on templates. Table 4.1 summarizes the different report types that are available.

Table 4.1 Report Experts Available in Crystal Reports	
Report Type	**Description**
Standard	A report that lists information in rows and columns, enabling you to sort and total data.
Listing	A straight list of data with no summary or totaling fields. You might use this kind of report to print telephone directories.
Cross-Tab	A summary of data in two dimensions. (See Chapter 2, "Queries," for information on crosstab queries.)
Mail Label	A report designed to print data in columns for mailing labels.
Summary	A report showing only totals or other aggregate figures, without the detailed data.
Graph	A visual representation of data.
Top *N*	A report that enables you to specify a certain number of records to display.
Drill Down	A report that enables you to double-click summary data to see the detail behind that data.
Another Report	A report that uses as a template a report you've previously created as a template.

Business Case 4.3: Outputting Business Data Using Crystal Reports

The sales force of Jones Novelties Incorporated has requested information on which products are selling well.

Using Crystal Reports, you decide to create a report that will show how much total revenue each item in inventory has generated. To do this, follow these steps:

1. Start Crystal Reports and create a new report. Choose the Standard expert.

2. In step one of the Standard expert, click the Data File button.

3. In the file dialog box, select the Novelty database, NOVELTY.MDB. Click Add to add the database's tables to your report, then click Done.

The list of tables is populated. The Standard expert moves to step two, which shows relationships among tables in your database. Figure 4.10 shows step two of the Standard expert.

Figure 4.10
Step 2 of the Standard expert shows relationships among tables in your database.

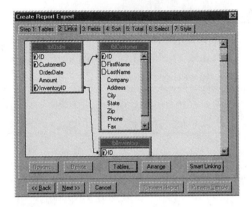

Because predefined relationships for this database have been defined at the database engine level, you don't have to define them again here. But if you did need to establish or delete a relationship at the report level instead of the database engine level, you'd follow these steps:

1. Click the relationship line joining the tblOrder and tblInventory tables.

2. Click the Delete button. The relationship is deleted.

3. Click-drag from the ID field in the tblInventory table to the InventoryID field in the tblOrder table, then click-drag the tables themselves to arrange them in the window. The Links step looks like Figure 4.11. The relationship is restored.

Note: It's easy to click-drag onto the wrong field when you're creating a relationship in this dialog box. If Crystal gives you an error message stating that the field you dragged onto is "missing an index," try click-dragging again, making sure to drag-drop directly onto the foreign key field.

4. Click the Next button.

You're now in step three of the Standard expert. In this step, you determine which fields will appear in your report. From the tblInventory table, select the Product field. From the tblOrder table, select the Amount field.

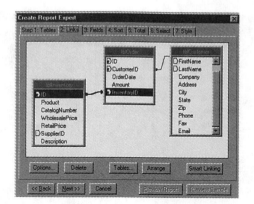

Figure 4.11
*The Links page
looks like this after
you establish rela-
tionships between
the tables.*

5. Click the Sort tab. This step enables you to determine how to sort your data. Select the Product field.

6. Click the Total tab. The Total page enables you to determine how the report will sum up your data. It selects the Amount field by default because it's a numeric field.

Note: For this example, there's no need to go to the Select step because you want all the data to be reported. But if you wanted to limit the type of data to display, you could do so in this step.

7. Click the Style tab. The Style page enables you to determine how the report will look. Choose a report style that strikes your fancy. (I like the Shading style.)

8. In the Title text box, type **Product Summary Report**.

9. Click the Preview Report button.

The report previews. The screen looks like Figure 4.12.

This example is intentionally simplified and designed to give you an idea of how easy it is to get started with Crystal Reports. Because creating reports is relatively straightforward, you don't need to go into much more detail here.

However, at this point, you should save your report so you can incorporate it in your application later. To do this, follow these steps:

Figure 4.12
*Here's the report
after you've gone
though all the
expert's steps.*

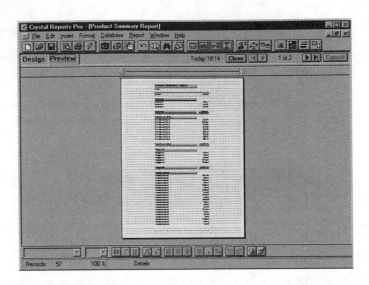

1. From the Crystal Reports File menu, choose Save.

2. The file dialog box appears. Give the report the filename `product.rpt`.

3. Click OK.

4. Exit Crystal Reports by choosing File, Exit.

In the next business case, you'll create a Visual Basic application that enables the user to run this report at will.

Running the Report in Your Application with the Crystal Reports ActiveX Control

After writing your report, you need a way to run it from within your application. The Crystal Reports ActiveX control provides a method to do this.

Enabling users of your applications to run Crystal Reports is quite simple; it involves adding the Crystal ActiveX control to your project and writing a few lines of code. To see how this works, follow these steps:

1. Create a new Visual Basic application with a single command button.

2. Add the Crystal Active X control to your project through the Project Components menu.

3. Create an instance of the Crystal Report control on your form by double-clicking it in the toolbar. The resulting control is called CrystalReport1.

4. In the command button's Click event, enter the following code:

```
Private Sub cmdReport_Click()

    CrystalReport1.ReportFileName = App.Path & "\product.rpt"
    CrystalReport1.PrintReport

End Sub
```

5. Run the application and click the Run button. The report runs, displaying its output to the user in a preview window. At this point, the user can output the report to a printer by clicking the Print button.

Note: By using the Crystal Report control's Destination property, you can send data directly to the printer, bypassing the preview window.

Code Example: The code discussed in this section can be found in the project CReport.vbp, located in the directory \vbdb\code\04-Report\CReport. For information on how to install the sample files on the CD that accompanies this book, see the section "Installing the Example Files" in the introduction at the beginning of this book.

Obtaining and Using Newer Versions of Crystal Reports

Version 4.6 of Crystal Reports ships with Visual Basic. There's a newer version of Crystal Reports available; for information on it, check out the Seagate Software Web site at http://www.img.seagate.com.

The commercial version of the system, Crystal Reports 6.0, offers several new features. These include the following:

▶ *Subreports,* which are similar to the subreport feature in Microsoft Access that enables you to show one-to-many relationships

▶ *New formatting options,* including the ability to run reports in columns and display different types of reports side by side

▶ *Conditional reports,* which can display differently based on the status of your data

▶ *Direct database drivers* for many major platforms (including Oracle, Informix, and Microsoft SQL Server) that enable you to bypass conventional Open Database Connectivity (ODBC) drivers, eliminating the need to set up ODBC data sources on client computers

▶ *Export* to Microsoft Word and Microsoft Excel formats

▶ *Web support,* including the ability to export to Hypertext Markup Language (HTML) Web pages and create reports that reside on a server

▶ *Support for nonrelational data sources* such as Microsoft Exchange Server activity and Windows NT event logs

CHARTING USING THE MSCHART CONTROL

You can use the MSChart control to visually represent data in your Visual Basic application. You've always been able to do this in code; new to VB6 is the ability of the chart control to directly bind to the database. This functionality is covered in Chapter 12, "User-Interface Controls."

USING THE VISUAL BASIC *PRINTER* OBJECT

You can use the Visual Basic Printer object to print data from your database access application. This is a code-intensive way of reporting, but it can give you more flexibility in situations where you need complete control over your printed output.

The Printer object is an intrinsic Visual Basic object; like the other Visual Basic intrinsic objects (such as the Clipboard, Screen, and Debug objects), the Printer object is always available to your applications. It's an abstract way to access the printer to which the user's computer is connected. It's helpful to think of the Printer object as a printed page; it has Width and Height properties, as well as other properties that enable you to print text and graphics.

Although it takes more code to create a database report using the Printer object, you gain access to more capabilities of your printer. You also don't have to distribute any additional files or purchase any third-party products, as you do with some of the other reporting solutions described in this chapter.

To create a custom output solution involving database access and the Visual Basic Printer object, follow these general steps:

1. Determine the coordinate system you want to use with the Printer object.

2. Create a design layout for the report.

3. Write code to create a Recordset object using whatever data access library you prefer.

4. Iterate through the records retrieved in the Recordset object, sending data to the Printer object using its properties and methods.

The following sections explore these steps in detail.

Setting Up the Printer's Coordinate System

You interact with the Printer object by assigning text and graphics to its coordinate system. The printer's coordinate system is an imaginary grid that divides a page into horizontal and vertical units.

You use the ScaleMode property of the Printer object to define the coordinate system used when you print. You can set the coordinate system to several English- or metric-based measurement systems. You can also set it to a custom-defined system. The choice of measurement systems determines the granularity of control you have over the page; a less granular system (such as centimeters or inches) gives you less control than a more granular system (such as twips or points).

By default, Visual Basic uses twips as the basis of its coordinate system; one twip is equivalent to one-twentieth of a point, and 72 points equal one inch.

If you're an American who is familiar with desktop publishing software, you might be most comfortable using points to plot custom reports using the Printer object. If you're one of our international friends outside the Land of English Measurement, then you may prefer to use metric measurements. It doesn't matter what type of coordinate system you use, because the Printer object supports many different types through the ScaleMode property.

Table 4.2 shows the different settings for the ScaleMode property and what they mean.

Table 4.2 Settings for the ScaleMode Property of the Printer Object		
Constant	**Value**	**Meaning**
vbUser	0	The coordinate system is user-defined
vbTwips	1	Twip (1/20 of a point or 1/1440 of an inch)
vbPoints	2	Point (72 points to the inch)
vbPixels	3	Pixel (exact size varies according to the resolution of the user's screen)
vbCharacters	4	Character (120 twips per unit horizontally and 240 twips per unit vertically)
vbInches	5	Inch
vbMillimeters	6	Millimeter
vbCentimeters	7	Centimeter
vbHiMetric	8	HiMetric
vbContainerPosition	9	Units used by the control's container to determine the control's position.
vbContainerSize	10	Units used by the control's container to determine the control's size.

The constants vbHiMetric, vbContainerPosition, and vbContainerSize are new in VB 6.0. Like many new features of VB 6.0, they're poorly documented.

Designing the Report

It's helpful to have an idea ahead of time about what your report will look like, because database reporting using the Printer object is such a code-intensive way to output data. So in addition to creating a written design that maps out what your report will look like (I've always been partial to graph paper for this kind of thing), you'll also want to create an *architectural* design for the report. The architectural design will determine exactly how your code will send data to the Printer object.

If you want to print your results in columns contained in boxes, you can create a subroutine (or, better yet, a class module) that knows how to draw boxes exactly the way you like. Then you can call that subroutine or class each time you print a record. (For more information on classes and why they're useful, see Chapter 7, "Database Access with Classes.")

Unless your code always works right the first time it's run, you'll always find that devoting time to design pays off in the long run, when you have to debug and maintain your code. That goes for any software you write, but particularly for a code-intensive solution involving the Printer object.

Outputting a Recordset to the *Printer* Object

After you have your data in place and an idea as to how to construct it, creating the report becomes a matter of sending data from a Recordset object to the Printer object.

The Printer object offers several properties and methods that can help you render data on the page and control the print job. These include the following:

▶ *The* CurrentX *and* CurrentY *properties* control the current print position on the page. CurrentX refers to the horizontal position on the page, whereas CurrentY refers to the vertical position. The position of everything you print is a function of these two values.

▶ *The* Font *object* of the Printer object controls the textual properties of text printed on the page.

▶ *The* Print *method* of the Printer object renders text on the page. Oddly, the *Visual Basic Language Reference* doesn't list the Printer object's Print method, even though it's the Printer object's most important method. (This was the case in VB 5.0 and is still the case in VB 6.0.) See Business Case 4.4 for an example of how to use the Print method.

▶ *The* NewPage *method* inserts a page break in the print job, the Page property returns the current page of the print job, and the KillDoc method cancels a print job.

▶ *Graphics methods* such as Line, Point, and Circle can help you add organization and flair to the report.

▶ *The* EndDoc *method* sends the entire print job to the printer. You execute this method at the end of a print job that uses the Printer object.

Note: The `Printer` object is an abstract way to communicate with whatever printer the user has designated as his or her default printer. Users can designate a printer as the default in the Printers control panel. If your application needs to get access to all the printers installed on a user's computer (for example, to present a list of available printers or to change the printer to which you're printing), use Visual Basic's `Printers` collection.

Business Case 4.4: Creating a Custom Database Report Using the Printer Object

The database denizens of Jones Novelties have once again asked you to create a database report for the company's sales force. They're interested in creating a report to display lists of their customers with customers in certain regions highlighted. Because this request demands a high degree of control over the display of each record, you decide to create a custom reporting using VB's `Printer` object.

To do this, follow these steps:

1. Start a Visual Basic project. On the project's main form, create a command button (or similar user-interface component). This button will enable the user to run the report. Use the Project, References dialog box to create a reference to DAO 3.51.

2. In the Declarations section of the form, set up some module-level variables that will store some of the frequently used information in the project:

```
Option Explicit

' References DAO 3.51

' Printer object variables.
' All measurements are in *points*
' (72 points = 1 inch)

Private mlngTopMargin As Long
Private mlngLeftMargin As Long
Private mlngHeaderFontSize As Long
Private mlngBodyFontSize As Long
Private mstrHeaderFontName As Long
Private mstrBodyFontName As Long
```

```
' DAO variables
Private db As Database
Private rs As Recordset
```

3. In the form's Load event, initialize the module-level variables, set the Printer object's coordinate system to points, and create a DAO Database object. The Load event procedure should look like the following:

```
Private Sub Form_Load()

    ' Set printer's coordinate system
    Printer.ScaleMode = vbPoints

    ' Set report defaults
    mlngTopMargin = 72
    mlngLeftMargin = 72
    mlngHeaderFontSize = 18
    mlngBodyFontSize = 12
    mstrHeaderFontName = "Arial"
    mstrBodyFontName = "Times New Roman"

    ' Open database
    Set db = Opendatabase("..\..\DB\novelty.mdb")

End Sub
```

4. Create a subroutine that prints the page header. This subroutine will be called at the beginning of each page of your report. The subroutine should look like the following:

```
Private Sub PrintHeader()

    ' Margins
    Printer.CurrentX = mlngLeftMargin
    Printer.CurrentY = mlngTopMargin

    ' Set font
    With Printer.Font
        .Name = mstrHeaderFontName
        .Size = mlngHeaderFontSize
        .Bold = True
    End With
```

```
Printer.Print "Customer Report"

' Draw a line under the title
Printer.Line (mlngLeftMargin, _
            mlngTopMargin + 24)-(Printer.ScaleWidth - 72, _
            mlngTopMargin + 24)


End Sub
```

5. Create a subroutine that opens a recordset and sends the data to the database one record at a time:

```
Private Sub PrintData()

    Set rs = db.OpenRecordset("Select FirstName, LastName, State " & _
                            "from tblCustomer")


    ' Set font.
    With Printer.Font
        .Name = mstrBodyFontName
        .Size = mlngBodyFontSize
        .Bold = False
    End With

    Do Until rs.EOF

        Printer.CurrentX = mlngLeftMargin

        ' Note the semicolon here -- it tells the Printer
        ' object not to advance CurrentX and CurrentY to
        ' the next line
        Printer.Print rs!FirstName & " " & _
                    rs!LastName;

        Printer.CurrentX = mlngLeftMargin + 144

        ' Advance to state column
        Printer.CurrentX = mlngLeftMargin + 144

        ' Highlight the state if it's in
        ' the west coast region.
```

```
            If rs!State = "CA" Or _
               rs!State = "OR" Or _
               rs!State = "WA" Then
                    With Printer.Font
                          .Bold = True
                          .Underline = True
                    End With
            End If

            Printer.Print rs!State

            ' Shut off special formatting
            With Printer.Font
                .Bold = False
                .Underline = False
            End With

            rs.MoveNext
        Loop

        rs.Close
        Set rs = Nothing

    End Sub
```

6. In the click event of the Print button, make references to all the subroutines you created, ending the code by executing the EndDoc method of the
Printer object. The click event should look like the following:

```
    Private Sub cmdPrint_Click()

        ' Print page header
        PrintHeader

        Printer.CurrentY = Printer.CurrentY + 24

        ' Print data
        PrintData

        Printer.EndDoc

    End Sub
```

To earn extra credit, you might modify this code by enabling it to print multipage reports. To do so, monitor the state of the Printer object's CurrentY property. When CurrentY gets to be within an inch or so of the ScaleHeight property, you execute the NewPage method of the Printer object, execute your PrintHeader subroutine again, and continue outputting records.

Code Example: You can find the code discussed in this section in the project PRObj.vbp, located in the directory \vbdb\code\04-Report\PRObj. For information on how to install the sample files on the CD that accompanies this book, see the section "Installing the Example Files" in the introduction at the beginning of this book.

One of the obvious shortcomings of the Printer object technique for database reporting is that it's difficult to determine what the report will look like—or even how many pages it will take up—before it's printed. You might solve this problem by writing a print preview facility for your reporting application. Instead of developing a print preview feature from scratch, though, it makes more sense to use an off-the-shelf tool that is suited to the job. The vsPrinter control, described in the next section, fits that bill nicely.

REPORTING USING VIDEOSOFT VSVIEW

You can use VideoSoft VSVIEW to create reports using code similar to that which you'd use with the Printer object, but with a more robust programming interface and more features, including print preview.

VSVIEW is a suite of ActiveX controls that includes vsPrinter. Although the vsPrinter control is similar in some ways to the Visual Basic Printer object, it offers several additional features, including the following:

- ▶ Automatic text wrapping
- ▶ Printing headers and footers on each page
- ▶ Printing in columns
- ▶ The capacity to arrange data in tables
- ▶ Automatic page numbering
- ▶ Print preview, including zooming
- ▶ The ability to save a previewed document to a file

For More Information: VideoSoft frequently releases maintenance updates to its products to fix bugs and add features. You can read about the latest version of VSVIEW and download a trial version from VideoSoft's Web site at `http://www.videosoft.com`. (The release of VSVIEW as of this writing was version 3.0.) A trial version of VSVIEW is also on the CD that accompanies this book; you'll need to install it before attempting any of the examples in this section.

Printing Tables with the vsPrinter Control

The vsPrinter control is well suited to printing database tables because it has explicit support for printing data in a row-and-column format. You can print data in this table by assigning data to the vsPrinter object's Table property.

To create a vsPrinter table, you first create a string that contains formatting information that determines how to print the table. This string determines the number of columns in the table, the alignment of text within each cell in a column, and the width of each column.

To denote the number of columns in a vsPrinter table, you supply the columns' widths in twips, or 20ths of a point (there are 1,440 twips to the inch). To denote the number of columns in a table, you separate the column measurements with a pipe character (|). You end the formatting string with a semicolon (;)—this is also the way you tell vsPrinter that you've come to the end of a row.

Note: You can change the meaning of the semicolon and pipe characters by altering the vsPrinter control's TableSep property. You might do so if you want your data output to display actual pipe characters or semicolons.

Table 4.3 lists the formatting characters you can use to set up a vsPrinter table.

Table 4.3 Formatting Characters Used in vsPrinter Tables	
Character	**Effect**
<	Left-align the column
>	Right-align the column
^	Center the column
=	Justify the text
+	Center the column vertically
–	Align the text vertically along the bottom of the cell
~	Don't wrap text in cells
!	Set a vertical border

For example, to set up a table that has three centered columns that are one inch wide, you use this formatting string:

```
^1440¦^1440¦^1440;
```

Business Case 4.5: Printing Data Using the VideoSoft vsPrinter Control

The marketing staff of Jones Novelties wants to print a catalog of the company's rapidly growing inventory regularly, but lacks the ability to do so. Asking for your help, the marketing department requests a utility that is fast, easy to use, and flexible, envisioning that the company's needs could change over time. The department is also interested in saving the reports that it generates to a file for future reference.

You decide to address the problem by creating a printing utility using the vsPrinter control, contained in the VSVIEW package.

To create a printing utility using the vsPrinter control, follow these steps:

1. Create a new Visual Basic project.

2. Add the VSVIEW tools to your project by using the Project, Components dialog box. Add a standard command button and an instance of the vsPrinter control to the project's main form. The interface should look like Figure 4.13.

Figure 4.13
The user interface of the vsPrinter database reporting application looks like this.

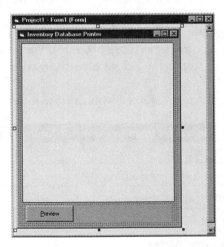

3. By choosing Project, References, make a reference to the Microsoft DAO 3.51 Project Library.

4. In the form's Declarations section, create the object variables you'll need to access the database:

```
Dim db As Database
Dim rs As Recordset
```

5. In the main form's Load event, establish the connection to the database:

```
Private Sub Form_Load()

    Set db = OpenDatabase("..\..\DB\novelty.mdb")

End Sub
```

6. In the Preview button's Click event, enter code that renders the page on the vsReport control. Listing 4.3 shows this code.

Listing 4.3   Viewing Data in the Print Preview Window of the vsPrinter Control

```
Private Sub cmdPreview_Click()
Dim strTable As String

  Set rs = db.OpenRecordset("tblInventory")
  vsPrinter1.Preview = True


  vsPrinter1.StartDoc

  vsPrinter1.MarginTop = 720   ' twips
  vsPrinter1.MarginLeft = 720

  With vsPrinter1.Font
    .Bold = False
    .Name = "Arial"
    .Size = 18
  End With

  ' This is formatting information
  strTable = "<2880¦<1440¦<4880;"

Do Until rs.EOF
  strTable = strTable & _
```

continues

Listing 4.3   Viewing Data in the Print Preview Window of the vsPrinter Control (Continued)

```
                    rs!Product & "¦" & _
                    rs!RetailPrice & "¦" & _
                    rs!Description & ";"
        vsPrinter1.Table = strTable
        rs.MoveNext
    Loop

    vsPrinter1.EndDoc

    rs.Close
    Set rs = Nothing

End Sub
```

7. Run the application and click the Preview button. The data appears on the vsPrinter control, as shown in Figure 4.14.

Figure 4.14
The print utility looks like this after the application populates it with data from the database.

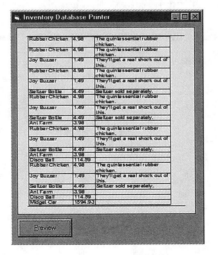

8. To give your application the ability to save the documents it creates, add two command buttons to the form. Label one command button Save, the other Load.

9. In the Save button's click event, add the following code:

```
Private Sub cmdSave_Click()

    vsPrinter1.SaveDoc App.Path & "\myreport.rep"

End Sub
```

10. In the Load button's `Click` event, add the following code:

```
Private Sub cmdLoad_Click()
On Error GoTo ErrHandler

    vsPrinter1.LoadDoc App.Path & "\myreport.rep"

Exit Sub

ErrHandler:
    MsgBox "The file 'myreport.rep' was not found.", _
           vbExclamation, _
           "File Load Error"
    Resume Next

End Sub
```

In the applications you build with the vsPrinter control, you'll probably want to give the user some way to choose the filename to save to, most likely by using the Windows file common dialog control.

Note also that when you save a report with the vsPrinter control, it's saved in a proprietary format that can be reloaded only through the vsPrinter's `LoadDoc` method.

> **Code Example:** You can find the code discussed in this section in the project **VSPrint.vbp**, located in the directory **\vbdb\code\04-Report\VSPrint**. For information on how to install the sample files on the CD that accompanies this book, see the section "Installing the Example Files" in the introduction at the beginning of this book.

Creating Ad-Hoc Reports Using the VideoSoft Data Report Component

An ad-hoc report lets the user customize the layout and parameters of the report at runtime.

The VSVIEW package contains a component, called VideoSoft Data Reporter that works in conjunction with the vsPrinter control described in the previous section. This component permits users to alter the way they view and print data. The component is packaged as an ActiveX component called VIEWUTIL.DLL.

Note: The VideoSoft Data Reporter is not to be confused with VideoSoft's VSREPORTS product. The former permits users to create and alter reports at runtime; the latter is a conversion utility that lets you run reports created in Microsoft Access within your Visual Basic application. Furthermore, the `DataReporter` object (provided by the VideoSoft Data Reporter component) is not to be confused with the DataReport designer included in VB 6.0.

It's not obvious where to find the documentation for the VideoSoft Data Reporter component, since it's not included in the VSVIEW online help file. The Data Reporter has its own online help file, `VIEWUTIL.HLP`. This file gets installed in the `Help` folder under your default `Windows` folder.

Creating and Formatting a VideoSoft Data Reporter

Because the Data Reporter is designed to be an end-user tool, the user has the ability to launch it at runtime. Users have the ability to load database files, or you can supply a DAO `Recordset` object for them. Users can also use the Data Reporter to specify custom formats in addition to arranging, grouping, and sorting fields the way they want.

To use the VideoSoft Data Reporter component in your application, follow these steps:

1. Create a new VB project. In the Project References menu, create a reference to :-) `VideoSoft Data Reporter`.

2. In the Project Components menu, check :-) VideoSoft vsView 3 Controls.

3. On the form, create a command button labeled Design.

4. In the form's `Load` event, create an instance of the `DataReporter` object, as well as a DAO `Database` object and a `Recordset` object. Assign the `Recordset` object to the `Recordset` property of the `DataReporter` object:

```
Option Explicit

' References DAO 3.51.
' References VideoSoft DataReporter.

Dim db As Database
Dim rs As Recordset

Dim dr As DataReporter
```

```
Private Sub Form_Load()
    Set dr = New DataReporter
    Set db = OpenDatabase("..\..\DB\novelty.mdb")
    Set rs = db.OpenRecordset("select * " & _
                              "from tblCustomer " & _
                              "where ID < 300")
    dr.Recordset = rs
End Sub
```

Note: The `Recordset` property of the `DataReporter` object is, for some reason, not settable using conventional syntax for object properties. This unamusing peculiarity means that instead of assigning a `Recordset` object to the Data Reporter using the normal syntax:

```
Set dr.Recordset = rs
```

You must use this syntax instead:

```
dr.Recordset = rs
```

5. In the Design button's `Click` event, write code to launch the report designer by executing the `DataReporter` object's `DoReport` method. To give the user access to the design facilities of the Data Reporter, set the `ShowLayoutWindow` and `ShowDataReporter` properties to True.

```
Priv ate Sub cmdDesign_Click()
    dr.ShowLayoutWindow = True
    dr.ShowDataReporter = True
    dr.DoReport
End Sub
```

6. Run the application and click the Design button. The Data Reporter design windows appear, as shown in Figure 4.15.

Figure 4.15
The VideoSoft Data Reporter design windows are displayed.

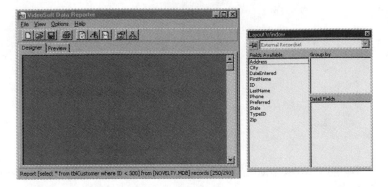

Now that you've assigned your recordset to the DataReporter object, you can design a report. To do this, follow these steps:

1. In the Layout window, drag fields from the Fields Available list to the Detail Fields list. Drag the following fields in order: LastName, FirstName, Address, City, State. Each time you drag a field to the Detail Fields list, the Designer window updates to show you what the report looks like, as shown in Figure 4.16.

Figure 4.16
The Designer window shows the result of adding Detail Fields to the report design.

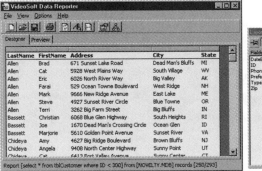

2. Next group the data by state. To do this, drag the State field from the Detail Fields list onto the Group By list. The Designer window updates to show the customers according to what state they live in.

3. Adjust the display of the report by selecting the menu command View, Global Settings in the VideoSoft Data Reporter window.

4. Click the Styles tab, then select Heading 1 Top. This is the style used for group headers (in this report, it's used for display of state names). Use the Font and Back Color buttons to alter the font size, color, and background color.

5. In the Settings dialog box, click OK. The report is reformatted to your specifications, as shown in Figure 4.17.

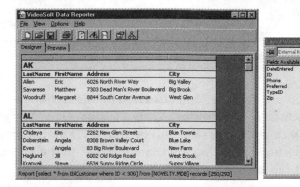

Figure 4.17
Report data is grouped by state by applying custom formatting to the report.

Now that you've created a custom format, you'll want to save it so you can run it later. Here's how to do this:

1. From the Data Reporter window, select the menu command File, Save Report.

2. Give your report the filename `myreport.vrd`.

3. Close the Data Reporter window by selecting the menu command File, Exit.

Previewing and Printing the Formatted Report

Once you've created a VRD file, you can load it programmatically in your application. You do this by passing the VRD file as an argument to the `Data Reporter` object's `DoReport` method. To see how this works, follow these steps:

1. Create a vsPrinter control and a command button on your form. Give the command button the label Run.

2. Write code in the Run button's `Click` event to launch the data reporter with the custom format file you created in the previous example. This code assigns the print preview to the form's vsPrinter control:

```
Private Sub cmdRun_Click()
    dr.DoReport App.Path & "\myreport.vrd", vsPrinter1
End Sub
```

3. Run the application and click the Run button. The data reporter appears, permitting you to arrange and sort fields any way you like. Notice that the fields are formatted according to the color and font selections you stored in the file `myreport.vsd`.

4. From the DataReporter's File menu, select Print. The formatted data is sent to the printer.

Code Example: You can find the code discussed in this section in the project `VSAdHoc.vbp`, located in the directory `\vbdb\code\04-Report\VSAdHoc`. For information on how to install the sample files on the CD that accompanies this book, see the section "Installing the Example Files" in the introduction at the beginning of this book.

Exporting to Text Using the Microsoft Scripting Runtime Library

New in VB6 was the addition of the Microsoft Scripting Runtime Library. This library is shared across multiple development environments and is designed to extend the functionality of scripting operations, such as that provided by Windows Scripting Host.

For Visual Basic developers, the addition of the scripting runtime means that you can bypass the archaic, inconsistent syntax of Visual Basic's old file-handling syntax. Instead, you can export data to files in a clean, object-oriented manner.

To use the Scripting Runtime library in your VB project, you make a reference to Microsoft Scripting Runtime in VB's Project References menu. Once you've done that, you can write code against the objects provided by the scripting runtime. The object provided by this library is shown in Figure 4.18.

As you can see, the object model provides access to a number of elements of the file system, including drives and folders. It also provides a `Dictionary` object, which gives you the ability to create associative arrays that work in a similar manner to collections or conventional arrays. However, in the case of exporting data, the only objects we're interested in are the `FileSystemObject` and the `TextStream` objects.

Here's how to create a file using the `FileSystemObject` and `TextStream` objects:

1. Create an application with a text box and two command buttons.

2. Use the Project References menu to make a reference to Microsoft Scripting Runtime.

3. Write the code shown in Listing 4.4.

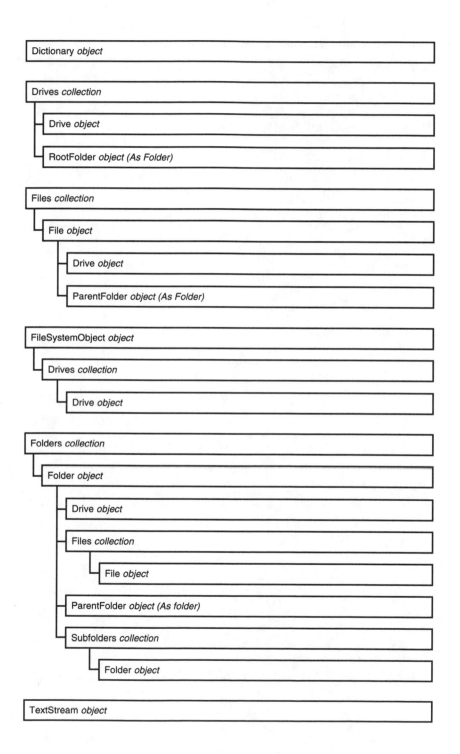

Figure 4.18
The Microsoft Scripting Runtime library provides this object model.

Listing 4.4   Saving and Reloading a One-Line Text File

```
Private Sub cmdOpen_Click()
    Dim MyFile As Scripting.FileSystemObject
    Dim txt As Scripting.TextStream

    Set MyFile = New Scripting.FileSystemObject

    ' Open the file.
    Set txt = MyFile.OpenTextFile(FileName(), ForReading)

    ' Retrieve data from the file and close.
    txtData.Text = txt.ReadLine
    txt.Close

End Sub


Private Sub cmdSave_Click()
    Dim MyFile As Scripting.FileSystemObject
    Dim txt As Scripting.TextStream

    Set MyFile = New Scripting.FileSystemObject

    ' Open the file.
    Set txt = MyFile.OpenTextFile(FileName(), ForWriting, True)

    ' Send data to the file and close.
    txt.WriteLine txtData.Text
    txt.Close
End Sub


Private Function FileName() As String
    Dim strPath As String

    strPath = App.Path

    If Right(strPath, 1) <> "" Then
        strPath = strPath & "\"
    End If

    FileName = strPath & "testfile.txt"
End Function
```

Notice that the `FileSystemObject`'s `OpenTextFile` method acts as a factory method, returning a `TextStream` object. This is analogous to the relationship between the `Database` object's `OpenRecordset` method in DAO. You can't create a `TextStream` object outside of the context of a `FileSystemObject`.

The True argument passed as the third parameter to the `OpenTextFile` method indicates that if the file doesn't exist, it should be created.

The application has the ability to save and retrieve anything entered into the text box. Once you have the ability to do this, you can integrate this functionality into a database-driven application. The next few sections discuss ways to do just that.

> **Code Example:** You can find the code discussed in this section in the project `FileSys.vbp`, located in the directory `\vbdb\code\04-Report\FileSys`. For information on how to install the sample files on the CD that accompanies this book, see the section "Installing the Example Files" in the introduction at the beginning of this book.

Exporting a Recordset Using the *TextStream* Object

Once you have opened a file, the next step is to create a recordset and send data from the recordset to the file. Listing 4.5 gives a minimal example of how you can use this technique to print the names of all the items in your inventory.

Listing 4.5   Sending Information from a Recordset to a File Using the *Textstream* Object

```
Dim db As Database
Dim rs As Recordset

Private Sub Form_Load()

Set db = OpenDatabase("..\..\DB\novelty.mdb")
Set rs = db.OpenRecordset("tblEmployees")

Open App.Path & "\people.txt" For Output As #1

Do Until rs.EOF
    Print #1, rs!FirstName & " " & rs!LastName
    rs.MoveNext
Loop

Close #1

End Sub
```

Note that this example happens to use DAO, but the data access technology you use is unimportant—this would work equally well with an RDO resultset or an ADO recordset.

Creating Delimited Database Output

You can concatenate various characters to values from database fields in order to delimit output. Delimited text files are used by a variety of applications as a common import and export format. Microsoft Excel, for example, can open various types of delimited text files directly.

One common and easy-to-implement format is the tab-delimited format. In a tab-delimited format, every record becomes a row of text, and fields are separated from each other by the tab character. Since the ASCII code for the tab character is 9, you can use VB's Chr function to create tab-delimited output.

Listing 4.6 shows how to do this using a TextStream object. The interface of the application contains a command button called cmdExport and a label called lblStatus.

Listing 4.6   Code to Export Sales Information from the Database to a Tab-Delimited Text File

```
Option Explicit

' References DAO 3.51.
' References Microsoft Scripting Runtime.

Private db As Database
Private rs As Recordset


Private Sub cmdExport_Click()

Dim fs As Scripting.FileSystemObject
Dim txt As Scripting.TextStream
Dim strSQL As String
Dim lngCount As Long

    strSQL = "SELECT FirstName, LastName, OrderDate, OrderAmount " & _
             "FROM tblCustomer " & _
             "INNER JOIN tblOrder " & _
             "ON tblCustomer.ID = tblOrder.CustomerID"

    Set db = OpenDatabase("..\..\DB\novelty.mdb")
    Set rs = db.OpenRecordset(strSQL)
```

```vb
    Set fs = New Scripting.FileSystemObject
    Set txt = fs.OpenTextFile(FileName(), ForWriting, True)

    Do Until rs.EOF
        txt.Write rs!FirstName & Chr(9)
        txt.Write rs!LastName & Chr(9)
        txt.Write rs!OrderDate & Chr(9)
        txt.WriteLine rs!OrderAmount & Chr(9)


        ' Update counter
        lngCount = lngCount + 1
        If lngCount Mod 10 = 0 Then
            Status lngCount & " orders exported."
            DoEvents
        End If


        rs.MoveNext
    Loop

    txt.Close

    Set txt = Nothing
    Set fs = Nothing

End Sub


Private Function FileName() As String
    Dim strPath As String

    strPath = App.Path

    If Right(strPath, 1) <> "" Then
        strPath = strPath & "\"
    End If

    FileName = strPath & "output.txt"
End Function


Private Sub Status(strText As String)
    lblStatus.Caption = strText
End Sub
```

This application takes all the orders in the database and outputs them into a text file called output.txt. (It takes a few seconds to run, even on a fast computer, so the application also includes a status label that shows how much work the export process has accomplished.)

Code Example: You can find the code discussed in this section in the project Delimit.vbp, located in the directory \vbdb\code\04-Report\Delmit. For information on how to install the sample files on the CD that accompanies this book, see the section "Installing the Example Files" in the introduction at the beginning of this book.

To view the text file generated by this application, you can open it in Microsoft Excel. The latest versions of Microsoft Excel include a Text Import Wizard that recognizes text files and enables you to specify data types of information in delimited text files.

To do this, follow these steps:

1. Use the Visual Basic application from the previous example to generate the tab-delimited text file output.txt.

2. Launch Microsoft Excel.

3. In Excel, choose File, Open.

4. In the Open dialog box, change the Files of Type combo box to Text Files so that the file dialog box displays text files.

5. Locate and select the file output.txt.

6. Click the Open button.

The Text Import Wizard runs, as shown in Figure 4.19.

Figure 4.19
Microsoft Excel 97's Text Import Wizard enables you to import delimited text files.

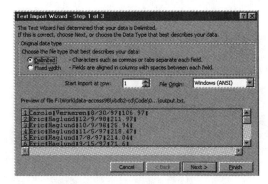

7. The Text Import Wizard recognizes that this is a delimited text file and provides a preview of your data. Click the Next button.

8. The wizard recognizes that your data is delimited with tabs. (Pretty smart, this wizard.) Click Next.

9. The wizard displays your data in columns. At this step, you have the option to denote data types for each column. The third column, which contains dates, should be stored in Excel's date format. To do this, select the column by clicking it (if it hasn't been selected already), then choose Date from the Column data format panel. The wizard should look like Figure 4.20.

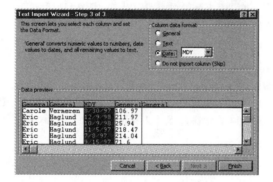

Figure 4.20
The Text Import Wizard is used to import a text file with a column containing dates.

10. Click Finish. Excel creates a new spreadsheet with your data in it. You can work with this spreadsheet the same way you work with any other Excel worksheet. Note that if you used the version of the Novelty database that came on the CD that accompanies this book, the import process will take a little while—it's bringing in about 30,000 records.

Exporting to HTML Web Pages

You can export from a database to an HTML file to produce Web pages from your database application. Because Web pages are really just text files, the technique you use to export to HTML is similar to the method you use for exporting to text (as explained in previous sections in this chapter).

You write procedures to export to static HTML files in the following situations:

▶ Several different types of users—potentially with different operating systems—are interested in viewing the data in a Web browser.

▶ You're interested in taking advantage of the features of a Web browser that are not offered by a plain text file, such as formatting, embedded graphics, and hyperlinks.

▶ You want to display information that does not become obsolete very often, such as an employee phone directory or the catalog of a company's products.

▶ You are uninterested in or unable to deploy Active Server Pages on your Web server—either because you're not running a Microsoft Web server or because Active Server Pages just don't fit into your organization's scheme for presenting data to users.

Note: The number of options for exporting data to HTML is increasing by leaps and bounds. If you're interested in a no-brainer solution for HTML export, check out the new exporting features of the Sheridan SSDBGrid control, described in Chapter 15, "Using Sheridan DataWidgets."

HTML Export Versus Active Server Pages

If you are interested in providing up-to-the-minute accuracy—that is, you want to give users access to "live" data through a Web browser—then the HTML export procedure described in this section might not be a good choice for you. You might instead consider a solution based on Active Server Pages (ASP), which does have facilities for enabling users to query data.

For example, if your company has a catalog of products to which you add new products once a month, you might consider exporting the whole catalog to HTML whenever you enter new data. Alternatively, you might write code that dumps only new or changed database records to HTML files; this solution is trickier to implement, but more efficient. Either way, with monthly updates, your data is probably stable enough to warrant using HTML export rather than ASP.

The biggest advantage of using ASP is that it can generate on-the-fly output in pure HTML, so that any user on any platform with any Web browser can view query results. The drawback is that you need to be using a Web server that supports ASP, such as Microsoft Internet Information Server 3.0 or 4.0.

For more information on developing Active Server Pages that connect to your databases, see Chapter 11, "Internet Database Applications."

Creating an HTML Template

To write a procedure that exports to HTML, it's helpful to have an idea of what you're shooting for before you write Visual Basic code. This is because when you export to HTML, you're using a query language (SQL) within a programming language (Visual Basic) to export to a document markup language (HTML). When you live in this complicated world, things can get confusing quickly.

To reduce the confusion, start by creating an HTML file the way you normally would. This file will become the pattern, or template, that your Visual Basic program will attempt to re-create—in effect, a prototype.

When you're creating your template, use whatever HTML editing tools you feel comfortable with. There is no shame in using Notepad to create HTML files, particularly if you know what you are doing. In fact, Notepad's popularity as an HTML editor has caused it to garner the name "Visual Notepad." (The people who call it this are, of course, making a little joke.)

> **For More Information:** If you are new to this Web stuff and you don't understand how HTML works, never fear. It's not difficult to learn, and there are a million books out there that can help you get started. The best are written by the fabulous Laura Lemay. Her *Sams Teach Yourself Web Publishing with HTML 4.0 in 14 Days* (Sams.net, 1997) is a beautiful, thousand-page behemoth of HTML goodness.

Listing 4.7 displays the code for a typical HTML report template. Note that the parts of the data generated by your Visual Basic application, such as the date and time the page was exported as well as the actual sales data taken from the database, are inserted in the template in all-uppercase letters. You'll replace these when you translate the template into Visual Basic code.

Listing 4.7   An HTML Template That Serves As the Design Prototype of Your Export Procedure

```
<html>
<head>
<title>
Sales Report - OUTPUT DATE
</title>
</head>

<body bgcolor="white">
<font face="Arial, Helvetica">
<p align=right><b>Jones Novelties Incorporated</b><br>
                                Sales Report<br>
                Last updated: OUTPUT DATE<br>
```

continues

Listing 4.7   An HTML Template That Serves As the Design Prototype of Your Export Procedure (Continued)

```
</font>

<hr>

<center>
<font face="Courier New, Courier">
<table border>
<tr>

<!- these are column headers->

    <td>
    <b>Catalog #</b>
    </td>

    <td>
    <b>Product</b>
    </td>

    <td>
    <b>Units sold</b>
    </td>

    <td>
    <b>Wsle price</b>
    </td>

    <td>
    <b>Retail price</b>
    </td>

    <td>
    <b>Total profit</b>
    </td>
</tr>

<tr>

<!- database data goes here ->

    <td>
    CAT#
    </td>

    <td>
    PRODUCT
```

```
        </td>

        <td>
        UNITS
        </td>

        <td>
        WHOLESALE
        </td>
        <td>
        RETAIL
        </td>

        <td>
        PROFIT
        </td>

</tr>
</table>

</font>
</center>

</body>
</html>
```

Figure 4.21 shows the template as viewed in a Web browser.

Figure 4.21
*The HTML tem-
plate file is viewed
in a Web browser.*

Writing Visual Basic Code to Export Data to HTML

After you have an idea of what you want your HTML file to look like, you can create Visual Basic code to write the file to disk. This is a process of dismantling the HTML file and putting Visual Basic code around it; the Visual Basic application you create takes care of everything having to do with database access and file handling.

> **Note:** As with most things, there's no one "right" way to write a procedure like this. However, if you export to HTML frequently, you may find it helpful to place the HTML export code in a Visual Basic class module. Putting frequently used code into a class makes it extremely easy to reuse. We haven't discussed classes yet, so the following example doesn't use that technique. However, for more information on using classes to create export functions, see Chapter 7.

Listing 4.8 shows the code to create a minimal HTML file. This code contains everything except the part that involves database access.

Listing 4.8 Exporting a Minimal HTML File from Within a Visual Basic Application

```
Private Sub cmdExport_Click()
Dim fs As Scripting.FileSystemObject
Dim txt As Scripting.TextStream

    Set fs = New Scripting.FileSystemObject
    Set txt = fs.OpenTextFile("c:\windows\desktop\test.html", _
                              ForWriting, True)


    txt.WriteLine "<html>"
    txt.WriteLine "<head>"
    txt.WriteLine "<title>"
    txt.WriteLine "Welcome to my HTML world."
    txt.WriteLine "</title>"
    txt.WriteLine "</head>"
    txt.WriteLine "<body bgcolor=#ffffff>"
    txt.WriteLine "This is my first HTML page created using Visual Basic."
    txt.WriteLine "</body>"
    txt.WriteLine "</html>"


    txt.Close

End Sub
```

This code example formats the output neatly by using the `WriteLine` method, which includes a carriage return after each line of output. If you ever want to export data without a carriage return after each line, use the `Write` method instead.

Remember, too, that HTML ignores white space characters such as tabs and spaces, as well as carriage returns. This is not to say that you shouldn't format your exported HTML code—white space in your HTML code can make it much easier to read. But remember that such formatting has no bearing on how the page displays.

Business Case 4.6: Publishing HTML Database Reports to the Web

Jones Novelties' chief financial officer likes the work you've done on exporting data to text files. But he's beginning to realize that this data is difficult for him to reach all the time. He travels a lot, and he works from home. He's now interested in seeing weekly financial report data on a Web page, so he can access it from anywhere, at any time, on any computer.

You decide to create an HTML export function that automatically copies its output to an HTML file that can be stored on the company's Web server. To do this, follow these steps:

1. Start a Visual Basic project. To the project's main form, add the Export button.

2. In Project References, make a reference to DAO 3.51 and Microsoft Scripting Runtime.

3. In the Declarations section of the form, create the variable declarations:

```
Option Explicit

' References MS DAO 3.51
' References MS Scripting Runtime

Private db As Database
Private rs As Recordset
Private fs As FileSystemObject
Private txt As TextStream
```

4. In the form's `Load` event, open the database and initialize the `FileSystemObject`:

```
Private Sub Form_Load()
```

```
        Set db = OpenDatabase("..\..\DB\novelty.mdb")
        Set fs = New Scripting.FileSystemObject

    End Sub
```

5. Write code to take data from a recordset and output HTML to the text file. Listing 4.9 shows the code that does this.

Listing 4.9   Code That Exports Data from the Orders Query to an HTML Table

```
Private Sub cmdExport_Click()

    Set txt = fs.OpenTextFile(App.Path & "\orders.html", _
                              ForWriting, True)

    HTMLPageStart "Jones Novelties - Customers - Florida"

    HTMLDataExport

    txt.WriteLine "</body>"
    txt.WriteLine "</html>"

    txt.Close
    Set txt = Nothing

End Sub

Private Sub HTMLPageStart(strTitle As String)

    With txt
        .WriteLine "<html>"
        .WriteLine "<head>"
        .WriteLine "<title>"
        .WriteLine "<h1>"
        .WriteLine strTitle
        .WriteLine "</h1>"
        .WriteLine "</title>"

        .WriteLine "<body bgcolor=#ffffff>"
        .WriteLine "<font face=Tahoma, Arial, Helvetica>"
    End With

End Sub

Private Sub HTMLDataExport()
```

```vba
    Dim f As DAO.Field

    Set rs = db.OpenRecordset("select FirstName, LastName, " & _
                              "Address, City, State " & _
                              "from tblCustomer " & _
                              "where State = 'FL' " & _
                              "order by LastName, FirstName")

    txt.WriteLine "<table border>"

    ' Export column headers
    With txt
        .WriteLine "<tr>"
        For Each f In rs.Fields

            .WriteLine "   <td bgcolor=#CCCCCC>"
            .WriteLine "   <b>" & f.Name & "</b>"
            .WriteLine "   </td>"
        Next f
        .WriteLine "</tr>"
    End With

    ' Export the data
    With txt
        Do Until rs.EOF
            .WriteLine "<tr>"
            For Each f In rs.Fields
                .WriteLine "   <td>"
                .WriteLine "   <b>" & f.Value & "</b>"
                .WriteLine "   </td>"
            Next f
            .WriteLine "</tr>"
            rs.MoveNext
        Loop
    End With

    txt.WriteLine "</table>"

    rs.Close
    Set rs = Nothing

End Sub
```

6. Run the application and click the command button. The HTML file ORDERS.HTML is created. When you open the file in a Web browser, it looks like Figure 4.22.

Figure 4.22
Database informa-tion exported to an HTML file is viewed in a Web browser.

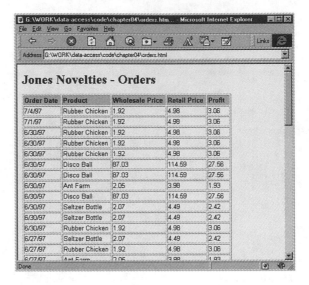

One cool thing about the HTMLExport subroutine is the fact that it dynamically iterates through the Fields collection of the Recordset object. That means that this code will work for any table, regardless of how many fields are in the table or what they're called. All you need to do to make the export subroutine work with other data is to change the code that sets up the recordset.

You could add many additional cosmetic and functional adornments to this application. For example, you could include hyperlinks with each product so that when you click a product name, the browser loads a page of information on sales of that product; you could do the same thing with customer information.

Code Example: You can find an example of the code discussed in this section in the project WebXPort.vbp, located in the directory \vbdb\code\ 04-Report\WebXPort. For information on how to install the sample files on the CD that accompanies this book, see the section "Installing the Example Files" in the introduction at the beginning of this book.

Sending Your Files to the Web Server

If your server is using the same local area network (LAN) as the computer you use, putting your exported HTML files on the Web requires only that you copy them to the Web server's directory. (For Microsoft Internet Information Server, this directory is any directory under the \WWWROOT directory.)

But if you don't own the server, you'll need to take a few extra steps to publish your exported HTML files on the Web. These steps usually entail sending the files to the Web server using Internet File Transfer Protocol, or *FTP*. You can use the Internet Transfer Control that comes with Visual Basic for this purpose, or you can use a commercial FTP control.

> **Note:** The Mabry FTP control, part of the Mabry Internet Pack, is a good control for sending and retrieving files over the Internet using FTP. You can get more information on the Mabry FTP control from Mabry Software's Web site at `http://www.mabry.com`.

EXPORTING TO TEXT FILES USING VB'S CLASSIC FILE FUNCTIONS

Before the Microsoft Scripting Runtime was included in VB6, you had the ability to manipulate text files using ancient, cryptic syntax inherited from the earliest days of the Basic programming language. Exporting to a text file using VB's "classic" file-handling operations involves the following steps:

1. Use the Open statement to open a file.

2. Use the OpenRecordset method to create a recordset.

3. Loop through a recordset one record at a time.

4. Use the Print # statement to send data from the recordset to the text file.

5. Use the Close statement to close the file.

The next few sections give details on how you accomplish these steps.

> **Note:** If you're happy with manipulating the file system using the Microsoft Scripting Library as discussed in previous sections, there's no need to learn how to use the "classic" file-handling syntax provided by VB. It's more cumbersome and less flexible than the Scripting Library way of handling files.

Using the *Open* Statement to Create a File

To create a file on disk, you use the Visual Basic Open statement. The Open statement has many forms, including forms that enable you to read files and write binary files. But in this case, you're interested only in outputting text, so you use this form of the Open statement:

```
Open filename For Output As #filenumber
```

The argument filename is any valid filename, enclosed in double quotation marks.

The argument *filenumber* can be any number between 1 and 511; it's used as shorthand to identify the file later when you send information to it using the Print # statement.

> **Note: In previous versions of Visual Basic, you could open only files numbered 1 to 255 using the Open statement. See the discussion on the FreeFile function later in this chapter for information on how to access file numbers in the range 256 to 511.**

For example, to create a file called CHEESE.TXT, you use the following code:

```
Open "cheese.txt" For Output As #1
```

At this point, the file is created and you can send data to it; in code, you refer to this file as file #1.

Using *FreeFile* to Determine the Next Available File

When you're using VB's classic file-handling syntax, you must keep track of the files your application has opened through a cumbersome system based on numbers. In addition to placing an artificial limit on the number of files you can open at once, this means you need a way to assign numbers to files in situations where you want to have more than one file open at a time.

The FreeFile function accomplishes this. When you call FreeFile, it returns the next available file number. If your application hasn't opened any files, this number will initially be 1.

Listing 4.10 shows an example of how to open a file with a file number generated by FreeFile.

Listing 4.10   Determining the Next Free File Number Using the *FreeFile* Function

```
Dim intFile As Integer
intFile = FreeFile()
Open "export.txt" For Output As intFile
```

Note that if you call FreeFile with its optional argument (the number 1), the function returns the next free file number in the range 256 to 511, as shown in Listing 4.11.

Listing 4.11   Using *FreeFile*'s Optional Argument to Access Higher-Numbered Files

```
Dim intFile As Integer
intFile = FreeFile(1)
Open "export.txt" For Output As intFile
```

The two forms of the FreeFile function exist to maintain backward compatibility with previous versions of Visual Basic.

Using *Print* # to Format Output

You have several options that enable you to format textual output with the Print # statement in VB's classic file-handling syntax. Table 4.4 lists these options.

Table 4.4 Formatting Options Used with Print #	
Setting/Operator	**Meaning**
Spc(n)	Insert a fixed number of spaces
Tab(n)	Insert the text at a fixed point in the row
Semicolon (;)	Do not break a line after the print expression

So, for example, if you want to print several database fields delimited by spaces, you might use code like this:

```
Print #1, rs!FirstName; Spc(1); rs!LastName
```

This can, in some cases, be more clear than doing the same thing with standard Visual Basic concatenation, which looks like this:

```
Print #1, rs!FirstName & " " & rs!LastName
```

If you want fields to start at a particular column in the exported text file, you use code like this:

```
Print #1, Tab(5); rs!FirstName; Tab(20); rs!LastName
```

This formatting expression exports the FirstName field at column 5 and the LastName field at column 20. (This means that there are five blank spaces at the beginning of each line.)

Using the `Tab(n)` expression to export data to a particular column in the text file should not be confused with embedding delimiter characters in the exported text. You use concatenation to embed delimiter characters in an exported text file.

For example, to create a tab-delimited text file, you use `Print†#` expressions that look like this:

```
Print #1, rs!FirstName; Chr(9); rs!LastName
```

The expression `Chr(9)` is the BASIC way to denote the tab character; you must use the `Chr` function to do this because you can't type a tab directly into a concatenated expression.

One advantage of tab-delimited output is the fact that it can be readily imported into many applications. For example, when you open a tab-delimited text file in Microsoft Excel, it will recognize and convert the text file into spreadsheet format. (There's an example of this earlier in this chapter.)

Using the *Close* Statement to Close the File

When using VB's classic file-handling syntax, you close a file using the `Close` statement. Closing a file indicates to the system that you're done sending output to it.

To close a file, you simply use the `Close` statement, followed by the number of the file you want to close, like this:

```
Close #1
```

When your code is done sending output to a text file, it's important for the sake of efficiency to close the file explicitly using the `Close` statement. Visual Basic buffers the output you send to an open file using the `Print` statement; this buffer is not "flushed" (or completely written to the disk) until you execute a `Close` statement. So, in cases where you write a small text file to the disk and forget to use the `Close` method, the data in the file might not appear at all; the file will be created, but it will have a length of zero bytes.

EXPORTING TO MICROSOFT OFFICE APPLICATIONS

You can send database data to Microsoft Office applications from your Visual Basic application. You do this through a Windows technology known as Automation. Automation is a process that enables applications to communicate and exchange data with each other.

> **Note:** Automation was formerly known as *OLE Automation*, in the days before OLE became a four-letter word.

To target an Automation server for database output, you go through the following steps:

1. In your Visual Basic project, set a reference to the object library of the Automation server you want to use.

2. Create an instance of the Automation server object in your Visual Basic application using the `Dim` and `Set` statements.

3. Declare and instantiate any subordinate objects (such as documents) provided by the Automation server.

4. Create a `Recordset` object that retrieves that data you're interested in exporting.

5. Send data from the `Recordset` object from your application to the Automation server using the properties and methods of its objects.

The exact code you use to create documents, enter data, and do formatting in a document depends on the Automation server's object model. This chapter gives examples for Word, but if you're creative, you should have no trouble setting up procedures that will send data to any Automation server at all. Other Automation servers include all the Microsoft Office applications (including Microsoft Outlook) as well as some third-party applications (such as the drag-and-drop graphics application Visio).

Exporting to Microsoft Word

Because Microsoft Word is an Automation server, you can write Visual Basic code to send database data to it. The product of an Automation session with Microsoft Word is typically a Word document, although you can also use Word as a sort of print engine—creating a document with data stored in the database, then printing it. Through Automation, you can also use Word from within your Visual Basic application to perform nearly any task Word can handle.

You can access Word's programmable features because it is an Automation server. An Automation server exposes a set of objects (which in turn have properties and methods) that you can program. This example uses DAO, but you can use any data access library to perform automation operations.

To program Word as an Automation server, you begin by making a reference to Word in Project References.

> **Note:** Automation has been a feature of Microsoft Word for a while, but only since Word 97 has the program supported a robust object model. Previous versions of Word exposed a single object, the WordBasic programming language, which is similar to, but not 100 percent compatible with, Visual Basic. Microsoft Word, on the other hand, has Visual Basic for Applications as well as a far more robust object model. The point is that if you're using an older version of Word, you might have trouble adapting the examples in this section to work with the version of Word you're using.

Business Case 4.7: Exporting Data to Word Through Automation
In their ceaseless effort to completely run you through the wringer, your taskmasters at Jones Novelties have asked that you once again reformulate the order reporting system so that it can generate Word documents.

To do this, follow these steps:

1. Create a new Visual Basic project. In the Project References menu, make references to DAO 3.51 and the Microsoft Word 8.0 Object Library.

2. Create a command button on the application's main form.

3. In the Declarations section of the form, declare the following variables:

```
Option Explicit

' References DAO 3.5
' References Microsoft Word 8.0 Object Library

Private WordApp As Word.Application
Private doc As Word.Document
Private sel As Word.Selection

Private db As Database
Private rs As Recordset
```

4. In the `click` event of the command button, include code to instantiate the object variables and send data to Word:

```
Private Sub cmdExport_Click()

    Set db = OpenDatabase("..\..\DB\novelty.mdb")
    Set rs = db.OpenRecordset("select * from tblCustomer " & _
                              "where State = 'ND'")
    Set WordApp = New Word.Application

    WordApp.Documents.Add
    Set doc = WordApp.ActiveDocument
    Set sel = WordApp.Selection

    doc.Tables.Add Range:=sel.Range, NumRows:=1, NumColumns:=4

    Do Until rs.EOF
        sel.TypeText Text:=rs!OrderDate
        sel.MoveRight Unit:=12              ' 12 = next cell

        sel.TypeText Text:=rs!Product
        sel.MoveRight Unit:=12

        sel.TypeText Text:=rs!WholesalePrice
        sel.MoveRight Unit:=12

        sel.TypeText Text:=rs!RetailPrice
        sel.MoveRight Unit:=12

        rs.MoveNext
    Loop

    WordApp.Visible = True

    Set WordApp = Nothing

End Sub
```

You'll notice that many of the assignment statements in this code use named arguments. Named arguments are useful in programming complicated object models that have many properties and methods with a large number of arguments; instead of having to remember which argument comes in which order, you can instead name the argument directly.

Code Example: You can find the code discussed in this section in the project `WordAut.vbp`, located in the directory `\vbdb\code\04-Report\WordAut`. For information on how to install the sample files on the CD that accompanies this book, see the section "Installing the Example Files" in the introduction at the beginning of this book.

When looking at Automation code, you might ask yourself how anyone is expected to garner information on the complicated object models exposed by Automation server, considering how many Automation servers there are in the world and how many interrelated objects they expose. There are three answers to this question:

▶ The least time-intensive solution is simply to make a reference to the Automation server and start writing code, allowing Visual Basic's Auto List Members feature to show you the objects, properties, and methods of each object in its drop-down list. This method is rather hit-and-miss, but it can work, particularly in a situation where you know what you want to do but you simply can't remember the proper syntax.

▶ Visual Basic's Object Browser lets you see the objects, properties, methods, events, and enumerations provided by a library. This is useful for virtually any kind of object server. You must make a reference to the object server (using the Project Components menu or the Project References menu) before you can use the Object Browser to view a library's contents.

▶ If you're just experimenting, or if you want a fast track to a solution, you can do what you did when developing the code for business case 4.7, which is to run Word's Macro Recorder. The versions of Visual Basic for Applications that exist in the Microsoft Office applications today are so similar to the code used in Visual Basic, it's easy to exchange code between the two development environments. (The changes between the Macro Recorder version of this code and the version you see in this chapter mostly involve the declaration of object variables.)

For More Information: If you're the kind of person who has to know simply everything about a component before you incorporate it into your application, you'll want to get your hands on the *Microsoft Office 97 Visual Basic Language Reference* (Microsoft Press, 1997). This reference has information on programming Visual Basic for Applications in Word, Access, Excel, and PowerPoint. Because the book weighs in at 4,192 pages, you can either use it to build cool applications or to prop open your door—it's your choice.

SUMMARY

This chapter was designed to give you (hopefully) all the solutions you'll ever need for extracting data from database applications. The chapter didn't cover many new database concepts; rather, it provided practical applications of the existing database concepts introduced in previous chapters.

Bear in mind when reviewing the database solutions in this chapter that although the examples were all written using DAO, they'll work with minimal modification with other database technologies (such as RDO, introduced in the next chapter). This is because both DAO and RDO expose recordsets in a navigational model that enables your applications to iterate through recordsets from beginning to end.

QUESTIONS AND ANSWERS

Q. This chapter seems like quite the *tour de force*. It seems as if it has included information on virtually every kind of reporting and exporting technique available to a Visual Basic programmer. Are there any others?

A. No.

Q. Really?

A. Well, pretty much. Perhaps the chapter missed some things, such as graphing. (Most of the top third-party graphing packages provide database-aware ActiveX implementations, however, so they don't require code. One, the MSChart control, is covered in Chapter 10.) But basically, after you see five or six different examples of iterating through a recordset or binding to a control, you pretty much get the idea of how to do it in any situation.

Q. **I think Automation is the greatest thing since hairless cats. What are some drawbacks?**

A. There are three main drawbacks: slow performance, unacceptably slow performance, and, occasionally, mind-bogglingly slow performance. I've done a bunch of work with Visual Basic applications that send data to Word through Automation. (This was how one of my books was formatted—I've also used Automation to provide solutions for clients.) In many cases where I've attempted to write a serious application using Automation, though, I've run into situations where Word runs out of memory (complaining that there are "too many edits" in the document, even though the document I was creating seemed ridiculously small). The moral of the story is that when you're creating solutions involving Automation, be sure to test rigorously and save your work frequently.

Q. **Can I use Automation with older versions of Microsoft Office applications?**

A. Yes, although not all of the older Office applications support Automation in the same way. For example, Word didn't include Visual Basic for Applications until the current version, Word 97; to interact with Word, you had to create an instance of its procedural macro language, WordBasic. And the current version of Microsoft Outlook doesn't include Visual Basic for Applications at all (although you can program it as an Automation server). As Microsoft licenses Visual Basic for Applications to more and more vendors (which it is doing aggressively), your options for providing solutions involving third-party applications will continue to grow. You'll want to consult the documentation for the application you're interested in using so that you can determine the robustness and functionality of the object model it exposes.

Getting Started with SQL Server

SETTING UP AND RUNNING MICROSOFT SQL
SERVER

MIGRATING FROM MICROSOFT ACCESS TO
SQL SERVER

In the past, many Visual Basic programmers got their first exposure to database programming through the Jet database engine shared between Visual Basic and Microsoft Access. As soon as your database application grows beyond a few hundred records or a few users, it's common to run into limitations. Multiuser contention for data, poor performance, and lack of advanced data and server-management features cause many programmers to turn to a more heavy-duty architecture to resolve their database problems. That architecture is *client/server computing.*

Client/server is not to be confused with multiuser computing, which Jet supports just fine. In a multiuser architecture, a number of users share the same data over a LAN.

In order to have a client/server architecture, you have to have some sort of *back end.* This doesn't refer to the body part of a programmer who sits in a chair for eighteen hours a day; rather, it refers to a piece of software responsible for retrieving and caching data, arbitrating contention between multiple users, and handling security. While Microsoft Access supports multiple users, it's not a client/server system because all requests for information are processed by individual client computers. There's no intelligence on the other side of the network that is responsible for processing requests and returning data.

If you have the Enterprise Edition of Visual Basic, then Microsoft SQL Server is your obvious choice for a database back end, since SQL Server comes along with VB. But bear in mind that much of the information in this chapter pertains to you, even if you aren't using SQL Server. This is the case for two reasons:

▶ Most database back ends use a common language, known as Structured Query Language, or SQL, to access data.

▶ In Visual Basic, you most commonly access a database back end through Remote Data Objects—a database-independent method of performing client/server programming.

This chapter focuses on getting started with SQL Server. This chapter intentionally overlooks the emerging client/server trend known as three-tier architecture. Instead, this chapter's intention is to give you a whirlwind introduction to client/server programming using Visual Basic and SQL Server—the architectural material is covered in Chapter 7, "Database Access with Classes," Chapter 8, "Remote Database Access," and Chapter 9, "Multiuser Jet Databases."

The Drama of the Gifted Server Programmer

Here's a typical scenario: You're working as the member of a client/server development team. You have a database server that is 95 percent functional— which is to say that it isn't really functional at all. You still need to get your work done, but the server component of the application just isn't happening at the moment.

What's more, you may only have one or two server-side programmers at your disposal. Because server-side programmers tend to have the most rarefied set of skills, this tends to happen often in client/server development organizations. They're the hardest kind of programmer for companies to hire and retain, and as a consequence, they can be the most stressed-out bunch of people you'd ever want to lay eyes on. Consequently, they are the hardest to get hold of when something goes wrong.

A big problem with this situation is that client-side programmers often can't get their work done until server-side programmers fix what's wrong with the server.

This is *The Drama of the Gifted Server Programmer*.

If you've ever been in a client/server development project involving more than two developers, you'll understand The Drama of the Gifted Server Programmer. One solution to The Drama is to prototype your client-side application using a mocked-up Jet data source first and then hook up your application to the server when the server is ready. Designating an ODBC data source (as described in Chapter 6, "Open Database Connectivity and Remote Data Objects") or using an

OLE DB data link (as described in Chapter 10, "ActiveX Data Objects") are two easy ways to do this. The layer of abstraction offered by ODBC or OLE DB permits you to easily create and use a prototype version of the database in your application, switching to the "live" database whenever you want.

Placing one or more layers of abstraction between the client and the server also keeps your client-side programmers from overburdening the server-side programmer. For the server-side programmer, that means exposing views or stored procedures that provide data services to clients; for VB programmers, it means creating ActiveX code components that do much the same thing. For information on strategies involving stored procedures and views, see the section "Creating and Running Stored Procedures" in this chapter; for more on ActiveX code components, see Chapter 8.

SETTING UP AND RUNNING MICROSOFT SQL SERVER

Running a true database server is a significant departure from sharing a Microsoft Jet database file. You have new things to worry about, new concepts to get your head around, and you don't get as much help from friendly user interfaces. (Although to its credit, Microsoft SQL Server is much easier to set up and maintain than its competitors.)

This section is intended to get you started with the bare minimum required to get a database up and running under SQL Server.

Note: A development version of Microsoft SQL Server comes with the Enterprise Edition of Visual Basic. This version gives you a full installation of SQL Server, but restricts you to 15 client connections. To create a production application using SQL Server, you'll need to obtain licenses for additional connections.

Determining Installation Requirements for SQL Server

To install SQL Server 6.5, Microsoft says you'll need a Windows NT computer with a 486 processor, 16MB of memory, 80MB of hard disk space, a CD-ROM drive, and Windows NT 3.51 or later.

If you've actually tried to run SQL Server on a 486 computer with 16 megs of memory, you have my permission to stop laughing and resume reading now. The fact of the matter is that these specifications are minimum requirements for running SQL Server. SQL Server may very well run on a machine this anemic.

But in the real world, the minimum requirement is the biggest, baddest computer you can realistically afford. This is supposed to be the computer that runs your entire business; scrimping on the hardware will only cause you grief later.

If there's one area you want to consider maxing out your computer, it's memory. Here's a totally anecdotal and unscientific example: The Windows NT Server used to build some of the examples in this chapter started with 56MB of memory. By the time the chapter was completed, I'd dropped an additional 128MB into the machine, and it was running in a much perkier manner. This is definitely not to say that you need 184MB for development on an SQL Server machine; rather, you may want to experiment with different configurations and consider upgrading if the performance on your machine isn't what you'd like.

> Note: Because this book is designed to be a survey of database-oriented solutions in Visual Basic, it doesn't go into every SQL Server feature. If you're looking for a book that goes into more detail about how to use SQL Server with Visual Basic, check out Bill Vaughn's *Hitchhiker's Guide to Visual Basic and SQL Server* (Microsoft Press).

Installing SQL Server

After you've designated a computer for use with SQL Server, you can proceed with installation. The installation of SQL Server is fairly straightforward (double-click the program `setup.exe` in the \i386 folder on the CD-ROM, if you're working with an Intel box). That is, the process is straightforward with a few minor exceptions:

▶ It takes a really long time.

▶ It asks you a lot of really weird questions that most conventional applications don't ask.

This book can't help you with the fact that it takes a long time, but it can give you some pointers about the questions posed by SQL Server's setup application.

First, the setup application asks you for the location of the directory where you want to install SQL Server. This can be any directory on the server.

Next, setup asks you where you want to create a file called `master.dat`. This is a database file SQL Server uses to keep track of all of the databases it manages. Accordingly, you want to install this file in a place normal users can't get to it (use Windows NT security to ensure this) and on a disk that is not about to run out of disk space (because 25MB is the minimum size for the master database).

The setup application then asks you about the code page and sort order you want to use. The *code page* refers to the set of alphabetic characters available to the application. Choose the code page that's appropriate for your international locale.

Sort order determines how data is sorted when it's queried from SQL Server. Unless you have some unusual requirement for sorting, choose the default case-insensitive sort order.

SQL Server supports a number of network protocols. In this step, simply choose the network protocol that your LAN users will be utilizing. If you're not sure which choice to make, you'll need to get in touch with your LAN administrator or check your network's settings yourself in the Network control panel.

You next determine whether SQL Server should start automatically when Windows NT is started. If you select this option, bear in mind that SQL Server will be started as a service from Windows NT. Services act as if they're part of the operating system; they don't appear in the Task Manager, and they can't be shut down like normal applications can. The next section gives more information on how to manage a service running under Windows NT, but you might also see the section "Controlling the Way SQL Server Starts Up" later in this chapter.

Starting and Stopping SQL Server Using SQL Service Manager

You use the SQL Service Manager to start and stop SQL Server. You do this in situations where you need to take down the server to perform certain tasks, or if you just don't want to run SQL Server on a particular machine (on a development machine, for example).

You don't have to stop SQL Server under normal circumstances. This goes along with SQL Server's role as an *enterprise* database system. The idea is that you're supposed to start it up and leave it running all the time, come heck or high water.

Yet there are certain rare situations where you must stop the server to perform certain tasks, such as changing configuration options on the server or performing a hardware upgrade to the computer on which the server resides. When one of these situations comes up, you use SQL Service Manager to take down SQL Server and bring it back up again.

SQL Service Manager does not have to be running in order for SQL Server to do its work. The SQL Service Manager exists merely to give you control over the activation and deactivation of your server. After your server is in production mode, you probably won't often use SQL Service Manager.

When you launch it (by selecting its icon in the SQL Server program group), SQL Service Manager looks like Figure 5.1.

Figure 5.1
*SQL Service
Manager in its
pristine state, in
which SQL Server
is running and all
is well with the
universe.*

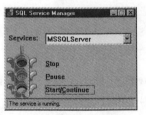

If SQL Server is running, the traffic light is green; if it's not running, the light is red. To start SQL Server, double-click the green light; to stop it, double-click the red light. It's really easier than making toast.

Controlling the Way SQL Server Starts Up

After you set up SQL Server, the operating system automatically launches SQL Server when your server computer is started. Through the Services control panel, you can control whether SQL Server always starts when your computer starts. To view the current state of SQL Server and control how it runs when your computer is started, follow these steps:

1 Launch the Windows Control Panel. Select Services from the Control Panel.

2 The Services control panel appears. Scroll through the list of services until you find MSSQLServer.

If you just installed SQL Server on your machine, the MSSQLServer service status is Started and its startup is Automatic. To stop the MSSQLServer service from the Services control panel:

1 Click the Stop button.

2 The control panel asks if you really want to stop SQL Server. Click Yes.

3 After a few seconds, SQL Server is stopped.

4 To restart SQL Server, click the Start button in the Services control panel.

Note: Starting and stopping SQL Server using the Services control panel is essentially the same thing as starting and stopping it from the SQL Service Manager, although you don't get to see the festive traffic light provided by the Service Manager.

Also notice that another SQL Server-related service, SQLExecutive, appears in the Services control panel. This service exists specifically to support the SQL Enterprise Manager application described later in this chapter. It's only activated when needed, so if you're not using SQL Server, you don't have to worry about it consuming memory on your computer.

Getting Started with SQL Server: The Basics

After it's installed, you have a number of minimum tasks to complete before SQL Server begins storing and retrieving data:

▶ Creating one or more disk devices

▶ Creating one or more databases on a particular disk device

▶ Creating tables in a database

▶ Creating views and stored procedures that govern how data is retrieved from a database

▶ Setting up user accounts and security groups

All the tasks you need to perform are described in this section. Most can be handled without writing code by using the SQL Enterprise Manager utility in SQL Server 6.5.

Running SQL Enterprise Manager

You can perform many of the most common database configuration and setup tasks in SQL Server using a utility called SQL Enterprise Manager. Because of its power and ease of use, SQL Enterprise Manager is one of the most important additions to Microsoft SQL Server 6.5. The utility makes the database administrator's task easier by putting an easy-to-use graphical interface on top of a number of chores that were formerly accomplished (and can still be accomplished) using somewhat arcane SQL commands.

You launch SQL Enterprise Manager from its icon in your SQL Server program group. After you've launched it, you'll gain access to the SQL Server(s) available on your network. The following sections in this chapter describe some of the most common tasks you perform with SQL Enterprise Manager in a production application.

Creating a New Database Device Using SQL Enterprise Manager

Before you can start creating databases in SQL Server, you must first create a *database device*. A database device is where databases reside in the SQL Server universe. Each database device can store multiple databases.

SQL Server makes you create disk devices in part because it's possible for a SQL Server disk device to span more than one physical hard disk. So you can have one *logical* database device that spans multiple *physical* hard disks. This is an advantage because you can have a database that spans dozens of gigabytes; it also means that if one disk drive fails, you can still have access to data stored on other disk drives.

While it's possible to create database devices using SQL code, in SQL Server 6.5 it's far easier to create them using Microsoft SQL Enterprise Manager. To do this, follow these steps:

1 Select SQL Enterprise Manager from the SQL Server 6.5 Program Group.

2 The first time you run SQL Enterprise Manager, you must register your SQL Server installation. This lets SQL Enterprise Manager know which SQL Server you want to work with; it also lets you administer more than one SQL Server installation.

Note: In a new SQL Server installation, you have only one username, sa, and it has no password. You'll obviously want to change this situation at your earliest convenience, because a username without a password is like a Buick without a back seat. For more information on how to manage user accounts and security in SQL Server, see the "Managing Users and Security in SQL Enterprise Manager" section later in this chapter.

You register a SQL Server in the Register Server dialog box, shown in Figure 5.2.

Figure 5.2
Microsoft SQL Enterprise Manager's Register Server dialog box.

Note: If you're attempting to register a SQL Server running on the machine you're working on, use the server name (local), including the parentheses. If you're trying to connect to a SQL Server located over a LAN, it's easiest to use the Servers button to browse the servers available on your network.

3 When you've registered the server you want to work with, click the Close button in the Register Server dialog. (You only have to do this once. After you've registered the server, SQL Enterprise Manager remembers how to connect to the server you want to work with.)

After you've registered your server, it appears in the Server Manager window (along with any other servers you may have also registered). On a machine with a connection to a local SQL Server, the Server Manager window looks like Figure 5.3.

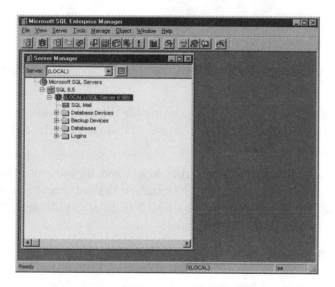

Figure 5.3
Server Manager window with a local SQL Server in SQL Enterprise Manager.

Now that you've launched Enterprise Manager and registered the server you want to work with, you can proceed to create a database device. To do this, follow these steps:

1 In SQL Enterprise Manager's Server Manager window, open the Database Devices folder underneath your SQL Server.

2 You should see a number of default database devices (such as master and temp_data) that were created for you by SQL Server's setup application.

3 Right-click the Database Devices folder, then select New Device from the pop-up menu.

4 The New Database Device dialog appears, as shown in Figure 5.4.

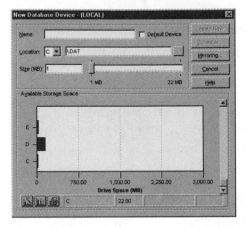

Figure 5.4
SQL Enterprise Manager's New Database Device dialog, which lets you create new database devices.

To create a new database device from the New Database Device dialog, follow these steps:

1 In the Name dialog box, type in a name for the new device; this can be any valid filename. (In the examples shown in this chapter, the database device is called business.)

2 From the Location combo box, choose a disk drive on which the new database device will be stored. The graph at the bottom of the New Database Device dialog shows you which disks are available to you and how much free space each one has.

3. In the Size text box, select the size of the database device you want to create (in megabytes). The slider control (to the right of the Size text box) gives you an idea of how large your database device is going to be in relation to the amount of free disk space you have on the drive; it also permits you to adjust the size of the device graphically.

If you're just creating a database device for the purposes of practicing techniques in this book, 10 megabytes should be a sufficient size. If you need to, you can always expand the size of the database device later.

4 To create the database device immediately, click the Create Now button.

5 SQL Enterprise Manager tells you that the database device is created by displaying a message box. When you close the New Database Device dialog, you should be able to see the new database device in the Database Devices folder of the Server Manager window.

Note: The Server Manager window of the SQL Enterprise Manager makes it easy to change how SQL Server runs. For example, if you want to make a database device smaller or larger, it's easy to do—simply double-click the device and change it in the dialog box.

Scheduling the Creation of a Database Device

Because the creation of a new database device—particularly a very large database device—can take a lot of time, you may want to put off the creation of the new device for another time. If you don't want to create the new database device immediately, you can schedule it to take place automatically at a time you choose (for example, during a time when few or no users are accessing the database).

To schedule the creation of the database device for another time, follow these steps:

1 In the New Database Device dialog, set the properties of the new database device, and then click the Schedule button. The Schedule Database dialog appears, as shown in Figure 5.5.

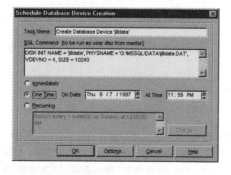

Figure 5.5
Scheduling the creation of a new database device in SQL Enterprise Manager.

2 Click the One Time button.

3 In the text boxes, specify the date and time you want SQL Server to create the database device, then click OK.

Note: The Schedule dialog box has an interesting side effect: it displays the SQL command that will be executed to create the new database device. Does this mean that it's possible to create new database devices by issuing SQL commands to the server in ISQL/w? Yes, but even experienced database administrators tend to forget the syntax of the SQL DISK INIT command. Unless you have a photographic memory for arcane SQL syntax, or you want to create a more sophisticated type of database device (such as the kind that spans multiple physical disks) you'll probably want to stick with the graphical way of creating database devices provided by SQL Enterprise Manager.

Designating a Database Device as the Default

It's important to designate a particular database device as the *default database device*. This is because the default database device is initially *master*, which is the device SQL Server uses for its own administrative purposes. If you don't change this, it's possible your new databases will accidentally be created on the master device. Changing the default database device from master to a database device of your own should be one of your first orders of business in a new SQL Server installation.

At any time during the device's existence, you can designate it as the default database device.

You can designate a database device as the default at the time you create it by clicking the Default Device check box in the New Database Device dialog. Or, to designate an existing database device as the default, follow these steps:

1 Double-click your database device in the Server Manager window.

2 The Edit Database Device dialog appears, as illustrated in Figure 5.6.

3 Click the Default Device check box, then click Change Now. The database device is set to be the default.

Creating a Database Using SQL Enterprise Manager

After you've installed SQL Server and created a database device, you're ready to get down to business. The next step is to create a database on a database device and begin populating it with database objects—tables, views, stored procedures, and so forth.

Although you can create databases using SQL code, it's easier to create them using SQL Enterprise Manager. This is because SQL Enterprise Manager lets you design the most common types of database objects graphically, shielding you from the complexity of SQL code.

To create a new database using SQL Enterprise Manager:

1 Right-click the Databases folder in the SQL Enterprise Manager's Server Manager window.

2 Select New Database from the pop-up menu.

3 The New Database dialog appears, as shown in Figure 5.7.

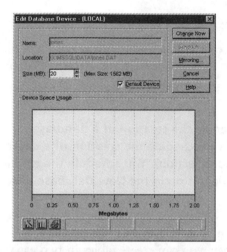

Figure 5.6
The Edit Database Device dialog box in SQL Enterprise Manager.

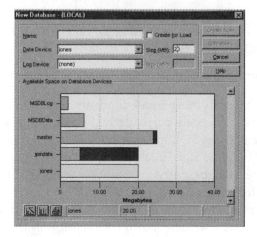

Figure 5.7
SQL Enterprise Manager's New Database dialog box, showing the available database devices and how much space they contain.

4 Type the new database's name in the Name text box. (The examples in this chapter use the name novelty.)

5 In the Size dialog, enter the size you want the new database to be in megabytes. The database can be as large as the database device it is stored on, but no larger. For your production databases, you'll want to make the database as large as you can to comfortably accommodate the data you're ever likely to store. You can increase the size of the database later, but it requires the intervention of the database administrator, which might prove inconvenient.

6 Click Create Now.

7 The new database is created and the New Database dialog box closes. You should be able to see your new database in the Databases folder of the Server Manager window.

Note: You can schedule the creation of a database for an off-peak period the same way you can schedule the creation of a database device (as discussed in the previous section). You schedule the creation of a database by clicking the Schedule button in the New Database dialog.

Creating Tables in a SQL Server Database

In Microsoft SQL Server, you can create tables in two ways:

▶ Use SQL Data Definition Language (DDL). This technique was introduced for Microsoft Jet databases in Chapter 2, "Queries." The code is nearly identical for SQL Server databases.

▶ Use the graphical table-building features of SQL Enterprise Manager.

Both techniques have advantages and disadvantages. SQL DDL commands are somewhat more complicated, particularly if you haven't worked with SQL extensively in the past; using SQL forces you to write and maintain code to create your database. Using the SQL Enterprise Manager, on the other hand, enables you to create a database structure quickly and easily, using all the graphical user interface advantages.

But some server programmers prefer using SQL code to create their databases because they always have a written record (in the form of their SQL DDL code) of what went into creating the database. The technique you use is a function of your personal preference, your organization's standards for development, and the kinds of database applications you're likely to create. Both techniques are introduced in the following sections.

Using SQL Enterprise Manager to Create Tables in SQL Server

After you've created a database in SQL Server, you can use SQL Enterprise Manager to create tables in the database.

To create a table in a database, follow these steps:

1 In SQL Enterprise Manager's Server Manager outline window, expand the outline node that represents the database in which you want to create a table.

2 Two folders appear underneath the database node: Groups/Users and Objects. Right-click the Objects folder.

3 Choose New Table from the pop-up menu.

4 The Manage Tables dialog box appears, as illustrated in Figure 5.8.

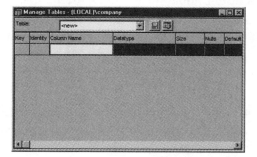

Figure 5.8
SQL Enterprise Manager's Manage Tables dialog, which lets you create tables in a database.

5 Start by creating a table to store customers. To do this, in the Manage Tables dialog, click in the column labeled Column Name. Then type the name of the first field for this table: **FirstName**.

6 Press Tab to move to the next column, Datatype. In this column, make the data type a variable-length text field, or varchar. The varchar data type is generally used in SQL Server to store relatively small pieces of string data.

7 In the next column, enter the number 50. This limits the number of characters in the FirstName field to 50.

8 The Nulls column determines whether a field allows null values. If the box is checked, then null values can be entered into the field. For the FirstName field, the Nulls box should be *unchecked*.

9 Enter additional field definitions and data types into the grid one at a time. When the table definition is done, it should look like Figure 5.9.

Figure 5.9
The Manage Table dialog box containing the field definitions for the new table.

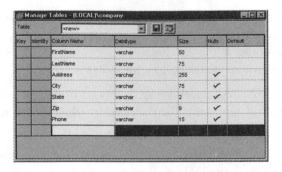

Note: At this point, you might want to create a field that acts as a unique identifier for each record in the table. (In SQL Server, this type of field is referred to as an identity column.) Now is the time to do this, because you can't create an identity column for the table after the table has already been created. This is because key fields cannot store null values, and you can only designate non-null fields in a table at the time the table is created. SQL Server is not as flexible as Microsoft Access is in this respect, but it's the price you pay for the increased performance and scalability SQL Server offers.

For more information on creating identity columns at the time the table is created, see the section "Creating Identity Columns to Uniquely Identify Records" later in this chapter.

10 When you're done designing the table, click Save at the top of the dialog box.

11 The Specify Table Name dialog appears. Type the table's name in the box; then click OK. You can use nearly any name you want, but for the examples in this chapter, the table name is tblCustomer.

12 The new table is created. You should be able to see the new table in the Server Manager window.

Creating an Identity Column to Uniquely Identify Records

It's useful (although not required) for every record to have a piece of information that uniquely identifies it. Often, this unique identifier has nothing intrinsically to do with the data represented by the record. For example, nobody knows your driver's license number by looking at your face; it's an essentially bogus number assigned to you to differentiate you from all the other Brad Joneses in the world.

The AutoNumber field in Microsoft Jet databases is introduced in Chapter 1, "Database Basics." SQL Server has an analogous concept known as an *identity column*. An identity column automatically assigns a unique numeric value to a column in each record as the record is created.

A SQL Server identity column is different from, and in some ways more flexible than, a Jet AutoNumber field. Identity columns in SQL Server have the following attributes:

▶ They can be of any numeric data type (in Jet, they can only be long integers).

▶ They can increment themselves by any amount you specify (in Jet, they can only increment themselves by one—or a random amount).

▶ They can start numbering at any value you specify (in Jet, they always begin at the value 1).

▶ They can be overridden. This allows you to insert specific numbers into identity columns—to reconstruct a record that was accidentally deleted, for example. (In Jet, identity columns are always read-only.)

There is one area where a SQL Server identity column is less flexible than a Jet AutoNumber field: If you're going to create an identity column for a table, you must do it at the time you create the table. This is because SQL Server requires that any field created later must allow null values; non-null fields can only be created at the time the table is created.

To create an identity column using SQL Enterprise Manager, follow these steps:

1 In the Manage Tables dialog box, create a new field called ID. Make its data type int. Remember that the SQL Server int data type is four bytes long, just like the Visual Basic Long data type, so a SQL Server int is really a long integer.

2 Uncheck the Nulls box. This ensures that null values can't be inserted into this column; it also makes this column eligible to act as an identity column.

3 Click the Advanced Features button at the top of the Manage Tables dialog box. This causes the bottom of the dialog box to pop open.

4 In the Identity Column combo box, select the name of the field you want to serve as the identity column. Optionally, you can set values in the Seed Value and Increment boxes; these boxes govern where automatic numbering starts and by what value each successive number increases.

When your identity column has been set, the Manage Tables dialog box looks like Figure 5.10.

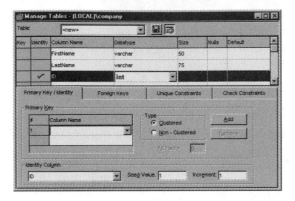

Bear in mind when using identity columns in SQL Server that they're not guaranteed to be sequential. For example, if Kevin tries to create a record that is designated ID number 101, then Laura creates the next record (ID number 102), and Kevin's insert transaction fails, a record with ID number 101 will never be created.

This may not be such a big deal, especially in a database application that never exposes the value of a primary key to the user (a design principle you should strive for). But remember that "lost" identity values are a possibility. If you use identity columns to give each record uniqueness, don't be surprised if you browse your data someday and you discover that there's no invoice number 101.

Using Other Methods to Generate Primary Keys

There's nothing that says you have to use an identity column to generate primary keys in your database applications. In fact, there's nothing that says your tables have to have primary keys at all. You'll probably find, however, that having a primary key—even if it's a bogus value made up by the server at the time the record was created—is a really good idea. This is because, as discussed in previous chapters on database design and queries, you need a primary key to do important things like joining multiple tables in queries. Primary keys are also handy ways to refer to records in the user interface. Rather than passing the whole record from one procedure to the next, having a primary key means that you can pass a minimal amount of data pertaining to the record.

Some of the alternative tactics for generating primary keys include

▶ Generating a completely random value in the primary key field for each record as it is created. This is the tactic used by tables containing AutoNumber fields that have been converted, or *upsized*, from Microsoft Access to SQL Server. It's also the technique used by replicated Access databases in order to avoid collisions between records that are entered by remote disconnected users. This is described in Chapter 9.

▶ Storing a counter value in a temporary table and using that value to seed each new record's primary key column as the record is created. This involves a transaction that reads the counter table's current value, using it to populate the primary key of the new record, then increments the value in the counter table in one atomic operation. This technique has the advantage of providing a sequential numbering system over which you have complete control. The disadvantage (when compared to the simpler technique of creating an identity column) is that you need to write a stored procedure and add tables to your database to implement it.

▶ Deriving a key from cues supplied by the data; for example, the key for a record for a person named Vito Polito might be VP001. If another person with the initials VP comes along, the system would give that record the key VP002, and so forth. This tactic has the advantage of providing a key that isn't totally dissociated from the data, but it does require more coding on your part (in the form of a stored procedure executing as a trigger, described later in this chapter).

Marking a Column as the Primary Key

When you create an identity column, you'll almost certainly want to designate that column as your table's primary key. You can do that in SQL Enterprise Manager's Manage Tables dialog box.

To designate a column as a table's primary key, follow these steps:

1 If you haven't done so already, open the Advanced Features section of the Manage Tables dialog box by clicking the Advanced Features button.

2 In the Primary Key panel of the Primary Key/Identity tab, select the name of the column you want to serve as the table's primary key.

Note: You have the capability to designate multiple fields as a table's primary key; this is known as a concatenated key. You do this in situations where, for example, you want the first and last names of every person in the table to be unique. This would prevent the name "Amy Rosenthal" from being entered in the table twice, but it wouldn't prevent other people named Amy from being entered into the table.

3 Click Add. The primary key index is added to the table definition, and the Manage Tables dialog looks like Figure 5.11.

Figure 5.11
Designating a column as a table's primary key in SQL Enterprise Manager.

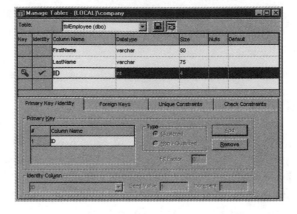

You can only designate a primary key for a table once. If you change your mind, you have to drop the table and start over. Therefore, you want to plan ahead and create the primary key at the time you create the table.

Note also that any field can serve as a table's primary key, not just an identity column.

Using ISQL/w to Access a Database

You can issue commands to SQL Server through a utility called ISQL/w. With ISQL/w, you can not only run SQL queries, but can perform updates, deletions, and other actions on records. You can also use ISQL/w to perform sophisticated database and server management tasks such as creating database devices, databases, views, and stored procedures.

If you're familiar with the SQL syntax, getting started with ISQL/w is easy. (Mastering it, on the other hand, can be tricky—which is why many of the more complicated examples in this chapter rely on ISQL/w's graphical cousin, SQL Enterprise Manager.)

To issue commands to the database using ISQL/w, follow these steps:

1 Launch ISQL/w from the SQL Server 6.5 program group.

2 ISQL/w launches, displaying the Connect Server dialog box.

3 Choose the server you want to connect to, type in a username and password, and then click Connect.

4 The ISQL/w main window appears, as illustrated in Figure 5.12.

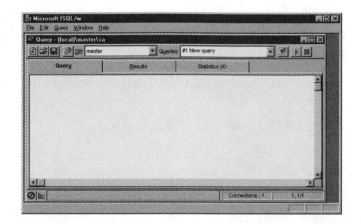

Figure 5.12
The main window of ISQL/w, which contains tabs for creating queries, returning results, and metering performance.

Once ISQL/w has launched, you can begin issuing commands to the database in SQL. To make sure this is working properly, though, it makes sense to test the connection to the database before attempting to do anything else. You can do this by accessing the pubs database that ships with SQL Server. To do this, follow these steps:

1 Tell SQL Server which database you want to use. To do this, execute the SQL USE command, followed by the name of the database you want to use. In ISQL/w's Query tab, type the following command:

```
USE pubs
```

Note: SQL commands can be entered in either uppercase or lowercase, but by convention, SQL keywords are entered in uppercase. This chapter follows that convention.

2 Execute the command by selecting Query, Execute, or by using Ctrl+E.

3 ISQL/w switches to the Results tab so you can view SQL Server's response. If everything worked properly, SQL Server responds with the terse message:

```
This command did not return data, and it did not return any
rows
```

4 Return to the Query window by clicking it (or by using the keystroke shortcut Alt+Y).

5 You should be able to see the previous command you issued to SQL Server. Clear the window by selecting Query, Clear Window (or by using the keystroke shortcut Ctrl+Shift+Delete).

Next, run a simple query against the pubs database to make sure it's returning data. To do this:

1 Type the following SQL code in the Query window:

```
SELECT *
FROM authors
```

2 Execute the query by pressing Ctrl+E.

3 If everything worked correctly, ISQL/w shows you the results of the query in the Query window, as illustrated in Figure 5.13.

Figure 5.13
Results of a test query against the pubs database as displayed in the ISQL/w window.

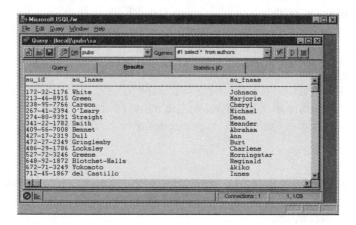

Viewing All the Objects in Your Database Using *sp_help*

SQL Server enables you to see all the objects available in any database. The system gives you this capability through a *stored procedure*—a bit of code stored and executed on the server.

sp_help is the stored procedure that enables you to browse databases. You execute sp_help the same way you execute any SQL query—entering it using ISQL/w's Query tab.

To get a road map to the objects in your database using sp_help, follow these steps:

1 Switch to the Query tab in ISQL/w; clear the query box using Ctrl+Shift+Delete if necessary.

2 In the query box, type the following:

```
sp_help
```

3 Execute the command. SQL Server responds by generating a listing of database objects similar to Figure 5.14.

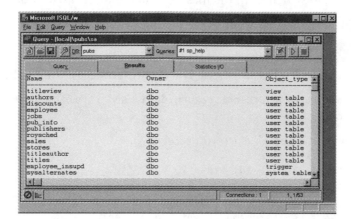

Figure 5.14
Typical response to an sp_help command for the pubs database.

Note: You can write your own stored procedures in SQL Server. For more information on this, see "Creating and Running Stored Procedures" later in this chapter. Also, while the stored procedures you create are usually local to an individual database, there are a number of other stored procedures provided by the system and available to every database in a SQL Server. For another example of such a system-provided stored procedure, see "Displaying the Text of an Existing View or Stored Procedure" later in this chapter.

Using an Existing Database

You can work with a particular database by executing the USE command in ISQL/w. When you designate a particular database with USE, all the subsequent SQL commands you issue are performed against that database. This is important to remember, because it's easy to inadvertently issue commands against the wrong database if you're not careful.

Note: Inadvertently issuing commands against the wrong database is one reason you should designate a database other than master to be your server's default database. (This is because only server configuration data should go into the master database.) You can change the default database at the time you create the database or anytime thereafter; the technique for accomplishing this is described in "Designating a Database Device as the Default" earlier in this chapter.

For example, to switch from the master database to the novelty database:

1 In ISQL/w's Query window, enter the following code:

```
use novelty
```

2 If the novelty database exists, SQL Server responds by issuing this message:

```
This command did not return data, and it did not return any
rows
```

3 If the database doesn't exist, you receive:

```
Msg 911, Level 16, State 2
Attempt to locate entry in Sysdatabases for database 'novelty'
by name failed - no entry found under that name.
Make sure that name is entered properly.
```

Remember, if you forget the name or spelling of a database, you can look it up in SQL Enterprise Manager or list the available databases using the `sp_help` stored procedure, as described earlier in this chapter.

Issuing SQL Commands to ISQL/w

You can execute any type of SQL command against a database by using ISQL/w. Using ISQL/w has a few advantages over other methods of sending commands to SQL Server. While it can be more difficult to remember SQL syntax than using SQL Enterprise Manager—particularly when using seldom-executed commands like creating databases—ISQL/w has the advantage of being interactive. The utility responds immediately to commands you issue. ISQL/w also has a number of features not offered by SQL Enterprise Manager, such as the capability to run queries and stored procedures.

Chapter 2 discusses the syntax of most basic SQL commands you're ever going to want to issue against a relational database. Most of this information is applicable to running queries and creating database structures in SQL Server as well.

Business Case 5.1: Writing a SQL Batch That Creates a Database

When a client/server database design is in development mode, it's common to write a SQL batch to create (and re-create) the database. Although writing a database batch to create your database design prevents you from taking advantage of the easier-to-use interface of SQL Enterprise Manager, it gives you a complete look at every command used to create every aspect of the database.

The stalwart developers of Jones Novelties, Incorporated have decided to take this approach to create the client/server version of their company database. The script they develop makes but a single assumption: that a database called novelty exists on the server.

The database schema that comprises the novelty database is illustrated in Figure 5.15.

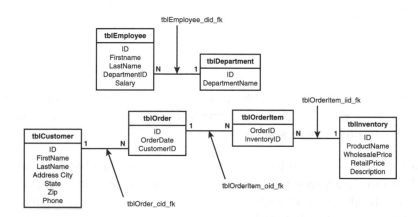

Figure 5.15
The schema of the Jones Novelties novelty database.

The batch that creates the database is executed in ISQL/w. In order to minimize bogus error messages, the batch destroys any old database objects each time it's run. This means that whenever you make a change in the design of the database in design mode, you can re-create the entire database from scratch by simply executing the entire batch again. This ensures that all the changes you've made in the database design get applied to the database each time you rebuild it.

The drawback of this technique, of course, is the fact that if you're not careful, the batch will wipe out all the tables in the database, and the data contained in the tables as well. So you may want to consider disabling or deleting such scripts from your system after you have put your database server into production. Alternatively, you can simply let the script check to see if a table already exists before deleting and re-creating it.

Note: While this section introduces the batch in chunks, the idea behind writing a SQL batch is to execute it as one big procedure. Accordingly, when you're writing batches in real life, dump the whole thing into the ISQL/w Query window (either by loading it from a text file or by copying and pasting) and hit the Execute button to run the batch. When you're developing SQL batches for use with ISQL/w, you can use that time-tested development environment known as Notepad to edit your batch. When you need to run it, copy it from Notepad and paste it into ISQL/w's Query window. Then hit Execute.

To begin, your batch should switch to the novelty database. You do this with the USE command. Because this command is executed as part of a batch, you use the go command after it to indicate that this command should be executed before anything else happens:

```
use novelty

go
```

Note: You can create the tables in a database other than novelty if you want. To do this, change the first line of code (the USE command) of the script described in this section.

Next, begin creating tables. Before you create a table in a batch, however, it's a good idea to see whether the table you're about to create already exists. This gives you the ability to minimize bogus error messages when you run and rerun your database-creating batch. You can check to see whether a table already exists by querying the sysobjects table using the SQL EXISTS statement. If the name of the table is returned in the query on the sysobjects table, the table exists in the database and should be dropped.

This batch checks to see if tblCustomer exists. If it exists, it checks to see whether it has a foreign key. If so, the batch destroys it:

```
if exists (select * from sysobjects
            where name = 'tblCustomer')
    begin
        if exists (select * from sysobjects
                    where name = 'tblOrder_cid_fk')
            begin
            alter table tblOrder
            drop constraint tblOrder_cid_fk
            end
```

```
    drop table tblCustomer
    end

go
```

> **Note:** You can turn the EXISTS test around to prevent your script from dropping a table that contains data. You typically do this in a production database where you don't want to inadvertently destroy a table that contains data. For a database that's in development mode, however, it's appropriate to drop the database unconditionally if it exists.

The code in this section of the batch checks for the foreign key definition tblOrder_cid_fk; the code attempts to destroy the foreign key constraint in another table, if it exists. This is done because referential integrity dictates that you can't destroy a table if a foreign key in another table refers to it.

Next, the batch actually creates the tblCustomer table:

```
create table tblCustomer
(
  ID             int identity,
    constraint tblCustomer_IDPK primary key (ID),
  FirstName      varchar(50)  not null,
  LastName       varchar(70)  not null,
  Address        varchar(100) null,
  City           varchar(50)  null,
  State          varchar(2)   null,
  Zip            varchar(9)   null,
  Phono          varchar(20)  null
)

print 'Creating tblCustomer.'

go
```

This code does a number of things in addition to simply creating the table. First, the batch declares the ID field as an identity column, meaning that it automatically generates a unique number for each record. Next, it declares the ID column as the table's primary key. This provides an index for queries on the ID column and insures that there will be no duplicate values in the column.

The FirstName and LastName columns are declared with the not null qualifier; this ensures that it is impossible to insert null values into these columns.

Finally, use a PRINT command to display a piece of text to the ISQL/w Results window. This gives a visible indication of the batch's progress. You can also use the printed output as a debugging tool that can help you determine where errors in your batch might be. Using the PRINT command is optional and has no direct bearing on the creation of the database.

Now that the first table has been created, create the other five tables in the database roughly the same way, using the code in Listing 5.1.

Listing 5.1   The Remainder of the SQL Batch That Creates the Tables in the Novelty Database

```
if exists (select * from sysobjects
          where name = 'tblEmployee')
   begin
   drop table tblEmployee
   end

go

create table tblEmployee
(
  ID            int identity,
    constraint tblEmployee_IDPK primary key (ID),
  FirstName     varchar(50) not null,
  LastName      varchar(70) not null,
  DepartmentID int          null,
  Salary        money        null
)

print 'Creating tblEmployee.'

go

if exists (select * from sysobjects
          where name = 'tblDepartment')
   begin
   if exists (select * from sysobjects
              where name = 'tblEmployee_did_fk')
       begin
       alter table tblEmployee
           drop constraint tblEmployee_did_fk
       end
   drop table tblDepartment
   end

go
```

```
create table tblDepartment
(
  ID              int identity,
     constraint   tblDepartment_IDPK primary key (ID),
  DepartmentName  varchar(75) not null
)

print 'Creating tblDepartment.'

go

if exists (select * from sysobjects
           where name = 'tblInventory')
    begin
    if exists (select * from sysobjects
              where name = 'tblOrderItem_iid_fk')
       begin
       alter table tblOrderItem
          drop constraint tblOrderItem_iid_fk
       end
    drop table tblInventory
    end

go

create table tblInventory
(
  ID              int identity,
     constraint   tblInventory_IDPK primary key (ID),
  ProductName     varchar(75) not null,
  WholesalePrice  money        null,
  RetailPrice     money        null,
  Description     text         null
)

print 'Creating tblInventory.'

go

if exists (select * from sysobjects
           where name = 'tblOrder')
    begin
    if exists (select * from sysobjects
              where name = 'tblOrderItem_oid_fk')
```

continues

Listing 5.1 The Remainder of the SQL Batch That Creates the Tables in the Novelty Database (Continued)

```
        begin
        alter table tblOrderItem
            drop constraint tblOrderItem_oid_fk
        end
    drop table tblOrder
    end

go

create table tblOrder
(
  ID            int identity,
    constraint tblOrder_IDPK primary key (ID),
  OrderDate     datetime  null,
  CustomerID    int       not null
)

print 'Creating tblOrder.'

go

if exists (select * from sysobjects
           where name = 'tblOrderItem')
drop table tblOrderItem

go

create table tblOrderItem
(
  OrderID       int not null,
  InventoryID   int not null
)

print 'Creating tblOrderItem.'

go
```

Now that the tables have been created, your batch creates four referential integrity constraints on the tables. You use the alter table command to do this, as shown in Listing 5.2.

Listing 5.2   Referential Integrity Constraints Among Tables in the Novelty Database

```
alter table tblEmployee add
    constraint tblEmployee_did_fk
    foreign key (DepartmentID)
    references tblDepartment (ID)

alter table tblOrder add
    constraint tblOrder_cid_fk
    foreign key (CustomerID)
    references tblCustomer (ID)

alter table tblOrderItem add
    constraint tblOrderItem_oid_fk
    foreign key (OrderID)
    references tblOrder (ID)

alter table tblOrderItem add
    constraint tblOrderItem_iid_fk
    foreign key (InventoryID)
    references tblInventory (ID)
```

Next, the batch creates a view that prevents unauthorized users from retrieving employees' salary information. The view accomplishes this by simply not returning the contents of the Salary column from the Employee table:

```
if exists (select * from sysobjects
            where name = 'qryEmployee')
drop view qryEmployee

go

create view qryEmployee
as
   select ID, FirstName, LastName, DepartmentID
   from tblEmployee

go

print 'Creating qryEmployee.'

go
```

Next, another view is created. This view simplifies the process of retrieving employees in situations where you want to retrieve both employees and department:

```
if exists (select * from sysobjects
           where name = 'qryEmployeeDepartment')
drop view qryEmployeeDepartment

go

create view qryEmployeeDepartment
as
  select e.ID, FirstName, LastName, DepartmentName
  from tblEmployee e, tblDepartment t
  where e.ID = t.ID

go

print 'Creating qryEmployeeDepartment.'

go
```

Next, the batch creates a view that enables you to access records in the tblCustomer table:

```
if exists (select * from sysobjects
           where name = 'qryCustomer')
drop view qryCustomer

go

create view qryCustomer
as
  select *
  from tblCustomer

go

print 'Creating qryCustomer.'

go
```

Finally, the batch populates the tblDepartment table with the names of the four departments in the Jones Novelties organization:

```
insert tblDepartment
  (DepartmentName)
values
  ("Administration")
```

```
go

insert tblDepartment
  (DepartmentName) ·
values
  ("Engineering")

go

insert tblDepartment
  (DepartmentName)
values
  ("Sales")

go

insert tblDepartment
  (DepartmentName)
values
  ("Marketing")

go
```

Remember, when you're using batches like this, feel free to run and rerun them whenever you want. The batch is written in such a way that it completely destroys and re-creates the database when it is executed. If you load sample data into your database during testing, you don't have to worry about that data inadvertently hanging around when you put your database into production mode. In addition, creating a database from a batch lets you easily migrate your database design to multiple servers. This enables you to have two physically distinct database servers, one for development, and another for production.

> **Code Example:** You can find the completed version of the script discussed in the previous business case in the `create-db.sql` text file, located in the directory `\vbdb\code\05-SQLServer`. For information on how to install the sample files on the CD that accompanies this book, see the section "Installing the Example Files" in the introduction at the beginning of this book.

Using Database Views to Control Access to Data

A *view* is a query definition stored in a database. It is conceptually similar to a query definition in the Microsoft Jet database engine, in the sense that it is a stored definition that resides in the database and gives client applications access to data.

You use views in situations where you want to give users access to data, but don't want to give them direct access to the underlying tables. The fact that a view looks exactly like a table to a client application gives you a number of advantages.

For example, when users access data through views rather than through direct access to tables

▶ You can change the table's design without having to change the views associated with it.

▶ You can restrict the number of rows or columns returned by the view.

▶ You can provide simple access to data retrieved from multiple tables through the use of joins contained in the view.

In order to take full advantage of views, you should have a security strategy for your database. This permits you to attach security permissions to views instead of tables, which makes it easier to grant and revoke permissions from different types of users. Security is discussed in the "Managing Users and Security in SQL Enterprise Manager" section later in this chapter.

Creating Views in SQL Enterprise Manager

As with many of the database objects you can create in SQL Server, you can create views in either ISQL/w or SQL Enterprise Manager. Both techniques are fundamentally similar; SQL Enterprise Manager's technique is slightly more graphical, while ISQL/w's technique is interactive, permitting you to test a view as soon as you create it.

To create a view in SQL Enterprise Manager, follow these steps:

1 From the Server Manager window, right-click the Views folder in the database you want to create a view.

2 Select New View from the pop-up menu.

3 The Manage Views window appears, as shown in Figure 5.16.

4 Replace the text <VIEW NAME> with the name of the view you want to create, such as qryEmployeeList.

Note: If you're accustomed to dealing with Microsoft Access query definitions, you might want to use Access's naming conventions (prefixing the name of a stored query that returns records with the letters "qry"). This makes it clearer to clients that what they're working with is a view rather than a table. Of course, you can use any naming convention you want, or none at all.

5 Enter the query statement shown in Listing 5.3 in the window.

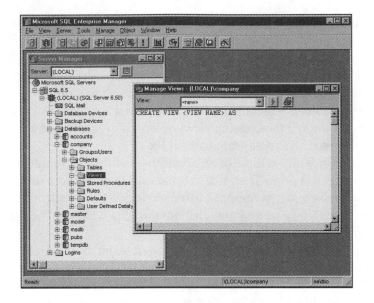

Figure 5.16
Creating a new view in SQL Enterprise Manager.

Listing 5.3   A Basic Select Query That Sorts by Two Fields

```
CREATE VIEW qryEmployeeList AS
  SELECT LastName + ', ' + FirstName AS Name, ID
  FROM tblEmployee
```

6 Click the Save button (the green arrow at the top of the Manage Views window). The view is saved into your database and the Manage Views form is cleared.

The appearance of the Save buttons in the Manage Views window and the other database object windows is different for your convenience—it isn't an inconsistency. The Manage Views window is set up to let you create a number of views in a rapid-fire fashion. When you're done with one view, you can start creating another one immediately. When you're done with the Manage Views dialog, close it by clicking on its close button in the upper-right corner of the window.

Using Views in a Production Application

A view is a construct that lets you have greater control over the retrieval of data in your SQL Server database. This control manifests itself in a number of ways.

By limiting the number of rows or columns retrieved by the view, you control the data a particular user can retrieve. This can enable you to do neat tricks, such as create selection criteria that are known only to the database designer or lock out users from particular subsets of your data based on their security permissions. You can do this because each object in the database—including tables, views, and stored procedures—can be associated with individual users or security groups. In a database that takes advantage of views and stored procedures, direct access to tables is generally limited to the database administrator; client applications are limited to accessing views or stored procedures that are, in turn, responsible for retrieving data from base tables.

A Hide column is an example of an application of this technique. If the Hide column of a record is set to True, that row is never returned to a user; it's filtered out by the view that is responsible for retrieving the data from the database. Client applications never know that anything has changed, because they're always issuing requests to the same view.

Accessing databases through views, rather than through direct access to tables, is an important component of any robust production SQL Server database installation. In addition to enabling you to limit the number of rows and columns retrieved, shielding your database tables with views gives you the capability to change things without breaking client applications.

This process of inoculating your database design from the change brought on by changing business rules can be taken a step further by introducing *middle-tier components*. Such components are philosophically similar to views and stored procedures in that they shield your database design from changes in your software application's mission, but they have advantages over views and procedures stored in SQL Server. Among these are the fact that they're easier to program, they return data in the form of objects instead of rows and columns, and they aren't tied to any one database management system or programming language. See Chapter 7 for more information on such middle-tier components.

Creating Views Using an ISQL/w Batch

You can create views using ISQL/w. The process for doing this is similar to creating views in SQL Enterprise Manager, but in ISQL/w you have the advantage of being able to test your view immediately by running it.

To create a query in ISQL/w, follow these steps:

1 Enter the code in Listing 5.4 in the ISQL/w query window. (This batch is written in such a way that it will create the view whether it currently exists or not.)

Listing 5.4   A SQL Batch That Creates and Selects Records from a SQL Server View

```
use novelty
go


drop view qryEmployee
go


create view qryEmployee as
    SELECT *
    FROM tblEmployee
go


SELECT * FROM qryEmployee
```

2 Either click the Execute Query button, or select the menu command Query Execute.

3 The view is created and executed.

In addition to being an example of how to create a view using ISQL/w, this code is another example of executing a batch in ISQL/w. You can see from the previous code example that the batch not only creates the view, but switches to the correct database and runs the view when it's done creating it. This confirms that the view is doing what you think it's supposed to be doing.

You create batches to simplify the process of creating database objects using ISQL/w; in most cases when you're creating database objects, you want to do more than one thing at once. Dropping a table, then creating a table, then populating it with sample data is a typical use for a SQL batch; checking to see if a user account exists, then creating that user account with a default password is another. There are many other uses.

Creating and Running Stored Procedures

While views give you a great deal of control over how data is retrieved from your SQL Server database, an even more powerful technique involves the use of *stored procedures*. A stored procedure is similar to a view, except that it gives you the capability to perform more complex operations on data.

For example, stored procedures let you do the following:

▶ Sort data

▶ Perform calculations on data

▶ Take or return parameters

▶ Return data in a way that is easy and more efficient to program from the client side

None of these features are available with traditional views.

While this section is by no means an exhaustive description of all the commands available to you in the world of stored-procedure programming, it should give you enough information on how stored procedures work, why they're useful, and how you can incorporate them into your applications built on SQL Server.

Creating Stored Procedures in SQL Enterprise Manager

You can create stored procedures in SQL Server's Enterprise Manager. To do this, follow these steps:

1 In SQL Enterprise Manager's Server Manager window, right-click the Stored Procedures folder under the database with which you're working.

2 From the pop-up menu, select Create Stored Procedure. The Manage Stored Procedures dialog appears.

3 Replace the text with the name of the procedure you want to create.

4 Write the text of the procedure, as illustrated in Figure 5.17.

Figure 5.17
Creating a stored procedure in SQL Enterprise Manager.

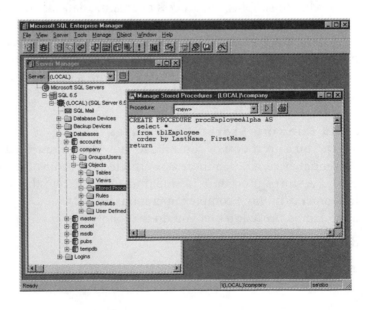

5 When you're done with the procedure, click the Save Object button at the top of the Manage Stored Procedures window. As in the Manage Views window, saving a stored procedure doesn't close the window; instead, it clears the window so you can enter another stored procedure.

6 When you're done with the Manage Stored Procedures window, click its close button in its upper-right corner.

Running a Stored Procedure from SQL Enterprise Manager

You can run stored procedures (as well as views and other SQL commands) from within SQL Enterprise Manager. This is helpful in situations where you want to test procedures or views you've created.

To test a stored procedure in SQL Enterprise Manager, follow these steps:

1 Select SQL Query Tool from SQL Enterprise Manager's Tools menu.

2 The Query window appears; it looks nearly identical to ISQL/w's command interface.

3 In the Query tab, type the name of the stored procedure you want to execute. For example, to execute the stored procedure you created in the last example, type the following:

```
procEmployeeAlpha
```

4 Execute the query by selecting the menu command Query Execute or by using the keystroke shortcut Ctrl+E.

5 The procedure executes and (if there is any data in the table) returns a result set.

When you're done with the SQL Enterprise Manager Query window, click its close button.

Creating Stored Procedures in ISQL/w

The steps to creating stored procedures in ISQL/w are nearly identical to the way you create them in SQL Enterprise Manager. The only difference is that ISQL/w doesn't set up the procedure's syntax the way SQL Enterprise Manager does.

To create a stored procedure in ISQL/w, you execute the `create proc` command. This command creates a procedure that returns data when given a numeric argument.

To do this, follow these steps:

1 In ISQL/w, enter the following code in the Query window:

```
create proc GetCustomerFromID
    @custID int
    as
    select * from tblCustomer
    where ID = @custID
```

This code creates a stored procedure called GetCustomerFromID. The procedure takes an argument, @custID, and returns a record for the customer that matches the @custID argument. (Because the ID field is tblCustomer's primary key, this procedure will always return either zero or one records.)

2 Execute the command. The stored procedure is created.

3 Return to the Query tab and test your stored procedure by running it. To run it, try to retrieve the first record in the table. Do this by typing the code:

```
GetCustomerFromID 1
```

SQL Server responds by returning the record for customer ID 1, as illustrated in Figure 5.18.

Figure 5.18
A single customer record returned by the stored procedure GetCustomerFromID in ISQL/w.

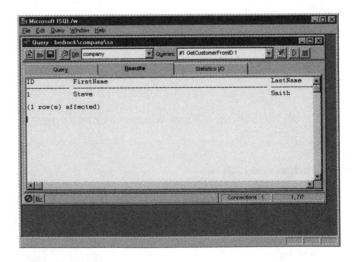

The procedure obviously only returns data if there is data in the table to retrieve.

> **Note:** Be sure you've created the stored procedure in the novelty database. It's easy to forget to switch to the correct database (using the USE command in ISQL/w) before issuing commands against it. Creating stored procedures in SQL Enterprise manager makes it harder to commit this error.

Displaying the Text of an Existing View or Stored Procedure

You can use the stored procedure sp_helptext to display the code for a view or stored procedure. In order to display this data, you issue the command sp_helptext, followed by the name of the database object you're interested in viewing. The SQL Server processor then returns the full text of the view or stored procedure.

For example, to see a code listing of the view qryEmployee you created in the previous section on views:

1 In ISQL/w's Query box, type this command:

```
sp_helptext qryEmployee
```

2 Execute the stored procedure by using the menu command Query Execute (or the keyboard shortcut Ctrl+E).

3 The query processor returns the code that defines the view, as illustrated in Figure 5.19.

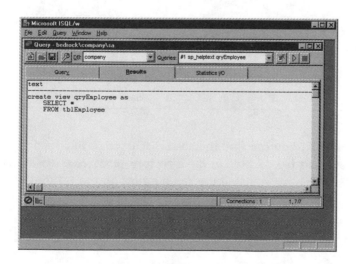

Figure 5.19
Displaying the text of a view using the stored procedure sp_helptext.

Creating Triggers

A *trigger* is a special type of stored procedure that's executed when data is accessed in a particular table. As a Visual Basic programmer, you can think of triggers almost as event procedures that execute when data is updated, deleted, or inserted into a table.

You generally use triggers when you need to do something complicated to your data in response to some kind of data access. For example, you might use a trigger to keep a log every time certain information in the database is changed, or you might use one to create a complicated default value for a field in a new record based on queries of one or more tables.

You shouldn't use triggers for simple defaults; instead, you should use rules. You shouldn't use them to maintain referential integrity; you should use SQL Server's inherent referential integrity constraint features for that. When you need to do something that goes beyond what's possible using SQL Server's feature set, you should consider using a trigger.

For example, you can use triggers to provide a unique value in a column to serve as a record's primary key; this tactic is used by Microsoft Access Upsizing Tools, which generates a random primary key for each record using a trigger. (You can also use identity columns for this purpose, as discussed later in this chapter.) An example of the code generated for such a trigger by the Upsizing Tools is shown in code Listing 5.5.

Listing 5.5   A Trigger That Provides a Random Value for the Primary Key of a Record at the Time the Record Is Created

```
CREATE TRIGGER tblCustomer_ITrig ON dbo.tblCustomer
FOR INSERT
AS
DECLARE @randc int, @newc int

SELECT @randc = (SELECT convert(int, rand() * power(2, 30)))
SELECT @newc = (SELECT ID FROM inserted)
UPDATE tblCustomer SET ID = @randc WHERE ID = @newc
```

Code Example: You can find the code discussed in this section in the `soundex.sql` text file, located in the directory `\vbdb\code\05-SQLServer`. For information on how to install the sample files on the CD that accompanies this book, see the section "Installing the Example Files" in the introduction at the beginning of this book.

Creating a random number to uniquely identify a record is by far the simplest technique for generating a primary key. This technique, however, suffers from two drawbacks. First, the primary keys are generated in no discernable order. This may seem like a cosmetic problem, but if you're trying to create an invoicing system, it's helpful to know that invoice 20010 follows invoice 20009.

The other, and potentially more serious problem, is the fact that there's no guarantee that the randomly generated primary key is actually going to be unique. This is because the trigger doesn't check to see if the random number it came up with has been used by some other record in the database. Granted, a random integer has a very small chance of being generated twice by the system (because a SQL Server integer data type is equivalent to a Visual Basic Long data type; that is, it is a four-bit whole number that can store values in the range of about negative 2.1 billion to about positive 2.1 billion).

Business Case 5.2: Creating a Trigger That Enables Soundalike Searches
In databases that involve queries on people's names, it can be difficult to deal with the problem of misspellings and homophones. Are you searching on Smith when the person spells it Smythe? Was it McManus or MacManus? If you have a last name that's the least bit unusual, you know what a problem this can be.

The intrepid database developers of Jones Novelties, Incorporated realize that they're going to run into this problem as well, so they decide to take advantage of a function of SQL Server to resolve this problem. This function, soundex(), converts a word into an alphanumeric value that represents its basic sounds. If you store the soundex value of a name at the time you create it, you can then search on the soundex value of the name in a query. The query returns more records, but it returns all the records that match the criterion.

Implementing this feature in the Jones Novelties company database requires several steps:

▶ Altering the tblCustomer table to accommodate a new LastNameSoundex field

▶ Running an update query to supply soundex values for existing records in the tblCustomer table

▶ Creation of a trigger that populates the LastNameSoundex field at the time the record is created or changed

▶ Creation of a stored procedure that returns all the customers whose last name sounds like a particular value

Begin by altering the tblCustomer table to accommodate a soundex value for each record in the database. Do this by issuing the following command to ISQL/w:

```
alter table tblCustomer add
   LastNameSoundex varchar(4) null
```

Next, run an update command that gives soundex values to records that are already in the database. You only have to do this once. Run the update by issuing the following SQL command to ISQL/w:

```
update tblCustomer
set LastNameSoundex = soundex(LastName)
go
select LastName, LastNameSoundex
from tblCustomer
go
```

Including the select statement in the batch after the update isn't necessary, but it's there if you want to confirm that the operation worked and see what data it changed.

Now you can create the trigger that will insert a soundex value for each customer as he's entered into the database. The code for this trigger should be entered in ISQL/w; it is listed in Listing 5.6.

Listing 5.6   An Insert/Update Trigger That Uses Soundex

```
create trigger trCustomerI
on tblCustomer
for insert, update
as
   update tblCustomer
   set tblCustomer.LastNameSoundex = soundex(tblCustomer.LastName)
   from inserted
   where tblCustomer.ID = inserted.ID
```

The reason this trigger seems a bit more complicated than it needs to be has to do with how triggers are executed. The rule with triggers is that they're executed once and only once, even if the insert, update, or delete that caused the trigger to execute is some kind of crazy batch process involving thousands of records. As a result of this rule, the triggers you write must be capable of handling a potentially unlimited number of records.

The key to handling the appropriate set of records in a trigger is to perform an update based on all the possible records that were changed by the procedure that caused the trigger to execute in the first place.

How does a trigger know what records were affected by this procedure? Triggers have access to this information through virtual tables called *inserted* and *deleted*. The inserted virtual table contains the record(s) that are inserted (or updated) by the procedure that launched the trigger; the deleted virtual table contains the data that is deleted by the procedure that launched a delete trigger.

Because the trigger you're building in this example is both an insert and an update trigger, referencing the records in the inserted virtual table sufficiently covers all the inserted or updated records, no matter how they were inserted or updated. Every record is assured to have a soundex value generated for it by the trigger.

Now that you have a bulletproof trigger that creates a soundex value for any record in your tblCustomer table, test it by inserting a record that fools a conventional query. Assuming you have a number of people named Smith in your database, the following insert command should suffice:

```
insert into tblCustomer (FirstName, LastName)
  values ('Abigail', 'Smythe')
```

You can confirm that the trigger created a soundex value for this record by immediately querying it back from the database:

```
select LastNameSoundex, LastName
from tblCustomer
where LastName = 'Smythe'
```

Now that you've confirmed that your trigger works, you can create a stored procedure that takes advantage of the LastNameSoundex column. This procedure takes a parameter—the last name of the person you're looking for—and returns all the people in the tblCustomer table whose names sound like the name for which you're looking. The code to create the stored procedure is in Listing 5.7.

Listing 5.7. Code to Create the *LastNameLookup* Stored Procedure

```
create proc LastNameLookup
  @name varchar(40)
as
select * from tblCustomer
where soundex(@name) = LastNameSoundex
```

Finally, you're ready to retrieve records from the database based on their soundex values. To do this, execute the LastNameLookup stored procedure:

```
LastNameLookup 'smith'
```

After executing this procedure, ISQL/w returns a result set composed of every person whose last name is similar to Smith in the database, including Abigail Smythe, as shown in Figure 5.20.

Figure 5.20
Resultset returned by the LastNameLookup stored procedure.

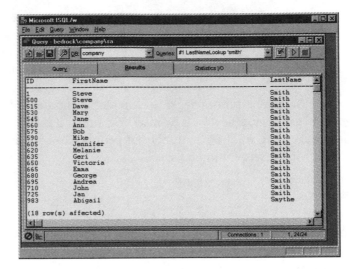

Managing Users and Security in SQL Enterprise Manager

One of the most important reasons you use SQL Server is to manage multiple users attempting to access the same data at the same time. Although a number of problems arise from this situation (such as users accessing privileged information and two users attempting to update the same record at the same time), you can resolve many of these problems with server-side settings.

Through its security features, SQL Server gives you a great deal of flexibility in determining who gets access to data.

Each database can have its own set of users, and each user can have his or her own set of permissions. A permission set gives users the capability to access and change data and (if you choose) potentially create and destroy database objects themselves.

SQL Server's security also enables you to put individual users into groups to more easily facilitate the assignment of permissions. For example, you may choose to create a developers group that has permission to access all the objects in the database, a managers group that has the capability to access sensitive information such as salary and sales information about the company, and a users group for normal users without extraordinary permissions in the database. How you divide users into groups is up to you, but you should use groups even in a simple database in order to make it easier to manage access.

Note: Another important multiuser issue pertains to locking, the process whereby no two users may access the same data in a table at the same time. For information on how locking works, see Chapter 9.

Managing Groups Using SQL Enterprise Manager

You can create groups in SQL Enterprise Manager, then assign permissions to the groups you create. After you create groups, you have the capability to add users to the group; any user added to a group inherits the permissions of that group. And changing the permissions of a group changes the permissions of all the users assigned to that group. That way, in order to add or revoke a large number of permissions for a particular user, you simply change which groups the user belongs to.

To create a group in SQL Enterprise Manager, follow these steps:

1 In SQL Enterprise Manager's Server Manager window, right-click the Groups/Users folder for the database you want to alter.

2 From the pop-up menu, select New Group. The Manage Groups dialog appears.

3 In the Group box, type the name of the new group. The group we'll create here will be a group for ordinary users, so type the name users, then click Add.

4 The new group is added to your database. Close the Manage Groups dialog by clicking its Close button.

5 In the Server Manager window, you should be able to see your new group, as shown in Figure 5.21.

Now that you've created a group, you need to assign permissions to it. To do this, follow these steps:

1 In the Server Manager window, right-click the group you want to assign permissions to.

2 From the pop-up menu, choose Permissions. The Object Permissions dialog appears, as shown in Figure 5.22.

Figure 5.21
A new group in the Server Manager window of SQL Enterprise Manager.

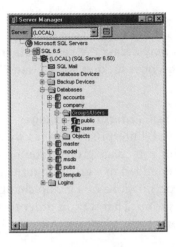

Figure 5.22
Using SQL Enterprise Manager's Object Permissions dialog box to assign permissions to a group.

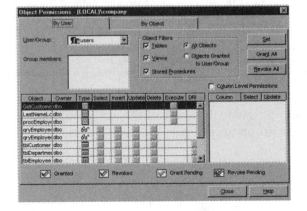

You'll recall from our discussion of views and stored procedures earlier in this chapter that it's a bad idea to give users direct access to tables. Accordingly, you'll use the Object Permissions dialog box to revoke all permissions for the table objects in the database from members of the users group. To do this, follow these steps:

1 Scroll down the list of objects in the novelty database until you get to the table objects.

2 Click twice on each column (select, insert, update, and delete) for the six table objects (Customer, Department, Employee, Inventory, Order, and OrderItem) in the database. Clicking the permission column once grants the permission; clicking it a second time revokes the permission. (Although the permission is currently "pending," it isn't officially revoked until you click the Set button.)

3 Grant select, insert, update, and delete permissions to all the views in the database.

4 Grant execute permissions to the stored procedures in the database.

5 Click the Set button to execute your permission changes.

6 The permission changes are executed. The Object Permissions dialog box should look like Figure 5.23.

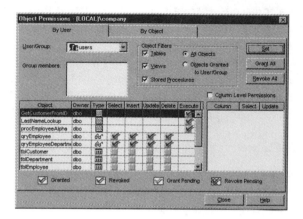

Figure 5.23
The Object Permissions dialog box after you've secured the database.

7 When you're done with the Object Permissions dialog box, click its close button.

There are currently no users in the users group, so the permissions you've just applied don't mean anything yet. You'll create users and add them to the user group in the next section.

Creating and Maintaining Logins and Users

In order to have a security system that is robust and flexible, it's important to give users their own identities. SQL Server gives you this ability by letting you designate logins and users.

A *login* represents an individual human being who has access to your SQL Server.

You use logins to create *users*. Creating a user permits you to give a login specific permissions for a particular database. You can also add users to groups, in order to give them a broad group of permissions all at once.

If the difference between a login and a user doesn't make sense to you, think about it this way: a login is created at the server level. A user is created at the database level. You must have a login before you can become a user of a particular database.

Note: This chapter covers what SQL Server refers to as standard security; that is, security that is managed by SQL Server as opposed to the operating system. Standard security has the advantage of working in all types of SQL Server installations, and it is the default security mode for SQL Server. However, if your users utilize Windows NT, you have the option of using integrated security, in which users and groups are managed by Windows NT rather than SQL Server. This has the advantage of only requiring users to log on once—when they first turn their computers on each day. This type of security can also be easier to administer because it gives you a single place to manage everything having to do with users and groups.

You can use a utility called SQL Security Manager to make it easy to map Windows NT users and SQL Server users using integrated security. For more information on integrated security, see Chapter 8, "Security Concepts," in SQL Server Administrator Companion.

To begin creating a user, create a login for an individual:

1 In SQL Enterprise Manager, right-click the Logins folder at the very bottom of the Server Manager window. (Logins don't belong to any individual database; instead, they belong to the server itself.)

2 Select New Login from the pop-up menu.

3 The Manage Logins dialog box appears.

4 In the Login Name box, type the name the person will use to log in. Optionally, enter a password and select a default language.

Note: In the client applications you build, consider establishing a procedure whereby a person can establish and change his or her password. You can implement this through the use of the `sp_password` stored procedure.

5 You can add this login as a user to a particular database at this time. To do this, click in the Permit column of the Database Access grid at the bottom of the Manage Logins dialog box. The user is given permission to access the database in the public group, as shown in Figure 5.24.

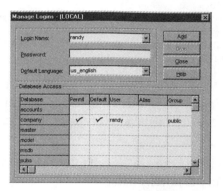

Figure 5.24
Creating a new login and adding user access to a database.

6 To add this user to a particular group other than public, select the group from the drop-down list in the Group column.

7 Click Add when you're done assigning this login to users in databases. The login is created, and any users you created for the login are added to the appropriate database. This is displayed immediately in SQL Enterprise Manager's Server Manager window, as shown in Figure 5.25.

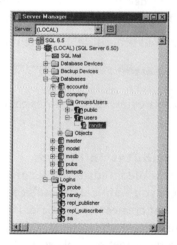

Figure 5.25
A new login and a new user displayed in the Server Manager window.

Testing Security Features in ISQL/w

You might be curious to see what happens when a "civilian" user attempts to use database objects for which he or she doesn't have permissions. Because ISQL/w lets you log in as any user, you can test how this works in the Query dialog of ISQL/w:

1 Log out of ISQL/w by choosing the menu command File Disconnect.

2 Use the menu command File Connect to log back in to SQL Server through ISQL/w. This time, rather than logging in as sa, log in as the user you created in the previous demonstration.

Rather than starting in the master database as you do when you logged in as sa, you're in the novelty database (or to whatever database your login defaults).

3 Execute the stored procedure sp_help. ISQL/w gives you a list of all the database objects in the novelty database.

4 Now try to run a query on a table you don't have permission to access. Execute the following query:

```
select *
from tblCustomer
```

SQL Server responds with this message:

```
Msg 229, Level 14, State 1
SELECT permission denied on object tblCustomer,
database company, owner dbo
```

5 Now try executing a stored procedure. Execute the following procedure:

```
LastNameLookup 'smith'
```

SQL Server responds by retrieving all the names that sound like Smith in the tblCustomer table.

Applying Security Attributes in ISQL/w

You can perform operations related to database security in ISQL/w. You generally do this in situations where you want a database's security features to be created by the same SQL batch that creates the database. If you always append the commands pertaining to security to the same SQL batch that creates the database object, it's less likely you'll forget to apply security features to new database objects you create.

Create a login in ISQL/w using the sp_addlogin stored procedure. For example, to create a login for the user randy (as you did in SQL Enterprise Manager in the previous example), you execute the following command:

```
sp_addlogin randy
```

To give the login randy the password "prince," add the password as an additional argument to the sp_addlogin procedure:

```
sp_addlogin randy, prince
```

To make the login randy a user of the novelty database, use the sp_adduser procedure:

```
use company
go
sp_adduser randy
go
```

To show a list of all the logins in your SQL Server installation in ISQL/w, use the SQL command:

```
use master
go
select suid, name
from syslogins
```

To create a group, you use the sp_addgroup stored procedure:

```
sp_addgroup users
```

You can display a list of all the groups in the database using the stored procedure sp_helpgroup.

You apply and remove permissions for a particular database object using the SQL grant and revoke commands. The grant command permits a user or group to have access to a database object, while the revoke command removes a permission.

For example, to grant members of the users group complete access to the tblCustomer table, use the following SQL command:

```
grant all
on tblCustomer
to users
```

To restrict members of the users group to the ability to select data from the tblCustomer table, qualify the grant command with the select option:

```
grant select
on tblCustomer
to users
```

To revoke permissions on a database object, use the revoke command. For example, to revoke permission to access tblCustomer table from members of the users group, use the SQL command:

```
revoke all
on tblCustomer
to users
```

You can grant or revoke permissions for update, select, delete, and insert on tables and views. You can grant or revoke permissions to execute stored procedures.

Determining Who Is Logged In with *sp_who*

You have the capability to determine which users are logged into a database at any time by using stored procedure sp_who. This procedure returns information on the users who are logged into the system as well as what database they're working in.

To use sp_who, execute it in ISQL/w's Query window. ISQL/w returns a list of current users, as shown in Figure 5.26.

Figure 5.26
Results of running the sp_who *stored procedure.*

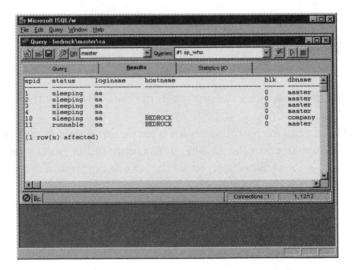

Viewing a list of currently logged-in users gives you the ability to do a number of things, such as terminate user sessions from the server, as described in the next section.

Ending a Process with the *kill* Command

In SQL Server, the system administrator has the ability to kill a process—such as a user session or a database lock—with the kill command. You generally do this in a situation where a user's session terminated abnormally and you want to get rid of his *hung* session, or when a client procedure has initiated a lock on a piece of data and won't let go. (These situations are rare, but they do happen, particularly in development.)

To use the kill command, you must first run the `sp_who` stored procedure (if you're trying to kill a user session) or the `sp_lock` procedure (if you're trying to kill a database lock). Both procedures return a column called spid, the procedure ID of the process. After you know the spid, you can kill the process by using the `kill` command.

For example, say you run `sp_who` and notice that there's a hung session from a user who you know for certain won the lottery three weeks ago and won't be returning to work. Notice that the bogus session's spid is 10. To kill spid 10, you issue the following command in ISQL/w.

```
kill 10
```

The bogus session is immediately killed.

Note: It's a good idea to run `sp_who` periodically, particularly during development, just to see what's going on in your database.

Removing Objects from the Database

The SQL Server term for removing an object from the database is to *drop* the object. When you drop an object from the database, it is deleted permanently. For tables that contain data, the structure and the data are deleted permanently.

To drop a database object—a table, for example—in SQL Enterprise Manager, simply right-click it. In the pop-up menu, select Delete. The object is deleted.

To drop a database object in ISQL/w, use the drop command. For example, to drop the tblCustomer table, use this command:

```
drop table tblCustomer
```

Migrating from Microsoft Access to SQL Server

If you're a psychic software developer, you'll always have a good idea of how big your database application needs to be, how many users it needs to support, and what kind of performance it needs to provide. If you're like most people, you need a way out when confronted with a situation in which your database needs to grow outside of the window box you planted it in.

For many Visual Basic developers, this means scaling a database application from a Microsoft Access/Jet-style database into SQL Server. Microsoft recognized early on that developers would have a need to do this, so it provided a wizard known as Microsoft Access Upsizing Tools. Microsoft has diligently upgraded the upsizing tools for each version of Access as new versions are released.

Because the tools are written as a Microsoft Access add-in, the Upsizing Tools aren't available to you if you're using straight Visual Basic. In this section, it's assumed that if you have Visual Basic and SQL Server, you'll likely also have Microsoft Access. (If you don't have Access, you should get a copy; it's a great tool for bridging the gap between VB and SQL Server.) Whether you have Access or not, the following sections give you some ideas for easing the transition from Jet to SQL Server.

Using Microsoft Access Upsizing Tools

To use the Microsoft Access Upsizing Tools to move your Access database to SQL Server, you must first download and install the tools. You can obtain the Microsoft Access Upsizing Tools for Access 97 as a free download from Microsoft. The tools are at

`http://www.microsoft.com/AccessDev/ProdInfo/Exe/AUT97.EXE.`

After you've downloaded and installed the add-in, you can launch it from Microsoft Access. Perform the following steps to run the Upsizing Tools:

1 First make sure that a database for storing the exported data exists on the SQL Server.

2 Make sure that the SQL Server database has a valid ODBC data source associated with it. (If you don't choose to create an ODBC data source at this time, you can create one using the Upsizing Tools.)

3 Select Add-Ins from Microsoft Access' Tools menu. Select Upsize to SQL-Server from the submenu.

4 The Upsizing Wizard launches, giving you the choice of creating a new database or migrating the current database to SQL Server. Choose Use Existing Database; then click Next.

5 The ODBC Select Data Source dialog box appears. Select the ODBC Data Source that corresponds to your SQL Server database; then click OK.

6 If your ODBC Data Source requires that you log in, you see the SQL Server Login dialog box. Log in; then click OK.

7 The Upsizing Wizard displays a list of the tables in your local Access database. Double-click each table you want to export to SQL Server. Click Next when you're done.

8 The next step allows you to choose a number of options that control how your data is exported to SQL Server. These options include the following:

▶ Which elements of the table, besides the field structure, you want to export to SQL Server. This includes indexes, validation rules, default values, and relationships.

▶ Whether the exporter should create a timestamp field in your exported table. (Timestamp fields let you keep multiple generations of data in the same table; to retrieve the most recent generation of data, you retrieve the one with the most recent timestamp. Timestamp fields also give you an audit trail that lets you know when a record was last changed.)

▶ Whether the exporter should export the entire table, including its data, or merely its structure.

▶ Whether the exported table should be linked back to your Access database.

9 Choose the option you want; then click Next.

10 In the final step, decide whether you want the Upsizing Wizard to create a report explaining what it did. You should always do this. Check the box, then click Finish.

11 The table is exported to SQL Server. The Upsizing Wizard report appears, giving you a summary of what the Upsizing Wizard did. (Because it isn't automatically saved in your Access database, you should print this report.)

You should be aware that there are certain situations in which the Upsizing Wizard won't be able to convert your table to a structure that SQL Server likes. It creates fields you might not want in your table and gags on OLE Object fields. Additionally, it doesn't export AutoNumber fields the way you might expect; instead, it tries to create a trigger that generates a random value in the field, which might not be what you'd expect.

The Upsizing Wizard is fine when you want a quick way to send data to SQL Server from Access, but you shouldn't have to rely on it (and suffer under its limitations) as long as you have a handle on the SQL Server topics presented in this chapter.

Exporting Data from Access to SQL Server Using Linked Tables

If you prefer to have more control over how data is moved from your Microsoft Access tables to SQL Server, you have the option of linking SQL Server tables into your Access database, then exporting data to the SQL Server tables by using an append query in Access.

You need to perform this activity in Microsoft Access because Access uses the Jet database engine, which is singularly adept at integrating data from disparate database engines. Because this technique assumes that you've already created tables on a SQL Server database, it's more time-consuming than using the Access Upsizing Tools. However, because you have complete control over the table design, you can bypass some of the questionable decisions made by the Upsizing Tools, such as converting AutoNumber fields to a field populated with a random number (rather than a column designated as an identity column).

> **Note:** In order for this technique to work, you need to have a handle on how to create an ODBC data source, because Access connects to SQL Server through ODBC.

Transferring data from Access to SQL Server involves three steps:

1 Creating tables on a SQL Server database to store your Access data

2 Linking those SQL Server tables to your Access database

3 Running an append query to transfer the data from Access to SQL Server

The first step in this technique is described in the section "Creating Tables in a SQL Server Database," earlier in this chapter. The second and third steps are described in the following sections.

Linking SQL Server Tables to Microsoft Access

One of the easiest ways to transfer data from Access to SQL Server (or to simply use SQL Server data in an Access applications) is through the use of *linked tables.* Linked tables are a Microsoft Access feature that enables you to use and browse data from an ODBC database (such as SQL Server) as if the table were stored locally in the Access database.

Perform the following steps to transfer data in a particular table from Access to SQL Server using this technique:

1 In Microsoft Access 97, open the database from which you want to export data.

2 Select Get External Data from the File menu. Select Link Tables from the submenu.

3 The link dialog box appears, as shown in Figure 5.27.

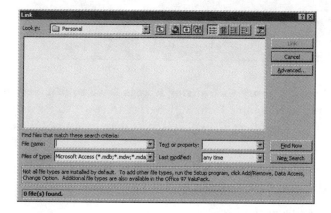

4 Select ODBC Databases in the Files of Type combo box.

5 The ODBC Select Data Source dialog box appears. Select the data source for your SQL Server database; then click OK.

6 The SQL Server Login dialog box appears. Log in to SQL Server with your username and password; then click OK.

7 The Link Tables dialog box appears. Select the table (or tables—the dialog box accepts multiple selections) you want to link to; then click OK.

8 The SQL Server table you've linked to appears in the Database window, as shown in Figure 5.28.

Figure 5.28
A SQL Server table linked into Microsoft Access.

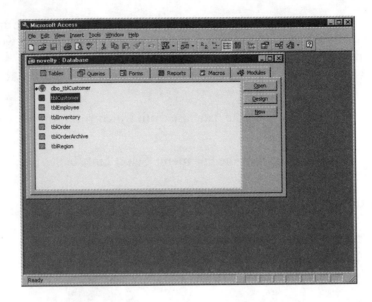

Creating an Append Query to Transfer Access Data to SQL Server

Now that you've linked a table from SQL Server to your Access database, you can construct an action query to export Access data to your SQL Server database:

1 In Microsoft Access' database window, click the local (not linked) version of your database table to select it.

2 Select Query from the Insert menu.

3 Choose Design View from the New Query dialog box; then click OK.

4 A new query definition window appears. Your local table should appear at the top of the window.

5 Select Append Query from the Query menu. This changes the query you're creating from a select query to an append query.

6 The Append dialog box appears. In the Table Name combo box, select dbo_tblCustomer (or whatever you named your linked SQL Server table). Leave the Current Database button highlighted. (Although the tables are stored in another database, since they're linked, they're treated as if they exist in the current database for the purposes of this query.)

7 Click OK.

8 In the Field row of the query design grid, select all the fields you want to export to the SQL Server database.

9 Select the menu command Query, Run. Access tells you how many records will be copied from the Access table to the SQL Server table. Click OK.

10 The append query executes, and data is copied into the SQL Server table.

Problems Exporting Null Data to SQL Server with Access Append Queries

Access 97 has difficulty communicating the concept of a null value to SQL Server in an append query. This is probably a limitation specific to Access 97, because this same thing has been successfully accomplished in previous versions of Access. This section includes a description of some of the problems as well as a workaround.

In a situation where you are attempting to export data to SQL Server through a Microsoft Access append query (as described in the previous section), when Access attempts to send a field that contains null data to SQL Server, you may get an error message that says, "You tried to assign a null value to a variable that isn't a Variant data type."

The workaround for this is to change the query so any field that might contain a null value is treated explicitly as a string value. The way to do this is to concatenate the contents of the field to empty strings.

So, in the Field row of the query grid in Access, instead of denoting the field name Address, use the following expression:

```
Address & ""
```

Access will prepend an expression label to the left of this expression when you enter it into the grid, which you can then ignore.

Never generate a null value when expressing fields this way; always pass an empty string. The even more perplexing and fascinating thing about this shortcoming in Access 97 is the fact that SQL Server does not make this distinction between an empty string and a null value; when you pass SQL Server an empty string, it stores it as a null.

An example of a Microsoft Access append query that has been modified to be "null safe" is shown in Figure 5.29.

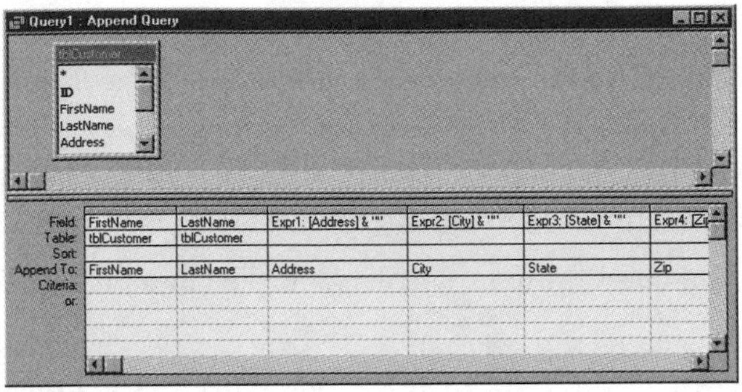

Figure 5.29
An append query that has been converted to be "null safe."

Exporting AutoNumber Fields to Identity Columns

One tricky thing about the process of exporting data from Microsoft Access is the fact that there's no easy way to export an Access AutoNumber field to a SQL Server identity column. However, you can hot-wire a SQL Server identity column so that it will accept any value. This allows you to insert rows into a table with an identity column set to a specific value you choose.

You do this by using the option in a SQL Server insert command. This option, which can be set to on or off, determines whether you're allowed to specify the value in a table's identity column. This value is set to off by default; you should only turn it on in a transaction specifically involving setting a value in an identity column.

For example, the SQL code to perform an insert involving an identity column in the tblCustomer table is shown in Listing 5.8.

Listing 5.8   Inserting a Value into an Identity Column Using the *identity_insert* Setting

```
set identity_insert tblCustomer on

insert tblCustomer (ID, FirstName, LastName)
      values (60559, "Mikki", "Halpin")

set identity_insert tblCustomer off

go
```

This batch inserts a record into the tblCustomer table with a customer ID of 60559.

Note: Overriding an identity column this way resets the identity column's internal counter. For example, after you've run the command in Listing 5.8, the next record you insert into the Customer table (assuming you don't override the counter again) has an ID of 60560.

SUMMARY

This chapter gives you the basics to get started doing client/server applications using Microsoft SQL Server.

You should bear in mind that although this chapter focuses on how to configure SQL Server, the sections in this book pertaining to client/server programming are applicable to any client/server system—Oracle, Sybase, Informix, whatever. As long as there is an ODBC driver or an OLE DB provider that can get to your back-end data, you should be able to get to the server from Visual Basic.

Chapter 6 is one way to program such servers, but as I mentioned at the beginning of this chapter, you probably only want to use it if you have an existing RDO code base. For information on how to program client/server databases using the latest techniques and technologies, see Chapter 10.

QUESTIONS AND ANSWERS

Q. **I've always been petrified to fool around with SQL Server. It always seemed like a black art to me. I once knew a guy whose brain exploded after doing a week of constant server-side programming. Will the topics covered in this chapter enable me to create serious database applications using SQL Server and keep my brain from exploding?**

A. Yes and no. This chapter wasn't designed to cover hard-core, day-to-day database administration, performance tweaking, or anything like that, and it's definitely not designed to be a comprehensive guide to SQL Server, just an introduction. The summary of getting started with SQL Server provided for you in the first half of this chapter was designed specifically so you can feel comfortable with the SQL Server. Migrating from the single-user and small-workgroup computing world up to client/server isn't trivial, but it shouldn't be a black art, either. That fear is what this chapter is designed to dispel. (As for your brain exploding, that's between you and your psychiatrist.)

Open Database Connectivity and Remote Data Objects

CONFIGURING AND USING OPEN DATABASE
   CONNECTIVITY (ODBC)

ACCESSING DATA USING THE REMOTE DATA
   CONTROL

USING REMOTE DATA OBJECTS IN CODE

WRITING YOUR OWN DATABASE OBJECT
   SERVER

Visual Basic 6.0 marks a radical change in client/server strategy. All of the new tools, technologies, and features related to databases point to ActiveX Data Objects—some don't even work with anything but ADO. ADO, covered in Chapter 10, "ActiveX Data Objects," provides an object model for database access that works well whether you're working with "desktop" or client/server databases; it also promises to give access to nonrelational data sources. But ADO wasn't the first object model used by VB developers to get access to client/server databases. In the beginning, there was Remote Data Objects, or RDO.

RDO was first included with Visual Basic 4.0. It was a lightweight object wrapper around the Open Database Connectivity (ODBC) API, designed to provide VB developers the client/server functionality they'd been asking for in an easy-to-program package similar to the popular DAO library. It succeeded, although the object library didn't come into its own until RDO 2.0, which was bundled with Visual Basic 5.0 and added a number of bug fixes and performance enhancements. In the VB5 era, RDO 2.0 was considered to be the most advanced, most efficient object model for client/server database access.

But RDO's fifteen minutes of fame are definitely over in VB6. There aren't many compelling reasons to use RDO now that ADO has asserted itself as the 800-pound gorilla of the database object library world. If you're starting a new client/server project, you'll want to use ADO—skip this chapter and go right to Chapter 10. (The first topic in this chapter, "Configuring and Using Open Database Connectivity," may still be useful to you even if you're going straight to ADO.) But if you're working on a project that hasn't migrated off of RDO yet, if you need to maintain an existing RDO code base, or if you want to migrate an RDO-based project to ADO, read on.

Also bear in mind that nearly all the techniques described in this chapter are exclusively for use with the Enterprise Edition of Visual Basic. The one exception to this is the ODBCDirect technique for database access. ODBCDirect is specifically designed for developers who don't have the Enterprise Edition of VB, or who are creating solutions in non-VB development environments (such as Microsoft Office VBA). This technique is covered in the section "Configuring and Using Open Database Connectivity (ODBC)" in this chapter.

Note: Nothing about RDO changed in Visual Basic 6.0. Programming RDO is exactly the same as it was in VB5.

CONFIGURING AND USING OPEN DATABASE CONNECTIVITY (ODBC)

In order to start programming with RDO, you'll need to have an understanding of Open Database Connectivity. ODBC is a Windows technology that lets a database client application connect to a remote database. Residing on client-side computers, ODBC seeks to make every relational data source generic from the viewpoint of the client application. This means that your application doesn't need to know about what specific type of database it's connecting to, giving you the ability to write client applications against one standardized version of SQL.

Note: Because it's a client-side technology, ODBC doesn't require that you do anything to your database server.

ODBC is composed of three parts:

▶ A driver manager

▶ One or more drivers

▶ One or more data sources

The architecture of ODBC is illustrated in Figure 6.1.

Figure 6.1
ODBC architecture showing the connection between the client application and the server database through the ODBC Driver Manager.

> **Note:** ODBC data sources created for use with RDO can be used as-is with ADO—in fact, ODBC is ADO's native provider, which makes migration from RDO fairly straightforward. For more information, see Chapter 10.

CREATING AN ODBC DATA SOURCE

In order for a client application to connect to a client/server database using ODBC, you must first supply information about an ODBC data source on the client. Every server requires a different package of information in order to connect a client. ODBC lets you give this information a single name so you can make reference to it, rather than constructing the package of information from scratch each time you need it. This gives client applications the capability to easily refer to a combination of a driver, a database, and optionally a username and password. This name is a *data source name,* or DSN.

> **Note:** The examples in this section were created with Version 3.51 of the ODBC Driver Manager and Version 3.6 of the SQL Server driver. If you're using an older version of ODBC, you might notice some cosmetic differences in the dialog boxes provided by the driver manager, as well as some features missing. Most notably, the ability to test a connection within the driver manager (described later in this section) isn't present in older versions of ODBC. You can download the latest version of the ODBC driver manager as part of Microsoft Data Access Components (MDAC), located at `http://www.microsoft.com/data/`.

To create an ODBC data source name on the client, follow these steps:

1. Make sure you have a SQL Server database up and running, and make sure it's accessible from the client computer. This ensures that you've ruled out any non–ODBC-related problems having to do with network connectivity, security, and so forth.

2. Launch Control Panel from your computer's Start menu.

3. From Control Panel, launch the ODBC control panel applet. The ODBC Data Source Administrator dialog box appears, as shown in Figure 6.2.

Figure 6.2
The ODBC Data Source Administrator dialog box.

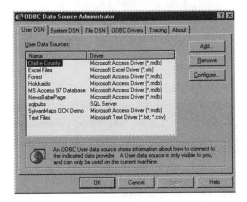

(The exact list of data sources that appear when you launch the ODBC applet will vary from one computer to the next.) At this point, you can create one of three types of ODBC data source names:

▶ A *user DSN*, which is usable only by you and only on the machine you're currently using.

▶ A *system DSN*, which anyone using your machine can use. Additionally, this is the kind of data source you need to create if you're setting up a Web database application (for more information on this, see Chapter 11, "Internet Database Applications.").

▶ A *file DSN*, which can be easily copied and used by other computers.

Because system DSNs are a bit easier to manage for some of the examples you run though later, create one of those now. To do this, follow these steps:

1. If it isn't selected already, click the System DSN tab in the ODBC Data Source Administrator window.

2. Click the Add button.

3. The Create New Data Source dialog box appears. Click the name of the database driver (in this case, SQL Server) you want to use.

4. Click Finish. The Create a New Data Source to SQL Server wizard appears.

5. In the Name box, enter the name of your data source. This name can be (essentially) anything you want. Because this is the name you use to refer to your database in your client applications, make it something memorable and consistent. Using the name of the database (Novelty) as the name of the DSN isn't a bad idea.

6. Filling in the Description box is optional. This gives you the ability to supply additional information pertaining to the ODBC data source name. This information is for your benefit only—it only shows up in the ODBC control panel, and serves to document the data source name.

7. In the Server combo box, choose the SQL Server upon which your database resides.

If your computer is connected to the SQL Server, the server's name should appear in the drop-down list. If you're working on the same computer on which your SQL Server resides, you can use the old reliable (local) to stand in for the name of your server.

8. Click Next. The next screen of the wizard appears, asking you how you want to log in to your server. You can either choose SQL Server authentication, in which your user ID must be explicitly created on the server (using the technique described in Chapter 5, "Getting Started with SQL Server,"), or Windows NT authentication, in which your network login is used as your database user ID. If you set up the database using the steps described in Chapter 5, you can use SQL Server authentication. Select this option, then enter your username and password in the boxes and click Next.

Note: If you're uncomfortable inserting your password into the ODBC data source name, you needn't supply it here. You have the option of supplying your password to the ODBC driver in your application, at the time you open a connection to the database. This prevents a potential security issue, since any information you supply as part of an ODBC DSN is stored in your computer's registry.

9. The next screen of the wizard appears. Click the "Change the default database to" check box, then select the Novelty database from the combo box. Although this step is technically optional, you should generally always associate a database name with an ODBC data source name. Your screen should look like Figure 6.3.

Figure 6.3
Choosing a default SQL Server database using the ODBC control panel.

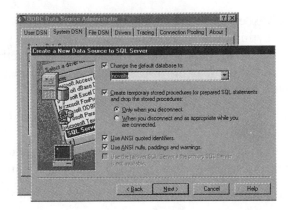

10. Click Next. The next screen appears, prompting you to choose a character set translation. You don't normally need to change anything here unless you're using an alternate character set on the server, so click Next.

11. The next screen gives you the option to activate logging. This lets you display the internal actions that ODBC takes to resolve a query. Normally you'd only turn this option on if you're troubleshooting or searching for performance bottlenecks in your application.

    Note: Switching on query logging, then forgetting to switch it off, is an extremely common source of degraded query performance when using ODBC. Logging is essentially a debugging tool—be sure to remember to switch it off when you move your application into production.

12. Click Finish. A dialog box appears describing the details of the data source you're about to create. Just to make sure everything's kosher, click the Test Data Source button. The driver should respond by telling you that a connection was successfully established.

    After you click OK, the new data source name appears in the ODBC Data Source Administrator window. It's now available for use by your applications.

TESTING A DATABASE CONNECTION WITH ODBCPING

Amazingly, earlier versions of ODBC didn't have the ability to actually connect to the data source to verify whether the connection information you supplied to the driver manager was valid. You had to go through the entire process of creating the DSN, then cross your fingers and hope that the connection was valid.

Current ODBC drivers have the ability to test the data source as you create the DSN, which lets you verify the connection information immediately. However, if you want to test an ODBC connection without using the driver manager, you can use the odbcping utility to determine whether a DSN is valid. This command-line utility instructs the ODBC driver manager to create a connection to the back-end database and return information about whether the connection was successful. This can be helpful in situations where you're attempting to determine whether a problem with your client/server connection lies on the server, in the network connection, in ODBC, or in your client application. The odbcping utility won't solve your problems for you, but it will at least tell you if you have connectivity to the server through ODBC.

Here's the syntax of odbcping:

```
odbcping /Uusername /Ppassword /Sserver
```

So, for example, to ping the SQL Server called BEDROCK using the login name randy and the password prince, you use this command line:

```
odbcping /Urandy /Pprince /SBEDROCK
```

To use odbcping to test your connectivity to the server, follow these steps:

1. From the Start menu, launch a new MS-DOS command prompt.

2. The command prompt window appears. In the command prompt window, type this:

```
odbcping /Urandy /Pprince /SBEDROCK
```

3. The odbcping utility establishes a connection to the server and then exits. If everything functions properly, your command prompt window should look like Figure 6.4.

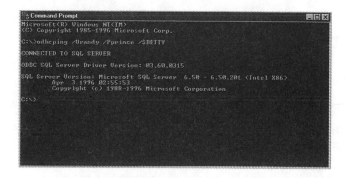

Figure 6.4
Results of a successful odbcping against a SQL Server.

ACCESSING A DATA SOURCE WITH THE DAO DATA CONTROL AND ODBCDIRECT

Creating a Visual Basic application with the DAO Data control makes connecting to an ODBC data source easy. In fact, it doesn't require any code at all to set up. You can use the Data control to quickly test a connection to a client/server database, or you can use it to create a user interface prototype with a direct connection to the database. For performance reasons, though, you may want to consider using the Remote Data Control (or *RDC*, described in the next section of this chapter) or the ADO Data control (introduced in Chapter 1, "Database Basics,") rather than the DAO Data control, since these data controls are geared specifically at accessing client/server data. Better yet, you may wish to do away with data controls altogether and write your own code to access the database (this is the tactic I'd recommend).

In versions of Data Access Objects prior to 3.5, DAO loaded the Jet database engine automatically whenever it accessed client/server data—even if you weren't actually using a Jet/Access database. In VB5, you gained the option of using ODBCDirect to access client/server data. ODBCDirect is simply a switch that tells DAO to access the server directly through DAO without loading the Jet database engine. This conserves memory and decreases your application's load time on the client computer. It's appropriate in situations where you have to use DAO to get access to client/server data but you're not terribly worried about flexibility, reusability, or maintainability of your code.

Code Example: You can find the code in this section in the sample project ODBCDAO.vbp, located in the directory \vbdb\code\06-rdo\ODBCDAO. For information on how to install the sample files that come on the CD that accompanies this book, see the section "Installing the Example Files" in the introduction at the beginning of this book.

To set up a quick VB application that tests a SQL Server DSN, do the following:

1. Make sure you've created an ODBC data source name called Novelty as described in the previous section.

2. Launch Visual Basic and create a Standard EXE project.

3. From the Project Components menu, add a reference to the Microsoft Data Bound Grid Control to your project.

Note: In this demonstration, you use the DBGrid control simply as a way to browse data. It has a variety of other uses. For more information on how to program the DBGrid control, see Chapter 13, "Using the DBGrid and Apex True DBGrid Controls."

4. The DBGrid control appears in your project's toolbox. Add an instance of the DBGrid control and a standard Data control to your project's form.

5. Change the Data control's `DefaultType` property to 1 - Use ODBC. This causes the text application to bypass the Microsoft Jet engine, which makes your application start more quickly and consume less memory.

6. In the Data control's `Connect` property, enter the following text:

```
ODBC;UID=randy;PWD=prince;DSN=Novelty;
```

Replace the string "prince" with your password. If necessary, replace the username randy with your username. (These should have been created in SQL Enterprise Manager when you initially set up the database back in Chapter 5.) Note that it isn't necessary to specify the login ID and password to ODBC here if you did so when you created the Novelty DSN earlier in this chapter.

Note: Although the syntax of an ODBC connection string may seem somewhat Byzantine, connection strings are expressed this way to give maximum flexibility to the particular database driver you're using. This is because some database drivers use ODBC connection string settings that others don't. The order in which you pass the elements of an ODBC connection string is irrelevant; however, the `ODBC;` clause should always come first when you're using the DAO Data control in ODBCDirect mode.

7. In the Data control's `RecordSource` property, enter the following SQL string:

```
select * from qryCustomer
```

Remember that when you set up the database in Chapter 5, you restricted users' permissions to access tables directly. So rather than selecting records from tblCustomer, you use the corresponding view, qryCustomer.

8. Set the DBGrid control's `DataSource` property to Data1.

9. Run the application. The grid should display all the data in the tblCustomer table (assuming there is data in the table). The running application is shown in Figure 6.5.

Figure 6.5
A Visual Basic application using the DBGrid control to test an ODBC database connection.

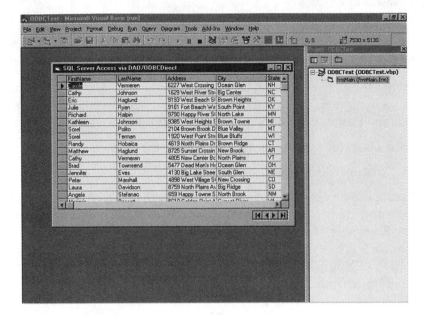

Accessing Data Using the Remote Data Control

The Remote Data Control (RDC) is another way to access remote data in a Visual Basic application. This control uses a programmable interface similar to that of the ADO Data control, introduced in Chapter 1, or the DAO Data control, introduced in the previous section. With a few minor exceptions, the Remote Data Control works the same as the other data controls—you give the control some information about where the data is stored and it retrieves data and supplies it to other data-aware user interface controls. The user can then interact with the data through these user interface controls—browsing data, performing updates, and adding records—and you don't have to write a single line of code to make it happen.

Note: Remember that you're not restricted to RDO when you want to use client/server data. VB6 introduces a new data control for ADO data sources designed to replace the Remote Data Control. For more information, see Chapter 10.

USING THE REMOTE DATA CONTROL IN YOUR PROJECT

To use the Remote Data Control in your Visual Basic project, do the following:

1. In Visual Basic, select the menu command Project, Components.

2. From the list of components, select Microsoft RemoteData Control. Also add a reference to the Microsoft Data Bound Grid Control.

3. Click OK. The Remote Data and Data Bound Grid controls appear in the Visual Basic toolbox, as illustrated in Figure 6.6.

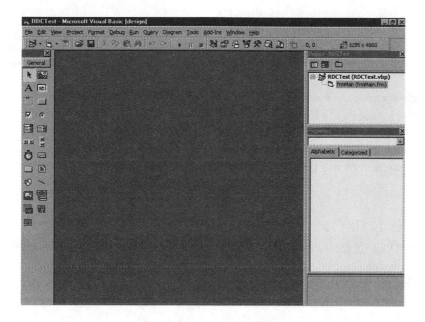

Figure 6.6
The icons for the Microsoft Remote Data Control and the Microsoft Data Bound Grid Control as they appear in the Visual Basic toolbox.

4. Use the toolbox to create instances of the Remote Data control and the Data Bound Grid on the form in your project.

5. If you didn't incorporate the username and password when you created the ODBC data source name earlier in this chapter, change the Remote Data Control's UserName property to a username with access to the database, such as "randy" or "sa."

6. Change the Remote Data Control's Password property to the user's password.

7. Set the Remote Data Control's SQL property to this:

```
select * from qryCustomer
```

8. In the DataSourceName property of the Remote Data Control, pick the DSN for your SQL Server database. The DSN you created earlier should appear in the drop-down list.

9. Set the DBGrid control's DataSource property to MSRDC1, the name of the Remote Data Control.

10. Run the application. The application retrieves the contents of the tblCustomer table and displays it in the data grid.

If you are perusing this chapter you've probably gotten the impression that using the Data control with the ODBCDirect option and the Remote Data Control to access data is essentially the same thing. This is the case. Both controls give you access to an ODBC database without writing Visual Basic code.

Code Example: You can find the code in this section in the sample project RDCTest.vbp, located in the directory \vbdb\code\06-rdo\RDCTest. For information on how to install the sample files that come on the CD that accompanies this book, see the section "Installing the Example Files" in the introduction at the beginning of this book.

USING REMOTE DATA OBJECTS IN CODE

Remote Data Objects are arranged in an object hierarchy similar to that of Data Access Objects. Figure 6.7 illustrates this hierarchy.

Notice that RDO's object model is simpler than that of DAO. This reflects the fact that much of DAO's functionality (such as responsibility for security and the capability to make changes in the database schema) is handled by the database engine itself. In RDO, on the other hand, this functionality is handled by the server.

Note: ADO provides an object model that's even simpler than RDO, while providing all of RDO's functionality. For more information, see Chapter 10.

This limitation means that you can't use RDO to create database objects such as tables, views, and stored procedures (at least, you can't do it using objects— you can, however, use RDO to pass procedural SQL commands directly to the server, which means that almost anything you're able to do in ISQL/w, you can do using RDO).

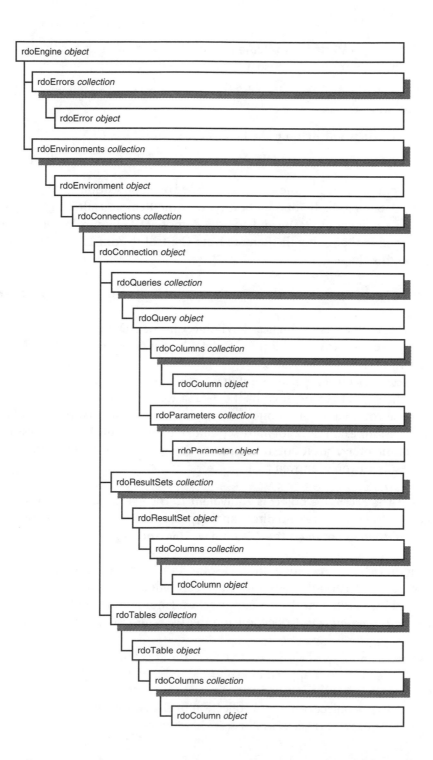

Figure 6.7
The complete structure of Remote Data Objects 2.0.

In order to get started with Remote Data Objects, you must first make a reference to the library in your Visual Basic project:

1. Select References from Visual Basic's Project menu. The References dialog box appears.

2. Select Microsoft Remote Data Object 2.0 from the list.

3. Click OK. Remote Data Objects are now available to your application.

Remember to perform these steps any time your application needs to access Remote Data Objects. If your application uses the Remote Data Control, you must add a reference to RDO and add the Remote Data Control to your project, as described in the "Using the Remote Data Control in Your Project" section earlier in this chapter.

SETTING DATABASE ENGINE PROPERTIES WITH THE *RDOENGINE* OBJECT

The `rdoEngine` object is the highest-level object in the RDO object model. You generally use the `rdoEngine` object to set default properties for the other RDO objects your application creates.

The `rdoEngine` object is also useful in situations where you want to set or inspect the type of cursors used by the database engine. A cursor is a way of accessing a row in a result set one row at a time. Different cursors have different capabilities; for example, a forward-scrolling cursor permits you to access rows, one after the other, but it doesn't permit you to go backward and reference rows in the result set you've moved past.

> **Note:** The `rdoEngine` object is equivalent to the `DBEngine` object in Data Access Objects. There's no direct analogy to `rdoEngine` in ADO; its functionality is divided between the ADO `Connection` and `Recordset` objects.

In addition to representing the data source, the `rdoEngine` object also contains an `rdoErrors` collection that lets you iterate through all the error messages generated by a particular database transaction (more on this in "Handling Errors with the *rdoErrors* Collection and the *rdoError* Object" later in this chapter).

The `rdoEngine` object belongs to no collection; it is a singleton object that can't be instantiated by your application (it just simply exists, in a Zen-like sort of way; it comes into existence the first time your application accesses RDO).

The `rdoEngine` object contains a collection of `Environment` objects, as well as a collection of `rdoError` objects, as illustrated in Figure 6.8.

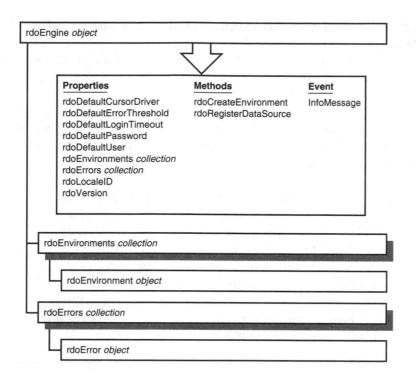

Figure 6.8
The Environments collection and Environment object in the Remote Data Object hierarchy.

For example, if your application needs to create a number of data objects based on a common user login and password, you can specify these when you start using remote data objects in your application. The defaults you set (using the `rdoDefaultPassword` and `rdoDefaultUser` properties) are in force for any `rdoEnvironment` objects created in your application.

You can also use the `rdoEngine` object to control how cursors are created and maintained by your application.

In addition to supplying defaults for other objects created in RDO, the `rdoEngine` object automatically creates an `rdoEnvironment` object. You can refer to this object in code as `rdoEnvironments(0)`.

Note that the properties of the `rdoEngine` object aren't used often, because by the time you have access to the `rdoEngine` object, it's already created the only `rdoEnvironment` object you're ever likely to need—`rdoEnvironments(0)`. If you want to change the database environment, you're probably better off simply adjusting the properties of `rdoEnvironments(0)` directly, as described in the next section.

ACCESSING THE ENVIRONMENT WITH THE *RDOENVIRONMENT* OBJECT

The rdoEnvironment object represents the database environment. It is a way to refer to a set of database connections (in the form of rdoConnection objects, discussed in the next section).

> **Note: The rdoEnvironment object is analogous to the Workspace object in Data Access Objects. In ADO, rdoEnvironment is somewhat similar to the ADO Connection object.**

As with the rdoEngine object, it's unlikely that your application would ever need to create more than one instance of an rdoEnvironment object—unless you needed to support multiple simultaneous transactions that spanned database connections. Rather than instantiating a new instance of the rdoEnvironment object, it's more likely that you'll access the existing rdoEnvironment object, rdoEnvironments(0), created for you by the rdoEngine object when you initially make a reference to Remote Data Objects in your VB application.

The rdoEnvironment object belongs to an rdoEnvironments collection and contains a collection of rdoConnection objects, as illustrated in Figure 6.9.

Figure 6.9
The rdoEnvironments collection and rdoEnvironment object in the Remote Data Object hierarchy.

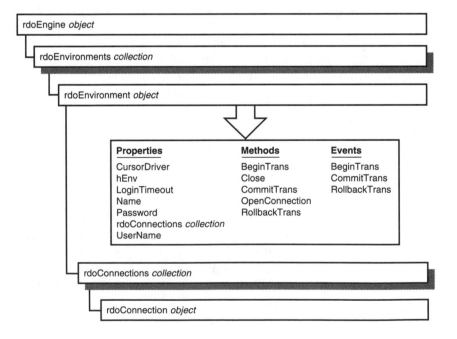

ESTABLISHING A CONNECTION USING THE *RDOCONNECTION* OBJECT
You use the rdoConnection object to establish a connection to a remote database
server in RDO. After you have a valid rdoConnection object, your application can
begin interacting with the database in earnest.

Note: The rdoConnection object is analogous to the Database object in Data
Access Objects programming. It's also similar in some ways to the ADO
Connection object.

rdoConnection objects belong to an rdoConnections collection and contain collections of rdoQuery objects, rdoResultset objects, and rdoTable objects, as illustrated
in Figure 6.10.

To create a connection using the rdoConnection object, you begin by creating
an ODBC connection string, as described at the beginning of this chapter.
Unlike with the Data control, though, you omit the ODBC; clause of the
rdoConnection object's connection string. (It's implied that since you're using
RDO, you're using ODBC.)

Your connection string can consist of as little as a data source name, assuming you supplied all the information required to log on (including login name
and password) at the time you created the ODBC DSN. However, if you don't
care to include your login name and password in the DSN, you can include it as
part of the connection string. You can also supply additional information in the
connection string—in fact, if you provide enough information in the connection string, you don't have to create an ODBC DSN at all.

Table 6.1 lists some of the most commonly used elements of an ODBC connection string when connecting to SQL Server.

Table 6.1 Typical Elements of an ODBC Connection String	
Argument	**Description**
UID=	The user's login name
PWD=	The user's password
DSN=	The data source name you created in the ODBC Driver Manager
DRIVER=	The ODBC driver you want to use
DATABASE=	The name of the database to which you want to connect
APP=	The name of the application connecting to the database
LANGUAGE=	The international language used by the server
SERVER=	The name of the SQL Server the application is connecting to

Figure 6.10
The rdoConnections collection and rdoConnection object in the Remote Data Object hierarchy.

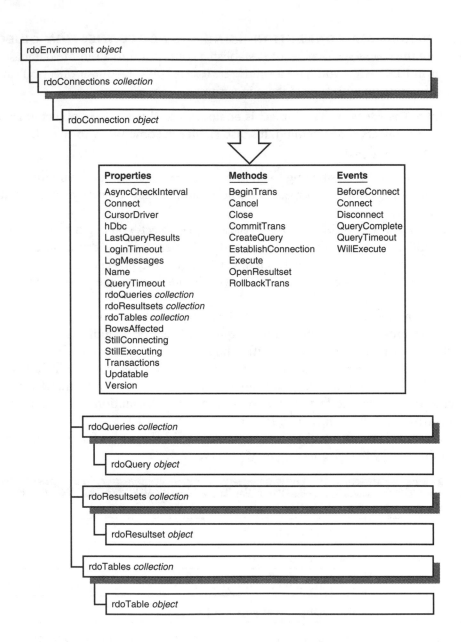

Again, bear in mind that this isn't a complete list of connect string arguments for every database. And not all of these arguments are required in every circumstance. The database back end you use may provide (or require) more or fewer arguments.

> **Note: In order to connect to an ODBC data source using a data source name (in other words, the DSN= parameter of the connection string), the data source must first be properly configured in the ODBC Control Panel. For information on how to do this, see "Configuring and Using Open Database Connectivity," earlier in this chapter.**

So, for example, to connect to the SQL Server database called Novelty using the login name randy and the password prince, you use this connect string:

```
DSN=Novelty;UID=randy;PWD=prince;
```

This string uses the Novelty DSN created earlier in this chapter, but assumes that you did not include your user ID and password when you created the DSN.

Bear in mind that if you bungle something in the connection string—forgetting to supply a login or a password, for example,—your user will be greeted with a potentially unpleasant surprise. When the application attempts to connect to the server, the ODBC driver displays a dialog box asking the user to supply the missing login information, as shown in Figure 6.11.

Figure 6.11
The SQL Server Login dialog displayed when you don't supply enough information to log in to the database.

Although you might be tempted to take advantage of the dialog as a standard way to permit your users to log in to the database, it probably isn't a good idea. It's simple enough to create a login form (or use the standard VB login dialog template displayed when you create a new form) yourself. This gives your application complete control over the login process and inoculates your app from login-related skullduggery.

CREATING DSN-LESS CONNECTION STRINGS

In addition to creating a connection string that takes advantage of a preconfigured ODBC data source name, you have the option of creating a connection string that does not require a DSN at all. To create such a so-called "DSN-less connection," you use a connect string that includes all the information required to log in, including an ODBC driver name. Such a string looks like this:

```
DRIVER={SQL Server};SERVER=bedrock;DATABASE=bedrock;UID=randy;PWD=prince;
```

Remember, the order in which the parts of the connection string appear isn't important, but spelling is. One of the most common mistakes developers make when constructing a DSN-less connection is to leave out a character (such as a semicolon or a curly brace) or insert an extra character (such as a space before or after an equal sign) in the connection string. ODBC is picky when it comes to the format of the connection string, so be careful.

> **Note:** You use a DSN-less connection in situations where you don't need or want complete control over client-side configuration. It's also a bit faster to log on to a database using a DSN-less connection. This is because DSNs are stored in the Windows registry, which is expensive to access.

Opening the Database   After you have the information you need to establish the connection to the database, you have two options to establish the connection:

▶ Use the OpenConnection method of the rdoEnvironment object

▶ Use the EstablishConnection method of the rdoEnvironment object

Both methods do exactly the same thing, although they work in slightly different ways. To demonstrate, Listing 6.1 shows an example of the rdoEnvironment object's OpenConnection method.

Listing 6.1   Connecting to a Database Using the *rdoEnvironment* Object's *OpenConnection* Method

```
Option Explicit

' References RDO 2.0

Private MyConn As rdoConnection

Private Form_Load()

    Dim strConnect As String

    strConnect = "DSN=Novelty;UID=randy;PWD=prince;"
```

```
    Set MyConn = rdoEnvironments(0).OpenConnection("Novelty", , , strConnect)

End Sub
```

The OpenConnection method has five arguments; the first one (which represents the data source name) is not optional. The other four arguments (Prompt, Readonly, Connect, and Options) are optional. This explains the strange syntax of the method— the missing parameters are placed in between the commas. (Note that this code uses the implicitly created rdoEnvironment object, referred to as rdoEnvionronments(0), to create the connection to the database.)

The EstablishConnection method, on the other hand, does the same thing as OpenConnection. But it does its work in a more straightforward way, as Listing 6.2 demonstrates.

**Listing 6.2   Connecting to a Database Using the *rdoEnvironment* Object's
EstablishConnection Method**

```
Option Explicit

' References RDO 2.0

Private MyConn As rdoConnection

Private Sub Form_Load()

    Set MyConn = New rdoConnection

    MyConn.Connect = "DSN=Novelty;" & _
                     "UID=randy;" & _
                     "PWD=prince;"

    MyConn.EstablishConnection

End Sub
```

Code Example: You can find the code discussed in this section in the sample project Connect.vbp, located in the directory \vbdb\code\06-rdo\Connect. For information on how to install the sample files on the CD that accompanies this book, see the section "Installing the Example Files" in the introduction at the beginning of this book.

Though Remote Data Objects makes it easy to connect to a database in code using the `rdoConnection` object, there's an even easier way—using a UserConnection Designer. This is demonstrated in "Creating a Connection with the UserConnection Designer" later in this chapter.

RESPONDING TO EVENTS IN RDO

RDO objects have the ability to generate events. This gives you a great deal of flexibility for writing code that is associated with the object, like you do with other types of objects in Visual Basic.

Events also permit your application to perform actions that can take a long time (such as connecting to the database or running a query) without holding up execution of your application. Instead of waiting around for the RDO action to take place, your application goes about its business until the connection is established or the query is done. This is called asynchronous execution. Events are how RDO objects notify your application that an asynchronous operation has completed.

To cause a particular data object to generate events, you must declare it in a special way: using the `WithEvents` keyword. For example, to declare a `rdoConnection` object called `MyConn` that generates events, you use the following code:

```
Private WithEvents MyConn As rdoConnection
```

After you've declared an object using `WithEvents`, its events become available in the Visual Basic code window, as shown in Figure 6.12.

Figure 6.12

Accessing event procedure of an RDO object declared with the WithEvents keyword.

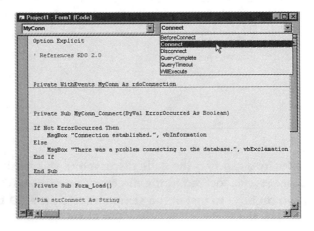

After you have an object that generates events, you can then write event procedures that perform actions based on the events generated by the object in question. These event procedures are identical to the other event procedures you've written in Visual Basic, such as the Click event of the command button or the Load event of the form.

One of the easiest ways to demonstrate how RDO events work is to write an event procedure that displays a message when a connection to the database is established. An example of a complete procedure that displays such a message in response to the rdoConnection object's Connect event is shown in Listing 6.3.

Listing 6.3   Using the *Connect* Event of the *rdoConnection* Object

```
Option Explicit

' References RDO 2.0

Private WithEvents MyConn As rdoConnection

Private Sub Form_Load()

    Set MyConn = New rdoConnection

    MyConn.Connect = "DSN=Novelty;" & _
                     "PWD=prince;" & _
                     "UID=randy;"

    MyConn.EstablishConnection

End Sub

Private Sub MyConn_Connect(ByVal ErrorOccurred As Boolean)

    If ErrorOccurred Then
        MsgBox "There was a problem connecting to the database.", _
               vbExclamation
    Else
        MsgBox "Connection established.", _
               vbInformation

    End If

End Sub
```

Code Example: You can find the code discussed in this section in the sample project `Connect.vbp`, located in the directory `\vbdb\code\06-rdo\Connect`. For information on how to install the sample files on the CD that accompanies this book, see the section "Installing the Example Files" in the introduction at the beginning of this book.

Note: The `Connection` and `Recordset` objects in ADO 2.0 also have the ability to generate events. For details, see Chapter 10.

CREATING A CONNECTION WITH THE USERCONNECTION DESIGNER

UserConnection designers make it easier for your VB applications to connect with a client/server database using RDO. Their purpose is to give you a design-time, graphical, reusable way to maintain information pertaining to a connection to a client/server database. The ultimate purpose of a UserConnection designer is to generate an `rdoConnection` object with a minimum of code.

UserConnection designers behave similar to forms in VB projects; you add a UserConnection designer to your project and use it as you'd use a form. When you compile an executable file in VB, the UserConnection designer is compiled along with it, just as forms are.

Note: In ADO under Visual Basic 6.0, you have a new type of designer to help you create database connections. This designer is called the *DataEnvironment*, and it's discussed in Chapter 10. It exceeds the capabilities of the UserConnection designer in several interesting ways.

If you're accustomed to writing code in Visual Basic with class modules, you have a leg up when you're learning how to use designers. Designers are actually a type of class module. If you're unfamiliar with how to use class modules to make your code more reusable and easier to maintain, check out Chapter 7, "Database Access with Classes."

To use a UserConnection designer, follow these general steps:

1. Add a new UserConnection designer to your project.

2. Using the UserConnection's graphical interface, indicate which ODBC data source you want to connect to, and how you want to connect to it.

3. In code, create an instance of an rdoConnection object from the
UserConnection designer.

For example, here's how to use the UserConnection Designer to connect to a
particular ODBC database:

1. In a VB project, choose the menu item Project, More ActiveX Designers.
From the submenu, choose Microsoft UserConnection.

2. A new UserConnection designer is added to your project, and the
UserConnection Properties dialog box is displayed, as illustrated in
Figure 6.13.

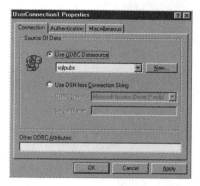

Figure 6.13
The Properties dialog box of a new UserConnection designer.

3. In the Connection tab, choose an ODBC data source or build a DSN-less
connection string.

4. Click the Authentication tab and enter a valid username and password.
Check the boxes labeled Save Connection Information for new Run-Mode
Class and Save Connection Information for Design Time, so you'll be able
to access the connection whenever you need to.

Note: In the UserConnection designer, as with the ODBC DSN, you have the
option of intentionally leaving out information pertaining to authentication. Leaving out the authentication information means that your username
and password won't be compiled into the application and it won't be saved
along with the UserConnection designer. Remember, though, that if your
UserConnection designer stores no authentication information, and you
don't provide that information in code at runtime, the ODBC driver will display a login dialog every time your application attempts to connect to the

database. (You can shut off this login dialog in the UserConnection designer by using the ODBC Prompt Behavior combo box in the Authentication tab of the designer's Properties dialog box.)

In your applications, you might want to approach the problem of user authentication in a different way—by retrieving the user's name and password at the time a user starts your application, or (for decision-support applications) creating a special read-only user account expressly for the purpose of browsing data.

5. Click OK.

6. The Properties dialog box closes. You are left with the UserConnection designer, as shown in Figure 6.14.

Figure 6.14
The UserConnection designer after you've set its initial properties.

7. In the Visual Basic Properties window, give the UserConnection designer a name. You use this name to refer to the UserConnection designer in code. For example, you might want to name a UserConnection designer that connects to the company database conCompany.

ACCESSING QUERIES WITH A USERCONNECTION DESIGNER

After you've created a UserConnection designer, you can use it to retrieve data based on views or stored procedures on the server. You can also use the designer to generate client-side SQL queries on-the-fly, although if you have control over both the client and server, it's preferable for performance and maintainability reasons to restrict your client applications to accessing stored procedures that reside on the server.

You can create queries stored in the UserConnection designer in one of three ways:

▶ Call a stored procedure or view on the database server that returns records.

▶ Issue a command to the database server in the form of a SQL string generated on the fly.

▶ Build a query in the UserConnection designer using Microsoft Query. This technique is similar to the on-the-fly query technique, but it's graphical, so it's a bit easier to construct at design time.

Calling a Stored Procedure in a UserConnection Designer In order to call a stored procedure from a connection object created from a UserConnection designer, you must add the stored procedure to the UserConnection designer at design time. After you've done this, you can access the stored procedure as a method of the connection object.

In this example, you add a reference to the LastNameLookup stored procedure in the company database:

1. In the toolbar of a UserConnection designer, click the Insert Query button. ("Query," in this context, refers to either a SQL string you generate on the client side or a stored procedure or view that resides on the server.)

2. The Query Properties dialog box appears. In the Query Name box, give the query a name; it can (and probably should) be the same name as the stored procedure to which you're referring.

3. The Based on Stored Procedure combo box provides a list of all the stored procedures in the company database. In this combo box, select the name of the LastNameLookup procedure you created in Business Case 5.2.

4. Click the Parameters tab. Note that the LastNameLookup procedure takes a parameter, name, that corresponds to the name of the person you're trying to look up.

5. Click OK. The LastNameLookup stored procedure is added to your UserConnection designer, as shown in Figure 6.15.

Figure 6.15
*The conCompany
UserConnection
with a reference
to the stored pro-
cedure
LastNameLookup.*

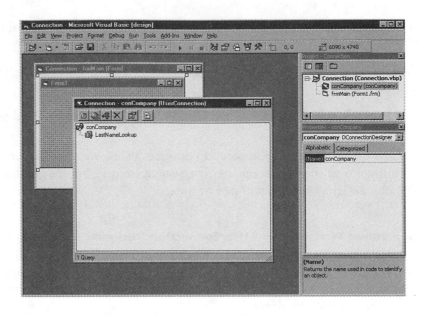

Code Example: You can find the code discussed in this section in the sample project UserConn.vbp, located in the directory \vbdb\code\06-rdo\
UserConn. For information on how to install the sample files on the CD that
accompanies this book, see the section "Installing the Example Files" in the
introduction at the beginning of this book.

To see how to call a query referenced in a UserConnection, you must create
an instance of the UserConnection in code, then execute the stored procedure as
a method of the rdoConnection object created by the UserConnection:

1. Add a standard list box, a standard command button, and a standard text
   box to the form in your project containing the UserConnection. You use
   the text box to enter a parameter for the query, while the list box stores the
   results of the query. The code to run the query is triggered by a click on
   the command button.

2. In the Declarations section of the form, declare a variable that stores the
   rdoConnection and an rdoResultSet. (The rdoConnection is created from the
   UserConnection designer, as the code in Listing 6.4 demonstrates.)

```
Private Conn As conCompany
Private rs As rdoResultset
```

3. In the command button's `Click` event procedure, write code that creates an instance of the UserConnection, connects to the database, and runs the stored procedure. The code is in Listing 6.4.

Listing 6.4   Code That Runs a Stored Procedure and Returns Its Results to a Standard List Box

```
Private Sub Command1_Click()

Set Conn = New conCompany

    Conn.EstablishConnection

    Conn.LastNameLookup Text1.Text

    Set rs = Conn.LastQueryResults

    List1.Clear

    Do Until rs.EOF
        List1.AddItem rs!LastName & " " & rs!FirstName
        rs.MoveNext
    Loop

    Conn.Close

End Sub
```

Notice that when you type a dot after the `Conn` object, the stored procedure referenced by the UserConnection appears in the drop-down list of members of the object, as shown in Figure 6.16.

4. Run the application. Type a name such as Smith in the text box, then click the command button. The list box is populated with a list of names that are similar to what you typed, as shown in Figure 6.17.

Using Microsoft Query to Build an SQL String in a UserConnection Designer
You've seen how easy it is to refer to a query stored on the server side using the UserConnection designer. In some cases, the query you want to run doesn't exist on the server, in which case you may want to generate the SQL on the client side and submit it to the server. The query is then executed on the server; the results are returned to the client.

To build a SQL string to submit to the server, you can either hand-code the SQL (the hard way) or use one of a number of client-side graphical query tools (the easy way). Microsoft Query is the tool most closely integrated with the UserConnection designer.

Figure 6.16
Running a stored procedure referenced by a UserConnection as a method of the rdoConnection object.

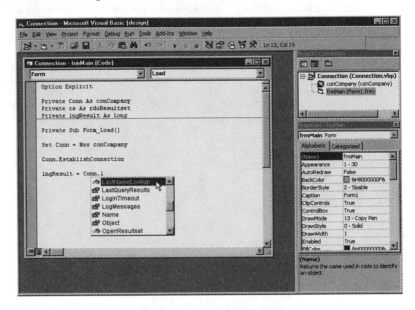

Figure 6.17
Results of a query in the application based on the UserConnection designer.

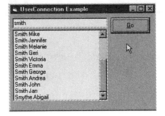

Note: Microsoft Query doesn't provide access to stored procedures stored in SQL Server, only tables and views.

To add a SQL query in the UserConnection designer using Microsoft Query, follow these steps:

1. Click the Insert Query button on the UserConnection designer's toolbar.

2. The query properties dialog box appears, as shown in Figure 6.18.

3. Type the name of the query you want to build in the Query Name text box. The query you're building retrieves everyone in the database named Jones, so call this query qryJones.

4. Select the Based on User-Defined SQL option, then click Build.

5. Microsoft Query launches and displays a Choose Data Source dialog box. Locate the data source you want to connect to, then click OK.

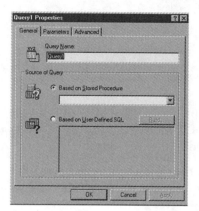

Figure 6.18
The UserConnection designer query's Properties dialog box.

Note: It might seem silly that you have to designate a data source again when you've already done so in the UserConnection designer. To make matters worse, you may have trouble getting Microsoft Query to recognize that you have a user DSN set up for the company database. For some reason, it really seems to want a file-based DSN rather than a user DSN or a system DSN. Fortunately, MS Query gives you the ability to create a DSN from within the program, so it's no major problem. It might, however, make you wish you could set up the whole shebang from one place.

Another problem you might have with MS Query stems from the fact that it's set up to look in the `\Program Files\Common Files\Microsoft Shared\Vba` directory for DSN files, and for some reason the ODBC applet creates file-based DSNs in `\Program Files\Common Files\ODBC\Data Sources`. In MS Query's Choose Data Source dialog box, you can resolve this problem by clicking the Options button to specify which directory to search for DSNs in. To do this, in the Data Source Options dialog box, click Browse, select the correct directory, click OK, then click Add. The new directory is then recognized by MS Query in the future.

6. The Query Wizard runs, displaying the data available in the data source you just selected. The first dialog box in the Query Wizard is illustrated in Figure 6.19.

Figure 6.19

The initial screen of the Query Wizard, which lets you pick data to retrieve.

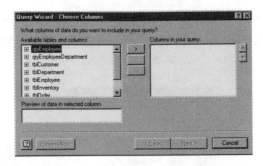

7. Double-click the query or view you want to use (for this demonstration, select the view qryCustomer). The query or view expands to show a list of the fields contained in the view or table.

8. Double-click each field you want to retrieve. Select the FirstName and LastName fields, as well as any other fields you want to retrieve.

9. Click the Next button.

10. The Filter Data step appears. In this step, you can determine how the query filters out records. To retrieve only those customers named Jones, select the LastName field from the list of fields. Then, in the combo box to the right of the list of columns, choose equals. In the next combo box, choose Jones (the combo box performs a query on the data to determine the data that exists in the column you choose). The Filter Data dialog box should look like the one shown in Figure 6.20.

Figure 6.20

Filtering out data according to a particular criterion in Microsoft Query.

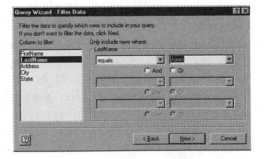

11. Click the Next button. The next step enables you to sort data. In the Sort combo box, choose FirstName.

12. Click the Next button. When you're done, you have the option of viewing the data you've retrieved or going back to the UserConnection designer. (If you choose to view the data in Microsoft Query, you can still return to the

UserConnection designer later.) Choose View Data or Edit Query in
Microsoft Query, then click Finish.

13. The data you've retrieved appears in Microsoft Query, as shown in
Figure 6.21.

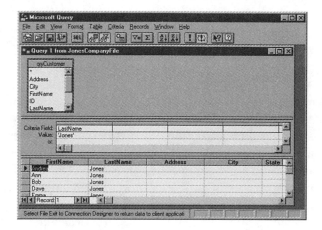

Figure 6.21
*Data retrieved by
the Query Wizard
displayed in
Microsoft Query.*

Code Example: The project discussed in this section is called `Query.vbp`. It's
located in the directory `\vbdb\code\06-rdo\Query`. For information on how
to install the sample files on the CD that accompanies this book, see the
section "Installing the Example Files" in the introduction at the beginning
of this book.

When you're done viewing the data in Microsoft Query, select the menu
command File, Exit to Connection Designer. Microsoft Query exits and returns
the query you built to the UserConnection designer's query properties dialog
box in the form of a SQL string. The Query Properties dialog box looks like the
one shown in Figure 6.22.

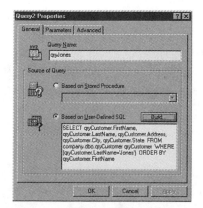

Figure 6.22
*Query Properties
dialog box of the
UserConnection
designer, after it's
been populated
with a query string
built in Microsoft
Query.*

When you're done with the Query Properties dialog box, click OK. The query is stored in the UserConnection designer for your use in code.

There are several advantages to storing SQL queries in UserConnection designers. Among these is the fact that you can reuse designers across multiple projects and multiple developers without having to make changes on the server side.

Additionally, queries stored in UserConnection designers help you manage complexity in your application because there is less code to maintain—after you have the query working and have stored it in the UserConnection designer, you can put it out of your way and work on something else.

However, the problem with incorporating SQL strings in UserConnection designers is the fact that they're not universally accessible from every client application. This can lead to a situation where different client applications access server data in different ways, potentially leading to inconsistencies, especially in situations where the design of the database evolves over time. If you find yourself creating custom SQL queries on the client side, you may want to consider migrating that code to the server if you can.

After you've created a query in a UserConnection designer, you refer to it the same way you refer to a stored procedure—as a method of the connection object created by the UserConnection designer. This technique is described earlier in this chapter.

UTILIZING DATA WITH THE *RDORESULTSET* OBJECT

You use the rdoResultset object to manipulate data returned by an interaction with the server.

Each rdoResultset object belongs to an rdoResultsets collection. The rdoResultset object contains a collection of rdoColumn objects, as illustrated in Figure 6.23.

The rdoResultset object is nearly identical to the Recordset object provided by Data Access Objects. You can create a rdoResultset object a number of ways; typically it's created as the result of a query (which can include a SQL string generated on the client, or the execution of a stored procedure or view on the server).

The following sections on queries and parameters give examples of the use of the rdoRecordset object in conjunction with queries generated on both the client and server side.

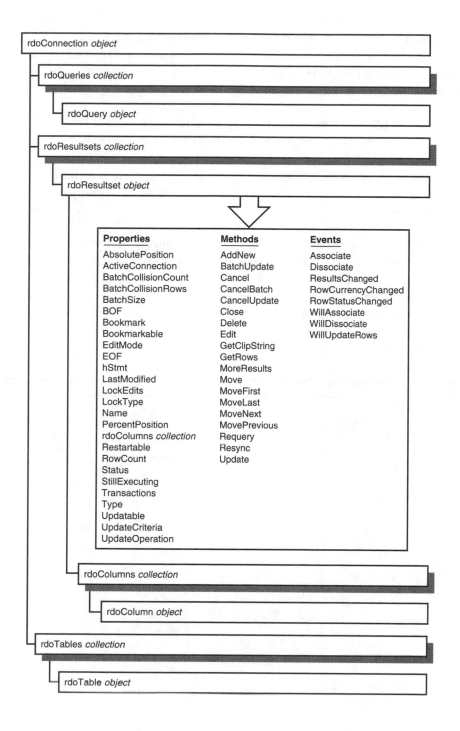

Figure 6.23
The rdoResultsets collection and rdoResultset object in the Remote Data Object hierarchy.

rdoConnection *object*

rdoQueries *collection*

rdoQuery *object*

rdoResultsets *collection*

rdoResultset *object*

Properties	**Methods**	**Events**
AbsolutePosition	AddNew	Associate
ActiveConnection	BatchUpdate	Dissociate
BatchCollisionCount	Cancel	ResultsChanged
BatchCollisionRows	CancelBatch	RowCurrencyChanged
BatchSize	CancelUpdate	RowStatusChanged
BOF	Close	WillAssociate
Bookmark	Delete	WillDissociate
Bookmarkable	Edit	WillUpdateRows
EditMode	GetClipString	
EOF	GetRows	
hStmt	MoreResults	
LastModified	Move	
LockEdits	MoveFirst	
LockType	MoveLast	
Name	MoveNext	
PercentPosition	MovePrevious	
rdoColumns *collection*	Requery	
Restartable	Resync	
RowCount	Update	
Status		
StillExecuting		
Transactions		
Type		
Updatable		
UpdateCriteria		
UpdateOperation		

rdoColumns *collection*

rdoColumn *object*

rdoTables *collection*

rdoTable *object*

RUNNING QUERIES WITH THE *RDOQUERY* OBJECT

You can run queries in RDO using the rdoQuery object. You typically do this in situations where the query in question is a parameterized query or an action query (a query that updates or deletes data).

> **Note:** In RDO 2.0, the rdoQuery object is a replacement for the rdoPreparedStatement object that existed in RDO 1.0. (RDO 1.0 shipped with Visual Basic 4.0.) You can technically still use rdoPreparedStatement objects in your RDO 2.0 code; rdoPreparedStatement objects were included in RDO 2.0 for backward compatibility. However, for new RDO code you should use rdoQuery objects.

Each rdoQuery object belongs to an rdoQueries collection. The rdoQuery object contains collections of rdoColumn objects and rdoParameter objects, as illustrated in Figure 6.24.

You can use the rdoQuery object to create a SQL query on the fly without the use of the UserConnection designer or any other outside assistance. Listing 6.5 gives an example of how to do this, using an application composed of a text box, a list box, and a command button.

Listing 6.5   Generating a Parameterized Query on the Fly Using the *rdoQuery* Object

```
Option Explicit

' References RDO 2.0

Dim Conn As rdoConnection
Dim qy As rdoQuery
Dim rs As rdoResultset

Private Sub Form_Load()

Set Conn = New rdoConnection

    With Conn
        .Connect = "uid=randy;pwd=prince;dsn=Novelty"
        .EstablishConnection rdDriverNoPrompt, True
    End With

End Sub

Private Sub Command1_Click()
```

```
Set qy = New rdoQuery

    qy.SQL = "select * from qryCustomer " & _
             "where LastName = '" & txtValue.Text & "'"

    Set qy.ActiveConnection = Conn
    Set rs = qy.OpenResultset

    lstResult.Clear

    Do Until rs.EOF
        lstResult.AddItem rs!LastName & " " & rs!FirstName
        rs.MoveNext
    Loop

    Set qy = Nothing
    Set rs = Nothing

End Sub
```

You can see that this code is quite similar to the code you'd write in Data Access Objects to generate SQL queries at runtime. The only difference between this code and DAO code is that you'd encounter this code somewhat less frequently in RDO. This is because RDO applications generally make greater use of server-based queries.

Code Example: You can find the code discussed in this section in the sample project QueryFly.vbp, located in the directory \vbdb\code\06-rdo\ QueryFly. For information on how to install the sample files on the CD that accompanies this book, see the section "Installing the Example Files" in the introduction at the beginning of this book.

The code also demonstrates how the rdoQuery object can be instantiated independently of its connection. (This is in contrast to DAO, where you must instantiate a Recordset or QueryDef object from a Database object.) The capability to dissociate the rdoQuery object from its connection can lead to more flexibility in the code you write, because you're not forced to establish a database connection before you construct an rdoQuery object; instead, you can associate a query with a database connection at any time by assigning its ActiveConnection property.

There is another way to create parameterized queries in RDO: through the use of the `rdoParameter` object. This provides a more object-oriented way to create parameterized queries on the fly in your client applications. The `rdoParameter` object is introduced in the next section.

Figure 6.24
The rdoQueries collection and rdoQuery object in the Remote Data Object hierarchy.

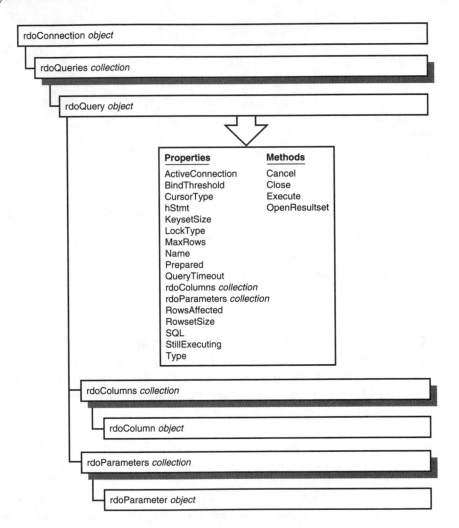

Creating Parameterized Queries Using the *rdoParameter* Object You can write parameterized queries using the `rdoParameter` object. Using `rdoParameter` objects gives you the ability to generate SQL queries in code and assign values to them in a manner that is neater and more object-oriented than generating a long concatenated SQL string (as described in the previous section).

Each `rdoParameter` object belongs to an `rdoParameters` collection. The position of the `rdoParameter` object in the RDO object-model hierarchy is illustrated in Figure 6.25.

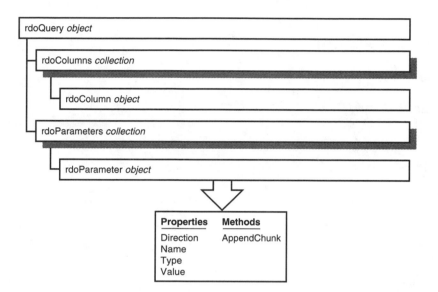

Figure 6.25
The rdoParameters collection and rdoParameter object in the Remote Data Object hierarchy.

Listing 6.6 demonstrates a query that uses an `rdoParameter` object. The parameter is set up in the query's SQL string through the use of the question mark character; in SQL Server, the question mark is a placeholder for a parameter.

Listing 6.6 Creating a Parameterized Query Using the *rdoParameter* Object

```
Option Explicit

' References RDO 2.0

Dim Conn As rdoConnection
Dim qy As rdoQuery
Dim rs As rdoResultset

Private Sub Form_Load()

Set Conn = New rdoConnection

    With Conn
        .Connect = "uid=randy;pwd=prince;dsn=Novelty"
        .EstablishConnection rdDriverNoPrompt, True
```

continues

Listing 6.6   Creating a Parameterized Query Using the *rdoParameter* Object (Continued)

```
    End With

End Sub

Private Sub Command1_Click()

Set qy = New rdoQuery

    qy.SQL = "select * from qryCustomer " & _
            "where LastName Like ?"

    Set qy.ActiveConnection = Conn
    qy.rdoParameters(0) = "%" & txtValue.Text & "%"
    Set rs = qy.OpenResultset

    lstResult.Clear

    Do Until rs.EOF
        lstResult.AddItem rs!LastName & " " & rs!FirstName
        rs.MoveNext
    Loop

    Set qy = Nothing
    Set rs = Nothing

End Sub
```

 Code Example: You can find the code discussed in this section in the sample project `Param.vbp`, located in the directory `\vbdb\code\06-rdo\Param`. For information on how to install the sample files on the CD that accompanies this book, see the section "Installing the Example Files" in the introduction at the beginning of this book.

One difference between this version of the query test application and the versions described previously in this chapter is the fact that this version uses the SQL LIKE operator to retrieve data. (The LIKE operator is introduced in "Operators in *WHERE* Clauses," in Chapter 2, "Queries.") Remember that when you use the LIKE operator, the query retrieves data that partially matches the criterion you specify ("sm" retrieves all the customers named Smith, for example). You can try this in the example application by typing in **jo** to retrieve all the customers named both Jones and Johnson.

Note that in SQL Server, you use the percent sign as the wildcard with the LIKE operator. This is in contrast to DAO's dialect of SQL, which uses an asterisk.

Retrieving Values Using the *rdoColumns* Collection The rdoColumns collection gives you access to the columns involved in an rdoResultset or rdoQuery object.

Each rdoColumn object belongs to an rdoColumns collection. The position of the rdoColumn object in the RDO object model hierarchy is illustrated in Figure 6.26.

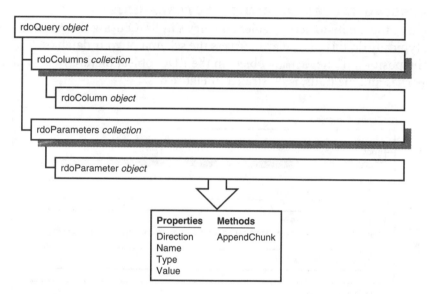

Figure 6.26
The rdoColumns collection and rdoColumn object in the Remote Data Object hierarchy.

Because the rdoColumns collection is the default property of an rdoQuery or rdoResultset object, you don't often refer to the rdoColumns collection or rdoColumn object directly. More frequently, you refer to it implicitly. In fact, the query and resultset in this chapter's previous examples have made implicit reference to the rdoColumns collection in order to retrieve values from individual columns.

For example, if you've queried the database and retrieved an rdoResultset object called rs, you use this code to populate a list box with its data:

```
Do Until rs.EOF
    List1.AddItem rs!FirstName & ? ? & rs!LastName
    rs.MoveNext
Loop
```

This code is actually shorthand for a reference to the rdoColumns collection contained in the rdoResultset object. If you were to write out the code without any shortcuts, it would look like this:

```
Do Until rs.EOF
    List1.AddItem rs.rdoColumns("LastName") & " " & _
                      rs.rdoColumns("FirstName")
    rs.MoveNext
Loop
```

You can see that using the default conserves a significant amount of code and doesn't make the code any less readable.

ACCESSING TABLES WITH THE *RDOTABLE* OBJECT

You have the ability to access tables and views in RDO using the rdoTable object. You typically do this to display or access the schema of your database.

The position of the rdoTable object in the RDO object hierarchy, as well as its properties and methods, is illustrated in Figure 6.27.

Figure 6.27
The rdoTables collection and rdoTable object in the Remote Data Object hierarchy.

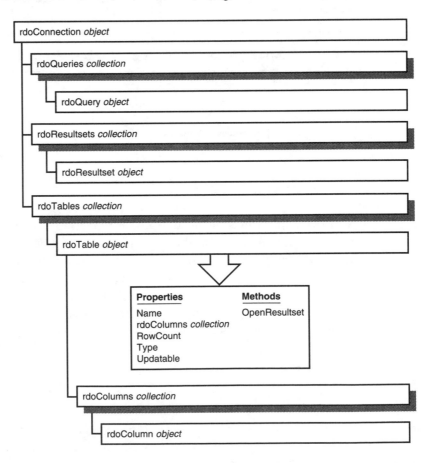

You can use the `rdoTables` collection to iterate through all the tables available in a particular database. To do this, use the code in Listing 6.7.

Listing 6.7   Retrieving a List of Objects in the Database Using the *rdoTables* Collection

```
Option Explicit

' References RDO 2.0

Dim Conn As rdoConnection
Dim rs As rdoResultset
Dim t As rdoTable
Dim qry As rdoQuery

Private Sub Form_Load()

Set Conn = New rdoConnection

    With Conn
        .Connect = "uid=randy;pwd=prince;dsn=Novelty"
        .EstablishConnection rdDriverNoPrompt, True
    End With

End Sub

Private Sub cmdTable_Click()

    Conn.rdoTables.Refresh

    lstResult.Clear

    For Each t In Conn.rdoTables
        lstResult.AddItem t.Name
    Next

End Sub

Private Sub cmdSys_Click()

Set qry = New rdoQuery

qry.SQL = "select * from sysobjects"

    Set qry.ActiveConnection = Conn
    Set rs = qry.OpenResultset

    lstResult.Clear
```

continues

Listing 6.7   Retrieving a List of Objects in the Database Using the *rdoTables* Collection (Continued)

```
    Do Until rs.EOF
        lstResult.AddItem rs!Name
        rs.MoveNext
    Loop

End Sub
```

Code Example: You can find the code discussed in this section in the sample project `Table.vbp`, located in the directory `\vbdb\code\06-rdo\Table`. For information on how to install the sample files on the CD that accompanies this book, see the section "Installing the Example Files" in the introduction at the beginning of this book.

Remember that it's impossible to alter the structure of the database using objects in RDO; consequently, the `rdoTable` object is read-only. (You can alter table structures using conventional DDL calls, though.) This means that the `rdoTable` object is much less important and less frequently used than DAO's `TableDef` object. Note also that the tables displayed in the `rdoTables` collection are limited to the tables accessible to the currently logged-on user (based on the user's security permissions). So if your application needs a procedure that inspects the structure of all of the objects in the database, it's probably better to query the sysobjects table of your database instead. The `click` event of the cmdSys button in the previous code example shows how to do this.

HANDLING ERRORS WITH THE *RDOERRORS* COLLECTION AND THE *RDOERROR* OBJECT

The `rdoErrors` collection is used to identify and handle errors in Remote Data Object programming.

Each `rdoError` object belongs to an `rdoErrors` collection, as illustrated in Figure 6.28.

It's important to utilize the `rdoErrors` collection (as opposed to conventional Visual Basic error-handling) to evaluate and act on errors that take place in your application. This is because it's possible that your application will encounter more than one error message when performing a single operation.

This is possible because of the bucket-brigade nature of client/server computing. When your application does something, it passes that something on to the ODBC driver, which then passes it on to middleware, which passes it on to the server. An error can be generated at any (or all) of these stages, so having access to a collection of errors instead of a single error (such as the `Err` object provided by VB) can go a long way toward helping you figure out exactly what went wrong.

The code to implement this involves iterating through the rdoErrors collection, as shown in Listing 6.8.

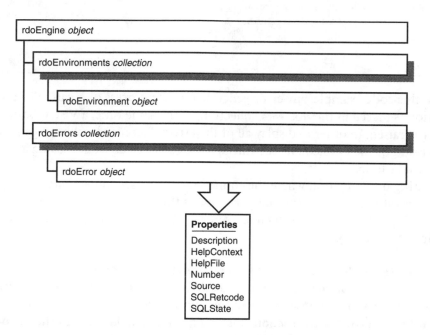

Figure 6.28
The rdoErrors collection and rdoError object in the Remote Data Object hierarchy.

Listing 6.8   Iterating Through the *rdoErrors* Collection in Response to a Data Access Error

```
Option Explicit

' References RDO 2.0

Dim Conn As New rdoConnection
Dim rerr As rdoError

Private Sub Form_Load()

    On Error GoTo ErrHandler

    With Conn
        .Connect = "uid=randy;pwd=prince;dsn=Novelty"
        .EstablishConnection rdDriverNoPrompt, True
    End With

Exit Sub
```

continues

Listing 6.8   Iterating Through the *rdoErrors* Collection in Response to a Data Access Error (Continued)

```
ErrHandler:
    lstResult.Clear
    For Each rerr In rdoEngine.rdoErrors
        lstResult.AddItem rerr.Number & " - " & rerr.Description
    Next

End Sub
```

In this code example, any error generated by the process of creating a connection is placed in the rdoErrors collection; at the same time, a Visual Basic error is raised. In order to display all of the errors that may have been generated as a result of the problem, iterate through the rdoErrors collection using a For Each...Next loop.

Setting up a situation where the connection to the server generates multiple errors is difficult to do easily, but you can test this code by changing the connection string. Change the user ID to a username that doesn't exist, for example, or remove the password.

Code Example: You can find the code discussed in this section in the sample project Error.vbp, located in the directory \vbdb\code\06-Basics\Error. For information on how to install the sample files on the CD that accompanies this book, see the section "Installing the Example Files" in the introduction at the beginning of this book.

WRITING YOUR OWN DATABASE OBJECT SERVER

Using Visual Basic, it's possible for you to create a database server component of your own. You do this using a combination of Component Object Model (COM) and the database engine of your choice (including Microsoft Access, SQL Server, or whatever else you have access to), in conjunction with data access libraries such as DAO, RDO, or ADO. This solution gives you a true client/server database application without necessarily having to use an actual client/server back end.

Why would you want to do this? Performance on the client side, for one thing—if you're using an Access MDB file, your clients don't have to load the Jet database engine on each client, then each client conserves memory. This also means that you don't have to distribute Jet or configure ODBC drivers or other middleware on each client. Database access solutions that seek to minimize the amount of business logic, processing and software components on the client side are sometimes referred to as thin client solutions. Such solutions are seen as desirable because in a corporate environment, the client computer is typically (but not always) the least powerful computer in the organization. These so-called "thin clients" are also desirable because it makes it easier for organizations to standardize on technology and business logic—the fewer changes you need to install on individual client computers, the easier it is to maintain and upgrade a system. This is the case regardless of what data access library you use or what database technology exists on the back end.

In order to create a solution like this, you must have a handle on programming with classes and objects in Visual Basic. This is introduced in Chapter 7.

For more details on how to build a thin-client solution based on ActiveX servers, see Chapter 7, "Database Access with Classes," and Chapter 8, "Remote Database Access."

SUMMARY

This chapter gives you everything you need to get started doing client/server applications using ODBC and Remote Data Objects.

You should bear in mind that although this chapter focuses on client/server programming using SQL Server, the sections in the chapter on Remote Data Objects are applicable to any client/server system—Oracle, Sybase, Informix, whatever. As long as there is an ODBC driver that can get to your back-end data, you should be able to use Remote Data Objects.

In Chapter 7, you take the idea of accessing databases in an object-oriented way a step further by introducing the concepts of classes and ActiveX/COM components. These technologies permit you to create your own application servers to abstract database access from your client-side applications.

QUESTIONS AND ANSWERS

Q. I'm accustomed to writing applications using Data Access Objects. Because DAO supports client/server data sources, I'm having trouble finding a compelling reason for changing my existing code to use RDO. Can you give me a good reason?

A. Performance, for one thing. Robustness, for another. Because Remote Data Objects is designed to be a thin layer around the ODBC API, it's capable of bypassing the Jet database engine entirely. Unless you're using ODBCDirect (which you should start doing unless you need to do something tricky, like link server data with a local Jet database), your existing application must load the Jet database engine whenever it makes a call to the SQL Server database. This doesn't make sense anymore, especially because DAO and RDO are so conceptually similar.

Beyond its performance benefits, RDO provides support for a number of compelling new features (establishing asynchronous connections, batch updates, and more) that go particularly well with client-server systems. At the same time, these new features are also provided by ActiveX Data Objects, discussed in Chapter 10. For new client/server development, ADO is an even more compelling choice than RDO because of its ease of use and flexibility.

Q. Should I use the Remote Data Control or the Data control with ODBCDirect to create data-bound controls?

A. My first instinct is to avoid the whole thing entirely if you can, since the Data control and Remote Data Control can cause architectural and performance problems in database applications. If you must have data-bound controls in your user interface, the trade-off is between the slightly increased performance of the Remote Data Control versus the better reputation for stability provided by the Data control with ODBCDirect (the Remote Data Control in Visual Basic 4.0 had a particularly bad reputation for "bugginess"). Depending on the architecture of your application, consider prototyping with both types of data controls to determine which gives you the best combination of performance and stability. (While we're on the topic—if you're going to use the DAO Data control with client/server data, don't make the mistake of forgetting to use ODBCDirect. There's no point in loading Jet anymore in situations where your Data control is going after data on a server.)

Database Access
with Classes

WORKING WITH CLASSES AND OBJECTS

USING CLASSES AND OBJECTS WITH DATABASE
    ACCESS

CREATING DATA-AWARE CLASSES

CREATING CLASSES THAT EXPORT DATA

DEPLOYING CLASSES AS ACTIVEX SERVERS

D atabase access applications can be complicated—much more so than other types of applications. One reason Visual Basic gives you access to technologies such as Data Access Objects, ActiveX Data Objects, and Open Database Connectivity is to help you manage this complexity.

Yet these database access technologies only go part of the way in helping you deal with complicated issues that arise in software development. A database object model such as ADO, for example, helps you by abstracting the database and therefore making it easy for you to update a record or change a table definition in code. It doesn't help you calculate tax on a sale of merchandise or reject a piece of customer data because it isn't associated with a valid customer ID.

These types of operations go beyond the bare minimum of what's required to get your data from point A to point B; they go even further than what is traditionally known as validation, in which your application checks a piece of data before it is committed to the database. These operations instead fall into a category known as business rules.

Visual Basic lets your applications enforce business rules through the use of classes. A class is a special kind of code module that enables you to create objects. The objects you create with classes are similar to the data access objects you use to communicate with databases, except they can be used for any purpose. In the context of database access, you typically use classes along with database objects to create a database access application.

For example, say you're creating an application to deal with orders and customers. In a non–object-oriented or procedural application, you'd attack the problem by writing functions that record customer and order information, retrieve such information from the database, print the information, and so forth. If you're writing the code in Visual Basic, it's likely that the code will be scattered hither and yon across perhaps a dozen or more event procedures. Each procedure would be hooked up to some esoteric function in your user interface such as a button click.

An object-oriented programmer, on the other hand, would begin by analyzing and designing components, or objects, that abstract the problem of dealing with customers and orders. He or she would determine what information a customer object owns and what actions that customer object performs with that data; likewise with the order object. After the basic objects involved in the business problem are analyzed and expressed as classes, it becomes a simple matter (most of the time) to express customers and orders as objects in the application. You can then reuse the customer and order object in any application that requires them in the future. Because the source code of these objects exists in an easy-to-access container—the class module—rather than existing in a dozen event procedures scattered throughout the application's source code, you can more easily debug and maintain these objects.

In addition to making for good organization and reuse, classes and objects permit you to take advantage of powerful language features in Visual Basic. For example, there's a relationship between customers and orders—you can say that a customer "belongs" to an order, or more accurately, that a collection of orders belongs to a customer. As you see later in this chapter, there is support in the Visual Basic language for collections—a set of objects that can be handled elegantly and efficiently in code.

Were it not for the fact that these concepts were represented by objects, it would be much more difficult for you to conceptualize the problem, discuss it with others, and create a software application that solves the problem.

Object-oriented systems, then, help you conceptualize problems by letting you work backward—starting at the solution, proceeding to the objects involved in that solution, and then going on to the business rules that govern those objects. You may find that working this way represents a bit of a mental stretch if you're accustomed to procedural programming, but in time you'll likely find that focusing on the problem rather than the solution is a more natural way to program.

An object-oriented system contains language elements that provide these elements:

▶ *Abstraction.* Entails reducing a problem to an easy-to-understand metaphor.

▶ *Polymorphism.* Involves enabling an object to perform the same actions or store the same data other objects can. This eases your programming tasks because you don't have to relearn how to program each new object that comes along because disparate objects have similarly named properties and methods.

▶ *Encapsulation.* The mechanism by which program logic and data are grouped together.

▶ *Inheritance.* The idea that a new object can be created from existing objects. The feature of inheritance as implemented in Visual Basic is limited; it's provided in the form of interfaces and through delegation.

For more information: There are a number of books that can help you go further with classes and objects. Deborah Kurata's *Doing Objects in Visual Basic 6.0* (Sams, 1998) is a great reference to object-oriented programming in Visual Basic; Kurata's book also contains a one-of-a-kind design methodology geared toward object-oriented development in VB. There's a Web page for this book at `http://www.insteptech.com/Books.htm`.

My *How to Program Visual Basic Control Creation Edition* (Ziff-Davis Press, 1997) is a step-by-step guide to creating ActiveX user-interface controls using any edition of Visual Basic. The book also contains a chapter on creating data-aware controls. The Web page for this book is `http://www.redblazer.com/cce`.

WORKING WITH CLASSES AND OBJECTS

Because working with classes represents a serious departure from traditional Visual Basic programming, for this section you don't concentrate on accessing the database. Instead, the intention is to get you started creating your own custom classes and to let you worry about integrating them with the database later.

If you've never used classes before, don't be surprised if some of the topics discussed in this section feel a little wrong to you. It's the instinct of every VB programmer to want to reduce the amount of code in his or her application; on the face of things, classes seem to run counter to that instinct, adding what appear at first glance to be pointless additional lines of code to your project.

Remember as you start working with classes that it's all about encapsulation and reusability. The code you write in a class module today is more maintainable because it's encapsulated into one logical structure (the class module itself), and it's more reusable because you can utilize class modules in more than one project (as is discussed in "Deploying Classes as ActiveX Servers" later in this chapter).

BUILDING CUSTOM CLASSES

You start creating an object-oriented application in Visual Basic by adding a class module to your application. After you've done that, you define the interface of objects to be created by that class. An object's properties and methods comprise its *interface*.

Classes can be composed of the following items:

▶ *Private member variables*, which store data

▶ `Property Let` *procedures*, which let users of your classes assign and change private member variables

▶ `Property Get` *procedures*, which let users of your classes read the values of private member variables

▶ *Methods*, which cause your classes to perform actions

▶ *Events*, which allow your classes to broadcast messages to host applications

▶ *Collections*, which allow you to store references to groups of objects

All the basic elements of classes are discussed in this section. Later in this chapter, you'll see how to utilize database objects with classes.

To give you an example of how to set up and use a class, start with something easy—a order-handling class that stores all the information required to take and process an order for a single item. (For this example, you ignore the fact that an order can be composed of more than one product, as well as the fact that the order needs to be stored in the database; you want to focus on the order itself, for now.) After you create the cOrder class in code, you can create and use cOrder objects in the application.

Note: To more accurately reflect a real application, the examples in this chapter use ActiveX Data Objects. You don't have to use ADO for object-oriented data access applications, however. You can use whatever data access technology you wish, including DAO. For more information on ADO, see Chapter 10, "ActiveX Data Objects."

The examples in this chapter assume you have an ODBC Data Source Name called JetNovelty set up on your computer. For information on how to create an ODBC data source, see Chapter 6, "Open Database Connectivity and Remote Data Objects."

Creating the Class Module   To create the corder class, do the following:

1. In Visual Basic, create a new Standard EXE project. The project, called Project1, is created. Initially, it contains a single form.

2. Close Form 1; you won't need it for now.

3. In the Visual Basic Project Explorer, right-click Project1. From the pop-up menu, select Add. From the submenu, select Class Module.

4. The Class Module dialog box appears; Class Module is selected. Click Open.

5. A new class module appears, as illustrated in Figure 7.1. Note that the class module is composed of code only; unlike a form, it has no visible user interface.

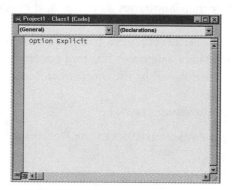

Figure 7.1
You see a new class module in a new Visual Basic project.

6. Finish creating the class by giving the class a name and typing it in the Visual Basic properties window. Change the name of the class from `Class1` to `COrder`. (Prepending the letter C before the name of the object is a standard convention for naming classes.)

Adding Properties to the Class Module   Any time you create a public data element in your class, the objects created in that class expose the data element as a *property* of the object.

Properties are the bread and butter of classes; very few classes without properties exist. You have two options for exposing properties in the classes you write:

▶ Declare a public variable in your class

▶ Declare a private variable in your class, then expose it publicly using `Property Get` and `Property Let` procedures

The public variable technique has the advantage of being easy to program; however, it's extremely inflexible because you have no control over what values get assigned to a public variable.

With a private variable and `Property Let` and `Get`, on the other hand, you have complete control over what gets assigned to a property. Your code can elegantly reject invalid values that users of your class attempt to assign, and it can manipulate data as it is retrieved from the property of your class.

> **Note:** `Property Let` and `Property Get` procedures in Visual Basic are sometimes referred to in other languages as *writer* and *reader functions*.

In our example, the `COrder` object needs to store a number of data items pertaining to orders—order date, customer ID, item ordered, and total cost of the order. These data items are stored by the `COrder` object in the form of properties, which you create in code.

To add properties to the `COrder` class:

1. Add four private member variables to the Declarations section, as shown in Listing 7.1.

Listing 7.1   Code to Declare Private Member Variables in the *COrder* Class

```
Option Explicit

' Private member variables
Private mdatOrderDate As Date
Private mlngCustomerID As Long
Private mstrItemOrdered As String
Private mcurPrice As Currency
```

2. Next, write code to expose the first private member variable, mdatOrderDate, as a public property called OrderDate. You do this with Property Let and Property Get code, as shown in Listing 7.2.

Listing 7.2   Code to Implement a Public *OrderDate* Property in the *COrder* Class

```
Public Property Get OrderDate() As Date
    OrderDate = mdatOrderDate
End Property

Public Property Let OrderDate(ByVal datNew As Date)
    mdatOrderDate = datNew
End Property
```

This is how the code works: The variable mdatOrderDate stores the actual date of the order in the object. The Property Get procedure is executed whenever the application needs access to the order date; it returns the value of mdatOrderDate. The Property Let, on the other hand, is executed when the application needs to assign a value to the order date property.

Using Property Get and Property Let gives you more control over how data is stored in objects you create from classes. What if you want to make a property read-only? Simple—delete the Property Let. What if you want to perform validation on date values assigned to the OrderDate property to make sure they're not four years in the past? No problem—write code in the Property Let to reject date values that are less than the current date.

To round out the properties of the COrder class, add the code shown in Listing 7.3. This provides objects created by this class the properties of CustomerID, ItemOrdered, and Price.

Listing 7.3   Implementing the Remaining Property Procedures in the *COrder* Class

```
Public Property Get CustomerID() As Long
    CustomerID = mlngCustomerID
End Property

Public Property Let CustomerID(ByVal lngNew As Long)
    mlngCustomerID = lngNew
End Property

Public Property Get ItemOrdered() As String
    ItemOrdered = mstrItemOrdered
End Property

Public Property Let ItemOrdered(ByVal strNew As String)
    mstrItemOrdered = strNew
End Property

Public Property Get Price() As Currency
    Price = mcurPrice
End Property

Public Property Let Price(ByVal curNew As Currency)
    mcurPrice = curNew
End Property
```

Your class is now fully functional; you can begin creating objects from it immediately. To test your new class, use the Immediate window to instantiate an object from it:

1. From the View menu, select Immediate window (or use the keystroke shortcut Ctrl+G).

2. The Immediate window appears. In the window, type this code:

```
Set MyOrder = New COrder
```

After you type the keyword New, you should be able to see the list of objects in your current project drop-down box; you should be able to choose COrder from the list.

Note: The Auto List Members feature seems to work inconsistently in the Immediate window; sometimes it doesn't display a list of properties and methods for an object unless the project you were working on is actually

running. This is a limitation of how you instantiate objects in the Immediate window. Don't worry about this—it will work as expected when you write code to instantiate the object in a form.

After you enter this line of code, the Immediate window instantiates a cOrder object, MyOrder, from your class. To assign a property to it, execute the following code in the Immediate window:

```
MyOrder.OrderDate = #6/5/98#
Print MyOrder.OrderDate
```

The Immediate window should respond by printing the date value you stored in the cOrder object.

This isn't the most impressive demonstration of how to create and use objects, but it's a good first step. You'll expand and modify the cOrder class in the next few sections.

Code Example: The code discussed in this section can be found in the project First.vbp, located in the directory \vbdb\code\07-Classes\First. For information on how to install the sample files on the CD that accompanies this book, see the section "Installing the Example Files" in the introduction at the beginning of this book.

Creating Custom Methods   In addition to public properties, most classes contain methods. Your component's users execute methods to get objects created by your classes to do work.

When you create a procedure in a class that is declared Public, it becomes a method of that class.

Methods can be implemented as either functions or subs; a method declared as a function can return a value. You run into methods that return values every so often in the world of object-oriented programming. The OpenDatabase method in DAO is an example of a method that returns a value; this method opens a Jet database and returns a Database object. For more on how you can use such methods in your own classes, see "Using Factory Methods" later in this chapter.

For an example of how you can create a method in the cOrder class, add a method that calculates sales tax for an order.

Perform the following steps to add the AddSalesTax method to the COrder class:

1. In the COrder class, enter the code in Listing 7.4.

Listing 7.4   Code to Add the *AddSalesTax* Method to the Order Class

```
Public Function AddSalesTax() As Currency

    ' Adds sales tax to the price and
    ' returns the amount of sales tax.

    Dim sngSalesTaxRate As Single
    Dim curTax As Currency

    'California is expensive
    sngSalesTaxRate = 0.085

    ' Figure out what the tax is
    curTax = Price * sngSalesTaxRate

    ' Add sales tax to the price
    Price = Price + curTax

    ' Return the sales tax you added
    AddSalesTax = curTax

End Function
```

2. In the Immediate window, enter the following code to test your new method:

```
Set MyOrder = New COrder
```

This creates a new instance of the COrder class.

3. Next, type the following code to set the value of the Price property of the MyOrder object:

```
MyOrder.Price = 3.98
```

4. To add the sales tax, enter the code:

```
Print MyOrder.AddSalesTax
```

This returns the value of the sales tax computed on a $3.98 order, which is 0.3383.

5. Finally, enter the code:

```
Print MyOrder.Price
```

The Immediate window should respond with the new price of the item ordered, which is $4.3183.

After you interact with an object this way, you begin to see why programming with objects makes your job simpler. Objects hide complexity from you, letting you concentrate on the problem instead of the details of how that problem is solved. When you're calculating a sales tax using the MyOrder object, you don't need to know that the sales tax rate is 0.085. Instead, you simply tell the object to add sales tax, and you're done with it.

CREATING COLLECTIONS AND COLLECTION CLASSES

A *collection* is a special data type designed to store references to other objects. You can use collections to easily manage a number of related objects all at once.

The Visual Basic language provides support for manipulating objects in collections. This makes it easier for you to perform operations that affect all the objects in a collection; this can involve anything from changing one or more properties of the objects in a collection to saving objects to a database as a group.

For example, if you have an Orders collection that contains a collection of Order objects, you can calculate the order's total by using the following code:

```
Dim curTotal As Currency

For Each Order in Orders
    curTotal = curTotal + Order.Price
Next
```

If you've already been through the chapters in this book on Data Access Objects and Remote Data Objects, you've seen examples of how to use collections to elegantly handle data structures. For an example of this, see "Working with Collections in Code" in Chapter 3, "Data Access Objects." (ActiveX Data Objects, covered in Chapter 10, also use collections to express one-to-many relationships between database objects.)

Using collections is easier than using arrays, because collections provide a predefined set of methods for manipulating data. For example, when you have an array of five elements and you want to add a sixth element, you have to write several lines of code, redimensioning the array and then adding the new element. The collection, in contrast, has an Add method. So to add a new element to the Orders collection, you simply use this code:

```
Orders.Add MyOrder
```

You don't have to write any code to implement the Add method of a collection, so adding a new element to the collection requires a grand total of one line of code. Adding new elements to a collection using the collection's Add method is also far more efficient than redimensioning and adding a new element to an array.

There are a number of ways to implement a collection in the classes you build.

The easiest (yet least flexible) method is to declare a public variable of the data type Collection in your class. Like public member variables (described earlier in this chapter), this ease of programming comes at a cost of control and flexibility. You don't have the ability to extend the properties or methods of an intrinsic Collection object, and you don't have any control over what type of object can be added to a Collection object—unless you protect the collection object by wrapping it in a class module.

You do this by building collection classes. The collection class is to collections what Property Let and Property Get procedures are to properties—they protect the data from unauthorized access, permit you to control and extend your collection's functionality, and enable you to perform additional processing (such as validation) when data is stored or retrieved.

The relationship between your application, a collection class, and the private collection object it contains is illustrated in Figure 7.2.

Figure 7.2
Relationship between an application and a collection class looks like this.

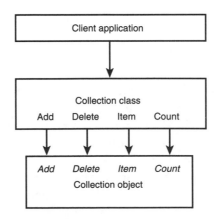

In order to implement a class that wraps a collection, follow these general steps:

1. Create a class with a private member variable declared as the Collection data type.

2. Create property procedures for the four elements of the interface of the collection objects: Add, Delete, Item, and Count. These trigger the Add, Delete, Item, and Count methods of the private collection member variable.

3. If you want, add any additional code your collection class needs. This can include modifications to enhance the default behaviors of the Add, Delete, Item, and Count methods of the collection, as well as any additional properties or methods the collection class needs to expose. For example, in a collection class, the Add method typically performs type validation, preventing inappropriate objects from being added to the collection.

If the idea of writing code in order to wrap a collection doesn't appeal to you, check out the Class Builder utility. In addition to generating code for classes (including Property Let and Get procedures), this VB add-in automatically writes the basic code for wrapping a collection; all you have to do is tell it what objects belong in the collection. There is an example of building an object hierarchy with Class Builder in the next section.

CREATING CLASS HIERARCHIES WITH VB CLASS BUILDER UTILITY

When you're setting up classes that contain other classes—particularly classes that wrap collections—the code can be tedious to write and difficult to keep track of. You can use Visual Basic's Class Builder Utility to make the task of setting up and managing the relationship between a collection and its class wrapper easier.

For example, to create a collection class that enables you to work with collections of Order objects, do the following:

1. Start Visual Basic and load the project that contains the COrder class.

2. From Visual Basic's Add-Ins menu, choose Add-In Manager.

3. Click VB 6 Class Builder Utility in the Add-In Manager dialog box. In the Load Behavior panel, click Loaded/Unloaded.

4. Click OK. The Class Builder Utility loads and becomes available to you.

5. To launch the Class Builder Utility, select the menu command Add-Ins, Class Builder Utility.

6. The Class Builder Utility gives you a warning that the current project contains existing classes not built with the Class Builder Utility. Click OK.

7. The Class Builder Utility window appears, as shown in Figure 7.3.

8. Now use the Class Builder Utility to create a collection class. To do this, start by clicking the Add New Collection button in the toolbar, as shown in Figure 7.3.

Figure 7.3
You can use the Class Builder Utility's New Collection button to create a collection class.

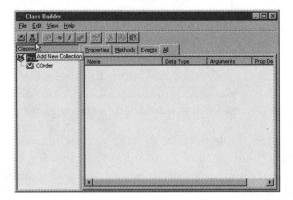

9. The Collection Builder dialog box appears. In the Name box, type the name of your collection class—**colOrder**.

10. Select corder in the panel labeled "Collection Of." This indicates that this collection class is a collection of corder objects. Doing this makes your collection class "type safe"—unlike a conventional collection, only corder objects can be added to this collection.

11. Click OK. The collection class is added to the Class Builder Utility, as shown in Figure 7.4.

12. You can see that the Class Builder Utility has generated properties and methods to support the four methods of the collection (Add, Count, Item, and Remove) as well as NewEnum.

Note: The NewEnum property is created by the Class Builder Utility to enable your collection class to support iteration through the collection using the For Each...Next code construct. It's not usually necessary to do anything with the NewEnum property in your code, but you should know it's necessary to have in a collection class if your class is to support For Each...Next.

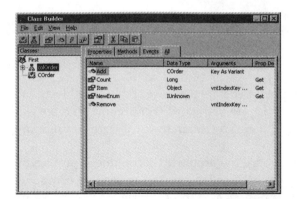

Figure 7.4
*The Class Builder
Utility window
looks like this after
it has created a
collection class.*

13. Now that you've defined your collection class, you can tell the Class Builder Utility to generate code for you. To do this, choose the menu command File Update Project (or use the keystroke shortcut Ctrl+S).

14. The Class Builder Utility silently constructs the collection class in the background. Close the utility by choosing File, Exit. You should be able to see the Orders class that was created by the Class Builder Utility.

You also should be able to see that the Class Builder Utility redefined the syntax of the collection's Add method. Instead of taking an object as an argument, like the Add method of a conventional collection, the new Add method takes variables as arguments. These variables map to the properties of the COrder object. This lets you create the object, add it to a collection, and assign values to it in one fell swoop—a big improvement over doing it the conventional way.

The way the code works now, you add an item to the collection using this syntax:

```
Dim MyOrder As COrder
Dim MyOrders As colOrder
Set MyOrders = New colOrder
Set MyOrder = MyOrders.Add(2.99, "Cheese", 201, #6/5/99#)
```

This might not be the best syntax for adding an item to the collection, though, since it's not immediately obvious to someone who reads your code what the arguments to the Add method mean. A tidier way of doing the same thing would be to use this code:

```
Dim MyOrder As COrder
Dim MyOrders As colOrder
Set MyOrders = New colOrder
Set MyOrder = MyOrders.Add()
```

```
MyOrder.Price = 2.99
MyOrder.ItemOrdered = "Cheese"
MyOrder.CustomerID = 201
MyOrder.OrderDate = #6/5/99#
```

Both code snippets generate the same result: An object is added to the collection and its properties are populated. The second example, which uses properties instead of arguments, is clearer, so you'd want to use it in most situations.

One situation where the argument technique is preferable to the property technique is when the collection class exists in a component deployed remotely over a network. In this scenario, each call to a property of an object generates a round-trip across the network. Accordingly, for performance purposes you should populate the object's properties with a single call rather than several. The argument technique accomplishes this (at the expense of code clarity).

To alter your collection class so it doesn't require arguments to the Add method, change the Add method so it looks like Listing 7.5.

Listing 7.5 Altering the *Add* Method of a Collection Class to Omit Arguments

```
Public Function Add(Optional sKey As String) As COrder
    Dim objNewMember As COrder
    Set objNewMember = New COrder

    If Len(sKey) = 0 Then
        mCol.Add objNewMember
    Else
        mCol.Add objNewMember, sKey
    End If

    Set Add = objNewMember
    Set objNewMember = Nothing

End Function
```

Your collection class is now ready to go, but you'll need to build an application in order to test it. That is described in the next section.

Code Example: You can find the code described in this section in the project First.vbp, located in the directory \vbdb\code\07-Classes\First. The evolved version of the Add method exists in the next project, Order.vbp,

found in the directory `\vbdb\code\07-Classes\Order`. For information on how to install the sample files on the CD that accompanies this book, see the section "Installing the Example Files" in the introduction at the beginning of this book.

Business Case 7.1: Manipulating Data Items Using a Collection Class Hard at work in their dank basement cubicles, the intrepid programmers of Jones Novelties, Incorporated are busy converting the entire corporation's business rules to objects. They're ready to build their first prototype—an order-entry application that transfers data from the user interface to an Order object stored in a collection. Storing the object in a collection enables the application to easily calculate a total on demand.

To build an application that utilizes the `COrder` class and the `colOrder` collection, do the following:

1. Start a new Standard EXE project. Add the `COrder` and `colOrder` classes you created in the previous example.

2. In the project, create a form that enables the user to enter Date, Customer ID, Item, and Price. Additionally, add two command buttons to the interface—the first button enters data, while the second one calculates a total of all the orders entered so far. The interface should look like Figure 7.5.

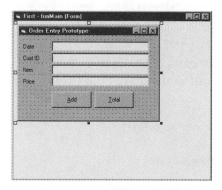

Figure 7.5
The interface of the prototype object-oriented order entry system includes two command buttons.

3. In the form, begin by declaring two module-level variables, one corresponding to a single `COrder` object, the other for the `colOrder` collection:

```
Option Explicit

Private ThisOrder As COrder
Private AllOrders As colOrder
```

4. Instantiate a `colOrder` collection in the form's `Load` event:

```
Private Sub Form_Load()
    Set AllOrders = New colOrder
End Sub
```

5. In the Add button's `Click` event, write code that adds the order to the collection, then resets the application's user interface:

```
Private Sub cmdAdd_Click()

    ' Creates a new order and adds
    ' it to the collection
    Set ThisOrder = AllOrders.Add

    ThisOrder.OrderDate = txtOrderDate.Text
    ThisOrder.CustomerID = txtCustomerID.Text
    ThisOrder.ItemOrdered = txtItemOrdered.Text
    ThisOrder.Price = txtPrice.Text

    ' Reset the user interface
    txtOrderDate.Text = ""
    txtCustomerID.Text = ""
    txtItemOrdered.Text = ""
    txtPrice.Text = ""
    txtOrderDate.SetFocus

End Sub
```

6. Finally, in the `Click` event of the Total button, write code that returns the total value of the orders that have been entered so far using a `For Each…Next` loop.

```
Private Sub cmdTotal_Click()

Dim curTotal As Currency

    For Each ThisOrder In AllOrders
        curTotal = curTotal + ThisOrder.Price
    Next

    MsgBox "The total is " & curTotal, vbInformation

End Sub
```

One cool thing about this code is the fact that it doesn't change when the internal procedures involved in the cOrder object and colOrder collection class change. Even if you change your class modules to support features such as database access, the programmable interface of your objects remains the same.

Code Example: You can find an example of the code discussed in this section in the project Order.vbp, located in the directory \vbdb\code\ 07-Classes\Order. For information on how to install the sample files on the CD that accompanies this book, see the section "Installing the Example Files" in the introduction at the beginning of this book.

Referring to Items in a Collection   Iterating through the collection with a For Each…Next loop isn't the only thing you can do with a collection. After you have the collection set up and populated with objects, you can retrieve individual items from the collection as well. If you add objects to the collection with a key or with a unique text value, you can retrieve the objects without having to know which position in the collection the object occupies—another distinct advantage over arrays.

For instance, in the previous business case example, you created a collection of cOrder objects. To retrieve the fourth order in the collection of orders, use this code:

```
Set MyOrder = AllOrders(4)
```

To refer to a property of the fourth Order object in the collection, simply make a reference to it by its index in the collection, as this line of code demonstrates:

```
AllOrders(4).OrderDate = #6/5/98#
```

This works because the default procedure of a collection returns a reference to the numbered item. This default procedure is the Item method. Because Item is the default method of a collection, you never have to explicitly write it out. If you choose to, though, the previous line of code would look like this:

```
AllOrders.Item(4).OrderDate = #6/5/98#
```

Caution: The first item in a collection is item number one, not item number zero. This is different than arrays, which begin numbering their members at zero. Confusingly, it's also different than Visual Basic collections of things like Form and Control objects; these collections begin numbering their items at zero. The rule is that collections you create are one-based, while collections VB creates are zero based. This is also the case for collections of data-access objects, such as the `TableDefs` collection of the `Database` object.

To retrieve an item from the collection using a key, you must first add it to the collection with a key. To do this with a collection class, pass a unique string value to the `Add` method:

```
AllOrders.Add "ORD1193"
```

You get a runtime error if this string value is not unique. To refer to a property of this object after it's been created in the collection, use the code:

```
MsgBox AllOrders("ORD1193").Price
```

It's important that you don't use a numeric value for an object's key value, even if you pass it to the `Add` method in the form of a string. This is because the `Item` method can return an object from the collection by key or by ordinal position; it determines whether to return an object by key or by ordinal position by what data type it gets. If the `Item` method gets a number n, it returns the nth item in the collection. If it receives a string, it returns the object with a key equal to that string. If your strings can be cast as numbers, though, you're setting yourself up for a problem.

USING FORMS AS CLASSES

You can use forms in your application the same way you use classes. This is useful in situations where you want to create instances of the same form repeatedly. It's also useful in situations where a particular data value or procedure is tightly bound to the user interface.

The login form is an example of this in the database access world. This form allows the user to enter a login name and password. There's no reason why that user-interface component can't also store the information pertaining to the user, making that information available to other procedures in the application. Such a form would also be reusable across other applications that require the user to log in to the same database.

To create and use a login form that exposes custom properties, do the following:

1. In a VB project, right-click the Project Explorer.

2. Select Add from the pop-up menu. Choose Form from the submenu.

3. The Form dialog box appears. Choose Login form, as shown in Figure 7.6.

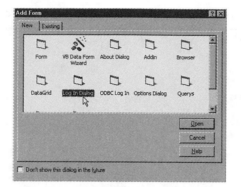

Figure 7.6
*Visual Basic's Add
Form dialog box
lets you choose
from a variety of
predefined form
templates.*

4. In the Form dialog box, click Open. A new form is created.

5. In the form's code, enter the property procedures in Listing 7.6.

Listing 7.6   Code to Supply Custom Properties and a Method to the Login Form

```
Public Property Get UserName() As String
    UserName = txtUserName.Text
End Property

Public Property Let UserName(ByVal strNew As String)
    txtUserName.Text = strNew
End Property

Public Property Get Password() As String
    Password = txtPassword.Text
End Property

Public Property Let Password(ByVal strNew As String)
    txtPassword.Text = strNew
End Property

Public Sub Login()
    MsgBox "Logging in user " & UserName & "."
End Sub
```

6. The standard Visual Basic login form contains code in the `Click` events of
the OK and Cancel buttons to log the user in to the system. Remove this
code and replace it with code in Listing 7.7; it takes advantage of your custom properties and method.

Listing 7.7   Code for the *Click* Events of the Login Form's OK and Cancel Buttons

```
Private Sub cmdCancel_Click()
    Me.Hide
End Sub


Private Sub cmdOK_Click()
    UserName = txtUserName.Text
    Password = txtPassword.Text
    Login
    Me.Visible = False
End Sub
```

Although expressing this code in terms of properties and methods may not seem like a radical departure from the default code provided by Visual Basic's login form template, it has a number of important advantages. Among these is the fact that the login form can be more easily reused across multiple applications. It's also easier to get information out of this form; you can use code like `frmLogin.Password` and `frmLogin.UserName` from anywhere in the application. Finally, placing a single public `Login` method in your login form means that it can be called from anywhere in your application. Having a single point of access to a database is very important when you're trying to conserve resources in a client/server application, as discussed in "Using Factory Methods" later in this chapter.

Code Example: You can find an example of the code discussed in this section in the project `Login.vbp`, located in the directory `\vbdb\code\ 07-Classes\Login`. For information on how to install the sample files on the CD that accompanies this book, see the section "Installing the Example Files" in the introduction at the beginning of this book.

CREATING MULTIPLE INSTANCES OF FORMS

You can create multiple instances of forms just as you create multiple instances of objects from classes. Each additional instance of the form has its own identity in the context of your application, with a copy of all the properties, methods, and user-interface controls that exist on the original design of the form.

It doesn't make sense to have more than one instance of a user login form, but it's common to have multiple instances of other types of forms. To do this, create a new instance of the form using the same code you'd use to create new instances of objects from a class. Listing 7.8 shows an example of how to do this.

Listing 7.8   Creating Multiple Instances of a Form Using Object-Oriented Code

```
Dim f as frmMain
Set f = New frmMain
f.Show
```

You can execute this code as many times as you want. Each time you create a new instance of frmMain and show it using its Show method, a new form—with its own interface, controls, properties, and methods—appears.

USING CLASSES AND OBJECTS WITH DATABASE ACCESS

Creating your own objects can go a long way toward managing complexity and reusing of code. Using object-oriented techniques for accessing databases, however, can be tricky. Developers who create their own custom classes and collections in Visual Basic initially want to take all their recordsets and convert them into collections. After all, collections are objects, and object-oriented programming is a good thing, right?

To a certain extent, this strategy makes sense. If you have a single object or set of objects that manage database access in your application, your application is easier to debug and modify, because you always know where the database access portion of your program is. You don't have to reinvent the wheel repeatedly in order to simply retrieve data and write it back to the data store.

The problem with database access in classes has to do with the fact that the object model and the relational model are at odds with each other. In many cases, treating a database record as an object is like sticking a round peg in a not-so-round hole. Most databases you're likely to use in the foreseeable future don't have the capability to store and retrieve custom-made objects (although database vendors are hard at work creating such "object-oriented databases").

To let your objects do database access using the mainstream database engines available to you today, you have to write code to translate, or map, data stored in a database to the set of properties exposed by the objects you create.

There are a number of means for applying object-oriented techniques to database access in VB. These include the following:

▶ *Mapping a single record to an object.* This is the simplest technique, requiring the least amount of code. Each field in the record becomes a property of the object; retrieving and saving the data to and from the database is handled by the object itself.

▶ *Delegating the handling of data to a* Recordset *object owned by your object.* This is the best technique to use when you have to deal with a potentially unlimited number of records. This technique can also be a bit easier to code, because much of the data management functionality is provided for you by the object model (either DAO or RDO) your class utilizes. The technique is particularly effective when you're using ActiveX Data Objects, since ADO gives you the ability to disconnect from the data source, permitting a client application to manipulate a chunk of data without maintaining a connection to the server. Since the number of simultaneously connected users is typically one of the big bottlenecks of client/server computing, disconnecting means that your solution will be more scalable.

▶ *Mapping a small group of records to a collection.* This is more difficult to code than mapping one object to one record at a time, but it's more useful if you have to deal with small related groups of records at a time. You can run into performance problems with this technique if you aren't careful to limit the number of records you handle at one time.

▶ *Dividing data access between client and server.* This technique is best when you want to achieve maximum scalability and efficiency in your application. It involves splitting the middle-tier logic of your application into two parts: a server-side component that performs data access and returns data chunks to the client and a client-side component that receives these chunks and maps them to properties of business objects.

These aren't the only techniques you can use for data access, and different methods are appropriate for different situations. The examples in the remainder of this chapter should give you an idea of which technique to use for your situation.

USING SINGLE-RECORD-HANDLING CLASSES

A *record-handling class* retrieves a single record from the database and makes it available to your application in the form of an object. The fields in the record are exposed as the object's properties. Any actions performed by the data (such as saving its data back to the database, printing, or performing calculations) are exposed as methods of the record-handling object.

To enable the class to populate its properties, give the class a method (named something like GetData) that knows how to perform a single-record query from the database. When the GetData method queries the data from the database, it uses the fields in the record it retrieves to populate the properties of the object.

When you give the object the responsibility of retrieving a record from a database, you'll need to give that object something to uniquely identify that record—preferably that record's primary key. The easiest way to do this is to make the primary key a property of the record-handling object; the object's GetData method uses this key data to retrieve the record it needs.

In addition to retrieving data from the database, you probably also want to give your record-handling class a method—most likely called save—that enables the user of the component to save the record back to the database.

Business Case 7.2 gives a more detailed example of such a class.

Business Case 7.2: Using a Single-Record-Handling Class   Jones Novelties has expanded its Information Services division. New applications are being planned monthly in response to increasing demand for data services by managers and users.

The intrepid database programmers of Jones Novelties decide to meet the need for reusable components that provide access to the corporate database by creating a class library that gives standardized access to the corporate database.

As with any database access in Visual Basic, you'll use a database object library—in this case, ActiveX Data Objects. (This technique works equally well with DAO or RDO, if you prefer to use those libraries.)

To start, create a cCustomer class that enables your applications to deal with customers in an object-oriented way. Each Customer object will have all the properties a customer has, including first name, last name, address, city, state, and ZIP Code. These values correspond to fields in the tblCustomer table in the company database, but in the object-oriented world, they are expressed as properties of the cCustomer object.

In order to provide connectivity to the company database, the Customer class uses a DataEnvironment designer named deNovelty. (DataEnvironment designers are introduced in Chapter 2, "Queries.") This designer contains a connection called cnNovelty used to get access to the database. All the database access code involved in retrieving and manipulating customers is kept away from the user of the Customer class, however. The gory details are "under the hood," in the guts of the cCustomer class.

Mapping a single record to an object requires that you write code to retrieve and store the record in the database; each field in the record becomes a property of the object created from your class. In ADO, single-record-handlers typically contain a private Recordset object. This object is not exposed to the user of the class in order to make the class module itself the one true way of accessing data.

That way, if some implementation detail changes in the future, you only have to make a change in the class.

Additionally, the Customer object needs to know how to save itself to the database (through the execution of a Save method) and perform other tasks related to accessing the database.

Listing 7.9 shows the properties of a single-record-handler in a class called CCustomer.

Listing 7.9   A Single-Record-Handler Class That Exposes Fields in a Record as Properties of an Object

```
Option Explicit

' References ADO 2.0.

' Private member variables for
' object properties
Private mstrFirstName As String
Private mstrLastName As String
Private mstrAddress As String
Private mstrCity As String
Private mlngID As Long                 ' Primary key
Private mstrState As String
Private mstrZip As String
Private mstrPhone As String


' Error constants
Const srCouldNotGetData = vbObjectError + 512 + 2
Const srCouldNotSaveData = vbObjectError + 512 + 3



Private Sub Class_Initialize()
    ' Open connection via
    ' DataEnvironment designer
    deNovelty.cnNovelty.Open
End Sub


Private Sub Class_Terminate()
    deNovelty.cnNovelty.Close
End Sub


Public Property Let Address(ByVal strNew As String)
    mstrAddress = strNew
```

```
End Property

Public Property Get Address() As String
    Address = mstrAddress
End Property


Public Property Let City(ByVal strNew As String)
    mstrCity = strNew
End Property

Public Property Get City() As String
    City = mstrCity
End Property


Public Property Get ID() As Long
    ID = mlngID
End Property

Public Property Let ID(ByVal lngNew As Long)
    mlngID = lngNew
End Property


Public Property Let FirstName(ByVal strNew As String)
    mstrFirstName = strNew
End Property

Public Property Get FirstName() As String
    FirstName = mstrFirstName
End Property


Public Property Let LastName(ByVal strNew As String)
    mstrLastName = strNew
End Property

Public Property Get LastName() As String
    LastName = mstrLastName
End Property
```

continues

Listing 7.9   A Single-Record-Handler Class That Exposes Fields in a Record as Properties of an Object (Continued)

```
Public Property Let Phone(ByVal strNew As String)
    mstrPhone = strNew
End Property

Public Property Get Phone() As String
    Phone = mstrPhone
End Property


Public Property Let State(ByVal strNew As String)
    mstrState = strNew
End Property

Public Property Get State() As String
    State = mstrState
End Property


Public Property Let Zip(ByVal strNew As String)
    mstrZip = strNew
End Property

Public Property Get Zip() As String
    Zip = mstrZip
End Property


Public Sub GetData(lngID As Long)

    Dim rs As ADODB.Recordset
    Set rs = New ADODB.Recordset

    If lngID <> 0 Then
        rs.Source = "select * from tblCustomer " & _
                    "where ID = " & lngID
        rs.MaxRecords = 1
        Set rs.ActiveConnection = deNovelty.cnNovelty
        rs.Open

        ' Make sure a record
        ' actually came back.
        If rs.EOF = True And rs.BOF = True Then
            Err.Raise srCouldNotGetData, _
                    "CCustomer - GetData", _
                    "Customer not found."
```

```
        End If

        ' Populate properties with
        ' results of the query.
        FirstName = rs!FirstName & ""    ' cheesy null-safe trick
        ID = lngID
        LastName = rs!LastName & ""
        Address = rs!Address & ""
        City = rs!City & ""
        State = rs!State & ""
        Zip = rs!Zip & ""
        Phone = rs!Phone & ""
    Else
        Err.Raise srCouldNotGetData, _
                "Customer - GetData", _
                "Customer not found."
        Exit Sub
    End If

End Sub


Public Sub Save()

    Dim rs As ADODB.Recordset
    Set rs = New ADODB.Recordset

    rs.LockType = adLockOptimistic
    rs.CursorType = adOpenKeyset
    Set rs.ActiveConnection = deNovelty.cnNovelty
    rs.source = "select * " & _
                "from tblCustomer " & _
                "where ID = " & ID
    rs.Open

    ' Insert or update?
    If ID = 0 Then
        ' Insert!
        rs.AddNew
    Else
        ' Update! No need for Edit
        ' method like in DAO.
    End If
```

continues

Listing 7.9   A Single-Record-Handler Class That Exposes Fields in a Record as Properties of an Object (Continued)

```
    rs.Fields("FirstName") = FirstName
    rs.Fields("LastName") = LastName
    rs.Fields("Address") = Address
    rs.Fields("City") = City
    rs.Fields("State") = State
    rs.Fields("Zip") = Zip
    rs.Fields("Phone") = Phone
    rs.Fields("Zip") = Zip

    rs.Update

    rs.Close
    Set rs = Nothing

End Sub
```

The initialization of the database connection happens in the class's `Initialize` event. The primary key, which is used in the `GetData` and `Save` methods, allows the record-handler class to look up all the information in the database pertaining to the information requested by the user.

The real benefit of placing database access in a single-record-handler class becomes evident when you look at the class's `Save` method. This method requires quite a bit of code to perform a simple update, and the method shown here (a SQL command constructed on the fly in code) isn't even the most sophisticated way to perform updates in ADO. (Calling a stored procedure would be more efficient.)

What if you decide to be ambitious and revise the `Save` method to actually call a stored procedure using ADO? Does your application care that you changed the code? Heck, no. All your application cares about is the fact that the data was actually saved in the database. The code used to call the class's `Save` method remains the same regardless of the code involved to perform the save.

The point here is that the details of the technique used to save the data shouldn't matter to your application. Separating the functionality of your application from its specific implementation is an important object-oriented technique that can go a long way toward making your programs easier to maintain and improve over time without breaking related code.

To use this class, write code in the project's form that retrieves a record and permit the user to save it back to the database:

1. Add eight text boxes to the project's form. The first text box stores the customer's ID number and is used for querying; the other seven text boxes display the customer's properties. Add two command buttons, one for retrieving data, the other for saving data.

2. Declare a CCustomer object variable in the form's Declarations section. In the form's Load event, instantiate the object, as shown in Listing 7.10.

Listing 7.10   Code to Declare an Object Variable and Create an Instance of the Customer Object

```
Option Explicit


Private CurrentCustomer As CCustomer



Private Sub Form_Load()
    Set CurrentCustomer = New CCustomer
End Sub
```

3. Next, add code to retrieve data for the CCustomer object according to the ID entered by the user, as shown in Listing 7.11.

Listing 7.11   Mapping Properties of User-Interface Controls to Properties of the *CurrentCustomer* **Object**

```
Private Sub cmdGet_Click()

    CurrentCustomer.GetData txtCustomerID.Text

    txtFirstName.Text = CurrentCustomer.FirstName
    txtLastName.Text = CurrentCustomer.LastName
    txtAddress.Text = CurrentCustomer.Address
    txtCity.Text = CurrentCustomer.City
    txtState.Text = CurrentCustomer.State
    txtZip.Text = CurrentCustomer.Zip
    txtPhone.Text = CurrentCustomer.Phone

End Sub
```

4. Enter code to save the record after the user changes it, as shown in Listing 7.12.

Listing 7.12   Saving a Customer Object From Within a Form

```
Private Sub cmdSave_Click()

    CurrentCustomer.FirstName = txtFirstName.Text
    CurrentCustomer.LastName = txtLastName.Text
    CurrentCustomer.Address = txtAddress.Text
    CurrentCustomer.City = txtCity.Text
    CurrentCustomer.State = txtState.Text
    CurrentCustomer.Zip = txtZip.Text
    CurrentCustomer.Phone = txtPhone.Text


    CurrentCustomer.Save

    MsgBox "The current customer has been saved.", vbInformation

End Sub
```

5. Finally, add code to destroy the Customer object when the form is
unloaded, as shown in Listing 7.13.

Listing 7.13   Destroying the Instance of the Customer Object Used by the Form

```
Private Sub Form_Unload(Cancel As Integer)
    Set CurrentCustomer = Nothing
End Sub
```

Now the advantage of using classes to access records in a database really
becomes apparent. The code in the form is so straightforward, looking at it
makes you sleepy. And that's exactly the point.

**Code Example: You can find the code discussed in this section in the pro-
ject Customer.vbp, located in the directory \vbdb\code\07-Classes\Customer.
For information on how to install the sample files on the CD that accompanies this book, see the section "Installing the Example Files" in the introduction at the beginning of this book.**

USING ARRAY-HANDLING CLASSES

You can create classes that query the database, then pass data back to client
applications in the form of arrays. The advantage to this technique is that if
your array-handling class is compiled to an ActiveX server DLL or EXE, it's

possible to create a client application that requires no references to the database engine. All the client requires is a reference to your ActiveX server component. This makes the footprint of your client-side application much smaller; it also makes the application much easier to distribute and configure.

Creating a server-side component that returns a construct such as an array means that client applications don't need to maintain a persistent connection to the server, which can increase scalability in your client/server applications.

For more information on creating ActiveX components that pass data in the form of arrays, see "Using GetRows to Return Data in an Array" in Chapter 8, "Remote Database Access."

USING FACTORY METHODS

An *object factory* is a method that creates other objects. You use object factories in situations where one object takes responsibility for creating other objects. Objects create other objects through the use of methods; such methods are called *factory methods*.

Although this might seems like one of those alien object-oriented concepts, you've probably used it already—in Data Access Objects, for example. The DAO Database object, for instance, has a number of factory methods that produce objects. By way of example, Table 7.1 gives some more examples of factory methods of the DAO Database object.

Table 7.1 Factory Methods of the DAO Database Object	
Method	**Description**
CreateQueryDef	Creates a QueryDef object
CreateRelation	Creates a Relation object
CreateTableDef	Creates a TableDef object
OpenRecordset	Creates a Recordset object
CreateProperty	Creates a Property object

In addition to using the factory methods provided by Visual Basic, you can create factory methods in the classes you build yourself. You do this in a number of situations, generally pertaining to simplifying and extending the capabilities of object instantiation in your application.

One common reason to use factory methods has to do with the way objects are created in VB. Other programming languages that use objects (such as Visual C++) have constructors responsible for creating instances of the object from the class; these constructors can also perform other tasks, such as supplying initialization data for the class. Classes can have multiple constructors from which programmers can choose, and constructors can take and return parameters.

There's no direct correlation, however, to constructors in Visual Basic. Instead, VB classes have an Initialize event. You can write code in the Initialize event as you can in a Visual C++ constructor, but unfortunately, you can't pass arguments to the VB Initialize event, and you only get one Initialize event per class. This makes the usefulness of the Initialize event extremely limited for all but the most basic, hard-coded default values. Factory methods provide an alternative that overcomes these limitations.

Business Case 7.3: Using a Factory Method to Create Record-Handling Objects

The stalwart developers of Jones Novelties Incorporated have really taken to using database-driven classes in their applications. Now they wish to simplify the process of working with the CCustomer object by creating a factory method, CCustomerFactory, to produce CCustomer objects whenever their applications require them.

The CCustomerFactory object has one method: CreateCustomer. This method takes an optional argument. If the argument is present, CreateCustomer retrieves an existing customer from the database. If it is missing, it creates a new Customer object. The code for the CCustomerFactory class is shown in Listing 7.14.

Listing 7.14   Code for the *CCustomerFactory* Class

```
Option Explicit

' Requires CCustomer class

Public Function CreateCustomer(Optional lngID As Variant) As CCustomer

Dim Cust As CCustomer

    If IsMissing(lngID) Then
        ' Create new customer
        Set CreateCustomer = New CCustomer
    Else
        ' Retrieve customer from DB
        Set Cust = New CCustomer
```

```
        Cust.GetData (lngID)
        Set CreateCustomer = Cust
    End If

End Function
```

The object factory makes creating a fully-populated customer object even simpler. The code to create a CCustomer object now looks like this:

```
Dim MyCust As CCustomer
Dim cf As CCustFactory
Set cf = New CCustFactory

' Retrieve data
Set MyCust = cf.CreateCustomer(txtID.Text)
```

Code Example: You can find an example of the code discussed in this section in the project Factory.vbp, located in the directory \vbdb\code\ 07-Classes\Factory. For information on how to install the sample files on the CD that accompanies this book, see the section "Installing the Example Files" in the introduction at the beginning of this book.

This project uses a CCustomer class similar, but not identical, to that introduced in Business Case 7.2, "Using a Single-Record-Handling Class." The main difference between the CCustomer class used in that business case and the CCustomer class used here is the fact that this CCustomer class uses code instead of a DataEnvironment designer to establish a connection to the database.

Another reason for using factory methods in Visual Basic database programming is to conserve connection resources. It's in your interest to make as few connections to the database as possible, because connecting to the database is computationally expensive; it requires time and memory resources on the client and on the server.

If you use a class that acts as an object factory, it's easier to limit the number of connections you make to the server. You do this by creating the connection object once, in the object factory class, instead of within each individual class module.

Note: The concept of the factory method introduced in this section is described in more detail in *Design Patterns: Elements of Reusable Object-Oriented Software* (Addison-Wesley, 1995). This book provides a number of scenarios for using objects in your applications in addition to the concept of the factory method. While not all the concepts introduced in the book are applicable to Visual Basic because of limitations of the language, many of the object-oriented programming (OOP) concepts in the book can help you grasp the Zen of OOP.

CREATING DATA-AWARE CLASSES

Classes have the ability to directly bind to databases. This feature is new in VB6. No longer are you limited to data controls as data sources for your database applications.

In addition to providing new data sources, VB6 also removes limitations on how your application connects to data sources. No longer do you have to establish data binding at design-time, as you did with the DAO Data control. Instead, you can assign a data source (such as an ADO Data control, DataEnvironment designer, or data provider class) to a data consumer (such as a bound user-interface control) at runtime. This gives you a great deal of flexibility when determining how your application runs. More importantly to object-oriented programmers, it permits you to encapsulate the code pertaining to data access and business rules in the place where such code belongs—the class module.

Note: This section isn't designed to be a complete discussion of data-bound user-interface controls in VB. That topic is covered in more depth in Chapter 12, "User-Interface Controls."

CREATING CLASSES THAT ACT AS DATA SOURCES

You can create a class that provides data to your application. Such a class, called a *data source* or a *data provider*, is better than a data control because you control the class's implementation in code. You're also not forced to insert the data source in a form, as you must do with a data control, so the class becomes more reusable.

Note: Data source classes are new in VB6. They aren't available in previous versions of VB.

To create a data source class to provide access to the Novelty database, do the following:

1. Create a Standard EXE project.

2. Use the Project menu to add a class module to your project. Name the new class module CCustData.

3. Use the Properties window to change the class's DataSourceBehavior to 1 - vbDataSource.

4. Using the Project, References menu, make a reference to Microsoft ActiveX Data Objects.

Note: You'll notice when you open the Project References menu that a reference to a library called Microsoft Data Source Interfaces has been made for you. This reference was made by VB automatically when you assigned the class module's DataSourceBehavior property in the previous step.

5. In the declarations section of the class, create a private Recordset object. This object will handle database access.

```
Private mrsCustomer As ADODB.Recordset
```

6. In the class' Initialize event, write code to create the Recordset object.

```
Set mrsCustomer = New ADODB.Recordset
mrsCustomer.Source = "select * from tblCustomor"
mrsCustomer.CursorType = adOpenKeyset
mrsCustomer.LockType = adLockOptimistic
mrsCustomer.ActiveConnection = "DSN=JetNovelty;"
mrsCustomer.Open
```

Using a keyset cursor isn't absolutely required here, but you'll find it necessary if you want your data source to work with complex bound controls such as grids. (You could substitute another scrolling cursor type if you wanted.) Also, specifying an editable lock type (such as adLockOptimistic) isn't required either, but it is necessary if you want the data provided by the control to be editable.

There's no reason why you can't make the connection string a public property of your class module; we've hard-coded it here for simplicity.

7. Also in the class's `Initialize` event, write code to register this data source with the `DataMembers` collection provided by the Microsoft Data Binding library. This will permit data consumers (such as bound controls) to use this class as a data source:

```
DataMembers.Add "Customers"
```

8. Write code in the class's `GetDataMember` event to return a `Recordset` object based on the event's `DataMember` parameter. (The `GetDataMember` event became available when you set the class's `DataSourceBehavior` property previously.) Because the `GetDataMember` event is parameterized in this way, you can connect your application to a potentially unlimited number of recordsets; however, this class will return only a list of customers.)

```
Private Sub Class_GetDataMember(DataMember As String, Data As Object)
    Select Case DataMember
        Case ""
            Set Data = Nothing
        Case "Customers"
            Set Data = mrsCustomer
        Case Else
            ' Raise your error here
    End Select
```

Notice that the `Data` argument of the `GetDataMember` event is an object, not a recordset. This suggests that you could give access to other types of objects in place of an ADO `Recordset` object from the event.

9. Next, write public methods in the `CCustData` class to control the recordset. You can write as many methods as you wish in your data-bound class; in this example we'll create the four "move" methods provided by a data control:

```
Public Sub MoveFirst()
    mrsCustomer.MoveFirst
End Sub
```

```
Public Sub MoveLast()
    mrsCustomer.MoveLast
End Sub
```

```
Public Sub MoveNext()
    mrsCustomer.MoveNext
    If mrsCustomer.EOF Then
        mrsCustomer.MoveLast
    End If
End Sub


Public Sub MovePrevious()
    mrsCustomer.MovePrevious
    If mrsCustomer.BOF Then
        mrsCustomer.MoveFirst
    End If
End Sub
```

10. Using VB's Project Components menu, add the control Microsoft DataGrid Control 6.0 (OLEDB) to your project. This will enable you to display the data in a grid. Create an instance of the grid control on your form.

11. On the form, create four command buttons to navigate through the data. Name these buttons cmdFirst, cmdPrevious, cmdNext, and cmdLast.

12. In the form's Load event, declare and create an instance of the data-source class. Write code in the command buttons' Click events to call the class's move methods.

```
Private mCustData As CCustData

Private Sub Form_Load()
    ' Create the data source object
    Set mCustData = New CCustData

    ' Bind the object to grid
    Set DataGrid1.DataSource = mCustData
    DataGrid1.DataMember = "Customers"
End Sub


Private Sub cmdFirst_Click()
    mCustData.MoveFirst
End Sub
```

```
Private Sub cmdPrevious_Click()
    mCustData.MovePrevious
End Sub


Private Sub cmdNext_Click()
    mCustData.MoveNext
End Sub


Private Sub cmdLast_Click()
    mCustData.MoveLast
End Sub
```

13. Run the application. You should be able to navigate through the data in the grid by using the command buttons. You should even be able to edit data. Edits are saved to the database automatically when you move off the edited record, just as if you were using a data control. But this application requires no data control to function; all the data-handling code exists in the data-source class.

Code Example: You can find an example of the code discussed in this section in the project `Source.vbp`, located in the directory `\vbdb\code\` `07-Classes\Source`. For information on how to install the sample files on the CD that accompanies this book, see the section "Installing the Example Files" in the introduction at the beginning of this book.

When you build a data source class, you're not limited to using them for bound controls. In fact, classes can act as data consumers as well as providers, as described in the next section.

CREATING CLASSES THAT EXPORT DATA

When you have a good general idea of how you want to export data, it makes sense to take that export logic and place it in a class. This is because classes make it easy to reuse code, and export code is among the most reused in the world of database programming.

Chances are that if you write one procedure that takes a database table and converts it into a delimited text file, you're going to have to do it again at some point in your life. This section shows you how to create such procedures once, get them right the first time, and never have to worry about them once you've deployed them.

This section builds on the HTML export function described in Chapter 4, "Reporting and Exporting Data," to demonstrate how easy it is to provide a programmable export object using classes. In that chapter, you built a function to take a database and map its fields to the properties of an object. The product of this process was the Customer class.

To give the CCustomer class export capabilities, you add one additional property and one method to the class. The new property, HTMLText, takes properties of the CCustomer object and formats them as an HTML page. This property procedure calls a private function, HTMLTableRow, that formats each individual row of the table. This code is shown in Listing 7.15.

Listing 7.15   The *HTMLText* Property of the Customer Class

```
Public Property Get HTMLText() As String
Dim str As String

    str = "<html>" & vbCrLf
    str = str & "<head>" & vbCrLf
    str = str & "<title>" & "Customer: " & _
                FirstName & " " & _
                LastName & _
                "</title>" & vbCrLf


    str = str & "<body bgcolor=#ffffff>" & vbCrLf
    str = str & "<font face=Tahoma, Arial, Helvetica>" & vbCrLf


    str = str & "<table border>" & vbCrLf


    str = str & HTMLTableRow("First name:", FirstName)
    str = str & HTMLTableRow("Last name:", LastName)
    str = str & HTMLTableRow("Address:", Address)
    str = str & HTMLTableRow("City:", City)
    str = str & HTMLTableRow("State:", State)


    str = str & "</table>"


    str = str & "</font>" & vbCrLf
    str = str & "</body>" & vbCrLf
    str = str & "</html>" & vbCrLf
```

continues

Listing 7.15   The *HTMLText* Property of the Customer Class (Continued)

```
    HTMLText = str

End Property


Private Function HTMLTableRow(strLabel As String, vValue As Variant) As String

' Returns a row of a two-column HTML table

Dim str As String

    str = str & "<tr>" & vbCrLf
    str = str & "  <td>" & vbCrLf
    str = str & "   " & strLabel & vbCrLf
    str = str & "  </td>" & vbCrLf
    str = str & "  <td>" & vbCrLf
    str = str & "   " & vValue & vbCrLf
    str = str & "  </td>" & vbCrLf
    str = str & "</tr>"

HTMLTableRow = str

End Function
```

You'll notice that this code doesn't actually export the HTML to a file; it simply formats it. This is done because you want the flexibility to do anything with the HTML data, not necessarily just export it to a file. The process of exporting is really two things: first, formatting the data in HTML, and second, writing it to a file. Accordingly, you write separate procedures to perform each task.

The SaveHTML method of the Customer object is responsible for saving the formatted HTML data to a file. Its code is shown in Listing 7.16.

Listing 7.16   The *SaveHTML* Method of the Customer Object, Which Saves the HTML Version of the Customer Data to a File

```
Public Sub SaveHTML(strFileName As String)
Dim fs As Scripting.FileSystemObject
Dim txt As Scripting.TextStream

    Set fs = New Scripting.FileSystemObject
    Set txt = fs.OpenTextFile(strFileName, ForWriting, True)
```

```
      txt.Write HTMLText
      Set fs = Nothing

End Sub
```

It's best to make these procedures part of the CCustomer class. This supports the object-oriented concept of encapsulation. Classes whose functionality is properly encapsulated are trivially easy to reuse in other projects.

To use the export functionality of the CCustomer class, create an application that allows the user to supply a customer ID and an export filename. When the user clicks a command button, the selected customer is exported to the HTML file specified by the user, as shown in Listing 7.17.

Listing 7.17   Code in a Form That Calls the Export Functionality of the *Customer* Class

```
Option Explicit

Private Cust As CCustomer

Private Sub Form_Load()
    Set Cust = New CCustomer
End Sub


Private Sub cmdExport_Click()
    Cust.GetData txtID.Text
    Cust.SaveHTML App.Path & "\" & txtFilename.Text

    MsgBox "File saved.", vbInformation
End Sub
```

The important thing to note about this code is its brevity, as well as the fact that it doesn't have to communicate with the database directly in order to perform its work. This makes it extremely easy to program, even for programmers who don't have any database expertise.

The HTML file created by the export method is illustrated in Figure 7.7.

Code Example: You can find an example of the code discussed in this section in the project Export.vbp, located in the directory \vbdb\code\ 07-Classes\Export. For information on how to install the sample files on the CD that accompanies this book, see the section "Installing the Example Files" in the introduction at the beginning of this book.

Figure 7.7
Exported HTML data is viewed in Microsoft Internet Explorer.

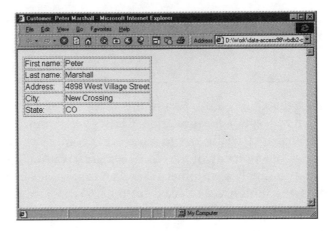

Deploying Classes as ActiveX Servers

You can use Visual Basic to compile class-based projects as ActiveX components. These components, which can take the form of either DLLs or EXEs, give you the ability to provide the functionality of objects without having to redistribute or duplicate the source code of your classes. This makes it easier for you to reuse code across multiple projects as well as multiple developers. Creating ActiveX components from the classes you build also lets you take advantages of other technologies such as remote distribution of objects, as described in Chapter 8.

To create an ActiveX component project in Visual Basic, you start by creating a new project. When Visual Basic asks you what kind of project to create, choose ActiveX DLL or ActiveX EXE. A new project is created with a single class module. You can then add additional classes to the project if you wish and write code for the classes. The final step is to compile the project into an ActiveX DLL or EXE.

You compile an ActiveX project the same way you compile a conventional project. The difference between compiling an ActiveX project and a standard EXE is that for ActiveX DLL, the product of the compilation is (obviously) a DLL rather than an EXE. However, ActiveX DLLs and EXEs are used differently than conventional executables. ActiveX components are object servers, designed to be used (and reused) with other applications.

While both ActiveX DLLs and EXEs can provide objects to other applications, ActiveX EXEs have the capability to execute on their own, a feature that ActiveX DLLs lack. For this reason, ActiveX EXEs are sometimes called "out-of-process servers." Conversely, ActiveX servers are sometimes called "in-process servers" because they can only run in the context of some other process.

To compile an ActiveX component, select the File Make menu command as you would with a standard EXE. The project is then compiled to an ActiveX DLL or an ActiveX EXE, as appropriate. Additionally, after it is compiled, the component is registered on your computer, so you have the ability to use objects created from its classes in other applications. The technique you use to accomplish this is described in the next section.

USING AN ACTIVEX COMPONENT IN A STANDARD EXE PROJECT

After you've compiled an ActiveX component, you can make a reference to it from another Visual Basic project. When you do this, you can use the classes contained in the ActiveX component to create objects in your project. This permits you to take advantage of the functionality of the ActiveX component in a simple, consistent way, without having to bother yourself with the code that went into the component.

To do this, begin by making a reference to the ActiveX server component from your project. This technique is exactly the same as making a reference to a database access library such as DAO or RDO; you use the menu command Project References.

To compile an ActiveX server and use it in a standard EXE application, do the following:

1. Create a new Visual Basic project. When VB asks you which type of project to create, select ActiveX DLL.

2. In the Properties window, change the Name property of the ActiveX DLL project from Project1 to CustSvr.

3. Visual Basic added a blank class, called Class1, to the ActiveX DLL project by default. Remove it by right-clicking it, then selecting Remove Class1 from the pop-up menu.

4. Because the class you're going to add to this project will use ADO, use the Project References menu to add a reference to Microsoft ActiveX Data Objects 2.0. If you're using the version of CCustomer you built in the previous section covering HTML Export, you'll need to make a reference to Microsoft Scripting Library as well.

5. Next add the class you created previously to the ActiveX DLL project. To do this, right-click the ActiveX DLL project CustSvr. Select Add from the pop-up menu. Choose Class Module from the submenu.

6. The Add Class Module dialog box appears. Click the Existing tab. Locate the CCustomer class you created in the previous example and select it.

7. In the properties for the CCustomer class, set the Instancing property to 5 - Multiuse.

Note: The Instancing property of a class controls how users of an ActiveX component can instantiate objects from it. Only classes within an ActiveX project have the Instancing property.

8. If necessary, add the DataEnvironment designer you created previously to your project. Do this by selecting the menu command Project, Add File, then selecting the file deNovelty.Dsr from the file dialog box.

9. The DLL project is now ready to be compiled. To compile it, select File, Make CustSvr.dll.

10. The Make Project dialog box appears. Choose a folder to save the DLL in and click OK.

The ActiveX DLL is compiled and registered on your computer. Its filename is CustSvr.dll. You can now use this component from within any of your projects.

Note: Not only can you use an ActiveX server from any Visual Basic project, you can use them from any development environment that knows about ActiveX components. This includes Visual C++, Microsoft Office applications, and even non-Microsoft development environments such as PowerBuilder and Delphi.

Perform the following steps to see how to use an ActiveX server from a Visual Basic project:

1. Start a new Standard EXE project.

2. Locate and check the CustSvr in the Project References menu, as illustrated in Figure 7.8.

3. In the form, enter the code in Listing 7.18. This instantiates an object from the ActiveX server and returns information from the database in the form of an object.

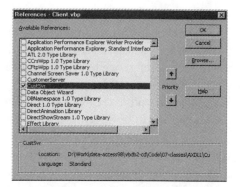

Figure 7.8
Adding a reference to an ActiveX server created in a standard EXE project.

Listing 7.18   Creating an Object from the ActiveX Server and Displaying Data from It

```
Option Explicit

' References CustSvr

Private Cust As CCustomer


Private Sub Form_Load()
    Set Cust = New CCustomer
End Sub


Private Sub cmdGetData_Click()

    Cust.GetData txtID.Text

    MsgBox Cust.FirstName & " " & _
           Cust.LastName & " " & _
           Cust.Address & " " & _
           Cust.City & " " & _
           Cust.State
End Sub
```

4. Run the application. It should display data from the database when you enter a valid number in the text box and click the command button.

The important thing to note about this application is that it doesn't need to know anything about the database. In fact, to function, it doesn't even need to know that there's a relational database on the other end. Additionally, the client application doesn't need to have a reference to ActiveX Data Objects or any other database library. That's taken care of by the ActiveX component. That's not a very important benefit when you're creating single-user, standalone applications, but when you enter the world of distributed systems, it can be a very significant benefit.

Components have the ability to be deployed remotely, over networks. You can remotely deploy an ActiveX EXE component on its own. You can also deploy an ActiveX DLL remotely using Microsoft Transaction Server. Such distributed systems using ActiveX components are discussed at length in Chapter 8.

Code Example: You can find the code for the ActiveX DLL discussed in this section in the project CustSvr.vbp, **located in the directory** \vbdb\code\ 07-Classes\AxDll. **The client application that calls this component is located in project** Client.vbp, **located in the directory** \vbdb\code\07-Classes\ AxClient. **For information on how to install the sample files on the CD that accompanies this book, see the section "Installing the Example Files" in the introduction at the beginning of this book.**

REGISTERING ACTIVEX COMPONENTS ON USERS' COMPUTERS

An ActiveX component must be registered on a particular computer in order to be usable on that computer. Registration ensures that the operating system is aware of the existence of the component whenever an application attempts to instantiate objects from it.

When you're working with ActiveX servers on a development computer, registration is no problem. That's because components are registered automatically by Visual Basic at the time they are compiled. When you distribute a component to a user, you must ensure that the ActiveX component is registered on the user's computer. There are a few methods you can use to accomplish this.

If you use the Visual Basic Package and Deployment Wizard to distribute your applications, registration of ActiveX components on a user's machine is done automatically by the Setup application. When you build a Setup application, the wizard adds any ActiveX components referenced by your project to your Setup application. When the user runs the Setup application created by the Setup Wizard, the components are registered transparently.

Note: You can also register (and unregister) ActiveX components manually using the `Regsvr32.exe` utility. You can find this command-line utility in the `\OS\SYSTEM` directory of the Visual Basic 6.0 Enterprise Edition CD.

CONVERTING STANDARD EXE PROJECTS TO ACTIVEX PROJECTS

You can convert a Standard EXE project into an ActiveX component project. You do this in a situation where you've built a project based on classes and you realize that you want to compile it as an independent ActiveX component.

Additionally, you can convert between the two types of ActiveX components (ActiveX DLL and ActiveX EXE) by changing a property of the project:

1. In Visual Basic, open the project you want to convert.

2. Select Project Properties from the menu.

3. Choose the project type you want your project to be, as illustrated in Figure 7.9.

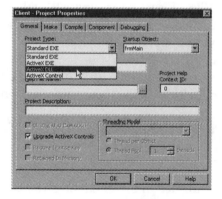

Figure 7.9
You can change a standard EXE project to an ActiveX project using the Project Properties dialog box.

USING ACTIVEX COMPONENTS REMOTELY

The ability to compile sets of classes independently as ActiveX components is an important element of remote database access. In a client/server environment, you can use ActiveX servers to mediate the interaction between client applications and database servers.

For more information on how this works, see Chapter 8.

CREATING MULTITHREADED COMPONENTS

Visual Basic has the ability to create multithreaded ActiveX components. With multithreading, your components execute in a more responsive way. This is because the operating system can allocate processor resources to individual threads; if your component is running on multiple threads, it's less likely that the functions your component is responsible for will be blocked by other threads (some of which may be assigned higher priority by the operating system). You can think of a thread, then, as the smallest unit of execution the operating system is capable of scheduling.

Additionally, on a multiprocessor machine, the operating system has the ability to assign particular threads of execution to separate processors. Giving your components multithreading capability is one way to maximize the power of a computer with multiple processors.

Visual Basic 5.0 introduced support for multithreaded ActiveX components, but the multithreading was limited to certain types of components. The components had to be marked for unattended execution, meaning they were the kind of components designed to run on a server box in a closet somewhere, and could not, therefore, contain any user-interface elements such as forms. (In VB5 Service Pack 2 and later, the option for running an ActiveX component in unattended mode now has nothing do with its multithreading capabilities. This continues to be the case in VB6.) Visual Basic supports multithreading across all the types of ActiveX components you can build with Visual Basic, including ActiveX DLLs, ActiveX EXEs, and ActiveX controls.

Adding support for multithreading in your components requires only that you change a project property at compile time. No change to your code is necessary. To add support for multithreading to a component project:

1. In Visual Basic, open a component project (an ActiveX EXE, ActiveX DLL, or ActiveX control project).

2. Select Properties from the Project menu.

3. Select Apartment Threaded in the Threading Model panel.

4. Click OK. When the project is compiled, it will take advantage of multithreading.

You have an additional option for ActiveX EXEs: Thread per Object or Thread Pool. Thread per Object means that your ActiveX EXE will spawn one thread for every object that is instantiated from it. This provides the best performance, but can consume more computational resources.

Thread Pool, on the other hand, enables you to control how many threads your ActiveX component is capable of instantiating at once, enabling you to limit the amount of resources consumed by the component. However, if the number of object requests exceeds the number of threads in a component server's thread pool, subsequent requests for objects from that server will be blocked until a client process frees up a thread. In other words, when a thread is no longer needed by a client process, control over the thread is returned to the pool of threads managed by the component server.

> **Note:** Setting a thread pool ActiveX server with one thread is the same as making the component "single threaded."

The option you choose for your ActiveX component, depends a great deal on the power of the computer it will run on and your application's behavior; you should perform extensive prototyping before making a decision about which route to take when deploying components based on this technology.

RESTRICTIONS ON MULTITHREADED COMPONENTS

Although it's easy to create multithreaded components in VB6, there are a number of considerations to keep in mind:

▶ *Limited language support for multithreading.* It's a compiler switch, and that's basically it. You can't write code to do anything with it except through Windows API calls, which is an extremely dicey proposition. (You can use the `ThreadID` property of the intrinsic VB `App` object to determine which thread your application has been allocated.)

▶ *No debugger support for multithreading.*

▶ *No support for multithreading in multiple-document interface (MDI) applications.*

▶ *No support for single-threaded ActiveX controls in multithreaded applications.* This restriction is imposed by Visual Basic because of big performance problems created by the combination of a single-threaded control in a multithreaded container. This means that if you're attempting to create a multithreaded ActiveX control that uses single-threaded constituent controls, you're out of luck—it won't work.

The good news is that most of the controls that come with Visual Basic now take advantage of multithreading.

▶ *Properties and methods declared* `Friend` *can't be called across threads.* In order to call a property or method of a particular object, the property or method must be declared Public.

▶ *ActiveX EXE projects that support ActiveX documents need to have the Thread per Object or Thread Pool options (with a thread pool greater than one).* You do this if you're interested in taking advantage of the capabilities of a multithreaded container (such as Internet Explorer 4.0).

▶ *When a component displays a modal form, that form is modal in the context of that component.* This prevents a particular thread from blocking execution of another thread.

▶ *You can only exchange information between forms using dynamic data exchange (DDE) if both forms are on the same thread.* This is only an issue for you if you're still using DDE—that dawn-of-time method of inter-process communication—but it's an important issue nevertheless.

Note: Visual Basic Books Online contains a deeper discussion of what multithreading is and how it relates to ActiveX component creation (in the topic "Scalability and Multithreading" in the VB *Component Tools Guide*.).

SUMMARY

The world of classes and objects represents a whole new frontier in Visual Basic programming—a frontier that many experienced VB programmers resist. "My procedural code works just fine," some programmers say. "I have a good handle on what's going on in my projects. Why should I spend the extra time writing all these `Property Let` and `Get` procedures?"

This chapter gives you the information to put advanced object-oriented techniques into action, not only to take advantage of advanced technologies such as multithreading and components, but to make your life simpler and more stable over time. The techniques discussed in this chapter—including classes, objects, collections and ActiveX components—are key to this strategy.

QUESTIONS AND ANSWERS

Q. **All this stuff about class modules and objects seems like a lot of work. It seems counterintuitive to me that you could make an application simpler by adding more code and more modules to it. The object information seems like it's a lot to get my head around. Am I missing something?**

A. You're right that building an application with objects and classes takes more time—the first time you build it. Remember one of the main goals of programming with objects—reusability. The implication here is that if you create a widget-handling application, you'll almost certainly have to deal with widgets again at some point in your career. If you already have an ActiveX DLL lying around that knows what widgets are, what information they use, and how they work, then you've saved yourself an enormous amount of time.

The fact of the matter is that it does take more work—and more planning—to write code in classes than it does to write it the old procedural way. The payoff in the long run, however, is easier maintainability, ease of debugging, and the ability to reuse code. In a sense, it's fair to say that while using classes and objects is a bigger time investment up front, it can save you an enormous amount of time in the long run if utilized properly.

Even if you don't foresee an obvious opportunity for reusing your code, it makes sense to use classes and objects for reasons of maintainability. If you find a bug having to do with customers in your application, the fact that you have a CCustomer class in your application means that you know just where to start looking in code for the problem.

If this stuff seems abstract and pointless to you, give it a try and stick with it. It is counterintuitive to the typical Visual Basic programmer. At first glance it seems backward to add more modules and more code to your application in the name of control, flexibility, and simplicity. After adopting the mindset of object-oriented programming over the course of a few projects, you'll likely wonder how you got along without it.

Remote Database Access

This book has given you insights into how database access works in Visual Basic. However, until now, you haven't delved into the architectural issues surrounding how data gets from point A to point B in a networked environment.

You've been able to skirt this issue because, by and large, you don't have to take very much into account when accessing a database over a network. The database object models (and, to a greater extent, the operating system) mask the complexity of remote database access from you. In general, it does not matter if your database resides on a machine across the network or on your own, local machine.

However, Visual Basic does give you a few ways to move data from a database across a network. These involve a bit more preparation and planning and are the subject of this chapter.

This chapter covers two major topics: three-tiered client/server database access using remotely deployed ActiveX servers, and database replication with Microsoft Jet databases. The objectives of these topics are to let you maintain reliable, consistent access to data across a network and to enable you to set up systems that intelligently duplicate records in Jet databases to multiple computers in your organization.

Note: ActiveX components were originally introduced in Chapter 7, "Database Access with Classes." You'll revisit them in Chapter 11, "Internet Database Applications."

This chapter is sort of an advanced version of the basic client/server technologies introduced in Chapters 5, "Getting Started with SQL Server," and 6, "Open Database Connectivity and Remote Data Objects." In order to understand it, you also must have the object-oriented programming concepts discussed in Chapter 7 under your belt. If you aren't at least somewhat familiar with the concepts introduced in those chapters, go back and take a look at them first. Don't worry, this chapter will still be here when you get back.

ABOUT CLIENTS, SERVERS, AND CODE COMPONENTS

The terminology surrounding middle-tier components has changed since these techniques were originally introduced—not only because Microsoft has this funny habit of changing its jargon every few months, but because of confusion surrounding how the technologies are applied.

For example, if you adhere strictly to the terminology used by Visual Basic, you could say that it's possible to create an ActiveX control embedded in a client application that talks to an ActiveX server component that resides on the client, which in turn talks to an ActiveX server that resides on a middle-tier machine, which in turn talks to a database server located on a Windows NT server. If you're shooting electric beams of hate at my brain for having just written that sentence, then you understand the extent of the problem. Here's a little primer that should help you sort things out:

▶ *ActiveX* is a broad term that generally pertains to software objects that communicate with each other. It's not a product, and it's not a technology. It's more of a blanket term for a bunch of (ostensibly) related technologies generally having to do with objects and interprocess communication.

▶ An *ActiveX control* is a visual component—usually (but not always) a user-interface component. The database grid components that ship with Visual Basic (described in more depth in Chapters 12, "User-Interface Controls," and 13, "Using the DBGrid and Apex True DBGrid Controls") are examples of ActiveX components. As you're doubtless aware, many other such components ship with the Professional and Enterprise Editions of Visual Basic. Visual Basic programmers tend to be most familiar with ActiveX controls, although ActiveX means much more than simple user-interface controls.

▶ An *ActiveX server* (also called an *ActiveX code component* and, in Visual Basic 4.0, an *OLE server*) is a component that exposes one or more classes in a compiled package. Your applications can use objects provided by the classes contained in the ActiveX component. The compiled package can also be accessed over a network through a technology known as Distributed Component Object Model (DCOM)

This chapter focuses on using ActiveX servers in a remote context and focuses even more specifically on setting up an ActiveX server on a network so that client computers can instantiate objects from it.

Note: This book does not cover the topic of creating ActiveX controls. You can use VB to create your own controls, however. There's a super book on the topic of ActiveX control creation written by a fine, hard-working author named Jeffrey P. McManus. It's called *How to Program Visual Basic 5.0 Control Creation Edition* (Ziff-Davis Press, 1997). It gives you all the information you need to create controls in any edition of VB (not just the Control Creation Edition). There's a Web page for the book at `http://www.redblazer. com/books/`.

ENCAPSULATING BUSINESS RULES WITH A THREE-TIER CLIENT/SERVER ARCHITECTURE

The Drama of the Gifted Server-Side Programmer dictates certain dynamics that any client/server developer is always going to contend with. These dynamics include the following:

▶ Maintaining a stable system in the face of business rules that change from time to time

▶ Providing a single, consistent entry point into data, while at the same time protecting the database from client-side applications—and, conversely, protecting client-side applications from the complexity and mutability of the server

▶ The desire to build business rules in any programming language, not just SQL

▶ The desire to deploy business rules onto a machine other than the database server, in order to conserve the database server's processing power

▶ The desire to deploy some business rules onto the client, in order to minimize network traffic

▶ Deploying business rules to a single point in the system (as opposed to having to deploy them to every client computer every time a change is implemented)

A three-tier client/server architecture solves this problem. In a three-tier architecture, business rules are encapsulated in a component that sits between the client application and the database server.

Such components are therefore referred to as *middle-tier components*. Middle-tier components accept requests from client applications, responding by making requests and issuing commands to the database server.

Because the word *component* describes what's on the middle tier, you may have already surmised that in the Visual Basic universe, the middle-tier is an ActiveX component. Middle-tier ActiveX components work the same way as other types of ActiveX components in the sense that they chew up data and spit out objects. Middle-tier components are specifically geared toward client/server database access.

In addition to providing an object-oriented interface into databases, ActiveX components can be accessed remotely over a network. This is possible through a technology known as *Distributed Component Object Model* (*DCOM*). With DCOM, a client application has the ability to instantiate objects from an ActiveX server, whether or not the server resides on the same computer as that client application. (In geek-speak, this is referred to as *instantiation across machine boundaries.*)

As with many aspects of programming in Visual Basic, there's very little having to do with the internals of DCOM that you can access directly. It's like trying to shift the gears of a car with automatic transmission. For the remainder of this section, you walk through the practical steps involved in setting up an ActiveX server for remote access by client computers.

Setting Up a Hardware Architecture for DCOM

There are potentially endless combinations of client and server computers you can put together in order to implement a client/server hardware architecture. This chapter's goal is to keep things as simple as possible in order to provide a solution that works for you in the most common situations you encounter.

This chapter assumes that you have two computers and that the first is a Windows NT Server. This computer is referred to as the server from here on out. The client machine used in the examples happens to be Windows 95 computer, but it could just as well be Windows 98 or Windows NT.

> **Note: Don't sweat it if you don't have immediate access to all the software and hardware described in this section. If you don't have two computers connected over a network, the demonstrations should work fine on a single computer. If you don't have a Windows NT machine, you should be able to fake it by using a Microsoft Jet database. The examples in this chapter are all written in ADO to accommodate this.**
>
> **Although this chapter was written with a Windows NT server in mind, you can set up DCOM on Windows 95 as well. The files that let you do DCOM on Windows 95 are on the Visual Basic Enterprise Edition CD Disc 1, in the \TOOLS\DCOM98 directory. For more information and access to the downloadable DCOM files, check out the DCOM for Windows 95 Web page at http://www.microsoft.com/com/dcom/dcom1_2/dcom1_2.asp.**

The premise of the demonstrations in this chapter is that users on the network need to get access to customer data. In the interest of consistency, code reuse, and ease of programming and maintenance, it's to your advantage to channel access to the database through an ActiveX component. This component is compiled and set up on the network so client applications can access it remotely.

A typical three-tier client/server architecture is expressed graphically in Figure 8.1.

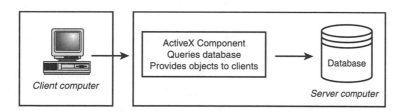

Figure 8.1
This diagram of a generic three-tier architecture merges the physical architecture (two computers) with the logical architecture (tiers that provide different types of functionality).

Figure 8.1 gives you an idea of how you'd split the logic of your application across two computers. There's no reason why you have to stop there; you can split middle-tier components across any number of computers. For this reason, three-tier client/server architecture is increasingly being referred to as *n-tier architecture*, as illustrated in Figure 8.2.

Figure 8.2
This example of n-tier client/server architecture shows the middle tier deployed to a machine of its own.

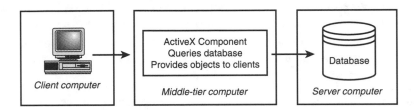

You deploy middle-tier components on a computer of their own in the following situations:

▶ The database server runs an operating system that does not support ActiveX.

▶ You want to conserve processing power on the database server.

▶ You want to enhance your application's scalability by deploying multiple copies of the same ActiveX server to more than one computer.

The disadvantage of giving your ActiveX component a computer of its own is that such a setup requires an additional network hop to get from client to database and back again. This can degrade performance and cause increased network traffic. Whether this situation is acceptable to you is a function of your specific network configuration and the prototyping you do during the design phase of your project.

Even if you don't have control of the operating system on which your database runs, you can still use an ActiveX middle tier—if you deploy it to a computer of its own. The database tier is a UNIX box or a corporate mainframe. This is no big deal to DCOM or to your client applications for two reasons. First, your client applications never get access to the database server; instead, they access data through the ActiveX component. Second, and more importantly, DCOM shields the application from the specific implementation of network protocol, platform, and machine boundary.

In some respects, deploying a client/server system in which the database server is on a non-Windows platform is easier in the world of three-tier, because you don't have to configure the *middleware* (the collection of drivers that handles cross-platform communication and network protocols) on every client computer. In three-tier, you only have to configure this software once—in the section of the architecture between the middle tier and the database server. This can save you quite a bit of time and trouble when you're configuring and deploying your application to many clients.

Using DCOM on Other Platforms

By the time you read this, DCOM might be happening on platforms other than Windows. Microsoft has partnered with other operating-system vendors to make COM happen on their platforms.

At some point COM and DCOM will begin to appear on UNIX computers. The ActiveX Software Development Kit for Macintosh has been around since late 1996; it's possible that using ActiveX on a Macintosh computer will be a reality by the time you read this.

> Note: Microsoft's Web site is the best source of information on what's happening with the portability of ActiveX components. The site you want to keep your eyeballs on is `http://www.microsoft.com/com/`.

Creating Your First DCOM Application

Now that you have a sense of why DCOM is useful and wonderful, it's time to get started using the technology to provide a real-world business software solution. To keep this example as simple as possible, do it using a version of the CustSvr project you created in Chapter 7. This simple ActiveX component has a single class, `CCustomer`, designed to query the database and return a `Customer` object.

> Code Example: The version of the CustSvr project you'll find in the code examples you installed on the CD is slightly different than the CustSvr project you created in Chapter 7. This project, called CustSvr2 adds support for a `GetList` property. `GetList` displays a brief list of customers based on the state in which they live. (The ODBC DSN required by the component is called JetNovelty.)

> **You can find this code in the project CustSvr2.vbp, located in the directory \vbdb\code\08-Remote\AxDLL. For information on how to install the sample files on the CD that accompanies this book, see the section "Installing the Example Files" in the introduction at the beginning of this book.**

ActiveX EXEs Are Tools of the Devil

In the first edition of this book, I described how to remotely deploy components packaged as ActiveX EXEs. The step-by-step description took seven pages of text, literally days of my time to set up and test, and untold amounts of frustration.

When I revised this chapter for the second edition of the book (the one you're reading now), I got even more frustrated. Not only did the revised demonstration take an additional half-day to set up, the result was totally unimpressive when placed next to the Microsoft Transaction Server demonstration you'll see in the next section.

It was, by far, the most difficult demonstration of the book to set up, mainly because the documentation for remotely deployed ActiveX EXEs is limited, the configuration tools provided by Microsoft are poor, and there are a million picky little things you have to get right before it'll work correctly. And even then, what you wind up with can stretch your definition of the term "works correctly."

There are dozens of support articles pertaining to DCOM on support.microsoft.com explaining the byzantine machinations of ActiveX EXE configuration under DCOM. I, your faithful author, was left with a choice between whether to regurgitate them here and somehow make sense of them for you, or pitch the whole thing entirely. I decided that rather than regurgitating all this valuable information on how to use remotely distributed ActiveX EXEs, I could give you a more important piece of advice:

Don't use remotely deployed ActiveX EXEs. For any reason.

Don't use them to take advantage of the multithreading compiler switch that became available in VB5 Service Pack 2. (MTS handles multithreading itself.) Don't use them to avoid having to use MTS (it's free with Windows NT, and it's actually easy to use, as the next section demonstrates). Don't use them to take advantage of DCOM's ability to manage security on an object-by-object basis (MTS handles this more effectively).

Note: If you're a developer who has consistently, successfully deployed a production solution using ActiveX EXEs, email me at `jeffreyp@sirius.com`. I'd love to hear how you're doing it.

Deploying ActiveX DLLs Remotely Using Microsoft Transaction Server

You can use Microsoft Transaction Server to deploy ActiveX DLLs. Once you've created the DLL, deployment under MTS becomes trivial; in fact, deploying a component under MTS is one of the easiest ways of creating a distributed application.

Microsoft Transaction Server runs under Windows NT and Windows 95/98. It runs more effectively under Windows NT, both from a performance and from a feature standpoint.

Microsoft Transaction Server will ship out of the box with Windows NT 5.0. If you have NT 4.0 (which this section assumes), you install the latest version of MTS using Windows Option Pack, which comes on the Visual Basic CD. It's located on Enterprise Edition Disc 2, in the `\Ntoptpak` directory.

If you'd instead like to download NT Option Pack, you can get it from the Microsoft Web site. It's located at `http://www.microsoft.com/windows/downloads/contents/Updates/NT40ptPk/`. Note that the Option Pack is applicable to Windows 95/98—when you install NT Option Pack on a non-NT machine, you get Personal Web Server for Windows 95 and a limited version of Microsoft Transaction Server. This is handy, because it means you can use your Windows 95/98 machines for development and testing, then use your NT Server to deploy your production application, if you want.

Note: This section covers Microsoft Transaction Server 2.0, which is the current version as of this writing.

This chapter only attempts to cover MTS in its role as an object request broker and management console for remotely distributed components. It doesn't attempt to cover MTS features that enable transactions between components, nor does it cover the MTS security model.

> **For more information on MTS, check out the Microsoft web site at**
> `http://www.microsoft.com/ntserver/basics/appservices/transsvcs/`.
>
> **My favorite book on these topics is Alex Homer and David Sussman's *MTS, MSMQ with VB and ASP* (Wrox, 1998). In addition to being a great reference to building distributed applications with VB, it wins the Acronym Award for the book with more acronyms than actual words in its title.**

Deploying a remote component under MTS 2.0 entails three steps:

1. Creating an MTS Package to house your component

2. Placing the component in the package

3. Exporting the package from MTS and installing it on client machines

The following sections explore these steps in detail.

Creating an MTS Package

A Microsoft Transaction Server *package* is a logical container for one or more class modules contained in ActiveX DLLs. Creating a package gives you the ability to manage all of the classes contained in the package, even if the classes came from different components.

To see how this works, follow these steps:

1. Launch Microsoft Transaction Server from the Windows Start menu. (It exists in different program groups depending on which version you have and how you installed it.)

2. MTS appears in Microsoft Management Console, as shown in Figure 8.3.

Figure 8.3
You view Microsoft Transaction Server through the Microsoft Management Console.

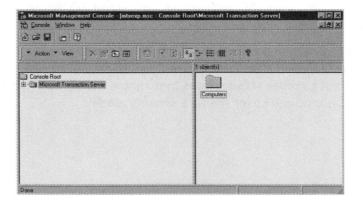

Note: Microsoft Management Console (MMC) provides a simple, integrated tool for administration of server resources. MTS, Microsoft Internet Information Server 4.0, and other NT tools are managed through MMC. More tools are slated be added to MMC in the future, including SQL Server 7.0. (MMC will enhance or replace the SQL Enterprise Manager in version 7.0.)

MMC provides extensibility through *snap-ins*. An MMC snap-in is a software component that acts as a conduit between MMC and the server tool. MMC snap-ins are packaged as ActiveX DLLs, but you can't (yet) build MMC snap-ins in Visual Basic. So if you have a software tool that you want to manage through MMC, you'll either have to wait for it to support VB or write your snap-in in Visual C++.

3. Using the outline pane on the left, open the Microsoft Transaction Server folder, then open Computers, then My Computer. You should be able to see a folder called Packages Installed.

4. Click the Packages Installed folder. You should be able to see several packages that came pre-installed (although the packages you see may vary from system to system). These are shown in Figure 8.4.

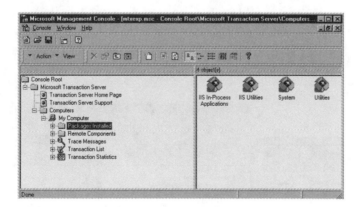

Figure 8.4
Click the MTS Packages Installed folder to see preinstalled MTS packages.

5. Right-click the Packages Installed folder. From the pop-up menu, select New, Package.

6. The Package Wizard appears. Select Create an empty package. Give the package the name Novelty.

7. The Set Package Identity screen appears. Since you won't be using security with this component, leave this set to Interactive user, then click Finish.

8. You should be able to see your new package in the Packages Installed folder.

Although you've successfully created a package, this package won't do anything yet, because you haven't added any components to it. You'll do that in the next section.

Placing a Component in an MTS Package

Placing a component in an MTS package is simplicity itself. You simply drag your ActiveX DLL onto a previously created MTS package. To see how this works, follow these steps:

1. In MTS, open the Novelty folder under the Packages Installed folder.

2. You should see two folders, Components and Roles. Click the Components folder. The folder should be empty, since you haven't added anything to it yet.

3. Arrange the windows on your screen so Windows Explorer and MTS appear side by side, as shown in Figure 8.5.

Figure 8.5
Two windows are open in preparation for adding an ActiveX DLL to an MTS package.

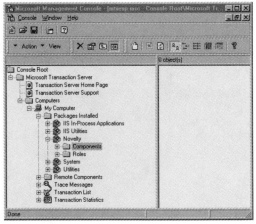

4. Click-drag the ActiveX DLL file to the right side of the MTS window. The classes provided by the component are added to the MTS package, as Figure 8.6 illustrates.

 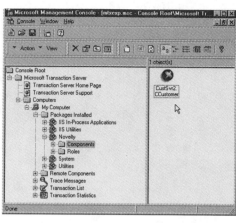

Figure 8.6
A component is added to an MTS package.

The green and black "pool ball" displayed in the Components folder is more than just an indication that the component is installed under MTS. It also serves as an indicator that the component is servicing a request. Here's how to test how this works:

1. Start a new Visual Basic Standard EXE application.

2. Using the Project References menu, make a reference to the CustSvr component you placed under MTS. (The name of the library used in this chapter's examples is CustSvr2.)

3. Write the following code in the application:

```
Private mCust As CCustomer

Private Sub Form_Load()
    Set mCust = New CCustomer
End Sub



Private Sub Form_Unload(Cancel As Integer)
    Set mCust = Nothing
End Sub
```

This application doesn't actually do anything with the component, it just holds open an instance of an object so you can examine MTS servicing its request.

4. Run the application. If you arrange the windows as shown in Figure 8.7, you should be able to see the mesmerizing MTS pool ball rotating, indicating that it's servicing your application's request.

Figure 8.7
The pool ball goes around and around and around.

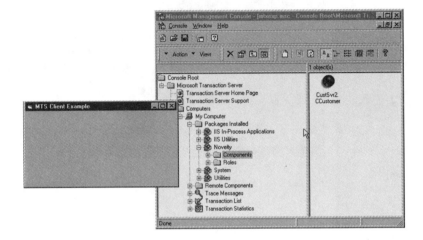

5. Close the application. The pool ball stops rotating, indicating that it's no longer servicing your application's request.

While the rotating pool ball is impressive, the MTS console can be used for more than personal amusement. For example, by right-clicking the package icon, you reveal a package properties dialog box, which lets you do a number of important things. For example, in the properties dialog's Advanced tab, you can control how many minutes MTS will keep your component loaded in memory after it's first accessed. This setting is illustrated in Figure 8.8.

This setting can be as little as zero, in which case the component is removed from memory as soon as the client application releases it, or as long as 1,440 minutes, which means that the component will be cached in memory for 24 hours after the last client access. If you want the component to be loaded in memory regardless of whether clients access it or not, select the option button labeled "Leave running when idle." This will increase performance and server-side memory consumption.

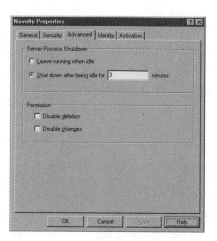

Figure 8.8
*The MTS package
properties dialog
box offers several
options.*

You have to make the decision as to which setting is appropriate for your application, depending on the relative importance of each package and the memory and processing resources your server machine has.

Exporting and Installing the MTS Package on Client Computers

In order to give client applications access to your component running under MTS, you must make an entry in the client computer's registry to tell it that the component is running remotely.

Making client computers aware of remotely distributed MTS components requires the following actions:

▶ *Export the MTS package.* This creates an installable executable which performs all the operations necessary to make the client application aware of the remotely deployed component.

▶ *Install the exported package on the client machine.*

To see an example of this, do the following:

1. In the MTS console, right-click your Novelty package. From the pop-up menu, select Export.

2. The Export Package dialog box appears. Use the Browse button to select an empty folder to export your package. Enter the filename `Novelty`, then click Save.

3. You're returned to the Export Package dialog box. Click Export. After a moment, the message box "The package was successfully exported" appears.

The folder into which your package was exported now contains a number of things:

▶ A file called novelty.PAK.

▶ A copy of the ActiveX DLL, CustSvr2.dll.

▶ A folder called clients. This folder contains a file called novelty.exe.

The files novelty.PAK and CustSvr2.dll are used to replicate the installation of the Novelty package to another Microsoft Transaction Server machine. The file novelty.exe is executed on a client machine to redirect requests for objects contained in CustSvr2.dll to the MTS machine. Once you run novelty.exe on a client machine, applications that reference the CustSvr2 component will access it over the network instead of accessing it locally.

To remove a component from Microsoft Transaction Server, you simply right-click it, then select Delete from the pop-up menu. This doesn't delete the ActiveX DLL from your system; it simply unregisters it. It will be unavailable to applications until you register it again.

USING ACTIVEX COMPONENTS TO FACILITATE DATABASE ACCESS

In Chapter 7 you learned how to access databases using classes and objects. This technique lets you encapsulate the logic of your programs into easily reusable class modules. The ability to independently compile class modules you write in the form of ActiveX DLLs and EXEs makes your classes even easier to reuse, giving you the ability to create extremely flexible and powerful database access applications.

This technique is also used when you need to squeeze every ounce of performance out of your client-side applications. This performance stems from the fact that your client applications don't have to load a database engine or other middleware when they are started. If you're using some other libraries, such as ADO or ODBC, you gain the same benefit, since you don't have to distribute those libraries or configure them on client machines either. This saves a significant amount of memory and makes the applications start much more quickly.

Another benefit of this technique is the fact that your application's distributable footprint becomes much smaller, because you don't have to load the lumbering Jet database engine DLLs onto every client computer.

If your client application is part of a client/server solution, you gain a number of benefits. You don't have to distribute and configure ODBC data sources and client/server middleware on client computers, which can be a source of mind-numbing grief for client/server developers and system administrators alike.

Additionally, by passing arrays instead of objects over the network, your application doesn't have to maintain a persistent connection to the server. This is because when you pass an object over the network, the object actually exists on the server machine (as the architectural diagrams at the beginning of this chapter demonstrate). However, when you pass a chunk of data such as an array over the network, the data doesn't exist on the server. Instead, it's completely passed to the client. This means that the client doesn't need to maintain a connection to the server while it's working with the data. And this, in turn, means that your application can service more users at once, because (for example) instead of having fifty users idly connected to the server, you have five hundred users who are only connected ten percent of the time.

> Note: Passing data to the client in the form of an array is only one way of creating so-called *stateless servers*. There are other ways of accomplishing this, depending on which data access technology you use. If you're using ActiveX Data Objects, you can achieve the same effect by using disconnected recordsets. See Chapter 10, "ActiveX Data Objects," for more information on how these work.

The following section describes how to use this technique with an ActiveX component. This component would be appropriate for remote deployment.

Using *GetRows* to Return Data in an Array

You can use the GetRows method of the Recordset object to return data from an ActiveX server to a client application in the form of a two-dimensional array of Variants. This technique is desirable because it keeps you from having to deploy any database engine libraries or perform any client-side database configuration. The client only knows about the arrays provided by the ActiveX server, which is remotely deployed over a network.

You typically follow these steps when using the GetRows method:

1. Create a Recordset object (typically as the result of a client request to a remotely deployed ActiveX component).

2. If you're using DAO, you must determine the number of rows in the Recordset object. (In ADO, GetRows automatically determines the size of the recordset for you.)

3. Declare a Variant to store the array.

4. Execute the GetRows method of the Recordset object to assign the data in the Recordset to the Variant array.

5. Execute code to convert the data in the resulting Variant array to something your application can use.

Listing 8.1 shows an example of a method that returns a Variant array after making a database call. This method, contained in a class module called CCustData, is designed to populate a list box with customer information.

Listing 8.1   Retrieving a Record from a Database and Providing It in the Form of a Variant Array

```
Option Explicit

' References DAO 3.51

' Private variables
Private db As Database
Private rs As Recordset
'

Private Sub Class_Initialize()
    Set db = OpenDatabase("..\..\DB\novelty.mdb")
End Sub

Public Function GetList(strState As String) As Variant
' Retrieves a list of employees and
' places it into a variant array
' using GetRows.

Dim strSQL As String

    strSQL = "SELECT ID, FirstName, LastName " & _
             "FROM tblCustomer " & _
             "WHERE State = '" & strState & "' " & _
             "ORDER BY LastName, FirstName"

    Set rs = db.OpenRecordset(strSQL)
```

```
    ' RecordCount isn't valid until
    ' you move to the end of the recordset
    ' in DAO
    rs.MoveLast
    rs.MoveFirst
    GetList = rs.GetRows(rs.RecordCount)

End Function
```

A client application that uses this class to populate a list box using this class looks like Listing 8.2.

Listing 8.2   Using a Variant Array–Handling Class in an Application

```
Option Explicit

' References CustSrvA.

Private mCustData As CCustData

Const FIRSTNAME = 1
Const LASTNAME = 2

Private Sub Form_Load()

    Set mCustData = New CCustData

    With cboState
        .AddItem "CA"
        .AddItem "WA"
        .AddItem "NV"
    End With

End Sub

Private Sub cboState_Click()
Dim vData As Variant
Dim x As Long

    vData = mCustData.GetList(cboState.Text)

    lstCustomer.Clear
```

continues

Listing 8.2   Using a Variant Array–Handling Class in an Application (Continued)

```
    For x = 0 To UBound(vData, 2)
        lstCustomer.AddItem vData(FIRSTNAME, x) & _
                            " " & vData(LASTNAME, x)
    Next x

End Sub


Private Sub Form_Unload(Cancel As Integer)
    Set mCustData = Nothing
End Sub
```

As you can see, this code is a bit difficult to follow. The disadvantage of this technique is that you have to write extra code to deal with the Variant array returned by the ActiveX component on the client side. One solution to the problem is to write a client-side ActiveX component to deal with the array, as demonstrated in the next section.

To add a method to retrieve data for a single customer using a Variant array, use the GetData method:

```
Public Function GetData(lngID As Long) As Variant

Dim strSQL As String

    strSQL = "select * from tblCustomer " & _
             "where ID = " & lngID
    Set rs = db.OpenRecordset(strSQL)

    GetData = rs.GetRows

    rs.Close
    Set rs = Nothing

End Function
```

Code Example: You can find an example of the code discussed in this section in the directory \vbdb\code\08-Remote\GetRows. **The code is split between two projects, an ActiveX DLL called** CustSrvA.vbp **and a Standard EXE client called** CustA.vbp. **You can open both projects simultaneously by using the group file** CustA.vbg.

For information on how to install the sample files on the CD that accompanies this book, see the section "Installing the Example Files" in the introduction at the beginning of this book.

Creating a Class to Decode Variant Arrays

When you make calls to an ActiveX server that returns data in the form of Variant arrays, you have a problem. How do you determine which column of the array maps to which field in the database? More importantly, how do you use your new best pal, object-oriented programming, to make your life simpler and make your code more reusable in conjunction with this technique?

One solution is to deploy a second ActiveX component, this time on the client side, to decode the Variant array served up by the middle tier. This component knows how to do only two things: place calls to CCustData and return an object constructed from the data in the Variant array passed back from the middle tier.

This class, CCustomer, is implemented as part of the client application. It contains no reference to any database library and exists solely for the purpose of retrieving Variant arrays from CCustData and mapping them to properties of a Customer object.

The beauty of this technique is that the client application deals exclusively with the Customer object. No direct database access takes place on the client computer; the client-side programmer doesn't even need to know what kind of database exists on the back end. He or she only needs to know how to code against CCustomer. The code for the CCustomer class is shown in Listing 8.3.

Listing 8.3 The *CCustomer* Class, Modified to Decode Variant Arrays Generated by the *CCustData* Class

```
Option Explicit

' References CustSrvA2.

' Private member variables for
' object properties
Private mstrFirstName As String
Private mstrLastName As String
Private mstrAddress As String
Private mstrCity As String
Private mlngID As Long   ' Primary key
Private mstrState As String
```

continues

Listing 8.3   The *CCustomer* Class, Modified to Decode Variant Arrays Generated by the *CCustData* Class (Continued)

```
Private mstrZip As String
Private mstrPhone As String

Private mCustData As CCustData

Private Sub Class_Initialize()
    Set mCustData = New CCustData
End Sub

Public Sub GetData(lngID As Long)

Dim vData As Variant

    vData = mCustData.GetData(lngID)

    ' Populate properties with
    ' results of the query.
    FirstName = vData(1, 0) & "" ' cheesy null-safe trick
    ID = lngID
    LastName = vData(2, 0)
    Address = vData(3, 0)
    City = vData(4, 0)
    State = vData(5, 0)
    Zip = vData(6, 0)
    Phone = vData(7, 0)

End Sub

Public Property Let Address(ByVal strNew As String)
    mstrAddress = strNew
End Property

Public Property Get Address() As String
    Address = mstrAddress
End Property

Public Property Let City(ByVal strNew As String)
    mstrCity = strNew
End Property

Public Property Get City() As String
    City = mstrCity
End Property

Public Property Get ID() As Long
    ID = mlngID
```

```
End Property

Public Property Let ID(ByVal lngNew As Long)
    mlngID = lngNew
End Property

Public Property Let FirstName(ByVal strNew As String)
    mstrFirstName = strNew
End Property

Public Property Get FirstName() As String
    FirstName = mstrFirstName
End Property

Public Property Let LastName(ByVal strNew As String)
    mstrLastName = strNew
End Property

Public Property Get LastName() As String
    LastName = mstrLastName
End Property

Public Property Let Phone(ByVal strNew As String)
    mstrPhone = strNew
End Property

Public Property Get Phone() As String
    Phone = mstrPhone
End Property

Public Property Let State(ByVal strNew As String)
    mstrState = strNew
End Property

Public Property Get State() As String
    State = mstrState
End Property

Public Property Let Zip(ByVal strNew As String)
    mstrZip = strNew
End Property

Public Property Get Zip() As String
    Zip = mstrZip
End Property

Private Sub Class_Terminate()
    Set mCustData = Nothing
End Sub
```

After you have the CCustData class performing database access and the CCustomer class converting its arrays into objects, you can write code in a form to retrieve customers and work with them. Listing 8.4 is an example of code in a form that uses the CCustomer class to retrieve a Customer object. It assumes you have a list box populated with customers and several text boxes to display customer details.

Listing 8.4   Client-Side Code to Retrieve Data by Using the *CCustomer* Class

```
Option Explicit

' References CustSrvA2.

Private mCustData As CCustData

Const FirstName = 1
Const LastName = 2


Private Sub Form_Load()

    Set mCustData = New CCustData

    With cboState
        .AddItem "CA"
        .AddItem "WA"
        .AddItem "NV"
    End With

End Sub


Private Sub cboState_Click()
Dim vData As Variant
Dim x As Long

    vData = mCustData.GetList(cboState.Text)

    lstCustomer.Clear

    For x = 0 To UBound(vData, 2)
        lstCustomer.AddItem vData(FirstName, x) & _
                            " " & vData(LastName, x)
        ' Add primary key to list
        lstCustomer.ItemData(lstCustomer.NewIndex) = vData(0, x)
```

```
    Next x

End Sub



Private Sub lstCustomer_Click()
    Dim mCust As CCustomer
    Set mCust = New CCustomer
    mCust.GetData lstCustomer.ItemData(lstCustomer.ListIndex)
    txtAddress.Text = mCust.Address
    txtCity.Text = mCust.City
    txtState.Text = mCust.State
End Sub



Private Sub Form_Unload(Cancel As Integer)
    Set mCustData = Nothing
End Sub
```

When you run the application, the user selects a state in order to view customers residing in that state. When the user clicks an individual customer, detailed information about the customer appears.

Notice how little code goes into the retrieval of data from the database using this class; all the complicated stuff is under the hood, safely out of your way—contained in the classes CCustomer and CCustData.

When you combine this technique with the ActiveX/DCOM technique described earlier in this chapter, you gain significant benefits. By compiling the CCustData class in an ActiveX component and deploying it over a network, you gain the benefit of centrally located business rules accessible from anywhere on your network. And because this component passes data to client applications over DCOM in the form of arrays, you don't need to deploy a database access library (of any kind) onto individual client machines. This can make client-side software faster to execute and easier to configure and manage.

Conversely, bear in mind that if you don't deploy the database access component remotely, there isn't much point to this technique.

Code Example: You can find an example of the code discussed in this section in the directory \vbdb\code\08-Remote\GetRows2. The code is split between two projects, an ActiveX DLL called CustSrvA2.vbp and a Standard EXE client called CustA.vbp. You can open both projects simultaneously by using the group file CustA2.vbg.

> For information on how to install the sample files on the CD that accompanies this book, see the section "Installing the Example Files" in the introduction at the beginning of this book.

Transferring Data with Database Replication

Centrally located databases can be both a blessing and a curse. Because all your business data is in one place, it's hypothetically possible to access it from anywhere on your corporate network. In order for that centralization to work, it means that the data must be rooted to the spot. It's difficult to move or modify your database without breaking client applications, and it's tricky to permit users whose computers aren't on your corporate LAN to gain access to the data they might need.

For example, if your company has a field sales force, it's possible (even likely) that some of your salespeople will never set foot in your office. In a situation like this, your salespeople can't easily get access to the database by simply hooking up their laptops to your LAN.

To get around this problem, Microsoft Jet gives you the ability to replicate a database from one computer to another. Rather than duplicating all the components of a database (as you would if you simply copied the database file), replication applies a bit more logic. Jet has the ability to perform *synchronization* on databases—comparing them record by record to ensure that they contain the same data, then copying the changes from the *master* database to any one of a number of *replica* databases.

> Note: The master database is also referred to as the *design master*, because it stores the design of the database as well as serves as a central repository for shared data. In a replicated system, design changes to the database—such as adding or deleting fields, tables, and query definitions—can be done only in the design master. However, when you make a change to a database object that resides in a design master, those changes can be distributed to replicas at the time the databases are synchronized. This is the only way to make a change to a replica database.

For example, say you're a user of a corporate database application. You want to take work home, but the database application resides on a server in your office. Replication gives you the ability to "check out" a copy of the database—by loading it on your laptop, for example—so you can work on it at home. The copy of the database you load onto your laptop is referred to as a *replica*.

When you return to the office, you check the database back in. At that time, Jet replication compares the records in your replica with the records in the master database. If you added any records, they are copied to the main system; if you made any changes to records, these changes are also made in the main system. Likewise, if any new data appeared in the master, it is copied to your replica at this time.

Now consider this scenario: What happens when your database grows to be 200MB in size? Backing up the database would be a colossal pain; it would require quite a bit of downtime to simply copy the file across the network, during which time other users would be denied access to the database to avoid the database being made inconsistent.

Replication solves this problem as well by enabling copying of only those records that have changed since the last backup. Because it only copies new and changed files, you don't have to back up the entire database each time you want to back up.

You can also use replication to perform updates to your database applications. This might be appropriate in situations where some of your application's logic is embedded in the database in the form of query definitions. If the query definition needs to change to reflect a change in the application or a change in your business practices, replication can automatically push the change out to all the clients who require it.

Designing a Database with Replication in Mind

As with any multiuser database, you must take several things into consideration when you're designing a database that will be replicated. This doesn't mean that you can't convert your existing single-computer databases into replicable databases, but planning ahead will make the transition go more smoothly.

One of the most important issues to consider is your table's primary key. This is particularly the case when a table's primary key is based on an AutoNumber field.

For example, consider a new database with tables whose primary keys are all based on AutoNumber fields. By default, AutoNumber fields begin numbering at 1 and increment themselves, one number per record. So if several users enter records in database replicas and then synchronize their data back to the master database, it's very likely that two or more users will have entered a record with the ID of 1. To avoid this, you should design your database's primary key fields using one of the following techniques:

▶ Set the AutoNumber field's New Values property to Random.

▶ Set the AutoNumber field's Field Size property to Replication ID.

Setting the primary key field to Random ensures that each new record gets a primary key in the range of a long integer. A Replication ID, on the other hand, is a 128-bit number that, because of its size, is much more likely to be unique from one replica to the next.

Although a the Replication ID data type takes more storage space than an AutoNumber, it's a good idea to use this data type when you're designing new tables slated for replication. Replication IDs almost totally negate the chance for collision of records during synchronization. However, because it's expressed as a long hexadecimal number, a Replication ID can be difficult to refer to conveniently. If you want a primary key to serve double duty in the real world (as an invoice number or employee ID, for example), you might want to consider using a random long integer AutoNumber instead.

> **Note: Because of the changes a database goes through when it's converted into a design master, it should go without saying that you should back up a database before converting it. Replication makes permanent, irreversible changes in your databases. Fortunately, when you convert a database into a design master in Microsoft Access, Access performs a backup for you automatically.**

When you designate a database as a design master, Jet makes a number of changes to your database under the hood. For example, Jet must create a number of new hidden system tables to your database to support such things as conflicts between multiple users who attempt to update the same record and then check their data back into the system. Replication can also add fields to each table in your system, which can cause problems if you've written code (or developed a user interface) that expects a set number of fields. The basic moral of the story is that you should make your database replicable as early in the development cycle as possible, to make it easier to work around these kinds of problems.

As an example of how much larger a database gets when you convert it into a design master, I created a database with a single table containing no data at the time it was replicated. This database swelled from 92K in size to a whopping 248K after it was converted to a design master. However, that size increase is not necessarily proportional for larger databases.

Doing Replication in Microsoft Access

In order to begin with a replicable database system, you must first determine how the databases will be synchronized and where the master database will reside. The particulars involve determining how remote users can connect to the design master (over a wide area network, for example, or through dial-up networking—potentially even over the Internet, as described later in this section). The important part here is to plan ahead in an effort to maintain accessibility to reasonably recent versions of data for most (if not all) of your users.

After you've planned the structure of your replicable database system, you're ready to set it up. When you're setting up replication, you go through the following general steps:

1. Create a database (or use an existing database).

2. Designate a database as the design master.

3. Create one or more replicas from that design master.

You can perform the steps to set up replication using either Microsoft Access, or in code, using Data Access Objects. Both techniques are described in the following sections.

Creating a Design Master and Replica in Microsoft Access

While you can perform replication using DAO code, Microsoft Access is the easier way to get started with database replication. This is because Access has menu commands that govern the creation of design masters and database replicas automatically.

To create a design master using Microsoft Access, you must have a feature called Briefcase Replication installed. You're given the option to install Briefcase Replication when you first install Access; if you don't have it installed, Access will let you know what you need to do when you attempt to create a design master.

To create a design master and a database replica in Access, do the following:

1. Definitely, absolutely, without question back up your database. If you're working with the Jones Novelties database `novelty.mdb`, you might want to give it a name such as `nmaster.mdb`. (A design master database called `NMaster.mdb` already exists in the `\Code\DB` directory of the files you installed from the CD that accompanies this book.)

2. Open the database in Microsoft Access.

3. Choose the Tools, Replication menu. Select Create Replica from the submenu.

4. Access issues a warning that the database must be closed before you can create a replica from it. It asks if you want to close this database and convert it into a design master. Choose Yes.

5. The database closes. Access next warns you to create a backup of the database and asks if you want do so before proceeding. Click Yes.

6. Access converts the database into a Design Master and creates a replica from it, asking you to name the replicated database. If you're using the Novelty database, you might want to give it a name like `nreplica.mdb`.

7. When the replication procedure is done, Access displays a message explaining what it did, as shown in Figure 8.9.

Figure 8.9
An extremely verbose message box is provided by Access after a successful initial replication.

To be precise, the replication process in Access actually creates two new files—the replica and the backup of the original database. When this process is complete, you can create additional replicas, enter data into either database, and perform synchronization between them, copying new or altered records back to the design master.

Adding Replicable Objects to a Database in Microsoft Access

When you initially add a new object (such as a table or query definition) to a design master database, it's not replicated by default. In Microsoft Access, this is obvious because the different types of database objects (replicable and non-replicable) have different icons in Access's Database window, as shown in Figure 8.10.

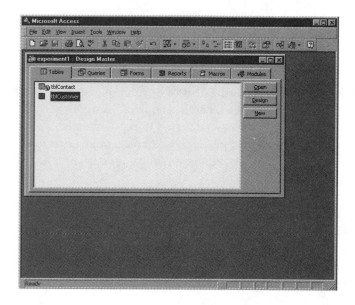

Figure 8.10

A replicable table (tblContact) and a nonreplicable table (tblCustomer) are displayed in the Microsoft Access Database window.

It's simple to make a new database object replicable in Access:

1. In the Database window, right-click the database object whose replication status you want to change.

2. From the pop-up menu, select Properties.

3. The Database Object Properties dialog box appears, as shown in Figure 8.11.

4. Click the Replicable check box, then click OK.

The database object's icon changes to reflect its new status as a replicable object. The next time you perform a database synchronization, the new database object is copied into the replica database.

Figure 8.11
Microsoft Access's Database Object Properties dialog box lets you change the replication status of a database object.

You can change the replication status of any database object at any time using this technique. In order to make a database object nonreplicable, you simply uncheck the replicable box in the Database Object Properties dialog box. Note, however, that when you make a particular database object nonreplicable, any objects previously copied into a database replica are deleted when the next synchronization takes place.

> **Note: You can also create new database objects and mark them as replicable using Data Access Objects programming. This approach is used in situations in which you do not want to use Microsoft Access to manage replication. For more information on this technique, see the section "Setting Up Replication in DAO" later in this chapter.**

Performing Synchronization in Microsoft Access

After you've created your first replicable database in Microsoft Access, you may want to test it. The simplest way to do this is to enter a single record in the design master, then synchronize the databases. This will cause the new record to be copied to the replica:

1. Open the design master database and enter a record into one of its tables. If you used Replication ID as the data type of its primary key, you should notice that the ID is generated as you enter the record, This is shown in Figure 8.12.

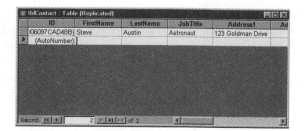

Figure 8.12
An automatically generated replication ID is added to a new data entry in Microsoft Access.

2. Close the table. Database objects must be closed in order to perform synchronization.

3. From Microsoft Access's Tools menu, select Replication. Select Synchronize Now from the submenu.

4. The Synchronize Database dialog box appears, displaying the name of the replica database.

Note that the Synchronize Database lets you select an existing replica or choose from a list of replicas (using the combo box's drop-down list). Because presumably you haven't created more than one replica so far, you can accept the proposed filename and click OK.

5. After a short delay, Access reports that the synchronization was completed successfully. It also asks if you want to close and reopen the current database in order to ensure that all the synchronized data appears. It's not necessary in this case because you know that no new data was copied from the replica to the design master.

6. To confirm that the new record was transmitted from the design master to the replica, close the design master database and open the replica. You should see that the data you entered in the design master has been copied to the replica.

At this point you can try reversing the process, adding a record, or making a change in the record that resides in the replica and resynchronizing the replica with the design master. This reveals an important point about synchronization: You can initiate synchronization from either the replica (in which case records are "pulled" into the replica from the design master), or you can synchronize from the design master (in which case data is "pushed" into the replica from the design master). As long as there is database connectivity between the replica and the design master, and no open database objects, replication will succeed.

Doing Replication in Data Access Objects

In Visual Basic, you can control how databases are replicated using Data Access Objects. DAO, introduced in Chapter 3, "Data Access Objects," is an object-oriented technique for accessing databases. When you use DAO to control replication, you gain the ability to control how replicable database are set up, configured, and synchronized in code. The DAO objects that contain properties relevant to replication are listed in Table 8.1.

Table 8.1 DAO Objects and Their Features Pertaining to Replication		
Replica Functionality	**Object**	**Description**
`KeepLocal` property	`TableDef` and `QueryDef` (as well as other Microsoft Access objects such as forms and reports)	Determines whether the object can be made replicable.
`Replicable` property	`Database` object, `TableDef`, and `QueryDef` (as well as other Access database objects such as reports and code modules)	Determines whether the object (and for `TableDefs`, the data it stores) is replicated at synchronization time.
`MakeReplica` method	`Database`	Makes a replica from a Design Master.
`Synchronize` method	`Database`	Synchronizes a replica database with its design master.
`ReplicaFilter` property	`TableDef`	Enables you to supply a SQL WHERE clause that governs which records from the table are replicated (this property supports partial replicas). For more information, see the section "Using Partial Replication" later in this chapter.
		continues

Replica Functionality	Object	Description
`PartialReplica` property	`Relation`	In a partial replica, it enables you to determine which relationship governs the replication of records.
`ReplicableBool` property	`Database`	Equivalent to the `Replicable` property, but easier to set.

Note: You want to make sure you back up your database before fiddling with its replication properties in DAO, because there are a few seemingly innocent things you can do with replication that can mess up your database permanently.

Setting Up Replication in DAO

To begin using replication with DAO code, you must make your database replicable. To do this, add a dynamic property to the `Database` object that represents the database. The idea of dynamic properties is crucial to understanding how to do replication in DAO; custom properties permit extensibility of the DAO object model.

Note: Because the `Replicable` property is a dynamic property of a Jet database, in order to use it, the property must first be appended to the `Properties` collection of the database object in question. Every Jet database object, including the database itself, has its own `Properties` collection.

Jet database's dynamic properties were introduced in Chapter 3 in the section titled "Creating and Using Custom Properties of Database Objects." Using DAO, you can write code to determine which properties a particular database object has. As a refresher of how this code works, Listing 8.5 shows how to list all the properties for a particular table in a design master.

Listing 8.5   Listing All the Custom Properties for a Particular Database Object

```
Option Explicit

' References DAO 3.51

Dim db As Database
Dim td As TableDef
Dim pr As Property

Public Sub ListProps()

    Set db = OpenDatabase("..\..\DB\nmaster.mdb")
    Set td = db.TableDefs("tblCustomer")

    For Each pr In td.Properties
        Debug.Print pr.Name
    Next

End Sub
```

You make a database replicable by creating a `Replicable` property, then setting that property to the string value "T." Making the database replicable converts it into a design master; this is different than making individual objects within the database replicable (as described in subsequent sections). It's different in DAO than it is in Access because, as with most things, Access does a bunch of the replication for you behind the scenes. When you ask Access to make a replica, it makes the database replicable in addition to the database objects you select.

Use code similar to that in Listing 8.6 to make your database replicable in DAO.

Listing 8.6   Making a Database Replicable by Adding a Dynamic *Replicable* Property

```
Option Explicit

' References DAO 3.51.

Dim db As Database
Dim pr As Property
Dim td As TableDef

Const DBPath = "..\..\DB\novelty.mdb"
Const MasterDBPath = "..\..\DB\nmaster.mdb"
Const ReplicaDBPath = "..\..\DB\nreplica.mdb"
```

```
Private Sub cmdMakeDBRep_Click()
On Error GoTo ErrHandler

    ' The "True" parameter in the OpenDatabase method
    ' tells Jet to open the database for exclusive
    ' access, which is required for creating properties.

    FileCopy DBPath, MasterDBPath

    Set db = OpenDatabase(MasterDBPath, True)

    With db
        Set pr = .CreateProperty("Replicable", dbText, "T")
        .Properties.Append pr
        .Properties("Replicable") = "T"
    End With

    MsgBox "The database has been copied to " & _
            db.Name & _
            " and its Replicable property is now " & _
            db.Properties("Replicable").Value

    db.Close
    Set db = Nothing      ' Release exclusive lock on db.

    Exit Sub
ErrHandler:
    Select Case Err.Number
        Case 3367          ' Replicable property already exists
        Exit Sub           ' So ignore the error and exit

        Case Else          ' Something unforeseen happened
        MsgBox "Error: " & Err & " - " & Error

    End Select

End Sub
```

Note that this code works whether the current database has a dynamic Replicable property or not. If the current database has a Replicable property, the code does not attempt to create it.

However, there's something tricky about creating a Replicable property for a database—when you create it, you can't get rid of it. You might think you could get rid of it using code like this:

```
db.Properties.Delete "Replicable"
```

But you can't. This code generates runtime error 3607: "The replication property you are attempting to delete is read-only and cannot be removed." This is the reason why you were so strenuously instructed to make backups of your database before fooling around with replication. Aren't you glad?

Code Example: You can find an examples of the replication code discussed in this section in the project `Replica.vbp`, located in the directory `\vbdb\code\08-Remote\Replica`. For information on how to install the sample files on the CD that accompanies this book, see the section "Installing the Example Files" in the introduction at the beginning of this book.

Making Objects Within the Database Replicable

After you've made the database replicable, you must make individual objects (such as tables) within the database replicable. You do this by creating dynamic `Replicable` properties for them, the same way you did for the database itself. Those database objects whose `Replicable` property is set to "T" are replicated at synchronization time.

To do this, you use code like that shown in Listing 8.7. This code assumes that the database itself has already been made replicable; it takes an existing table in a database and makes it replicable.

Listing 8.7   Making a Single Table Replicable

```
Private Sub cmdMakeTable_Click()
On Error GoTo ErrHandler

    Set db = OpenDatabase(MasterDBPath, True)
    Set td = db.TableDefs("tblCustomer")
    td.Properties("Replicable") = "T"

    On Error GoTo 0

    MsgBox "The Replicable property of " & _
        td.Name & _
        " has been set to " & _
        td.Properties("Replicable")

    Set db = Nothing     ' Release exclusive lock on DB

    Exit Sub

ErrHandler:
```

```
    If Err.Number = 3270 Then
        Set pr = td.CreateProperty("Replicable", dbText, "T")
        td.Properties.Append pr
    Else
        MsgBox "Error " & Err & " - " & Error
    End If

End Sub
```

This code is fairly similar to the code that set up the initial Replicable property for the database. In this case, the error trapping takes care of the situation where the Replicable property has not been created for the object. The code uses error trapping to determine whether the Replicable property for a database object exists; if it doesn't exist, it creates it and sets the custom property to the string value "T." Setting a database object's Replicable property to "T" causes the object (and any data it contains) to be copied to replica databases at synchronization time.

Setting a database object's Replicable property to "T" automatically causes its KeepLocal property to be set to "F."

Making an Object Replicable Using the *ReplicableBool* Property

You might have noticed that the custom properties used so far in this chapter all take text arguments—the letters T or F instead of the actual Boolean values True or False. That's because when they were introduced to Jet, custom database properties could only store text values. In Jet 3.51, custom properties can store a richer set of data types. This may make it easier for you to create properties pertaining to replication in DAO if you prefer to work with True and False instead of T and F.

If you want to set the Replicable property of a database object using Boolean values, you can create and set the ReplicableBool property rather than the Replicable property. ReplicableBool takes a Boolean value, obviously, rather than a string.

The code to make a database object replicable using the ReplicableBool property is shown in Listing 8.8. Note that the code is startlingly similar to the code that uses the Replicable property.

Listing 8.8   Making a Particular Database Object Replicable Using the
ReplicableBool **Property**

```
Private Sub cmdMakeTableBool_Click()
On Error GoTo ErrHandler

    Set db = OpenDatabase(MasterDBPath, True)
    Set td = db.TableDefs("tblCustomer")
    td.Properties("ReplicableBool") = True


    On Error GoTo 0

    MsgBox "The Replicable property of " & _
           td.Name & _
           " has been set to " & _
           td.Properties("Replicable")

    Set db = Nothing     ' Release exclusive lock on DB

    Exit Sub

ErrHandler:

    If Err.Number = 3270 Then
        Set pr = td.CreateProperty("ReplicableBool", dbBoolean, True)
        td.Properties.Append pr
    Else
        MsgBox "Error " & Err & " - " & Error
    End If

End Sub
```

When you create and set the ReplicableBool property, the Replicable property also becomes available, and the two properties return the same value. That is, when you set ReplicableBool to True and then read the Replicable property, it returns the value "T."

Creating a Replica Database Using DAO Code
You make a replica database from a design master by executing the MakeReplica method of the Database object. The MakeReplica method has the following syntax:

```
db.MakeReplica filename, [description], [options]
```

In this syntax, `filename` is the new database replica file you want to create, and `description` is a textual description for the new replica. This argument is optional.

The `options` argument can be one of two values. The first option, `dbRepMakePartial`, creates a partial replica, which means you can control which records are copied from the design master to the replica. The other option, `dbRepMakeReadOnly`, permits you to make the replica read-only to replica users. (You can still send data and new data objects to the replica through synchronization, however.)

> **Note: You can make a replica both a partial replica and a read-only replica by adding the values `dbRepMakePartial` and `dbRepMakeReadOnly` together in the options argument.**
>
> **Also, I tried my darnedest, but I couldn't figure out what that *description* argument is used for. You'd think that it would become a dynamic property of the replicated database, but it doesn't. I'm sure it's useful for something, but I wasn't able to figure out what, and none of the documentation I have access to is any help. (Naturally, if you're interested in adding custom properties to your own replicated databases, there's nothing to keep you from doing so; that's what dynamic properties are for.)**

In order to replicate an existing design master, you use code like that shown in Listing 8.9.

Listing 8.9   Creating a Replica Database Using Data Access Objects Code

```
Private Sub Command4_Click()

Private Sub cmdSpawn_Click()
    Dim db As Database
    Set db = OpenDatabase(MasterDBPath, True)

    db.MakeReplica ReplicaDBPath, "MyReplica"

    db.Close
    Set db = Nothing

End Sub
```

Code Example: You can find an example of the code discussed in this section in the project `Replica.vbp`, located in the directory `\vbdb\code\08-Remote\Replica`. For information on how to install the sample files on the CD that accompanies this book, see the section "Installing the Example Files" in the introduction at the beginning of this book.

Performing Synchronization in DAO

In order to synchronize a replica and a design master using DAO code, follow these steps:

1. In code, create a `Database` object variable that represents the replica database.

2. Execute the `Database` object's `Synchronize` method in order to synchronize the replica to its design master. The `Synchronize` method takes the filename of a design master database as an argument.

Listing 8.10 gives an example of code that synchronizes two databases. In the example, `nreplica.mdb` is the replica, whereas `nmaster.mdb` is the design master.

Listing 8.10   Synchronizing a Replica and a Design Master Database

```
Private Sub cmdSynch_Click()
    Dim db As Database
    Set db = OpenDatabase(MasterDBPath)

    Screen.MousePointer = vbHourglass
    db.Synchronize ReplicaDBPath
    Screen.MousePointer = vbNormal
End Sub
```

User-interface code (using the `Screen` object's `MousePointer` property) is used to tell the user that the replication is in progress.

Using Partial Replication

Often you don't want to transmit a complete set of data from the design master to the replica. This happens in situations where it's inappropriate and impractical to send the entire contents of the master database to remote users.

Examples of information that shouldn't be transmitted include confidential business information such as salaries, as well as any security-oriented information pertaining to your database, such as user IDs and passwords. Your database may also simply be set up such that only data pertaining to an individual user is replicated to that user's computer. This kind of replication is more efficient than full replication because it only copies the data that a particular user is likely to use.

A *partial replica* is a database that doesn't replicate all the data in the design master. In order to create a partial replica, you follow these general steps:

1. Create a partial replica using the MakeReplica method of the Database object, specifying the dbRepMakePartial option.

2. Set the TableDef object's ReplicaFilter property to restrict the records copied to the partial replica. ReplicaFilter lets you set a criterion SQL WHERE clause to limit the number of records that are copied into the partial replica from the source database.

3. Optionally, set the Relation object's PartialReplica property to restrict records copied to the replica based on joins between tables.

4. Execute the Database object's PopulatePartial method to copy data from the design master to the partial replica.

In partial replication, you can filter out records, but you can't filter out fields. In order to restrict the columns visible to the user, you may want to consider using database security to restrict user access to database objects. For more information on this, see Chapter 9, "Multiuser Jet Databases."

Creating a Partial Replica Using the *MakeReplica* Method

In Data Access Objects, you use the Database object's MakeReplica method to create a partial replica database from either a design master or another full replica. (You can't create a partial replica from another partial replica.)

Use code like that in Listing 8.11 to create a partial replica.

Listing 8.11   Creating a Partial Replica Database from a Design Master Database

```
Option Explicit

' References DAO 3.51

Private db As Database
Private td As TableDef

Const MasterDBPath = "..\..\DB\nmaster.mdb"
Const ReplicaPath = "..\..\DB\npartial.mdb"

Private Sub cmdMakePartial_Click()
    Set db = OpenDatabase(MasterDBPath)
    db.MakeReplica ReplicaPath, "Partial", dbRepMakePartial
    db.Close
    Set db = Nothing
End Sub
```

When you create a partial replica using the code in the previous listing, the partial replica initially contains the structure of the replicated database, but no data.

When you've created a partial replica, you can't convert it into a full replica. However, it is possible to replicate all the data in a design master into a replica by setting the ReplicaFilter property to True (as described in the next section).

Performing a Partial Replication

After you've created a partial replica, you can copy records from another full replica or design master by following these general steps:

1. In Data Access Objects code, declare and set a Database variable for the partial replica database.

2. Declare TableDef variables for the tables in the partial replica that will store replicated data.

3. Set the ReplicaFilter property of each TableDef object to a valid SQL WHERE criterion. This determines which records are copied into the partial replica.

4. Execute the PopulatePartial method of the Database object, specifying the path and filename of the design master or full replica database from which you want to copy records.

You use the ReplicaFilter property of the TableDef object to replicate a partial set of records from a database to a partial replica database. The ReplicaFilter property can be set to one of three values:

▶ If ReplicaFilter is set to True, all the records in the source database are copied to the partial replica database.

▶ If ReplicaFilter is set to False, no records in the source database are copied to the partial replica.

▶ If ReplicaFilter is set to a string, the database engine assumes that the string is a SQL WHERE clause.

To assign a replica filter and copy records from a design master or full replica into a partial replica, use code similar to that in Listing 8.12.

Listing 8.12   Copying Records That Meet a Specific Criterion into a Partial Replica

```
Option Explicit

' References DAO 3.51

Private db As Database
Private td As TableDef

Const MasterDBPath = "..\..\DB\nmaster.mdb"
Const ReplicaPath = "..\..\DB\npartial.mdb"

Private Sub cmdMakePartial_Click()
    Set db = OpenDatabase(MasterDBPath)
    db.MakeReplica ReplicaPath, "Partial", dbRepMakePartial
    db.Close
    Set db = Nothing
End Sub

Private Sub cmdReplicate_Click()

    ' Open partial replica in exclusive mode
    Set db = OpenDatabase(ReplicaPath, True)
    Set td = db.TableDefs("tblCustomer")

    td.ReplicaFilter = "State = 'CA'"

    ' Populate with data from design master
    db.PopulatePartial MasterDBPath

    ' Release exclusive lock on database
    Set db = Nothing

End Sub
```

After you run this code, only customers living in the state of California are copied to the partial replica.

Performing Database Replication over the Internet

Microsoft Jet Replication gives you the ability to synchronize data with a design master located on a Web server on the Internet. Note, however, that you can only use this technique if you have a utility called the Replication Manager, a utility that comes with the Developer Edition of Microsoft Office 97.

In order to set up a system like this, you follow these general steps:

1. Create a design master and one or more replicas as you normally would.

2. Place the design master on a Web server using whatever technique you normally use to place a file on a Web server. This can involve a simple file copy to a public directory (if the Web server machine is located on a machine accessible to your machine over a LAN) or an FTP upload (if the Web server machine isn't directly accessible).

3. When it's time to synchronize data, use the `dbRepSyncInternet` argument with the `Synchronize` method of the `Database` object. This argument lets you pass a uniform resource locator (URL) to the `Synchronize` method, causing the database to be replicated over the Internet.

The advantage of this technique is that anyone can get access to this data from anywhere on earth at any time. This can be a disadvantage as well, but presumably you'll take care to secure your replicated database in such a way that your valuable data doesn't fall into the hands of your enemies.

SUMMARY

This chapter covers two major topics having to do with distributing data over a network to multiple users. In the first section, you learned how to use ActiveX components to gain object-oriented access to data. This included a discussion of DCOM deployment of ActiveX components, permitting you to deploy business objects across a LAN.

In the second section, you learned how to replicate Jet databases across a network in order to distribute data across two or more database files.

Although the discussion of ActiveX middle-tier components and replication represent separate major sections of this chapter, they're by no means mutually exclusive. In a production application, you could take advantage of both techniques in concert to distribute your data far and wide. Which technique you use depends on your application's architecture, the number of users you need to support, and the degree of consistency your data requires.

In the next chapter, you continue reading a discussion of multiuser Jet databases, which extends to such topics as record-locking and security.

QUESTIONS AND ANSWERS

Q. I have a whole carload of database-accessing ActiveX DLLs I've created. Do I need to recompile them as ActiveX EXEs in order to access them remotely over a network?

A. Heavens, no. If you use Microsoft Transaction Server, you can package those pesky little ActiveX DLLs right up and access them remotely. Remote deployment of components under MTS is covered in this chapter.

Q. When I'm doing database replication, my database system is essentially offline. How can I know how long it's going to take?

A. That's a tricky question to answer, because there are so many variables—the amount of data you have to convey, your network bandwidth, the speed of the computers crunching records. If you're running into performance problems with replication you may want to consider automating the process if you can (preferably by writing a VB application to synchronize data when the database isn't being used much—like in the middle of the night). You also might want to consider using partial replication in order to minimize the amount of data being copied hither and yon.

Q. Because partial replication gives you the ability to replicate none, some, or all records, given the fact that you can't convert back and forth between partial replicas and full replicas, why not make all replicas partial?

A. You can only do synchronization between design masters and full replicas, not between partial replicas and other replicas. This gives you more flexibility in situations where you want to synchronize multiple replicas to each other to offload the processing crunch from the computer that contains the design master.

Q. Is it true that your nickname in high school was "Package Wizard?"

A. Yes. Yes, it was.

Multiuser Jet Databases

Locking Data in Microsoft Jet

Using Microsoft Jet Database Security

When your database applications require access by multiple users at the same time, you need to make special accommodations. From the planning and design stage to the development and deployment of your database application, multiuser applications demand much more of the software developer—it's not just a matter of throwing a multiuser switch and copying client applications to all the computers in your organization.

Previous chapters scratched the surface of what goes into a multiuser database system. Previous chapters have covered the deployment of components that enable users to gain access to your program logic over a network using ActiveX and DCOM technology, as well as the database replication technology made available to you by the Microsoft Jet database engine.

This chapter covers two techniques that are crucial to making a Jet multiuser database run smoothly—locking data and the security model provided with the Microsoft Jet database engine.

LOCKING DATA IN MICROSOFT JET

When two or more users have access to data in a database system, those users can cause problems for each other. For example, when one user opens a record in a table, then another user opens the same record and makes a change to it, the first user is working with an out-of-date record. And this is just one scenario; there are several others.

Your software must manage contention between users. To do this, your software, in conjunction with the database engine, has the capability to lock various parts of the database. An error occurs when a user attempts to gain access to a part of the locked database; how your application deals with that error is up to you.

In order to give you flexibility and control, the Microsoft Jet database permits you to lock the database on a number of levels. Listed in order from the most restrictive to the least restrictive, here are the levels of locking available in Jet:

▶ *Database-level locking*. This is also known as *exclusive mode*. This involves opening the database in such a way that no other user can edit records in any table in the database.

▶ *Table-level locking*. In this mode, a single user has exclusive access to a particular table in a database. All the records in that table are locked, preventing other users from editing records.

▶ *Pessimistic page-level locking*. A lock is placed on data at the time the user begins to edit it. The lock is released when the edit is committed to the database or when the user aborts the edit.

▶ *Optimistic page-level locking*. The record is locked the instant it is committed to the database, and released when the update is complete.

The following sections in this chapter discuss each locking option in detail, giving you code examples so you can use the locking techniques in your applications.

Before you proceed, note that none of these techniques permit you to lock an individual record. This is because the Jet engine locks pages of records, rather than individual records. (This is the page-locking strategy used by SQL Server 6.5 as well, although SQL Server 7.0 offers row-level locking.)

A page is 2048 bytes of memory. If a particular record comprises less that 2048 bytes worth of data, the record, and potentially one or more records adjacent to it, will be locked as well.

Jet database locks are implemented through the use of a locking file. This file is given the same name as the database, but with an .LDB extension. (You can see this file in the directory where your database is stored when you open the database for read-write access.) In Jet 3.*x*, unlike previous versions of Jet, the locking file is automatically deleted by the database engine when all users have closed the database.

LOCKING THE ENTIRE DATABASE USING DATA ACCESS OBJECTS

You have the ability to lock the entire database using Data Access Objects code. You do this in situations where you need to perform maintenance on the database, when you're performing design changes on the database, or when it's simply not appropriate for other users to have access to the database for a period of time.

To restrict access to the entire database using DAO, you supply a parameter to the OpenDatabase method, as shown in Listing 9.1.

Listing 9.1 Placing a Lock on the Entire Database Using Data Access Objects Code

```
Option Explicit

' References Microsoft DAO 3.51

Private db As Database


Private Sub cmdExclusive_Click()
On Error GoTo ErrHandler

Dim rs As Recordset

    ' Open the database in exclusive mode.
    ' No other users will be able to change
    ' records when you do this.
    Set db = OpenDatabase("..\..\DB\novelty.mdb", True)

Exit Sub
ErrHandler:
    MsgBox Err & " - " & Error
End Sub
```

The Database object is declared in the Declarations section of the form, not in the Click event procedure. While you wouldn't normally declare a Database variable in a procedure, in this test application it's particularly important that the Database variable have module-level scope. That's because the database lock only persists as long as the database variable is in scope. If the object variable db was declared within the procedure, it would go out of scope as soon as the procedure finished executing.

This isn't to say that you'd never want to have a procedure-level declaration for a Database variable; it just means that you need to carefully consider where and how you declare variables when performing actions with them in database access.

When your application attempts to open a database that is already opened exclusively by another user (or another application), an error occurs: number 3045, "Couldn't open X, file already in use." (The easiest way to test this for yourself is to attempt to open the Novelty database in Access while it's opened in your VB application in exclusive mode.) By trapping this error in your applications, you can ensure that your applications won't inadvertently attempt to open a database that is exclusively locked by another user.

Code Example: You can find examples of all the database locking modes discussed in this chapter in the project DBLock.vbp, located in the directory \vbdb\code\09-Multiuser\DBLock. For information on how to install the sample files on the CD that accompanies this book, see the section "Installing the Example Files" in the introduction at the beginning of this book.

USING RECORDSET-LEVEL LOCKING

You can use Data Access Objects to place a lock on an entire table (or multiple tables, in the case of a Recordset based on a join between more than one table). You might do this in a situation where you need to perform maintenance on the table or if you need to change the table's design, but you don't want to deny users access to the entire database.

Listing 9.2 gives an example of DAO code that locks a database table, returns its record count, and unlocks it by releasing its object variable.

Listing 9.2   Data Access Objects Code to Lock an Entire Database Table

```
Private db As Database


Private Sub cmdTable_Click()

    Dim rs As Recordset

    ' Open database in multiuser mode
    ' with no database-level lock
    Set db = OpenDatabase("..\..\DB\novelty.mdb")

    ' Open table exclusively
    Set rs = db.OpenRecordset("tblCustomer", dbOpenTable, _
                              dbDenyWrite + dbDenyRead)

    ' Required to get an accurate record count
```

```
    rs.MoveLast

    MsgBox "The table contains " & rs.RecordCount & " records."

    ' Now you can test to see whether you
    ' really have a table lock
    Stop

End Sub
```

One quick way to test this code is to run this code in Visual Basic and then attempt to open the table in Microsoft Access (the stop statement in the procedure permits you to do this). If it worked properly, Access should refuse to open the table, instead of generating an error message indicating that the table is exclusively locked.

USING PAGE-LEVEL LOCKING

Page-level locking is the least restrictive level of locking available in the Jet database engine. With page-level locking, records that are being updated are locked for some period of time to ensure that other users' operations don't interfere with the update.

Remember that Jet locks pages (of 2,048 bytes each) rather than records. This means that when a page is locked, it's likely that more than one record will be locked. This can be a source of frustration for database programmers who like to have complete control over what's going on with their data. But after you become accustomed to it, you may find that it isn't such a big deal.

You have two options to enforce page-level locking: optimistic and pessimistic locking. Optimistic locking is turned on at the instant a record is being committed to the database; pessimistic locking is activated as soon as you open a record for editing. Both techniques have their own advantages and disadvantages.

Using Optimistic Locking   You use optimistic locking when you need to minimize the number of locks on records in your database. It's particularly appropriate when a large number of users need access to all the records in your database at all times. Optimistic locking might also be appropriate for an application whose purpose is primarily inserting, rather than updating, information in a database.

To explicitly specify that you want to open a recordset with optimistic locking, supply the dbOptimistic flag to the options parameter of the OpenRecordset method:

```
db.OpenRecordset("tblPerson", dbOpenDynaset, False, dbOptimistic)
```

Optimistic locking requires an error trap associated with the process of updating a record. An Update method on an optimistically locked recordset generates an error if another user makes a change to a record between the time you started editing and when you committed it back to the database.

Listing 9.3 shows an example of such a collision using optimistic locking.

Listing 9.3   Retrieving and Updating a Record from a Database Using Optimistic Locking

```
Option Explicit

' References Microsoft DAO 3.51

Private db As Database
Private rsOp As Recordset


Private Sub cmdOpOpen_Click()

    Set db = OpenDatabase("..\..\DB\novelty.mdb")

    ' Optimistic lock is the default
    Set rsOp = db.OpenRecordset("tblCustomer", _
                                dbOpenDynaset, _
                                False, _
                                dbOptimistic)

    ' Go into edit mode to make the
    ' optimistic lock happen.
    rsOp.Edit

    ' Populate the user interface with
    ' data from the first record.
    txtFirstName.Text = rsOp!FirstName
    txtLastName.Text = rsOp!LastName
    txtAddress.Text = rsOp!Address

End Sub
```

```
Private Sub cmdOpSave_Click()

    If rsOp Is Nothing Then
        Exit Sub
    End If

    rsOp!FirstName = txtFirstName.Text
    rsOp!LastName = txtLastName.Text
    rsOp!Address = txtAddress.Text

    ' If this is the 2nd instance of the app,
    ' this should cause an error
    rsOp.Update

End Sub
```

Follow these steps to demonstrate a collision between two applications attempting to edit the same record at the same time using optimistic locking:

1. Compile the DBLock application using Visual Basic's File, Make menu command.

2. Launch two copies of the application by double-clicking DBLock.exe twice in Windows Explorer.

3. Click the Optimistic Open command button in the first copy of the application. A record is loaded into the application.

4. Click Optimistic Open in the second copy of the application. The same record is loaded.

5. Make a change in the data in the application's first copy and click Optimistic Save. The data is written to the database.

6. Make a change in the data in the application's second copy and click Optimistic Save.

7. The second application generates an error, as illustrated in Figure 9.1.

To avoid this situation, trap the error and report it back to the user. Optionally, you could also provide a service in the user interface to preserve the data entered by the user until it's entered at a later time, comparing the latest version of the record with the data entered by the user.

Figure 9.1
This is an example of a collision between two applications accessing data using optimistic locking.

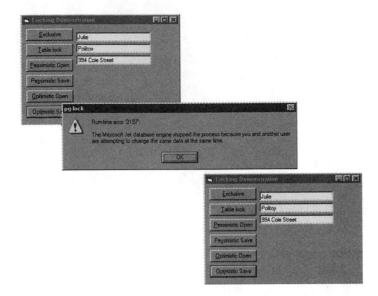

Using Pessimistic Locking   You use pessimistic locking when you want to make sure that no other user accesses data while you're working with that data. When pessimistic locking is activated, a lock is placed on the database page containing the record you're editing as soon as you execute the Edit method against the record. If other users attempt to retrieve a record that's on the locked page containing your record, their application generates an error.

You activate pessimistic locking by using the dbPessimistic flag when executing the OpenRecordset method. Listing 9.4 shows an example of a procedure that opens a recordset with pessimistic locking.

Listing 9.4   Opening a Recordset in Data Access Objects Using Pessimistic Locking

```
Option Explicit

' References Microsoft DAO 3.51
'
Private db As Database
Private rsPess As Recordset

Private Sub cmdPess_Click()

    Set db = OpenDatabase("..\..\DB\novelty.mdb")
```

```
        Set rsPess = db.OpenRecordset("tblCustomer", _
                                      dbOpenDynaset, _
                                      False, _
                                      dbPessimistic)

        ' Get a lock on the data. If this
        ' is the 2nd copy of the app,
        ' this should cause an error
        rsPess.Edit

        ' Populate the user interface
        txtFirstName.Text = rsPess!FirstName
        txtLastName.Text = rsPess!LastName
        txtAddress.Text = rsPess!Address

End Sub


Private Sub cmdSave_Click()

    If rsPess Is Nothing Then
        Exit Sub
    End If

    rsPess!FirstName = txtFirstName.Text
    rsPess!LastName = txtLastName.Text
    rsPess!Address = txtAddress.Text

    rsPess.Update

End Sub
```

Note: Any page lock—either optimistic or pessimistic—is released after the successful execution of the Update method.

You can test pessimistic locking with this application by doing the following:

1. Compile the application.

2. Launch two copies of the application (by double-clicking the file DBLock.exe twice in Windows Explorer).

3. In the first copy of the application, click Pessimistic Open to load the first record in the recordset.

4. The data appears in the application's interface. Click Pessimistic Open in the second application's copy.

5. The second application generates an error, as illustrated in Figure 9.2.

Figure 9.2
Two applications contending for the same record generates an error in pessimistic locking.

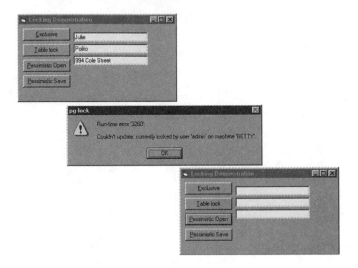

The moral of this story is that although pessimistic locking keeps you from having to worry about data changing while you're working, you must include additional error handling to account for situations in which two users attempt to open the same record at the same time. Pessimistic locking also puts your database in a situation where your data isn't available to as many users. Carefully consider the implications of locking before implementing it in your applications—stringent locking is almost never required, and it's not needed as often as most programmers think it is.

USING MICROSOFT JET DATABASE SECURITY

One compelling reason to use the Microsoft Jet database engine is the fact that it supports multiple concurrent users. But database locking is only one way in which Jet supports multiple users.

You can use Jet's database security features to identify individual users and groups of users. This lets you control access to various parts of your database. When you restrict access to a database, that database is described as secure—although the Jet security model allows for many different shades of meaning within the word secure. The level of security you choose to implement in your databases depends on your needs, the needs of your users, and the amount of effort you want to expend.

You have the ability to secure a database using the graphical user interface in Microsoft Access. This has the advantage of being easy to implement. But even with Access you can't create secure databases unless you have a handle on the Jet security model. Accordingly, this section focuses on how to manage the security of your database using DAO code.

One advantage of Data Access Objects 3.*x* is that, unlike previous versions of DAO, you can now access the Jet security model in Visual Basic code (either in Visual Basic, or in the version of Visual Basic for Applications found in Microsoft Access and other Microsoft Office applications). The ability to write code to access the database's security features gives you a great deal of flexibility to create and maintain a secure database system.

> **Note:** You can use Data Access Object programming to perform all but one task pertaining to managing database security—the creation of a workgroup information file. For this, you need a utility provided with Microsoft Access. More on this in "Creating a Workgroup Information File" later in this chapter.
>
> This chapter focuses on DAO as a way to programmatically access Jet security because, as of this writing, it isn't possible to control most Jet security features from ActiveX Data Objects. Accordingly, if you're creating a secure Jet database application, you'll almost certainly want to stick with DAO for now.

The Visual Basic documentation is extremely deficient in the area of documenting how Microsoft Jet security works. This section gives you a complete introduction into how security works, including examples of how to perform security operations using Data Access Objects.

Because security from the Microsoft Access perspective is fairly well documented, this section seeks to avoid a discussion of using Access as a security-enabling tool (with one exception: creating a workgroup information file, the single Jet security operation that requires a utility found only in Microsoft Access).

Understand, however, that Access provides a simple set of menus and dialog boxes to implement security. If you're interested in setting up security for an existing application on a one-time basis and you don't need programmatic access to Jet's security model, you may find it more efficient to take advantage of Access's interface into Jet database security.

ACCESSING A SECURED JET DATABASE IN CODE

In order to gain access to a secured database, you must identify yourself with a username, a password, or both (depending on how your database was secured). If your code attempts to access a secure database, it will generate an error unless it supplies this information to the database engine.

To specify a username and password in Data Access Objects code, use the `connect` parameter of the `OpenDatabase` method. As you've seen in previous chapters' discussions involving ODBC databases, the connect string permits you to supply additional information to the database engine about the user's identity and how he should be connected to the database.

As introduced in Chapter 6, "Open Database Connectivity and Remote Data Objects," connect strings are composed of a series of settings separated by semicolons. This syntax, while unwieldy at times, permits the connect string to convey a potentially unlimited amount of information about how the user should be connected to the database.

Normally when you build a connect string in code, the first setting is `ODBC;`. This indicates that you want to connect to a remote database using an ODBC driver.

However, when you want to connect to a Jet database, you supply a connect string solely for the purpose of indicating a username and a password. In this case, replace the ODBC setting with a blank.

The database name is the next connect string setting. The `DATABASE` setting provides the path and filename of a Jet database.

For example, a connect string to open the Jones Novelties database would look like this:

```
";DATABASE=c:\data\novelty.mdb"
```

Use the `PWD` value to provide a password in the connect string. This logs you into the database whether you use simple password protection or user-level security. For example, if the Jones Novelties database had a password of prince, you'd use the following connect string:

```
";DATABASE=c:\data\novelty.mdb;PWD=prince"
```

Remember that in Jet, passwords can be up to 20 characters in length, and they are case sensitive.

In a database that contains user-level security (described later in this chapter), all users must identify themselves to the system with a unique username (of up to 14 characters). You include this information in the connect string using the connect string's USR value. To extend the previous example, the connect string to get into the Jones Novelties database with a username of randy and a password of prince is this:

```
";DATABASE=c:\data\novelty.mdb;USR=randy;PWD=prince"
```

The order in which the connect string values appear is unimportant, with the exception of the first value, which specifies which type of data source you're opening (ODBC or non-ODBC). The previous connect string could also have been expressed as this:

```
";DATABASE=..\..\DB\npass.mdb;PWD=prince;USR=randy"
```

Listing 9.5 demonstrates how to gain access to a password-protected database using a connect string passed as a parameter to the OpenDatabase method.

Listing 9.5   Logging into a Secured Database Using a Connect String

```
Option Explicit

Private db As Database

' References DAO 3.51

Private Sub Command1_Click()
On Error Resume Next

Dim strConnect As String
strConnect = ";DATABASE=..\..\DB\npass.mdb" & _
            ";PWD=" & txtPassword.Text

    ' Open in non-exclusive mode and pass connect string
    Set db = OpenDatabase("", True, False, strConnect)

    If Err Then
        MsgBox "Error: " & Err.Description & _
                " [" & Err.Number & "]", vbExclamation
        Exit Sub
    Else
        MsgBox "Database successfully opened.", vbInformation
    End If

    db.Close
    Set db = Nothing

End Sub
```

Code Example: You can find the code discussed in this section in the project `Login.vbp`, located in the directory `\vbdb\code\09-Multiuser\Login`. This code uses a version of the Novelty database called `npass.mdb`. This version of the database is exactly the same as the normal version except that it's password protected. For information on how to install the sample files on the CD that accompanies this book, see the section "Installing the Example Files" in the introduction at the beginning of this book.

There are two important differences between this code and the code you've used previously to open databases using DAO.

First, the DATABASE= value in the connect string replaces the filename parameter you typically supply to the OpenDatabase method. In this scenario, you pass the OpenDatabase method an empty string (as a placeholder) in place of the filename parameter.

Error handling is used to deal with a situation where the database can't be opened. You should have an error handler active whenever you perform file access, but it's particularly important when you're accessing a secure database. This is because login information is typically supplied by the user, and it's quite common for the user to supply incorrect information (such as a misspelled username or an expired password). An error trap is the only way your application can gracefully recover from this situation.

ASSIGNING A PASSWORD TO A DATABASE

Assigning a password to a Jet database is one of the easiest ways to restrict access to a database. When you password-protect a database, only authorized users can get access to the database.

Merely assigning a password to a database does not provide airtight security. In fact, it's one of the least rigorous security measures you can apply to a Microsoft Access database. Simply assigning a password to a database is used primarily because it's easy to implement. And for many systems, locking unauthorized users out of the database with a password check is all the security that is required.

Note, however, that this technique does not require users to log in with a unique username. Consequently, it does not permit you to restrict particular users' access to particular database objects (to do this, you must implement user-level security, as described later in this chapter).

In Data Access Objects programming, you assign a password to a database by opening the database in exclusive mode and then using the Database object's NewPassword method. The NewPassword method's syntax is as follows:

```
db.NewPassword oldpassword, newpassword
```

oldpassword is the database's current password, and *newpassword* is the password you want to apply. If the database doesn't currently have a password (by default, it does not), you supply an empty string in place of *oldpassword*. (Similarly, if you're interested in removing a password from a previously password-protected database, supply an empty string to the *newpassword* argument.)

To assign a password to a database that currently doesn't have a password, use code similar to that in Listing 9.6.

Listing 9.6 Assigning a Password to a Database That Doesn't Currently Have a Password

```
Private Sub cmdPassword_Click()
On Error Resume Next

' NB: The database password is
' either "tool" or "shed"

    Dim strConnect As String

    strConnect = ";DATABASE=" & "..\..\DB\npass.mdb" & _
                 ";PWD=" & txtOld.Text

    ' Open in exclusive mode with existing password, if any
    Set db = OpenDatabase("", True, False, strConnect)

    If Err Then
        MsgBox "Error opening database: " & _
                Err.Description & " [" & Err.Number & "]", _
               vbExclamation
        Exit Sub
    End If


    ' Change password
    db.NewPassword txtOld.Text, txtNew.Text

    If Err Then
        MsgBox "Error changing password: " & _
               Err.Description & " [" & Err.Number & "]", _
               vbExclamation
        Exit Sub
    Else
        MsgBox "The database password was changed!"
    End If


End Sub
```

Code Example: You can find the code discussed in this section in the project `Password.vbp`, located in the directory `\vbdb\code\09-MultiUser\Password`. For information on how to install the sample files on the CD that accompanies this book, see the section "Installing the Example Files" in the introduction at the beginning of this book.

Remember from the discussion of the `Database` object in Chapter 3, "Data Access Objects," that the `OpenDatabase` method takes several arguments. In this context, the `True` and `False` arguments supplied to `OpenDatabase` indicate that the database should be opened in read-write, exclusive mode (the `True` argument means open the database in read-write mode; the `False` argument means open it in exclusive mode). You must open a database in read-write, exclusive mode before you can assign the database a password.

You should make judicious use of error-handling when your code manipulates a database's security information, or when you open a database that has been secured with a password. Just as with other data access and file operations, a number of things can go wrong when you access a database. In this case, the likeliest problems are the following:

▶ Another user already has the database open.

▶ The user attempted to change to an invalid password.

Remember also that passwords are case sensitive and must be 20 characters or less. After you've assigned a password to a database, remember it. If you forget it, you'll never be able to open the database again.

Note: The topics pertaining to security in the rest of this chapter cover user-level security, in which you create user accounts and groups that can have permissions to access objects in the database. In order to set up this type of security, you must go through a complicated series of steps, including creating a special type of external database that manages information pertaining to users, groups, and permissions. This database is called a _workgroup information file_, and it's covered later in this chapter. Bear in mind, though, that you don't need a workgroup information file if you only want to assign a password to the database. When you assign a password to the database using the technique described in this section, the password is stored in the database itself (in encrypted form, of course).

The concept of assigning a password to a database was a new feature added to Jet 3._x_.

When you attempt to use Microsoft Access to open a password-protected database, Access displays a password dialog box, as shown in Figure 9.3.

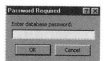

Figure 9.3
The logon dialog box displayed by Microsoft Access for databases secured at the share level.

Access displays a similar dialog for databases that have been secured with user-level security, as shown in Figure 9.4.

Figure 9.4
The logon dialog displayed by Microsoft Access for databases secured at the user level.

IDENTIFYING THE CURRENT USER IN CODE

In a secure database, users identify themselves to the database engine by supplying a username and a password. This is the case whether you've explicitly done anything to secure your database or not. If the database is unsecured, the user is always identified with a username of Admin and a blank password. You might not have encountered this because in an unsecured Jet database, the username Admin is supplied as a default.

You can see this for yourself by creating an application that inspects the username in the default Jet workspace, known as Workspaces(0). Remember that Workspaces(0) is created automatically when you run an application that contains a reference to Data Access Objects. The code to return the name of the current user in Jet is shown in Listing 9.7.

Listing 9.7   Displaying the Current User in Microsoft Jet Security

```
Option Explicit
Private db As Database

' References DAO 3.51

Private Sub Form_Load()

    MsgBox Workspaces(0).UserName, vbInformation

End Sub
```

Again, note that even though this is DAO code, you don't have to declare or set any object variables for it to work, because Workspaces(0) is always available to you.

LOGGING INTO THE DATABASE USING THE *WORKSPACE* OBJECT

In an unsecured Jet database, you are implicitly logged on as the Admin user. When logging on to a secured database using DAO code, however, you must identify yourself as a database user. You typically do this by creating a new workspace, passing your username and password to the CreateWorkspace method of the DBEngine object. Listing 9.8 shows how to do this.

Listing 9.8   Opening a Secured Database Using the *CreateWorkspace* Method of the *OpenDatabase* Object

```
Option Explicit

' References DAO 3.51

Private ws As Workspace
Private db As Database
Private rs As Recordset

Private Sub Form_Load()
    DBEngine.SystemDB = App.Path & "\mygroup.mdw"
    Set ws = DBEngine.CreateWorkspace("", "johnny", "johnny")

    Set db = ws.OpenDatabase(App.Path & "\nsecure.mdb")
    Set rs = db.OpenRecordset("tblCustomer")

    rs.MoveLast
    MsgBox "The table contains " & rs.RecordCount & " records.", vbInformation

End Sub
```

The CreateWorkspace method takes three arguments here: a blank string that represents the name of the workspace, a username, and a password. (In the secured sample database, users' names and passwords are all the same.) When you open the database using this technique, you use the Workspace object's OpenDatabase method, instead of the way you'd normally do it—using OpenDatabase by itself:

```
OpenDatabase(App.Path & "\nsecure.mdb")
```

When you use OpenDatabase this way, you're really executing the DBEngine object's OpenDatabase method, which doesn't permit you to include security login information generated by the DAO workspace object. Remember when you're logging into a secured database to use the OpenDatabase method of the Workspace object, not the DBEngine's OpenDatabase method.

Note also that if the user johnny doesn't have permission to open the tblCustomer table, the application generates an error (number 3112, "Record(s) can't be read, no read permission on 'tblCustomer'.") Accordingly, make sure that this error is trapped and handled appropriately in your applications that use secured databases.

CREATING A WORKGROUP INFORMATION FILE

A *workgroup information file* is a type of database that stores information about users and groups. This information is stored in a different file (as opposed to within your database) because it's possible you'd want to share security information across multiple databases.

> Note: Before you begin the process of securing a database by creating a workgroup information file, you may wish to back up your database. The version of the Novelty database used for security-related examples in this chapter is called nsecure.mdb.

The workgroup information file is typically named SYSTEM.MDW (although it doesn't have to have this filename). You use the Workgroup Administrator utility, WRKGADM.EXE, to create a workgroup information file. Irritatingly, though, this utility does not come with Visual Basic; it only comes with Microsoft Access. This is the only component of Jet security you can't manipulate using Visual Basic alone.

To create a workgroup information file, follow these steps:

1. If you're running Microsoft Access, exit it.

2. Launch the Workgroup Administrator utility WRKGADM.EXE. This file is located in the Windows system folder.

3. The Workgroup Administrator launches, as shown in Figure 9.5.

4. To create a new workgroup information database, click Create. The Workgroup Owner Information dialog box appears, as shown in Figure 9.6.

Figure 9.5
*The Microsoft
Access Workgroup
Administrator dis-
plays the current
default workgroup
information file.*

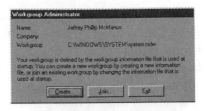

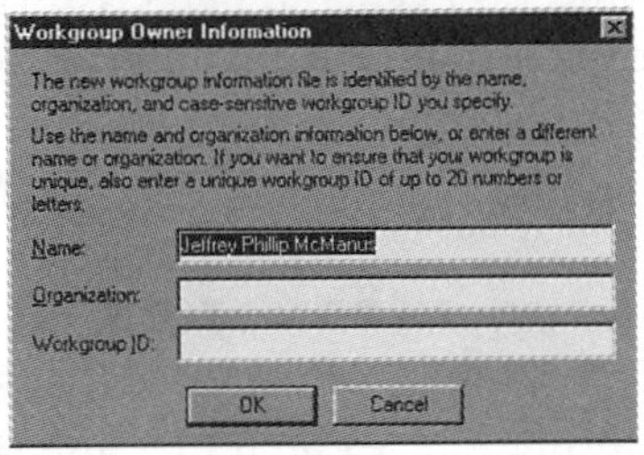

Figure 9.6
*The Workgroup
Owner
Information dialog
box lets you supply
information used
to create a new
workgroup infor-
mation file.*

5. Enter your name and company name in the appropriate text boxes. (If you
entered these when you set up Microsoft Access, they are entered into the
text boxes for you.) Additionally, in order to make your workgroup information file unique, enter a workgroup ID of up to 20 alphanumeric characters. When the Workgroup Owner Information dialog box is complete, it
should resemble Figure 9.7.

Figure 9.7
*Here's the
Workgroup Owner
Information dialog
box containing the
owner's informa-
tion and a work-
group ID.*

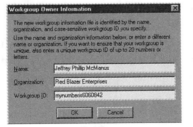

6. Click OK. A dialog box appears, asking you for the folder into which you
want to save your workgroup information file. Choose a folder and click
OK.

7. The Confirm Workgroup Information dialog box appears, as shown in
Figure 9.8.

Figure 9.8
The Confirm Workgroup Information dialog box shows you the information you entered.

The Confirm Workgroup Information dialog box displays the information you entered; this information is used to create a unique workgroup information file. It's important to record this information; otherwise, your workgroup information file can't be replaced if it becomes destroyed or deleted in the future. Because all the information you need is being displayed for you in the Confirm Workgroup Information dialog box, now is a good time to record the information and put it away for future reference.

Note: You might want to take a screen shot of this dialog box and print it out so you have a permanent copy of your user information and workgroup ID. You can do this by pressing the Print Screen key on your keyboard. This places a copy of the screen on the Windows Clipboard. You can then print out the screen shot by pasting the image into any application that accepts images. Microsoft Word and Windows Paint both work well for this purpose.

You should also keep your workgroup ID secret. If an unscrupulous person obtains your workgroup ID, he or she can re-create your workgroup information file and gain access to your secure databases.

8. Click OK to create the new workgroup information file. You'll receive a confirmation message; then you're returned to the original Workgroup Administrator utility dialog box.

9. Click Exit to exit the Workgroup Administrator application.

It's important to note that creating a new workgroup information file also makes it your default workgroup file. This can have implications for existing secured databases. If you're currently using security based on the default SYSTEM.MDW file located in your Windows system directory and you create a new workgroup information file, you may have to switch back to your original .MDW file (using the Workgroup Administrator utility) in order to access databases secured with the original workgroup information file.

ASSIGNING A WORKGROUP INFORMATION FILE USING DAO CODE

You can designate a specific workgroup information database for your Visual Basic application. Your applications should do this where possible to avoid inadvertently utilizing whatever default workgroup file a user may have set up on his or her computer.

You direct the database engine to use a particular workgroup information database by assigning the workgroup file's filename to the DBEngine object's SystemDB propertyy:

```
DBEngine.SystemDB = "..\..\DB\mygroup.mdw"
```

Remember that you don't have to instantiate the DBEngine object; it's one of those DAO objects that's always available to you. But if you're going to assign an alternate workgroup information database using this technique, ensure that it's the first DAO operation your application makes. You need to do this because the DBEngine object is initialized as soon as you create a DAO object. If you don't assign a workgroup database to the DBEngine first, it will use whatever is set up as the default on your computer (or, it will use no workgroup information database at all). If that happens, you have to restart your application to get the database engine to recognize the new workgroup database.

CREATING AND DELETING USERS

After your application has a unique workgroup information database, you can create user accounts (usually referred to as *users*). A *user account* allows an individual to log into and use a database. An account also uniquely identifies a user, permitting the database administrator to permit and deny that user access to specific elements of the database.

Remember that user information is stored in the workgroup information database (as opposed to the database itself). This means that the same sets of users, groups, and permissions can be applied to many databases, as long as the databases share the same workgroup information database.

You can access the list of user accounts by iterating through the Workspace object's Users collection. Remember that you can always access a default Workspace object by using the expression Workspaces(0); this workspace is always available to you, and you don't have to instantiate it.

An example of DAO code that uses a list box to display all user accounts in the Users collection is shown in Listing 9.9.

Listing 9.9   **Adding the Contents of the *Users* Collection to a List Box**

```
Option Explicit

' References DAO 3.51

Private ThisUser As User

Private Sub Form_Load()
    DBEngine.SystemDB = "..\..\DB\mygroup.mdw"
End Sub


Private Sub cmdUser_Click()
    List1.Clear

    For Each ThisUser In Workspaces(0).Users
        List1.AddItem ThisUser.Name
    Next

End Sub
```

Code Example: The code examples pertaining to user and group security discussed in this section are located in the project `UsrGrp.vbp`, located in the directory `\vbdb\code\09-Multiuser\UsrGrp`. For information on how to install the sample files on the CD that accompanies this book, see the section "Installing the Example Files" in the introduction at the beginning of this book.

To create a new user account, create a `User` object using the `Workspace` object's `CreateUser` method. You then assign its name, password, and a unique identifier called a personal identifier (PID). The PID is a string of between 4 and 20 characters that provides uniqueness to a user account. If your workgroup information file is lost, you can use the username and personal identifier to re-create the user's account. (Users should accordingly keep their PIDs secret.)

Listing 9.10 shows an example of how to create a new user account using DAO code.

Listing 9.10   Creating a New User Account

```
Option Explicit

' References DAO 3.51

Private ThisUser As User
Private ThisGroup As Group

Private Sub cmdNewUser_Click()
Dim strName As String
Dim strPID As String
Dim strPassword As String

    strName = InputBox("Enter the new user's name.", "New User")
    strPassword = InputBox("Enter the new password.", "New User")
    strPID = InputBox("Enter a personal ID.", "New User")

    Set ThisUser = Workspaces(0).CreateUser(strName)
    ThisUser.PID = strPID
    ThisUser.Password = strPassword

    Workspaces(0).Users.Append ThisUser

    ' Extra step required in DAO but
    ' done automatically in Access
    Set ThisGroup = ThisUser.CreateGroup("Users")
    ThisUser.Groups.Append ThisGroup

    ' Refresh list of users
    cmdUser_Click

End Sub
```

The code that adds the user to the default Users group is described more fully in "Adding Users to Groups" later in this chapter. The process of adding a new user to the default Users group is done automatically when you use Microsoft Access to manage security. However, in DAO code, users aren't automatically added to any groups. You must write code to give the user access to the database.

To delete a user account, simply delete the User object from the Users collection, as shown in Listing 9.11.

Listing 9.11   Deleting a New User Account

```
Option Explicit

' References DAO 3.51

Private Sub cmdDeleteUser_Click()
Dim strUser As String

    strUser = InputBox("Enter the user to delete.", "Delete user")
    Workspaces(0).Users.Delete strUser

    ' Refresh list of users
    cmdUser_Click

End Sub
```

Note: Don't delete all the user accounts from the Admins group. If you do this, you won't be able to administer the database, which means that you won't be able to create new users, assign ownership of objects, or assign permissions to users and groups.

Adding a Password to a User   Normally you assign a password to a user account when you create the user's account, but occasionally you need to add a password to a user after the fact. You also may need to change a user's password or permit the user to change his or her own password.

Use the User object's NewPassword method to do this, as shown in Listing 9.12.

Listing 9.12   Changing a User's Password Using the *NewPassword* Method

```
Private Sub cmdChangePwd_Click()
On Error Resume Next

Dim strOld As String
Dim strNew As String

    strOld = InputBox("Enter this user's current password:", _
            "Password Change")
    strNew = InputBox("Enter this user's new password:", _
            "Password Change")

    Set ThisUser = Workspaces(0).Users(List1.Text)
    ThisUser.NewPassword strOld, strNew
```

continues

Listing 9.12   Changing a User's Password Using the *NewPassword* Method (Continued)

```
    If Err = 0 Then
        MsgBox "Password changed.", vbInformation
    Else
        MsgBox Err.Description
    End If

End Sub
```

This code assumes that the application has populated a list box called List1 with the list of users in the workgroup information database. To change the password, select a user in List1 and click Change Password. The procedure asks for the existing password and the new password and then changes the password.

If you're logged on to the database as an administrative user, you can change a user's password whether or not you know his existing password. To do this, pass an empty string as the first parameter of the NewPassword method.

Default Accounts Created by the Jet Database Engine   In addition to the default Admin account discussed earlier in this chapter, Jet creates two additional accounts by default. These accounts are called Creator and Engine, and they're used to support internal operations by the database engine. You can't use these objects in your code.

CREATING AND DELETING GROUPS

You make the process of assigning permissions to users easier by assigning sets of users and permissions to groups. Although you can assign permissions to either individual users or groups, it's generally better to assign permissions to groups only. The process of assigning a large number of permissions to a large number of users can grow very burdensome very quickly. Assigning permissions to groups and then assigning users to groups makes the process of managing permissions exponentially simpler.

When you create a new user, for example, you need simply assign the user to whichever groups are appropriate for that user, as opposed to having to remember all nine million permissions appropriate for that type of user. The process of assigning permissions to both users and groups is discussed in the next section.

You can access the list of groups that exist in a database by iterating through a Workspace object's Groups collection. Listing 9.13 shows an example.

Listing 9.13   Assigning the Groups in the *Groups* Collection to a List Box

```
Option Explicit

' References DAO 3.51

Private ThisGroup As Group

Private Sub cmdGroup_Click()
    List1.Clear

    For Each ThisGroup In Workspaces(0).Groups
        List1.AddItem ThisGroup.Name
    Next

End Sub
```

To create a group, create a `Group` object using the `Workspace` object's `CreateGroup` method; then append it to the `Groups` collection using code similar to that in Listing 9.14.

Listing 9.14   Creating a New Security Group Using Data Access Objects

```
Option Explicit

' References DAO 3.51

Private ThisGroup As Group

Private Sub cmdNewGroup_Click()
Dim strName As String

    strName = InputBox("Enter the name of the new group.", "New group")
    Set ThisGroup = Workspaces(0).CreateGroup(strName)
    ThisGroup.PID = InputBox("Enter a unique PID for this group.", "New group")
    Workspaces(0).Groups.Append ThisGroup

    cmdGroup_Click

End Sub
```

To delete a group, you delete it from the `Groups` collection, as shown in Listing 9.15.

Listing 9.15   Deleting a Group from the *Groups* Collection Using DAO Code

```
Option Explicit

' References DAO 3.51


Private Sub cmdDeleteGroup_Click()
Dim strGroup As String

    strGroup = InputBox("Enter the group to delete.", "Delete group")
    Workspaces(0).Groups.Delete strGroup

    ' Refresh list of groups
    cmdGroup_Click

End Sub
```

This is another one of those procedures that doesn't require you to declare any database object variables, because it uses the implicit Workspace object that's always available to you through the database engine.

ADDING USERS TO GROUPS

You can add users to groups to give users access to the database. When you add a user to a group, that user inherits all the permissions assigned to the group.

To determine which groups a user belongs to, iterate through the User object's Groups collection. To add a user to a group, create a Group object using the CreateGroup method of the User object; then append the Group object to the User object's Groups collection. Listing 9.16 shows an example of how to display lists of groups and add a user to a group.

Listing 9.16   Adding a User to a Group Using the *CreateGroup* Method of the *User* Object

```
Option Explicit

' References DAO 3.51

Private ThisUser As User
Private ThisGroup As Group

Private Sub Form_Load()
    DBEngine.SystemDB = "..\..\DB\mygroup.mdw"
End Sub

Private Sub cmdUser_Click()
    List1.Clear
```

```
    For Each ThisUser In Workspaces(0).Users
        List1.AddItem ThisUser.Name
    Next

    Label1.Caption = "Users"

End Sub

Private Sub cmdUserGroup_Click()
On Error Resume Next

Dim strGroupName As String

    If Label1.Caption <> "Users" Or List1.Text = "" Then
        Exit Sub
    End If

    strGroupName = InputBox("Enter the group to add " & _
                    List1.Text & " to.", _
                    "Add user to group")

    Set ThisUser = Workspaces(0).Users(List1.Text)
    Set ThisGroup = ThisUser.CreateGroup(strGroupName)
    ThisUser.Groups.Append ThisGroup

    If Err = 0 Then
        MsgBox "User added to group.", vbInformation
        ShowUserGroups
    End If

End Sub

Private Sub ShowUserGroups()

    ' List groups for this user
    Set ThisUser = Workspaces(0).Users(List1.Text)

    List2.Clear
    Label2.Caption = "Groups"

    For Each ThisGroup In ThisUser.Groups
        List2.AddItem ThisGroup.Name
    Next

End Sub
```

This code works by populating a list box with the contents of the Users collection. After the list box is populated, click a user in the list to display the groups to which that user belongs, as shown in Figure 9.9.

Figure 9.9
An application can display the list of groups associated with a user.

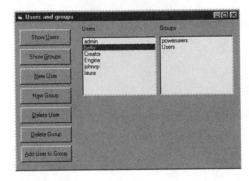

After the application displays a list of users, you can click a user to select that user. Clicking cmdUserGroup adds the selected user to a group you specify.

DEFAULT GROUPS CREATED BY THE JET DATABASE ENGINE

The Microsoft Jet database engine creates two groups by default. These groups have special attributes you should keep in mind as you design your database application's security model.

Members of the Admins group have the ability to create and delete users and groups and to assign permissions to database objects. They also have the ability to change users' passwords, thereby denying users access to the database and restoring access to the database when a user forgets a password.

The Users group is the default group to which all new users are added when they are created. Members of the Users group have full permissions for any new database objects you create. The Jet database engine does this to support the idea of maintaining easy database access, even in light of the fact that database security is always turned on—if it weren't for the fact that all new users were added to this default group, you'd have to assign permissions to new users (or assign them to a group you created) in all your Jet databases, even if you weren't really taking advantage of Jet security features.

ASSIGNING AND REMOVING OWNERSHIP OF DATABASE OBJECTS

Every object in the database has an owner. By default, the owner of a database object is the user who created it. In an unsecured database, the owner of every object is the Admin user; however, ownership in an unsecured database doesn't mean much because every user has full access to every database object.

Owners of objects can always assign permissions to the objects they own. This power can't be revoked, even by database administrators. Accordingly, if you must maintain control over objects in the database, you need to do one of two things:

▶ If you're creating a new database, create the database using your own administrative user account. This ensures that you own the database, as well as all the objects in the database.

▶ If you're securing an existing database, transfer ownership of all the objects in the database to an administrative account under your control. You can do this by creating a new database using your administrative account and then importing all the objects from the existing database into the new database.

Note: Microsoft Access is an extremely handy tool in situations where you want to take ownership of a database. This is the case because Access provides a utility called the User-Level Security Wizard, which automates the task of taking ownership of all the objects in a database.

You can manage ownership of an object in a Jet database through the Document and Container objects associated with each database object. Document and Container objects are accessible through the Containers and Documents collections. These containers exist to provide database extensibility, so your database can conceivably have an unlimited number of types of containers and documents that perform various functions in addition to managing security.

A Jet database created in Microsoft Access has the containers listed in Table 9.1.

Table 9.1 Containers That Exist in a Jet Database Created Using Microsoft Access	
Container Name	**Description**
Databases	Contains the database document.
Forms	Contains a collection of Microsoft Access form documents (not accessible through DAO).
Modules	Contains a collection of Microsoft Access code module documents (not accessible through DAO).
	continues

Table 9.1   Containers That Exist in a Jet Database Created Using Microsoft Access (Continued)

Container Name	Description
Relationships	Contains a collection of relationship documents.
Reports	Contains a collection of Microsoft Access report documents. Access reports aren't accessible through DAO, but they are accessible through Automation (see Chapter 4, "Reporting and Exporting Data," for more information).
Scripts	Contains a collection of Microsoft Access macro documents (not accessible through DAO).
SysRel	Used internally by Jet; undocumented.
Tables	Contains a collection of table documents.

Remember that because containers and documents exist to provide application extensibility to a Jet database, the only way to know which containers exist in a particular Jet database is to inspect the Containers collection using code similar to that shown in Listing 9.17.

Listing 9.17   Iterating Through the *Containers* Collection, Displaying the Names of Containers in a Database

```
Dim Thiscon As Container
Dim db As Database

Set db = OpenDatabase("..\..\DB\novelty.mdb")

For Each Thiscon In db.Containers
    Debug.Print Thiscon.Name
Next
```

You can inspect the Document object's Owner property to determine the owner of a database document. To change the owner, you simply change the Owner property. Listing 9.18 is an example of how to change the owner of a table using DAO code.

Listing 9.18 Changing a Database's *Owner* Property

```
On Error Resume Next

   With db.Containers("Tables").Documents("tblCustomer")
      .Owner = InputBox("Enter the new owner.", "New Owner")
      If Not Err Then
         MsgBox "The database owner was changed to " & .Owner
      End If
   End With
```

As with previous code examples in this chapter, this code assumes you've already created a valid Database object and opened it in code.

ASSIGNING PERMISSIONS TO USERS AND GROUPS

Permissions enable a user to gain access to database objects and data. By assigning and revoking permissions to users and groups, you can take control of who has access to what in the database.

In an unsecured database, all users are logged in as the Admin user, with no password. Because the Admin user is a member of the Users and Admins group, that user has full access to all the objects in the database by virtue of the permissions granted to those groups.

When you secure a database, you gain the ability to identify each user and add users to groups. Users inherit permissions from groups—although it's possible to assign permissions directly to users, it's easier to manage a set of permissions when all users' permissions are inherited through a group.

If you need to revoke a particular set of permissions for a particular user within a group, you simply remove the user from the group. This prevents you from having to keep track of information pertaining to which users have which permissions on which database objects. This technique is also better from a security standpoint because you're less likely to inadvertently assign permissions to groups than to users.

Table 9.2 provides a summary of the permissions available for Jet database objects.

Table 9.2 Permissions for Objects in Microsoft Jet

Permission	Description	Applies To
dbSecNoAccess	No access	All database objects except Document objects
dbSecFullAccess	Full access	All database objects

continues

Table 9.2   Permissions for Objects in Microsoft Jet (Continued)

Permission	Description	Applies To
dbSecDelete	Can delete the object	All database objects
dbSecReadSec	Can read object's security information	All database objects
dbSecWriteSec	Can change access permissions	All database objects
dbSecWriteOwner	Can change Owner property	All database objects
dbSecCreate	Can create new documents	All database objects except Document objects
dbSecReadDef	Can read the table definition	Table's Container object
dbSecWriteDef	Can modify or delete the table definition	Table's Container object
dbSecRetrieveData Document objects	Can query records	Table's Container object;
dbSecInsertData Document objects	Can add records	Table's Container object;
dbSecReplaceData Document objects	Can modify records	Table's Container object;
dbSecDeleteData Document objects	Can delete records	Table's Container object;
dbSecDBCreate	Can create databases	Database's Container object; Document objects
dbSecDBExclusive	Can open the database in exclusive mode	Database's Container object; Document objects

Permission	Description	Applies To
dbSecDBOpen	Can open the database	Database's `Container` object; `Document` objects
dbSecDBAdmin	Can replicate the database or change the database's password	Database's `Container` object

To change a permission associated with a user account, you first log into the database with a username that has administrative privileges. You then set the appropriate `Document` object's `UserName` property to the name of the user for whom you want to set the permission.

After you've set the `UserName` property, you can either add or revoke a permission for the database object in question. To add a permission, you perform a logical `Or` operation on the `Permissions` property. Perform a logical `And Not` operation on the `Permissions` property to revoke a property. Listing 9.19 gives an example.

Listing 9.19   Using the *Permissions* Property of a *Document* Object to Grant a User Access to a *Database* Object in DAO

```
Option Explicit

' References DAO 3.51

Private ws As Workspace
Private db As Database
Private rs As Recordset

Private Sub Form_Load()

    DBEngine.SystemDB = "..\..\DB\mygroup.mdw"

    ' To log in as admin, uncomment this line
    Set ws = DBEngine.CreateWorkspace("", "johnny", "johnny")

    ' To log in as johnny, uncomment this line
    'Set ws = DBEngine.CreateWorkspace("", "admin", "")

    Set db = ws.OpenDatabase("..\..\DB\nsecure.mdb")
```

continues

Listing 9.19   Using the *Permissions* Property of a *Document* Object to Grant a User Access to a *Database* Object in DAO (Continued)

```
    lblUser.Caption = "Logged in as " & Workspaces(0).UserName

End Sub


Private Sub cmdGrant_Click()
On Error Resume Next

    With db.Containers("Tables").Documents("tblCustomer")
        .UserName = "johnny"
        .Permissions = .Permissions Or dbSecRetrieveData
        If Err = 0 Then
            MsgBox "Permission granted to user johnny."
        Else
            MsgBox "Permission not granted (" & Err.Description & ")."
        End If
    End With

End Sub


Private Sub cmdRevoke_Click()

    With db.Containers("Tables").Documents("tblCustomer")
        .UserName = "johnny"
        .Permissions = .Permissions And Not dbSecRetrieveData
        If Err = 0 Then
            MsgBox "Permission revoked from user johnny."
        Else
            MsgBox "Permission not revoked (" & Err.Description & ")."
        End If
    End With

End Sub


Private Sub cmdShow_Click()

' This fails if the user doesn't have
' retrieve permissions on this table

    Set rs = db.OpenRecordset("tblCustomer")

    rs.MoveLast
```

```
    MsgBox "The table contains " & rs.RecordCount & _
           " records.", vbInformation

End Sub
```

Remember that you must log on as a user with administrative privileges (that is, a member of the Admins group) in order to add or revoke permissions for another user.

You assign permissions with groups the same way you assign permissions to users; the only exception is replacing the name of the user with the name of the group. Listing 9.20 shows a modified version of the procedure that grants a permission on the table to the PowerUsers group.

Listing 9.20   Granting a Permission to a Group, Rather Than to an Individual User

```
Private Sub cmdGrant_Click()
On Error Resume Next

With db.Containers("Tables").Documents("tblCustomer")

    ' Grant permission to all users in PowerUsers group
    .UserName = "powerusers"
    .Permissions = .Permissions Or dbSecRetrieveData
    If Err = 0 Then
        MsgBox "Permission granted to " & .UserName & "."
    Else
        MsgBox "Permission not granted (" & Err.Description & ")."
    End If
End With

End Sub
```

This example assumes you've declared, set, and opened a Database object variable earlier in your code.

Determining a Document's Permissions for a User   You can determine which permissions a user has for a particular database object by using the AllPermissions property of that object's underlying Document object. A document's AllPermissions property is a function of a particular username; you can set or retrieve the username associated with a document through a document's UserName property.

Note: Document objects have a `Permissions` property in addition to an `AllPermissions` property. The `Permissions` property returns the user's permissions for the database document. The `AllPermissions` property returns the permissions granted to the user, in addition to the permissions the user inherited by virtue of his or her membership in groups that have permissions on the database document in question. In other words, if you're looking to figure out what permissions a user really has for a particular database document, use `AllPermissions`, not `Permissions`.

The `AllPermissions` property was added in Jet version 3.*x*.

You determine if a user has a particular permission on a database object by performing a logical `And` comparison on the database document's `AllPermissions` property and the particular permission you want to know about (using the permission constants listed in Table 9.2). If the value of the `And` comparison is not 0, the user has the permission in question.

For example, use the code in Listing 9.21 to determine whether the currently logged-in user has permission to delete the database table tblCustomer.

Listing 9.21   Code to Determine Whether a User Has Permission to Delete a *Database* Object

```
With db.Containers("Tables").Documents("tblCustomer")
    If .Permissions And dbSecFullAccess Then
        MsgBox "This user can delete the object."
    Else
        MsgBox "The user can't delete the object."
    End If
End With
```

This code assumes you've already defined and created a `Database` object and used the `Database` object to open the database successfully. If the username does not exist in the current workgroup information file, this code generates an error.

Preventing Users from Opening the Database in Exclusive Mode   Only administrative users should have the ability to open a database in exclusive (single-user) mode. To enforce this restriction in a multiuser environment, you can withhold permission to open the database in exclusive mode to members of the Users group. Listing 9.22 shows an example.

Listing 9.22   Removing Permission from Opening the Database in Exclusive Mode to Members of the Users Group

```
Private Sub cmdExclusive_Click()
' Keeps members of the Users group from
' opening the database in exclusive mode.

    With db.Containers("Databases").Documents("MSysDB")
        .UserName = "Users"
        .Permissions = .Permissions And Not dbSecDBExclusive
        If Err = 0 Then
            MsgBox "Permission revoked from user " & .UserName & "."
        Else
            MsgBox "Permission not revoked (" & Err.Description & ")."
        End If

    End With

End Sub
```

Note: The constant dbSecDBExclusive is referred to in the *Jet Database Engine Programmer's Guide* as dbSecDBOpenExclusive. This is a documentation error—it should be dbSecDBExclusive.

This code works the way it does because there's a special Document object, MSysDB that represents the database itself. You can assign or remove the dbSecDBOpen and dbSecDBAdmin permissions from MSysDB as well. For more information on these permissions, refer to Table 9.2.

Disabling the Admin User   It's important to disable the Admin account when you're securing a database. This is because the Admin user is the same in every workgroup information database created by Microsoft Access. As a result, if you don't disable the Admin account, anyone could replace your workgroup information file with his own and then, using the Admin account, take ownership of the database and proceed to wreak untold havoc on your database.

To disable the Admin account, simply remove it from the Admins group.

In addition to removing the Admin user from the Admins group, you should also add a password to the Admin user. Although it may seem less than meaningful to add a password to a user that has no permissions, it's important in Access. That's because Admin is the default user. If the Admin user has no password, Access users won't see a login dialog box and are automatically logged in as Admin when they open the database. This means that they will have a hard time doing anything because, at this point, the Admin user has no permissions.

Note: This may seem like an awful design, but it's done this way to support two concepts: a consistent security system that is always on, whether you need it or not, and the ability to log in to the database using a default identity (that of the Admin user) with no password, in situations where security isn't important.

You supply a password to a user account using the User object's NewPassword method, as described in "Adding a Password to a User" earlier in this chapter.

ENCRYPTING A MICROSOFT JET DATABASE

Encrypting a database is an important final step in securing a database. Although your database may be password protected, the database can be opened and viewed with any application that has the capability to open large data files. Though the database can't be used, chunks of its data may still be discernable by pesky intruders.

To resolve the problem, you can encrypt your database. To do this using DAO code, use code similar to that shown in Listing 9.23. This code takes an existing database, called novelty.mdb and creates an encrypted copy called nencrypt.mdb.

Listing 9.23 Encrypting a Database Using the *CompactDatabase* Method of the *DBEngine* Object

```
Option Explicit

' References DAO 3.51

Private Sub cmdGo_Click()
On Error Resume Next

    Dim strTarget As String

    strTarget = "..\..\DB\novelty.mdb"

    DBEngine.CompactDatabase "..\..\DB\nencrypt.mdb", _
                             strTarget, "", _
                             dbEncrypt
    If Err Then
        MsgBox "Encryption failed. (" & _
               Err.Description & ")", vbExclamation
    Else
        MsgBox "Database encrypted as " & strTarget, vbInformation
    End If

End Sub
```

The original database is not altered in this operation. The blank string passed to the `CompactDatabase` method indicates the database's international locale; this is important for sorting purposes. Passing a blank string as the locale parameter means that you want the new, encrypted database to have the same international locale settings as the original database.

Given the benefits of encryption, why wouldn't you always encrypt the database? The answer is performance—an encrypted database runs 10 to 15 percent slower than an unencrypted database. Encryption is an important aspect of a secured database, however, so take advantage of it in order to make it harder for unauthorized users to gain access to your information.

CHECKLIST FOR IMPLEMENTING JET DATABASE SECURITY

Many developers who use secure Jet databases find it useful to have a checklist to follow when securing the database. Accordingly, this section introduces a step-by-step list of instructions for securing a Jet database (see Table 9.3).

It's important to follow these instructions in order. For example, if you remove the default Admin user from the Admins group before creating an administrative account for your own use, you'll be locked out of the database. If you use Microsoft Access as a security tool, you get a warning message when you try to remove the last user from the Admins group; if you use DAO, the database engine happily locks you out of the database when you delete the last user from the Admins group. Be careful.

Table 9.3 Checklist for Securing a Microsoft Jet Database	
Operation	**Completed**
Using the `Workgroup` object, create a new workgroup Administrator utility information database with a unique and secret workgroup ID. Record the workgroup ID for future use in case you need to re-create it.	❏
Assign a password to the Admin user.	❏
Create a new user for administrative use. Add an account for this user to the Admins and Users groups.	❏
Remove the Admin user group from Admins.	❏

continues

Table 9.3 Checklist for Securing a Microsoft Jet Database (Continued)	
Operation	**Completed**
If the database objects, such as tables and queries, contain database definitions, take ownership of all the objects in the database by creating a new database and importing all the database objects from the original database.	❑
Create groups.	❑
Assign permissions to groups.	❑
Create users.	❑
Assign users to groups.	❑
Encrypt the database.	❑

The details on how to implement each of these steps appear earlier in this chapter. Note that "Assign a password to the database" does not appear in this checklist. That's because this is a checklist for user-based security, and in user-based security, assigning a password to the database is irrelevant.

SUMMARY

In this chapter, you learned how to implement two important components of a multiuser Jet database: record locking and security. With these important topics under your belt, you now have the ability to create database applications using Jet that permit more than one user to have access to your database at the same time.

While the theoretical limit on the number of users that can work with a Jet database seems large—Microsoft says that a maximum of 255 users can be hooked up at the same time—in a practical sense, you're asking for trouble whenever your Jet database needs to support more than about a dozen users inserting and updating records simultaneously. That's because Jet isn't a true client/server database management system. There's no centralized intelligence to handle contention between users. In a situation where you need to support more users simultaneously updating and inserting records, or when you need to implement a stronger security model, consider migrating your database to a true client/server architecture such as Microsoft SQL Server or Oracle.

QUESTIONS AND ANSWERS

Q. **How strong is the encryption provided by the Microsoft Jet engine?**

A. When you encrypt a Jet database, it encrypts the database one page at a time. Each database page has a 32-bit encryption key (remember that a page of data in a Jet database is 2,048 bytes of data). Microsoft Jet uses an RSA encryption algorithm to work its magic.

Q. **I have an application that uses optimistic locking. What would you suggest I do in a situation where my users are running into an unacceptable number of collisions while updating records?**

A. I'd suggest that you not use optimistic locking. Redesign your application to use pessimistic locking or set things up so it doesn't use locking at all. It's my opinion that in a large number of software designs that use locking, it's possible to redesign the application so it doesn't use locking at all. Eliminating locking gets you a number of performance and scalability benefits, in addition to the fact that it decreases contention between users.

Q. **If I go with pessimistic locking, how do I deal with the situation where some users need to update while other users are reporting?**

A. What are your reporting users doing with read-write access to the database anyway? Reports should be run against read-only, forward-scrolling snapshots, unless you have a good reason to do otherwise. Not only is locking not an issue in a read-only recordset, but you may notice increased performance—both for your report-running users and your record-updating users.

Q. **Why would I want to perform security work in a VB application instead of using Access?**

A. Use Access in situations where you need to set up your application's security system once and never touch it again. Use Visual Basic when your application needs programmatic access to the Jet security model.

ActiveX Data Objects

Building Visual Basic Applications with
   ActiveX Data Objects

Using ADO Remote Data Services

H alfway through Visual Basic 5.0's lifetime, ActiveX Data Objects (ADO) became the cornerstone of Internet database access for those of us who live on Planet Microsoft. In VB6, ADO 2.0 is even more important—and powerful. As you'll see from the demonstrations in this chapter, you can use ADO for more than just getting access to your database through a Web page—you can use it to get to your data from a Visual Basic application as well.

In addition to being yet another object model for database access, ADO is an object-based interface to an emerging data technology called OLE DB.

OLE DB is designed to supplant ODBC as a method of accessing data. ODBC is currently a pervasive Windows client-side standard for accessing relational data because it makes relational database servers as generic as possible to the client application. OLE DB attempts to take that a step further, by making all data sources generic to client applications.

BUILDING VISUAL BASIC APPLICATIONS WITH ACTIVEX DATA OBJECTS

Microsoft ActiveX Data Objects (ADO) is an object-oriented database access technology similar to Data Access Objects (DAO) and Remote Data Objects (RDO) (both of which are described in chapters of their own earlier in this book). It is part of Microsoft's Universal Data Access initiative, which seeks to make all data sources generic in the way that, currently, all relational data sources are generic—by virtue of ODBC.

> **Tip:** To get the latest information on Microsoft's Universal Data Access initiatives, including a link to the download page for the files that comprise ActiveX Data Objects, check out the Data Access Components Web page at `http://www.microsoft.com/data/`. For more specific information on Active Data Objects, check out `http://www.microsoft.com/data/ado/`.

ADO is currently being positioned by Microsoft as a technique for accessing databases from a Web server. Because ADO is provided in the form of an ActiveX Server library (just as DAO and RDO are), you can use ADO in your Visual Basic application with no problem. In fact, in many ways, you'll find that it's easier to get to a client/server database using ADO than the other alternatives discussed earlier in this book. Even though ADO is one of the newest technologies for database access, you'll find that in almost every case its performance rivals that of RDOs.

The first part of this chapter focuses on building conventional Visual Basic applications with ADO, including a discussion of the ADO object model. This leads into Chapter 11, "Internet Database Applications," in which I'll show you how to build a simple Web application based on Active Server Pages accessing an ADO database.

UNDERSTANDING THE OLE DB/ADO ARCHITECTURE

Most Visual Basic Developers never interact with OLE DB directly. Instead, they program against ActiveX Data Objects, the object model that provides interfaces into OLE DB. This architecture is illustrated in Figure 10.1.

> **Note:** If you're having trouble getting your head around the idea of a data "provider," you might want to think of it simply as a "driver." The two are conceptually analogous in their roles when you put the ODBC and OLE DB architectures side by side.

There aren't as many OLE DB providers as there are ODBC drivers, but the number increased significantly when ADO 2.0 was released in 1998. This release, which is included in Visual Basic 6.0, includes native providers for SQL Server, Oracle, and Microsoft Jet/Access.

It's very likely that you will be able to get to a relational data source you prefer using ADO and OLE DB even if there aren't native OLE DB providers for it. This is because there is a generic OLE DB provider for ODBC relational databases. The (rather convoluted looking) architecture for this is illustrated in Figure 10.2.

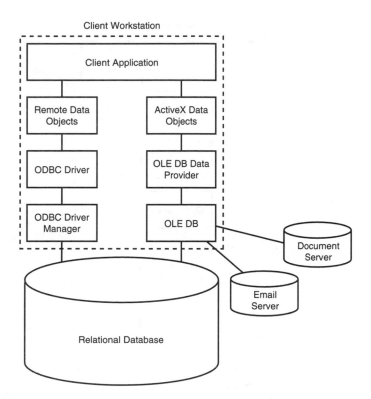

Figure 10.1
This is how you gain access to information in a database using ADO and OLE DB.

Microsoft has stated that ADO is tuned for Internet use, with the capability to serve a large number of users simultaneously from a server that is rebooted infrequently. The easiest way to use ADO from a Web application is in the form of Active Server Pages.

Because you can also access ADO from an application or ActiveX component built in Visual Basic, you can create a single source for access to your data and business logic that is accessible from Visual Basic as well as from Web applications. Figure 10.3 gives an illustration of this architecture.

In this scenario, all the logic pertaining to your business is placed in class modules and compiled in the form of an ActiveX component. That way, the amount of code that needs to exist on the client side is minimal. You should only need user-interface code on the client side. Because data access for both the Web browser and the VB application is channeled through the ActiveX server, you can be sure that your program logic is always applied consistently, no matter what kind of application is used.

Figure 10.2

*Here is the archi-
tecture for access-
ing an ODBC data-
base using the
ODBC OLE DB
provider.*

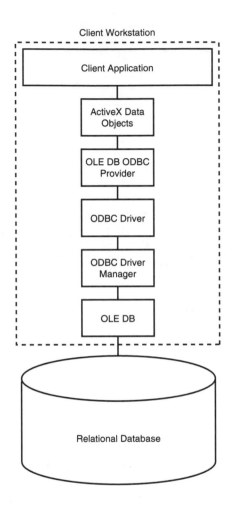

Figure 10.3

*This architecture
permits you to use
a common ActiveX
code component
with both Web
browser and
Visual Basic client
applications.*

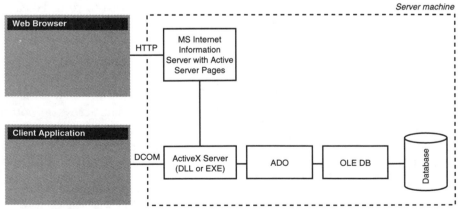

INSTALLING AND CREATING A REFERENCE TO ADO IN YOUR VISUAL BASIC APPLICATION

Before you can begin working with ADO in your Visual Basic application, it must be installed on your computer. ADO is installed as part of the normal install of Visual Basic 6.0.

> **Note:** ADO is installed with Visual Basic 6.0. The latest version of ActiveX Data Objects is available as a free download from the Microsoft Web site at `http://www.microsoft.com/data/ado/`. As Microsoft releases updates and additional capabilities to ADO, you'll be able to download them from the Web. And remember that ADO functions with any development environment that can deal with ActiveX/COM objects, including Visual Basic, Visual C++, the Microsoft Office suite, and Active Server Pages Web scripting.

If ADO is installed on your computer, you can begin using it by making a reference to the ADO library in your VB application, the same way you make references to the DAO or RDO libraries:

1. In your Visual Basic project, choose Project, References.

2. The References dialog box appears.

3. Check the box for Microsoft ActiveX Data Objects 2.0 Library and then click OK.

You can now use ADO in your code.

When you reference the ADO library in your project, make sure you don't inadvertently make a reference to Microsoft ActiveX Data Objects 2.0 Recordset library. This is a lightweight version of the ADO library that's designed for use on the client side of a client/server application. It only supports the Recordset and Field objects. If you find yourself unable to instantiate a Connection or Command object in your ADO application, this might be the reason why.

USING ADO WITH OTHER DATA ACCESS OBJECT LIBRARIES

If you're creating an application designed to use ADO in conjunction with another data access object library, such as DAO, you need to be careful to differentiate between, for example, the DAO Recordset object and the ADO Recordset object. They aren't interchangeable.

If you have references to both DAO and ADO in your project and you create a Recordset variable, how do you know whether you have a DAO- or ADO-style Recordset? The answer has to do with the order in which you added the reference to your project. If you add a reference to the DAO library first, creating a Recordset object gives you a DAO-style Recordset; you need to use the full class name ADODB.Recordset to explicitly create an ADO-style Recordset. (The spelled-out name of a class is also known as its *ProgID*.)

> **Note: Some development environments, such as Active Server Pages and older versions of Microsoft Office applications, don't support early binding. This means that they can't make references to object libraries the way they can with the References dialog in Visual Basic. For environments similar to these, you always have to use the library object syntax to create objects from the ADO library.**

If you don't want to make a direct reference to the object library in your code, you have an alternative. You can control which object library is accessed by default by using the priority setting in the References dialog box. For example, to give the DAO Object Library priority over the ADO Object Library, do the following:

1. In your VB project, choose Project, References.

2. References to both the Microsoft DAO 3.51 Object Library and Microsoft ActiveX Data Objects 2.0 Library should appear in the list of references (assuming they're installed on your computer).

3. Click (but don't uncheck) the reference to the DAO object library.

4. Click the upward-pointing arrow labeled Priority. The reference to the DAO object library moves up in the list. This means that DAO will be used when you create an object (such as the Recordset object) that has the same name as an object in the ADO library.

Having control over the priority of the object models ensures that whenever you create a Recordset object variable in your code, it's a DAO Recordset, not an ADO Recordset. (In this scenario, to create an ADO Recordset, you have to explicitly specify in code that you want an ADODB.Recordset—see Listing 10.1 for an example.)

While assigning priorities to object libraries gives you the ability to manage name space collisions between libraries, an even better technique is to explicitly denote which object library you're using when you create the object. Listing 10.1 shows an example of a procedure that creates two Recordset object variables — one from the ADO library, the other from the DAO library.

Listing 10.1   Creating Both DAO and ADO *Recordset* Objects in Visual Basic Code Using ProgID Syntax

```
Option Explicit

' References DAO 3.51
' References ADO 2.0

Dim db As DAO.Database

Private adoRS As adodb.Recordset
Private daoRS As DAO.Recordset

Private cn As adodb.Connection
Dim strSQL As String

Private Sub Form_Load()
    Set cn = New adodb.Connection
    strSQL = "SELECT * FROM tblCustomer"
End Sub

Private Sub cmdShow_Click()
    ' ** Create DAO recordset
    Set db = OpenDatabase("..\..\DB\novelty.mdb")
    Set daoRS = db.OpenRecordset(strSQL)
    MsgBox "DAO query returns " & daoRS.Fields("FirstName")

    ' ** Create ADO recordset
    Set cn = New adodb.Connection
    cn.ConnectionString = "DSN=JetNovelty;"

    cn.Open
    Set adoRS = cn.Execute(strSQL)

    MsgBox "ADO query returns " & adoRS.Fields("FirstName")

End Sub
```

Code Example: You can find an example of the code discussed in this section in the project `AdoDao.vbp`, located in the directory `\vbdb\code\ 10-Ado\AdoDao`. For information on how to install the sample files on the CD that accompanies this book, see the section "Installing the Example Files" in the introduction at the beginning of this book.

USING THE ADO *CONNECTION* OBJECT TO CONNECT TO A DATA SOURCE

In ActiveX Data Objects, you use the Connection object to establish a connection to a data source. At the same time, as code examples later in this section demonstrate, you don't need to use a Connection object to perform useful work with ADO—this aspect of ADO is one of its advantages over RDOs, which is far more dependent on the concept of a Connection object.

The position of the ADO Connection object in the ADO object model, as well as its properties and methods, is shown in Figure 10.4.

Figure 10.4
The ADO Connection object and its properties and methods are shown here in the context of the ADO object.

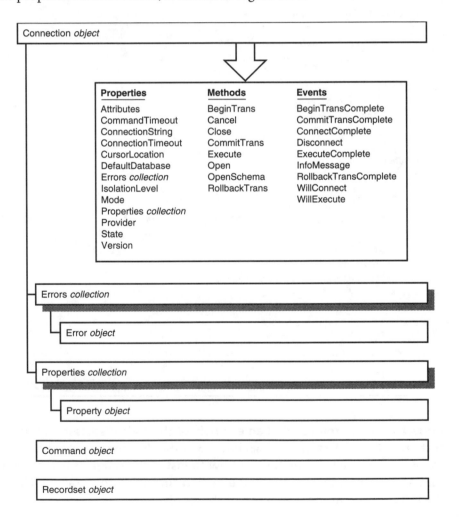

You use the ADO `Connection` object's `Open` method to establish the connection with the data source. In order to tell ADO how to get to the data source, you must provide information in the form of a connect string identical to the ODBC connect string. You use the `Connection` object's `ConnectionString` property to do this. You also have the option of choosing which provider you want to use by setting the `Connection` object's `Provider` property. The next few sections in this chapter give code examples that demonstrate how to do this.

Specifying an OLE DB Provider and Connection String   You specify an OLE DB provider using the `Provider` property of the ADO `Connection` object. This property tells ADO which OLE DB provider to use in order to execute commands against the server. (If you don't specify a provider, or if you don't use a `Connection` object, you get the default provider, which is the ODBC provider for OLE DB, also known as `MSDASQL`.)

The `Connection` object's `Provider` property is a text string that tells the connection which OLE DB provider to use. To use the ODBC provider for OLE DB, you don't need to specify a provider because the ODBC provider is the default. However, you can specify it for clarity if you want.

You use a *connection string* in ADO to provide information about how to connect to the database server. When you're using the ODBC provider for OLE DB, the connection string is the same as an ODBC connect string. This means that the exact information expected by the ODBC driver can vary from implementation to implementation. For other providers, the connection string can be of an entirely different syntax.

When you're using the ODBC provider, the `ConnectionString` property can be a Data Source Name (DSN) or it can be a DSN-less connection. Here's an example of a connection to a database using the ODBC provider with a DSN:

```
cn.Provider = "MSDASQL"
cn.ConnectionString = "DSN=Novelty;"
```

Using a DSN in the connection string obviously requires that a DSN called Novelty must actually exist on the client computer.

Note: ODBC connection strings, DSNs, and DSN-less connections were introduced in Chapter 6, "Open Database Connectivity and Remote Data Objects."

Here's an example of the same connection with a DSN-less connection:

```
cn.Provider = "MSDASQL"
cn.ConnectionString = "DRIVER={SQL Server};DATABASE=novelty;UID=randy;PWD=prince;"
```

This connection will connect to the server more quickly because it doesn't have to read the DSN information out of the Windows registry. However, it is less flexible because it hard-wires the connection information into your compiled code.

This next example tells the `Connection` object to use the Microsoft Jet OLE DB provider. For the Jet provider, the connection string is the path and filename to an MDB file:

```
cn.Provider = "Microsoft.Jet.OLEDB.3.51"
cn.ConnectionString = "c:\data\novelty.mdb"
```

To connect to a secured database using ADO and the Jet provider, you must supply additional information through the `Connection` object's `Properties` collection. This usually involves a password, a username, and the location of a special workspace database that stores information on security. Here's an example of how to set these values in ADO:

```
cn.Provider = "Microsoft.Jet.OLEDB.3.51"
cn.ConnectionString = "c:\data\mydata.mdb"
cn.Properties("Jet OLEDB:System database") = "c:\data\system.mdw"
cn.Properties("Password") = "mypass"
cn.Properties("User ID") = "myname"
cn.Open
```

To connect to a SQL Server database, you use the provider SQLOLEDB.1:

```
cn.Provider = "SQLOLEDB.1"
cn.ConnectionString = "DATABASE=mydata;SERVER=mysvr;UID=user;PWD=mypass;"
```

Notice in this case that the connection string is the same for SQL Server as it is for a DSN-less ODBC connection string, except for the DRIVER= parameter:

To connect to Oracle, you use the Oracle driver, called MSDAORA:

```
cn.Provider = "MSDAORA"
cn.ConnectionString = "user/mypass@servicename"
```

Notice that for the Oracle driver, the connection string is a standard Oracle connection string, combining the user name, password, and service name. You can also log on to Oracle by supplying the server, username, and password as arguments to the `Connection` object's `Open` method:

```
Dim cn As ADODB.Connection
Set cn = New ADODB.Connection
```

```
cn.Provider = "MSADORA"
cn.Open "SERVER", "USERID", "PASSWORD"
```

You can also assign a connect string to a parameter of the Recordset object's Open method, as described in the section "Using the ADO Recordset Object to Manipulate Data" later in this chapter.

Working with Cursors Just as with RDO and DAO, ADO provides support for a number of types of cursors. In addition for providing support for navigating through the recordset one record at a time, different types of cursors permit you to control how the management of a recordset takes place.

You set the location of the cursor by assigning a value to the CursorLocation property of the Recordset object. Table 10.1 lists the types of cursors available with the ADO Connection object.

Table 10.1 Cursor Locations Available in ActiveX Data Objects		
Cursor Type	**Constant**	**Description**
Client-side	adUseClient	Creates the cursor on the client side
Server-side	adUseServer	Creates the cursor on the server

Choosing a client-side cursor means that ADO and OLE DB handle cursor operations. Client-side cursors often have abilities that aren't available on the server. For example, in ADO, you can create a disconnected recordset, which permits you to manipulate records without a persistent connection to the server. This capability is a function of the client-side cursor library.

In ADO, the CursorLocation property is applicable to both the Recordset and Connection objects. If you assign the CursorLocation property of a Connection object, all recordsets you create from that connection have the same cursor location as its associated Connection object.

In addition to specifying the cursor's location, you have the ability to create four different types of cursors in ADO. Your choice of cursor is generally governed by a balance between functionality and performance.

You specify a cursor type by assigning the CursorType property of the Recordset object. Table 10.2 lists the types of cursors you can create in ADO.

Table 10.2 Cursor Types Available Using the ADO *Recordset* Object		
Cursor Type	**Constant**	**Description**
Forward-only	adOpenForwardOnly	No cursor at all—you can only move forward in the recordset; the `MovePrevious` and `MoveFirst` methods generate an error.
Keyset (known in DAO as a *dynaset*)	adOpenKeyset	You can't see records that have been added to the recordset by other users, but updates and deletes performed by other users do affect your recordset; can be the most efficient kind of cursor, particularly when the recordset is large.
Dynamic	adOpenDynamic	You can see all changes to the data performed by other users while your recordset is open; this is usually the least efficient, but most powerful, type of cursor.
Static (known in DAO as a *snapshot*)	adOpenStatic	A copy of all the data for a recordset; particularly useful when you're looking up data or running reports; can be very efficient when your recordset is small.

Of course, the reason you'd choose a forward-only cursor rather than a keyset or dynamic cursor is performance—if you're simply populating a list box or printing a list of items stored in the database, a forward-only cursor makes more sense and will give you better performance.

Note that if the data provider can't create the specific type of cursor you ask for, it will create whatever type of cursor it can. It will not, generally, generate an error unless you attempt to do something that's specifically prohibited with the kind of cursor you have (for example, a MovePrevious method on a forward-only cursor). Determining which cursors are supported by a particular provider is discussed in the next section.

Determining the Cursors and Other Features a Provider Supports Because OLE DB and ADO are designed to give you access to a broad spectrum of data sources, your application may need to determine which features a particular provider supports. It's possible that while an enterprise relational database management system might let you create a server-side, forward-only cursor, a desktop or file-based database might not.

The Supports method of the ADO Recordset object determines which cursors a data provider supports. Table 10.3 is a list of values you can pass to the Supports method to determine which features a particular Recordset object supports.

Table 10.3 Constants Used by the *Supports* Method	
Constant	**Description**
adAddNew	New records can be added to the recordset.
adApproxPosition	The AbsolutePage and AbsolutePosition properties are available; they are used in conjunction with the PageSize and PageCount properties of the Recordset object to permit you to determine on which page the current record is located.
adBookmark	You can set bookmarks in the recordset.
adDelete	Records can be deleted from the recordset.
adHoldRecords	Records can be retrieved from the database without committing existing changes.
adMovePrevious	The recordset can be scrolled backward as well as forward.

continues

Table 10.3	Constants Used by the *Supports* Method (Continued)
Constant	**Description**
adResync	The Resync method is available.
adUpdate	The recordset is updateable.
adUpdateBatch	The recordset is batch updateable using the UpdateBatch method. With batch updates, you can commit changes to many records in a single operation, improving client/server efficiency.

For example, to determine whether a data provider has the capability to provide a scrolling cursor, you use this expression:

```
rs.Supports(adMovePrevious)
```

Here, rs is a Recordset object. If the expression evaluates to True, the data provider supports a scrolling cursor.

Using VB's IntelliSense Features with ADO An advantage ADO has over other database access object models is the fact that its constants are publicly enumerated. For the VB developer, this means you get a drop-down list of constants in the integrated development environment while you're writing code.

An example is shown in Figure 10.5. As you can see, when you're typing code in ADO, there's no need to hit F1 every time you want to use a method of an object or determine which constant is appropriate

Figure 10.5
This is an example of the extremely helpful list of constants provided by ADO.

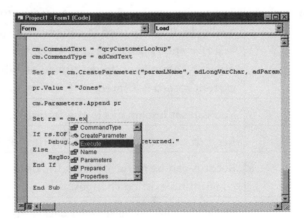

Considering the popularity of this Visual Basic feature, for some developers, the presence of these drop-down lists by themselves is a powerful argument in favor of migrating to ADO.

Record Locking in ADO   As with other database access object models, ADO permits you to set different types of record-locking modes. You do this in situations where you need control over how records are updated by multiple users in the database. (For more information on the appropriateness of the different record-locking modes and how they work, see the discussion of record locking in Chapter 9, "Multiuser Jet Databases.")

You set the locking mode for an ADO Recordset object through its LockType property. Table 10.4 lists the four types of record locking available.

Table 10.4 Record-Locking Modes Available through the ADO *LockType* Property	
Constant	**Description**
adLockReadOnly	No updates to the recordset are permitted.
adLockPessimistic	Pessimistic locking. Records in the recordset are locked when editing begins, and remain locked until you execute the Update method or move onto another record.
adLockOptimistic	Optimistic locking. Records are locked only at the instant you execute the Update method or move to another record.
adLockBatchOptimistic	Optimistic batch locking. Provides support for updating multiple records at once.

It's extremely important to understand that the default lock method in ADO is adLockReadOnly. This is one of the most significant differences between ADO and DAO programming, since in DAO, recordsets are editable by default. This means that if you don't bother to set the LockType and CursorType properties, your ADO recordsets will always be read-only.

The availability of different types of locking is dependent on what the data provider supports. You can determine whether a provider supports a particular type of locking by using the Supports method of the Recordset object (described earlier in this chapter).

Remember, too, that ADO recordsets can be disconnected from their source. This is discussed in "Creating Disconnected Recordsets," later in this chapter.

Opening and Closing a Connection to the Data Source   To issue commands to a data source using ADO, you open a connection to that data source. You typically do this using the ADO Connection object's Open method. When you're done with the data source, you close it using the Connection object's Close method. Here's the ADO Connection object's Open method syntax:

```
cn.Open [connect], [userid], [password]
```

All the arguments to the Open method are optional. If you don't supply a connection string as an argument to the Open method, you can instead supply it using the ConnectionString property of the Connection object. The effect is the same.

The syntax of the connection string is determined by the provider. Listing 10.2 gives an example of opening a connection to an ODBC database using an ADO Connection object.

Listing 10.2   Opening a Connection to a Data Source Using the ADO *Connection* Object

```
Option Explicit

' References ADO 2.0

Private cn As Connection

Private Sub Form_Load()
    Set cn = New Connection
    cn.Open "DSN=JetNovelty;"

End Sub
```

This code assumes you have an ODBC data source name (DSN) called JetNovelty set up on your computer (Chapter 6 discusses how to do this). If you don't have this DSN set up, or you don't care to create it on the client computer, you can instead supply all the connection information at once in the form of a DSN-less connection.

When you're finished with an ADO Connection object, you should always close it using its Close method.

```
cn.Close
```

Explicitly closing the connection to the data source ensures that any resources (either on the client or the server, or both) associated with the connection are released in a timely fashion.

USING THE ADO *RECORDSET* OBJECT TO MANIPULATE DATA

The ADO Recordset object, similar to DAO's Recordset and RDO's rdoResultset object, is the way to access information retrieved from the data provider. The ADO Recordset has many of the same properties and methods as the other object models' recordset objects, so you can work with it the same way.

The position of the ADO Recordset object in the ADO object model, as well as its properties and methods, is shown in Figure 10.6.

The procedure for creating an ADO Recordset object is similar to creating an rdoResultset object in RDO. However, ADO adds an interesting twist: the ability to create a Recordset object that does not require an implicit Connection object. (This is different than having a disconnected recordset—the connection is there, there's just no object variable to represent it.)

As an example, Listing 10.3 shows how to create an ADO Recordset object in a traditional manner. This technique will be familiar to RDO programmers—first create a Connection object, then run a query against the connection by passing a SQL query to the Connection object's Execute method.

> **Note:** A command string that creates an ADO Recordset can be a table name, the name of a stored query, or a SQL statement —it works the same way as the OpenRecordset method in DAO.

Listing 10.3 **Creating an ADO *Recordset* Object Using a *Connection* and *Recordset* Object**

```
Option Explicit

' References ADO 2.0

Private cn As Connection

Private Sub Form_Load()
    Set cn = New ADODB.Connection
    cn.ConnectionString = "DSN=JetNovelty;"
    cn.Open
End Sub
```

continues

Listing 10.3   Creating an ADO *Recordset* Object Using a *Connection* and *Recordset* Object (Continued)

```
Private Sub cmdQueryCN_Click()

    Dim rs As ADODB.Recordset
    Set rs = New ADODB.Recordset

    rs.Source = "select * " & _
                "from tblCustomer " & _
                "where State = 'DE' " & _
                "order by LastName, FirstName"

    Set rs.ActiveConnection = cn
    rs.Open

    lstData.Clear

    Do Until rs.EOF
        lstData.AddItem rs.Fields("FirstName") & " " & _
                        rs.Fields("LastName") & " " & _
                        rs.Fields("Address")

        rs.MoveNext
    Loop

End Sub

Private Sub Form_Unload(Cancel As Integer)
    cn.Close
    Set cn = Nothing
End Sub
```

As an alternative to this technique, ADO lets you create the Recordset without creating a Connection object first. You do this by passing a connect string to the Open method of the Recordset object, as shown in Listing 10.4.

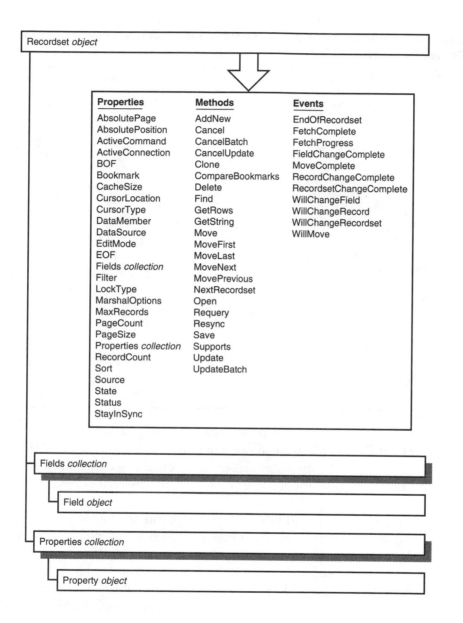

Figure 10.6
Properties and methods of the ADO Recordset object are listed in the ADO object model.

Listing 10.4   Creating an ADO *Recordset* Object Without First Creating an ADO *Connection* Object

```
Private Sub cmdQueryRS_Click()

    Dim rs As ADODB.Recordset
    Set rs = New ADODB.Recordset

    rs.Source = "select * " & _
                "from tblCustomer " & _
                "where State = 'DE' " & _
                "order by LastName, FirstName"

    rs.ActiveConnection = "DSN=JetNovelty;"
    rs.Open

    lstData.Clear

    Do Until rs.EOF
        lstData.AddItem rs.Fields("FirstName") & " " & _
                        rs.Fields("LastName") & " " & _
                        rs.Fields("Address")

        rs.MoveNext
    Loop

End Sub
```

This code works, unmodified, on any type of relational data source for which there are ODBC drivers. You could easily modify it to work with one of the native OLE DB provider discussed earlier in this chapter—only a single additional line of code, to set the `Provider` property of the `Connection` object, is necessary.

This technique is best used in situations where you don't need a persistent connection to the database—you're simply interested in getting in, getting the data, and getting out with a minimum of fuss. If your application needs to maintain a persistent connection to the database, on the other hand, you may want to consider opening and maintaining a `Connection` object. It's often better to hold open a connection to the database rather than open and close it repeatedly.

UPDATING AND INSERTING RECORDS USING THE *RECORDSET* OBJECT

Performing inserts and updates of records in ADO is almost precisely the same as in DAO. To insert a record, follow these steps:

1. Open a recordset.

2. Execute the AddNew method of the Recordset object.

3. Assign values to the fields in the Recordset object.

4. Save the record by executing the Update method of the Recordset object.

To update an existing record using the ADO Recordset object, follow these steps:

1. Open a recordset.

2. Assign values to the fields in the Recordset object. (Notice that you don't have to execute the Edit method of the Recordset as you did in DAO—ADO does away with that.)

3. Save the record by executing the Update method of the Recordset object.

The application that demonstrates entering and updating records permits the user to first populate a list box with customer data, and then select a particular customer to edit. When running, the application resembles Figure 10.7.

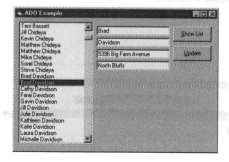

Figure 10.7
This application demonstrates entering and updating records.

Listing 10.5 displays the code in the application.

Listing 10.5   Updating Records in ActiveX Data Objects

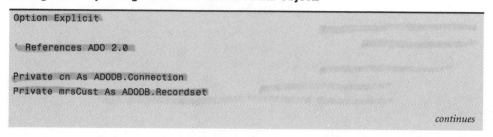

```
Option Explicit

' References ADO 2.0

Private cn As ADODB.Connection
Private mrsCust As ADODB.Recordset
```

continues

Listing 10.5   Updating Records in ActiveX Data Objects (Continued)

```
Private Sub Form_Load()
    Set cn = New ADODB.Connection
    cn.ConnectionString = "DSN=JetNovelty;"
    cn.Open

    Set mrsCust = New ADODB.Recordset
    mrsCust.LockType = adLockOptimistic
    mrsCust.CursorType = adOpenKeyset
End Sub

Private Sub cmdList_Click()

    Dim rs As ADODB.Recordset
    Set rs = New ADODB.Recordset

    rs.Source = "select * " & _
                "from tblCustomer " & _
                "where State = 'DE' " & _
                "order by LastName, FirstName"

    Set rs.ActiveConnection = cn
    rs.Open

    lstData.Clear

    Do Until rs.EOF
        lstData.AddItem rs.Fields("FirstName") & " " & _
                        rs.Fields("LastName")
        lstData.ItemData(lstData.NewIndex) = rs.Fields("ID")
        rs.MoveNext
    Loop

    rs.Close
    Set rs = Nothing

End Sub

Private Sub lstData_Click()
Dim strSQL As String

    strSQL = "select * " & _
             "from tblCustomer " & _
             "where ID = " & lstData.ItemData(lstData.ListIndex)

    mrsCust.Source = strSQL
```

```
        Set mrsCust.ActiveConnection = cn
        mrsCust.Open

        txtFirstName.Text = mrsCust.Fields("FirstName")
        txtLastName.Text = mrsCust.Fields("LastName")
        txtAddress.Text = mrsCust.Fields("Address")
        txtCity.Text = mrsCust.Fields("City")

        mrsCust.Close

End Sub

Private Sub cmdUpdate_Click()
Dim strSQL As String

        strSQL = "select * " & _
                "from tblCustomer " & _
                "where ID = " & lstData.ItemData(lstData.ListIndex)

        mrsCust.Source = strSQL
        Set mrsCust.ActiveConnection = cn
        mrsCust.Open

        mrsCust.Fields("FirstName") = txtFirstName.Text
        mrsCust.Fields("LastName") = txtLastName.Text
        mrsCust.Fields("Address") = txtAddress.Text
        mrsCust.Fields("City") = txtCity.Text

        mrsCust.Update
        mrsCust.Close

        ' Refresh list of customers
        cmdList_Click

End Sub

Private Sub Form_Unload(Cancel As Integer)
    cn.Close
    Set cn = Nothing
End Sub
```

To use this application, run it, and then click the Show List button to display the list of customers. When the user clicks on a customer in the list, the detail appears in the text box. To change a record, alter the values of one of the text boxes, and then click Update.

To apply the update, the code in the Click event of the Update button requeries the data and then performs an Update on it. This isn't the most efficient way to do things in a client/server environment, but it works splendidly when you're going against an Access database. (A more efficient, but more complicated way of performing the update would be to use a SQL UPDATE command. These are introduced in Chapter 2, "Queries.")

Remember that in ADO, the default locking mode is read-only (as discussed in the locking section earlier in this chapter), so you must set the LockMode property of the Recordset object to an editable mode before you can perform updates or inserts on it.

Other than that, the only significant difference between this code and the equivalent code in DAO is the fact that ADO doesn't have (or need) an Edit method. If the Recordset is editable, you need only change the contents of a field and then execute the Update method to write the information back to the database.

To insert records, you add an Add As New button to the application:

```
Private Sub cmdAddNew_Click()

Dim strSQL As String

    ' Open empty recordset
    strSQL = "select * " & _
             "from tblCustomer " & _
             "where ID = 0"

    mrsCust.Source = strSQL
    Set mrsCust.ActiveConnection = cn
    mrsCust.Open

    mrsCust.AddNew

    mrsCust.Fields("FirstName") = txtFirstName.Text
    mrsCust.Fields("LastName") = txtLastName.Text
    mrsCust.Fields("Address") = txtAddress.Text
    mrsCust.Fields("City") = txtCity.Text
    mrsCust.Fields("State") = "DE"

    mrsCust.Update
    mrsCust.Close

End Sub
```

In a real application, you want to try and fold the "Update" and "Insert" functionality into the concept of a Save command. You can do this by examining the state of the recordset—if it contains a value in its primary key field, for example, it's a good bet that the recordset needs an update rather than an insert.

Code Example: The code discussed in this section is in the project `Update.vbp`, located in the directory `\vbdb\code\10-Ado\Update`. For information on how to install the sample files on the CD that accompanies this book, see the section "Installing the Example Files" in the introduction at the beginning of this book.

CREATING DISCONNECTED RECORDSETS

When you use the ADO client-side cursor library, you have the ability to disconnect from the server and continue to work with data. This can go a long way toward making your application more scalable because many more users can be working with data if they don't all have to be connected to the server at any given moment.

To disconnect from the server in ADO, you set the Recordset object's ActiveConnection property to Nothing. The client will continue to be able to work with data even though it is not connected to the server.

Listing 10.6 shows an example of a method of a server-side component that returns a disconnected ADO Recordset. This method might be appropriate in situations where you want to display a list of customers in the user interface.

Listing 10.6   Returning a Disconnected ADO *Recordset*

```
Public Function GetList(strState As String) As ADODB.Recordset
' Retrieves a list of employees and
' places it into a disconnected ADO recordset.

Dim strSQL As String
Dim rs As ADODB.Recordset

    strSQL = "SELECT ID, FirstName, LastName " & _
             "FROM tblCustomer " & _
             "WHERE State = '" & strState & "' " & _
             "ORDER BY LastName, FirstName"

    ' Create an initialize recordset
    Set rs = New ADODB.Recordset
    Set rs.ActiveConnection = cn
```

continues

Listing 10.6   Returning a Disconnected ADO *Recordset* (Continued)

```
rs.CursorLocation = adUseClient
rs.LockType = adLockReadOnly
rs.CursorType = adOpenForwardOnly

rs.Open strSQL

' Disconnect
Set rs.ActiveConnection = Nothing

' Return recordset
Set GetList = rs

' Dereference object variable
Set rs = Nothing

End Function
```

To perform the same operation on a single customer record, alter the SQL statement, as shown in Listing 10.7.

Listing 10.7   Returning a Single Record in the Form of a Disconnected ADO *Recordset*

```
Public Function GetData(lngID As Long) As ADODB.Recordset

Dim rs As ADODB.Recordset
Dim strSQL As String

    strSQL = "SELECT * " & _
             "FROM tblCustomer " & _
             "WHERE ID = " & lngID

    ' Create and initialize recordset
    Set rs = New ADODB.Recordset
    Set rs.ActiveConnection = cn
    rs.CursorLocation = adUseClient
    rs.LockType = adLockBatchOptimistic
    rs.CursorType = adOpenKeyset

    rs.Open strSQL

    Set rs.ActiveConnection = Nothing
    Set GetData = rs

    Set rs = Nothing

End Function
```

In this function, the cursor and lock types are made editable. The `LockType` property is set to `adLockBatchOptimistic`, so the recordset can be reconnected to the database and updated later (a batch lock type is the only ADO type that supports updating a reconnected recordset). Listing 10.8 demonstrates this.

Listing 10.8   Updating a Disconnected ADO *Recordset*

```
Public Sub Save(rsDis As ADODB.Recordset)
    ' Updates a disconnected ADO
    ' recordset.

    Dim rs As ADODB.Recordset
    Set rs = New ADODB.Recordset
    Set rs.ActiveConnection = cn

    ' reopen the recordset
    rs.Open rsDis, cn

    rs.UpdateBatch

End Sub
```

This subroutine takes a disconnected ADO `Recordset` object as an argument. It creates another ADO `Recordset` object using the disconnected recordset as its source argument. You use this method because you can't reconnect a disconnected recordset directly—you have to go in using a fresh `Recordset` object. After establishing the connection, the `Recordset` object performs a batch update, and the data is saved back to the database.

The real value of this code becomes apparent when you call it from a client-side component. For example, say the previous code examples that return disconnected recordsets are placed in a class called `CCustData`, packaged in a server-side component. You'd then be able to write a class called `CCustomer` packaged in a client-side component that used `CCustData`'s services. The relevant code in the client-side `CCustomer` class is in Listing 10.9.

Listing 10.9   A Client-Side Class That Calls a Server-Side Data Access Class

```
Private mData As CCustData
Private mrs As ADODB.Recordset


Private Sub Class_Initialize()
    Set mData = New CCustData
End Sub
```

continues

Listing 10.9   A Client-Side Class That Calls a Server-Side Data Access Class (Continued)

```
Public Sub GetData(lngID As Long)
' Retrieves data for an
' individual customer

    Set mrs = mData.GetData(lngID)

    FirstName = mrs!FirstName & ""
    ID = lngID
    LastName = mrs!LastName & ""
    Address = mrs!Address & ""
    City = mrs!City & ""
    State = mrs!State & ""
    Zip = mrs!Zip & ""
    Phone = mrs!Phone & ""

End Sub


Public Function GetList(strState As String) As ADODB.Recordset
' Retrieves a list of customers
Dim rs As ADODB.Recordset

    Set GetList = mData.GetList(strState)
    Set rs = Nothing

End Function

Public Sub Save()

    mrs.Fields("Address") = Address
    mrs.Fields("City") = City
    mrs.Fields("FirstName") = FirstName
    mrs.Fields("LastName") = LastName
    mrs.Fields("State") = State
    mrs.Fields("Phone") = Phone
    mrs.Fields("Zip") = Zip

    mData.Save mrs

End Sub
```

The `CCustomer` class also contains all the `Property Let` and `Property Get` procedures that any good class module should have; those aren't listed here, but they are in the code installed from the CD.

Code Example: You can find an example of the code discussed in this section in the project CustSvr3.vbp, located in the directory \vbdb\code\ 10-Ado\Disconn. This project, an ActiveX component, is called by the Standard EXE client application, contained in the project file Cust.vbp in the same directory. (You can open both projects at once by using the group file Disconn.vbg.)

For information on how to install the sample files on the CD that accompanies this book, see the section "Installing the Example Files" in the introduction at the beginning of this book.

The client application that uses the component described in the previous examples displays lists of records, permitting users to select from and update records. The code for this Standard EXE application is shown in Listing 10.10.

Listing 10.10   A Standard EXE Application That Uses the Disconnected Object Server

```
Option Explicit

' References CustSvr3.
' References ADO Recordset Library.

Private mrs As ADOR.Recordset
Private mCust As CustSvr3.CCustomer

Private Sub Form_Load()
    Set mCust = New CustSvr3.CCustomer
    DisplayList
End Sub

Private Sub DisplayList()
    Set mrs = mCust.GetList("NV")

    Do Until mrs.EOF
        lstCust.AddItem mrs.Fields("FirstName") & " " & _
                    mrs.Fields("LastName")
        lstCust.ItemData(lstCust.NewIndex) = mrs.Fields("ID")
        mrs.MoveNext
    Loop

End Sub
```

continues

Listing 10.10   A Standard EXE Application That Uses the Disconnected Object Server (Continued)

```
Private Sub lstCust_Click()
    mCust.GetData lstCust.ItemData(lstCust.ListIndex)
    txtAddress.Text = mCust.Address
    txtCity.Text = mCust.City
    txtState.Text = mCust.State
    txtZip.Text = mCust.Zip
End Sub

Private Sub cmdUpdate_Click()

    mCust.Address = txtAddress.Text
    mCust.City = txtCity.Text
    mCust.State = txtState.Text
    mCust.Zip = txtZip.Text

    mCust.Save

End Sub

Private Sub Form_Unload(Cancel As Integer)
    Set mCust = Nothing
End Sub
```

This project references ADOR, the Microsoft ActiveX Data Objects Recordset library. This lightweight library is ideal for this type of client because it needs to process recordset objects, but it doesn't need any of the advanced functionality contained in the Connection or Command objects. (These are managed by the server-side component.)

As you might imagine, disconnecting from the server is most effective when you have a server-side component serving up disconnected recordsets. For more information on this, check out Chapter 7, "Database Access with Classes," which covers programming with classes and objects, and Chapter 8, "Remote Database Access," which discusses remote deployment of components based on classes.

EXECUTING A QUERY USING THE ADO *COMMAND* AND *PARAMETER* OBJECTS

After you've successfully achieved a connection to your data source using the Connection object, you can begin issuing commands against the data source. You do this by using the ADO Command object.

The position of the ADO Command object in the ADO object model, as well as its properties and methods, is shown in Figure 10.8.

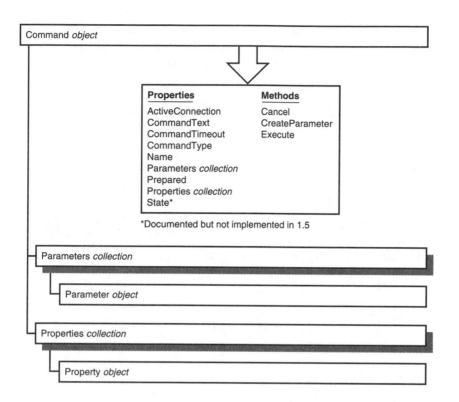

Figure 10.8
Here are the properties and methods of the ActiveX Data Objects Command object.

Bear in mind that you don't have to use a `Command` object to issue commands against a data source (the previous few code examples that use the `Connection` and `Recordset` objects demonstrate this). You generally use `Command` objects in situations where you want to execute a stored procedure, or when you need to issue a parameterized query.

As discussed in the introduction to Chapter 2, "Queries," queries stored in the database are generally superior to queries generated in your Visual Basic code. This is the case for many reasons, most of which have to do with efficiency—the database engine can optimize the query in advance of its execution.

Note: One promise of the OLE DB and ADO technology is that other data providers will, in the future, provide other types of commands. For example, a spreadsheet might provide a recalculate command, or an email store might provide some type of send command. The abilities of future OLE DB providers are aggressively hypothetical at this point because very few providers exist today. The point, though, is that ADO doesn't have to be wound up in relational database technology and structured query language the way DAO and RDO are.

Listing 10.11 shows an example of the GetData procedure from the previous example, enhanced to use a Command object that calls a parameterized, stored query. Similar to the GetData method in the previous version of the CCustData class, this function returns a Recordset when it is executed.

Listing 10.11   Returning a *Recordset* Using the *Command* Object

```
Public Function GetData(lngID As Long) As ADODB.Recordset

Dim cm As ADODB.Command
Dim rs As ADODB.Recordset
Dim p As ADODB.Parameter

    ' Create ADO Command
    Set cm = New ADODB.Command
    Set cm.ActiveConnection = cn
    cm.CommandType = adCmdStoredProc
    cm.CommandText = "qryCustomerByID"

    ' Supply parameter
    Set p = cm.CreateParameter("pID", adInteger, adParamInput, , lngID)
    cm.Parameters.Append p

    Set rs = cm.Execute

    Set GetData = rs

    Set rs = Nothing

End Function
```

Parameterized queries give you the ability to have the best of both worlds—the flexibility of a query that your application can alter at runtime, along with the efficiency of a precompiled query.

The position of the ADO Parameter object in the ADO object model, as well as its properties and methods, is shown in Figure 10.9.

Code Example: You can find an example of the code discussed in this section in the project CustSvr4.vbp, located in the directory \vbdb\code\ 10-Ado\Command. For information on how to install the sample files on the CD that accompanies this book, see the section "Installing the Example Files" in the introduction at the beginning of this book.

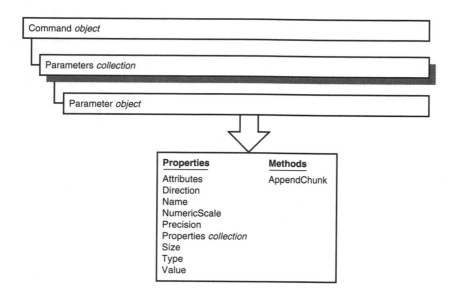

ACCESSING RECORDSET DATA USING THE ADO *FIELD* OBJECT

Use the `Field` object and the `Fields` collection when you have an ADO `Recordset` object and you're interested in reading or setting a field's value in the current record. This technique is nearly identical to the similarly named collections of fields in DAOs and RDOs.

The position of the ADO `Field` object in the ADO object model, as well as its properties and methods, is shown in Figure 10.10.

The sections earlier in this chapter on editing and updating records in a `Recordset` object give examples on how to use the `Field` object in code. In short, if you're accustomed to accessing values of fields in DAO `Recordset` objects, you'll find nothing new in ADO.

HANDLING ERRORS USING THE ADO *ERRORS* COLLECTION

In ActiveX Data Objects, as in the other database access object models, a variety of errors can take place. They can occur particularly in client/server applications, in which a number of software layers must cooperate in order to shuttle data between the client and the server—a single fault can generate a number of error messages. As a result, ADO provides an `Errors` collection, which makes each error available to you when something goes wrong.

The position of the ADO `Error` object in the ADO object model, as well as its properties and methods, is shown in Figure 10.11.

Figure 10.10
Properties and methods of the ActiveX Data Objects Field object are seen in the ADO object model.

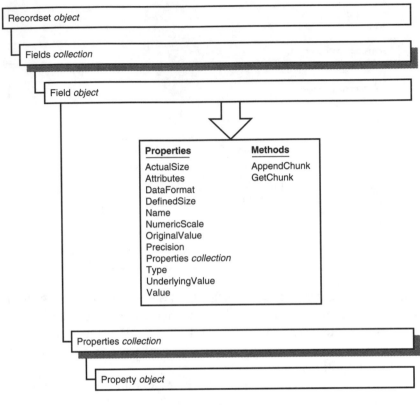

Figure 10.11
Properties and methods of the ADO Error object are viewed in the ADO object model.

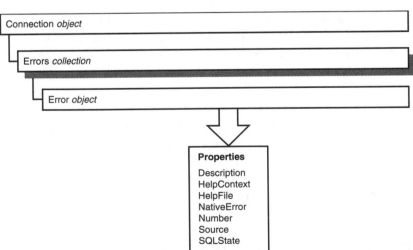

In Visual Basic, a trappable error is raised when ADO encounters an error. As with DAO and RDO, you can iterate through the Errors collection to display or act on all the error messages that were generated between the client and the server.

Inspecting Provider-Specific Attributes Using the ADO *Properties* Collection

In addition to the conventional objects and properties, DAO provides for an extensible Properties collection that can be assigned to each object in its object model. ADO provides for similar collections of properties, but with one important difference—ADO Property objects can't be created and modified by your applications. Instead, they're under the control of the data provider.

The position of the ADO Property object in the ADO object model, as well as its properties and methods, is shown in Figure 10.12.

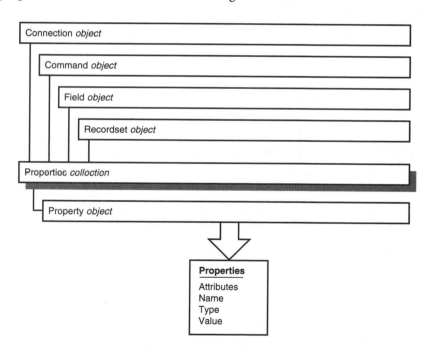

Figure 10.12
Here is the ADO Property object, and its properties and methods, in the ADO object model.

Listing 10.12 gives an example of code that dumps the contents of a Connection object's Properties collection to a list box.

Listing 10.12   Displaying the Contents of a *Connection* Object's *Properties* Collection

```
Option Explicit

' References ADO 2.0

Private cn As Connection

Private Sub Form_Load()
    Set cn = New ADODB.Connection
    cn.Provider = "MSDASQL"    ' ODBC
    cn.ConnectionString = "DSN=JetNovelty;"
    cn.Open
End Sub


Private Sub cmdProp_Click()
    Dim pr As ADODB.Property

    lstProps.Clear

    For Each pr In cn.Properties
        lstProps.AddItem pr.Name & " = " & pr.Value
    Next

End Sub

Private Sub Form_Unload(Cancel As Integer)
    cn.Close
    Set cn = Nothing
End Sub
```

With the ODBC provider for OLE DB, the number of provider properties is quite extensive. Remember that the type and value of these properties changes from provider to provider.

Code Example: You can find an example of the code discussed in this section in the project `Props.vbp`, located in the directory `\vbdb\code\10-Ado\Props`. For information on how to install the sample files on the CD that accompanies this book, see the section "Installing the Example Files" in the introduction at the beginning of this book.

USING ADO REMOTE DATA SERVICES

You can use Remote Data Services (RDS) to get ADO recordsets from a Web server. This library, which comes with ADO, essentially lets you use HTTP (the network transport of the Web) as the network transport for your database application. While this was originally intended for use with Web browser clients, it works perfectly well with Visual Basic clients.

> **Note:** RDS was formerly referred to as Advanced Data Connector, or ADC. You can get more information on RDS online at `http://www.microsoft.com/data/ado/rds/`.

You can retrieve an ADO Recordset object over the Internet using the RDS DataControl object. This object, which is served from a computer running Microsoft Internet Information Server 3.0 or later, has the ability to return disconnected ADO Recordset objects to any client over HTTP. The easiest way to demonstrate how to use RDS is to perform a query from a Web server using the RDS DataControl object. To do this, follow these steps:

1. Create a new Standard EXE project.

2. In the Project References menu, make a reference to Microsoft Remote Data Services 2.0 Library and Microsoft ActiveX Data Objects 2.0 Recordset Library.

3. Create a text box, a command button, and a list box on the form.

4. Enter the code shown in Listing 10.13 into the form.

Listing 10.13 Querying a Database Through ADO Remote Data Services

```
Option Explicit

' References RDS.

Private rdc As RDS.DataControl

Private Sub cmdQuery_Click()

    Screen.MousePointer = vbHourglass

    Set rdc = New RDS.DataControl
```

continues

Listing 10.13   Querying a Database Through ADO Remote Data Services (Continued)

```
    rdc.SQL = "select * from tblCustomer where state = 'IN'"
    rdc.ExecuteOptions = adcExecAsync
    rdc.Connect = "DSN=JetNovelty;"
    rdc.Server = "http://localhost/"
    rdc.Refresh

    ' Wait until server responds
    While rdc.ReadyState = adcReadyStateLoaded  ' busy
        DoEvents
    Wend

    Do Until rdc.Recordset.EOF
        With rdc.Recordset
            lstCustomer.AddItem .Fields("FirstName") & " " & _
                                .Fields("LastName")

            .MoveNext
        End With
    Loop

    Set rdc = Nothing

    Screen.MousePointer = vbNormal

End Sub
```

In this example, the server "localhost" is used. This is Web-server shorthand for "the computer I'm working on right now." It's handy for testing and examples; it also has the benefit of working on any computer that has a Web server installed on it.

The only thing unusual about this code is the While…Wend loop used to wait for the server to respond. This reflects the high-latency, asynchronous nature of an HTTP call. You can't be certain of how long the server will take to respond, so you have to sit around and wait. (The RDS DataControl object is capable of listening to events if you declare it using the WithEvents keyword; however, this didn't work consistently in my tests.)

Code Example: You can find an example of the code discussed in this section in the project RDSQuery.vbp, located in the directory \vbdb\code\ 10-Ado\RDSQuery. For information on how to install the sample files on the CD that accompanies this book, see the section "Installing the Example Files" in the introduction at the beginning of this book.

Summary

You learned how to take advantage of the power of ActiveX Data Objects (ADO). This chapter also gives you a crash course in creating dynamic Web sites using Active Server Pages, in conjunction with ADO, to permit Internet users to access your database.

In this chapter, you also learned how to use ADO within a Visual Basic application. If you develop software targeted for the corporate LAN and the Web, this will make it easy for you to share database access code between your VB applications and your Active Server Pages.

The remaining chapters in this book explore the challenges of creating database-enabled user interfaces with Visual Basic. In Chapter 11, you're shown how to use ADO and ActiveX components in a Web application. The final few chapters show you how to use Visual Basic's Professional and Enterprise Edition controls—as well as their commercial counterparts—to create the zippiest user interfaces imaginable.

Questions and Answers

Q. Would you recommend using ADO for single-user applications based on the Jet database engine?

A. If you never plan to scale the application up to client/server, no. DAO is a much better choice for database access against Jet today. In 1999, that may well change. A new version of the Jet engine, a new version of the Jet provider for OLE DB, and performance enhancements in OLE DB itself might make the equation change.

OLE DB and ADO are great choices for client/server and Web programming today. The technologies hold great promise for providing access to non-relational data sources in the future. But for right now, if you're creating a single-user Jet application, I recommend sticking with DAO.

Internet Database Applications

SETTING UP AND CONFIGURING MICROSOFT
INTERNET INFORMATION SERVER FOR ACTIVE
SERVER PAGES

You can use Visual Basic to create applications that are accessible through the World Wide Web. At the end of Chapter 10, "ActiveX Data Objects," you saw an example of this with the Remote Data Services (RDS) library. That example used RDS to retrieve a recordset from an HTTP Web server, but HTTP was just used as the network transport—that wasn't really a Web application because you still had an EXE on the client side. With that configuration, you're hypothetically able to get access to your data from anywhere in the world, but you can't access it from any *computer* in the world. If you have a Visual Basic client, your client operating system must be Windows.

This chapter departs from the idea of a Visual Basic Standard EXE client application, permitting you to apply your Visual Basic knowledge to the creation of a Web application that can service any kind of Web browser client on any kind of platform. That includes Netscape, Macintosh, UNIX, and anything else you can think of.

SETTING UP AND CONFIGURING MICROSOFT INTERNET INFORMATION SERVER FOR ACTIVE SERVER PAGES

You must be running a Microsoft Web server in order to use Active Server Pages (ASP). Microsoft Internet Information Server (MS IIS) version 2.0 came with Windows NT 4.0; IIS version 3.0 is the version that includes ASP. The current version of IIS (as of this writing) is 4.0. Conveniently, this version ships with the Enterprise edition of VB6. If you don't have the Enterprise edition, you can download IIS as part of Windows NT Option Pack from `http://www.microsoft.com/windows/downloads/contents/Updates/NT40ptPk/`. Note that you can install NT Option Pack on Windows 95/98 as well; doing so gets you Personal Web Server, a lightweight version of IIS that supports ASP.

Because Active Server Pages are scripts instead of normal HTML Web pages, they must be placed in a directory on the Web server that is marked as executable. Locating or creating a scriptable directory is the first step you take when creating an ASP application.

You mark a directory as executable using the Internet Service Manager utility found in your Internet Information Server (IIS) program group. (In IIS 4.0, this utility is a part of Microsoft Management Console, the same tool used to manage Microsoft Transaction Server (MTS). MTS is covered in Chapter 8, "Remote Database Access.")

By default, the \scripts directory under your IIS directory is marked as executable, but you may not want to use the default directory. Follow these steps to create a different script directory:

1. Launch Internet Service Manager.

2. Open the folder labeled Internet Information Server, and then open the folder labeled Default Web Site. The directories available to your Web server are shown in Figure 11.1.

Note: Your machine may have different directories available—Figure 11.1 shows something close to the default settings.

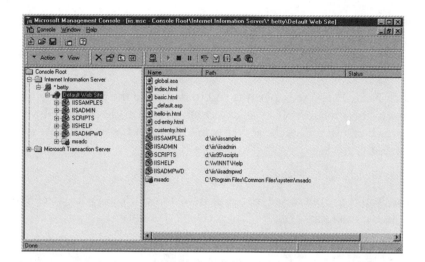

3. To create a new scriptable directory, right-click on Default Web Site. From the pop-up menu, choose New, Virtual Directory. The New Virtual Directory Wizard appears, as shown in Figure 11.2.

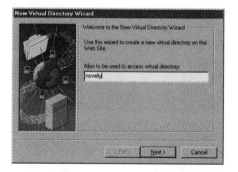

Figure 11.2
You can create a new directory using the New Virtual Directory Wizard.

4. Type the name **novelty**. This is the name that users will use to access your directory through their Web browsers. This is a virtual folder; it does not necessarily correspond to a physical folder on your computer, as you'll see in the next step.

5. Click Next. In this screen, type (or browse for) the physical folder where you want your Web application to reside. For simplicity, you will probably want to make this a folder underneath the wwwroot directory created by default when you installed IIS, but you can use any folder you want.

Note: Note that the browse dialog provided by this wizard annoyingly does not permit you to create new folders. If you want to create a separate folder for your Web application, you must switch to Windows Explorer to do it.

6. Click Next. This screen permits you to designate the access levels users will have to this directory. It's very important that you check the Allow Execute Access box; otherwise, the server won't interpret the ASP and your application won't work.

7. Click Finish.

You should be able to see that your new script directory has been created, as shown in Figure 11.3.

Figure 11.3
Internet Information Server displays your new script directory.

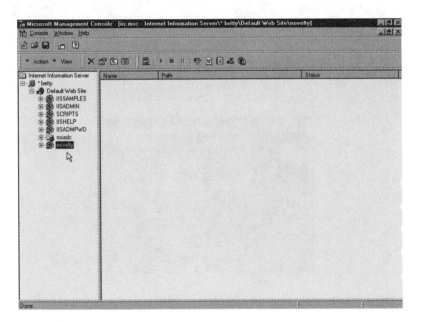

You must go through this process only if you're interested in creating a new script directory. If you're happy putting all your ASPs in the default \scripts directory, that's fine, although it's better to have each Web application in a directory of its own.

Writing Scripts with ASP

When you're writing an Active Server Page, the script's execution takes place on the server. None of the code is sent to the client application unless you indicate you want it to be sent.

In order to make a differentiation between client- and server-side code, you enclose the code that is to be executed on the server in special brackets. The brackets are comprised of a chevron and percent sign and resemble the following:

```
<html>

At the tone the time will be:<br>

<%
    Response.Write(Time
%>

</html>
```

Note: In the previous example, the expression that is marked as executed on the server is in the VBScript language, a subset of Visual Basic. For more information on VBScript, including online documentation, see the Microsoft Scripting Technologies Web site at `http://msdn.microsoft.com/scripting/vbscript/`.

Code Example: You can find the code discussed in this section in the script file `Time.asp`, located in the directory `\vbdb\code\11-Internet\Time`. For information on how to install the sample files on the CD that accompanies this book, see the section "Installing the Example Files" in the introduction at the beginning of this book.

Running an ActiveX Data Object Query in ASP

The simplest application of ActiveX Data Objects (ADO) and ASPs is to run a simple query against a data source. With the exception of the fact that your code is embedded in an HTML page, there's not much difference between database access in ASP and in Visual Basic.

One important difference, though, is in the area of object binding. In Visual Basic, you can make a reference to an object library (using the Tools References menu) to gain access to that library's objects. This isn't the case in ASP. In ASP, you must instead use the CreateObject method of the Server object to create instances of objects. For example, to create an ASP Recordset object using CreateObject, you use the following code:

```
set rs = Server.CreateObject("ADODB.Recordset")
```

The end result is the same, in the sense that an ADO Recordset object is created—the syntax is just different.

> **Note: Because the Server object is ASP's default object, you don't have to reference it directly when using CreateObject. This means that instead of using the syntax Server.CreateObject(), you can instead just use CreateObject().**

Now that you have the ability to create objects in code, it's time to do something useful with them. Listing 11.1 gives an example of an Active Server Page that uses ADO to display a list of names from the Novelty database.

Listing 11.1   Using ASP to Query and Display Data in a Web Browser

```
<html>
<head>
<title>
ADO Query Demonstration
</title>
</head>

<body bgcolor=#ffffff>
<font face='Tahoma, Arial, Helvetica'>

<%

set rs = Server.CreateObject("ADODB.Recordset")

rs.ActiveConnection = "DSN=JetNovelty;"
rs.Open "select * from tblCustomer where state = 'RI'"

Do Until rs.EOF
   Response.Write (rs.Fields("FirstName") & " ")
   Response.Write (rs.Fields("LastName") & " ")
   Response.Write (rs.Fields("Address") & "<br>")
```

```
    rs.MoveNext
Loop

%>

</font>
</body>
</html>
```

Code Example: You can find the code discussed in this section in the script file `Query.asp`, located in the directory `\vbdb\code\11-Internet\Query`. For information on how to install the sample files on the CD that accompanies this book, see the section "Installing the Example Files" in the introduction at the beginning of this book.

The server-side script is enclosed in ASP brackets (the angle bracket and percent sign thingamajigs). Notice also that when referring to fields in the `Recordset` object, you need to use the full syntax.

```
rs.Fields("FirstName")
```

You cannot use the Visual Basic shortcut:

```
rs!FirstName
```

This is another minor difference between the programmability features of VBScript in ASP versus Visual Basic.

When displayed in a browser, the query script looks similar to Figure 11.4.

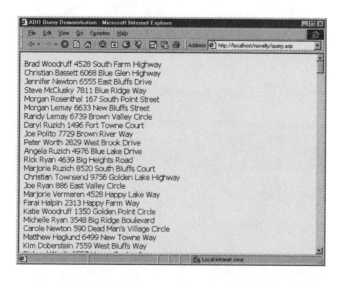

Figure 11.4
This is the output from the basic Active Server script query.asp.

If you find the idea of dumping the data to a textual HTML list unsatisfying, you have a number of formatting options. One of the most popular (and easiest to implement) is the HTML table. By inserting HTML table tags into the data generated by the database call initiated by the ASP script, you can make the data much easier to read. Listing 11.2 gives an example.

Listing 11.2   Modified Version of ASP Script to Output a Query in an HTML Table

```
<html>
<head>
<title>
ADO Query Demonstration
</title>
</head>

<body bgcolor=#ffffff>
<font face='Tahoma, Arial, Helvetica'>

<table border>

<!-- Header -->

<tr bgcolor=#CCCCCC>
  <td>
  <b>First</b>
  </td>
  <td>
  <b>Last</b>
  </td>
  <td>
  <b>Address</b>
  </td>
</tr>

<%

set rs = Server.CreateObject("ADODB.Recordset")

strSQL = "select FirstName, LastName, Address " & _
         "from tblCustomer " & _
         "where State = 'RI'" & _
         "order by LastName, FirstName"

rs.Open strSQL, "DSN=JetNovelty;"
```

```
Do Until rs.EOF
   Response.Write("<tr>")

   Response.Write("<td>")
   Response.Write(rs.Fields("FirstName"))
   Response.Write("</td>")

   Response.Write("<td>")
   Response.Write(rs.Fields("LastName"))
   Response.Write("</td>")

   Response.Write("<td>")
   Response.Write(rs.Fields("Address"))
   Response.Write("</td>")

   rs.MoveNext
   Response.Write("</tr>")
Loop

%>

</table>

</font>
</body>
</html>
```

This script's output is illustrated in Figure 11.5.

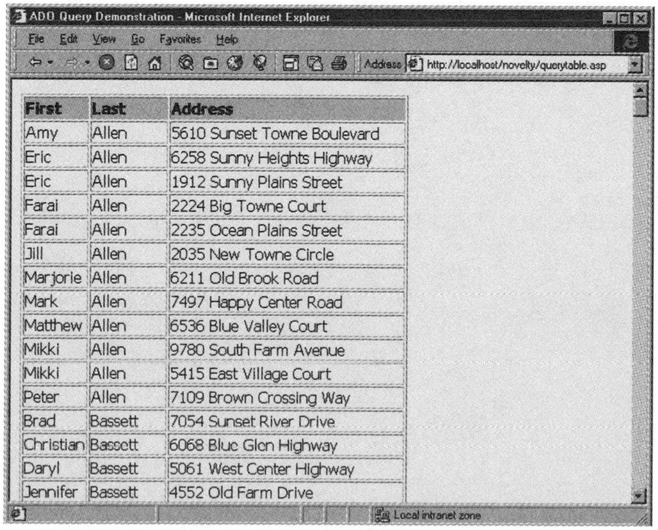

Figure 11.5
Here's the output from the enhanced version of the Active Server script querytable.asp.

Code Example: You can find the code discussed in this section in the script file `QueryTable.asp`, located in the directory `\vbdb\code\11-Internet\QueryTable`. For information on how to install the sample files on the CD that accompanies this book, see the section "Installing the Example Files" in the introduction at the beginning of this book.

Using ASP in Netscape and Other Browsers

Because ASP is a server-side technology, your scripts are oblivious to what's on the client side. As long as the client can process HTML, it works. You don't need to do anything special on the client side to make ASP work. This means you can use any Web browser on any platform to get to your script.

Figure 11.6 shows an example of the ADO query script `querytable.asp` from the previous section of this chapter displayed in a Netscape browser.

Figure 11.6
Now you see the miracle of server-side scripting with a Netscape client.

First	Last	Address
Amy	Allen	5610 Sunset Towne Boulevard
Eric	Allen	6258 Sunny Heights Highway
Eric	Allen	1912 Sunny Plains Street
Farai	Allen	2224 Big Towne Court
Farai	Allen	2235 Ocean Plains Street
Jill	Allen	2035 New Towne Circle
Marjorie	Allen	6211 Old Brook Road
Mark	Allen	7497 Happy Center Road
Matthew	Allen	6536 Blue Valley Court
Mikki	Allen	9780 South Farm Avenue
Mikki	Allen	5415 East Village Court
Peter	Allen	7109 Brown Crossing Way
Brad	Bassett	7054 Sunset River Drive
Christian	Bassett	6068 Blue Glen Highway
Daryl	Bassett	5061 West Center Highway
Jennifer	Bassett	4552 Old Farm Drive
Julie	Bassett	2688 Ocean Center Road

Note: You can get more information on the Netscape browser at
`http://home.netscape.com/computing/download/`.

Figure 11.7 shows the same script displayed in Lynx, a text-mode browser. Lynx has been ported to many platforms, but the implementation you're seeing here is running on Solaris. (I used Windows Telnet to get to the Solaris machine.)

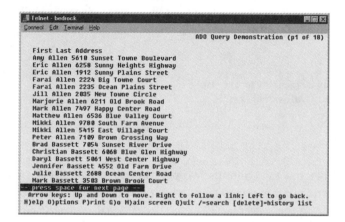

Figure 11.7
Here's the majesty of server-side scripting shown on a Lynx text-mode client.

Note: There are currently ports for Lynx that run on VMS, UNIX, Windows 95, Windows NT, and DOS, among others. You can get more information on the Lynx browser at `http://lynx.browser.org/`.

Inserting Records Using ASP and HTML Forms

You can use a Web browser to insert records in a database. If you're using ADO, a database insert involves creating several things:

▶ A Web page that provides a user interface into which users can enter data

▶ An HTML form—a collection of HTML tags embedded in a Web page that submits information from the browser to the Web server

▶ An Active Server Page that takes information from the HTML form and inserts it into the database using ADO

The following sections demonstrate how to build a minimal Web application, starting with a Web form, as well as creating the ASPs you need in order to perform the actual database update.

> **Note: The particulars of how to do HTML have been intentionally left out of this book. If you're interested in moving forward with HTML, there are a ton of great books out there. One of the best is Laura Lemay's *Teach Yourself Web Publishing With HTML 4.0 in 14 Days* (Sams.net, 1997).**

Creating an HTML Form

To submit information to the database server, begin by creating an HTML form. An *HTML form* is a group of HTML code tags inserted into an HTML Web page, all contained within the <FORM> tag:

```
<html>

<form method=post action="myscript.asp">
<input type=submit value="Run Me!">
</form>

</html>
```

In this example, this tag contains two parameters: METHOD and ACTION. You always set the METHOD parameter to post, which indicates that the form should send information to the server.

The ACTION parameter gives the server the name of a script to execute in response to the form submission. If you're using ASPs, this will be the name of an ASP script stored in an executable directory on the server.

> **Note: ASPs are not the only type of scripting available to you. Many other Web servers use other technologies, such as common gateway interface (CGI) scripts or scripts written in the Perl language.**

Listing 11.3 gives an example of an HTML page called custform.html that includes an input form.

Listing 11.3   HTML Code that Generates a Data Input Form for Display in a Web Browser

```
<html>
<head>
<title>
ASP/ADO Data Entry Form
</title>

</head>
```

```
<body bgcolor=#ffffff>
<font face="Verdana, Arial, Helvetica">
<p>Instructions: Enter the new customer's first and last name in the fields
    provided, then click on Save.

<form method=post action="/scripts/custsave.asp">

<!-- The table is here for formatting purposes -->

<table>
<tr>
<td>
First Name:
</td>

<td>
<input type=text name=txtFirstName>
</td>

</tr>

<tr>
<td>
Last Name:
</td>

<td>
<input type=text name=txtLastName>
</td>
</tr>

<tr>
<td>
Address:
</td>

<td>
<input type=text name=txtAddress>
</td>
</tr>

<tr>
<td>
```

continues

Listing 11.3   HTML Code that Generates a Data Input Form for Display in a Web Browser (Continued)

```
City:
</td>

<td>
<input type=text name=txtCity>
</td>
</tr>

<tr>
<td>
State:
</td>

<td>
<input type=text name=txtState>
</td>
</tr>

<tr>
<td>
 
</td>

<td align=right>
<input type=submit name=cmdSave value="Save">
</td>
</tr>

</table>
</form>

</font>
</body>
</html>
```

Figure 11.8 shows what this page resembles when loaded in Microsoft Internet Explorer.

Note that this page doesn't have to be deployed to an executable directory in order to be accessed. In this example, the file was placed in the WWWROOT directory and accessed using the URL http://localhost/custform.html.

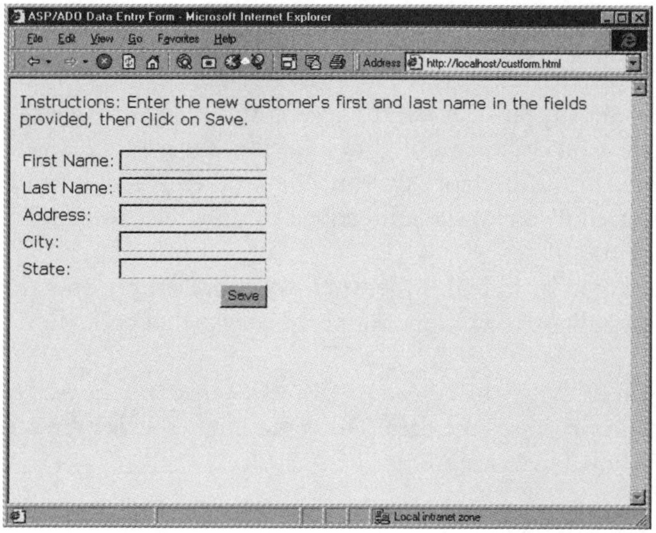

Figure 11.8
This Web page permits a user to perform data entry and submit the data to the server.

Submitting Data to the Server and Updating the Database

After the user has navigated to a Web page that contains a data entry form, he or she then clicks the command button (referred to in HTML as a *SUBMIT control*) to submit the form's data to the Web server.

Building on the example form in the previous section, when the Web server receives the form data, the form tag's action parameter tells the server to run the script custsave.asp. This script takes the data passed to it by the form, saves it to the database using ADO, and generates an output page indicating to the user what took place.

Before you get started writing the script file custsave.asp, your script will need to include a reference to ADO constants. Unlike Visual Basic, ASP can't make references to object libraries in advance of script execution. This means, among other things, that enumerated constants contained in the object libraries won't be available to your ASP scripts.

Fortunately, it's easy to include references to other files in ASPs. Use the #Include directive enclosed in an HTML comment. In order to write an Active Server Page that uses ActiveX Data Objects' predefined constants, you must reference a file, adovbs.inc, that is installed along with ADO. (If you can't locate the file on your system, a copy is included, along with the code you installed, on the CD-ROM that accompanies this book.)

In a Web page, the statement that includes this file looks like this:

```
<!-- #Include file="adovbs.inc" -->
```

This line should appear near the top of the Active Server Page that requires it (as shown in the next code example). In addition, the actual adovbs.inc file should be copied into a directory on your Web server, where it can be accessed by scripts that need it (an #Include directive can only refer to a file in the same directory as the page).

You didn't have to include this file when you were simply querying the database (in the example earlier in this chapter) because that code didn't require any ADO constants.

Now that you've set up the constants file, you can write the Active Server Page that actually processes the data. The remaining code for the script custsave.asp is shown in Listing 11.4.

Listing 11.4   Saving Data from a Form into a Database Using ADO

```
<!-- #include file="adovbs.inc" -->

<html>
<head>
<title>
ADO Insert Demonstration
</title>
</head>


<body>

<%

'***Set up data access

Set cn = Server.CreateObject("ADODB.Connection")
Set rs = Server.CreateObject("ADODB.Recordset")

cn.Open "DSN=JetNovelty;"

Set rs.ActiveConnection = cn
rs.CursorType = adOpenKeyset
rs.LockType = adLockOptimistic
rs.Source = "tblCustomer"
rs.Open

'***Create a record, assign values, and update
```

```
rs.AddNew
  rs.Fields("FirstName") = Request.Form("txtFirstName")
  rs.Fields("LastName") = Request.Form("txtLastName")
  rs.Fields("Address") = Request.Form("txtAddress")
  rs.Fields("City") = Request.Form("txtCity")
  rs.Fields("State") = Request.Form("txtState")
rs.Update

'***Generate output indicating what you did

Response.Write(Request.Form("txtFirstName") & " ")
Response.Write(Request.Form("txtLastName") & "<br>")
Response.Write(Request.Form("txtAddress") & "<br>")
Response.Write(Request.Form("txtCity") & ", ")
Response.Write(Request.Form("txtState") & "<br>")
Response.Write("<p>Response written to database!")

%>

</body>
</html>
```

After the data has been written to the database, the page displays the data it entered, as shown in Figure 11.9.

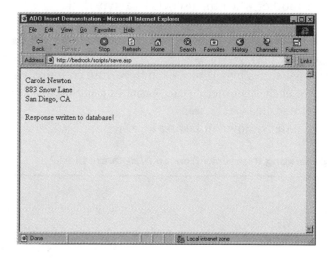

Figure 11.9
Now you see the result of the Active Server Page save.asp execution in the Web Browser.

Code Example: You can find the code discussed in this section in the directory \vbdb\code\11-Internet\FormSave. For information on how to install the sample files on the CD that accompanies this book, see the section "Installing the Example Files" in the introduction at the beginning of this book.

This particular Active Server Page performs no validation or error handling. It would be trivial to modify it to do so, however.

As an alternative, you could write a client-side script to validate the data. Validation based on client-side scripting has the advantage of keeping bad data off the server; it's particularly appropriate in situations where the user is very likely to make data entry mistakes and you need to keep as much bad data off the server as possible. It has the disadvantage of requiring a Web browser that understands scripting, which means that your potential audience is a bit smaller.

It's even better to include validation code in a reusable ActiveX DLL deployed to the server machine. This is demonstrated in "Using Components with ASP Scripting," later in this chapter.

Permitting Drill-Down Using the *QueryString* Property

While it's relatively simple to display static lists of information using an ASP script, it's even more impressive to use the features of HTML to permit users to drill-down on the data. One way to do this is to include parameters that enable one script to call another when the user clicks a hyperlink.

The script drill.asp does this. This script is an evolved version of the querytable.asp script created earlier in this chapter. It queries the customer database the same way that querytable.asp does, but instead of dumping the data to lifeless HTML, it generates hyperlinks. Each hyperlink contains a parameter—the primary key of each customer record—enabling the user to click and launch a second ASP script, called detail.asp.

The script drill.asp is shown in Listing 11.5.

Listing 11.5   Generating Hyperlinks from an ADO Query in ASP

```
<html>
<head>
<title>
ADO Query Demonstration
</title>
</head>

<body bgcolor=#ffffff>
```

```
<font face='Tahoma, Arial, Helvetica'>

<table border>

<!— Header —>

<tr bgcolor=#CCCCCC>
  <td>
    <b>Name</b>
  </td>
  <td>
    <b>Address</b>
  </td>
</tr>

<%

set rs = Server.CreateObject("ADODB.Recordset")

strSQL = "select ID, FirstName, LastName, Address " & _
         "from tblCustomer " & _
         "where State = 'RI'" & _
         "order by LastName, FirstName"

rs.Open strSQL, "DSN=JetNovelty;"

Do Until rs.EOF
   Response.Write("<tr>")

   Response.Write("<td>")

       ' Begin parameterized hyperlink
       Response.Write("<a href='detail.asp?CID=")
       Response.Write(rs.Fields("ID")) & "'>"

       Response.Write(rs.Fields("LastName") & " " & _
                      rs.Fields("FirstName"))

       ' End parameterized hyperlink
       Response.Write("</a>")

   Response.Write("</td>")
```

continues

Listing 11.5   Generating Hyperlinks from an ADO Query in ASP (Continued)

```
    Response.Write("<td>")
    Response.Write(rs.Fields("Address"))
    Response.Write("</td>")

    rs.MoveNext
    Response.Write("</tr>")
Loop

%>

</table>

</font>
</body>
</html>
```

The script `detail.asp` is shown in Listing 11.6.

Listing 11.6   Displaying Detail Using the Script *detail.asp*

```
<html>
<head>
<title>
ADO Drill-Down Demonstration
</title>
</head>

<body bgcolor=#ffffff>
<font face='Tahoma, Arial, Helvetica'>

<p>Here are the details for the customer you selected.

<p>

<%

set rs = Server.CreateObject("ADODB.Recordset")

strSQL = "select * " & _
         "from tblCustomer " & _
         "where ID = " & Request.QueryString("CID")

rs.Open strSQL, "DSN=JetNovelty;"
```

```
    Response.Write "First: " & (rs.Fields("FirstName")) & "<br>"
    Response.Write "Last: " & (rs.Fields("LastName")) & "<br>"
    Response.Write "Address: " & (rs.Fields("Address")) & "<br>"
    Response.Write "City: " & (rs.Fields("City")) & "<br>"
    Response.Write "State: " & (rs.Fields("State")) & "<br>"
    Response.Write "Zip: " & (rs.Fields("Zip")) & "<br>"

%>

</table>

</font>
</body>
</html>
```

You can see that the drill-down is accomplished with the QueryString property of the ASP Request object. This property represents the parameters included at the end of the URL submitted to the server. Your scripting code can act on these parameters in any way you want.

You pass a query string in a URL by appending a question mark and then including the query variable or variables. For example, to view the detail for customer 123 using detail.asp, you'd use the URL:

```
http://localhost/novelty/detail.asp?CID=123
```

These URLs are embedded in the page generated by drill.asp, preventing the user from having to enter them manually.

Figure 11.10 shows what the browser looks like after the user clicks on a customer to view its detail.

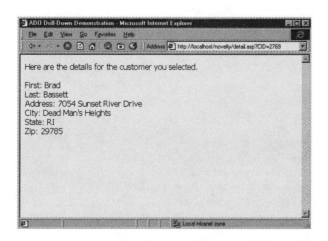

Figure 11.10
You can view the detail after clicking a hyperlink in the Web browser.

Code Example: You can find the code discussed in this section in the directory \vbdb\code\11-Internet\Drill. For information on how to install the sample files on the CD that accompanies this book, see the section "Installing the Example Files" in the introduction at the beginning of this book.

Using Components with ASP Scripting

ASP applications work best when they're used in conjunction with ActiveX components such as ActiveX DLLs. This is the case from both a performance perspective and from the perspective of ease of programming.

Since you already have a component that permits you to access the Novelty database, it should be trivial to write an ASP script to use the code in the component. This is indeed the case.

Listing 11.7 shows an example of a script that retrieves a customer from the database using the CustSvr2 component (created in Chapter 8).

Listing 11.7   Retrieving Detail on a Customer Using an ActiveX Component

```
<html>
<head>
<title>
ADO Drill-Down Demonstration
</title>
</head>

<body bgcolor=#ffffff>
<font face='Tahoma, Arial, Helvetica'>

<p>Here are the details for the customer you selected.

<p>

<%

    Set MyCust = CreateObject("CustSvr4.CCustomer")
    MyCust.GetData Request.QueryString("CID")

    Response.Write "First: " & (MyCust.FirstName) & "<br>"
    Response.Write "Last: " & (MyCust.LastName) & "<br>"
    Response.Write "Address: " & (MyCust.Address) & "<br>"
    Response.Write "City: " & (MyCust.City) & "<br>"
    Response.Write "State: " & (MyCust.State) & "<br>"
    Response.Write "Zip: " & (MyCust.Zip) & "<br>"
```

```
%>

</table>

</font>
</body>
</html>
```

Not only is this code easier to read and understand than the previous version of detail.asp, it also runs faster. This is because most of the work performed by the query is handled by the compiled ActiveX DLL component rather than the script. What's more, placing calls to components has an additional benefit: If something changes, either in the code that implements your business rules or in the structure of the database, you don't have to go searching through dozens (or even hundreds) of script files to change every reference to the database. Since all database access is channeled through one place—the ActiveX DLL compo-nent—your application becomes easy to change and evolve over time.

> **Code Example:** You can find the code discussed in this section in the script files Drillx.asp and Detailx.asp, located in the directory \vbdb\code\11-Internet\CustSvr. This directory also contains a copy of the ActiveX DLL component CustSvr2, originally introduced in Chapter 8.
>
> For information on how to install the sample files on the CD that accompa-nies this book, see the section "Installing the Example Files" in the introduc-tion at the beginning of this book.

SUMMARY

In Chapter 10, you learned how to take advantage of the newest database access object model, ActiveX Data Objects (ADO). This chapter takes that a step fur-ther, giving you a crash course in creating dynamic Web sites using Active Server Pages (ASP), in conjunction with ADO, to permit Internet users to access your database.

In this chapter, you also learned how to use ADO in conjunction with a Visual Basic component. If you develop software targeted for both the corporate LAN and the Web, this sets up a situation where you can share similar database access code between your VB applications and your ASP.

The remaining chapters in this book explore the challenges of creating database-enabled user interfaces with Visual Basic. In Chapter 12, "User-Interface Controls," you're shown how to use the basic user interface controls that ship with Visual Basic in your database client application.

QUESTIONS AND ANSWERS

Q. **I like the idea of using Active Server Pages, but using Notepad to create and manage my database-enabled Web site is driving me buggy. Is there an alternative?**

A. Microsoft Visual InterDev may be what you're looking for. This development environment gives you the ability to create and manage complex Web sites that contain both server- and client-side scripting. The scripts themselves can be written in either VBScript or JScript, Microsoft's flavor of JavaScript. One of Visual InterDev's big features is its capability to create basic data-enabled Web sites through the use of wizards. Visual InterDev is beyond the scope of this book, but it's definitely worth looking into if you're planning a large Web database development project. For more information on Visual InterDev, see the Microsoft Web site at
`http://msdn.microsoft.com/vinterdev/`.

User-Interface Controls

Using Intrinsic Data-Aware Controls

Using Data-Aware ActiveX Controls

Creating Database-Aware ActiveX Controls

12

The construction of a database-aware user interface isn't one of the most technically challenging tasks a database developer can take on. Visual Basic gives you so many options—not all of which are straightforward or intuitive—that it's helpful to have a guide to what's out there.

This chapter provides an overview of the user-interface components you typically use in your Visual Basic applications. The chapter's divided into two sections: *intrinsic controls*, which work with all versions and editions of Visual Basic, and *ActiveX controls*, which are add-on components available with the Professional and Enterprise editions of VB.

Note: A few of the user-interface controls that come with the Professional and Enterprise editions of VB are so chock full of features, they have their own chapters. Chapter 13, "Using the DBGrid and Apex True DBGrid Controls," covers the DBGrid control, while Chapter 14, "Using the MSFlexGrid, Hierarchical FlexGrid, and VideoSoft VSFLEX Controls," covers the MSFlex control.

USING INTRINSIC DATA-AWARE CONTROLS

Visual Basic comes with a number of user-interface controls out of the box. These controls, known as *intrinsic controls*, are the most basic and most commonly used controls in Windows applications. They are also easy to use and don't require much effort to deploy. Most of them can connect to a field in a database directly through a Visual Basic data control or other data source, such as a DataEnvironment designer.

This section takes you a step further than the introduction to the VB Data control in Chapter 1, "Database Basics." This section presents all the controls that are bindable to data sources and gives you some ideas about how to use controls that aren't intrinsically "database aware."

ENTERING DATA WITH THE TEXTBOX CONTROL

The TextBox control is most commonly used to display and permit users to edit textual and numeric data from a database. Because it's an intrinsic Windows control, the TextBox is available with every edition of Visual Basic. It does not require an additional file to be distributed to users when you deploy your application.

Chapter 1 shows you an example of how to hook up a TextBox control to a field in a database through a data control. This section demonstrates a few additional properties of the TextBox control related to database access.

> **Note:** The TextBox control can store a limited amount of data. If you're interested in permitting users to manipulate a large amount of data, you may want to consider using the RichTextBox control or a third-party data-aware textbox control instead. The RichTextBox control comes with the Professional and Enterprise editions of Visual Basic; it's introduced in the section "Displaying Formatted Data with the RichTextBox Control" later in this chapter.

Detecting a Change in Bound Data with the *DataChanged* Property   You can determine whether data has been changed in a bound control by inspecting the value of the control's DataChanged property. This is useful if your application needs to do some processing based on a user changing data at runtime.

Although this section's DataChanged example shows how to use the property with a bound TextBox control, the property exists for many data-aware controls.

Listing 12.1 gives an example of how to use the DataChanged property. In this example, the property indicates whether a user altered data in a database browser application using a DAO Data control. This code inspects the value of the DataChanged property of each TextBox control in the form's Controls collection, setting the dirty flag bChanged to True if it detects a text box whose data has been changed. In the command button's Click event, the application displays an alert that the data has been changed.

Listing 12.1   Using the *DataChanged* Property to Detect Changes in Bound Text Boxes

```
Option Explicit

' References DAO 3.51.

Private Sub Form_Load()
    Data1.DatabaseName = "..\..\DB\novelty.mdb"
End Sub


Private Sub cmdChanged_Click()
Dim t As Control
Dim bChanged As Boolean

    bChanged = False

    For Each t In frmTextBox.Controls
        If TypeName(t) = "TextBox" Then
            If t.DataChanged Then
                bChanged = True
            End If
        End If
    Next

    If bChanged = True Then
        MsgBox "The data has been changed. " & _
            "Be sure to save this record!", _
            vbExclamation
    Else
        MsgBox "There's no need to save this one."
    End If

End Sub
```

Code Example: You can find the code discussed in this section in the project TxChange.vbp, located in the directory \vbdb\code\12-UIControls\ TxChange. For information on how to install the sample files on the CD that accompanies this book, see the section "Installing the Example Files" in the introduction at the beginning of this book.

Validating Data Using Control Events It's common to provide some level of data-entry validation in a form. Although this code becomes more reusable if you take it out of the form and place it in a middle-tier component (as discussed in Chapter 7, "Database Access with Classes"), occasionally you'll want to perform light validation (such as data type-checking) at the UI level.

Visual Basic 6.0 provides a new event you can use to check data entry in the user interface. The Validate event is triggered when a control is about to lose the focus. Unlike the LostFocus event, this permits you to keep the focus on a field that has failed a validation rule.

For example, say your application prohibits users from entering a customer with a ZIP code of fewer than five characters. You might use the Validate event to inform the users when they've entered an invalid ZIP code. The code (using the control array-based user interface introduced in the previous section) looks like Listing 12.2.

Listing 12.2   Using the *Validate* Event to Check Data Entry

```
Private Sub TextBoxArray_Validate(Index As Integer, Cancel As Boolean)
    Select Case Index
        Case txtZip
            If Len(TextBoxArray(Index).Text) < 5 Then
                MsgBox "Please enter a five digit Zip code.", _
                        vbExclamation, _
                        "Validation Error"
                ' Don't move the focus
                Cancel = True
            End If

        '****Other text boxes would be
        '        validated here

        Case Else

    End Select

End Sub
```

This code checks to see if the ZIP code contains five characters. If it does not, it displays a message box and sets the Validate event's Cancel parameter to True, which prevents the focus from moving off the control.

Note, however, that this code does not automatically support the auto-select feature discussed earlier in this section. Because that functionality exists in the control array's `GotFocus` event, you would need to call it explicitly. To do this, insert the code

```
TextBoxArray_GotFocus Index
```

immediately after setting the `Validate` event's `Cancel` parameter to True.

All user interface controls in VB6 trigger the `Validate` event by default. If you don't want a particular control to trigger the `Validate` event, set the control's `CausesValidation` property to False. This will prevent you from having to write elaborate `Select Case` blocks to handle each field in your control array, whether or not the form handles validation.

Note also that while this example uses text boxes, these techniques apply to all controls in Visual Basic.

> **Code Example:** You can find the code discussed in this section in the project `Validate.vbp`, located in the directory `\vbdb\code\12-VSFlex\Validate`. For information on how to install the sample files on the CD that accompanies this book, see the section "Installing the Example Files" in the introduction at the beginning of this book.

Creating Faster Data Entry Interfaces Using Text Boxes   There are a variety of tricks you can use to make data entry faster using text boxes. Most of these techniques require very little coding.

Sometimes it's desirable to advance the focus from one text box to the next programmatically. You might do this in situations where you want data entry to go more quickly, preventing the user from having to type Tab to move to the next field. Of course, this technique might be useful in any application, but it's particularly common in database-driven applications where speed of data entry is crucial.

You can create a user interface such as this in VB by using the `Change` event of the text box control in conjunction with the control's `SetFocus` method. This works for any type of data-entry control, but it's most often used with text boxes.

For example, in an application that accepts data entry for customers, you might have text boxes for address, city, state, and ZIP code. The lengths of addresses and cities aren't predictable, but the lengths of states and ZIP codes are. You can write this code to cause the focus to advance automatically after the user inputs a two-character state code and a five-digit ZIP code:

```
Private Sub txtState_Change()
    If Len(txtState.Text) >= 2 Then
        txtZip.SetFocus
    End If
End Sub


Private Sub txtZip_Change()
    If Len(txtZip.Text) >= 5 Then
        cmdSave.SetFocus
    End If
End Sub
```

Although this code is functional, it depends on the ZIP Code text box following the state box and the save button following the ZIP Code box. If you later add a new text box to your form or change the order of text boxes on the form, this code may not work quite right. It might be better to assign the text boxes to a control array. This lets you handle the automatic focus-advancing centrally, using a single event handler for all the text boxes' change events, as shown in Listing 12.3.

Listing 12.3   Using a Control Array to Automatically Set the Focus in a Data Entry Application

```
' These constants map to
' indexes of the control array.
Const txtState = 4
Const txtZip = 5


Private Sub TextBoxArray_Change(Index As Integer)
Dim bAdvance As Boolean

    Select Case Index
        Case txtState
            If Len(TextBoxArray(Index).Text) > 2 Then
                bAdvance = True
            End If

        Case txtZip
            If Len(TextBoxArray(Index).Text) >= 5 Then
                bAdvance = True
```

```
            End If

        Case Else
            bAdvance = False

    End Select

    If bAdvance = True Then
        TextBoxArray(Index + 1).SetFocus
    End If
End Sub
```

To create a control array, you assign all the text boxes on the form the same Name property. When VB displays a message box asking you if you'd like to create a control array, answer Yes.

Creating a control array also lets you easily perform other common interface chores, such as automatically selecting the text when a text box gets the focus. This makes it much easier for the user to overtype a value in a text box without having to use the mouse.

To automatically select text in a text box, write code in the text box's GotFocus event that sets the control's SelStart property to zero and its SelLength property to the length of text in the field. Once again, if your text boxes are in a control array, as in the previous example, this code becomes very easy to implement. Code Listing 12.4 shows how to do this.

Listing 12.4   Using a Control Array to Automatically Select Text When the Text Box Receives Focus

```
Private Sub TextBoxArray_GotFocus(Index As Integer)
    With TextBoxArray(Index)
        .SelStart = 0
        .SelLength = Len(.Text)
    End With
End Sub
```

This code assumes your form has an array of text boxes called TextBoxArray. Note that because it's based on a control array, this code will work for any form containing a control array named TextBoxArray, no matter how many text boxes it contains.

Code Example: You can find the code discussed in this section in the project **FastUI.vbp**, located in the directory **\vbdb\code\12-UIControls\FastUI**. For information on how to install the sample files on the CD that accompanies this book, see the section "Installing the Example Files" in the introduction at the beginning of this book.

BINDING TO THE DATAENVIRONMENT DESIGNER

New to VB6 is the ability to create a data-bound user interface based on a DataEnvironment designer. Because you can share DataEnvironment designers across multiple forms and multiple applications, this gives you all the features and ease of programming found in a data-bound application with a greater level of reusability. Binding to a DataEnvironment designer is actually faster than binding to a data control because you don't have to bind each individual control to the data source. In fact, because the DE supports drag-and-drop, you don't even have to create the UI controls.

Follow these steps to create a data-bound user interface based on the DE designer:

1. In a new Visual Basic project, add a DataEnvironment designer by selecting the Project, Add DataEnvironment command. A DE designer appears.

2. Open the Data View window by choosing the menu command View, Data View Window. Drag a table (such as tblCustomer) from the data view window onto your DataEnvironment designer. (If your Data View window doesn't contain a link to a data source, you'll need to create one. Creating data links in the data view window is covered in Chapter 2, "Queries.")

3. The table appears under a new connection in the DataEnvironment designer.

4. Open a form.

5. Click-drag the table from the DataEnvironment designer onto your form. The database-bound data entry interface is generated automatically by Visual Basic, as shown in Figure 12.1.

6. Run the application. You should be able to see the first record in the tblCustomer table.

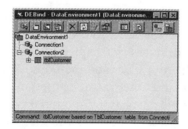

Figure 12.1
The data entry interface is created automatically by dragging and dropping from the DataEnvironment designer.

Note: You can bind a user interface control to a DataEnvironment designer by setting the control's `DataSource` property to the name of the DataEnvironment designer, then setting the control's `DataField` property to the name of the field the control you want to bind to. This technique is identical to the way you bind a user interface control to a data control.

Creating a Navigation Interface in a DataEnvironment-Bound Interface

While creating a user interface using the DataEnvironment designer is fast, it doesn't immediately provide all the functionality of the Data control. For example, there's no way to navigate from one record to the next. You can add this functionality easily, though, by writing code.

To do this, create four command buttons on the form. Assign them the captions First, Previous, Next, and Last.

In the form's code, write the code shown in Listing 12.5.

Listing 12.5 Code to Provide Navigation in a User Interface Bound to a DataEnvironment Designer

```
Private Sub cmdFirst_Click()
    DataEnvironment1.rstblCustomer.MoveFirst
End Sub

Private Sub cmdLast_Click()
    DataEnvironment1.rstblCustomer.MoveLast
End Sub

Private Sub cmdNext_Click()
    DataEnvironment1.rstblCustomer.MoveNext
End Sub

Private Sub cmdPrevious_Click()
    DataEnvironment1.rstblCustomer.MovePrevious
End Sub
```

In this example, `rstblCustomer` is the name the DataEnvironment designer gave to the `Recordset` object that represents your Customer table. This is a normal ADO `Recordset` object (introduced in Chapter 10, "ActiveX Data Objects"), which means it has all the properties and methods of any ADO `Recordset` object. The `MoveNext`, `MovePrevious`, and other methods used in the code, then, are using the `Recordset` object's normal navigation functionality to move through the recordset. You can use the other properties and methods of the `Recordset` object to provide additional functionality to your application—providing the ability to save data using the `Update` method, create new records using the `AddNew` method, and so forth.

Code Example: **This code discussed in this section exists in the project** **`DEBind.vbp`, located in the directory `\vbdb\code\12-UIControls\DEBind`. For** **information on how to install the sample files on the CD that accompanies** **this book, see the section "Installing the Example Files" in the introduction** **at the beginning of this book.**

You can make this code even more elegant and compact if you add all four buttons to a control array. This lets you handle all the navigational chores in one event, the `Click` event of the control array, instead of the `Click` events of four separate controls. If your control array is called CommandButtonArray, the code will looks like Listing 12.6.

Listing 12.6   Code Adding Four Buttons to the Control Array

```
Private Sub CommandButtonArray_Click(Index As Integer)

    With Novelty.rstblCustomer
        Select Case Index
            Case cmdFirst
                .MoveFirst
            Case cmdPrevious
                .MovePrevious
            Case cmdNext
                .MoveNext
            Case cmdLast
                .MoveLast
            Case Else
                MsgBox "Unhandled case in CommandButtonArray_Click."
        End Select
    End With

End Sub
```

Making Data in the DataEnvironment Designer Editable   When you bind data to a DAO Data control, records are editable by default. This is because DAO's philosophy is to make things as easy as possible on the programmer.

However, when you bind to a DataEnvironment designer, you're using ADO to get access to the data. In ADO, performance is given higher priority over convenience of programming. As a result, connections to data sources in ADO are generally in read-only mode by default. This is the case for the DataEnvironment designer. In fact, if you bind to a DataEnvironment designer using the techniques described earlier in this chapter and then attempt to change the data, you'll get a cryptic runtime error.

Here's how to make the data provided by the DataEnvironment designer available for read-write access:

1. In the DataEnvironment designer, right-click the table you want to access.

2. From the pop-up menu, select Properties.

3. Click the Advanced tab. In the Lock Type combo box, select Optimistic. This will lock the record only at the instant it's committed back to the database.

4. Click OK and run the application. You should now be able to edit records. (When you navigate from one record to the next, the changes you make in each record are automatically committed back to the database, just as with the data controls.)

ACCESSING BOOLEAN VALUES WITH THE CHECKBOX CONTROL

You can use the CheckBox control to display a true or false value from a field in a database.

Because it's an intrinsic Windows control, the CheckBox is available with every edition of Visual Basic. It does not require an additional file to be distributed to users when you deploy your application.

Figure 12.2 shows an example of a data entry interface that includes a CheckBox control.

In the database, each customer has a Preferred field that designates whether that customer is a normal or preferred customer. In the user interface, the field is represented by a CheckBox control bound to the field. You bind the CheckBox control to the data source as you would any other bound control, using its DataSource, DataMember, and DataField properties.

Figure 12.2
This data entry interface uses a CheckBox control to represent the Preferred field.

Displaying a Custom Graphical CheckBox   In addition to representing a Boolean field with a check box, you can use the CheckBox control to display images pertaining to the state of the field. You do this by using the Style and Picture properties of the CheckBox control.

By using the Style and Picture properties of the CheckBox control, you can make the control display any bitmap graphic you want. Figure 12.3 shows an example of a graphical CheckBox control with a custom image that makes it look like a command button.

Figure 12.3
A CheckBox control is altered to display custom graphics.

To convert a database-aware CheckBox control to display custom graphics, do the following:

1. Create a database-aware user interface with a CheckBox control bound to a Boolean field.

2. At design time, use the Properties window to set the CheckBox control's Style property to 1 - Graphical. The CheckBox becomes button-like in appearance.

3. Set the CheckBox control's DownPicture property to the filename of the bitmap you want displayed when the value of the field is True (that is, when the current record is for a preferred customer). You can use the bitmap file pref.bmp for this property; the file is in the directory \vbdb\code\12-UIControls\Check.

4. Set the control's Picture property to the bitmap you want displayed when the value of the field is False. You can use the bitmap file norm.bmp for this property; the file is also in \vbdb\code\12-UIControls\Check.

5. Optionally, you may want to set the control's Caption property to an empty string, particularly if the custom graphics contain text of their own. If you don't set the Caption property to nothing, it's possible that the graphic and the CheckBox's caption will interfere with each other.

In order to change the value of the graphical CheckBox control, the user simply clicks it, as he or she would with a normal CheckBox control.

> **Code Example:** You can find an example of a data-bound custom graphical check box in the project Check.vbp, located in the directory \vbdb\code\ 12-UIControls\Check. For information on how to install the sample files on the CD that accompanies this book, see the section "Installing the Example Files" in the introduction at the beginning of this book.

USING THE LISTBOX CONTROL TO DISPLAY DATA

You can use the ListBox control to display items in a user's choice list. You must be careful when using the ListBox control to display data from a database— although the control is database aware, there are limits to how much data it can store and display.

> **Note:** The ListBox control has the ability to bind to a field in the database, but it doesn't have the ability to use a recordset as the basis of the list of choices it displays. This limitation will come as a disappointment to Microsoft Access developers, since Access's combo and list box controls do have this capability. However, there are ActiveX controls that provide this functionality. The DBList control is discussed later in this chapter, and data-bound list controls are discussed later in this book.

The ListBox control is available in every edition of Visual Basic. It does not require an additional file to be distributed to users when you deploy your application.

Adding Items to the ListBox Control   To add items to the ListBox control, use its AddItem method. Here's the syntax of the AddItem method:

```
List1.AddItem data, [index]
```

The *data* argument represents the information you want added to the ListBox control.

The *index* argument indicates where in the list you want to insert the new item. This argument is optional; if you omit it, the item is added to the end of the list—unless the list is sorted, in which case the item is always added in the correct sorted order in the list. (You can automatically sort the items in a ListBox control by setting its Sorted property to True, but bear in mind that this will always be slower than sorting the data using the ORDER BY clause of a SQL statement.)

For example, to populate a list box named lstStockItem with the items Squirting Boutonniere, Plastic Vomit, and Fake Ants, you'd use the following code:

```
lstFruit.AddItem "Squirting Boutonniere"
lstFruit.AddItem "Plastic Vomit"
lstFruit.AddItem "Fake Ants"
```

Use this code to add an item to the top of the list:

```
lstStockItem.AddItem "Windup Dinosaur", 0
```

In order to display a database-generated list of information in a ListBox control, loop through the records in a Recordset object, adding information from each record to the ListBox control using the AddItem method.

Using the ListBox's *ListIndex* Property   Items in a ListBox control are numbered starting at 0; this number is referred to as the item's *index*. If no item is currently selected, the value of the ListBox's ListIndex property is –1.

Setting the ListIndex property to a value causes an item in the ListBox control to be selected; this is helpful in a database access application if you want to set a default value for the control. For example, in the list of stock items you populated earlier, if you wanted "Squirting Boutonniere" to be the default, you use the following code to populate the list box:

```
lstStockItem.AddItem "Squirting Boutonniere"
lstStockItem.AddItem "Plastic Vomit"
lstStockItem.AddItem "Fake Ants"

lstStockItem.ListIndex = 0
```

You can retrieve the value of the current item in the ListBox control by setting its ListIndex property, then inspecting its Text property. For example, to determine the textual value of the initial item in a ListBox control, use the following code:

```
lstStockItem.ListIndex = 0
strValue = lstStockItem.Text
```

This code would have the potentially undesirable side effect of altering the currently selected item in the list box. You can avoid this by using the `List` property. The `List` property returns the contents of a ListBox control in the form of an array. For example, use the following code to retrieve the initial value of a ListBox control using the `List` property:

```
strValue = lstStockItem.List(0).Text
```

Remember when you're using this kind of code that the index numbering of a ListBox control starts at zero.

Using a ListBox to Provide a Static List of Choices   You can use a ListBox control to provide the user with a list of choices from which to choose. Do this by binding the ListBox control to a field in the database, then populating the control using its `AddItem` method.

Figure 12.4 shows an example of such an application.

Figure 12.4
This data entry application has a ListBox control that provides a static list of choices.

You create a data entry application with a list box by following these general steps:

1. Create a bound database access application using a data source such as a data control or DataEnvironment designer and bound controls linked to fields.

2. For the field you want to link to a ListBox, create a ListBox control and set its `DataSource` and `DataField` properties as you would for a text box.

3. In code, populate the ListBox with a list of choices that are appropriate for the field.

Listing 12.7 shows a sample application that populates a ListBox control used for data entry.

Listing 12.7   Populating the List of Choices Provided by a ListBox Control

```
Option Explicit

Private Sub Form_Load()

    lstZip.AddItem "80448"
    lstZip.AddItem "81735"
    lstZip.AddItem "84493"
    lstZip.AddItem "88475"
    lstZip.AddItem "88944"
    lstZip.AddItem "94117"
    lstZip.AddItem "94483"
    lstZip.AddItem "99485"

End Sub
```

To finish this application, assign the DataSource property of the ListBox to a data source such as a data control or DataEnvironment designer. You then assign the ListBox control's DataField property to Zip (the name of the field that contains the customer's ZIP Code).

Using the ListBox control this way also has the side effect of performing airtight validation on the data-entry user. It's impossible to enter bad data if the bad data doesn't appear in the list of choices.

Code Example: You can find an example of the code discussed in this section in the project ListPop.vbp, located in the directory \vbdb\code\ 12-UIControls\ListPop. For information on how to install the sample files on the CD that accompanies this book, see the section "Installing the Example Files" in the introduction at the beginning of this book.

Of course, hard-coding a list of choices is unsatisfying if the list of choices changes frequently. Ideally, you'd provide some way for the list to be dynamically populated at runtime from a source other than your Visual Basic code. One of the most logical places for the list to reside is in the database itself. The following section gives an example of how to populate a ListBox with data from a database.

Creating a Recordset to Populate a ListBox Control   When you're using a control that displays a list of records, you generally present a list of choices to the user. However, if those choices are hard-coded, it becomes very difficult to alter the list over time. It's often better to store the list of choices in the database, then populate the list box controls at runtime.

Unfortunately, while connecting a database-aware control to a database requires no code, populating a ListBox control with the contents of a recordset requires code. Fortunately, the code required to perform this operation is not difficult to implement.

Listing 12.8 gives an example of an application that populates a ListBox control with the contents of an ADO Recordset object contained in a DataEnvironment designer called Novelty.

Listing 12.8   Populating a ListBox Control with the Items from a Recordset

```
Option Explicit

Private Sub Form_Load()
Dim rs As ADODB.Recordset

    Set rs = Novelty.rstblCustomer
    rs.Open

    Do Until rs.EOF
        lstCustomer.AddItem rs!LastName & ", " & rs!FirstName
        lstCustomer.ItemData(lstCustomer.NewIndex) = rs!ID
        rs.MoveNext
    Loop

    Set rs = Nothing

End Sub
```

This code adds the contents of the tblCustomer table to the ListBox control, as shown in Figure 12.5.

This code displays a message box showing the primary key of the record when you click it. (The technique used to do this is discussed in the section "Storing a Hidden Key Column in a ListBox Control Using the ItemData Property" later in this chapter.)

Note that if you add the results of a very large query to the ListBox control, you experience the misery of a system crash after the ListBox control attempts to blindly suck in all the data you give it. In this example, I cheated by adding a parameter to the DataEnvironment designer's CommandText property; it only queries the first hundred records from the database. This technique isn't as cheesy as you might think, though. Adding a WHERE clause to a query is one of the best and simplest ways to limit the amount of data displayed in the user interface. In a real application you'd call a parameterized query and display choices based on some user input, like the first few letters of the customer's last name or her ZIP code.

Ultimately, the primary rationale for using a data-aware control instead of a conventional control like the ListBox isn't its data storage capacity, but the fact that ListBox controls can take a really long time to populate. If you're interested in a control that stores or displays a large number of items—say, hundreds or thousands of items—consider using the DBList control, discussed in the section "Displaying Data in Lists with the DBCombo and DBList Controls" later in this chapter.

Figure 12.5
This ListBox control has been populated with data from a database.

 Code Example: You can find the code discussed in this chapter in the project ListRS.vbp, located in the directory \vbdb\code\12-UIControls\ListRS. For information on how to install the sample files on the CD that accompanies this book, see the section "Installing the Example Files" in the introduction at the beginning of this book.

Storing a Hidden Key Column in a ListBox Control Using the *ItemData* Property   The ListBox control has the ability to invisibly store a long integer alongside any element in the list. This lets you easily refer to the primary key of a record without actually displaying that record's primary key.

You store and retrieve this long integer value through the ItemData property of the ListBox control. To set the ItemData property of an item in a ListBox control, you must know its ListIndex. This syntax of the ItemData property is as follows:

```
List1.ItemData(List1.ListIndex) = keyvalue
```

This code assigns the value *keyvalue* to the currently selected item in the ListBox control.

You typically set this property at the time you're populating it with data, when no items in the list are selected. This leaves you with the alternative of assigning the ItemData property to the last item you added to the list. However, there's a problem here. To assign an ItemData value, you need to know the index of the item in the ListBox control to which you're assigning a key. How do you know what index number was assigned to the most recently added item in the list? You'd think that the index number would be equal to the number of items in the list, but that's not always the case. If the ListBox control's Sorted property is set to True, the last item you added could have any index number. This is because the control sorts the new entry before it adds it to the list; a new entry for a customer named Aaron that would normally take the thirtieth position in the list might be assigned index number 1 because of the way it alphabetizes in the list.

Fortunately, the ListBox control gets you out of this conundrum by providing a special property, NewIndex. This property always returns the index number of the most recently added item in the list. So, to assign the ItemData property to the item that was last added to the ListBox, you use the expression:

```
lstCustomer.ItemData(lstCustomer.NewIndex) = keyvalue
```

You saw an example of how to populate a ListBox control with a record's primary key back in Listing 12.8. Listing 12.9 gives an example of how to retrieve the primary key of a record displayed in a ListBox control using the ItemData property.

Listing 12.9   Retrieving a Record's Primary Key from a ListBox Using the *ItemData* Property

```
Private Sub lstCustomer_Click()
    MsgBox "The primary key of this item is " & _
           lstCustomer.ItemData(lstCustomer.ListIndex), _
           vbInformation
End Sub
```

This code displays a message box when the user clicks a customer in the ListBox. Figure 12.6 shows what happens when this code is run.

In a real application, you could use this value to populate the foreign key of a related table (such as the tblOrder table, if you were creating an order entry system), or you could simply use it as a way to drill down on the detail for the record the user clicked. In this case, the primary key stored in the ItemData property permits you to easily query each individual record as the user clicks it.

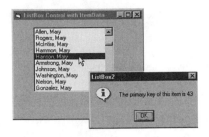

USING THE STANDARD COMBOBOX CONTROL

You can use Visual Basic's standard ComboBox control to display values in a manner nearly identical to the ListBox control. The main difference between the ListBox and the ComboBox control is the fact that the ComboBox control displays choices in a drop-down list.

The ComboBox control is available in every edition of Visual Basic. It does not require an additional file to be distributed to users when you deploy your application.

Although the ComboBox control is fully data aware, it makes more sense to use the DBCombo control to display the contents of large lists. This is for performance reasons, as well as because the ComboBox is limited in how much data it can store. (These limitations also affect the ListBox control.) Visual Basic's data-aware list controls are introduced in the "Displaying Data in Lists with the DBCombo and DBList Controls" section later in this chapter.

DISPLAYING READ-ONLY DATA WITH THE LABEL CONTROL

The VB Label control is data aware; however, it's inherently noneditable. As a result, it's ideal for displaying data in a situation where you don't want users to be able to alter data.

Because it's an intrinsic Windows control, the Label is available with every edition of Visual Basic. It does not require an additional file to be distributed to users when you deploy your application.

This example uses the ADO Data and Label controls to provide a pure, read-only database browser with a grand total of zero lines of code. To construct this application, do the following:

1. In Visual Basic, create a new Standard EXE project.

2. Using the Visual Basic toolbox, create a data source such as a data control or DataEnvironment designer.

3. On the form, use labels and text boxes to represent fields in the data source. (For a more realistic example, you can use a Label to represent the ID field of the tblCustomer table, since the ID field is noneditable. The remaining fields can be represented by text boxes.)

4. Set each control's DataSource property to the name of the data control or DataEnvironment designer.

5. Set each Label control's DataField property to the name of the field in the data source you want the label to display.

6. If you're using a DataEnvironment designer, set each control's DataMember property to the name of the table or command that populates the data source.

7. Run the application. Your noneditable data is displayed in soothing shades of noneditable black and gray, as shown in Figure 12.7.

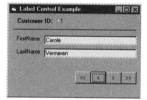

Figure 12.7
A simple database browser application will keep users from mucking around with data that can't be changed anyway.

Code Example: You can find the code discussed in this section in the project Label.vbp, located in the directory \vbdb\code\12-UIControls\Label. For information on how to install the sample files on the CD that accompanies this book, see the section "Installing the Example Files" in the introduction at the beginning of this book.

DISPLAYING BITMAP IMAGES USING THE PICTUREBOX CONTROL
The Visual Basic PictureBox control has the ability to store graphical data. It also has the DataField, DataMember and DataSource properties common to other data-aware controls. However, the PictureBox control can't bind to a Microsoft Access OLE Object field (the type of field that permits you to store binary data such as images). This is the case no matter which data access library (DAO, RDO or ADO) you're using. This makes it essentially useless for creating database-aware interfaces based on data binding.

When you bind a PictureBox control to an Access OLE Object field, things work fine until you hit a record that has data in the field. At that point, if you're using the DAO Data control, you get an Invalid Picture error. If you're bound to the database using the ADO-based DataEnvironment designer, nothing happens. This is the case even though it's trivial to create a Microsoft Access form containing a picture field bound to an OLE Object field.

Binding a PictureBox control to data stored in an OLE Object field has been a problem ever since controls become bindable to database fields in Visual Basic 3.0. As a workaround for this problem, you can instead bind the Visual Basic OLE control to the OLE Object field. This technique is introduced in the "Displaying Binary Objects with the OLE Container Control" section later in this chapter.

If you're brave, it's possible to write code to extract the data from the OLE Object field and assign it to the PictureBox control; Microsoft lists a code example showing how to do this on its Knowledge Base Web site at `http://support.microsoft.com/support/kb/articles/q147/7/27.asp`. Bear in mind, though, that not only is this technique technically tricky, it's also much slower than simply storing graphics in a directory on disk and storing references to their filenames in textual fields in the database.

> **Note:** The PictureBox and Image controls support GIF and JPEG graphics formats, as well as the native Windows BMP graphic format.
>
> There are also third-party picture controls that can bind directly to a Jet OLE Object field that contains images.

Using the Image Control to Display Bitmaps The Visual Basic Image control is designed to display graphics in a manner similar to the PictureBox control. Its main difference is that it's lighter and supports fewer features than that PictureBox control; in fact, it's faster in a number of ways. Frustratingly—but not surprisingly—it suffers from the same inability to bind to and display images from a Jet OLE Object field.

If you want to display images stored in a database without writing a bunch of complicated code, use the Visual Basic OLE Object control introduced in the next section.

DISPLAYING BINARY OBJECTS WITH THE OLE CONTAINER CONTROL

In Windows, Object Linking and Embedding (OLE) is a technology that permits applications to exchange and display each other's data. Using OLE, you can take information from any application that knows about OLE and display and edit it in any other application that knows about OLE.

In Visual Basic, you display OLE data using the OLE Container control. This control permits you to display data created in another application on a Visual Basic form. This control is also database aware, which means it has the ability to bind to an OLE Object field in a Jet database. However, this only works with the DAO Data control or the RDO Remote Data Control; it doesn't work with the ADO Data control or with the DataEnvironment designer.

To use the OLE Container control to display graphical images stored in an OLE Object field, do the following:

1. Create a Visual Basic user interface based on the Data control. Connect the data control to a table or query that contains an OLE Object field. (The table tblCustomerPicture in the novelty.mdb database has such a field.)

2. Create an OLE Container control on the form. When you create an OLE Container control, the Insert Object dialog box appears, as shown in Figure 12.8.

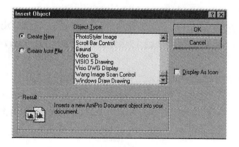

Figure 12.8
The Insert Object dialog box appears when you create an OLE Container control.

3. Dismiss this dialog box by clicking the Cancel button. You don't need to assign an object to this container at this time; instead, the container gets its data from the OLE Object field in the database.

4. Assign the DataSource property of the OLE Container control to the name of the Data control. Assign the DataField property of the container to the name of the OLE Object field in the database.

5. Run the application. For fields that contain data in the OLE Object field, you should see a picture displayed in the OLE Container control like that shown in Figure 12.9.

Figure 12.9
An application displays graphical data using an OLE Container control.

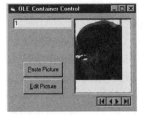

This technique gives you the ability to display information from an OLE Object field. But although you can display data using the OLE Container control without writing code, you must write code to permit the user to insert and edit data in the control. The next few sections describe how to do this.

Inserting Data into an OLE Container Control   Although the OLE Container control works great for displaying graphical data stored in an OLE Object field, you must write code to allow the user to insert data into the field bound to the control.

> **Note: This technique represents another difference between the ways Microsoft Access and Visual Basic let you handle OLE Object data; in Access, you simply create an OLE Object field, and it works correctly with no code.**

Applications that permit you to embed data using OLE typically do so through the Windows Clipboard. Listing 12.10 gives an example of the code your application must execute to permit a user to insert information from the Clipboard into an OLE Object field.

Listing 12.10   An Application That Displays Graphical Data Using the OLE Container Control

```
Option Explicit
'
' References DAO 3.51

Private Sub Form_Load()
    Data1.DatabaseName = "..\..\DB\novelty.mdb"
End Sub
```

```
Private Sub cmdPaste_Click()
    ' Pastes data from clipboard into
    ' Picture field represented by
    ' OLE Container control olePicture.

    ' Allow only embedded (not linked) data.
    olePicture.OLETypeAllowed = vbOLEEmbedded

    If olePicture.PasteOK = True Then
        olePicture.Paste
    Else
        MsgBox "The information on the clipboard can't be pasted.",_
               vbExclamation
    End If

End Sub
```

Follow these steps to insert an image using this application:

1. Create an image using any application that permits you to create or handle images. You can use the Paintbrush application that comes with Windows if you want to create your own image; otherwise, you can use another application such as Internet Explorer to find a prefabricated image.

2. Use the application's technique for copying an image to the Clipboard. For most image-handling applications, this entails selecting the image, then choosing the menu command Edit, Copy. For Internet Explorer, you can right-click the image, then select Copy from the pop-up menu.

3. Run your VB application and click the Paste Picture button. The image you copied should be pasted into the OLE Container control.

When you move off the current record using the data control, the data you pasted in the control is saved in the database.

> **Code Example:** You can find the code discussed in this section in the project `OLE.vbp`, located in the directory `\vbdb\code\12-UIControls\OLE`. For information on how to install the sample files on the CD that accompanies this book, see the section "Installing the Example Files" in the introduction at the beginning of this book.

Editing Data in an OLE Container Control   Use the OLE Container control's DoVerb method to edit the information contained in an OLE Container control. Executing the DoVerb method causes the server application responsible for the data to launch, providing an editing interface for the data. This is particularly handy, because your application doesn't have to take responsibility for providing an interface for every new type of data that comes along. It only needs a place to store OLE Objects.

There are a few ways to open an OLE Object using the DoVerb method. Listing 12.11 gives an example of a command button that simply launches the server application—one of the simplest ways of providing an OLE editing interface.

Listing 12.11   Launching the Server Application of an OLE Container Object for Editing

```
Private Sub cmdEdit_Click()
    ' Open the data in its own window
    olePicture.DoVerb vbOLEOpen
End Sub
```

The vbOLEOpen constant instructs the OLE Container to open the server application in its own window. There are other alternatives to this, most notably the option of in-place activation, in which your application's interface automatically trades places with the interface of the OLE server, but that's more complicated to implement.

To demonstrate how this code works, do the following:

1. Run your VB application.

2. Move to a record that contains something in its Picture field.

3. Click the Edit Picture button.

4. The Paintbrush application launches.

5. Using the Paintbrush application's tools, alter the picture in some way. You may notice that the representation of the data in your application changes as you alter the data in Paintbrush.

6. When you're done editing, select File, Exit and Return. The data in your VB application is updated.

If you hit the Edit Picture object for a record that has no picture, an error is generated. You'll want to trap that error and have your application do something intelligent in response to this situation.

Using Data-Aware ActiveX Controls

The controls discussed up to this point in this chapter are available to any Visual Basic developer. Most are basic controls that appear in any Windows application, and most are fairly unspectacular in appearance and behavior.

The controls in this section come with the Professional and Enterprise editions of Visual Basic. Unlike the user-interface controls introduced earlier in this chapter, the controls aren't provided by the operating system. Instead, you must distribute additional controls to users' computers for your applications to use them. This isn't a big deal (most of this is handled transparently for you by the Visual Basic Package and Deployment Wizard), but in some cases it can be an issue—particularly when you're trying to keep your application's distributable footprint small, or if you're concerned about issues pertaining to component versioning.

CONTROLLING TEXT INPUT WITH THE MASKEDEDIT CONTROL

In many situations when building a data entry interface, you need to give users a visual cue. For example, if the field they're entering is a phone number, are they supposed to type an area code? How about the parentheses around the area code? If they're supposed to type the parentheses, why? If the parentheses are the same for every record, why doesn't the computer provide them instead of making the user type them?

The MaskedEdit control provides a solution to those and other problems. In addition to providing a visual cue for users entering data in a field, it provides validation at the user-interface level, thus preventing users from entering bad information in the control.

The MaskedEdit control comes with the Professional and Enterprise editions of Visual Basic. Its filename is MSMASK32.OCX. To use the Masked Edit control in your Visual Basic project, do the following:

1. In Visual Basic, select Project Components.

2. The Components dialog box appears. In the list of components, scroll down until you see Microsoft Masked Edit Control 6.0.

3. Check the control in the list, then click OK. The Masked Edit control is added to your Visual Basic toolbox, as shown in Figure 12.10.

Figure 12.10
The Microsoft Masked Edit control is added to the Visual Basic toolbox.

Setting the Input Mask Using the *Mask* Property   When you're using the MaskedEdit control, you have the ability to force the user to enter information according to a certain pattern. For example, in a ZIP code field, you can force the user to enter five or more characters.

The rules that govern what a user can enter in a Masked Input control are called an *input mask*. You assign an input mask to a Masked Input control using the control's Mask property.

The Mask property is composed of a string of characters that indicate the pattern to be entered in the Masked Edit box. The characters you can use as part of this string are summarized in Table 12.1.

Table 12.1 Characters Used in the *Mask* Property of the Masked Edit Control	
Character	**Description**
#	Digit
.	Decimal
,	Thousands separator
:	Hours and minutes separator
/	Day and date separator
\	Escape code to treat the next character in the string literally
&	Character placeholder
>	Converts characters to uppercase
<	Converts characters to lowercase
A	Required alphanumeric character

Character	Description
a	Optional alphanumeric character
9	Optional numeric character
C	Optional character or space
?	Letter
Anything else	Displayed as entered

As an example, if you wanted to force the user to enter a seven-digit phone number, you'd set the Mask property to the following:

```
#######
```

For information on how to display data differently than the way it's entered, see the discussion of the Format property in the following section.

If you want the user to enter a value such as an inventory number beginning with a letter and ending in five numbers, and you want to make sure that the first character is always displayed in uppercase, use a Mask property such as the following:

```
>?99999
```

> **Note:** If you set the Mask property to an empty string, the Masked Input control behaves like a normal TextBox control.

When users violate the mask you've set, your application makes an audible beep, and the bad characters they entered are not accepted.

Changing the Display of Information Using the *Format* Property In addition to using the Mask property to require the user to enter information in a certain pattern, you can also specify how the information in the control should be formatted on the screen. You do this using the MaskedEdit control's Format property.

For example, if a field stores a telephone number that you want displayed with parentheses and dashes, you'd use a Format string such as the following:

```
(###) ###-####
```

This means that the user only needs to type the 10-digit telephone number, as shown in Figure 12.11. The extra formatting characters, such as the parentheses, show up automatically.

Figure 12.11
The user enters this data into a formatted field that's using the MaskedEdit control.

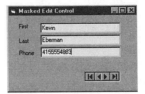

After the focus moves off the MaskedEdit control, the formatting kicks in and the data is displayed with the proper formatting, as Figure 12.12 shows.

Figure 12.12
The MaskedEdit control displays the formatted information.

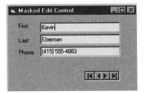

Code Example: You can find the code discussed in this section in the project `MaskEdit.vbp`, located in the directory `\vbdb\code\12-UIControls\MaskEdit`. For information on how to install the sample files on the CD that accompanies this book, see the section "Installing the Example Files" in the introduction at the beginning of this book.

Formatting Data Without Using the MaskedEdit Control New to VB6 is a feature that lets you take advantage of some of the functionality of the MaskedEdit control, but using a conventional text box. The `DataFormat` property lets you perform the data-formatting job of the MaskedEdit control, although it doesn't let you restrict user's input or provide a cue as to what's appropriate to enter into a text box the way the MaskedEdit control does.

Here's how to provide a data format for a conventional text box:

1. Create a normal text box control. Optionally, bind the control to a field provided by a data source, such as a data control or the DataEnvironment designer. (The Phone field in the tblCustomer table, used in the previous example, works perfectly for this.)

2. From the Properties window, click the ellipsis button to the right of the `DataFormat` property.

3. The property page for the `DataFormat` property appears. From the list of formats, select Custom.

4. The Format String text box becomes available. Enter a format string appropriate for a phone number, such as this:

```
(###) ###-####
```

The property page should look like Figure 12.13.

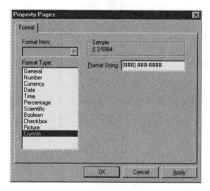

When you run the application, the data in the bound text box should be formatted exactly the same as the way the MaskedEdit control formats it.

Code Example: You can find an example of the code discussed in this section in the project `MaskEdit.vbp`, located in the directory `\vbdb\code\ 12-UIControls\MaskEdit`. For information on how to install the sample files on the CD that accompanies this book, see the section "Installing the Example Files" in the introduction at the beginning of this book.

DISPLAYING FORMATTED DATA WITH THE RICHTEXTBOX CONTROL

The RichTextBox control looks like a conventional TextBox control but has the ability to store much more text. In addition, the control can store and display text formatting. All that, coupled with the control's ability to bind directly to a database field, makes the RichTextBox control a formidable bit of ActiveX juju indeed.

The RichTextBox control comes with the Professional and Enterprise editions of Visual Basic. Its filename is RICHTX32.OCX. To use the RichTextBox control in your Visual Basic project, do the following:

1. In Visual Basic, select Project Components.

2. The Components dialog box appears. In the list of components, scroll down until you see Microsoft Rich Textbox Control 5.0.

3. Check the control in the list, then click OK. The Rich Textbox control is added to your Visual Basic toolbox, as shown in Figure 12.14.

Figure 12.14
The Microsoft RichTextBox control is added to the Visual Basic toolbox.

One of the nice things about the RichTextBox control is that it works nearly identically to the conventional TextBox control; the two controls share many of the same properties. However, the RichTextBox control has a number of additional properties that control text formatting. You can see a couple of them in the sample application shown in Figure 12.15.

Because the RichTextBox control supports the same properties that the TextBox control supports, this application doesn't require any code changes at all; the RichTextBox is, for all intents and purposes, a standard TextBox control.

In order for this control to really sing, you need to write code that permits the user to apply formatting. Listing 12.12 shows an example of how to permit users to apply boldfaced and italicized formatting to text they select in the field bound to the RichTextBox control.

Figure 12.15
Here's an interface of a data access application that contains a RichTextBox control.

Listing 12.12   Applying Boldfaced and Italicized Formatting to Text in a Field

```
Option Explicit

Private Sub cmdBold_Click()
    rtfDescription.SelBold = Not rtfDescription.SelBold
End Sub

Private Sub cmdItalic_Click()
    rtfDescription.SelItalic = Not rtfDescription.SelItalic
End Sub
```

The bold and italic buttons use a Not expression to reverse the current state of bold or italic. This permits the controls to be used to either apply or remove formatting, depending on what's present.

None of this has a direct bearing on the application's database access features. Even though formatted text is being saved to the database, the data binding handles it without any intervention from your code.

> **Code Example:** You can find the code discussed in this section in the project `RichEdit.vbp`, located in the directory `\vbdb\code\12-VSFlex\RichEdit`. For information on how to install the sample files on the CD that accompanies this book, see the section "Installing the Example Files" in the introduction at the beginning of this book.

DISPLAYING DATA IN LISTS WITH THE DBCOMBO AND DBLIST CONTROLS

The DBList control is designed to bind to a field in a table while it displays a list of data derived from elsewhere in the database. The DBCombo control is nearly identical to the DBList control, except it displays choices in a drop-down list.

The DBList and DBCombo controls come with the Professional and Enterprise editions of Visual Basic, in the file DBLIST32.OCX. Do the following to use the DBList or DBCombo controls in your Visual Basic project:

1. From the Visual Basic menu, select Project Components.

2. The Components dialog box appears. In the list of components, scroll down until you see Microsoft Data Bound List Controls 6.0.

3. Check the control in the list, then click OK. The two list controls are added to your Visual Basic toolbox, as shown in Figure 12.16.

Figure 12.16
The Microsoft Data Bound List controls are added to the Visual Basic toolbox.

You bind the DBList control to a data source the same way you do a conventional bound control—through its DataSource and DataField properties. Unlike the conventional ListBox control, you populate the list of choices using the RowSource and ListField properties instead of writing code.

Often when you're using a DBList control, you need at least two data sources—one to provide the list of choices and one to connect to the main recordset.

> **Note: The data source of the DBList and DBCombo controls can only be a DAO or RDO data control. You can't use a DataEnvironment designer or the ADO Data control to bind to these controls. If you want to use ADO to provide a data-bound list control, use the DataList or DataCombo controls, described in the next section.**

For example, say you have two tables in the database—tblCustomer to store customers and tblCustomerType to store a list of several types of customers. There is a one-to-many relationship between customer types and customers; the

CustomerID field in the customer table is a foreign key to the customer type table.

These tables and fields exist in the accompanying CD's Chapter 12 version of the Jones Novelties database, novelty.mdb. To express this relationship in a VB user interface using the DBList control, do the following:

1. Create a standard data-bound user interface based on the tblCustomer table using text boxes and a DAO Data control. Include the FirstName and LastName fields. Name the Data control datCustomer and set its RecordSource property to tblCustomer.

2. Create a DBList control on the form. Name it dblCustomerType.

3. Set the DataSource properties of the two text boxes and the DBList control to the Data control datCustomer.

4. Set the DataField properties of the two TextBox controls to FirstName and LastName, respectively.

5. Set the DataField property of the DBList control to TypeID, the name of the field in tblCustomer that stores the customer type. This binds the DBList control to the field in tblCustomer.

6. Create a second Data control to display the list of customer types. Name this control datCustomerType.

7. Set datCustomerType's RecordSource property to tblCustomerType and then set its Visible property to False.

8. Go back to the DBList control dblCustomerType and set its RowSource property to datCustomerType.

9. Set the dblCustomerType's ListField property to Type.

10. Set the dblCustomerType's BoundColumn property to ID.

11. In the form's Load event, write the following code to initialize the two Data controls:

```
Option Explicit

' References DAO 3.51

Private Sub Form_Load()
    datCustomer.DatabaseName = "..\..\DB\novelty.mdb"
    datCustomerType.DatabaseName = datCustomer.DatabaseName
End Sub
```

12. Run the application. The DBList control should be populated with the list of choices in tblCustomerType, as shown in Figure 12.17.

Figure 12.17
A list of choices is provided by the DBList control in this database access application.

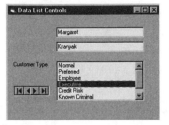

The trick to using these controls is getting a handle on what all the property names mean. There are five properties to keep track of:

▶ DataSource and DataField, which are the same for every bound control.

▶ RowSource, which indicates the name of the data control that is to provide the list of choices.

▶ ListField, which indicates which field from the RowSource data control is displayed in the list. This can be any field, as long as it's clear to the user what's being displayed. In the example, ListField is the name of tblCustomerType's Type field.

▶ BoundColumn, which indicates which field supplies the value that is inserted in the bound field. This has to be a piece of data that uniquely identifies the user's choice. In the example, BoundColumn is the name of tblCustomerType's primary key, ID.

Bear in mind as you're building applications using the DBList and DBCombo controls that their advantage lies not only in the fact that they let you create applications with very little code, but that much of the database access chores are handled transparently by the Data control.

Code Example: You can find an application that uses the DBList control in DBLst.vbp, located in the directory \vbdb\code\12-UIControls\DBLst. (Note that this example is different than the example in the DataList directory. That example covers the DataList control, discussed later in this chapter.) For information on how to install the sample files on the CD that accompanies this book, see the section "Installing the Example Files" in the introduction at the beginning of this book.

USING THE DATAGRID CONTROL

The DataGrid control is new in Visual Basic 6.0; it's similar to the data-aware DBGrid control that originally shipped with VB5. The DataGrid control has the ability to display data in a row-and-column format when bound to the ADO Data control or DataEnvironment designer, but it lacks a few of the features of the old DBGrid control. (DBGrid is still shipped with VB6 for backward compatibility, but is no longer installed by default). Specifically, the DataGrid control doesn't have the RowBuffer object, which supports the unbound mode offered by the DBGrid control. This makes sense, since the DataGrid control can't be used in unbound mode—nor can it be bound to data controls other than the ADO Data control.

Aside from compatibility with the ADO Data control, the only other advantage the control offers is size—the old DBGrid OCX is more than 500KB, whereas the new DataGrid control is a comparatively svelte 252KB.

To use the DataGrid control, simply create an ADO Data control, then assign the grid's DataSource property to the name of the ADO Data control. When you run the application, the data provided by the ADO Data control will be displayed in rows and columns in the grid.

USING THE DATALIST AND DATACOMBO CONTROLS

The DataList and DataCombo controls are new controls that replicate the functionality of the DBList controls that shipped with VB5 (described earlier in this chapter). The controls permit your application to bind to two data controls: one control supplies the list of choices provided by the list, while the second connects the data entered into the control into a field in the database.

Unlike the DataGrid control, which only works with ADO, the list controls are compatible with both the DAO Data control and the new ADO Data control. Aside from that, the controls work pretty much the same as the old DBList controls.

Here's how to bind a database field to a DataList control:

1. Use VB's Project Components menu to add the Microsoft Data List Controls 6.0 (OLEDB) to your project. The DataList and DataCombo controls appear in your VB toolbox.

2. Create an instance of the DataList control on a form, as well as a few standard text boxes.

3. Bind the text boxes to a data source such as an ADO Data Control or a DataEnvironment designer the way you normally would.

4. Set the DataList control's DataSource property to the name of a valid data source, such as a data control or a DataEnvironment designer.

5. If you're using a DataEnvironment designer, set the DataList control's DataMember property to the command in the designer that provides data. (In the example, the command tblCustomer is used.)

6. Set the control's DataField property to a foreign key field, such as CustomerID.

7. To display the list of customer types, create a second command in the DataEnvironment designer to represent the tblCustomerType table. This command should have the following SQL statement:

```
SELECT *
FROM tblCustomerType
```

8. To assign this new data control to the list portion of the combo box, assign the DataList control's RowSource property to the name of the DataEnvironment designer. (In the example, it's called Novelty.)

9. Set the DataList control's RowMember property to the name of the command you want it to display (tblCustomerType).

10. Set the control's ListField property to the name of the field you actually want to display in the list (the field called Type).

11. Finally, to indicate that the ID value from the customer list should be saved to the TypeID field of the tblCustomer table when the user makes a choice from the list, assign the BoundColumn property of the DataList to the field ID.

At this point the application displays a list of customer types, even though it's only storing their IDs in the database, as shown in Figure 12.18.

Figure 12.18

The application displays a data-driven list of choices using the DataList control.

Code Example: You can find the code discussed in this section in the project `DataList.vbp`, located in the directory `\vbdb\code\12-UIControls\DataList`. (This is not the same as the DBLst project described earlier in this chapter.) For information on how to install the sample files on the CD that accompanies this book, see the section "Installing the Example Files" in the introduction at the beginning of this book.

USING THE DATAREPEATER CONTROL TO VIEW DATA IN CUSTOM ROWS

The DataRepeater control is new in Visual Basic 6.0. It's a unique control that converts any ActiveX control into something like a grid control or a Microsoft Access subform.

If you've never worked with an Access subform, think of it as a way to represent the "many" of a one-to-many relationship between data elements. But rather than being stuck with using rows in a grid control to display the "many" relationship, the DataRepeater lets you use any ActiveX control or combination of controls to display related records. And you don't need to have a one-to-many relationship to use the DataRepeater. It's appropriate anytime you want to create a control that displays data in repeating rows.

Note: This section isn't designed to be a comprehensive description of how to create ActiveX controls. If you're looking for more information on how to create controls, check out my book, *How to Program Visual Basic Control Creation Edition*. You can get more information on the book online at `http://www.redblazer.com/cce/`.

To use the DataRepeater control to build a custom data list control, follow these steps:

1. In Visual Basic, create an ActiveX control project.

2. Name the UserControl designer CustList and give the project the name CLCtrl.

3. In the UserControl designer, create constituent text boxes to represent the FirstName and LastName fields.

4. Create public property procedures for the control that will correspond to the controls you've created on it. You implement these in code, as shown in Listing 12.13.

Listing 12.13   Providing Public Property Procedures for the UserControl

```
Option Explicit


Public Property Get FirstName() As String
    FirstName = txtFirstName.Text
End Property

Public Property Let FirstName(ByVal strNew As String)
    txtFirstName.Text = strNew
    PropertyChanged "FirstName"
End Property


Public Property Get LastName() As String
    LastName = txtLastName.Text
End Property

Public Property Let LastName(ByVal strNew As String)
    txtLastName.Text = strNew
    PropertyChanged "LastName"
End Property
```

5. Mark the property procedures you just created as data-bound by selecting the Tools, Procedure Attributes menu.

6. In the Procedure Attributes dialog box, click the Advanced button.

7. Indicate that both the FirstName and LastName properties are data-aware by clicking the check box labeled "Property is data-bound." Also click the box labeled "Show in DataBindings collection at design time." Do this for both the FirstName and LastName fields.

8. The control is now "data bindable." In order to use it in the context of a DataRepeater control, you must compile it. Do this by using the File, Make menu command.

9. Start a new Standard EXE project. In the Project Components dialog box, make a reference to Microsoft DataRepeater Control 6.0 (OLEDB).

10. Create an instance of the DataRepeater control on the form.

11. In the DataRepeater control's RepeatedControlName property, select the name of your control. It should appear in the list as CLCtrl.CustList.

12. The control is displayed again and again in the DataRepeater control, as shown in Figure 12.19.

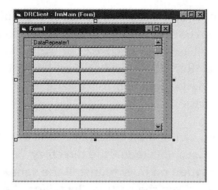

Figure 12.19
The DataRepeater control displays multiple instances of a contained control.

13. To bind the DataRepeater control to the database, add a DataEnvironment designer connected to the Novelty database.

14. Assign the DataRepeater's DataSource property to Novelty, the name of the DataEnvironment designer. Assign the control's DataMember name to tblCustomer.

15. Right-click the DataRepeater. In the property page dialog box, click the RepeaterBindings tab. In the PropertyName combo box, select FirstName, then select the corresponding data field in the DataField combo box.

16. Click Add.

17. Bind the LastName property to the LastName field the way you did for the FirstName field.

18. Run the application. You should be able to scroll through multiple records, as shown in Figure 12.20.

Figure 12.20
The DataRepeater control displays data at runtime.

Although this example uses an ActiveX control you build yourself to demonstrate the DataRepeater control, you don't need to use your own control to use a DataRepeater—any database-aware ActiveX control will do. If you're looking to get started with the DataRepeater quickly, try replacing the TitleList control in this example with the MaskedEdit control (a database-aware ActiveX control that ships with Visual Basic).

Code Example: You can find an example of the DataRepeater control in the project `Repeater.vbp`, located in the directory `\vbdb\code\12-UIControls\Repeater`. For information on how to install the sample files on the CD that accompanies this book, see the section "Installing the Example Files" in the introduction at the beginning of this book.

USING THE MONTHVIEW AND DATETIMEPICKER CONTROLS

The MonthView and DateTimePicker controls are new in Visual Basic 6.0. They give you the ability to graphically select date and time values from a calendar or scrolling list of values.

The MonthView control represents the graphical calendar itself, whereas the DateTimePicker is essentially a calendar-enabled combo box, permitting you to conserve space on a form while providing the same graphical date-picking functionality as the MonthView control. Both bind to the database the same way as any other data-bound control.

To use DateTimePicker or MonthView, first use the Project Components menu to add Microsoft Windows Common Controls-2 6.0 to your project. After you've done this, create an instance of the DateTimePicker control on your form.

The first thing you'll notice when you run the application is the appearance of the calendar (shown in Figure 12.21).

Figure 12.21
A DateTimePicker control calendar appears in a data-bound application.

The clunky bold lettering and childish-looking red circle denoting the current date aren't quite as elegant as similar UI widgets you see in Microsoft Outlook, for example (or in the third-party ActiveX calendar controls that have been around for years). But you can do a few things to make the control look cooler. For example, changing the `CalendarBackColor` property to &H8000000F& (the special color code corresponding to the Button Face setting in Control Panel) makes the drop-down calendar display in a shade of soothing gray.

In addition to dropping down a calendar, you can use the control to enable users to choose time values by setting the control's `Format` property to 2 - dtpTime. At the same time, you'll want to send the control's `UpDown` property to True. This gets rid of the calendar drop-down control, replacing it with a spin control. Using the spin control, users can adjust the value displayed in the control using the mouse instead of typing on one of those pesky old-fashioned keyboards.

The control also gives you the ability to do certain types of validation. The `MaxDate` and `MinDate` properties prohibit your users from entering dates that fall outside a specified range.

When you need to programmatically inspect the date or time entered by the user, use the control's `Value` property. The `Value` property returns a familiar Visual Basic Date value; if you'd prefer, you also have the ability to retrieve numeric values corresponding to the selected month, day of the week, week of the year, and so forth. The code to do this is a no-brainer:

```
Private Sub cmdDayOfWeek_Click()
    MsgBox DTPicker1.DayOfWeek
End Sub

Private Sub cmdMonth_Click()
    MsgBox DTPicker1.Month
End Sub

Private Sub cmdDay_Click()
    MsgBox DTPicker1.Day
End Sub
```

Code Example: You can find an example of the DateTimePicker control in the project **DateTime.vbp**, located in the directory **\vbdb\code\12-UIControls\ DateTime**. For information on how to install the sample files on the CD that accompanies this book, see the section "Installing the Example Files" in the introduction at the beginning of this book.

USING THE MSCHART TO DISPLAY DATA GRAPHICALLY

The MSChart control has been included with Visual Basic out of the box since time immemorial. You use the control to display data in a graphical chart format. New to VB6 is the ability to bind the MSChart control directly to a database through a data control.

To see how this works, follow these steps:

1. From the Project, Components menu, select Microsoft Chart Control 6.0 (OLEDB) and Microsoft ADO Data Control 6.0 (OLEDB).

2. Create an instance of the ADO Data control and the MSChart control on your form.

3. Connect the ADO Data control with your database by setting its ConnectionString and RecordSource properties. Typically for a chart, you'll want to use an aggregate SQL query such as this:

```
SELECT State, Count(ID)
FROM tblCustomer
GROUP BY State
```

4. Since you won't need it in this application, you may want to set the data control's Visible property to False.

5. Set the MSChart control's DataSource property to the name of the ADO Data control.

6. If you wish, you can change the appearance of the chart by changing its ChartType property.

7. Run the application. The chart displays summarized data showing how many customers you have in each state, as shown in Figure 12.22.

Figure 12.22
Using MSChart control, an application can display summarized data graphically.

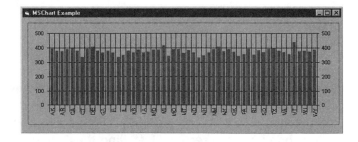

If you used the prepopulated `novelty.mdb` database installed from the CD that accompanies this book, the chart display shows that you have roughly 400 customers in each state. If you use your own database, your results will undoubtedly differ (unless you used random data to populate your database, as I did).

> **Code Example:** You can find the code discussed in this section in the project `DataChart.vbp`, located in the directory `\vbdb\code\12-UIControls\ DataChart`. For information on how to install the sample files on the CD that accompanies this book, see the section "Installing the Example Files" in the introduction at the beginning of this book.

USING THE DBGRID, MSFLEXGRID, AND HIERARCHICAL FLEXGRID CONTROLS

The DBGrid control permits you to display a recordset in row and column form. The MSFlexGrid control is also a data-aware grid, but it permits users to perform *ad hoc* analysis of data using drag-and-drop techniques. The Hierarchical FlexGrid control is new in Visual Basic 6.0. It gives you the ability to browse data in a row-and-column format.

Chapter 13 discusses the DBGrid control, as well as its commercial cousin, Apex True DBGrid, in depth. Chapter 14 discusses the MSFlexGrid and Hierarchical FlexGrid controls as well as their more mighty cousin, the VideoSoft vsFlexGrid control.

CREATING DATABASE-AWARE ACTIVEX CONTROLS

You have the ability to create your own data-aware ActiveX controls in Visual Basic. You typically do this in situations where you need to provide some additional functionality to an existing database-aware user-interface control.

You might create your own data-aware ActiveX control in situations where you need the following types of controls:

▶ A control that extends the functionality of an existing control. The TextBox control in particular is a common target of enhancement by ActiveX control developers.

▶ A control that combines the functionality of two controls into one. Visual Basic is particularly adept at creating these types of controls. This is because VB lets you create ActiveX controls graphically, based on one or more existing controls.

▶ A control that needs to graphically represent a unique aspect of your business. Say you're dealing with racks of industrial material, and each rack is five units long by six units wide. Each cell in the rack has its own set of a few dozen properties that need to be stored in the database and manipulated graphically in the user interface. This situation is an ideal candidate for ActiveX control.

Tip: If you're looking to take this a step further, pick up *How to Program Visual Basic Control Creation Edition (Ziff-Davis Press, 1997)*. This book gives you step-by-step information on creating ActiveX controls in any edition of VB5.

The Visual Basic Control Creation Edition, which is freely downloadable from Microsoft's Web site at `http://www.microsoft.com/vbasic/controls`, gives you the ability to create ActiveX controls but does not include database access libraries. This means that if you use the Control Creation Edition, it's possible to create a database-aware control you can't test.

SUMMARY

This chapter provides an introduction to the basic user-interface controls available in Visual Basic, as well as the additional ActiveX controls available in the Visual Basic Professional and Enterprise editions.

The next few chapters provide a more in-depth introduction into a number of third-party user-interface controls, including the MSFlexGrid and the DBGrid controls that ship with Visual Basic, as well as their enhanced commercial counterparts.

QUESTIONS AND ANSWERS

Q. **I need a control that binds to a Date/Time field in a Jet database and permits the user to select a day of the month graphically, without entering any data, but the display of the DateTimePicker control leaves something to be desired. Are there any alternatives?**

A. There are a few dozen third-party database-aware calendar controls that I know about. One of the best is mh3dCalendar, part of the BeCubed Software's OLETools suite. This control does everything but sit up and beg—it even formats days and months in Esperanto. The OLETools package that contains the calendar control also contains more than fifty other controls, many of which are also database aware. Check out more OLETools information at http://www.becubed.com.

By way of comparison, you might also want to check out Sheridan Calendar Widgets, which is slightly different than the calendar control in OLETools but is also quite good. You can read about them on Sheridan's Web site at http://www.shersoft.com/products/actvxlist.htm or download a demonstration from http://www.shersoft.com/download/trials.htm.

Q. **Are there any other cool third-party, database-aware controls weren't mentioned in this chapter?**

A. Sure, carloads of them. DynamiCube is a data analysis tool similar to VSFLEX (the topic of Chapter 14). It has the ability to summarize data in a few ways that VSFLEX can't, and it's also "Web friendly," so you can display data in a browser over your network or the Internet. Get more information on DynamiCube from the Data Dynamics Web page at http://www.datadynamics.com.

In addition, Formula One is one of the best spreadsheet-like data grids out there. If your application needs a grid interface and True DBGrid (the subject of the next chapter) doesn't do it for you, check this one out. You can get more information on Formula One from the Visual Components Web site at http://visualcomp.com.

Using the DBGrid and Apex True DBGrid Controls

The DBGrid control permits you to display information from a database in a row-and-column format. The effect is similar to the datasheet view provided in Microsoft Access—although applications built with Visual Basic and the DBGrid control generally have a much smaller distributable footprint and are, as a result, generally much peppier than Microsoft Access-based applications. Additionally, the DBGrid control has display properties, behaviors, and features not offered by Access, as this chapter demonstrates.

The DBGrid control ships with the Professional and Enterprise editions of Visual Basic, although it's no longer installed by default, as it was in Visual Basic 5.0. The commercial version of the grid control, True DBGrid, is available as a separate add-on to Visual Basic.

> **Note:** The commercial version of the control, True DBGrid Pro, was formerly called TrueGrid Pro. True DBGrid Pro is an updated version of the TrueGrid and DBGrid controls.
>
> By the time you read this, True DBGrid Pro 6.0 should be out. This chapter uses version 5.0d of the OLE DB flavor of the control, but the code examples should work with the new version as well.

This chapter introduces these two controls and demonstrates how you can use them to display and modify information in a database.

USING THE DBGRID CONTROL

This chapter gives you a brief overview of how to use the DBGrid control in your applications and provides a few examples of the extended capabilities of True DBGrid—the commercial version of the DBGrid control.

Unlike previous versions of Visual Basic, the lightweight version of the DBGrid control is no longer installed automatically when you install VB. If you installed VB 6.0 on top of VB 5.0, you have the DBGrid control already. If you've never installed VB on your system, though, you'll need to install the DBGrid control manually. To do this, follow these steps:

1. Locate the DBGrid control files on your Visual Basic CD. For the Enterprise Edition CD, the files are on Disc 1, in the folder `\COMMON\TOOLS\VB\CONTROLS`.

2. Copy the files `DBGRID32.OCX`, `DBGRID32.DEP`, and `DBGRID.REG` to your Windows system folder.

3. In your Windows system folder, double-click the file `DBGRID.REG`. This registers the control on your system and lets you use it in your VB projects.

Remember that you only have to do this if the DBGrid control wasn't installed on your system by a previous version of VB. If the DBGrid control is listed in Visual Basic's Project Components menu, you should be able to use it with no problem.

> **Note: If this installation procedure seems awkward and inconvenient, I suspect it's because Microsoft is trying to gently encourage you to use its new data-bound grid control, DataGrid, discussed in Chapter 12, "User-Interface Controls." While this control surpasses the DBGrid control's functionality (giving you the ability to bind to an ADO data source, for example), it doesn't come close to matching the feature set of the commercial True DBGrid control, introduced later in this chapter. For this reason, the DBGrid control is still worth familiarizing yourself with.**

GETTING STARTED WITH THE DBGRID CONTROL

This section walks you through the basics of the DBGrid control that comes with Visual Basic. If you're using the commercial True DBGrid Pro product, this section applies to you as well, because the basic techniques for both versions of the control are the same.

The DBGrid control contains a number of other objects used to manipulate the grid. The DBGrid control's object model is illustrated in Figure 13.1.

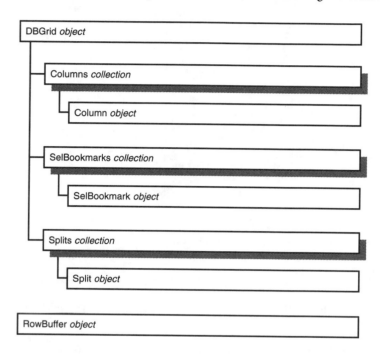

Figure 13.1
This is the object model of the Apex DBGrid control.

The DBGrid control is installed on your computer when you install either the Professional or Enterprise editions of Visual Basic. Its filename is DBGRID32.OCX.
To use the DBGrid in a Visual Basic project, do the following:

1. In Visual Basic, select Project Components.

2. The Components dialog box appears. In the list of components, scroll down until you see Microsoft Data Bound Grid Control. The exact version number may vary; for example, if you're using the version of DBGrid that came with the last version of VB 5.0, the control will appear in the list as Microsoft Data Bound Grid Control 5.0 (SP3).

Note: Apex Software periodically makes updates of the control available for download on its Web site. Check out http://www.apexsc.com for more details.

3. Check the control in the list; then click OK. The DBGrid control is added to your Visual Basic toolbox, as shown in Figure 13.2.

Figure 13.2
The DBGrid control now appears in the Visual Basic toolbox.

To display the contents of a recordset in the database grid, bind it to a data control just as with other data-aware controls. To do this, follow these steps:

1. Add a DAO Data control and a DBGrid control to a VB form.

2. Set the Data control's DatabaseName and RecordSource properties as you normally would.

3. Set the DBGrid control's DataSource property to the name of the Data control. (Because it displays many fields, the DBGrid control has no DataField property.)

4. Run the application. The data should be displayed in the grid, as shown in Figure 13.3.

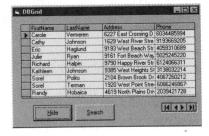

Figure 13.3
You can view information from a Data control displayed in the DBGrid control.

This application is easy to build because it requires very little code, but it has a few problems. First, the columns from the recordset are displayed in a random order. Second, the data is read-only. Those problems are resolved in the next few sections.

SELECTING COLUMNS TO DISPLAY AT DESIGN TIME

The DBGrid control has a powerful property sheet that permits you to determine several aspects of the grid's behavior and appearance. In this example, you use the property sheet to denote which columns to display and in which order. Follow these steps:

1. In the Visual Basic design-time environment, right-click the DBGrid control.

2. Select Properties from the pop-up menu.

3. The Properties dialog box appears, as shown in Figure 13.4.

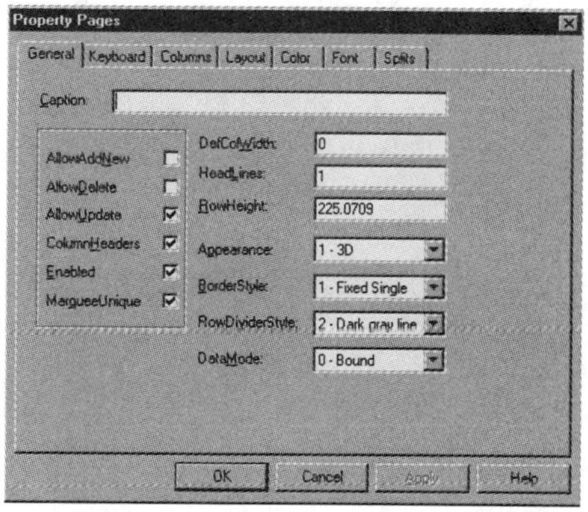

Figure 13.4
The DBGrid Property Pages dialog box enables you to make design-time changes to the control.

4. In the Properties dialog box, click the Columns tab. By clicking the Column combo, you can see that at design time, there are two columns by default: Column0 and Column1.

5. Assign the DataField property of Column0 to FirstName.

6. In the Column combo box, select Column1. Assign the DataField property of Column1 to LastName.

7. Click OK; then run the application again. Only the first and last names of customers should appear in the grid.

The appearance of a set of columns in a DBGrid control is referred to as a *layout*. In the commercial True DBGrid component, the control stores a collection of Layout objects. This permits you to easily manipulate and switch between multiple layouts.

In both the bundled and commercial versions of the grid control, you have the ability to manipulate grid columns at runtime, using code. This topic is covered in the section "Manipulating Grid Columns in Code" later in this chapter.

MANIPULATING COLUMNS AT DESIGN TIME

You can add columns to the DBGrid control at design time by using the control's context menu. After you've added columns, you can bind each new column to another field in the database using its Properties dialog box. Follow these steps:

1. In the Visual Basic design-time environment, right-click the DBGrid control.

2. Select Edit from the pop-up menu. The grid is now in edit mode (even though its appearance remains the same).

3. Right-click the DBGrid control again. This time the pop-up menu is different, reflecting the fact that the grid is in edit mode. This is shown in Figure 13.5.

Figure 13.5
The DBGrid's pop-up menu is different when the grid is in edit mode.

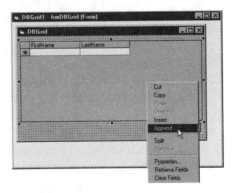

4. Select Append from the pop-up menu. A new column appears to the right of the two existing columns.

To delete a column, follow these steps:

1. While the grid is in edit mode, click on a column to select it.

2. Right-click the grid. Select Delete from the pop-up menu.

To resize a column, follow these steps:

1. While the grid is in edit mode, position your mouse pointer in the gray header area, directly on the boundary between two columns. The mouse pointer turns into a double-headed arrow, as shown in Figure 13.6.

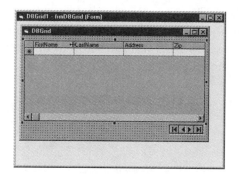

Figure 13.6
You can resize a column at design time using the mouse pointer.

2. Click-drag to resize the column.

Using a combination of mouse actions and the Properties dialog box, you should be able to set up the grid so it displays four fields: FirstName, LastName, Address, and Zip. This interface is shown in Figure 13.7.

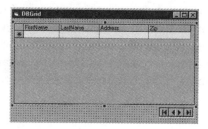

Figure 13.7
The DBGrid interface displays four fields from the recordset.

MAKING GRID DATA EDITABLE

By default, the DBGrid control permits users to alter the data it displays, but it doesn't let users delete or add records. You can manipulate properties of the grid control to control whether users can change data and insert or delete records.

Here are the properties that the DBGrid control uses to manage the editing of records:

▶ AllowAddNew. Determines whether the user can add new records (False by default)

▶ `AllowDelete`. Determines whether the user can delete records (False by default)

▶ `AllowUpdate`. Determines whether the user can edit existing data (True by default)

In order to be able to edit, append, and delete the data displayed in the grid, simply set all three of these properties to True at design time. When the `AllowAddNew` property is set to True, you can scroll to the bottom of the grid to add a new record, as shown in Figure 13.8.

Figure 13.8
The user can add a new record in a DBGrid whose AllowAddNew property is set to True.

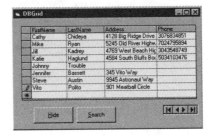

This is the same technique you use to add records in a Microsoft Access datasheet.

Note: It's generally better to manage the editing of records at the database-engine level rather than at the user-interface level. For example, don't create a read-write `Recordset` object and make it read-only by setting the DBGrid's `AllowUpdate` property to False. Opening database objects for write access is generally more computationally expensive than opening them for read-only.

INSERTING SPLITS AT DESIGN TIME

You can split a grid into multiple sections. This makes it easy for users to view a large amount of data in the grid without having to scroll back and forth in the grid.

Splits can be either horizontal or vertical. When a split exists in a grid, two sets of scrollbars become available, one to control each split. Splits don't affect the data in the grid, only the way it's displayed; you can think of them as separate viewports onto the set of data displayed by the grid.

Here's how to create and configure a split at design time:

1. Put the grid in edit mode.

2. Right-click the control. Select Split from the pop-up menu.

3. A vertical split appears, as shown in Figure 13.9.

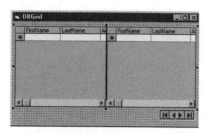

Figure 13.9
A vertical split is created at design time.

4. With the control still in edit mode, right-click and select Properties from the pop-up menu.

5. Select the Splits tab. You should be able to see two splits in the Splits combo box: Split0 and Split1. You can alter the properties of Split0 to make the first two columns visible at all times.

6. Change the `SizeMode` property of Split0 to 2 - Number of Columns. Then change its `Size` property to 2. This will cause the split to be two columns wide.

7. Finally, set the split's `ScrollBars` property to 0 - None; then click OK.

8. Run the application. It should look like Figure 13.10.

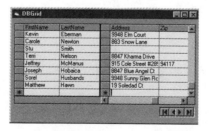

Figure 13.10
This DBGrid control has a nonresizable vertical split.

As with the other elements of the DBGrid control, you have the ability to create and manipulate splits at runtime, using code, as well as at design time. The next section gives an example of how to do this.

MANIPULATING SPLIT OBJECTS IN CODE

There's one problem with the interface you've built in the previous examples. The right split, Split1, initially displays the same information as the left split. It would be better if Split0 showed columns 0 and 1 by default, while Split1 showed columns 2 and 3.

Unfortunately, you can't designate the initial column for a particular split at design time. Here's where you get to delve into the DBGrid control's object model—specifically, the split object. You declare a split object in code the same way you declare any other object:

```
Dim sp As Split
```

Your grid control has two splits: Split0 and Split1. Because these objects are members of the splits collection, you can also refer to them ordinally, as splits(0) and splits(1). To assign the split object variable to one of your control's two splits, use the following code:

```
Set sp = DBGrid1.Splits(1)
```

This sets the object variable sp to the rightmost split. You can now manipulate the properties and methods of the rightmost split through the object variable sp. Listing 13.1 uses this technique to set the rightmost split's default column.

Listing 13.1   Assigning the Default Column of a Split Using the *Split* Object's *LeftCol* Property

```
Option Explicit

' References DAO 3.51

Private Sub Form_Load()
Dim sp As Split

    Data1.DatabaseName = "..\..\DB\novelty.mdb"

    Set sp = DBGrid1.Splits(1)
    sp.LeftCol = 2

End Sub
```

In addition to manipulating existing splits, you also can create and delete splits in code at runtime (using the Add and Remove methods of the grid's splits collection).

MANIPULATING GRID COLUMNS IN CODE

You have the ability to manipulate the columns of a grid in code. This technique is similar to the technique you used to access the properties of a split in the previous section. Create an object variable to represent the element of the grid you want to manipulate; then access the properties and execute the methods of the object variable.

For example, say you want to permit the user to easily hide a particular column of the grid and then make the column visible again later. You can do this by setting the Visible property of a Column object. Listing 13.2 shows you how to do this.

Listing 13.2   Manipulating the Properties of a DBGrid Control's *Column* Object

```
Private Sub cmdHide_Click()
Dim c As Column

    Set c = DBGrid1.Columns(1)   ' LastName column
    c.Visible = Not c.Visible

End Sub
```

Applying the Not operator to the Column object's Visible property means that the Hide button will display the column if it's hidden already.

In addition to manipulating existing columns, you also can create and delete columns in code at runtime (using the Add and Remove methods of the grid's Columns collection).

Code Example: You can find an example of the code discussed in this section in the project Basics.vbp, located in the directory \vbdb\code\ 13-DBGrid\Basics. For information on how to install the sample files on the CD that accompanies this book, see the section "Installing the Example Files" in the introduction at the beginning of this book.

NAVIGATING WITH THE *BOOKMARK* PROPERTY

You can refer to the currently selected row in the grid by the grid's Bookmark property. This property permits you to save the location of a particular record so you can return to it later.

Listing 13.3 gives an example of two command buttons—one to set a bookmark, the other to return to the bookmarked record.

Listing 13.3   Setting Bookmarks and Returning to Bookmarked Records

```
Private mstrBookmark As String

Private Sub cmdBookmark_Click()
    mstrBookmark = DBGrid1.Bookmark
End Sub

Private Sub cmdGo_Click()
    DBGrid1.Bookmark = mstrBookmark
End Sub
```

When the user clicks the Bookmark button, the value of the current record's bookmark is stored in the module-level variable mstrBookmark. When the user clicks the Go button, the value of mstrBookmark is assigned to the grid's Bookmark property, causing the grid to move to the row with that bookmark.

SELECTING RECORDS USING THE *SELBOOKMARKS* COLLECTION

In addition to bookmarking a record, you can use the Bookmark property in conjunction with the SelBookmarks collection to visibly select one or more rows in the grid. You select a row in order to highlight it to the user, or to prepare it for a later operation, such as deletion.

The SelBookmarks collection is a collection of bookmarks of selected rows of the grid. To select a row in the grid, you add its bookmark to the grid's SelBookmarks collection, using code like this:

```
DBGrid1.SelBookmarks.Add DBGrid.Bookmark
```

This code adds the current row to the SelBookmarks collection—with the side effect of selecting the current row.

As a practical example of this technique, say your application needs a search feature. This feature uses the FindFirst method of the Data control's Recordset object to locate a record. After it does that, it would be helpful if the application selected the record to make it easy for the user to see what took place. Listing 13.4 gives an example of code that does this.

Listing 13.4   Searching a Recordset and Highlighting a Found Record in the Grid Using the *SelBookmarks* Collection

```
Private Sub cmdSearch_Click()
Dim strFind As String
    strFind = InputBox("Enter the last name to find.", "Find")
    Data1.Recordset.FindFirst "LastName='" & strFind & "'"
```

```
    If Data1.Recordset.NoMatch Then
        MsgBox "The name was not found.", vbExclamation
    Else
        DBGrid1.SelBookmarks.Add DBGrid1.Bookmark
    End If

End Sub
```

Figure 13.11 shows the DBGrid application after it has found and selected a customer in response to a user query.

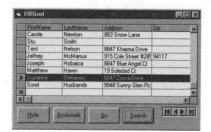

Figure 13.11
The DBGrid appli-cation displays a selected record.

The fact that `SelBookmarks` is a collection implies that a number of rows in the grid can be selected at the same time. This is, in fact, the case. You might do this in a situation in which the user performs a search on the records in the grid and the search retrieves a number of rows.

USING THE DBGRID CONTROL IN UNBOUND MODE

Until now, all the examples in this chapter have been predicated on the concept of a DBGrid control connected to a database through the Data control. You have the ability, however, to display and manipulate data in a DBGrid control without a Data control. This is referred to as *unbound mode.*

You use unbound mode when you need greater control over how information is retrieved and displayed in the grid control, or when you want to overcome the performance or flexibility shortcomings of the Data control. The DBGrid control provides a number of properties and events that support unbound mode.

To use a DBGrid control in unbound mode, start by setting the control's `DataMode` property to 1 - dbgUnbound. When you do this, you're telling the control that your code takes complete responsibility for manipulating and displaying data in the control.

In an unbound control, you write code that handles data manipulation in response to four events. These events include:

▶ UnboundAddData. Triggered when the grid needs to add a row to the data source

▶ UnboundDeleteRow. Triggered when the grid needs to delete a row from the data source

▶ UnboundReadData. Triggered when the grid needs to retrieve a row of data from the data source

▶ UnboundWriteData. Triggered when the grid needs to write data back to the data source

Note: The commercial True DBGrid control adds a new type of unbound mode, *unbound extended mode,* that is simpler to code against (because it requires fewer events) and is a bit more efficient. The technique described in this section, however, has the advantage of working in DBGrid as well as the commercial True DBGrid control.

The big disadvantage of using unbound mode is the fact that it's fairly complicated to code. To make it work, you need to write code to all the events, interacting with the RowBuffer object passed to your application from the grid through the events as an argument.

DEVELOPING DATABASE-AWARE APPLICATIONS USING TRUE DBGRID PRO

The commercial version of the DBGrid control is called True DBGrid Pro. This control contains all the features of the DBGrid control, is nearly 100 percent backward compatible with earlier versions of the control, and provides some significant additional features that permit you to customize the control's appearance and behavior. Significantly for VB6 developers, the commercial version of the control supports binding to ADO data sources.

Some of the features available in the commercial True DBGrid that aren't available in the version that ships with Visual Basic include the following:

▶ Support for extended unbound mode and storage mode, two unbound modes that permit the grid to display information without a Data control

▶ The ability to include unbound columns in a grid that's bound to a Data control

▶ The ability to embed user-interface controls and bitmap images in grid cells

▶ The ability to apply formatting to individual cells in the grid

▶ Support for *CellTips*, a feature similar to the ToolTips you find in a toolbar control, but assignable to each cell in the grid

▶ The ability to load and save predefined sets of formats called *layouts*, and to program layouts at runtime through the Layout object

Some of these features are demonstrated in the remainder of this chapter.

The object model of the commercial TrueDBGrid Pro control is a superset of the object model of the DBGrid control that ships with Visual Basic. Figure 13.12 shows the object model of True DBGrid Pro.

True DBGrid Pro does not ship with Visual Basic; it's a separate product. A trial version of the commercial control is available on the CD that accompanies this book, in the folder \Software\TrGrdPro.

The True DBGrid Pro product supports both DAO/RDO data binding, as well as ADO/OLE DB data binding. Like many commercial controls that are being updated to support OLE DB, supporting the new data binding modes requires a new distributable file.

Accordingly, the flavor of the True DBGrid control that supports DAO/RDO binding is called TDBG5.OCX. The OLE DB version is called TODG5.OCX. You'll need to make sure that you've installed and registered the correct flavor of the control for the type of project you're interested in building.

To use True DBGrid in your Visual Basic project, do the following:

1. In Visual Basic, select the Project Components menu.

2. The Components dialog box appears. In the list of components, scroll down until you see Apex True DBGrid Pro 5.0. It should appear in the list with Apex True DBGrid Pro 5.0 (OLE DB).

3. Check the control you wish to use from the list; then click OK. The True DBGrid and TDBDropDown controls are added to your Visual Basic toolbox, as shown in Figure 13.13.

Figure 13.12
This is the object model of the True DBGrid Pro control.

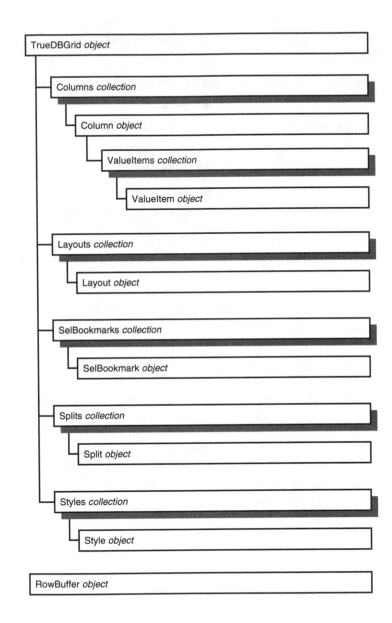

Figure 13.13
The True DBGrid control is added to the Visual Basic toolbox.

Note: Apex Software periodically makes updates of its controls available for download on the company's Web site. Check out `http://www.apexsc.com` for more details.

Bear in mind that this chapter is designed to give you a brief introduction to True DBGrid Pro's features—it's not even close to being a complete reference to the control. The current edition of the (very helpful and well-done) manual for the commercial version of the control runs about 400 pages and covers the features of the control in much more depth than this chapter has room for.

MIGRATING FROM PREVIOUS VERSIONS OF TRUE DBGRID

Because there have been changes in the programmable interface of the True DBGrid control over the years, the True DBGrid Pro package comes with a migration tool. This tool inspects your code, picking out incompatibilities and updating calls to the elements of the control's interface that have changed.

This migration tool is installed when you install True DBGrid. To use it, follow these steps:

1. Because the tool makes changes to your code, start by backing up your source code files.

2. Open a Visual Basic project based on a previous version of the True DBGrid control.

3. Activate the migration add-in by selecting Add-Ins, Add-In Manager.

4. The Add-In Manager dialog box appears. Check True DBGrid Pro 5.0 Migration Utility in the list; then click OK.

5. The Migration utility is loaded; it appears as a button in the Visual Basic toolbar (it does not appear as an item in the Add-Ins menu, as many add-ins do). This toolbar button is illustrated in Figure 13.14.

Figure 13.14
The True DBGrid Pro Migration utility now appears in the Visual Basic toolbar.

6. Run the migration utility by clicking the button in the toolbar. The Migration Utility dialog box appears, as shown in Figure 13.15.

Figure 13.15
Use the True DBGrid Pro Migration Utility dialog box to update your code.

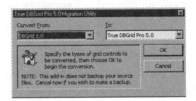

7. Using the combo box in the Migration Utility dialog box, select the version of the DBGrid control your current application uses; then click OK.

8. The Migration utility analyzes your code, commenting out any that doesn't conform to the new version of the control and replacing that code with the True DBGrid 5.0 version of the code.

STORING AND APPLYING FORMATTING WITH THE *STYLE* OBJECT

In True DBGrid Pro, you have the ability to manipulate sets of formatting attributes composed of such things as font, color, and alignment. These sets of attributes are called *styles*. Styles in True DBGrid Pro are conceptually similar to styles in the Microsoft Office applications—they can be named, applied to sections of the grid, and altered to suit your needs. When you change the definition of a style, all the grid elements that have that style change to reflect the new style definition.

You can create and manipulate grid styles using True DBGrid Pro's Property dialog box. You can also manipulate styles in code. You use the style object when you're working with styles in code.

You can create styles yourself; True DBGrid Pro comes with a number of pre-defined styles. These are listed in Table 13.1.

Table 13.1 Predefined Styles Available in True DBGrid Pro	
Name	**Description**
Normal	The basic style upon which other styles are based.
	Font: MS Sans Serif 8.25
	BackColor: Window Background
	ForeColor: Window Text
	Text Align: Left
Heading	Parent: Normal
	BackColor: System Button Face
	ForeColor: System Button Text
Selected	Parent: Normal
	BackColor: System Highlight
	ForeColor: System Highlight Text
Caption	Parent: Heading
	Alignment: Center
HighlightRow	Parent: Normal
	BackColor: System Window Text
	ForeColor: System Window Background
EvenRow	Same as the Normal style
OddRow	Equivalent to the Normal style

Note: System colors (such as System Button Face) are defined by the user through the Windows Control Panel. Accordingly, you can't predict with certainty to what those colors will be set.

Applying Styles in Code

You can apply style formatting to the entire grid by setting the `Style` property of the grid control. This property is a string that corresponds to an existing style in the grid's `Styles` collection.

For example, use the following code to set the grid's formatting to the preset EvenRow style:

```
Private Sub cmdStyleGrid_Click()
    TDBGrid1.Style = "EvenRow"
End Sub
```

This sets the entire grid's formatting to the Preferred style, but you can also apply styles to individual rows and columns in the grid. For example, use the following code to apply the EvenRow style to the first and third columns in the grid:

```
Private Sub cmdStyleCol_Click()
    TDBGrid1.Columns(0).Style = "EvenRow"
    TDBGrid1.Columns(2).Style = "EvenRow"
End Sub
```

Using the `Style` property, you can apply a style to the entire grid control, a single column within the control, or a split within the control.

Creating Your Own Styles in Code

You can create your own styles in code at runtime. You might do this in situations where you want to enable the user to apply style-based formatting to the grid, or if you simply prefer to describe your styles in code as opposed to using the control's property sheet.

To create a style, create a new `Style` object, add it to the grid's `Styles` collection, and assign its properties. For example, assume you need a style to highlight a particular type of customer. Listing 13.5 shows how to do this.

Listing 13.5   Creating the Preferred Style at Runtime

```
Option Explicit

' References ADO 2.0


Private Sub Form_Load()

Dim st As Style
    Set st = TDBGrid1.Styles.Add("Preferred")
```

```
    With st
        .Parent = "Normal"
        .Font.Bold = True
        .BackColor = vbYellow
        .ForeColor = vbRed
    End With

End Sub
```

Code Example: You can find an example of the code discussed in this section in the project `TrueDBG.vbp`, located in the directory `\vbdb\code\ 13-DBGrid\TrueDBG`. For information on how to install the sample files on the CD that accompanies this book, see the section "Installing the Example Files" in the introduction at the beginning of this book.

As soon as your custom style is created, you can apply it to grid elements (as demonstrated in the previous section).

Note: This just scratches the surface of what you can do with styles. True DBGrid Pro's style features are much more involved than this chapter has space to cover. The grid comes with additional documentation and sample applications that give you more information on how to use its extensive style features.

Applying Custom Styles Using the *FetchRowStyle* Event   The True DBGrid control provides a number of features that make it easy for you to apply custom style formatting based on the contents of cells. One way to do this is with the FetchRowStyle event.

The FetchRowStyle event is triggered whenever the grid control needs to display a row of data. In the event procedure, you can write code specifying how each row of data should be formatted, based on data contained in cells or any other criterion you specify.

Enable the FetchRowStyle event by setting the grid's FetchRowStyle property to True. You can then write an event procedure in the FetchRowStyle event that formats cells based on the criteria you specify. Listing 13.6 gives an example of this.

Listing 13.6 **Using the *FetchRowStyle* Event Procedure to Apply Styles to Cells**

```
Option Explicit

' References ADO 2.0

Private Sub Form_Load()

Dim st As Style
    Set st = TDBGrid1.Styles.Add("Preferred")

    With st
        .Parent = "Normal"
        .Font.Bold = True
        .BackColor = vbYellow
        .ForeColor = vbRed
    End With

    ' Enables row-by-row style formatting
    ' via FetchRowStyle event
    TDBGrid1.FetchRowStyle = True

End Sub


Private Sub TDBGrid1_FetchRowStyle(ByVal Split As Integer, Bookmark As _
            Variant, ByVal RowStyle As TrueOleDBGrid50.StyleDisp)
    If TDBGrid1.Columns("Preferred").CellText(Bookmark) = True Then
        RowStyle = "Preferred"
    End If
End Sub
```

This code highlights all of Jones Novelties' preferred customers with the Preferred style (created in the previous example). The result of this code is illustrated in Figure 13.16.

Figure 13.16
You can format data in the True DBGrid control with styles according to the data in each record.

CHANGING THE DISPLAY OF A COLUMN WITH THE *VALUEITEM* OBJECT

Occasionally, you need to alter the display of information in a column in order to clarify or highlight the data. TrueDBGrid Pro provides this functionality through the ValueItem object.

The ValueItem object has Value and DisplayValue properties. The Value property is the actual value of the cell, while DisplayValue is the information you want to display in the grid.

For example, by default, the Preferred column in the example application displays True and False values. It would be easier to make out this information if the column displayed the values Preferred and Normal. Listing 13.7. gives an example of how to use the ValueItem object to change the display of data in a column.

Listing 13.7   Using the *ValueItem* Object to Alter the Display of Information in a Column

```
Private Sub cmdValue_Click()
Dim Item As New ValueItem

    With TDBGrid1.Columns("Preferred").ValueItems
        Item.Value = True
        Item.DisplayValue = "Preferred"
        .Add Item

        Item.Value = False
        Item.DisplayValue = "Normal"
        .Add Item

        .Translate = True
    End With

End Sub
```

This causes the grid to display data as shown in Figure 13.17.

Because it's no longer displaying the numeric values True and False, but instead the textual values Preferred and Normal, applying this change to your application breaks your FetchRowStyle event procedure. To fix that, change the grid's FetchRowStyle event procedure as shown in Listing 13.8.

Figure 13.17
The grid displays data translated with the ValueItems object.

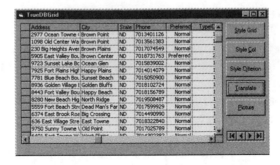

Listing 13.8   Changing to the *FetchRowStyle* Event Procedure to Accommodate the Translated Value

```
Private Sub TDBGrid1_FetchRowStyle(ByVal Split As Integer, Bookmark As _
            Variant, ByVal RowStyle As TrueOleDBGrid50.StyleDisp)
    If TDBGrid1.Columns("Preferred").CellText(Bookmark) = "Preferred" Then
        RowStyle = "Preferred"
    End If
End Sub
```

An interesting variation on the ValueItem object available in True DBGrid is the ability to display graphics in cells. To do this, simply set the ValueItem object's DisplayValue property to a picture retrieved with the Visual Basic LoadPicture function. Listing 13.9 gives an example of this.

Listing 13.9   Displaying Graphics in the Grid Using the *ValueItem* Object

```
Private Sub cmdValue_Click()
Dim Item As New ValueItem

    With TDBGrid1.Columns("Preferred").ValueItems
        Item.Value = -1
        Item.DisplayValue = LoadPicture(App.Path & "\pref.bmp")
        .Add Item

        Item.Value = 0
        Item.DisplayValue = LoadPicture(App.Path & "\norm.bmp")
        .Add Item

        .Translate = True
    End With

End Sub
```

Figure 13.18 shows what the grid looks like when this code is run .

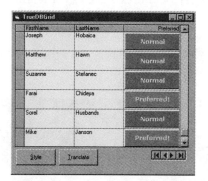

Figure 13.18
The grid displays a graphic instead of a text value in a column.

PROVIDING HELP FOR USERS WITH CELLTIPS

True DBGrid Pro has the ability to provide CellTips to users. CellTips are visual cues similar to the ToolTips in Microsoft Office applications, except CellTips can be different for each row, column, or cell in your application.

You set up CellTips in your True DBGrid application by setting the grid's CellTips property to something other than 0 (which is the default). When you've set this property, write code in the FetchCellTips event to supply text to the cell tip. Listing 13.10 gives an example.

Listing 13.10   Populating the Grid's CellTips

```
Private Sub TDBGrid1_FetchCellTips(ByVal SplitIndex As Integer, ByVal _
     ColIndex As Integer, ByVal RowIndex As Long, CellTip As String, _
     ByVal FullyDisplayed As Boolean, ByVal TipStyle _
     As TrueOleDBGrid50.StyleDisp)

' Set CellTips property to make this work

   Select Case ColIndex
       Case 0  ' First Name
       CellTip = "The customer's first name"


       Case 1  ' Last Name
       CellTip = "The customer's last name"


       Case 2  ' Preferred
       CellTip = "Preferred customers have this field set to -1."


   End Select

End Sub
```

The FetchCellTips event takes a large number of arguments, permitting you to supply CellTips in a variety of contexts. In this case, the code simply supplies a description of the various columns displayed in the grid by setting the CellTip argument to a text string.

Setting the grid's CellTips property to 2 - Floating produces the effect shown in Figure 13.19.

Figure 13.19
You can float CellTips over a True DBGrid control.

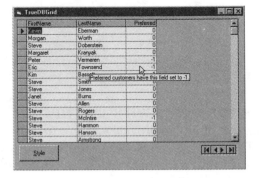

SUMMARY

This chapter gave a brief summary of the DBGrid and True DBGrid Pro controls' features. In addition to providing examples of using the control with a data control, you learned how to use the grid in unbound mode, as well as take advantage of techniques that permit you to display data differently based on the contents of a particular field.

The next chapter introduces another grid control, the MSFlexGrid control, and its commercial counterpart, the VideoSoft VSFLEX control. You can use this grid to work with data in a manner similar to the DBGrid control, but with a number of user-definable customization features.

QUESTIONS AND ANSWERS

Q. Is there an easy way to permit the user to select from a list of choices when entering information in a grid cell?

A. Yes. The True DBGrid control provides support for controls—such as a drop-down list box—to appear in a cell when a user is editing data. True DBGrid Pro provides a drop-down list called TDBDropDown. The benefit of using this control is the fact that it supports many of the properties and methods of the full grid control, including the display of data in multiple columns. You can even bind the TDBDropDown control to a different Data control than the True DBGrid control is bound to.

Q. **Can I apply an input mask to a grid cell the same way I can with a masked edit control?**

A. Yes. To do this, use the EditMask property of the grid's Column object. The same formatting characters supported in the Visual Basic Masked Edit control are supported in True DBGrid. (The Masked Edit control is introduced in Chapter 12.)

Using the MSFlexGrid, Hierarchical FlexGrid, and VideoSoft VSFLEX Controls

Using Online Decision Support

Using the MSFlex Control

Using the Hierarchical FlexGrid Control

Using VideoSoft VSFlexGrid Pro 6.0

The MSFlexGrid control is one of several grid controls to ship with Microsoft Visual Basic. Although you'd think that VB is "gridded out," you'll find that the FlexGrid control provides some significant features the others don't.

These features include the capability to display and analyze data by clicking and dragging with the mouse. When you do this, the FlexGrid control regroups data and combines it in ways that let you see trends across a large amount of data without forcing you to analyze every bit of information in your database.

USING ONLINE DECISION SUPPORT

Database tools are generally divided into two categories: transaction-processing tools and decision-support tools. *Transaction processing* involves entering and altering data in the database, while *decision support* involves evaluating data that's already in the database.

A database report is an example of a decision-support tool. In most cases, report data is non-interactive; a user can't generally edit the numbers (often because the report is presented to him or her in the form of printed numbers on a sheet of paper). Most importantly for the developer, if the report's consumer needs to see the data in a different way (sorted by date and grouped by region, for example), the developer must go back to the grindstone and create a whole new report.

An alternative to this is a process known as online analytical processing (OLAP). OLAP tools have the following characteristics:

▶ *Displaying data in multiple dimensions.* This generally involves a minimum of two dimensions (which makes a database grid ideal for use as an OLAP tool), but sometimes involves views of data that exceed three dimensions.

▶ *Drill-down.* This process permits you to expose detail about a specific statistic. For example, if your application displays a list of sales figures for each division of your company, you might want to see details on how each salesperson in each region fared. A drill-down feature makes this process a no-brainer. In a GUI, drilling down is typically accomplished by clicking the piece of data about which you want more detail.

▶ *Grouping.* This is the opposite of drill-down; it's also known as roll-up. This process involves hiding or summarizing information in situations where you don't need to know the detail. For example, if you're a company's CEO, it's unlikely that you'd need to know how many rubber chickens were sold in retail store #485 yesterday. Instead, you'd roll that data up into a regional or company-wide statistic. OLAP applications permit you to do that.

The MSFlexGrid control permits you to create highly effective decision-support applications. The commercial vsFlexArray control lets you do even more, particularly in the area of roll-up and drill-down. This chapter introduces both controls, showing how you can use them in applications both with and without the use of data controls.

USING THE MSFLEXGRID CONTROL

Microsoft Visual Basic comes with an ActiveX component that lets you incorporate OLAP capabilities into your VB applications. This component, the MSFlexGrid control, displays data in a grid that makes it easy for users to group information in order to view and summarize data.

Note: The MSFlexGrid control is a "light" version of the VSFLEX component developed by VideoSoft Corporation. For more information on the full version of VSFLEX, check out the VideoSoft Web site at http:// www.videosoft.com. A working demonstration version of the control is on the CD-ROM accompanying this book.

There is also more information on the commercial version of VSFLEX (including differences between it and the MSFlex control that comes with VB) in the "Using VideoSoft VSFlexGrid Pro 6.0" section later in this chapter.

The MSFlexGrid control ships with the Professional and Enterprise editions of Visual Basic. The MSFlexGrid control's filename is MSFLXGRD.OCX. To use the MSFlexGrid in your Visual Basic project, do the following:

1. In Visual Basic, select Project Components.

2. The Components dialog box appears. In the list of components, scroll down until you see Microsoft FlexGrid Control 6.0.

3. Check the control in the list and click OK. The MSFlexGrid control is added to your Visual Basic toolbox, as shown in Figure 14.1.

Figure 14.1
The MSFlexGrid control is added to the Visual Basic toolbox.

To start using the MSFlexGrid control, add an instance of the control to a Visual Basic form. You can then optionally bind the MSFlexGrid control to a Data control. This chapter takes you through the process of creating an application based on the MSFlexGrid control: first in unbound mode and then bound to a DAO data control.

Adding Data to the MSFlexGrid Control

When the MSFlexGrid isn't bound to a data control, you can add data to the control using its properties and methods. You start populating an unbound FlexGrid by setting the grid's Rows and Columns properties. This provides cells into which you can insert data. Here's an example:

```
FlexGrid1.Rows = 12
FlexGrid1.Columns = 4
```

This code creates a grid with 48 cells—12 rows by 4 columns. After you've created a number of rows and columns in the FlexGrid, you can navigate from one cell to the next in code, adding data to each cell. Navigate to the cell to which you want to add data by setting the Row and Col properties of the grid; this sets the position of the current cell. You can then assign data to the current cell by using the cell's Text property. The Text property returns or assigns data to the current cell (as set by the Row and Col properties).

Listing 14.1 gives an example of code that populates a single-row grid with data.

Listing 14.1   Populating a FlexGrid Control with Hard-Coded Data

```
Option Explicit

Private Sub Form_Load()
    MSFlexGrid1.Cols = 4
    MSFlexGrid1.Rows = 1

    ' Place text in header
    MSFlexGrid1.Row = 0
    MSFlexGrid1.Col = 1
    MSFlexGrid1.Text = "January"

    MSFlexGrid1.Col = 2
    MSFlexGrid1.Text = "February"

    MSFlexGrid1.Col = 3
    MSFlexGrid1.Text = "March"

End Sub
```

Code Example: You can find the application described in this section, including the modifications described in the next section, in the directory \vbdb\code\14-VSFlex\HardCode.vbp. For information on how to install the sample files on the CD that accompanies this book, see the section "Installing the Example Files" in the introduction at the beginning of this book.

This code produces a header for the grid, but doesn't add any data to it. The grid produced by this code is illustrated in Figure 14.2.

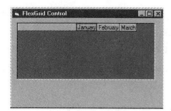

Adding Data to the FlexGrid Using the *AddItem* Method

As an alternative to determining the number of rows and columns in advance, you can use the AddItem method to populate the grid with as much data as you want, without having to know in advance how much data you have.

Listing 14.2 modifies the code example in the previous section, populating a FlexGrid control with three rows of hard-coded data using the AddItem method.

Listing 14.2   Populating the Grid Using the *AddItem* Method

```
Option Explicit

Private Sub Form_Load()
    FlexGrid1.Cols = 4
    FlexGrid1.Rows = 1

    ' Place text in header
    FlexGrid1.Row = 0
    FlexGrid1.Col = 1
    FlexGrid1.Text = "January"
    FlexGrid1.Col = 2
    FlexGrid1.Text = "February"
    FlexGrid1.Col = 3
    FlexGrid1.Text = "March"


    ' Place data in grid
    FlexGrid1.AddItem "Rubber chickens" & vbTab & "100" & vbTab & "200" & _
                   vbTab & "250"
    FlexGrid1.AddItem "Hand buzzers" & vbTab & "75" & vbTab & "125" & _
                   vbTab & "65"
    FlexGrid1.AddItem "Squirt flowers" & vbTab & "15" & vbTab & "35" & _
                   vbTab & "115"

End Sub
```

Note: The FlexGrid control is designed to be compatible with the (non–database-aware) Grid control, which has shipped with Visual Basic since time immemorial. Consequently, many of the techniques in this section of the chapter (pertaining to the Cols and Rows properties, for example, as well as the AddItem method) are applicable to the plain-vanilla Grid control as well.

The grid produced by this code is shown in Figure 14.3.

Figure 14.3
This grid is populated with hard-coded data by using the AddItem method.

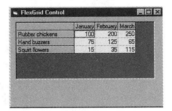

The tab character, expressed in code as the intrinsic constant vbTab, is used to delimit data when using the AddItem method. When you use AddItem, each piece of data separated by a tab character goes into a separate column.

In addition to using the AddItem method, you can also add information to cells in the grid using the TextMatrix property, described in the "Adding Data Using the *TextMatrix* Property" section later in this chapter.

Creating a Grid Header Using the *FormatString* Property

The FlexGrid control provides an additional method of creating a header row—the FormatString property. This is probably the simplest method of assigning text to the header row, and it has the advantage of being usable at design time. It also lets you align the cells in the grid at the same time you supply header text.

To format a grid's header, you assign a string that contains special formatting characters to the grid's FormatString property. You can do this at design time or at runtime, using code. For example, to enter data in the grid's header, you enter text separated by a pipe character . Using the semicolon character, you can assign values for the row header as well as the column header. You can also use formatting characters to specify the alignment of information in columns.

The formatting characters available in the FlexGrid's FormatString property are shown in Table 14.1.

Table 14.1 Formatting Strings Available in the FlexGrid's FormatString Property	
Character	**Meaning**
|	Delimiter; separates text that should be placed in different columns of the grid's header row
<	Left-align the column
>	Right-align the column
^	Center the column
;	Begin row information

For example, to create a grid with three columns labeled with the first three months of the year, use the following format string:

```
"January¦February¦March"
```

Use the following format string to create a grid to illustrate the sales of various products over a period of months:

```
"¦>January¦>February¦>March;¦Rubber Chickens¦Hand Buzzers¦Squirt Flowers"
```

This formatting string contains an extra pipe character (to the left of the month of January); this causes the upper-left cell of the grid to be blank.

Code Example: You can find an example of the `FormatString` property in the project `HardCode.vbp`, located in the directory `\vbdb\code\14-VSFlex\HardCode`. For information on how to install the sample files on the CD that accompanies this book, see the section "Installing the Example Files" in the introduction at the beginning of this book.

Adding Data Using the *TextMatrix* Property

In addition to adding information to the grid the old-fashioned way using the `AddItem` method, the FlexGrid control also provides a technique that the classic VB grid control doesn't support—the `TextMatrix` property. This property is an array that represents all the cells in the Grid control.

To assign a value to a cell in the grid using the `TextMatrix` property, you must first create the cell you're attempting to address. You've seen a number of techniques for creating grid cells in this chapter—the `AddItem` method, the `FormatString` technique (which creates cells as a side-effect of creating row and column headers), and the easiest method, which simply involves assigning the `Rows` and `Cols` properties of the grid.

After you've created cells, populate them by addressing their x-y coordinates using the grid's TextMatrix property. For example, use the following code to place a piece of information in Column 3, Row 2 of the grid:

```
FlexGrid1.TextMatrix(3, 2) = "Rubber Chicken"
```

Remember when you're assigning values to cells in the grid that rows and columns in a FlexGrid control begin numbering at zero.

Adding Pictures to a FlexGrid Control

Any cell in a FlexGrid control can contain a picture. You add a picture to a grid cell by using the grid's CellPicture property in conjunction with Visual Basic's LoadPicture function. Remember that LoadPicture returns an object variable, so you must assign it using the Set operator.

```
Set FlexGrid1.CellPicture = LoadPicture(App.Path & "\exclam.bmp")
```

Remember that, as with many of the properties of the MSFlexGrid control, you must select a cell you wish to change before assigning a picture to it. Select a cell using the Row and Col properties of the grid.

Code Example: You can find an example of the CellPicture property in the project Picture.vbp, located in the directory \vbdb\code\14-VSFlex\Picture. For information on how to install the sample files on the CD that accompanies this book, see the section "Installing the Example Files" in the introduction at the beginning of this book.

Figure 14.4 shows an example of a FlexGrid control with an image embedded in its upper-left cell.

Figure 14.4
You can embed a bitmap in a cell of an MSFlexGrid.

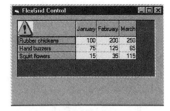

Sorting Data in the FlexGrid Control

You sort data in the FlexGrid control by selecting the column you want to sort by; then you set the grid's sort property to a sort constant.

The sort constants available with the FlexGrid control are listed in Table 14.2.

Table 14.2 Sort Constants Used with the FlexGrid's Sort Property		
Constant	**Value**	**Description**
flexSortNone	0	No sorting
flexSortGenericAscending	1	Sort in ascending (A to Z, 0 to 9) order; in a generic sort, the control guesses whether a piece of data is textual or numeric
flexSortGenericDescending	2	Sort generically, in descending order
flexSortNumericAscending	3	Sort in ascending order, treating strings as numbers
flexSortNumericDescending	4	Sort in descending order, treating strings as numbers
flexSortStringNoCase Ascending	5	Sort in case insensitive, ascending order
flexSortNoCaseDescending	6	Sort in case insensitive, descending order
flexSortStringAscending	7	Sort in case sensitive, ascending order
flexSortStringDescending	8	Sort in case sensitive, descending order
	9	Use a custom sort order determined by the grid's Compare event

Listing 14.3 gives an example of a Command button that sorts a list of products by product name.

Listing 14.3   Sorting a List of Items in the FlexGrid Control

```
Private Sub cmdSort_Click()
    ' Select the column you
    ' want to sort by
    FlexGrid1.Col = 0

    ' Apply the sort constant
    FlexGrid1.Sort = flexSortStringAscending
End Sub
```

The sorting capability becomes important in an application based on the FlexGrid control, because values that are adjacent to each other in the grid can be merged if they share the same value. However, the items in the grid tend to appear next to each other in the grid only if they're sorted. This is different than grouping, as you find in database reports. When data is merged, duplicate values in adjacent cells are displayed in one merged cell; in grouping, a number of records' values are added together, averaged, or combined in some other arithmetical way.

Merging the contents of cells makes for a more concise expression of data; it's introduced in the next section.

Note: Bear in mind that in a database access application, it's almost always faster to let the database engine sort data rather than sorting it in the user-interface level.

Merging Data in Cells Using the FlexGrid Control

In order to take advantage of the FlexGrid control's full capabilities, you must set it up to merge cells.

To set up your grid to merge cells, you follow these general steps:

▶ Set the grid's MergeCells property to a value that permits merging. By default, MergeCells is set to zero, which prohibits merging cells.

▶ Use the MergeRow and MergeCol properties to designate which rows and columns are eligible to be merged.

▶ Write code that responds to an action in the user interface—such as clicking a column—that indicates the user wants to merge data based on a particular field.

To begin creating an application with data cells that can be merged, you set the grid's MergeCells property. The MergeCells property dictates how cells are going to be merged. With the least restrictive setting, flexMergeFree, any cell that is adjacent to (that is, to the left or on top of) a cell with the same value is merged with that cell. The MergeCells property has five settings in all, shown in Table 14.3.

Table 14.3 Settings of the MSFlexGrid Control's MergeCells Property		
Setting	**Value**	**Description**
flexMergeNever	0	Don't permit merging. This is the default setting.
flexMergeFree	1	A cell can be merged with the value in the row or column adjacent to it.
flexMergeRestrictRows	2	Data can only be merged by rows.
flexMergeRestrictColumns	3	Data can only be merged by columns.
flexMergeRestrictAll	4	Data can be merged by both rows and columns.

Note: Visual Basic's online help topic for the MergeCells property lists the constant flexMergeRestrictBoth. This is an error; the constant is actually named flexMergeRestrictAll.

For example, suppose you start with the following basic data set:

Product	**Region**	**Units Sold**
Rubber chickens	North	100
Rubber chickens	South	125
Joy buzzers	North	75
Joy buzzers	South	85
Squirt flowers	North	25
Squirt flowers	South	65

With a data set like this, the first two columns can be merged (because it wouldn't make sense to group matching values in the Units Sold column). Use the following code to enable this:

```
FlexGrid1.MergeCol(0) = True
FlexGrid1.MergeCol(1) = True
```

Now you have the ability to set the MergeCells property to see the data in different ways. If you set MergeCells to flexMergeFree, the grid looks like this:

Product	Region	Units Sold
Rubber chickens	North	100
	South	125
Joy buzzers	North	75
	South	85
Squirt flowers	North	25
	South	65

Notice how much more compact and clear this data is than the previous data set. Now watch what happens when the Region column is moved to the leftmost side of the grid (remember that in this grid, MergeCells is set to flexMergeFree).

Region	Product	Units Sold
North	Rubber chickens	100
	Squirt flowers	125
	Joy buzzers	75
South		85
	Rubber chickens	125
	Squirt flowers	65

Because the grid is set to flexMergeFree and the Joy buzzers product appears twice in the Product column, Joy buzzers are merged across the North and South regions. It's still clear how many buzzers were sold by each region, but only because you suppressed merging in the Units Sold column. To prevent Joy buzzers from merging across regions like this, set the grid's `MergeCells` property to flexMergeRestrictRows. This prevents cells from merging vertically. The grid now looks like this:

Region	Product	Units Sold
North	Rubber chickens	100
	Squirt flowers	125
	Joy buzzers	75
South	Joy buzzers	85
	Rubber chickens	125
	Squirt flowers	65

This organization makes things a bit clearer.

Listing 14.4 gives a complete example of a grid application that populates itself with this data and permits you to rearrange its columns by double-clicking to see data differently.

Listing 14.4   Sales-Tracking Application That Permits You to Rearrange Data

```
Option Explicit

Private Sub Form_Load()

    Dim x As Integer

    FlexGrid1.FormatString = "Inventory Item Name¦Region¦Amount"

    FlexGrid1.FixedCols = 0
    FlexGrid1.Cols = 3
    FlexGrid1.Rows = 1

    With FlexGrid1
        ' Product sales data by region
        .AddItem "Rubber chickens" & vbTab & "North" & vbTab & "100"
```

continues

Listing 14.4   Sales-Tracking Application That Permits You to Rearrange Data (Continued)

```
            .AddItem "Rubber chickens" & vbTab & "South" & vbTab & "125"

            .AddItem "Joy buzzers" & vbTab & "North" & vbTab & "75"
            .AddItem "Joy buzzers" & vbTab & "South" & vbTab & "85"

            .AddItem "Squirt flowers" & vbTab & "North" & vbTab & "25"
            .AddItem "Squirt flowers" & vbTab & "South" & vbTab & "65"
        End With

        FlexGrid1.MergeCells = flexMergeRestrictRows

        ' Make the product and
        ' region columns mergable
        For x = 0 To 1
            FlexGrid1.MergeCol(x) = True
        Next x

End Sub

Private Sub FlexGrid1_DblClick()
    FlexGrid1.ColPosition(FlexGrid1.MouseCol) = 0

    ' Without the sort, the merge
    ' doesn't work
    FlexGrid1.Col = 0
    FlexGrid1.Sort = flexSortStringAscending
End Sub
```

 Code Example: You can find the code discussed in this section in the project `Merge.vbp`, located in the directory `\vbdb\code\14-VSFlex\Merge`. For information on how to install the sample files on the CD that accompanies this book, see the section "Installing the Example Files" in the introduction at the beginning of this book.

The important thing about this application is the fact that it is interactive—the user gets to determine which column is merged by double-clicking it. This is what OLAP is all about. When the grid's DblClick event is triggered, the column the user double-clicked (as determined by the grid's MouseCol property) becomes the leftmost column (as a result of the ColPosition property). The grid is then resorted, which causes adjacent cells with the same value to merge.

Figure 14.5 shows what this application looks like when it is running. In the figure, the user has moved the Region column to the leftmost side in order to aggregate sales by regions.

The one remaining unsatisfying aspect of this application is that it populates

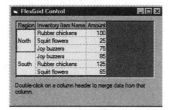

Figure 14.5
Data in this FlexGrid application has been sorted and merged.

itself with hard-wired data embedded in the code. This problem is fixed in the next section.

Using the FlexGrid with a Database

You can bypass the various programmatic techniques for populating the FlexGrid control with data by simply connecting it to a data control. When you do this, the data displayed by the grid is determined by the data control; you don't need to use the AddItem or any other property or method to populate the grid with data.

Bear in mind that you can't edit data displayed in the MSFlexGrid control. If you need the grid to be able to write information back to the database, use the commercial version of the control—vsFlexArray, introduced later in this chapter.

To bind a MSFlexGrid control to a data control, follow these steps:

1. Create a new VB project.

2. Create a DAO Data control, a MSFlexGrid control, a command button, and two text boxes on the project's main form. Name the text boxes txtFrom and txtTo, and name the command button cmdQuery.

3. Set the Data control's DatabaseName property to the location of the novelty.mdb database in your code directory.

4. Set the Grid's DataSource property to the name of the Data control, Data1.

5. In the form, write a subroutine called Query to set the Data control's RecordSource property to a SQL string. This string will use the parameters provided by the text boxes to limit the amount of data returned.

```
Private Sub Query()
```

```
        Screen.MousePointer = vbHourglass
        Data1.RecordSource = "SELECT OrderDate, State, " & _
                             "Sum(OrderAmount) As OrderTotal " & _
                             "FROM tblCustomer " & _
                             "INNER JOIN tblOrder " & _
                             "ON tblCustomer.ID = tblOrder.CustomerID " & _
                             "GROUP BY OrderDate, State " & _
                             "HAVING OrderDate BETWEEN #" & _
                             txtFrom.Text & "# AND #" & _
                             txtTo.Text & "#"
    Data1.Refresh
    Screen.MousePointer = vbNormal
End Sub
```

The SQL query assigned to the Data control in this subroutine returns three columns: OrderDate, State, and OrderTotal. The query returns this information by joining the two tables tblCustomer and tblOrder, aggregating the value of the OrderAmount field.

6. In the Click event of the Query button, call the Query subroutine:

```
Private Sub cmdQuery_Click()
    Query
End Sub
```

7. Because the user won't interact with the Data control, set its Visible property to False.

8. Set the grid's FixedCols property to 0; then run the application.

9. Enter the dates **1/1/98** and **1/7/98**; then click the Query button. The grid should display the data, as shown in Figure 14.6.

10. Make the cells in the grid mergable. To do this, set the grid's MergeCells property to 2 - flexMergeRestrictRows.

11. Enable merging for the first two columns by adding the following code to the form's Load event:

```
FlexGrid1.MergeCol(0) = True
FlexGrid1.MergeCol(1) = True
```

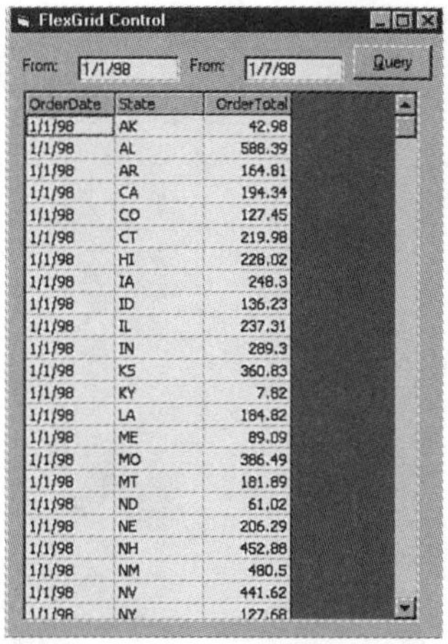

Figure 14.6
An MSFlexGrid control displays query results in an application.

12. Now permit the user to determine which column is merged by adding the following code to the grid's Click event:

```
Private Sub FlexGrid1_Click()

    FlexGrid1.ColPosition(FlexGrid1.MouseCol) = 0

    FlexGrid1.Col = 1
    FlexGrid1.ColSel = 0
    FlexGrid1.Sort = flexSortStringAscending

End Sub
```

13. Run the application. The grid sorts by date, showing you the purchases by each state from one day to the next.

14. Finally, click the State field's header. The grid rearranges itself to show which states contain customers who placed orders during the time period specified. This reveals new information about your data source that you may not have been able to infer before. For example, as Figure 14.7. shows, business was booming in Alabama on New Year's Day.

Figure 14.7
This FlexGrid control merging information is based on customer type.

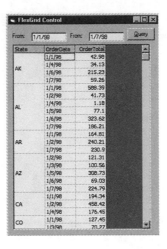

Code Example: You can find the code described in this section in the project `FlexData.vbp`, located in the directory `\vbdb\code\14-VSFlex\FlexData`. For information on how to install the sample files on the CD that accompanies this book, see the section "Installing the Example Files" in the introduction at the beginning of this book.

Using the Hierarchical FlexGrid Control

The Hierarchical FlexGrid control is new in Visual Basic 6.0. You can use the control to view related groups of data in a compact format.

To bind data to a Hierarchical FlexGrid control, you use the MSDataShape provider. This provider gives you the ability to execute a command using a superset of the SQL syntax. This syntax allows you to describe a relationship between two recordsets.

Although it's possible to describe a relationship between two tables using a SQL join, a hierarchical relationship can express the relationship more efficiently—instead of displaying multiple repetitive records on the "one" side of the join, you only pass the records once.

To set up the application, follow these steps:

1. Create a new VB application.

2. In the Project Components dialog box, add the controls Microsoft Hierarchical FlexGrid Control 6.0 (OLE DB) and Microsoft ADO Data Control (OLE DB) to your project.

3. Create an instance of the HFlexGrid and ADO Data controls on your form.

4. In the Load event of the form, prepare a connection string using the code:

```
Private Sub Form_Load()

Dim strCn As String
strCn = "Provider=MSDataShape.1;" & _
        "Data Source=Novelty;" & _
        "Data Provider=MSDASQL;" & _
        "UID=sa;"
```

5. While remaining in the Load event of the form, write code to create a Shape command that retrieves data. This command will retrieve a list of states and a related list of customers (if this command had been executed as a SQL join, it would be known as a self-join, since the data in the table is related to itself):

```
Dim strSQL As String

strSQL = "SHAPE {SELECT DISTINCT State FROM tblCustomer} AS States " &
_
         "APPEND ({SELECT * FROM tblCustomer} AS Customers RELATE " &
_
         "State TO State) AS Customers"
```

6. Finally, assign the connection string and the record source to the data control and set the data source of the grid to the data control:

```
With Adodc1
    .ConnectionString = strCn
    .RecordSource = strSQL
End With

Set MSHFlexGrid1.DataSource = Adodc1
```

The result is that you can see a list of states and all of the customers that live in each state. Because the related records are displayed in an outline format (as shown in Figure 14.8), you can expand and collapse the list easily. This gives you the ability to browse the data in a more compact format.

Figure 14.8
Related records are displayed in the Hierarchical FlexGrid control.

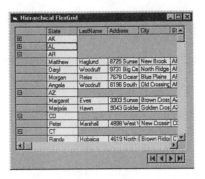

Code Example: You can find the code discussed in this section in the project `HFlex.vbp`, located in the directory `\vbdb\code\14-VSFlex\HFlex`. For information on how to install the sample files on the CD that accompanies this book, see the section "Installing the Example Files" in the introduction at the beginning of this book.

USING VIDEOSOFT VSFLEXGRID PRO 6.0

The commercial version of the MSFlexGrid control is called *VideoSoft VSFlexGrid Pro*. The VSFlexGrid Pro product actually consists of two controls—vsFlexArray, the commercial version of the FlexGrid control, and vsFlexString, used to find patterns and expressions in data.

Note: A trial version of the commercial VSFlexGrid Pro package is on the CD that accompanies this book. For more information on the commercial VSFlexGrid Pro package, visit the VideoSoft Web site at `http://www.videosoft.com`.

The full version of VSFlexGrid Pro offers a number of new features and performance enhancements over the MSFlexGrid control included with VB out of the box. The following features are include:

▶ The ability to bind to a data control in read-write mode (the MSFlexGrid control can bind to a data control, but the data is read-only)

▶ The ability to bind to an ADO Data control

▶ The ability to edit text inside a cell

▶ The ability to present subtotals and display data in outline format, similar to the way Windows Explorer displays folders and files

▶ Columns that resize themselves automatically to fit their contents

▶ The ability to mask input in a cell similar to the way a MaskedEdit control works

▶ Enhanced sort capabilities, including support for international sort orders

▶ Display of flood values in cells, giving you the ability to graphically display data similar to a progress meter

▶ Additional options for controlling the appearance of the control

▶ The ability to embed controls such as check boxes and combo boxes in grid cells

▶ The ability to save the entire contents of the grid to a file and reload the file into the grid later

▶ Increased performance

The VSFlexGrid Pro controls do not ship with Visual Basic; VSFlexGrid Pro is a separate product. There are two versions of the VSFlexGrid Pro controls; their filenames are VSFLEX6D.OCX (the DAO flavor of the grid) and VSFLEX6.OCX (the flavor that supports OLE DB and ADO).

Do the following to use the VSFLEX controls in your Visual Basic project:

1. In Visual Basic, select Project Components.

2. The Components dialog box appears. In the list of components, choose either :-) VideoSoft vsFlex3 Controls (DAO) or :-) VideoSoft vsFlex3 Controls (OLE DB), depending on which data access library your application uses. The libraries should conveniently appear toward the top of the alphabetical list of components, because of VideoSoft's crafty practice of placing an emoticon at the beginning of the names of each of their components.

3. Click OK. The vsFlexGrid and vsFlexString controls are added to your Visual Basic toolbox.

Many of the MSFlexGrid control enhancements provided by the vsFlexArray control are discussed in the remainder of this chapter. The commercial VSFLEX package also contains the vsFlexString control, which lets you perform lookups on data based on expressions.

Binding the vsFlexArray Control to a Data Source

You have the ability to bind a vsFlexArray control to either the DAO or ADO Data controls. To do this, create the appropriate data control on the form; then set the vsFlexGrid's DataSource control to the name of the data control.

Figure 14.9 shows a vsFlexArray control bound to an ADO Data control. The data shown is in the tblCustomer table in the database novelty.mdb.

Figure 14.9
This data is displayed by the vsFlexArray control bound to an ADO Data control.

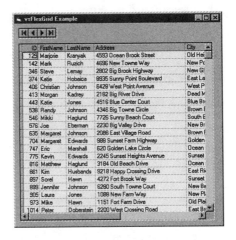

Code Example: The project described in this section is called VsfBound.vbp. It is located in the directory \vbdb\code\14-VSFlex\VsfBound. For information on how to install the sample files on the CD that accompanies this book, see the section "Installing the Example Files" in the introduction at the beginning of this book.

Editing Data in Cells

When your application uses the MSFlexGrid control, the only way you can change the contents of a cell at runtime is in code, by selecting the cell and altering its Text property. An important improvement in the vsFlexArray control over the MSFlexGrid control is the fact that users can edit data in cells directly. You don't need to write any code to support this feature. In-cell editing works whether the grid is bound to a data control or not.

In-cell editing is deactivated by default in vsFlexArray. To permit users to edit values directly in cells, you set the control's Editable property to True. You can do this at design time or runtime.

To permit users to perform in-cell edits on data when your grid is bound to a data control, you must also set the grid's DataMode property to 1 - flexDMBound. This tells the grid to commit edited data in cells back to the data source through the data control.

It's important to bear in mind that if the DataMode property isn't set correctly, the user can edit the contents of a grid cell, but the update won't be sent back to the database, and no error is triggered. Note also that the update won't take place until you move off the row containing the changed record.

Performing Automatic Searching

The vsFlexGrid control has the ability to permit users to search for data in the grid by typing. This feature is new in VSFLEX 6.0.

You can automatically search the grid by setting the AutoSearch property to something other than its default, which is 0 - flexSearchNone. If you set the property to 1 - flexSearchFromTop, you'll be taken to the first record that matches the characters you type. If you choose 2- flexSearchFromCursor, the control will locate the next record that matches what you type, based on where the cursor was located when you started.

Figure 14.10 shows an example of a vsFlexGrid control that has its AutoSearch feature activated. You can see how, as the user types data, the appropriate piece of information is selected.

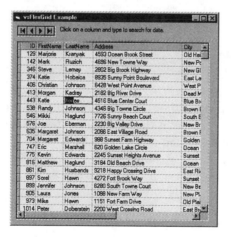

Figure 14.10
Begin typing to search the vsFlexArray control for data using the AutoSearch feature.

Code Example: The project described in this section is called `Search.vbp`. It is located in the directory `\vbdb\code\14-VSFlex\Search`. For information on how to install the sample files on the CD that accompanies this book, see the section "Installing the Example Files" in the introduction at the beginning of this book.

Automatic Sorting

You can automatically sort a column in the grid by setting the `ExplorerBar` property to 1- flexExSort. This causes the grid to behave in a manner similar to the Windows Explorer—if you click the column header, the column is sorted. If you click the same column header again, the data is sorted in reverse order. An example of this is shown in Figure 14.11.

Figure 14.11
Here is the result of automatic sorting in a grid whose ExplorerBar property is set to flexExSort.

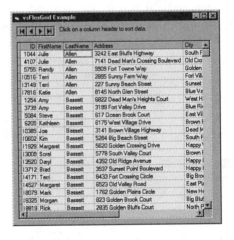

Code Example: A project that demonstrates the `ExplorerBar` property is called `Sort.vbp`. It is located in the directory `\vbdb\code\14-VSFlex\Sort`. For information on how to install the sample files on the CD that accompanies this book, see the section "Installing the Example Files" in the introduction at the beginning of this book.

Accessing Cell Properties

In previous versions of the vsFlexGrid control (including the MSFlexGrid flavor), you had to navigate to a particular cell using the grid's `Row` and `Column` properties before you could manipulate a cell's properties. New to version 6.0 of the vsFlexGrid control is the ability to address properties of a cell without having to navigate to it. You can use this feature to return or set properties of single cells or of ranges of cells.

You do this by using the `Cell` property of the grid control. Here's the syntax of the `Cell` property:

```
VsFlex1.Cell(Setting, [Row1], [Col1], [Row2], [Col2]) = Value
```

`Value` is the setting you want to apply to the range of cells. The value will be different depending on the value of the `Setting` parameter.

The row and column arguments let you to select a two-dimensional range of cells to affect. You use all four row and column properties when assigning a value to a range of cells. When you're reading the value of a cell, you use only the first row and column arguments.

The `Setting` argument refers to the type of property you want to set or retrieve. The options are listed in Table 14.4.

Table 14.4 Legal Values for the Setting Argument of the Cell Property	
Setting Value	**Corresponds to Property**
flexcpText	Text
flexcpTextStyle	
flexcpAlignment	CellAlignment
flexcpPicture	CellPicture
flexcpPictureAlignment	CellPictureAlignment
flexcpChecked	CellChecked
flexcpBackColor	CellBackColor
flexcpForeColor	CellForeColor
flexcpFloodPercent	CellFloodPercent
flexcpFloodColor	CellFloodColor
flexcpFont	Font
flexcpFontName	The name of the font (undocumented)
flexcpFontSize	The size of the font (undocumented)
flexcpFontBold	Whether the font is bold or not (undocumented)
	continues

Table 14.4 Legal Values for the Setting Argument of the Cell Property (Continued)	
Setting Value	**Corresponds to Property**
flexcpFontItalic	Whether the font is italic or not (undocumented)
flexcpFontUnderline	Whether the font is underlined or not (undocumented)
flexcpFontStrikethru	Whether the font is struck through or not (undocumented)
flexcpFontWidth	The width of the font (undocumented)
flexcpValue	Numeric value of the contents of the cell
flexcpTextDisplay	The formatted text
flexcpData	The Variant value attached to the cell
flexcpCustomFormat	Whether any formatting has been assigned to the cell

So, for example, if you were interested a 10 by 10 range of cells red in color, you'd use the code:

```
Private Sub cmdFormat_Click()
    vsFlexGrid1.Cell(flexcpBackColor, 1, 1, 10, 10) = vbRed
End Sub
```

If you wanted to apply a particular set of font formatting to the same range of cells, you use this code:

```
Private Sub cmdFont_Click()
    Dim f As stdole.StdFont
    Set f = New stdole.StdFont

    f.Bold = True
    f.Italic = True
    f.Name = "Tahoma"
    f.Size = 8

    Set vsFlexGrid1.Cell(flexcpFont, 1, 1, 10, 10) = f

End Sub
```

The object type `stdole.StdFont` is an object type that's available through the standard OLE library, which is referenced from every VB project by default. By instantiating an object of this type, you can refer to the properties and methods of the `font` object and then assign the object to the grid to apply formatting to it. This technique is much faster and more elegant than using the individual font properties of each cell.

After this code executes, the grid looks like Figure 14.12.

ID	FirstName	LastName	Address	City
129	*Marjorie*	*Kranyak*	*4593 Ocean Brook Street*	*Old He*
142	*Mark*	*Ruzich*	*4696 New Towne Way*	*New P*
346	*Steve*	*Lemay*	*2802 Big Brook Highway*	*New G*
374	*Katie*	*Hobaica*	*8935 Sunny Point Boulevard*	*East L*
406	*Christian*	*Johnson*	*6428 West Point Avenue*	*West J*
413	*Morgan*	*Kadrey*	*2182 Big River Drive*	*Dead I*
443	*Katie*	*Jones*	*4516 Blue Center Court*	*Blue B*
538	*Randy*	*Johnson*	*4346 Big Towne Circle*	*Brown*
546	*Mikki*	*Haglund*	*7726 Sunny Beach Court*	*South*
576	*Joe*	*Eberman*	*2230 Big Valley Drive*	*New B*
635	Margaret	Johnson	2086 East Village Road	Brown F
704	Margaret	Edwards	988 Sunset Farm Highway	Golden
747	Eric	Marshall	620 Golden Lake Circle	Ocean
775	Kevin	Edwards	2245 Sunset Heights Avenue	Sunset
816	Matthew	Haglund	3184 Old Beach Drive	Ocean
861	Kim	Husbands	9218 Happy Crossing Drive	East Ri
897	Sorel	Hawn	4272 Fort Brook Way	Sunset
899	Jennifer	Johnson	6280 South Towne Court	New Be
905	Laura	Jones	1088 New Farm Way	New Pl
973	Mike	Hawn	1151 Fort Farm Drive	Old Plai
1014	Peter	Doberstein	2200 West Crossing Road	East Br

Figure 14.12
Here are the results of a vsFlexGrid control that has been formatted using the Cell property and the standard OLE font object.

Code Example: You can find the code described in this section in the project `CellProp.vbp`, located in the directory `\vbdb\code\14-VSFlex\CellProp`. For information on how to install the sample files on the CD that accompanies this book, see the section "Installing the Example Files" in the introduction at the beginning of this book.

Displaying a Combo Box in a Cell

You have the ability to display a list of choices in the form of a combo box control in a vsFlexArray cell. You do this in situations where you want the user to pick from a list of choices.

You create the combo box control by using the grid's `ComboList` property. This property takes a string variable that permits you to designate the list of choices, delimited by pipe characters (|).

You write the code that assigns the `ComboList` property to the Grid control in the control's `BeforeEdit` event. This event is triggered at the time the user attempts to initiate an in-cell edit. This event receives the grid's current row and column as arguments, so you can display a different list of choices for each column.

Note: Providing combo boxes only makes sense if the grid is editable. For information on how to make a grid editable, see "Editing Data in Cells" earlier in this chapter.

For example, consider a vsFlexArray control that contains a list of customers. You want to enter each customer's name, address, and state of residence. Because there are a finite number of states, it might be nice to provide a list of states. Listing 14.5 shows an example of this.

Listing 14.5   Displaying a List of Choices Using the vsFlexArray's *BeforeEdit* Event and *ComboList* Property

```
Option Explicit

Private Sub Form_Load()
    Data1.DatabaseName = "..\..\DB\novelty.mdb"

    FlexGrid1.Editable = True
    FlexGrid1.DataMode = flexDMBound

End Sub

Private Sub FlexGrid1_BeforeEdit(ByVal Row As Long, ByVal Col As Long,
Cancel As Boolean)
    If Col = 3 Then
        FlexGrid1.ComboList = "AZ¦CA¦ID¦MT¦NM¦NV¦OR¦WA"
    Else
        ' Shut off list for other columns
        FlexGrid1.ComboList = ""
    End If
End Sub
```

This code assumes you've set the RecordSource property of the Data control to return data from the tblCustomer table. The code also includes only 8 of the 50 states for brevity.

In the BeforeEdit event, the list is displayed when the user edits column number 3 (the column that contains states, which is actually the fourth column in the grid since columns are numbered starting at zero). But it's set to an empty string when the user attempts to edit another column. This is important—if you don't do this, the list appears in every column after the user edits a value in the State column.

Figure 14.13 shows what the drop-down list looks like when it's being edited.

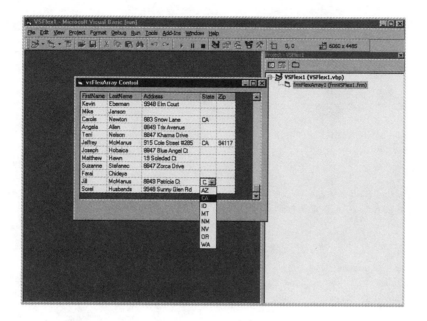

Figure 14.13
The ComboList property provides a list of choices for editing a vsFlexArray cell.

Saving Grid Contents to a Disk File

The vsFlexArray control enables you to save the control's entire contents to a disk file and reload the data from disk later. This is an exceptionally handy feature, particularly if you must minimize impact on a server in a client/server configuration. In this scenario, your application connects to the server, downloads the data it needs, adds it to the grid, and disconnects from the server. Users then save the data locally and begin to slice and dice the data. If they must use the data again at a later date, they reload the data from their disk file as opposed to reconnecting to the server.

Save the contents of a vsFlexArray grid by using its SaveGrid method. Load the contents of a previously saved file using the grid's LoadGrid method.

> **Note:** When using the SaveGrid and LoadGrid methods, you have the option of saving and loading just the data, just the formatting, or both.

Listing 14.6 gives an example of an application that loads data (through a link with the DAO Data control), saves the data to a file, disconnects from the Data control, and then reloads the data from the file. This application assumes that the Data control called Data1 has been connected to a database at design time.

Listing 14.6   A vsFlexArray Application That Saves and Loads Data Using the
SaveGrid **and** *LoadGrid* **Methods**

```
Option Explicit

Private Sub cmdLoadDB_Click()
    ' Data is displayed in faBound
    faBound.Visible = True
    faUnbound.Visible = False
End Sub


Private Sub cmdSaveFile_Click()
    faBound.SaveGrid App.Path & "\savegrid.dat", flexFileAll
End Sub


Private Sub cmdLoadFile_Click()
    faBound.Visible = False
    faUnbound.Visible = True

    faUnbound.LoadGrid App.Path & "\savegrid.dat", flexFileAll
    MsgBox "Local data loaded.", vbInformation
End Sub
```

The tricky thing about this application is the fact that when a control is
bound to a Data control, it's bound to the control forever—you can't disconnect
it. This is because the Data control's DataSource property isn't read-write at runtime. In addition, if you attempt to use the LoadGrid method with a bound control, you get a runtime error.

A possible solution to this problem is to include two identical vsFlexArray
controls in the application, one bound and one unbound. When the user asks to
save the data, the application takes the contents of the bound grid and writes it
to a disk file called savegrid.dat. When the user reloads savegrid.dat to the grid,
the application loads the data into the unbound grid. It's a kludge, but it
demonstrates how to save and load data in the grid.

Automatically Resizing Columns

One of the enhancements to the commercial version of the FlexArray control is
the fact that it automatically resizes columns to accommodate information in
cells—no more resizing columns in order to see what's there.

The grid does this through its AutoResize property, which by default is set to
True. This means that you don't have to do anything to take advantage of this
feature.

Binding to an Array

You can "bind" vsFlexGrid to a two-dimensional array of Variants. This is useful in situations where you want to view the data, but you don't want to incur the overhead of a constant connection to a data source.

There are a variety of ways to create an array that you can use to bind to a vsFlexArray control. It's not a coincidence that all three data access libraries available to the VB programmer (DAO, RDO, and ADO) have an extremely simple way of converting a recordset to a Variant array—the GetRows method. Since all three libraries' Recordset objects have a GetRows method, the technique is often used to manipulate data, particularly in a client/server scenario where you don't want to maintain a persistent connection to the database.

Listing 14.7 gives an example of an application that generates a Variant array and then binds it to the grid when a user clicks a command button.

Listing 14.7　Binding a vsFlexArray Control to a Variant Array Using the ADO
Recordset **Object's** *GetRows* **Method**

```
Option Explicit

' References ADO 2.0.

Private rs As Recordset
Private vData As Variant    ' array

Private Sub Form_Load()

    ' Open the recordset
    Set rs = New ADODB.Recordset
    rs.Source = "select * from tblCustomer " & _
                "where state = 'pa'"
    rs.ActiveConnection = "DSN=novelty;UID=sa;"
    rs.Open

    ' Convert the recordset into
    ' an array
    vData = rs.GetRows

    ' Prepare the grid
    vsFlexGrid1.FixedCols = 0

End Sub


Private Sub cmdBind_Click()
    vsFlexGrid1.BindToArray vData
End Sub
```

Code Example: You can find the code discussed in this section in the project `VSFArray.vbp`, located in the directory `\vbdb\code\14-VSFlex\VSFArray`. For information on how to install the sample files on the CD that accompanies this book, see the section "Installing the Example Files" in the introduction at the beginning of this book.

Summary

This chapter showed you how to analyze data using the MSFlexGrid and MSHFlexGrid controls that ship with VB6. It showed you examples of the control in bound and unbound mode, as well as the enhanced capabilities of the commercial vsFlexArray control, part of the VideoSoft VSFLEX control suite.

In the next chapter, you'll see how to construct a data-aware user interface with the ActiveX controls in the Sheridan DataWidgets suite. In addition to providing a grid that has slightly different capabilities than the MSFlexGrid and DBGrid controls, the package contains several additional user-interface controls, such as data-aware list boxes and command buttons.

Questions and Answers

Q. **I want to look up data in the Grid control, but the search facilities provided by SQL aren't sufficient. Do I have any other options?**

A. The commercial vsFlexArray version of the Grid control comes with a second control, vsFlexString, that permits you to search on regular expressions. The control's search facility could find, for example, the fifth occurrence of a word that contains a vowel in a FlexArray control. In addition to this kind of search, the control permits you to search on substrings that come at the beginning, end, or within a string, strings that contain uppercase or lowercase letters, or any type of number. The control also has the ability to evaluate expressions and provides search-and-replace functionality.

Q. **Is it possible to use this control as a reporting tool?**

A. There's not enough space in this chapter to go into many of these features, but yes, the Grid control provides a number of formatting features, including the ability to apply font formatting on a cell-by-cell basis and the ability to integrate with the Visual Basic `Printer` object. VideoSoft also makes another product, VSVIEW, introduced in Chapter 4, "Reporting and

Exporting Data," which provides print preview capabilities and serves as a replacement for the VB `Printer` object. VSFLEX integrates with VSVIEW, permitting you to use the controls together to print data after you've sliced and diced it.

Q. **Using the `GetRows` method of the `Recordset` object to convert the recordset into an array is a swell trick. Is there a `PutRows` method, too?**

A. Sorry, Sparky. You gotta write the code for this one yourself.

Using Sheridan DataWidgets

OVERVIEW OF THE SHERIDAN DATAWIDGETS
SUITE

The Sheridan DataWidgets suite contains a variety of user-interface controls that permit you to create database-aware applications. This chapter provides an introduction to each control, demonstrating how to get started using the control and giving an example of how it is used in applications.

OVERVIEW OF THE SHERIDAN DATAWIDGETS SUITE

The Sheridan DataWidgets suite is composed of six ActiveX controls. They are packaged as both 16- and 32-bit controls, so if you need to support Windows 3.1 development using the 16-bit version of Visual Basic 4.0 (the last version of VB that supported 16-bit development), you can use the same controls (or a reasonable facsimile thereof).

The controls in the DataWidgets suite include the following:

▶ *SSDBGrid.* A control to display a recordset in rows and columns

▶ *SSDataCombo.* A combo box that binds to a database field and displays values from another recordset

▶ *SSDBDropDown.* A combo box designed for use with the SSDBGrid control to provide the user with a list of choices when editing

▶ *SSDataOptSet.* A set of option buttons that can be bound to a database field

▶ *SSDBData.* A control designed to work with, as well as replace, the Visual Basic Data control

▶ *SSDBCommand.* A data-aware command button that can trigger certain data access actions (such as navigating through a recordset, creating and deleting records) without code

Each of these controls is demonstrated with a code example in this chapter.

NEW FEATURES OF DATAWIDGETS 3.1

Sheridan DataWidgets was updated twice since the release of Visual Basic 5.0. Version 3.1 of the package sports these new features:

▶ *ADO/OLE DB binding.* These are new versions of the controls that bind to OLE DB data sources.

▶ *Export to HTML.* You can use the data in a DataWidgets grid control to generate an HTML Web page or a plain text file. You also have the ability to use an HTML template to give your outputted page the exact look you want.

▶ *Printing.* The grid control supports the ability to output to a printer through the use of the control's contained ssPrintInfo object. A call to this object's PrintData method sends the grid data to the printer.

▶ *Custom formatting.* You can save the format of a grid to a file, then load that file later to instantly apply the formatting styles to the grid.

▶ *Data masking.* The controls in the suite have the ability to restrict the data entered by the user and to perform validation on that data (similar to the behavior of the MaskedEdit control, described in Chapter 12, "User-Interface Controls").

> **Note: The Sheridan DataWidgets suite is not shipped with Visual Basic; it's a separate product. For more information about DataWidgets and Sheridan's other ActiveX packages, check out Sheridan's Web site at http://www.shersoft.com.**

A trial version of Sheridan DataWidgets package is on the CD that accompanies this book (in the \Software\DataWdg directory). You can also download the latest version of Sheridan DataWidgets directly from the Sheridan Web site. The files can be found at http://www.shersoft.com/download/trials.htm.

The Sheridan DataWidgets controls are packaged in four OCX files. For binding to old-style data sources (the DAO Data control and Remote Data control), you use the file SSDW3A32.OCX for the SSDBGrid, SSDataCombo, and SSDBDropDown controls. The ADO/OLE DB equivalent of this file is SSDW3A0.OCX.

The file SSDW3B32.OCX contains the SSDBData, SSDBOptSet, and SSDBCommand controls for use with the DAO and Remote Data controls. The ADO/OLE DB version of this file is called SSDW3B0.OCX.

These files must be copied to your system and registered before you can use them in your Visual Basic projects or in a running application. (Normally the Sheridan DataWidgets installation program will do this for you on your development machine.)

Do the following to use the DataWidgets controls in a Visual Basic project using ADO/OLE DB:

1. In Visual Basic, select Project Components.

2. The Components dialog box appears. In the list of components, scroll down until you see Sheridan DataGrid/Combo/DropDown 3.1 (OLEDB) and Sheridan dbData/dbOptSet/dbCmd 3.1 (OLEDB).

3. Check the set of controls you want to use, then click OK. The controls you chose are added to your Visual Basic toolbox, as shown in Figure 15.1.

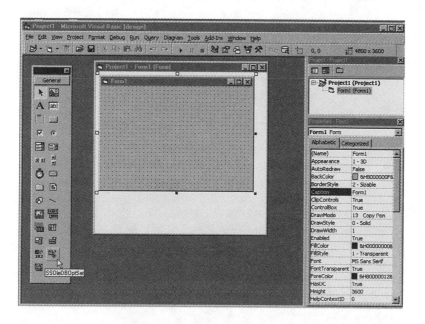

Figure 15.1
The DataWidgets controls are added to the Visual Basic toolbox.

Note: The different flavors of the Sheridan DataWidgets controls have different class names. For example, the DAO/RDO version of the grid control is called SSDBGrid. Its ADO/OLE DB counterpart is referred to as SSOleDBGrid. For simplicity, this chapter refers to only the old-style class names of these controls (for example, references to the SSDBGrid control apply to the SSOleDBGrid control as well).

Bear in mind that the controls should work identically no matter which data access library or flavor of control you use. There are a few exceptions to this, however. I've noted the differences in functionality along with each control's description in this chapter.

Although you can use ADO with any 32-bit version of VB, the ADO/OLE DB versions of the DataWidgets controls aren't supported in versions of Visual Basic prior to 6.0.

USING THE SHERIDAN SSDBGRID CONTROL

The Sheridan SSDBGrid control provides many of the features offered by the True DBGrid control (covered in Chapter 13, "Using the DBGrid and Apex True DBGrid Controls"). In fact, some of its properties and contained objects are identical to those of the DBGrid control.

Figure 15.2 shows an example of the Sheridan SSDBGrid control displaying data from the Jones Novelties database.

Figure 15.2
A bound Sheridan SSDBGrid control displays information from a database.

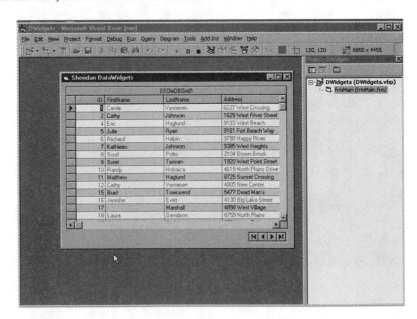

You use the same technique to bind the SSDBGrid to a data control as you use with the DBGrid control—simply create a data control, connect it to the database, and assign the control's DataSource property to the name of the data control. Like other grid controls, the SSDBGrid has no DataField property, because it is designed to display all the fields in a data source. You can create a basic data browser application based on the SSDBGrid with no code, as you'd expect from any self-respecting bound control.

You can see that by default, the SSDBGrid control shows rows of data in alternating colors. This is designed to help you read data in a row; it's particularly helpful if your application contains very long rows of data. If you'd prefer to view data in a single color, or a color of your choice, you can set the grid's ForeColorEven, BackColorEven, ForeColorOdd, and BackColorOdd properties to any colors you choose.

Like the DBGrid control, the SSDBGrid control permits you to determine whether the user can add, update, or delete data in the grid with a series of design-time properties. These properties even have the same names as their DBGrid counterparts—AllowAddNew, AllowDelete, and AllowUpdate. Setting the AllowAddNew property to True at design time adds a new, blank row to the bottom of the grid. You can use this row to insert new records, as shown in Figure 15.3.

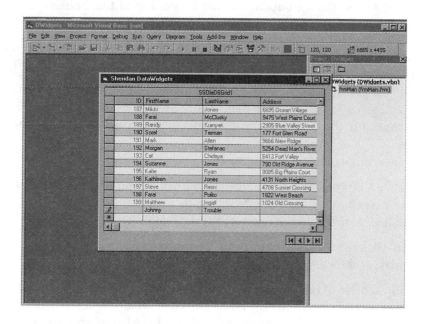

Figure 15.3
You can insert a new record in the SSDBGrid control after its AllowAddNew property is set to True.

Note that AllowAddNew is set to False by default. Also remember that just because the grid control is set to allow new records doesn't mean you have write access to the database. If you can't insert new records, it may mean that you've got a problem in your data source—if you're using the ADO data control, check to see that the LockType property isn't set to read-only and that the CursorType is set to an editable mode, such as optimistic.

Note: When you begin entering records into the Sheridan grid control, you may notice that fields that have defaults set in the database engine, as well as AutoNumber fields, don't display correctly in the grid. This is a limitation in the current version of OLE DB; it should be fixed in a future release. This problem isn't limited to the Sheridan grid control. It pops up in other contexts as well.

Code Example: You can find an example of the Sheridan grid control in the sample project DGrid.vbp, located in the directory \vbdb\code\ 15-DataWidgets\DWidgets. For information on how to install the sample files on the CD that accompanies this book, see the section "Installing the Example Files" in the introduction at the beginning of this book.

Altering the Grid's Design-Time Properties   The SSDBGrid control provides a design-time property dialog box that permits you to visually assign a large number of the grid's properties. Because this dialog box contains a very effective interface and gives you access to so many more properties than the Visual Basic property sheet, use the grid's own property dialog box to set its design-time properties.

To see how this works, do the following:

1. Create a VB project with a SSDBGrid control bound to a data control or other data source. Bind the data source to a database, and set the grid's DataSource property to the name of the data source.

2. Right-click the SSDBGrid control. The control's property dialog box appears, as shown in Figure 15.4.

3. As an example of how to change a property with this property sheet, select the Caption property in the list under the General tab. When you do so, the Caption property should appear to the right of the list of properties.

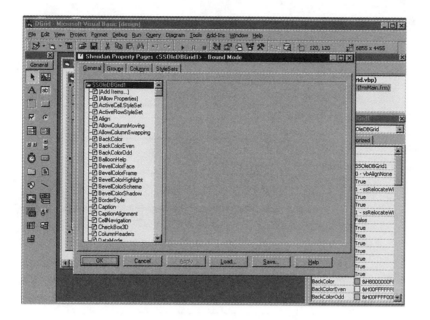

Figure 15.4
The Sheridan grid control's custom properties dialog box provides access to many of the grid's properties.

4. Change the `Caption` property to Jones Novelties Customers, then click OK.

5. You should be able to see that the grid control's caption has changed to the value you assigned.

Considering how involved a grid control's set of properties can be, it's nice to have an enhanced properties dialog box to minimize the complexity of working with the control at design time. In the next few sections of this chapter, you'll manipulate the design-time properties of the grid control using this property dialog to take advantage of some of its unique features.

Working with the Grid's Object Model   Like the DBGrid, the SSDBGrid contains subordinate objects that permit you to manipulate the control's properties and appearance in code. Figure 15.5 is a diagram of this object model.

Notice that elements in the SSDBGrid control's object model are suspiciously similar to the DBGrid's object model—there's a `Columns` collection, but there's also a `SelBookmarks` collection that permits you to select rows, and a variation of the `RowBuffer` object that permits you to receive rows as arguments to event procedures. It's clear that the SSDBGrid and DBGrid controls were designed to be at least conceptually similar to each other, which is good for you, because there are fewer differences to learn.

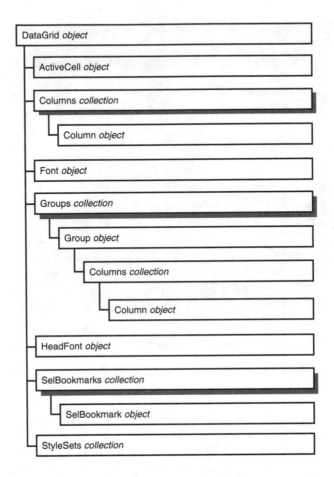

The `Group` object provided by the SSDBGrid control permits you to refer to and display a number of related columns as a group. For example, when displaying customers, you might place properties pertaining to the customers' addresses, cities, states, and ZIP codes in one group, while putting their customer status, credit rating, and order history in another group.

The `StyleSet` object is similar to the DBGrid `style` object. It permits you to create formatting objects (composed of background color, font, and foreground color) that can be assigned to cells, columns, groups, the active row, or the entire grid control.

The `PrintInfo` object was added in version 3.0 of the control. It gives you programmatic control over the grid's printing capabilities.

Dividing Columns into Groups at Design Time   You can divide your grid into groups of columns at design time. You do this in situations where you want to visually denote that a number of data fields fall into the same category. This is particularly useful when you want to indicate that a number of different columns are in the same recordset.

To assign groups to a SSDBGrid control at design time, follow these steps:

1. Connect the grid to the tblCustomer table in the database `novelty.mdb` using a data control or other data source. (You don't have to use a bound grid to take advantage of groups, but it makes this demonstration easier to follow.)

2. Right-click the grid and select Properties from the pop-up menu.

3. The control's Property Pages dialog box appears. Click the Groups tab. The Groups property page is displayed, as shown in Figure 15.6.

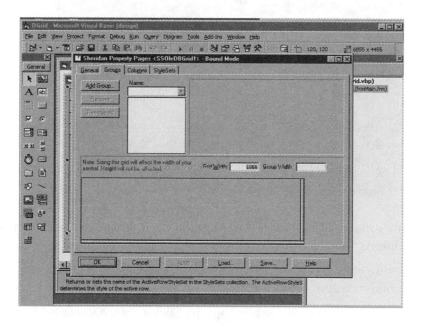

Figure 15.6
Click the Groups tab of the SSDBGrid Custom Property dialog box to display the Groups property.

4. Click the Add Group button. The Add Group dialog box appears. Type **Person**, and click OK.

5. The Person group appears in the property dialog box. Add another group, Address, using the same technique.

6. You should see two groups in the Custom Property dialog box. You have the ability to resize the width of these groups by click-dragging with the mouse. Resize the Person group so it's approximately 2,000 twips wide, then resize the Address group so it's approximately 4,000 twips wide. (A *twip* is the standard measurement unit in Visual Basic programming, equal to a twentieth of a point; there are 1,440 twips to the inch.) You can resize the overall grid control by click-dragging on the right edge of the sizing control, as shown in Figure 15.7.

Figure 15.7
You can resize groups and the grid in the Groups page of the SSDBGrid control's custom property sheet.

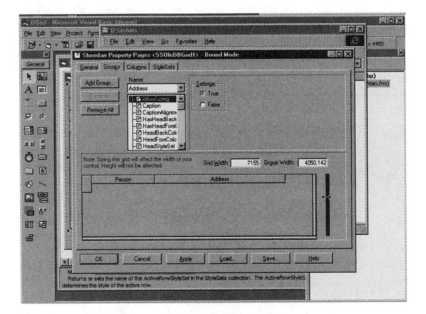

7. Now you can add columns to each group. To do this, start by clicking the Columns tab of the Custom Properties dialog box.

8. Because your grid is bound to a database, you can select columns from a list of data columns in the database. To do this, click the Fields button.

9. The Field Selection dialog box appears. Click the FirstName field, then hold down the Shift key and click the LastName field. The dialog box should look like the one shown in Figure 15.8.

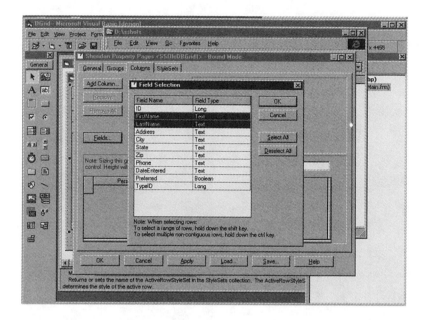

Figure 15.8
Select fields from a database to add to the columns in a SSDBGrid group.

10. Click OK. The fields are added to the Person group, as shown in Figure 15.9.

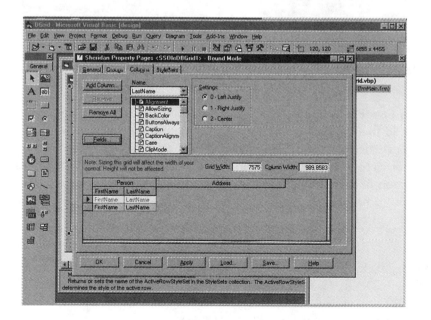

Figure 15.9
Fields are added to a group on the Columns page of the SSDBGrid's Custom Property dialog box.

11. Click the Address group, then use the Field Selection dialog box to add the Address, City, State and ZIP fields to the Address group. Use your mouse to resize the columns. When you're finished, the grid looks like Figure 15.10.

Figure 15.10
You can add and resize the columns of the SSDBGrid control in groups at design time.

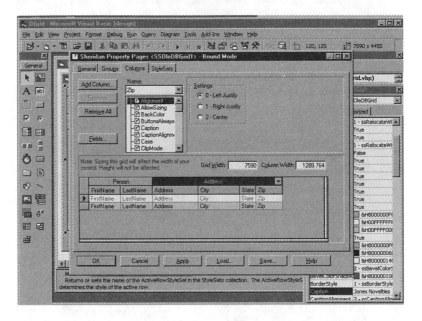

12. Click OK to close the property page dialog and run the application. Your data is displayed and organized in groups, as shown in Figure 15.11.

> **Note:** In addition to assigning groups to the grid at design time, you can also add them in code at runtime, by manipulating the SSDBGrid control's `Groups` collection. Additionally, when you have a grid that contains groups, you can access columns at runtime in code using either the grid's `Columns` collection or each `Group` object's `Columns` collection. This can make it easier for you to navigate through a grid in code when your grid contains a large number of columns.

Exporting Data to HTML Using the Sheridan Grid Control   New to version 3.0 of the SSDBGrid is the ability to export grid data to a Web page in HTML format. You can do this using the `Export` method of the grid control.

The `Export` method has the following syntax:

```
SSDBGrid1.Export type, exportflags, file, template, outputfilefields
```

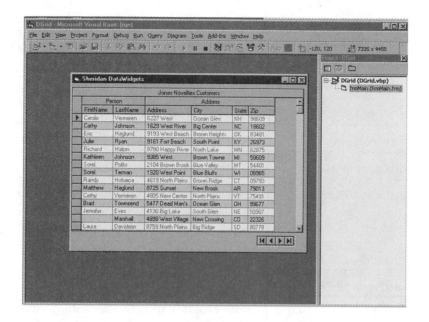

Figure 15.11
You can view data in a grid comprised of groups.

The type argument indicates the format you're exporting to. The legal values are listed in Table 15.1.

Table 15.1	Export Type Constants for the SSDBGrid Control's *Export* Method
Constant	**Meaning**
ssExportTypeText	Exports to a plain text file
ssExportTypeHTMLTable	Exports to a single HTML file
ssExportTypeHTMLRowFiles	Exports to multiple HTML files, one file per row in the grid

The *exportflags* argument of the Export method determines the data you want to export. The legal values for this argument are listed in Table 15.2.

Table 15.2	Export Type Constants for the SSDBGrid Control's *Export* Method
Constant	**Meaning**
ssExportCurrentRow	Exports the current row of data
ssExportSelectedRows	Exports all the selected rows

continues

Table 15.2   Export Type Constants for the SSDBGrid Control's *Export* Method (Continued)

Constant	Meaning
ssExportNonSelectedRows	Exports the unselected rows
ssExportAllRows	Exports all rows in the grid
ssExportFieldNames	For text files, exports the names of fields
ssExportColumnHeaders	For text files, exports column headers
ssExportInLayoutOrder	Exports columns in the order they appear in the grid, as opposed to their position in the control's Columns collection
ssExportHiddenColumns	Exports hidden columns
ssExportOverwriteExisting	Replaces the existing export file
ssExportAppendToExisting	Adds exported data to the existing export file

These constants can be combined. For example, if you want to export all the rows in the grid as well as their field names, set the exportflags argument to the expression ssExportAllRows + ssExportFieldNames.

The file parameter is the name of the file you want to export to. If you export to a file that already exists and you don't use the ssExportOverwriteExisting or ssExportAppendToExisting constants with the type argument, a runtime error occurs.

The template parameter indicates the name of an HTML template file used by the grid to format the output. Although this parameter is optional for text exporting, it's required for HTML exporting. To see how to build such a template, see the example later in this section.

The *outputfilefields* parameter is also optional. It indicates which field in the grid supplies filenames for a multifile export. This is typically the primary key of the table contained by the grid. It's only relevant when the type argument is set to ssExportTypeHTMLRowFiles.

To export the contents of a single grid to a single HTML file, follow these steps:

1. In Visual Basic, create a data-bound grid interface as demonstrated earlier in this chapter. It doesn't matter which flavor of the Sheridan grid control you use, or how you bind the control to the database.

2. Using any text editor (Windows Notepad will do), create a text file called `template.html` containing the following HTML tags:

```
<html>
<head>

<title>
Sheridan Data Export Example
</title>

</head>

<body bgcolor=#ffffff>

<font face='Tahoma, Arial, Helvetica'>
<h1>Sheridan Data Export Example</h1>

{SSREPLACE COLHEAD TABLE DATA}

</body>
</html>
```

This is identical to a standard HTML file, except for the SSREPLACE tag. This tag indicates that you want column headers and an HTML table comprised of the data contained in the grid to be exported to the HTML file.

3. In the VB application, create a procedure that executes the Export method of the grid control:

```
Private Sub cmdExport_Click()
    Screen.MousePointer = vbHourglass
    SSOleDBGrid1.Export ssExportTypeHTMLTable, _
                        ssExportAllRows + ssExportOverwriteExisting, _
                        App.Path & "\export.html"
                        App.Path & "\template.html"
    Screen.Mousepointer = vbNormal
End Sub
```

4. Run the application and click cmdExport to export the file.

5. The file export.HTML should appear on your disk. Open the file in your favorite Web browser. It should look like Figure 15.12.

Figure 15.12
*Use a Web brows-
er to view the
product of an
HTML export using
the SSDBGrid
control.*

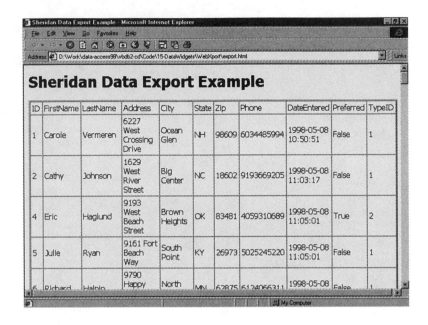

Note that this is the most basic example of what the SSDBGrid control can do. There are a number of other SSREPLACE tags you can use to vary the output of the Sheridan grid control. For more information on what tags are available and how they work, see the topic "HTML Template Codes" in the DataWidgets online help.

Code Example: You can find an example of HTML export from the Sheridan grid control in the project WebXPort.vbp, located in the directory \vbdb\code\15-DataWidgets\WebXPort. For information on how to install the sample files on the CD that accompanies this book, see the section "Installing the Example Files" in the introduction at the beginning of this book.

USING THE SSDATACOMBO CONTROL
The Sheridan SSDataCombo control is a combo box that binds to a database field and displays a list of choices from another recordset. The control gives you the ability to provide data-driven lists of choices without writing code.

Figure 15.13 shows an example of the Sheridan SSDataCombo control.

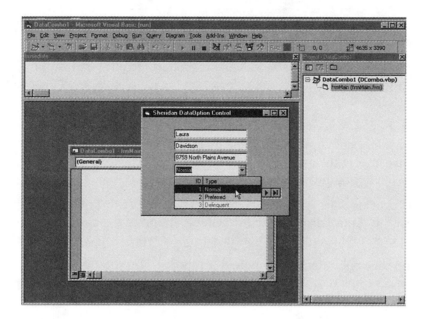

Figure 15.13
You can use the SSDataCombo control to create a data-entry interface.

Do the following to create this application:

1. Create a database access application using a data source such as a data control or DataEnvironment designer. (This example uses an ADO Data control bound to tblCustomer in the Novelty database.)

2. Create three text boxes bound to the FirstName, LastName, and Address fields.

3. Add a reference to the Sheridan DataWidgets controls in your project, if necessary.

4. Create a SSDataCombo control on your form. Because this control binds to the TypeID field in the tblCustomer table, name the control cboCustomerType.

5. Bind cboCustomerType to the TypeID field the way you would for any other bound control—by setting its DataSource property to the name of the data control and setting its DataField property to TypeID.

6. Populate the list of choices provided by this control. To do this, create a second data control named adcTypeList. Connect this control to the tblCustomerType table in the database.

7. Because the user won't be using this data control to navigate, set datCustomerType's `Visible` property to False.

8. Set cboCustomerType's `DataSourceList` property to adcTypeList. This property governs which data source provides the list of choices in the combo box's list.

9. Set the cboCustomerType's `DataFieldList` property to ID. This field represents the value copied into the main record when the user makes a selection—that is, the primary key of tblCustomerType to be inserted into the foreign key of tblCustomer.

10. Set cboCustomerType's `DataFieldToDisplay` property to Type. This ensures that the control displays the textual description of the customer type, as opposed to the numeric ID of the customer type.

11. Run the application and choose from the list. You should see the full list of choices displayed. Best of all, this application requires no code.

> **Code Example: You can find the project discussed in this section in the sample project `DCombo.vbp`, located in the directory `\vbdb\code\ 15-DataWidgets\DCombo`. For information on how to install the sample files on the CD that accompanies this book, see the section "Installing the Example Files" in the introduction at the beginning of this book.**

USING THE SSDBDROPDOWN CONTROL

The Sheridan SSDBDropDown control is a combo box specifically designed for use with the SSDBGrid control. It provides the user with a list of choices when editing data in a grid cell.

Figure 15.14 shows an example of the SSDBDropDown control in action, displaying a list of choices from the Jones Novelties customer database.

The technique for assigning a SSDBDropDown control to a column in the grid is similar to building a SSDataCombo control. To do this, follow these steps:

1. Create a project composed of a data control or other data source and a SSDBGrid control. If you're using a data control, name it datCustomer.

2. Bind the data control to the tblCustomer table in the Novelty database.

3. Name the grid dbgCustomer and connect it to the data control by setting its DataSource property to datCustomer. When you run this application, it displays the contents of the TypeID field as a number, as shown in Figure 15.15.

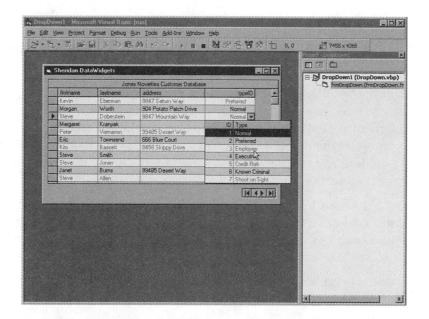

Figure 15.14
You can provide a list of choices in a SSDBGrid control using the SSDBDropDown control.

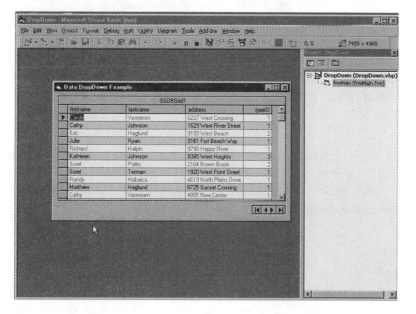

Figure 15.15
SSDBGrid control displays a numeric field before adding a SSDBDropDown control.

Instead of displaying the TypeID, you'll want to display the contents of the tblCustomerType table in order to let the user know what the type IDs mean. To do this, create a second data control. Name this control datCustomerType and bind it to the tblCustomerType table.

4. Create a SSDBDropDown control on the form. Name this control ddCustomerType. You can place this control anywhere on the form; its exact position on the form at runtime is determined by which cell the user edits.

5. Assign the SSDBDropDown's `DataSource` property to datCustomerType, assign its `DataFieldList` property to ID, and set its `DataFieldToDisplay` property to Type. This causes the control to display the textual customer type but store the numeric customer type ID in the database. (These settings are identical to the settings you used for the SSDataCombo control in the previous section's example.)

6. You must write a line of code in order to assign the SSDBDropDown control to a column in the SSDBGrid. Do this in the grid's `InitColProps` event. The code assigns the SSDBDropDown control's window handle to the `DropDownHwnd` property of one of the SSDBGrid's column objects:

```
Private Sub dbgCustomer_InitColumnProps()
    dbgCustomer.Columns(3).DropDownHwnd = ddCustomerType.hWnd
End Sub
```

Note: The *window handle*, or hWnd, of a control is a unique value the operating system uses to identify a control or other window. It isn't used much in Visual Basic programming, but you run across it every so often. It's used more often when you place calls to the Windows Application Programming Interface (API).

7. Run the application. You should be able to see that now, instead of the TypeID, the textual customer type is displayed. When you click on a Customer Type cell, the SSDBDropDown displays the list of customer types in tblCustomer, as shown in Figure 15.16.

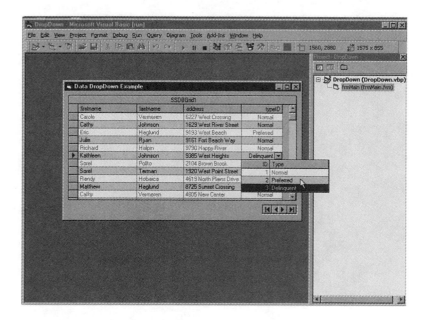

Figure 15.16
*SSDBDropDown
control displays a
database-bound
list of choices.*

Note: Remember to make the recordsets that populate lists read-only. This alteration greatly improves performance.

Code Example: You can find the project discussed in this section in the sample project DropDown.vbp, located in the directory \vbdb\code\ 15-DataWidgets\DropDown. For information on how to install the sample files on the CD that accompanies this book, see the section "Installing the Example Files" in the introduction at the beginning of this book.

USING THE SSDATAOPTSET CONTROL

The SSDataOptSet control provides a database-aware set of option buttons. You can bind as many option buttons as you want to the same database field; when the user chooses a particular button, the value associated with that button is stored in the field.

Figure 15.17 shows an example of the SSDataOptSet control displaying data from the Jones Novelties database.

Figure 15.17
*The SSDataOptSet
control at runtime
displays the con-
tents of the TypeID
field.*

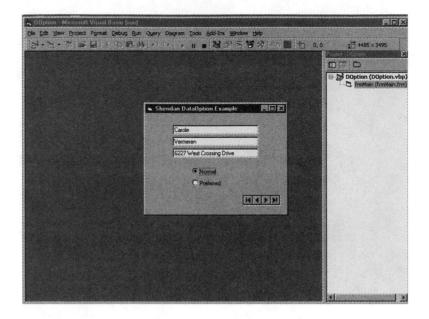

Do the following to create this application:

1. Create a database access interface based on a data control connected to the tblCustomer table in the Novelty database. Create text boxes bound to the FirstName, LastName, and Address fields.

2. Create two SSDataOptSet controls on the form. Give the first control the caption Normal and give the second control the caption Preferred.

3. Assign the OptionValue property of the first control to 1. Assign the second control's OptionValue property to 2. This will cause the option buttons to store the numeric values 1 and 2 in the database.

4. Assign both controls' DataSource properties to datCustomer and assign both controls' DataField properties to TypeID.

5. Run the application. You should be able to see that for the first record that appears, either the Normal or Preferred field is selected. To change this customer's status, simply click the appropriate option button.

The obvious disadvantage of the SSDataOptSet control is the fact that you have to hard-code the controls' values through the OptionValue property; you can't bind the list of option buttons to a Data control as you can with the SSDataCombo. However, the SSDataOptSet control contains a collection of

Button objects that you can use to add buttons to the control at runtime. You can use this to make the SSDataOptSet control more useful in situations where you need to make a set of buttons appear based on the value stored in a related database table.

USING THE SSDBDATA CONTROL

The Sheridan SSDBData Control isn't a replacement for the standard Visual Basic data control. Rather, it's designed to work alongside an existing VB data control to provide additional features.

These additional features include the following:

▶ The ability to display the control horizontally, like the conventional data controls, or vertically

▶ The ability to navigate through the recordset with bookmarks

▶ The ability to browse through records quickly by clicking and holding a button (a feature called *Speed Buttons*)

▶ A Find dialog box that tailors itself to your record source

Figure 15.18 shows an example of the Sheridan SSDBData control in an application that displays data from the Jones Novelties database.

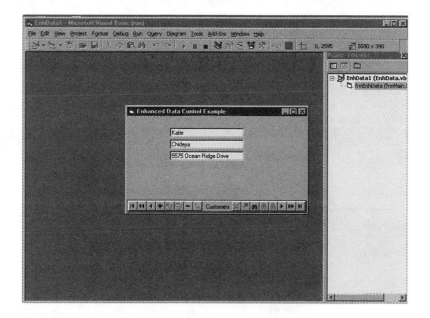

Figure 15.18
The Sheridan SSDBData control in an application at runtime looks like this.

Do the following to create this application:

1. Create a database access application using the Visual Basic DAO Data control.

2. Because you'll use the SSDBData control to navigate through the recordset, set the VB Data control's `Visible` property to False.

3. Add an instance of the Sheridan SSDBData control to your form.

4. Set the SSDBData control's `Caption` property to Customers and set its `DataSource` property to the name of your VB Data control.

5. Set the SSDBData control's `Align` property to 2 - vbAlignBottom. This causes the control to align to the bottom of your form and to resize along with the form.

6. Run the application. You can now use the SSDBData control to navigate through your recordset. Your application can now use the control's buttons to provide a number of features not offered by the standard Data control.

Code Example: You can find the project discussed in this section in the sample project `EnhData.vbp`, located in the directory `\vbdb\code\15-DataWidgets\EnhData`. For information on how to install the sample files on the CD that accompanies this book, see the section "Installing the Example Files" in the introduction at the beginning of this book.

Table 15.3 lists each of the SSDBData Control's buttons with descriptions of what each button does. The buttons are listed in the table as they appear on a default SSDBData control—from left to right.

Table 15.3 Description of the Buttons on a Sheridan SSDBData Control	
Button	**Description**
MoveFirst	Equivalent to the conventional Data control's MoveFirst button
Previous Page	Moves to the previous page of data
MovePrevious	Equivalent to the conventional Data control's MovePrevious button, except you can hold down the button to move through records in a rapid-fire fashion

Button	Description
Add	Adds a new record to the interface; the Cancel and Update buttons become available when you click this button
Cancel	Aborts the creation of a new record
Update	Commits the creation of a new record
Delete	Deletes the current record
Add Bookmark	Adds a bookmark to the current record, permitting you to return to it later using the Go To Bookmark button. The number of bookmarks that can be stored by the control is governed by its `BookmarksToKeep` property; the default is 10
Clear All Bookmarks	Clears any bookmarks you may have previously created
Go To Bookmark	Moves the current record to the next bookmark you've created
Find	Displays the SSDBData control's Find dialog box, permitting you to locate records based on criteria you specify
FindPrevious	Finds the previous record; available only if you've specified a Find criterion using the Find button
FindNext	Finds the next record; available only if you've specified a Find criterion using the Find button
MoveNext	Equivalent to the conventional Data control's MoveNext button (except you can hold down the button to move through records in a rapid-fire fashion)
Next Page	Moves ahead to the next page of data
MoveLast	Equivalent to the Data control's MoveLast button

You can disable the additional buttons on an SSDBData control. Do so by assigning the Boolean values of the control's `Show` properties at design time; for example, to suppress display of the control's Delete button, set the control's `ShowDeleteButton` to False. (All the control's `Show` properties are set to True by default.)

Note: As of this writing, the Update and Cancel buttons on the SSDBData control don't work as expected when bound to an ADO/OLE DB data source, according to Sheridan. They work correctly when bound to a DAO data control, however. Sheridan recommends disabling these buttons in an ADO/OLE DB application by setting the control's `ShowUpdateButton` and `ShowCancelButton` properties to False.

USING THE SSDBCOMMAND BUTTON

The Sheridan SSDBCommand control provides several common database access functions (such as navigation and the creation and deletion of new records) with a minimum of code. You can use it as an alternative to, or in conjunction with, the SSDBData control described in the previous section.

You use the SSDBCommand button by binding it to a data control, then assigning an action to it. The action taken by the SSDBCommand control is governed by its `DatabaseAction` property, as shown in Table 15.4.

Table 15.4   Values for the *DatabaseAction* Property of the Sheridan SSDBCommand Control

Value	Description
0	MoveFirst
1	Previous Page
2	MovePrevious
3	MoveNext
4	Next Page
5	MoveLast
6	Save Bookmark
7	Go To Bookmark
8	Refresh

Figure 15.19 shows an example of an application that uses SSDBCommand Button controls to navigate through a recordset. This isn't the most visually impressive control in the suite, but it does cut down on the number of lines of code you write in your application, which is usually a good thing.

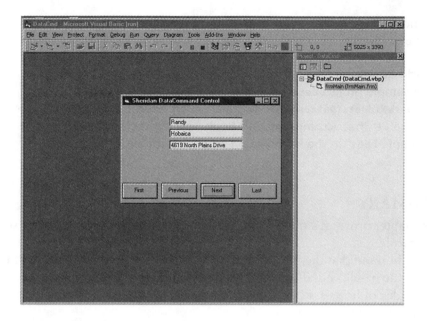

Do the following to create this application:

1. Build a database access interface based on the data control.

2. Create four SSDBCommand buttons on your form.

3. Set the buttons' Caption properties to First, Previous, Next, and Last, respectively.

4. Set the buttons' DatabaseAction properties to 0 - ssFirst, 2 - ssPrevious, 3 - ssNext, and 5 - ssLast, respectively.

5. Set the button's CaptionAlignment property to 7 - ssAlignmentCaptionCenterMiddle. (The buttons' captions are aligned to the bottom by default because the button supports a Picture property, which lets you assign a custom graphic to the button.)

6. Run the application. You should be able to navigate through the recordset using the SSDBCommand controls.

In addition to supporting database actions without code, the SSDBCommand buttons support automatic text wrapping (through the WordWrap property) as well as rapid-fire navigation through the recordset. To see how this works, run the sample application, then click and hold the mouse on the MoveNext button.

You should be able to see that the button moves you through one record at a time very quickly.

Code Example: You can find the project discussed in this section in the sample project `DataCmd.vbp`, located in the directory `\vbdb\code\15-DataWidgets\DataCmd`. For information on how to install the sample files on the CD that accompanies this book, see the section "Installing the Example Files" in the introduction at the beginning of this book.

Summary

This chapter provides a quick introduction to the Sheridan DataWidgets suite's six controls.

Bear in mind that the third-party controls discussed in this book aren't necessarily the be-all, end-all of database-aware controls—but hopefully they give you an idea of how easy it is to build a database-aware user interface with a minimum of code.

Questions and Answers

Q. **I'm interested in displaying data in a hierarchical format—not in rows in columns, but in more of an outline format, like the Visual Basic TreeView control. Is there a data-aware control that does this?**

A. I don't know of a TreeView-style control that connects directly to a database through a data control. However, Sheridan Software provides a control called ActiveTreeView, which is compatible with the VB TreeView control and supports a number of additional features (such as an event-driven virtual mode that lets you populate the control with only the data needed for display—as opposed to having to dump thousands of records in the control at once).

Q. **Is it possible to use the SSDBGrid control without binding it to a data control?**

A. Certainly. In fact, the control supports three data modes—bound, unbound, and AddItem. You set these modes through the grid control's `DataMode` property. When the grid is in `AddItem` mode, you can add items to the grid manually, at design time, through the grid's custom property dialog box.

Index

Hey, you've got enough worries.

Don't let IT training be one of them.

Get on the fast track to IT training at InformIT,
your total Information Technology training network.

 | **www.informit.com** | **SAMS**

■ Hundreds of timely articles on dozens of topics ■ Discounts on IT books from all our publishing partners, including Sams Publishing ■ Free, unabridged books from the InformIT Free Library ■ "Expert Q&A"—our live, online chat with IT experts ■ Faster, easier certification and training from our Web- or classroom-based training programs ■ Current IT news ■ Software downloads ■ Career-enhancing resources